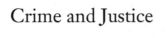

Crime and Justice

# Crime and Justice
## *A Review of Research*
### *Edited by Michael Tonry*

VOLUME 47

*The University of Chicago Press, Chicago and London*

The University of Chicago Press, Chicago 60637
The University of Chicago Press, Ltd., London

© 2018 by The University of Chicago
All rights reserved.
Printed in the United States of America

ISSN: 0192-3234

ISBN: 978-0-226-57704-3

LCN: 80-642217

The paper used in this publication meets the minimum requirements of American
National Standard for Information Sciences—Permanence of Paper for Printed
Library Materials, ANSI Z39.48-1984. ⊗

# Contents

# Preface

This is the forty-seventh in a series of volumes of commissioned essays on research on crime and justice, designed to survey the contours of knowledge of crime and of society's methods to understand and deal with it. Knowledge in criminology, as in other fields of research, grows by artificial isolation of a segment of a topic for close analysis and by the deliberate juxtaposition of insights gained from the study of other segments. We must both specialize and look across the borders of our own specialties. No one can see all the problems whole. No one can keep abreast of the major literature, for it far exceeds time and energy; but some effort at broad understanding is essential if only to lend direction to one's own specialty. Such an overview of research and knowledge about crime and justice is the purpose of this series.

More than 40 years have passed since Norval Morris and I in 1977 convened the initial editorial board meeting in Reston, Virginia, to plan the first volume. That's a long time. Almost everyone who attended has passed away: Norval Morris, dean of the University of Chicago Law School; Blair Ewing, director of the National Institute of Law Enforcement and Criminal Justice, and assistant director Paul Cascarano, whose joint idea *Crime and Justice* was and whose support made it possible; Daniel Glaser, professor of sociology at the University of Southern California; Ted Robert Gurr, chairman of the Political Science Department at Northwestern University; Wade McCree, solicitor general of the United States; Sheldon Messinger, professor of sociology at the University of California at Berkeley and the last dean of its School of Criminology; Patrick V. Murphy, president of the Police Foundation and former New York Police Department commissioner; and Albert J. Reiss Jr., professor of law and sociology at Yale. At that first meeting, we invited Nigel Walker, director of the Institute of Criminology at Cambridge; Lloyd Ohlin, professor of sociology at Harvard; and James Q. Wilson, professor of political science at Harvard to join the board. Of *Crime and Justice*'s founding principals, only Alfred Blumstein and I remain.

Much, however, has not changed. The core mission was, and remains, to commission leading scholars to write critical, state-of-the-art reviews of current knowledge concerning important subjects related to crime and the criminal justice system. We aimed, and still do, to be multidisciplinary, to recruit talented writers from many countries, and to be as internationally and cross-nationally comprehensive in coverage as available literatures allow.

The process has not changed. Quality control remains unusually rigorous for a social science journal. Most essays are commissioned, but not all those commissioned are published. All are reviewed by paid referees, many are discussed in detail at specially convened scholarly meetings, and almost all are extensively revised before they are published. The process is long and to writers must sometimes be frustrating; remarkably few have complained.

Norval Morris and I, or I, wrote prefaces to a fair number of volumes that felt like milestones—volume 10, volume 25, the 2002 volume that tolled a quarter century since that first meeting—each time with a mixed sense of delight that the series had survived and thriven for so long; bewilderment that we managed to obtain substantial financial support for it, primarily from the National Institute of Justice from 1977 to 2002 and since then from other sponsors in the United States and Europe; and apprehension that our run of luck could not continue indefinitely. The delight, bewilderment, and apprehension continue, but at least for the present, *Crime and Justice* is in good shape.

This volume contains a particularly happy mix of essays, drawing on a wide range of disciplines, written by established senior scholars and emerging younger ones. Writers come from four continents and Australia, and many countries.

The essays in this volume manifest continuity and change. Well over 400 have been published to date. Each in this volume proudly goes where others in *Crime and Justice* have gone before: on deterrence (John Braithwaite), juvenile justice (Barry Feld), prison life (Craig Haney), punishment philosophy (the editor), criminal history (Rhys Hester and colleagues), crime rates (Stefan Harrendorf), prospective longitudinal studies (Joseph Murray and colleagues), the history of crime (Rosemary Gartner and Liam Kennedy), and scholarly citation analyses (Ellen Cohn and colleagues). Each, however, offers new information and new ideas. Some offer new paradigms.

First-rate scholarly essays on topics new and old, writers young and not so young and from many countries, a wide range of disciplines and subjects—what's not to like? All these things are as *Crime and Justice* was meant to be. I believe this is one of the strongest volumes we have published. Readers will decide for themselves.

Michael Tonry
Isola D'Elba, February 2018

*Rosemary Gartner and Liam Kennedy*

# War and Postwar Violence

ABSTRACT

Wars are related to subsequent violence in complex and at times contradictory ways. The relationships between war and postwar violence, recognized throughout history, have attracted the attention and concern of researchers, state officials, and policy makers and the broader public. Methodological challenges, however, limit the potential for isolating the precise circumstances under which war and postwar violence are causally related. The weight of the evidence indicates that war is often followed by increases in violence, but there are important exceptions to this pattern. Potential theoretical explanations for this relationship abound. The harmful effects of wars on the minds and bodies of those participating in them are less influential on postwar violence than are the damages wars do to postwar societies' social and economic institutions, political legitimacy, and group relations. Preventing or reducing elevated rates of violence after wars is rarely a priority during peace negotiations. As a consequence, policies instituted as part of the peace-building process often fuel violent crime.

Although the end of war is typically celebrated as an end to violence and the arrival of peace, is this consistently the case? Or does war leave a legacy of violence in the postwar period? These questions have preoccupied many people for centuries, most of whom have argued that war—through the direct experience of it or its indirect effects on postwar society— raises the likelihood of violence of various types in its aftermath. Claims about the harms war does to individuals and to society in general were expressed by Sir Thomas More ([1516] 1967), Erasmus ([1517]1813), and Machiavelli ([1532] 2005) and have been echoed in scholarly and popular

Electronically published March 5, 2018
   Rosemary Gartner is professor emerita of criminology and sociolegal studies, University of Toronto. Liam Kennedy is assistant professor of criminology/sociology, King's University College, Western University Canada.

1

circles during many wars in the centuries since (e.g., Darrow 1922; von Hentig 1947; Durkheim [1950] 1957). Anecdotal evidence of ex-soldiers forming bandit gangs or massacring family members was a staple of wartime and postwar broadsheets in the eighteenth and nineteenth centuries (Adler 1996; Rogers 2012) and is mirrored in the attention the media have given to the military background and war experiences of mass shooters, particularly in the United States, in recent years (e.g., Klay 2016; Steele 2017).

More systematic evidence from the last century, however, shows that many, but certainly not all, postwar societies are plagued by high levels of violence. Archer and Gartner's (1976*b*) analysis of 29 nations participating in World Wars I and II, for example, found that 13 had postwar homicide rates that were significantly higher than their prewar rates; the other 16 showed either no significant change (12 nations) or significantly lower homicide rates (four nations). Since World War II, however, the nature of wars has changed, with intrastate or civil wars replacing interstate wars. Civil wars in recent decades are even more likely to have been followed by postwar increases in homicide and other violent crime (Call and Stanley 2001; Collier and Hoeffler 2004; Howarth 2014), but again there are exceptions to this pattern (Grandi 2013*a*; Rivera 2016). The question thus shifts from "Are wars followed by elevated rates of violence?" to "Under what circumstances are wars followed by elevated rates of violence?" If, as Berdal (2012, p. 313) states, there is "no simple or automatic relationship between even very high and protracted levels of atrocious violence [during war] and its persistence into the postwar period," then we need to know "how, to what degree and under precisely what circumstances one form of violence metamorphoses into another" (Binford 2002, p. 209).

Scholars from a number of disciplines—history, political science, sociology, criminology, psychology, and more—have contributed insight into this question. Our aim in this essay is to review their findings about the relationship between war and postwar violence. Because of its multidisciplinary nature, this literature approaches the topic from a range of methodological and theoretical perspectives. Psychologists and psychiatrists, for example, have been particularly interested in whether exposure to violence during war affects individuals' psychological functioning and mental health in ways that encourage or fail to constrain their violent behavior when the war ends. The context-rich case studies of societies in the aftermath of wars by historians and political scientists yield insight into how individual- and societal-level changes produced by war or by the transition to peace shape postwar violence. And social scientists' statistical analyses of data on homicide and other violent crimes from countries participating in wars identify both general patterns in the relationship between war and postwar violence and specific departures from them.

The diversity of this literature is both a weakness and a strength. Studies differ in how they define and measure participation in war, the length of the postwar period, and their measures of postwar violence, as well as in their choice of comparators for assessing whether postwar violence has increased. The mechanisms that could link wars to postwar violence—at either the individual or societal level—have been measured in a variety of ways (or not at all), limiting the ability systematically to test predictions about why war and postwar violence are (or are not) related. Nevertheless, this diverse literature reveals some consistent patterns, strengthening our confidence in identifying the factors most likely to lead to high rates of violence following wars and in our overall conclusion that increases in postwar violence are not inevitable but may be predictable.

Does war escalate postwar violence by harming the bodies or the psyches of those who engage in and/or are directly exposed to wartime violence? Combatants and noncombatants alike experience physical harm and traumatic experiences that could increase their likelihood of violence after war. Some research shows that some individuals with symptoms of post-traumatic stress disorder (PTSD) or other physical and psychological injuries from wartime violence are subsequently more violent than others. The evidence, however, is inconsistent, and causal connections between these harms and subsequent violence are difficult to establish. It therefore seems unlikely that this is a major contributor to postwar violence.

Does war increase postwar violence through a process of learning or habituation?[1] Military training, particularly during wartime, and a masculinized military culture teach soldiers to overcome their inhibitions to and fear of killing, how to kill, and, in some cases, how to enjoy killing. While this feeds popular concerns about brutalized veterans returning home inured and disposed to violence, those concerns are realized only rarely. Similarly, the possibility that the general population of warring

---

[1] The terms habituation, conditioning, brutalization, modeling, and mimesis are all used in the research we examine in this section. Although the processes implied by these terms are somewhat different and at times overlap with arguments regarding the effect of war trauma on violence, we treat the terms as similarly implying some sort of learning process.

countries becomes habituated to violence or adopts and adapts the state's legitimation of violence during war in ways that increase postwar violence lacks strong and direct empirical support. Neither the harms nor the lessons of war appear to be necessary or sufficient conditions for substantial increases in postwar violence.

War often damages a society's social, political, and economic institutions and its physical infrastructure, limiting the state's ability to provide for and protect its citizens after war. This "public security gap" can have two important consequences. First, it creates opportunities for violent predation, reprisal and revenge killings, and the continuation of illicit war economies that rely on the use or threat of violence. Second, it may undermine the legitimacy of a postwar society's political institutions, which in turn may foster violence. There is ample evidence from both the historical record and contemporary times that these conditions are associated with high levels of postwar violence.

Even when a society's institutional structures and legitimacy are not undermined, the transformation to peacetime can bring new opportunities and motivations for violence. The speed and nature of demobilization and reintegration processes may leave ex-combatants without work and aggrieved over their reception at home or—in the case of ex-combatants on the losing side in civil wars—their treatment by the victors. Peace accords and reconstruction policies can exacerbate economic inequality or destabilize local networks of social control. Postwar efforts to reverse changes in gender relations and the gender order that war often produces have the potential to stoke friction in families and workplaces. All of these features of the transformation to peacetime have been associated with postwar violence, particularly in recent decades.

Here it is important to stress that these explanations for increases in postwar violence are not incompatible with one another, and most who have studied violence in postwar societies see several processes operating together. Nevertheless, explanations focusing on the indirect effects of war on postwar societies appear to have the greatest support.

Postwar societies are not universally more violent than they were before a war and sometimes may be less violent. Most obviously, if a postwar society is not characterized by the sorts of conditions just described, it may escape the violent fallout of war. Decreases in postwar violence may also occur if there is a reduction in the population most at risk of violence (i.e., young males) or through a process of catharsis or war weariness, although evidence for either of these possibilities is very limited. To the extent wars are followed by an increase in social cohesion, trust, and civic engagement, postwar violence also may decline. Finally, there is evidence from recent intrastate wars of growth in women's participation in the political sphere in some postwar societies; among the consequences of this feminization of politics may be lower levels of postwar violence.

In this essay, we review research on the ways in which wartime violence may affect violence after wars. Section I outlines some of the methodological challenges in studying this relationship and how these have limited our capacity to draw causal conclusions. Sections II and III survey explanations for a positive relationship between war and postwar violence and the research related to those explanations. The ways in which the direct experience of war may raise the likelihood of postwar violence for individuals and societies are the focus of Section II. Section III explores how war may reshape postwar society, creating conditions that raise the motivations and opportunities for violence. Section IV considers arguments and evidence about how wars may reduce violence in their aftermath. Although these have received much less attention by scholars, they offer insight into why and how elevated rates of postwar violence can be avoided. We summarize our findings and offer some suggestions about how to avoid a postwar increase in violence in Section V.

## I. Challenges in Studying the Relationship between War and Postwar

Definitional and measurement issues challenge efforts to determine whether violence increases after wars and, if so, why. We begin by discussing issues relevant to the independent variable in this relationship—war—and then turn to those relevant to the dependent variable—postwar violence.

### A. Defining and Measuring War and Postwar

What qualifies as a war for purposes of studying its relationship to postwar violence is less straightforward than it might first appear. Societies and individuals wage war, but to varying degrees; these variations may be important for predicting postwar violence. Similarly, deciding when the postwar period begins and ends has implications for determining whether violence has changed and, if so, why.

1. *What Constitutes a War and Participation in It?*   When does armed conflict qualify as war? Many conflicts—World Wars I and II, several other major interstate wars (such as the Franco-Prussian War, the Sinai War, and the Vietnam War), as well as many intrastate or civil wars (such as the American Revolutionary and Civil Wars, the Salvadorian Civil War, and the Yugoslav Wars)—appear on all lists of wars compiled by scholars and have been included in studies of the relationship between war and postwar violence. Nevertheless, there are debates over the criteria for defining a civil war (as opposed to a rebellion, revolt, or coup) and for defining a country's participation in an interstate war (e.g., How many troops are sent? How long is the country involved? Does violence occur on the country's territory?) (Gleditsch et al. 2002; Collier and Hoeffler 2004; Rivera 2016). In the Correlates of War project (Singer and Small 1972; Small and Singer 1982), the leading source of global data on armed conflict since the early nineteenth century, for instance, a conflict with a minimum of 1,000 battle deaths annually qualifies as a war. The Troubles in Northern Ireland, then, would not be a war according to this definition. Consequently, some scholars use a much lower threshold, such as 25 battle deaths annually (Gleditsch et al. 2002).

Determining a war's start and end dates (and hence the beginning of the postwar period) can also be complicated. As Kurtenbach (2013) notes, civil wars can end through a negotiated peace settlement, outright surrender, or a de facto victory; but the dates on which any of these occur do not necessarily signal the end of fighting, and so "the boundary lines between war and peace are fluid" (Suhrke 2012, p. 6). Furthermore, some civil wars extend over decades, and some countries are involved in multiple, overlapping wars, making distinctions between pre- and postwar periods nearly impossible.

Similar issues arise when the focus is on how individuals' exposure to war affects postwar violence. Is military training in preparation for war sufficient to shape postwar behavior, or are any effects restricted to those who have been deployed to a combat zone or have killed and seen killing (Emsley 2014; Treadwell 2016)? For civilians, how much, if any, direct exposure to wartime violence and destruction is necessary to have an impact (and at what age or for how long)? Is mediated exposure—through images and language in the media or war propaganda—sufficient to influence postwar violence? Attention to such questions is vital, although usually lacking, when testing different explanations of postwar violence.

2. *What Constitutes the Postwar Period?* When does the postwar period begin and end? Clearly, if establishing when a war ends is difficult, then establishing when the postwar period begins is as well. Deciding on the end of the postwar period is, as Suhrke (2012, p. 6) notes, a matter of judgment: "The time element embedded in the term 'post' suggests the period cannot last too long, but how long is another matter." Some researchers argue that 5 years after the end of a war is an appropriate definition of the postwar period (Archer and Gartner 1976*b*; Boyle 2014), whereas others follow the UN convention of limiting "postwar" to 2 years (Grandi 2013*a*). Shorter periods, such as 2 years, may be insufficient if soldiers are not fully demobilized or occupying forces are still present. Even the 5-year convention can fail to capture the long-term effects of combat exposure or the effects on those who were children during a war (Emsley 2014; Couttenier et al. 2016). This is why some who study war's relationship to postwar violence consider effects as long as 10 years after a war's end (e.g., Collier and Hoeffler 2004),[2] while those who examine war's effects on veterans often use even longer time periods (e.g., Taft et al. 2009).

### B. Defining and Measuring Postwar Violence

Postwar violence takes many different forms, ranging from a state's use of violence in response to remnants of civil war fighting to protests by aggrieved veterans, collective violence motivated by revenge for wartime acts or by efforts to transform the postwar allocation of political power, and individual violence for reasons of personal gain or protection. We focus on research on individual and, to some extent, collective forms of postwar violence, rather than state violence, because the latter blurs what is often an indistinct line between wartime and peacetime.

1. *Conceptually Distinguishing among Types of Violence.* Some research on postwar violence is concerned primarily with interpersonal violence: violence motivated by personal goals or emotions and carried out by individuals, alone or in small groups of friends or acquaintances. Other research expands this to include nonpolitical forms of criminal violence committed by members of organized crime groups, gangs, and other or-

---

[2] Suhrke (2012, p. 7) goes even further, observing that the violent legacy of a war can extend for generations: "Contemporary racial violence in the United States, for instance, has roots in the civil war that ended more than 150 years ago and to that extent is postwar violence."

ganizations with illicit intent. These types of violence have been labeled expressive and instrumental (Boyle 2014) or opportunistic, vengeful, and anarchic (Grandi 2013*a*), and distinguished from strategic violence (Boyle 2014) or revolutionary, repressive, and revisionist violence (Grandi 2013*a*). Here, the extent to which violence is intended to serve political as opposed to personal ends is key.

These conceptual distinctions among types of violence are recognized as largely heuristic, because much postwar violence is "dual purpose," serving both collective, political goals and individual purposes (Green and Ward 2009). Lowe (2012) provides an example of this in describing a feud between two families that began in 1942 in occupied Greece and eventually left several people dead. A young man whose affections were not returned by a young woman sought revenge by telling Italian occupiers the woman was hiding weapons for a resistance group, leading to her being beaten by the occupiers. This set in motion a series of reprisals and revenge killings that extended into the postwar period. Similarly, postwar violence by state agents authorized to use it may also be motivated by personal interests. Because postwar violence can take varied forms and serve multiple purposes, it "eludes comprehensive theory-building" (Grandi 2013*a*, p. 310).

2. *Empirically Distinguishing among Types of Violence.* Some of this conceptual imprecision reflects the difficulties of operationalizing and measuring different types of postwar violence, especially after civil wars. Many societal-level studies, particularly statistical analyses of one or more countries, rely on official crime statistics on homicide or other violent crimes to measure postwar violence. Unfortunately, well-known problems with these statistics—for example, underreporting (especially of less serious violence or violence between intimates) and differential recording practices—often are exacerbated in postwar periods, because criminal justice agencies lack resources or citizens distrust the police or are afraid or unwilling to report victimizations for other reasons (e.g., Collier and Hoeffler 2004; Jarman 2004). Criminal justice agencies may also be under pressure to manipulate official statistics after a war, although for different reasons. For example, the state may have an interest in conveying the image of being in control and so may discourage the police and others from fully recording or reporting violent crimes (Berdal, Collantes-Celador, and Buzadzic 2012). Alternatively, to justify repressive tactics against certain groups, the state may encourage criminal justice agents to exaggerate

the threat of postwar violence or label politically motivated violent acts as apolitical crimes by criminal groups (Kurtenbach 2013).

In individual-level studies, postwar violence has been measured with an array of methods, including official records of arrest (or conviction), self-reports of victimization and perpetration, clinical interviews, and observations. These, too, have problems with validity and reliability that vary depending on the type or definition of violence. Some studies rely on measures of aggression, instead of violence (e.g., Roth, Ekblad, and Prochazka 2009; Nandi et al. 2015), particularly those examining the behaviors of children in postwar settings (e.g., Boxer et al. 2013; Gvirsman et al. 2014). In an unusually creative effort to determine the effects of exposure to civil war on subsequent violence, Miguel, Saiegh, and Satyanath (2011) measured propensity to use violence with the number of penalty cards for aggressive play given to soccer players from countries with recent histories of civil war. While such variation in the ways postwar violence is measured can increase ability to generalize beyond the most serious forms of violence, it also can limit the comparability of research findings and the reliability of any conclusions.

## C. Choosing Comparators

To what do we compare postwar violence to determine if it is higher than it would be had there been no war? Comparisons of levels of violence during war with violence after war, whether for individuals or societies, are inappropriate for a number of reasons (see, e.g., Mannheim 1941b; Willbach 1948; Archer and Gartner 1984). For example, violence in countries sending large numbers of soldiers to war in other countries is likely to drop because of the absence of young males, those most at risk of violence. In countries where fighting is taking place, the violence of war and other forms of violence may be indistinguishable in practice, even if not in theory; countries experiencing great loss of life and physical destruction are unlikely to have the resources to compile reliable data on criminal violence. Fortunately, there are a number of alternative comparators, at both the individual and societal levels.

1. *Comparing Violence at the Individual Level.* To determine whether exposure to or involvement in violence during war increases the likelihood of engaging in violence after war, one would ideally compare people before and after their wartime experiences. Not surprisingly, such longitudinal studies are rare. This is an important limitation in studies

of ex-combatants, in particular, because the military may attract, disproportionately recruit, or send into combat people who are prone to or have
histories of violence (Orcutt, King, and King 2003; MacManus et al.
2013). Indeed, during some wars convicted offenders have been offered
the option of joining the military rather than going to prison (Emsley
2014). Thus, if ex-combatants have higher rates of violence than noncombatants after wars, this could be due to selection effects rather than
any effects of war experience.[3] For these reasons, research on veterans
often compares levels of violence for those who served in combat and
those who did not or based on the length of exposure to combat (e.g.,
Calvert and Hutchinson 1990; Augsburger et al. 2015). Similarly, studies of civilians who experience war typically compare those who directly
observed or experienced violence with those who did not (e.g., Catani
2010; Saile et al. 2014).

 2. *Comparing Violence at the Societal Level.* Studying differences in
levels of prewar and postwar violence is often easier at the societal level
than it is at the individual level, especially in countries where statistics on
violent crime are regularly compiled. Many statistical analyses of one or
more countries are based on such comparisons (e.g., Mannheim 1955;
Rousseaux, Vesentini, and Vrints 2009). However, if the prewar period
is characterized by unusual conditions, such as social unrest or economic
crises that may be related to both the start of a war and high rates of violence, or is proximate to the end of an earlier war, comparisons to postwar years may underestimate any effect of war on violence. An alternative
approach is to compare postwar violent crime rates for countries involved
in a war with those of countries not involved in a war (e.g., Ghobarah,
Huth, and Russett 2003), a design strengthened by also comparing differences between pre- and postwar violence for each set of countries
(e.g., Sellin 1926; Archer and Gartner 1976b). Some researchers capitalize on subnational variations in wartime and postwar violence and ask
whether areas experiencing more violence and destruction during war
differ from areas less directly affected by wartime violence (Sánchez, Solimano, and Formisano 2005; Deglow 2016). These designs, however, are
limited in their ability to rule out selection effects: Wars are not randomly

---

 [3] Even when the violent behavior of people who fight in wars could be measured before
and after their war experience, the effects of aging could muddy the results. Hence, one
would need a second comparison: those of similar ages who did not fight in war. In this
case, selection bias again becomes an issue.

distributed among nations nor is wartime violence randomly distributed within nations, and so comparison groups may not be sufficiently similar to make strong causal claims. Furthermore, studies rarely consider the possibility that high levels of prewar violence make countries more prone to war (Collier and Hoeffler [2004] is an exception) or mean that the war was barely a "rupture with the previous universe" (Duclos 2012, p. 11) and so war itself was not a cause of postwar violence.

*D. Assessing Theoretical Mechanisms*

Identifying how and why war is related to postwar violence requires measuring the various mechanisms assumed to link the two, something research often falls short on. This is partially the fault of some of the explanations, which lack clarity about the specific processes by which war influences postwar violence, particularly those that feature concepts such as brutalization or habituation. Macro-level statistical studies probably are more prone to this limitation, because locating measures of constructs that are comparable across societies (for comparisons of warring and nonwarring countries) or over time (for pre- and postwar comparisons) is difficult, and these measures rarely capture key individual-level processes. Deglow (2016, p. 795), for example, notes that "in this study, the suggested causal mechanism linking war-related violence . . . to postwar violent crime is the erosion of legitimacy of local law enforcement agencies. . . . However, the causal mechanism cannot be directly measured in this study, and the theoretical implications of the observed patterns must be interpreted with caution."

Individual-level studies focusing on trauma or socialization processes, and context-rich case studies of particular countries after war, often do a better job of measuring or assessing intervening variables. Studies of ex-combatants, for example, often investigate whether PTSD symptomology mediates the relationship between exposure to or involvement in killing during war and postwar violence (e.g., Elbogen et al. 2014). Research on post–civil war violence in Latin America has documented changes in economic inequality after war or the extent to which public security has been militarized to support arguments about the conditions or processes responsible for high rates of postwar violence (Kurtenbach 2013; Howarth 2014). However, because the factors linking war and postwar violence frequently are assumed rather than directly measured, few of the explanations we discuss next have been systematically evaluated.

In sum, demonstrating the causal effect of war on individuals' or societies' postwar violence is fraught with methodological challenges. The wide variety of research designs and disciplinary approaches to studying this relationship limits our ability to compare studies systematically. Determining whether a society is more violent after a war than before a war is easier for more recent wars, because data on violence are more reliable and valid than in the past. But even for recent wars—particularly those in less economically developed countries—such data have considerable error. Identifying the conditions and processes responsible for a relationship between war and postwar violence suffers from similar difficulties. Nevertheless, the extensive scholarship on this relationship allows us to draw conclusions about general patterns as well as the complex processes that underlie them.

## II. The Experience of War Increases Postwar Violence

Individuals and societies that go through war undoubtedly are changed by the experience. Thus, high levels of violence in postwar periods are expected and explained by some as a consequence of war's effects on individuals' bodies and psyches and on a society's culture, effects that are present regardless of the outcome of a war. Erasmus captured this in *Complaint of Peace* when he wrote that "the injury done to the morals of the people, and the general good order and discipline of the state, is a loss which neither money, nor territory, nor glory can compensate" ([1517] 1813, p. 69). For some explanations, postwar violence is a consequence of the traumatic transformations wars produce in people who participate in or are directly exposed to war's violence. For others, wartime reorders cultural values inhibiting violence and teaches people that violence is justifiable, effective, and even enjoyable. The distinction between trauma-based and learning-based explanations is at times blurred in the research, as it may well be in reality, and so should not be overdrawn. Nevertheless, we discuss these two explanations separately, highlighting the scholars and work most closely associated with each.

### A. The Harms of War

War can damage people physically and psychologically, by subjecting them, their comrades, and their loved ones to violence, but also by allowing or compelling them to engage in violence. Much of the individual-level research on the trauma of war focuses on ex-combatants; however, with the growing number of civil wars in recent decades, studies of civilians caught up in and traumatized by war have increased. Societal-level studies tend not to distinguish between trauma-based and learning-based processes, in part because of the difficulties of empirically differentiating between the two with aggregate data. For this reason, we discuss how a society's wartime experiences may be linked to postwar violence in the section on lessons of war; in this section, we focus on studies of how individuals may be physically or psychologically harmed by war in ways that increase their violent behavior.

1. *Physical Harm.* Physical injuries, exposure to noxious substances, and drug use during war have been linked to postwar psychological and behavioral problems, including violent behavior, since at least the nineteenth century. Concussions and other brain injuries suffered during battle were suspected of causing mental derangement and criminal behavior, including violent offending, in some veterans of the American Civil War and World War I (Kleist 1934; Faust 2008). These suspicions were verified, to some extent, by subsequent research that found concussive and traumatic brain injury to be associated with "war neuroses" (Jones, Fear, and Wessely 2007), as well as aggression and violence (Brower and Price 2001). In the Vietnam Head Injury Study, for example, veterans with frontal lobe lesions due to penetrative head injuries were at elevated risk of aggression and, to some extent, violent behavior (Grafman et al. 1996). The long-term psychological and behavioral effects of exposure to the types of toxic chemicals often used in war—such as mustard gas, phosgene, and nerve agents—have received less attention (Wessely, Hyams, and Bartholomew 2001). However, at least one study of Vietnam veterans found that those exposed to Agent Orange were at higher risk of both PTSD and violent behavior (Levy 1988). Of course, civilians are often and increasingly exposed to such chemicals during war as well, with little-known long-term consequences for their violent behavior.

Drug use by soldiers during war stretches back to classical Greece. Throughout history a wide variety of psychoactive substances have been given to soldiers to increase stamina, reduce fear and pain, increase coping and physical strength, and reward good performance (Kamieński 2016). Amphetamines, opium, cocaine, and morphine were distributed to the armed forces during the Napoleonic Wars, the American Civil War, and both world wars, among others. The US military currently makes available "go pills" to pilots, steroids to those in the infantry, and anti-anxiety drugs and other psychopharmaceuticals to those with symptoms of PTSD (Lawver, Jensen, and Welton 2010; Drummond 2013; Wing and Ferner 2015). Some of these drugs on their own or in interaction with other drugs are associated with a host of psychological and behavioral problems, including increased violence and aggression, and may be addicting (Moore, Glenmullen, and Furberg 2010). To the extent their use continues after combatants return home, their risk of violence may increase (Breggin 2010). The provision of drugs to control recruits in some recent civil wars—such as that in Sierra Leone (Collier and Hoeffler 2004)—also has been linked to postwar violence. Similarly, Wright, Carter, and Cullen (2005), in their life course analysis of Vietnam veterans, contend that military service increased their drug use and subsequent offending rates. Other research on combat veterans of the Vietnam, Afghan, and Gulf Wars has found an association between postwar drug or alcohol abuse or dependence, which often began in the military, and intimate partner violence (Savarese et al. 2001; Cesur and Sabia 2016; Tharp et al. 2016b; for evidence regarding World War I, see Nelson [2007]).

2. *Psychological Harm.*  Directly witnessing and engaging in serious violence is psychologically distressing, and long-term exposure to and engagement in killing may lead to mental health problems that in turn are linked to behavioral problems, including violence. That combatants may suffer such harm was recognized as far back as the ancient Greeks and has been referred to as bullet wind, battle fatigue, and soldier's heart (Dean 1999; Schroder and Dawe 2007; Meineck 2016). As the term "soldier's heart" implies, the symptoms of psychological trauma were often linked to physical disability or damage and expected to diminish or disappear after war (Oppenheimer and Rothschild 1918). Near the end of the nineteenth century and with the rise of psychiatry, however, psychological trauma began to be recognized as a distinct diagnostic category (i.e., war neuroses; Young 1995) often unrelated to physical injury (such as concussive head injuries due to prolonged bombardment, or "shell shock") and as long-lasting.

Assessing the connection between psychological trauma in war and ex-soldiers' violent behavior afterward is difficult, if not impossible, with historical data. Systematic evidence of this relationship is therefore limited to more recent wars. Scores of studies of US and British veterans of various wars over the past 40 years have explored whether combat experi-

ences are related to PTSD and to postmilitary or postdeployment violence. Combat exposure, especially prolonged and heavy combat, has
been linked to PTSD and increased interpersonal violence, including intimate partner violence, among veterans of the Vietnam War (e.g., Boulanger 1986; Gimbel and Booth 1994; Beckham et al. 1997; Beckham,
Feldman, and Kirby 1998) and of the Afghan and Gulf Wars (e.g., Elbogen et al. 2012, 2013, 2014; MacManus et al. 2012). Furthermore,
specific wartime experiences—such as exposure to atrocities, fearing for
one's life, and participation in killing (rather than simply deployment to
a combat area)—also appear to raise the likelihood of both PTSD and violent behavior (Hiley-Young et al. 1995; Orcutt, King, and King 2003;
Taft et al. 2005). Importantly, however, not all studies find these relationships (e.g., Petrik, Rosenberg, and Watson 1983; Bouffard 2003; Tharp
et al. 2016a).

Drawing conclusions from this literature about whether war raises
postwar violence by traumatizing combatants is complicated by a number
of factors. Many of these studies do not take into account soldiers' prewar
experiences and orientations, particularly their propensity toward violence prior to joining the military. The concern that the military might
attract, disproportionately recruit, or send into combat individuals with
a propensity for violence or with preexisting troubles pervades the literature (e.g., Boulanger 1986; Calvert and Hutchinson 1990; Bouffard and
Laub 2004). In support of these concerns, some have found that those
with a history of criminal and violent behavior may be more likely to join
the military (Yager 1976; Wright, Carter, and Cullen 2005) or more likely
to be deployed in a combat role (Orcutt et al. 2003; MacManus et al.
2013). Furthermore, much of this research is based on small, select, and
often clinical samples, uses different conceptualizations and operationalizations of violence, and follows veterans for different lengths of time. If
we are to understand combat veterans' risk for postmilitary violence, then
we require more consistency with respect to measurement as well as a
more comprehensive picture of individuals' backgrounds prior to service,
experiences in the military, and lives afterward.

Whether psychological trauma, such as PTSD, mediates the relationship between combat exposure and postwar violence has also been de-
bated. For example, Elbogen et al. (2014) contend that the association
between PTSD and violence is weaker and less direct than is typically
believed (see also Emsley 2013) and suggest that comorbidity with alcohol misuse is critical. The strongest relationships between PTSD and ag-

gression or violence are associated with hyperarousal symptoms (i.e., the propensity to be hypervigilant, irritable, and quick to anger), whereas numbing or avoidance symptoms of PTSD appear not to be associated with subsequent violence (Savarese et al. 2001; Taft et al. 2007; MacManus et al. 2013). Nevertheless, the bulk of the research on Vietnam, Afghan, and Gulf War veterans from the United States and Britain points to an association between certain wartime experiences and feelings—particularly exposure to atrocities and mass killings, killing someone, and fearing for one's life—PTSD, and postwar aggression and violence.

Studies of the relationship between experience in combat, PTSD or psychological trauma, and postwar violence in non-Western countries have been less numerous by comparison, in part because many non-Western countries do not recognize or accept such Western-based mental health diagnoses (e.g., Schafer 2007; Le Huérou and Sieca-Kozlowski 2012). However, recent civil wars in Latin America and Africa have engendered interest in the topic. Some studies have found that adult ex-combatants, both male and female, have moderate to high levels of PTSD symptomology or trauma-related disorders, particularly among those who did not voluntarily join an armed force (e.g., Odenwald et al. 2007; de la Espriella, Sweetnam Pingel, and Falla 2010; Hecker et al. 2013; but see Schafer 2007). However, these symptoms or disorders are not consistently associated with subsequent aggression or violent behavior (Hecker et al. 2012), as illustrated by two studies of ex-combatants in the Burundian civil war. Augsburger et al.'s (2015) research comparing female ex-combatants and female civilians (some of whom had been exposed to wartime violence) found that the former suffered more severely from PTSD symptoms, but these symptoms did not predict their current aggression. In their comparison of active and former male combatants in Burundi on levels of and relationships among self-committed violence in war, trauma-related disorders, and current aggression, Nandi et al. (2015) also found higher levels of PTSD symptomology among ex-combatants, but lower levels of current appetitive aggression, when controlling for self-committed violence.[4] As these and other researchers note, studies of this sort are characterized by many of the same methodological problems identified in re-

---

[4] Appetitive aggression is defined as "the perpetration of violence and/or the infliction of harm to a victim for the purpose of experiencing violence-related enjoyment" (Weierstall and Elbert 2011, p. 1).

search on Vietnam, Afghan, and Gulf War veterans, which greatly limit the ability to make causal claims.

Child soldiers and their lives after war have attracted particular attention from politicians, the media, and researchers. Estimates suggest that over 300,000 boys and girls under the age of 18 participated in violent conflicts and wars in Asia, Africa, Europe, the Americas, and the former Soviet Union in recent years (Kerig and Wainryb 2013), and this group has been labeled a "time bomb" (BBC 2007) of "damaged and uneducated pariahs" (*New York Times* 2006) threatening postwar societies.

Some researchers have echoed these fears. Dickson-Gōmez (2003), for example, attributes the rise in gang violence in postwar El Salvador to youths who participated in and were traumatized by the country's civil war. Exposure to and involvement in severe violence during war has been shown to be traumatizing for child soldiers (relative to war-affected but noncombatant peers), as evidenced by elevated rates of psychiatric disorders, including PTSD (e.g., Kohrt et al. 2008; Klasen et al. 2010). However, the extent to which these disorders predispose ex–child soldiers to engage in violence is not clear, partly because research tends to focus on outcomes other than their postwar violent behavior, such as adjustment to school, the labor force, and family life.[5] Ertl et al.'s (2014) study of ex–child soldiers in northern Uganda is an exception, although they measured aggressiveness rather than violent behavior. They found that ex–child soldiers had been exposed to more traumatic events during the war and had higher levels of PTSD symptomology compared to youths exposed to war but who had not been combatants; furthermore, PTSD symptomology mediated the relationship between traumatic events and subsequent aggression. On the other hand, there are numerous studies, including ethnographic and longitudinal research, showing that ex–child soldiers are socially and psychologically resilient and do not differ from others in their aggression or involvement in violence in either adolescence or adulthood (e.g., Wessells 2006; Blattman and Annan 2010; Boothby and Thomson 2013).

Noncombatants, both adults and children, also experience violence during war—witnessing the killing of family members, living through aerial bombardment, being harmed by combatants—even if they do not en-

---

[5] Some research has considered "whether child soldiering in a previous dispute may increase both the willingness and opportunity to resume fighting in the post-conflict period" (e.g., Haer and Böhmelt 2016, p. 408).

gage in it. Here, too, some research has shown that the greater the exposure to these experiences, the more likely one is to develop symptoms
consistent with PTSD (e.g., Somasundaram and Sivayokan 1994; Macksoud and Aber 1996) and to engage in aggression or violence after the
war (e.g., Keresteš 2006; Qouta, Punamäki, and Sarraj 2008; Clark et al.
2010). However, only a handful of studies examine whether PTSD symptomology or other measures of psychopathology mediate the relationship between war experiences and subsequent violence or aggression. In
a two-generational study of children and their parents/guardians who
lived through civil war in Northern Uganda, Saile et al. (2014) found that
male guardians exposed to greater war trauma were more likely to develop PTSD symptoms and to engage in child maltreatment; the same
associations were not observed for female guardians (see also Catani,
Schauer, and Neuner 2008). Similarly, in their study of Albanian adults
mass-evacuated to Sweden during the Kosovo War, Roth, Ekblad, and
Prochazka (2009) also found positive associations between their experience of traumatic events and PTSD-related symptoms and between those
symptoms and subsequent physical aggression. In contrast, among minors from war-torn countries who became refugees in Germany, greater
exposure to violence in their home countries was associated with PTSD
symptom severity; however, these symptoms were not related to the
youths' aggression (Mueller-Bamouh et al. 2016). Another study of asylum seekers in Switzerland (Couttenier et al. 2016) concluded that the association between exposure to war trauma and subsequent violence among
this group was less likely to be due to psychological harm than to societal
changes caused by war.

The body of work examining the psychological harms of war and their
consequences for individuals' postwar violent behavior does not provide
a consistent picture of this association. This can be attributed, in part, to
the variety of methodological approaches and research designs used in
these studies and to difficulties in conducting research in societies recently riven by war. It may also be due to cultural differences in the understanding and experience of trauma and psychopathology, which could
explain why the evidence for trauma-based explanations of postwar violence is stronger in studies of US and British veterans. Most research in
this area has used Western-based concepts and operationalizations of
trauma-related psychological disorder that may be ill-suited to non-
Western contexts. In Russia after World War II, for example, there was

no expectation that the mass slaughter of war would lead to psychological disturbances in soldiers or civilians (Dale 2015), and Russian doctors and the broader public continue to be averse to this notion (Merridale 2001; see also Alexievich 1992; Le Huérou and Sieca-Kozlowski 2012). As Merridale (2001, p. 16) states, "They cannot picture it, this trauma, and they do not understand its privileged place in the Western understanding of violence and its consequences. It is also possible that this particular diagnosis and its treatment are so alien to the Russian way of thinking about life, death, and individual need that notions of psychological trauma are genuinely irrelevant to Russian minds." More generally, Western trauma-based perspectives on war have an individualistic focus that decontextualizes war experiences and ignores the broader cultural, economic, ethnic, and historical forces that shape their meaning (Bracken 1998; Barber 2009). The interplay of these forces, particularly in the postwar setting, along with individual differences in personality, coping styles, social support, and other personal characteristics, almost certainly affect whether and how horrific wartime experiences shape subsequent violent behavior.[6]

*B. The Lessons of War*

Participating in a war typically requires overcoming cultural prohibitions against the use of violence and learning to view violence as a necessary, effective, and even praiseworthy means to accomplish culturally desirable goals. Learning-based explanations of postwar violence can be applied to individuals, especially those in the military, in which case the lessons of war include gaining skills at and overcoming the disgust and fears of engaging in violence. Applied to societies as a whole, the learning process is less tangible, occurs through exposure to propaganda and other messages legitimizing violence, and can neutralize norms about nonviolence. Bonger ([1905] 1916, p. 518) referred to the effects war has on soldiers and societies alike when he wrote that "war arouses a spirit of violence not only in those who take part in it, but in the whole population." Because the skills and values learned in wartime do not disappear with the arrival of peace, the likelihood of postwar violence is greater.

---

[6] Others have critiqued trauma-based explanations of violence by veterans, noting that these pathologize veterans, such that "the violent disorder of veterans is not assumed to be normal for military personnel" (Murray 2016, p. 320).

1. *Military Service as a School for Violence.* The military as a social institution has a culture and structure designed to produce individuals able and willing to kill. On this topic Bonger (1916, p. 517) described the military, in war and peacetime, as characterized by "excessive discipline to the role of a machine" that debases and undermines men's moral qualities and arouses a "thirst for domination" not limited to combat situations. Military culture is also highly gendered and produces a form of "military masculinity" that extols toughness and aggressive heterosexuality and denigrates qualities—such as empathy—traditionally associated with femininity (Wadham 2016; Walklate and McGarry 2016). Emsley (2014, p. 17), among others (e.g., Nikolić-Ristanović 1996; Fregoso and Beharano 2010; McWilliams and Ní Aoláin 2013), links this form of masculinity not just to violence generally but specifically to violence against women: "The very nature of the armed forces fosters elements of aggressive masculinity that, in turn, can develop or encourage violent posturing and sexual boasting, both of which can prompt serious criminal behavior." These features of the military may be magnified for some if—because of their sex, age, personality, or family background—they are at elevated risk for violence when they join (Treadwell 2016).

All of these features of military culture are exaggerated during wartime, beginning with training in the use of violence, through the authorization of and rewards for extreme forms of violence intolerable in other contexts. The rewards of violence during war may not be limited to those officially bestowed on soldiers, but may also include a sensual pleasure in combat and face-to-face killing, as well as sexual release through rape during war (Broyles 1985; Bourke 1999). Civilian life may be numbingly boring by contrast, sending ex-soldiers in search of the thrill of risk taking and rule breaking they had experienced during war (Allport 2009; Emsley 2014).

That soldiers may return from war with a heightened taste for violence has incited popular fears and informed explanations of postwar violence by veterans for centuries. Hanawalt (1979, p. 234) notes that in fourteenth-century England, contemporaries blamed the lawlessness and violence of the day on men who had "learned pillage, rape, and murder during the wars," a claim repeated after England's late Elizabethan wars (Cockburn 1977), as well as its late seventeenth- and eighteenth-century wars (Beattie 1974; Hay 1982; Childs 1997). Indeed, popular concerns about violent crime by deserters and demobilized veterans led Parliament to ban "the impressment of convicts in 1596, but the post-demobilization crime waves continued," which Roth (2009, p. 32) attributes to "a brutal and profane military culture." Tallett (1992), too, cites evidence of postwar violence by ex-soldiers in many early modern European countries, where the violent habits soldiers had developed during war were faulted.

Whether this violence was more a product of postwar impoverishment and homelessness, or of prewar dispositions, than of the lessons of war is not clear. Indeed, the demobilization of soldiers following the Restoration in England in 1660 was a relatively calm affair, Tallett (1992, p. 146) notes, because the government paid ex-soldiers a substantial arrears that allowed them to avoid poverty and return to previous occupations. Furthermore, in the absence of more systematic evidence, Cockburn (1991) cautions against overstating demobilized veterans' contributions to postwar homicide rates in early modern England. Even so, similar concerns were expressed after the American Civil War—when veterans were seen as having developed not only a taste for violence but also the skills and expertise to use it effectively (Obert 2014)—and the Franco-Prussian War of 1870–71 (Starke 1884).

The world wars of the twentieth century provided more fodder for this argument. Mosse (1990), for example, a key proponent of the brutalization thesis,[7] argues that the effects of the valorization and legitimation of violence on soldiers was likely greater in the twentieth-century world wars because they were not fought primarily by professional armies, but by conscripts who were particularly vulnerable to exposure to military culture and wartime cruelties. The post–World War I increase in capital crimes in Germany by ex-soldiers with no previous criminal record is cited by Mosse (1990) in support of this thesis. Yet neither Liepmann (1930) nor Exner (1927), in their studies of (respectively) post–World War I Germany and Austria, saw the increases in murder and robbery as disproportionately due to veterans (see also Bessel 1993; Ziemann 2006). Similarly, the post–World War II wave of violent crime in Germany has not been linked to veterans, in particular, by either Mosse (1990) or others (Kramer 1988; Canoy 2007). Furthermore, after World War I, veterans in England and in British and French Africa did not show up in statistics of violent crime in unusual numbers (Emsley 2008; Fogarty and Killingray 2015; but see Nelson [2003] for evidence of vio-

---

[7] Mosse's (1990) brutalization thesis gives greater emphasis to how war changes attitudes and norms about violence than to how it traumatizes those who participate in it.

lent crimes by Australian veterans of World War I). On the basis of his study of prison records, Hakeem (1946) concluded there was no evidence of a "wish to kill" among US veterans after World War II. According to Emsley's (2013, p. 173) review of evidence from both world wars, then, "Brutalized, violent veterans who created crime waves made good stories for the press but . . . are hard to find."

For a number of civil wars of recent decades, however, there is suggestive evidence that brutalized veterans have contributed disproportionately to postwar violence. For example, according to Fregoso and Beharano (2010), the high rates of violence against women in post–civil war Guatemala and El Salvador are due to the "military machismo" of ex-soldiers and their use of violence against women as a terrorizing tactic during these wars. Samset (2012) makes a similar argument in explaining widespread sexual violence after the 1998–2002 war in Eastern Congo. Relatedly, Nikolić-Ristanović (1998, p. 474) asserts that former soldiers were responsible for high rates of serious violent crimes, including domestic violence, after the war in the former Yugoslavia: "The phenomenon of abstract hatred directed against other nationalities has been smoothly transformed into a hatred against very close persons, such as wives, children and relatives." That engaging in violence in combat may be experienced as exciting and appealing, and may increase the likelihood of appetitive aggression after war, has received some support from studies of male and female combatants in Burundi's civil war (e.g., Augsberger et al. 2015; Nandi et al. 2015). Perhaps intrastate wars, with their less distinct shifts from war to "not war" and from combatant to ex-combatant, create conditions particularly conducive to the lessons of war bleeding into peacetime.

In sum, although some and perhaps many ex-soldiers internalize the lessons of war and act on them in peacetime, the image of masses of veterans habituated to violence that has fed popular fears for centuries may be more mythic than real (Archer and Gartner 1976a). Furthermore, a narrow focus on ex-combatants as risky or at-risk subjects elides questions about the role of the state and the military in exposing men and women (and sometimes children) to training and combat experiences that have long-term consequences for their lives. As Brown, Stanulis, and McElroy (2016, p. 30) note, "it is much easier to simply assign the veteran who commits a crime into the 'selection error' category than to study the problem and develop prevention techniques" (see also Jamieson 1998).

2. *War's Effects on the Broader Culture.* The state's use and legitimation of violence during war has been blamed for weakening cultural values that constrain violent behavior both during and after war. For Mosse (1990), societies as well as soldiers are brutalized by war, an argument reflected in work by Steenkamp (2014, p. 6), who states that "war shapes the norms and values which govern the use of violence to create a 'culture of violence' which makes the use of violence in daily life possible and acceptable." Because of this change in the broader culture, violence in the postwar period will not be restricted to individuals or societies directly exposed to wartime violence. Indeed, the valorization and sanctioning of violence during war may be "more credible to civilians than to combat soldiers with direct experience of the realities of war," lowering "the threshold for using homicide as a means of settling conflicts in everyday life" (Archer and Gartner 1976*b*, p. 960). Males may be particularly susceptible to cultural messages about violence during wartime, because these are often linked to (re)constructions of masculinity that emphasize men's roles as protectors, providers, and warriors (Steenkamp 2014, p. 131). As a consequence, the socialization of male children during and immediately after wartime may tolerate and encourage aggression and violence as they grow into adolescence and adulthood.[8]

Studies of individuals exposed to war shed some light on these arguments. Like others who draw on social cognition and learning theories in studies of children exposed to wartime violence (e.g., Qouta, Punamäki, and Sarraj 2008; Dubow et al. 2010; Landau et al. 2010), Boxer et al. (2013) find weak but significantly positive effects of exposure to political violence on subsequent serious physical violence among Palestinian, Israeli Jewish, and Israeli Arab children. They link this to the effects of political violence on "the violence level in more proximal environments (e.g., community, school, peers, and family), which in turn affect a youth's socialization" (pp. 163–64). In an extension of this work, researchers have also studied adolescents and young adults who have grown up in countries experiencing wars. Beckley (2013), for example, looked at the criminal records of over 25,000 16–28-year-old male migrants to Sweden to determine whether their violent and property offending was related to exposure to war in their home countries. Those who were present in their countries during war had higher rates of violent offending; how-

---

[8] For evidence of relationships among war, socialization for aggression, and violent behavior outside of war in nonstate societies, see Ember and Ember (1994) and Armit (2011).

ever, those who came from countries with lengthier histories of war between 1946 and 1975 (before any of the migrants were born) did not. For
Beckley these findings are inconsistent with culture of violence arguments, because she did not find a positive relationship between presence
during wartime and property offending; however, her conclusion ignores
the possibility that cultural changes may be specific to violent behavior. In addition, Beckley cannot rule out alternative explanations for her
findings—such as the possibility that a culture of violence preexists war
and explains both war and higher rates of postwar violence—leaving her
results open to a number of interpretations.[9]

Studies of particular postwar societies offer some support for learning
explanations by identifying specific processes responsible for and representative of war's influence on the wider culture. World War I produced
an "escalating violence of language and visual representation . . . reflecting the process of brutalization" of postwar German society, according to Mosse (1990, p. 177). He pointed to the greater lenience with
which the legal system responded to "so-called patriotic acts of violence"
(p. 171) as further evidence of this cultural shift. Northern Ireland's
30-some-years-long Troubles had a similar cultural impact, Jarman
(2004, p. 435) argues:

> Apart from the more obvious influences that living through a sustained
> militarized conflict has on the people and their society, one can also
> point to the legitimizing impact of a wider culture of commemoration
> and celebration, the annual cycle of parades that are held to mark the
> anniversaries of wars, battles, risings and martyrs. There is also a
> growing popular culture of paramilitarism and resistance which has
> been elaborated through the media of writing, song, music and the
> painting of elaborate murals . . . [and which] helps to legitimize certain
> forms of violent or criminal activity.

The Guatemalan government's impressment of nearly a million civilians to serve in armed civil patrols during its recent civil war provides

[9] A number of macro-level studies use a country's history of war (measured, e.g., by
number of wars or battle deaths in wars) as a measure of a cultural orientation toward
violence to predict homicide rates (see, e.g., Gartner 1990; Fox and Hoelsher 2012;
Lappi-Seppälä and Lehti 2014) and generally find a positive relationship between the
two. In general, however, these studies do not interpret this as support for the idea that
wars are responsible for cultures of violence, but rather that wars are an indicator of cultural tolerance of violence.

another example, in Steenkamp's view (2011, p. 361), of how the legitimization of violence during war "taught civilians how to use violence and established a culture of violence that outlived the conflict." (See Bourgois [2001] for a similar argument regarding the civil war in El Salvador.) Archer and Gartner (1976*b*) also interpreted their finding that postwar homicide rates were significantly higher than prewar rates in the majority of the 50 "nation-wars" in their study as more consistent with a legitimation of violence model than other explanations. Postwar homicide rates were higher in both defeated and victorious nations, in nations with better and worse postwar economies, and after both large and small wars.

Brutalization, legitimization of violence, and other culturally based explanations face some important challenges, however. Because of the difficulties in measuring cultural values, these explanations are difficult to test directly and may be supported more by the absence of disconfirming evidence than through direct validation. Furthermore, these explanations do not account for why some nations do not experience high rates of postwar violence or why most combatants or civilians exposed to cultural messages extolling violence do not become violent after wars (Chaudhary 2012; Edele and Gerwarth 2015). As Kleck (1987, p. 246) suggests, one key question "is whether ordinary potential individual aggressors perceive representatives of their government, such as soldiers or policemen, as relevant behavior models." He concludes that "Americans apparently do not," on the basis of his analysis of homicide rates in the United States after World War II, the Korean War, and the Vietnam War. Brutalization or legitimation explanations also are vague as to how long war's effects on cultural attitudes toward violence last—clearly not indefinitely since interpersonal violence has declined over the centuries.

Critics of learning and culture-based explanations, then, see them as uninformative about the conditions under which war's violence transmutes into postwar violence. What is needed, then, is more attention to how long wars last (and thus the length of exposure to war's "lessons"), prewar levels of violence for individuals and societies (e.g., was a culture of violence already present?),[10] the type of war (e.g., inter- versus intrastate wars, where civilians are more profoundly affected), and many other

---

[10] Warner et al. (2007), e.g., do not find higher assault rates after war in eighteenth-century Portsmouth, England, which they attribute to the endemic nature of violence in this military town.

factors that would shape the extent to which a culture of violence extends beyond wartime. Equally as important is greater attention to the conditions of postwar society, which will affect the likelihood that the lessons of war will increase postwar violence.

### III. Postwar Conditions Increase Postwar Violence

Regardless of whether wars harm people and traumatize societies or teach lessons that legitimate violence, wars have a profound impact on postwar society and can create conditions under which war's trauma and lessons are more likely to be expressed through violent behavior. This is why, historically, scholars have blamed a range of "abnormal political, economic and social conditions born out of the war" (Sellin 1926, p. 34) for high rates of postwar violence. Explanations of postwar violence that emphasize war's indirect effects can be distinguished by whether they focus on war's damage to social, economic, and political institutions or on the social changes that accompany the transformation from war to peacetime. This distinction is rarely acknowledged in the literature and is largely heuristic: clearly any damages due to war shape how the transition to peace will play out. Nevertheless, we see it as a useful way to organize a series of interrelated arguments about the conditions under which postwar societies will be at increased risk of violence.

### A. War Damages Postwar Societies and Their Institutions

In societies that experience massive wartime destruction and loss of life, large numbers of displaced persons and orphaned young people, and the collapse of many state and social institutions that provide basic resources and services, traditional informal and formal social controls are likely to be weak or even nonexistent; motivations to use violence for protection, predation, and profit are likely to be strong; and weapons left over from the war may be widely available (Sutherland and Cressey 1960; Muggah 2006). For Boyle (2014, pp. 51, 53), postwar societies are similar to weak states because they "are beset by poor governance, violent crime, economic problems such as unemployment and inflation, and poor infrastructure," with the result that "many of the basic institutions of public life . . . are nonexistent or dysfunctional." In this section we explore how damage to infrastructure, economic instability, and weakened public security institutions caused by war could lead to an increase in violence. These conditions are particularly likely to affect the postwar context in defeated countries and countries coming out of civil wars.

1. *War's Damage to Physical Infrastructure and Economic Stability.* When war is fought on a country's soil, combatants do their best to destroy places where the enemy can hide, sources of food the enemy can feed itself with, roads and bridges the enemy can travel on, and factories that provide the enemy with weapons and matériel. Prior to aerial bombardment, which could wreak such havoc over vast tracts of land from a distance, soldiers would burn towns, fields, and orchards or pour poisons down wells and into rivers and streams. During the 100 Years' War in fourteenth- and fifteenth-century France, for example, these practices dislocated large swathes of the population, impoverished those living in rural areas, and caused starvation in urban areas well into the postwar period; for many, brigandage and robbery were the only means to survive after the war (Cohen 1996). This pattern has repeated itself with dreary regularity since then. In contrast, when invading forces do not penetrate and local leaders can protect and provide for their constituents—such as in the Shenandoah Valley during the American Revolution—increases in postwar violence can be avoided (Roth 2009, p. 173).

Because of technological advances in weaponry, such destruction during twentieth-century wars could be escaped only through geographic distance. During World War I, although England suffered through 51 bombing raids by German zeppelins, the extent of physical destruction and dislocation was much less than on the continent. Consistent with the expectations of war's destructive effects on postwar society, England was the only country in Sellin's (1926) study that did not experience increases in postwar homicide rates. Germany, France, and Italy each did. The devastation of World War I was nothing as compared to that of World War II, however, when entire cities were wiped out, millions of people left homeless, industrial centers and transportation networks obliterated, and rural areas deforested and left barren, rendering postwar Europe a "savage continent" prone to outbreaks of violence (Lowe 2012). Germany and Russia were particularly hard hit by both the destruction of war and postwar violence, according to Kramer (1988) and Dale (2015). In contrast, the damage from bombing during World War II does not appear to have raised homicide rates in Japan; however, robberies were seen as epidemic and often linked to the need for food or other basic goods caused by the physical destruction of the country (Dower 1999, pp. 108–10).

Even when a country does not experience physical destruction, the end of war can create economic instability and need, particularly when masses of demobilized men must earn a living. In addition, while wartime often increases opportunities for paid work, whether at home or in the military, many of these opportunities may disappear following the war's conclusion. Beattie (1977), for example, links the closing down of jobs that had emerged during the War of Austrian Succession in 1748 to increases in crime, both violent and nonviolent, in postwar England. Similarly, wartime also increases opportunities for illicit "employment" in black markets; if these are disrupted by the arrival of peace, motivations for violence may grow (Nussio and Howe 2016). Civil wars may be particularly prone to postwar economic instability because a country's economic resources have been depleted by both sides to the conflict; former enemies in competition within a reduced labor market can be a recipe for violent behavior (Binford 2002; Rivera 2016).

2. *War's Damage to Public Security and Political Legitimacy.*   A key obligation of a state is to protect its citizens through institutions of public security. When states fall short on this, their legitimacy in the eyes of citizens declines and people may be inclined or forced to provide their own protection through violence. Wartime can weaken institutions of public security by draining them of human resources (i.e., adult males) they typically rely on and, when occupying forces take over these institutions, by undermining their legitimacy. Rebuilding these institutions after war and regaining people's trust in them take time. This postwar "public security gap" and the resulting loss of the deterrent effect of the law and trust in the state have been blamed for high rates of postwar violence, particularly after revolutions or civil wars (Call and Stanley 2001; Cawthra and Luckham 2003; Steenkamp 2014). In America after the Revolutionary and Civil Wars, for example, the areas most distant and isolated from the reach of the legal system or where the law was held in disrepute were particularly prone to increases in both politically and personally motivated violence (Roth 2009).

The strongest evidence linking a postwar public security gap to postwar violence comes from more recent wars, perhaps because before the nineteenth century many states did not have well-developed public security institutions that were effective at preventing crime; hence, wars may have had only limited impact on the law's deterrent capacity. After the two world wars, rising levels of violence were linked to the state's diminished ability to protect citizens in many European countries. In Belgium in the years immediately after World War I, for example, banditry re-emerged as a major crime problem, in part because of war-weakened criminal justice and police agencies (Rousseaux, Vesentini, and Vrints 2009; Leloup, Rousseaux, and Vrints 2014). Similarly, for European nations that were occupied during or defeated in World War II, chaos often reigned during the immediate postwar period because of "the lack of any form of law and order [which] meant that murders went unreported, uninvestigated, and often unnoticed" (Lowe 2012, p. 92).

Civil wars since the mid-twentieth century offer numerous examples of public security gaps and their consequences. Several analysts of post–civil war Guatemala have described a general impunity for crimes that encouraged vigilante violence, lynchings, and gang activity. Torres (2008), for example, notes that only about 2 percent of the 5,000 or so murders occurring annually in Guatemala after the war were investigated by police (see also Godoy 2002; Fernández Garcia 2004). In post–civil war El Salvador, peace accords stipulated that existing police forces be dissolved and replaced with a national force; during the 2 years it took to put the new force in place, the country's violent crime rate soared (Call 2007; Höglund 2008). In contrast, the decline in Lebanon's homicide rate after its civil war has been attributed to "an enhancement of its coercive apparatus" and more effective crime detection and deterrence (Richani 2007). The Lebanese example raises questions, however, about potential costs of strengthening a postwar state's security sector. Cruz (2011), for example, argues that many Latin American countries did not have effective security institutions before their civil wars; and the strengthening of these institutions afterward sometimes has meant recruiting people from the groups involved in criminal activities during the war or ex–military personnel. In turn, this has enabled some postwar states to engage in highly repressive strategies to control crime and violence that may have the opposite effect (Kurtenbach 2013).

Ineffective or highly repressive institutions of public security can undermine the legitimacy of the law enforcement arm of the state, which may also lead to postwar violence. In her analysis of postwar violent crime in Northern Ireland, for example, Deglow (2016, p. 790) found support for the hypothesis that "violence by antigovernment groups [during a war] is particularly likely to contribute to the erosion of law enforcement legitimacy and hence to a postwar public security gap that facilitates violent crime" after the war (see also Jarman 2004). State legitimacy, which has been linked to trends in violent crime (LaFree 1998), can also be undermined where a war is unpopular, reinforces political divisions, or ends in defeat. For instance, in Roth's (2009) view the erosion of government legitimacy during and after the French and American Revolutions, the American Civil War, World War II in Germany, and US involvement in the Vietnam War explains the patterns of postwar homicide in these countries (see also Brown 2006). The legitimacy of the state in post–civil war societies is likely to be particularly precarious, which can set the stage for further violence, both political and personal (Babo-Soares 2012; Peou 2012).

3. *War Motivates Reprisals and Revenge.*   The suffering and losses experienced during war can be a strong motivator for revenge and reprisal violence after war; and the absence of strong public security institutions creates fertile grounds for its expression (Grandi 2013*a*). Boyle (2012) sees a value in distinguishing between these two types of violence in postwar societies. He defines revenge violence as "acts of expressive violence against a member of a targeted group with the intention of punishing them for a previous act of violence." Reprisal violence, in contrast, is "an act of strategic violence directed against a member of a targeted group in response to a prior or precipitate act" (p. 96). In other words, revenge violence tends to be motivated by emotion (e.g., sorrow, anger), be uncoordinated or loosely coordinated, target people on personal grounds, and be proportionate to the prior act; reprisal violence is more instrumental, is organized and engaged in by groups, is aimed at changing the balance of power in an area, and "is neither reciprocal or proportionate" (p. 98). Wars, especially when fought on an individual's or a group's home ground, promote both types of postwar violence.

Revenge impelled many men, combatants and noncombatants, to commit murders after the American Revolutionary and Civil Wars, according to Roth (2009). For some Revolutionary War patriots and loyalists, "it was clear that no cease-fire could put an end to the enmity between the two camps; it was too strong and too personal, and it would spill past the verges of the war and seep into the lives of the children and grandchildren of combatants" (p. 166). Likewise, in some parts of the US South, such as the Cumberland Plateau, "in the first years after the war, men killed mostly for revenge" (p. 337). What Lowe (2012, p. 77) terms the "forces of vengeance" also swept across Europe and were "a fundamental part of the bedrock on which postwar Europe was built" (see also Kramer 1988). Those who had collaborated with the Nazis were targeted everywhere, but particularly in Italy, where an estimated 12,000–20,000 people were killed very soon after the war's end before occupying forces arrived and established a form of law and order (Lowe 2012, p. 150; see also Grandi 2013*b*). Lack of trust in the willingness and ability of new police forces and courts to punish misdeeds during the war appropriately also drove violence against collaborators and members of some ethnic groups in postwar Yugoslavia (Lowe 2012, pp. 249–65). Elsewhere, some governments encouraged such reprisal violence. In Czechoslovakia, for example, the government in exile called for the rape of female collaborators and the murder of German and Hungarian minorities in retribution for their support for the Nazis (Frommer 2005).[11]

Reprisal and revenge violence has been well documented in many post–civil war societies, including Sri Lanka (de Silva 2008), Uganda (Rice 2009), and Colombia (Nussio and Howe 2016). One of the most in-depth analyses of these forms of postwar violence is Boyle's (2012) case study of Kosovo after its 1998–99 war. He argues that "the conceptual inter-relationship between revenge and reprisal violence confers a strategic advantage on actors who engage in carefully organized campaigns of reprisal after wars by allowing them to mask their actions as 're-venge' by individuals settling personal grievances" (p. 96). In the immediate postwar period, revenge killings by individuals and small groups predominated, but within a year reprisal attacks by the Kosovo Liberation Army (KLA)—with the goal of ousting Serbs and Roma from Albanian regions—largely had replaced these, despite the presence of a major UN peacekeeping mission. By "employing the metaphor of revenge" (p. 102), the KLA avoided blame and political responsibility for the violence, a strategy that highlights the difficulties of distinguishing between political and personal violence after wars.

4. *War Creates Opportunities for Illicit Economies.* During war, organized crime groups and networks of criminal entrepreneurs often turn to or increase their trafficking in arms, drugs, stolen goods, illegally extracted natural resources, humans, and more (Sánchez, Solimano, and Formisano 2005; Höglund 2008; Cockayne and Lupel 2009). For militias

---

[11] Lowe (2012, p. 56) also discusses the routine rape and exploitation of women by soldiers during and after World War II but questions the extent to which it reflected a desire for retribution: "The fact that the incidence of rape was high for several years after the war suggests that it was not motivated solely by revenge as many people contend—instead we are confronted with the far more worrying suggestion that many soldiers committed rape merely because they could."

or insurgents fighting civil wars, as well as for violent state leaders and warlords, collusion with organized crime groups provides a source of funding (Nordstrom 2004; Green and Ward 2009). They may have few incentives "to relinquish these networks and the profits it produces when the war is over" (Steenkamp 2014, p. 60). When weak postwar states cannot provide protection for their citizens, organized crime groups may be well positioned to step in—if they have not already done so during the war—by offering illegal protection systems to individuals, groups, and even state actors (Nussio and Howe 2016).

Organized crime groups and criminal gangs are not at a loss for new recruits after wars. Mercenaries and paramilitary soldiers with little or no political agenda and out of work once fighting ceases are easy converts to criminal organizations (Call and Stanley 2001; Rivera 2016). The combat skills and weapons they accrued during war may make veterans in general attractive to criminal gangs and organized crime groups that can offer greater financial rewards than does licit employment. These opportunities may be particularly attractive to convicted criminals who joined the military as an alternative to imprisonment or because they were released from prison to serve in the military (Mannheim 1941a; Emsley 2014; Dale 2015). Thus, the persistence of illegal war economies, especially where a public security gap exists, may result "in a homicidal peace in which post-war killings equal or exceed those in war" (Cooper 2006, p. 20).

There is no lack of historical evidence of demobilized soldiers—lacking work, in possession of weapons, and skilled at violence—forming armed groups following wars that robbed and pillaged to survive or that hired themselves out to private interests to protect, extort, or terrorize on command (see, e.g., Egmond 1993; Lange 2007; Obert 2014). By and large, however, these groups emerged after wars rather than from wartime illicit networks and organizations, at least until the nineteenth or twentieth century. In the twentieth century, however, wars often saw the growth of criminal organizations, which extended their reach and their violence into the postwar years. The years after the Russian Revolution of 1917 and the 1918 civil war, for example, became known as the country's "gangster period." Gilinskiy and Kostjukovsky (2007, p. 188) describe it this way: "Against the backdrop of general crisis and discontent, the weakening of state authority, and the Civil War that began in 1918, the activities of criminal organisations intensified. In addition to the current members, these organisations recruited new followers among the peasants ruined by the war, deserters, and criminals amnestied by the bourgeois Revolution of February 1917." Sometimes organized crime groups that were repressed prior to wartime are revived by the anarchy of war and the immediate postwar period. We saw this when the American invasion of Sicily in 1943 breathed new life into the Italian mafia, which had suffered during the Mussolini era. By the end of World War II, it had gained control of the thriving black market, drawing new recruits from bandit gangs, and reinserting itself into the political and economic life of Italy through its reputation for violence (Lupo 2009).

Civil wars in the last half of the twentieth century have had particularly strong connections to organized crime or have been funded by illegal activities that persist after war. The spike in serious and violent crimes in Northern Ireland in the early 2000s, according to Jarman (2004), was due to feuding over drug territory among Loyalist paramilitary groups that had developed links to organized crime during the Troubles. Similarly, after the Bosnian War, many forms of criminal violence escalated, which Boyle (2014) has attributed to the expansion of criminal gangs and organized crime—an expansion made possible in part by the appointment of members of criminal organizations to formal control agencies and political positions during the war (Nikolić-Ristanović 1998). Insurgents often are dependent on profits from illegal activities to finance their movements; in Colombia, for example, the Revolutionary Armed Forces of Colombia funded itself through kidnapping, extortion, and drug trafficking (Sánchez, Soliman, and Formisano 2005). But state actors, particularly those in the military, also often capitalize on the disruption of wartime to make money in illegal markets. For instance, the illegal trade in timber that enabled the Khmer Rouge to continue its military campaign did not end with the 1991 Paris Peace Accords; instead, it continued to flourish—as did the intimidation, kidnapping, and killing that went with it—with the support of military actors who personally profited from it (Le Billon 2000). As a consequence, Steenkamp (2014, p. 83) notes, "when war is perceived as being so conducive to profiteering and material gain, military leaders have little incentive to abandon it for peace and a return to legal existence."

In this section, we have reviewed the ways in which the waging of war—and particularly the devastation and chaos that accompany it—creates social, economic, and political conditions conducive to violence in the postwar period. The ravages of war can transform the relationship between citizens and their state, with ill effects on relationships among citizens when this transformation opens opportunities, increases incentives, and feeds motivations for violent behavior. The war-induced possibilities for violence described in this section are most likely to be realized in countries that directly experience fighting, destruction, and death on their own territory. How long these possibilities remain open depends on how the transition to peacetime unfolds, as we discuss next.

## B. The Transition to Peace and Postwar Violence

In her analysis of postwar violence in Central America, Kurtenbach (2013, p. 105) asserts that "it should be no surprise that violence does not necessarily end with the signature of a peace accord, a cease-fire or the fading out of organized warfare" given that "the transition out of war produces insecurity." Understanding the persistence of violence after a civil war, in her view, requires attention to how the war was terminated and the nature of peace accords, postwar reform policies aimed at alleviating societal grievances and cleavages (which often are the cause of the war), and institutional reconstruction, particularly of the security sector. It is not only after civil wars that the transition to peace may set the stage for criminal and other forms of violence, however. After interstate wars, differences in demobilization processes, economic agendas, and social relations altered during wartime also may explain differences in postwar violence.

1. *Postwar Demobilization and Reintegration of Combatants.* Demobilization creates a set of conditions, both psychological and structural, that are unrelated to ex-soldiers' experiences during war, but may be conducive to violence by ex-soldiers. The end of military service and combat may leave veterans without a sense of purpose or the supportive camaraderie they had previously known, and civilian life may seem directionless or empty (Allport 2009; Emsley 2014). If, in response, veterans seek each other out to recreate that camaraderie and in so doing reproduce the type of military masculinity described earlier, tendencies toward violence may be reinforced. Demobilized soldiers in the tens and even hundreds of thousands were regular and worrisome features of their home countries after the many European wars of the sixteenth, seventeenth, and eighteenth centuries (Hay 1982; Lawson 1986; Tallett 1992). Often regarded as little better than criminals, at times owed substantial arrears by their governments, and competing for work in what could be inflexible and overcrowded labor markets, ex-soldiers sometimes re-

sponded by turning to crime—particularly robbery and banditry—to survive (Childs 1997; Rogers 2012).

As noted above, however, postwar crime waves attributable to demobilized soldiers were neither inevitable nor as frequent as many contemporaries feared. Where the economy was strong and where governments took measures to ameliorate ex-soldiers' grievances or ease the transition to civilian life, increases in violent crime were likely to be avoided. Childs (1997, p. 12), for example, identifies a number of major disbandments in seventeenth-century England that "do not appear to have caused particular difficulties in absorbing veterans back into civilian life." He attributes the successful demobilizations in part to actions by the British Parliament, such as its enactment of statutes allowing disbanded soldiers to practice trades without having to complete an apprenticeship and exempting them from arrest for debt for 3 years.

The reception veterans receive by their families and intimate relations, as well as by society as a whole, can also influence their inclinations to violence. If, for instance, spouses or intimate partners have been involved with others or seek to end their relationships, veterans may respond with violence toward their partners or their rivals (Allport 2009; Emsley 2013). More recent wars have been followed by riotous and violent behavior by demobilized soldiers aggrieved at what they viewed as poor treatment by military and government officials on their return home, angry at those at home who appeared to have prospered (and, in the ex-soldiers' eyes, often illegally) during the war, or no longer willing to put up with discriminatory treatment based on class or race after serving their countries. When veterans feel their wartime sacrifices are not appreciated or when fears about "brutalized veterans" are stoked by the media or public figures, resentment, anger, and frustration may fuel aggression by ex-soldiers (Bourke 1999; Edele and Gerwarth 2015; Murray 2016). The same may occur where economic prospects for veterans are limited or where veterans believe certain groups have profited from the war while experiencing little hardship (Rosenbaum 1940; Cooper 2006; Leloup et al. 2014).

Several examples are demonstrative. Riots and mutinies by demobilized soldiers occurred immediately after the end of World War I in England, Canada, the United States, and Australia, among other countries (Morton 1980; Voogd 2008; Crotty 2017). In the United States, the Red Summer of 1919 saw a number of riots—most notably in Chicago (Williams 2007)—in which black veterans fought back against attacks by whites on black individuals and neighborhoods (Voogd 2008). Violence by Australian veterans of World War I was more well organized: the Returned Sailors' and Soldiers' Imperial League of Australia "strategically used violence" to gain concessions from the government, but also "deployed violence against 'outsider' or disloyal elements of Australian society with the tacit approval of the authorities" (Crotty 2017, p. 186). These conditions may be exacerbated after civil wars for combatants on the losing side, especially if they feel grievances they had with the state or powerful social groups prior to the war are not addressed.

As wars have shifted from interstate to intrastate conflicts, demobilization has become a focus of governments and international bodies because, as Rivera (2016, p. 87) notes, "in the wake of civil wars a large number of combatants are demobilized and are likely to participate in criminal activity, particularly because armed conflicts hinder countries' economies and former combatants face severe barriers to entry to the labor market." In El Salvador, for example, more than 60,000 guerrillas, soldiers, and civil defense guards were demobilized (and hence left without employment) all within a few weeks of the end of the civil war (Call 2003); homicide rates in the country soared to the highest levels in the western hemisphere soon after (Richani 2007). Among others (e.g., Call and Stanley 2001; Kurtenbach 2013), Binford (2002, p. 208) attributes this rise in violence in part to "high levels of postwar unemployment and underemployment, disgruntled former soldiers and guerrillas who were left out of the material settlement (land, etc.), the ready availability of military weaponry, [and] the involvement of former elements of the National Guard and National Police in well-organized and well-equipped criminal bands."

Demobilization does not inevitably lead to postwar violence, however. After the civil war ended in Uganda in 1992, 20,000 soldiers were transported back to their home areas, where they were required to set up bank accounts to receive government payments; as a consequence, demobilization reduced criminal violence among those who had access to land (Collier 1994). Mozambique's approach to demobilization after its civil war—which included heavy emphasis on local conflict resolution processes—has often been cited as a success story (Nordstrom 1997; Duclos 2012). The reintegration programs for ex-combatants established after the war were the "most comprehensive ever attempted at the time" (McMullin 2004, p. 626) and helped keep levels of postwar violence in check.

2. *Peace Settlements and Postwar Reconstruction.* The nature of peace settlements and efforts at reform and reconstruction, as Suhrke (2012,

p. 3) points out, can help explain patterns of postwar violence. States, both those experiencing a war and those playing a role in brokering a war's end, can increase the likelihood of violence after war through their actions and capabilities as much as through their inactions and weaknesses (Cooper 2006). If postwar states respond to violence through highly repressive policies and practices that target and demonize certain groups, this may backfire and encourage more violence. Likewise, peace agreements that fail to recognize and address grievances of the defeated country or rebel groups can lay the groundwork for both political and interpersonal forms of violence (Kurtenbach 2013).

In modern times, the number of governmental and nongovernmental organizations, international financial institutions, and multinational corporations that help broker peace and reconstruct postwar societies has grown exponentially. However, these entities have their own set of political and economic interests that can set the stage for postwar violence. For example, neoliberal economic policies foisted on a society after war may enrich elites at the expense of others (Pugh 2005), "produce inequality, [and] exacerbate perceptions of relative deprivation that cause a resurgence in post-conflict interpersonal violence and crime" (Howarth 2014, p. 261). In addition, outside interventions intended to stabilize the governance of postwar societies may undermine and weaken those societies' political and economic institutions and arrangements, set in place regimes unwilling or unable to address local crime problems, and increase the dependency of postwar states on international bodies (Paris 2010). Together these may undermine the legitimacy and effectiveness of governments in postwar societies and in turn increase interpersonal and political violence.

Many of these factors (along with the growth of narcotrafficking organizations) came together in both El Salvador and Guatemala after their civil wars and have been cited as reasons for their high rates of postwar homicide. Because the Salvadorian war ended after a political and military stalemate, grievances that engendered the war were not adequately addressed, leading to anger and frustration in large sections of the population (Kurtenbach 2013). At the same time, elites and the mass media they controlled sensationalized violent crime, attributing it to youthful predators and organized street gangs (*maras*). In turn, this raised support for repressive state strategies (*mano dura*) and for vigilante justice meted out by armed civilian groups and paramilitaries (Binford 2002; Kurtenbach 2013). Public security was also militarized, with ex–military officers moving into positions with civilian police forces. For Cruz (2011, p. 1), this "survival of violent entrepreneurs in the new security apparatus and their relationship with new governing elites foster the conditions for the escalation of violence in northern Central America." In both countries, economic inequality rose to the highest levels in the western hemisphere, pushed upward in part by fiscally austere neoliberal economic policies and privatization that weakened the state's distributive capacity (Richani 2007; Howarth 2014).

In reference to Guatemala, Suhrke (2012, p. 12) writes that "the violence seemed to reflect less the legacy of war than the pathologies of a development trajectory and a drug economy that continued to underwrite poverty, inequality, and impunity" (see also McNeish and López Rivera 2012).

In contrast, in other postwar societies the transition to peace has unfolded in ways that have limited violence. Nicaragua, for example, has been able to keep postwar violence in check, according to Kurtenbach (2013), because it has more effectively addressed many of the grievances underlying the war and has been more successful at demilitarizing and professionalizing its police. Similarly, Cruz (2011) believes the major factor distinguishing Nicaragua from its northern neighbors and responsible for its lower rates of postwar violence is the more limited role of the state in contributing to that violence. In addition, Liberia's experience after its civil war suggests that a massive international peacekeeping presence that helps demilitarize a country and inclusive peace negotiations that involve both government and rebel groups may constrain postwar violence.[12] However, to complicate this picture, the international peacebuilding intervention appears to have reinforced a political and economic system more beneficial to established elites than to the ex-combatants they demonized (Chaudhary 2012).

The post–civil war experience of Lebanon, where the war spanned the period 1975–90, is a departure from that of many other countries. Richani (2007) reports that the homicide rate in Lebanon in the year before the war was 6.5 per 100,000 and 3 years after the end of the war was 7.5 per 100,000, dropping to 2.2 per 100,000 by the early 2000s. Several

[12] The lack of reliable data on violent crime prior to the Liberian civil war means it is not possible to determine whether violence increased or decreased after the war. Chaudhary (2012, p. 261), however, cites data that "[do] not seem to suggest crime spiraling out of control, and overall crime rates compare favorably with other countries in the region."

factors worked together to lower violent crime rates, including a strong postwar security apparatus that was effective at detecting and punishing criminal violence, increased social spending by the government, and economic policies that kept employment rates relatively high. Thus, despite only a partial demobilization and widely available light weapons, post–civil war Lebanon appears to have avoided a wave of violent crime in part through enacting socioeconomic policies that raised the opportunity costs of crime (Richani 2007). This is generally consistent with Berdal's (2012, p. 311) argument that "post-war violence, while ubiquitous, is also diverse and of variable intensity, [which] suggests that policy intervention can influence, for better or worse, its trajectory. While escaping post-war violence is . . . plainly very difficult, it is equally true that such violence does not spring from a simple primordial source."

3. *Postwar Gender Relations and Gender Inequality.* War may affect postwar violence, particularly violence against women, through its transformation of gender relations and the gender order (Connell 2002; McWilliams and Ní Aoláin 2013). The postwar period can raise women's risks of violence for the same reasons it affects men's risks, but there are certain aspects of both wartime and the postwar period that may have distinctive effects on violence against women. Sexual violence targeted at women is a common—although not inevitable (Wood 2009; Cohen 2013)—feature of wartime (Buss et al. 2014);[13] when militaries use sexual violence against women strategically and extensively during war, this may affect gender relations in complex ways after the war and lead to further violence against women (Samset 2012). Indeed, "one stark reality of war is that although peace may be declared and weapons laid down, levels of sexual violence against girls and women do not necessarily diminish, but often escalate, even dramatically" (Sharkey 2014, p. 86).

In addition, when women gain greater autonomy and independence during war through increased participation in the labor force and their greater authority in the family, in the postwar period they may face hostility and violence from men, especially their intimate partners, who feel

---

[13] Sexual violence against men during armed conflict also has a long history and has been documented in 25 wars in the last decade (Russell 2007); it has only recently gained systematic attention by researchers and legal scholars, however (Sivakumaran 2007; Solangon and Patel 2012).

threatened by women's gains (Pankhurst 2008). Similarly, if large numbers of women are active participants in armed conflicts, as they often are in intrastate wars, the blurring of cultural boundaries around gender identities is likely to extend into the postwar period and may lead to gender conflicts and violence. Boutron (2012, p. 89), for example, argues that domestic violence increased in rural communities in Peru after the armed conflict between the government and leftist political parties ended in 2000: "Political violence is thus converted into interpersonal violence, not only with the goal of reproducing masculine identity but also of preventing the older fighters from losing the social mobility they won through their participation in the counter-subversive struggle."

The possibility of backlash violence against women after wars is typically seen as a consequence of war (Pankhurst 2008). In this section, however, our focus is on how the nature of the transition to peace—that is, demobilization processes, peace accords, and reconstruction policies—may affect gender relations and gender inequalities and thus raise the risks of violence. For instance, demobilization policies that grant ex-combatants (who are predominantly male) preferential treatment in the labor market can increase women's dependence on men even above pre-war levels—especially if women's traditional sources of livelihood have been undermined by war—making it more difficult for women to leave abusive relationships (Pankhurst 2008; Ní Aoláin, Haynes, and Cahn 2011). Moreover, if men returning from war are hailed as heroes by the wider society, women's willingness to report abuse by their partners and criminal justice officials' willingness to take those reports seriously may wane (Handrahan 2004). And postwar policies that increase women's dependency on men and men's impunity for domestic violence can put women at risk. On this topic, McWilliams and Ní Aoláin (2013, p. 20) note that "in post-conflict settings, dependency roles are frequently elevated to the level of national policy" such as when "families with many children are favoured in subsequent taxation and social policies, reinforcing the power of fathers and husbands within the family." Such pro-natalist policies often are put in place in societies experiencing high death rates during war or coming out of ethnically or religiously based civil wars and have been blamed for a rise in domestic violence in Croatia after the Yugoslav War (McWilliams and Ní Aoláin 2013).

Because women rarely have been granted formal roles in peace processes, they have had little opportunity to put in place measures to counteract these tendencies (Bloomfield, Barnes, and Huyse 2003). As a consequence, in many countries postwar reforms of the security sector prioritize the need to control public forms of violence and "masculine conceptualizations of safety" (Ní Aoláin, Cahn, and Haynes 2014) as well as neglect the vulnerability of women within the home. More generally, security sector reforms can reinforce the "militarized masculinities" that are encouraged in wartime but become "a root source of violence and conflict," including violence against women and gender conflicts, after wars (Clarke 2014, p. 217). Some countries coming out of civil wars have made efforts, often with the urging of international actors, to involve women in peace talks and postwar reconstruction processes, especially of the security sector (Call and Stanley 2001). In Liberia, for example, women's representation in the police force rose and a special Women and Child Protection Unit was established; and in Guatemala, women's participation in peace talks ensured that sexual and other forms of violence, especially against indigenous women, were the focus of policy reforms (Bouta, Frerks, and Bannon 2005). How successful these efforts have been at reducing violence against women in postwar societies is not clear, however.

The material reviewed in this section speaks to how policies and practices that emerge from the peace process and during postwar reconstruction can influence the likelihood that postwar violence will be higher than prewar levels. Policies that do not alleviate or that worsen systematic inequalities and the marginalization and exclusion of vulnerable groups are likely to promote postwar violence. This can occur regardless of how much damage and destruction a war has caused but is certainly heightened when economic conditions are poor, the physical infrastructure has been ravaged, or the state's legitimacy has been weakened. The good news is that where peace accords and institutional reforms are attentive not just to reducing the likelihood of more war but to creating more inclusive social, economic, and political conditions, postwar violence can be kept in check or even reduced below prewar levels. There are other conditions and processes that some argue can drive down violence in the postwar period; these are taken up in the next section.

## IV. The Experience of War Decreases Postwar Violence
War, as we have seen, is not always followed by elevated rates of violence. Where the individual- and societal-level transformations and conditions described in the previous two sections are absent, postwar violence may

return to levels that characterized the prewar period. Under some conditions, the experience of war may even reduce violence below prewar levels, although the literature on postwar violence devotes much less attention to this potential legacy of war.

## A. Deaths in War

The most direct and brutal way in which war may drive down postwar violence is the large-scale killing of people most at risk of engaging in violence, that is, adolescent and adult males. Germany, for example, lost over 15 percent of its male population aged 20–45 in World War I and about 4.5 million soldiers in World War II. The sex ratios of some countries' populations are profoundly affected as a consequence; for instance, after World War II there were over 13 million more women than men in the Soviet Union. Lowe (2012, p. 23), in describing this "demographic absence" after World War II, quotes a British major who wrote, "In our thousands of miles that we travelled in Germany, the most outstanding fact of all was the total absence of men between the ages of 17 and 40. It was a land of women, children, and old men." It is difficult, however, to square this loss of men with evidence that countries that experienced the most battle deaths per population during the two world wars were the most likely to experience postwar increases in homicide (Archer and Gartner 1976b). Another possibility is that skewed sex ratios due to the high death rates of males during war may indirectly affect postwar violence. After the civil war and genocide in Rwanda, the sex ratio (or number of men per 100 women) dropped to 88; in other words, women substantially outnumbered men. This limited women's choices in the marriage market and their relative power in intimate relationships after the war and, as a consequence, increased women's risks of intimate partner violence (La Mattina 2014).

## B. Catharsis or War Weariness

War may also reduce postwar violence through catharsis or war weariness.[14] According to this explanation, the butchery and brutality of war

---

[14] The term "war weariness" has also been used in reference to the physical and psychological exhaustion, at times bordering on incapacitation, that veterans sometimes feel after war (see, e.g., Schafer 2007). Our use of the term here differs from this usage.

drain people—both those who fight and those who do not—of their violent impulses, leaving them less inclined to engage in violence after war. War "exhausts the criminal passions scattered through every nation," according to Tarde ([1890] 1968, p. 422), and provides people with their "necessary quantum of violence" such that "no further violence may be needed" (Mannheim 1941*b*, p. 127). Although the concept of war weariness has typically been applied to the relationships between wars (see, e.g., Richardson 1960; Levy and Morgan 1986), it is also relevant to the relationship between war and postwar violence. As Richardson (1960, p. 232) observed, "[a] long and severe bout of fighting confers immunity on most of those who have experienced it," thereby theoretically reducing the likelihood of both postwar violence and a precipitate return to warfare.

A closely related argument is that the experience of war engenders greater appreciation for peaceful living. Willbach (1948), for example, concluded that US veterans of World War II were leaving behind their training and experiences in violent combat when they returned home and embracing their civilian roles and responsibilities, which their time at war imbued with renewed importance. His review of pre- and postwar arrest statistics for New York City supported his argument. Freud anticipated this process—at least for those on the winning side—shortly after the outbreak of World War I: "When the furious struggle of the present war has been decided, each one of the victorious fighters will return home joyfully to his wife and children, unchecked and undisturbed by thought of the enemies he has killed whether at close quarters or at long range" ([1915] 1957, p. 295). That the vast majority of German veterans on returning home did not engage in violence (Bessel 1993) suggests that this process may extend to defeated fighters as well. On the other hand, Germany appears to have experienced a rise in violence after World War I, including, as noted earlier, an increase in capital crimes by ex-soldiers without previous criminal records (Mosse 1990).

## C. Military Service Reduces Violence

In contrast to those who see the military as a school for violence, some have pointed to a number of benefits of military service that could reduce the likelihood that veterans would engage in violent crime after wars. In many wars, the vast majority of soldiers have been drawn from among the less advantaged in society and accused or convicted criminals have been able to avoid legal sanctions by joining the military. For that reason, Bonger (1916, p. 517), a harsh critic of militarism, acknowledged that "military service *can* have a favorable effect upon totally lawless individuals, who thus learn order and discipline" (emphasis in the original). To the extent military training teaches discipline and self-control, technical and work-related skills, and literacy, as well as providing a sense of identification with an honorable cause, it can reduce the likelihood that ex-soldiers turn or return to violent crime after war (Alker and Godfrey 2016). This depends to a considerable extent on the economic opportunities available to veterans and how they are perceived by the wider society on their return home, but there is historical evidence that at least some ex-soldiers were better off economically and socially than they had been before their participation in war and thus had fewer incentives to resort to violent crime (Tallett 1992).

Probably the best evidence from recent wars of the crime-reduction benefits of military service comes from research on US veterans of World War II. Laub and Sampson's (2003) follow-up study of men who had been remanded as teenagers to reform schools in 1940s Boston found that military service was a key turning point in the lives of many of them. While in the service, they were no longer under the influence of criminal peers from their past, were provided supervision and social support, and were able to form new, noncriminal identities. After the war, the GI Bill allowed them to afford further education and job training, reducing the stigma of their prewar criminal record. In interviews later in their lives, these men recalled how being in the military had taught them to control their tempers and gave their lives structure, purpose, and meaning that extended well after their service. Laub and Sampson, however, also acknowledge that some men were traumatized by their service in ways that negatively affected them after the war. Elder (1986, p. 245), in his study of the effects of military service on men born in California in 1928 and 1929, similarly concluded that "the least probable candidates for such personal enhancement are the surviving veterans who served in combat, were wounded or taken captive, who killed and observed the killing by others. Men with such experiences are likely to reflect a more tragic side of war and military duty." Furthermore, because neither of these studies compared men with different (or no) experiences of military service on their violent behavior after World War II, any effects on postwar violence are not known.

D. *War Increases Postwar Civic Engagement, Social Trust,*
   *and Social Cohesion*

The idea that wars increase social solidarity and in-group identification has a long history. For Charles Darwin and some of his followers
war was a "powerful evolutionary force that might foster social solidarity and altruism toward the fellow members of one's group" (Choi and
Bowles 2007, p. 636). In his classic work *Folkways*, Sumner (1906, p. 12),
although an opponent of imperialist wars, asserted that "the exigencies
of war with outsiders are what make peace possible, lest internal discord
would weaken the we-group." Even habitual criminals have been thought
to be favorably influenced by war. In 1914, an editorial in the *Times* of
London observed that "the criminal like the honest citizen is impressed
by the War conditions which make it every man's duty to give as little trouble as possible" (quoted in Mannheim [1941*b*, p. 108]). Social cohesion
and solidarity, mutual trust, and informal social control are all dimensions
of collective efficacy and have been linked to lower levels of criminal violence, including homicide and domestic violence, at the neighborhood
and national levels (Morenoff, Sampson, and Raudenbush 2001; Browning 2002; Lederman, Loayza, and Menéndez 2002).

Whether and how long social cohesion lasts after war, and what effects
it might have in societies going through civil wars—where in-group solidarity might be expected to both prolong the war and heighten conflict
afterward—complicate predictions about its effects on postwar violence.
However, an emerging body of scholarship on civic engagement, trust,
and prosociality following civil wars provides indirect evidence relevant
to this issue. In a study of male youths in northern Uganda, for example,
Blattman (2009) found that those who had been conscripted into the
Lord's Resistance Army (LRA) through abduction and those who had
been victims of LRA violence had higher levels of political engagement
after the 2006 truce—including a 73 percent increase in the likelihood
of being a member of a peace-promoting organization—than other youths.
Likewise, a survey of households in Sierra Leone after its civil war showed
that households that experienced more intense wartime violence had significantly higher levels of political mobilization and engagement (Bellows
and Miguel 2009). Similarly, according to a field experiment in Nepal after its 10-year civil war, members of communities that experienced more
fatal violence during the war had higher levels of "prosocial motivation,
measured by altruistic giving, public good contributions, investment in

trust-based transactions, and willingness to reciprocate trust-based investments" (Gilligan, Pasquale, and Samii 2014, p. 604; see also Voors et al. 2012). However, these positive post–civil war outcomes have not been observed in research in other countries, such as a study by Cassar, Grosjean, and Whitt (2013) of post–civil war Tajik (see also De Luca and Verpoorten 2015). Furthermore, none of this research has considered whether the increase in political participation, prosociality, and trust after these wars is associated with lower levels of violence. Nevertheless, the potential for war to decrease postwar violence by enhancing social cohesion, trust, and civic engagement deserves further investigation.

## E. War Feminizes the Political Sphere

The ways in which wars can transform gender relations to the detriment of women and their safety in the postwar period have been extensively discussed in the literature on gender and war. Recently, an alternative perspective has emerged that focuses on how wars can increase women's political representation, with potential benefits for women and for postwar societies as a whole. According to this perspective, ruptures in gender relations brought about during and after war can create opportunities for women to move into positions of political power, particularly after civil wars. In contrast to interstate war, in civil wars women are much more likely to be combatants, which can transform their identities—and men's perceptions of women's capabilities—and give them a sense of power and confidence (Bop 2001). Even where women do not fight, civil wars often push them into new roles outside of the home, with potentially similar consequences.

When peace arrives, women may have an advantage over men in the political process for several reasons. To the extent women are seen as less bellicose and less responsible for having encouraged war in the first place, they may have more political legitimacy than men in societies coming out of civil war. Where the sex ratio is skewed after wars because of high casualty rates among men, women also may have more opportunities to compete for political power. Partly as a consequence of their victimization and dislocation during war, women are often motivated to become involved in social movements designed to improve human rights, support refugees and victims of war, and expand women's rights (Bop 2001; Rehn and Sirleaf 2002); experiences in social movement mobilization in turn may spur more women into pursuing more formal political careers. In recent years, international organizations that assist with postwar reconstruction have provided considerable support both for these female-run movements and for greater representation of women in political offices.

How might these developments be related to postwar violence? In countries where women make up a larger proportion of national legislators, spending on social welfare—including child health care, education, and women's reproductive health (e.g., Bolzendahl and Brooks 2007)— is greater and public perceptions of the legitimacy and credibility of political elites are enhanced (Shair-Rosenfield and Wood 2017). Higher levels of both social welfare spending and political legitimacy have been linked to lower levels of homicide in both cross-national and historical research (e.g., Gartner 1990; Savolainen 2000; Roth 2009).

Evidence that women's political participation may increase after war is largely limited to recent years, intrastate wars, and low-income nations but is growing. Of 118 developing countries studied by Fallon, Smith, and Viterna (2012), women's legislative representation in the years between 1975 and 2009 increased the most in countries coming out of civil wars, especially prior to 1995 (see also Viterna and Fallon 2008). In her analysis of 36 high-income, 86 middle-income, and 63 low-income countries in the 1980s and 1990s, Hughes (2009) found that intrastate wars that were longer and more deadly, and those that contested government rather than territory, were the most likely to be followed by increases in women's representation in parliamentary seats. In subsequent research focused on African countries, Hughes and Tripp (2015) replicated these findings but also noted that the growth in women's legislative representation in these countries emerged only after 2000, when international and regional norms about the political inclusion of women had strengthened.

Although none of this work has considered the effects of women's greater political representation on postwar violence, one study has found (for the period 1946–2011) that a higher proportion of female representatives in national legislatures prolonged peace following wars that ended through a negotiated settlement (Shair-Rosenfield and Wood 2017). More generally, Pinker (2011, p. 688), after reviewing a vast literature on violence, argues that "several varieties of feminization—direct political empowerment, the deflation of manly honor, the promotion of marriage on women's terms, the right of girls to be born, and women's control over their own reproduction—have been forces in the decline of violence" over the last several centuries.

In contrast to the bulk of the literature on the relationship between war and postwar violence, the work reviewed in this section points to ways in which war might reduce postwar violence. The reasons for a negative relationship between war and postwar violence have received less attention in the literature largely because there is so little empirical evidence of such a relationship. For example, Archer and Gartner (1976b) identified only four (out of 29) countries that experienced significant decreases in homicide after their participation in World War I or II.[15] Nevertheless, many countries have not experienced substantial increases in postwar homicide rates. The processes described in this section may have played a role in reining in postwar violence in these countries, although the lack of systematic evidence about the mechanisms linking war and postwar violence does not allow for any definitive conclusions.

## V. Discussion and Conclusion

In this essay, we have identified a number of ways in which war's violence can translate into higher or, in rare cases, lower rates of postwar violence. Nevertheless, we still cannot fully answer Binford's (2002) questions about "to what degree and under precisely what circumstances" war will instigate violence in its aftermath. There is undoubtedly a relationship—albeit far from a perfect one—between war and postwar violence at both individual and societal levels: Many societies and some people that have gone through war tend to be more violent after war. There are also important exceptions to this pattern and serious limitations on our ability to make causal claims or isolate the mechanisms responsible for any relationship between war and postwar violence. Furthermore, these mechanisms almost certainly differ in their relevance and intensity depending on the characteristics of a war and of the societies and people participating in it.

The evidence reviewed in this essay indicates that although many people are traumatized or harmed in other ways by directly participating in or experiencing wartime violence, the vast majority does not become

[15] After World War I, the homicide rates in Australia, Canada, and Hungary were significantly lower than prewar rates; and after World War II the homicide rate in the United States was significantly lower than its prewar rate.

more violent as a consequence. A state's legitimation of violence during war may increase a society's tolerance for violence afterward, but there is limited direct validation of such a process of cultural change. In other words, the individual harms and larger lessons of wartime do not appear to be either necessary or sufficient conditions for elevated rates of postwar violence. Where, however, a war weakens a society's economic, political, and social institutions, undermines a state's ability to protect and provide for its citizens, heightens grievances that preexisted the war, or encourages the expansion of criminal organizations and illicit economies, an increase in violence afterward is likely. In addition, peace accords and reconstruction policies that reinforce systemic inequalities or that marginalize and repress vulnerable groups will have similar consequences. In sum, the conditions of the postwar period have greater influence on postwar crime rates than does the direct experience of war.

Not surprisingly, then, those who study violence in postwar settings agree on the need for peace negotiations and reconstruction policies to attempt to mitigate economic inequality, enhance state legitimacy, strengthen public security institutions, reduce the availability of firearms, and challenge cultural norms promoting violence (e.g., Suhrke and Berdal 2012; Kurtenbach 2013; Steenkamp 2014). Social scientists will recognize these as consistent with the kinds of policies suggested by criminological research and theory as effective at reducing violent crime. However, too often peace agreements and reconstruction efforts focus on the warring parties and the prevention of further conflict rather than on providing for the security, protection, and needs of the general public (Call and Stanley 2001; Braithwaite 2014). As Cooper (2006, p. 21) notes, "the interests of civil society are consequently treated as an afterthought, considered only once the parameters of postwar power and political economy have been established in agreements with warlords or militaries whose main concern is maintaining influence, rather than transforming the status quo." Where this is the case, the interests and security of women and children take a backseat, if they are considered at all (Handrahan 2004; McWilliams and Ní Aoláin 2013).

When international intervenors—whether other states, international organizations, or private bodies—are involved in peace negotiations (which they almost always are in contemporary wars), their own interests and ideologies inevitably shape the final accords. A number of negative consequences of this have been identified, particularly in relation to what has been called "the liberal peace." Liberal peace theory posits that post-conflict states should focus on the development of democratic institutions and processes, the rule of law and human rights, and a market economy in order to avoid the recurrence of war (Paris 2010). Its critics, however, see the liberal peace as ethnocentric, inattentive to the specific cultural and structural context of postwar societies, and primarily attuned to the economic and political concerns of international intervenors (e.g., Pugh 2005; Mac Ginty 2010). Among its consequences, "such liberalization can produce inequality, [and] exacerbate perceptions of relative deprivation that cause a resurgence in post-conflict interpersonal violence and crime" (Howarth 2014, p. 261). The neoliberal economic policies advocated by external bodies—such as privatization of public enterprises and state industries—more often than not "foster the illicit economy as an alternative to welfarism" (Cooper 2006, p. 21) and enrich organized crime groups, as well as elites, that benefited from the war economy and can continue to profit from postwar shadow trade in natural resources or trafficking in drugs, weapons, and people (Pugh 2005).

Concerns about the importation of policies and practices from the global North to the global South—where most wars are currently being waged—extend to the reform or rebuilding of the public security sector and its institutions (Höglund 2008; Kurtenbach 2013). Some scholars see the management of postwar violence, both political and interpersonal, as a prerequisite for the success of postwar political and economic reforms but warn against willy-nilly deployment of "the technocratic tools of criminology" (Braithwaite 2014, p. 70) and neglecting to consult with local groups and regional leaders. "In particular," Höglund (2008, p. 100) states, "successful violence management requires strategies that differ from those that are used in stable, democratic societies."

Nonetheless, there are lessons to be learned from research on crime about general principles and goals that could guide efforts to close the public security gap in postwar societies. Avoiding highly repressive and exclusionary criminal justice and legal responses to postwar violence will pay off in the longer term by increasing the legitimacy of these institutions and reducing the attractions of relying on nonstate actors—particularly organized crime groups—for security (Call and Stanley 2001; Richani 2007). Closing the public security gap also requires creating a context in which the opportunity costs of violence are high, by putting in place social policies that address structural conditions conducive to violence (Richani 2007; Steenkamp 2011). "Criminal violence in postwar societies is not merely a law and order issue," observes Steenkamp (2011, p. 379), "but is a legacy of war and peacemaking." This brings us full circle by pointing to the many and complex relationships between war, other forms of state violence, and interpersonal violence. Postwar violence needs to be seen and addressed not so much as a consequence of brutalized and traumatized individuals, but as a function of the state's role in perpetrating, encouraging, and tolerating many forms of violence before, during, and after war.

REFERENCES

Adler, Jeffrey S. 1996. "The Making of a Moral Panic in 19th Century America: The Boston Garroting Hysteria of 1865." *Deviant Behavior* 17(3):259–78.

Alexievich, Svetlana. 1992. *Zinky Boys: Soviet Voices from the Afghanistan War*. Translated by Julia and Robin Whitby. New York: Norton.

Alker, Zoe, and Barry Godfrey. 2016. "Soldiers and Victims: Conceptions of Military Service and Victimhood, 1914–45." In *The Palgrave Handbook of Criminology and War*, edited by Sandra Walklate and Ross McGarry. Basingstoke, UK: Palgrave Macmillan.

Allport, Alan. 2009. *Demobbed: Coming Home after the Second World War*. New Haven, CT: Yale University Press.

Archer, Dane, and Rosemary Gartner. 1976*a*. "The Myth of the Violent Veteran." *Psychology Today* 10:94–96, 110–11.

———. 1976*b*. "Violent Acts and Violent Times: A Comparative Approach to Postwar Homicide Rates." *American Sociological Review* 41(6):937–63.

———. 1984. *Violence and Crime in Cross-National Perspective*. New Haven, CT: Yale University Press.

Armit, Ian. 2011. "Violence and Society in the Deep Human Past." *British Journal of Criminology* 51(3):499–517.

Augsburger, Mareike, Daniel Meyer-Parlapanis, Manassé Bambonye, Thomas Elbert, and Anselm Crombach. 2015. "Appetitive Aggression and Adverse Childhood Experiences Shape Violence Behavior in Females Formerly Associated with Combat." *Frontiers in Psychology* 6:art. 1756.

Babo-Soares, Dionísio. 2012. "Conflict and Violence in Post-Independence East Timor." In *The Peace in Between: Post-war Violence and Peacebuilding*, edited by Astri Suhrke and Mats Berdal. Abingdon, UK: Routledge.

Barber, Brian K. 2009. "Glimpsing the Complexity of Youth and Political Violence." In *Adolescents and War: How Youth Deal with Political Violence*, edited by Brian K. Barber. New York: Oxford University Press.

BBC. 2007. "Child Soldiers Are a Time Bomb." February 5. http://news.bbc.co.uk/2/hi/europe/6330503.stm.

Beattie, J. M. 1974. "The Pattern of Crime in England 1660–1800." *Past and Present* 62:47–95.

————. 1977. "Crime and the Courts in Surrey 1736–1753." In *Crime in England, 1550–1800*, edited by J. S. Cockburn. Princeton, NJ: Princeton University Press.

Beckham, Jean C., Michelle E. Feldman, and Angela C. Kirby. 1998. "Atrocities Exposure in Vietnam Combat Veterans with Chronic Posttraumatic Stress Disorder: Relationship to Combat Exposure, Symptom Severity, Guilt, and Interpersonal Violence." *Journal of Traumatic Stress* 11(4):777–85.

Beckham, Jean C., Michelle E. Feldman, Angela C. Kirby, Michael A. Hertzberg, and Scott D. Moore. 1997. "Interpersonal Violence and Its Correlates in Vietnam Veterans with Chronic Posttraumatic Stress Disorder." *Journal of Clinical Psychology* 53(8):859–69.

Beckley, Amber. 2013. "Correlates of War? Towards an Understanding of Nativity-Based Differences in Immigrant Offending." *European Journal of Criminology* 10:408–23.

Bellows, John, and Edward Miguel. 2009. "War and Local Collective Action in Sierra Leone." *Journal of Public Economics* 93:1144–57.

Berdal, Mats. 2012. "Reflections on Post-war Violence and Peacebuilding." In *The Peace in Between: Post-war Violence and Peacebuilding*, edited by Astri Suhrke and Mats Berdal. Abingdon, UK: Routledge.

Berdal, Mats, Gemma Collantes-Celador, and Merima Zupcevic Buzadzic. 2012. "Post-war Violence in Bosnia and Herzegovina." In *The Peace in Between: Post-war Violence and Peacebuilding*, edited by Astri Suhrke and Mats Berdal. Abingdon, UK: Routledge.

Bessel, Richard. 1993. *Germany after the First World War*. New York: Clarendon.

Binford, Leigh. 2002. "Violence in El Salvador: A Rejoinder to Philippe Bourgois's The Power of Violence in War and Peace." *Ethnography* 3(2):201–19.

Blattman, Christopher. 2009. "From Violence to Voting: War and Political Participation in Uganda." *American Political Science Review* 103(2):231–47.

Blattman, Christopher, and Jeannie Annan. 2010. "The Consequences of Child Soldiering." *Review of Economics and Statistics* 92(4):882–98.

Bloomfield, David, Teresa Barnes, and Luc Huyse, eds. 2003. *Reconciliation after Violent Conflict: A Handbook*. Halmstad, Sweden: International Institute for Democracy and Electoral Assistance.

Bolzendahl, Catherine, and Clem Brooks. 2007. "Women's Political Resources and Welfare State Spending in 12 Capitalist Democracies." *Social Forces* 85: 1509–34.

Bonger, Willem A. 1916. *Criminality and Economic Conditions*. Translated by Henry P. Horton. Boston: Little Brown. (Originally published 1905 as *Criminalité et conditions économiques*.)

Boothby, Neil, and Blake Thomson. 2013. "Long Term Impacts of Involvement in Child Soldiering: Child Soldiers as Adults; the Mozambique Case Study." *Journal of Aggression, Maltreatment, and Trauma* 22:735–56.

Bop, Codou. 2001. "Women in Conflicts, Their Gains and Their Losses." In *The Aftermath: Women in Post-conflict Transformation*, edited by Sheila Meintjes, Anu Pillay, and Meredith Turshen. London: Zed.

Bouffard, Leana Allen. 2003. "Examining the Relationship between Military Service and Criminal Behavior during the Vietnam Era: A Research Note." *Criminology* 41(2):491–510.

Bouffard, Leana Allen, and John H. Laub. 2004. "Jail or the Army: Does Military Service Facilitate Desistance from Crime?" In *After Crime and Punishment: Pathways to Offender Reintegration*, edited by Shadd Maruna and Russell Immarigeon. Cullompton, Devon, UK: Willan.

Boulanger, Ghislaine. 1986. "Violence and Vietnam Veterans." In *The Vietnam Veteran Redefined: Fact and Fiction*, edited by Ghislaine Boulanger and Charles Kadushin. Hillsdale, NJ: Erlbaum.

Bourgois, Philippe. 2001. "The Power of Violence in War and Peace: Post–Cold War Lessons from El Salvador." *Ethnography* 2(1):5–34.

Bourke, Joanna. 1999. *An Intimate History of Killing in Twentieth-Century Warfare*. London: Basic Books.

Bouta, Tsjeard, Georg Frerks, and Ian Bannon. 2005. *Gender, Conflict, and Development*. Washington, DC: World Bank.

Boutron, Camille. 2012. "Reintegrating Civilian Life after Combat: Between Invisibility and Resistance; the Experience of the Ronderas in Peru." In *War Veterans in Postwar Situations: Chechnya, Serbia, Turkey, Peru, and Côte d'Ivoire*, edited by Natalie Duclos. New York: Palgrave Macmillan.

Boxer, Paul, L. Rowell Huesmann, Eric F. Dubow, Simha F. Landau, Shira Dvir Gvirsman, Khalil Shikaki, and Jeremy Ginges. 2013. "Exposure to Violence across the Social Ecosystem and the Development of Aggression: A Test of Ecological Theory in the Israeli-Palestinian Conflict." *Child Development* 84 (1):163–77.

Boyle, Michael J. 2012. "Revenge and Reprisal in Kosovo." In *The Peace in Between: Post-war Violence and Peacebuilding*, edited by Astri Suhrke and Mats Berdal. Abingdon, UK: Routledge.

———. 2014. *Violence after War: Explaining Instability in Post-conflict Societies*. Baltimore: Johns Hopkins University Press.

Bracken, Patrick J. 1998. "Hidden Agendas: Deconstructing Post Traumatic Stress Disorder." In *Rethinking the Trauma of War*, edited by Patrick J. Bracken and Celia Petty. London: Free Association Books.

Braithwaite, John. 2014. "Crime in Asia: Toward a Better Future." *Asian Criminology* 9:65–75.

Breggin, Peter. 2010. "Antidepressant-Induced Suicide, Violence and Mania: Risks for Military Personnel." *International Journal of Risk and Safety in Medicine* 22(3):149–57.

Brower, M. C., and B. H. Price. 2001. "Neuropsychiatry of Frontal Lobe Dysfunction in Violent and Criminal Behaviour: A Critical Review." *Journal of Neurological and Neurosurgical Psychiatry* 71:720–76.

Brown, Howard. 2006. *Ending the Revolution: Violence, Justice and Repression from the Terror to Napoleon*. Charlottesville: University of Virginia Press.

Brown, William B., Robert Stanulis, and Gerrad McElroy. 2016. "Moral Injury as a Collateral Damage Artifact of War in American Society: Serving in War to Serving Time in Jail and Prison." *Justice Policy Journal* 13(1):1–41.

Browning, Christopher R. 2002. "The Span of Collective Efficacy: Extending Social Disorganization Theory to Partner Violence." *Journal of Marriage and Family* 64(4):833–50.

Broyles, William. 1985. "Why Men Love War." *Esquire* (November):55–63.

Buss, Doris, Joanne Lebert, Blair Rutherford, Donna Sharkey, and Obijiofor Aginam, eds. 2014. *Sexual Violence in Conflict and Post-conflict Societies: International Agendas and African Contexts.* New York: Routledge.

Call, Charles T. 2003. "Democratisation, War and State-Building: Constructing the Rule of Law in El Salvador." *Journal of Latin American Studies* 35(4):827–62.

———. 2007. "The Mugging of a Success Story: Justice and Security Sector Reform in El Salvador." In *Constructing Justice and Security after War*, edited by Charles T. Call. Washington, DC: US Institute of Peace.

Call, Charles T., and William Stanley. 2001. "Protecting the People: Public Security Choices after Civil Wars." *Global Governance* 7:151–72.

Calvert, William E., and Roger L. Hutchinson. 1990. "Vietnam Veteran Levels of Combat: Related to Later Violence?" *Journal of Traumatic Stress* 3(1):103–13.

Canoy, Jose Raymund. 2007. *The Discreet Charm of the Police State: The Landpolizei and the Transformation of Bavaria, 1945–1965.* Leiden, Netherlands: Brill.

Cassar, Alexandra, Pauline Grosjean, and Sam Whitt. 2013. "Legacies of Violence: Trust and Market Development." *Journal of Economic Growth* 18:285–318.

Catani, Claudia. 2010. "War at Home: A Review of the Relationship between War Trauma and Family Violence." *Verhaltenstherapie* 20(1):19–27.

Catani, Claudia, Elizabeth Schauer, and Frank Neuner. 2008. "Beyond Individual War Trauma: Domestic Violence against Children in Afghanistan and Sri Lanka." *Journal of Marital and Family Therapy* 34(2):165–76.

Cawthra, Gavin, and Robin Luckham, eds. 2003. *Governing Insecurity: Democratic Control of Military and Security Establishments in Transitional Democracies.* London: Zed.

Cesur, Resul, and Joseph J. Sabia. 2016. "When War Comes Home: The Effect of Combat Service on Domestic Violence." *Review of Economics and Statistics* 98(2):209–25.

Chaudary, Torunn Wimpelmann. 2012. "The Political Economics of Violence in Post-war Liberia." In *The Peace in Between: Post-war Violence and Peacebuilding*, edited by Astri Suhrke and Mats Berdal. Abingdon, UK: Routledge.

Childs, John. 1997. "War, Crime Waves, and the English Army in the Late Seventeenth Century." *War and Society* 15:1–17.

Choi, Jung-Kyoo, and Samuel Bowles. 2007. "The Coevolution of Parochial Altruism and War." *Science* 318:636–40.

Clark, Cari Jo, Susan A. Everson-Rose, Shakira Franco Suglia, Rula Btoush, Alvaro Alonso, and Muhammad M. Haj-Yahia. 2010. "Association between Exposure to Political Violence and Intimate-Partner Violence in the Occupied Palestinian Territory: A Cross-Sectional Study." *Lancet* 375:310–16.

Clarke, Yaliwe. 2014. "Security Sector Reform in Africa: A Lost Opportunity to Deconstruct Military Masculinities?" In *Sexual Violence in Conflict and Post-*

*conflict Societies: International Agendas and African Contexts*, edited by Doris Buss, Joanne Lebert, Blair Rutherford, Donna Sharkey, and Obijiofor Aginam. New York: Routledge.

Cockayne, James, and Adam Lupel. 2009. "Introduction: Rethinking the Relationship between Peace Operations and Organized Crime." *International Peacekeeping* 16(1):4–19.

Cockburn, J. S. 1977. "The Nature and Incidence of Crime in England 1559–1625: A Preliminary Survey." In *Crime in England, 1550–1800*, edited by J. S. Cockburn. Princeton, NJ: Princeton University Press.

———. 1991. "Patterns of Violence in English Society: Homicide in Kent, 1560–1985." *Past and Present* 130:70–109.

Cohen, Dara Kay. 2013. "Explaining Rape during Civil War: Cross-National Evidence 1980–2009." *American Political Science Review* 107(3):461–77.

Cohen, Esther. 1996. "The Hundred Years' War and Crime in Paris, 1332–1448." In *The Civilization of Crime: Violence in Town and Country since the Middle Ages*, edited by Eric A. Johnson and Eric H. Monkkonen. Urbana: University of Illinois Press.

Collier, Paul. 1994. "Demobilization and Insecurity: A Study in the Economics of the Transition from War to Peace." *Journal of International Development* 6(3):343–51.

Collier, Paul, and Anke Hoeffler. 2004. "Murder by Numbers: Socio-economic Determinants of Homicide and Civil War." Working paper no. 2004-10. Oxford: Centre for Studies of African Economies, Oxford University.

Connell, Robert. 2002. "Masculinities, the Reduction of Violence and the Pursuit of Peace." In *The Post-war Moment: Militaries, Masculinities and International Peacekeeping*, edited by Cynthia Cockburn and Dubravka Zarkov. London: Lawrence & Wishart.

Cooper, Neil. 2006. "Peaceful Warriors and Warring Peacemakers." *Economics of Peace and Security Journal* 1(1):20–24.

Couttenier, Mathieu, Veronica Preotu, Dominic Rohner, and Mathias Thoenig. 2016. "The Violent Legacy of Victimization: Post-conflict Evidence on Asylum Seekers, Crimes and Public Policy in Switzerland." Discussion Paper no. 11079. London: Centre for Economic Policy Research.

Crotty, Martin. 2017. "The RSL and Post–First World War Returned Soldier Violence in Australia." In *Legacies of Violence: Rendering the Unspeakable Past in Modern Australia*, edited by Robert Mason. New York: Berghahn.

Cruz, José Miguel. 2011. "Criminal Violence and Democratization in Central America: The Survival of the Violent State." *Latin American Politics and Society* 53(4):1–33.

Dale, Robert. 2015. *Demobilized Veterans in Late Stalinist Leningrad: Soldiers to Civilians*. London: Bloomsbury.

Darrow, Clarence. 1922. *Crime: Its Causes and Treatment*. New York: Crowell.

Dean, Eric T. 1999. *Shook over Hell: Post-traumatic Stress, Vietnam, and the Civil War*. Cambridge, MA: Harvard University Press.

Deglow, Annekatrin. 2016. "Localized Legacies of Civil War: Post-war Violent Crime in Northern Ireland." *Journal of Peace Research* 53(6):786–99.

de la Espriella, R., E. Sweetnam Pingel, and J. V. Falla. 2010. "The (De)Construction of a Psychiatric Diagnosis: PTSD among Former Guerrilla and Paramilitary Soldiers in Colombia." *Global Public Health* 5(3):221–32.

De Luca, Giacomo, and Marijke Verpoorten. 2015. "Civil War and Political Participation: Evidence from Uganda." *Economic Development and Cultural Change* 64(1):113–41.

de Silva, Purnaka L. 2008. "Hatred and Revenge Killings: Construction of Political Violence in Sri Lanka." In *Matters of Violence: Reflections on Social and Political Violence in Sri Lanka*, edited by Jayadeva Uyangoda. Colombo, Sri Lanka: Social Scientists' Association.

Dickson-Gómez, Julia. 2003. "Growing Up in Guerrilla Camps: The Long-Term Impact of Being a Child Soldier in El Salvador's Civil War." *Ethos* 30 (4):327–56.

Dower, John W. 1999. *Embracing Defeat: Japan in the Wake of World War II.* New York: Norton.

Drummond, Katie. 2013. "This Is Your Military on Drugs." *New Republic*, February 5. https://newrepublic.com/article/112269.

Dubow, Eric F., Paul Boxer, L. Rowell Huesmann, Khalil Skikaki, Simha Landau, Shira Dvir Gvirsman, and Jeremy Ginges. 2010. "Exposure to Conflict and Violence across Contexts: Relations to Adjustment among Palestinian Children." *Journal of Clinical Child and Adolescent Psychology* 39(1):103–16.

Duclos, Natalie. 2012. "Introduction: Rethinking the Former Combatants' Return to Civilian Life." In *War Veterans in Post-war Situations: Chechnya, Serbia, Turkey, Peru, and Côte d'Ivoire*, edited by Natalie Duclos. New York: Palgrave Macmillan.

Durkheim, Emile. 1957. *Professional Ethics and Civil Morals.* Translated by C. Brookfield. London: Routledge & Kegan Paul. (Originally published 1950 as *Physique des moeurs et du droit.*)

Edele, Mark, and Robert Gerwarth. 2015. "The Limits of Demobilization: Global Perspectives on the Aftermath of the Great War." *Journal of Contemporary History* 50(1):3–14.

Egmond, Florike. 1993. *Underworlds: Organized Crime in the Netherlands, 1650–1800.* Cambridge: Polity.

Elbogen, Eric B., Sally C. Johnson, Virginia M. Newton, Sara Fuller, H. Ryan Wagner, VA Mid-Atlantic MIRECC Registry Workgroup, and Jean C. Beckham. 2013. "Self-Report and Longitudinal Predictors of Violence in Iraq and Afghanistan War Era Veterans." *Journal of Nervous Mental Disorders* 201(10): 872–76.

Elbogen, Eric B., Sally C. Johnson, H. Ryan Wagner, Virginia M. Newton, Christine Timko, Jennifer J. Vasterling, and Jean C. Beckham. 2012. "Protective Factors and Risk Modification of Violence in Iraq and Afghanistan War Veterans." *Journal of Clinical Psychiatry* 73(6):767–73.

Elbogen, Eric B., Sally C. Johnson, H. Ryan Wagner, Connor Sullivan, Casey T. Taft, and Jean C. Beckham. 2014. "Violent Behaviour and Post-traumatic Stress Disorder in US Iraq and Afghanistan Veterans." *British Journal of Psychiatry* 204(5):368–75.

Elder, Glen H., Jr. 1986. "Military Times and Turning Points in Men's Lives." *Developmental Psychology* 22(2):233–45.

Ember, Carol R., and Melvin Ember. 1994. "War, Socialization, and Interpersonal Violence: A Cross-Cultural Study." *Journal of Conflict Resolution* 38 (4):620–46.

Emsley, Clive. 2008. "Violent Crime in England in 1919: Post-war Anxieties and Press Narratives." *Community and Change* 23(1):173–95.

———. 2013. *Soldier, Sailor, Beggar Man, Thief: Crime and the British Armed Services since 1914.* Oxford: Oxford University Press.

———. 2014. "Crime During and After Military Service." In *Oxford Handbooks Online: Criminology.* New York: Oxford University Press.

Erasmus, Desiderius. 1813. *Complaint of Peace.* Translated from Latin. Boston: Charles Williams. (Originally published 1517 as *Querela Pacis.*)

Ertl, Verena, Anett Pfeiffer, Elisabeth Schauer-Kaiser, Thomas Elbert, and Frank Neuner. 2014. "The Challenge of Living On: Psychopathology and Its Mediating Influence on the Readjustment of Former Child Soldiers." *PLoS One* 9(7):e102786

Exner, Franz. 1927. *Krieg und Kriminalität in Oesterreich.* Vienna: Holder-Pichler-Tempsky.

Fallon, Kathleen M., Liam Swiss, and Jocelyn Viterna. 2012. "Resolving the Democracy Paradox: Democratization and Women's Legislative Representation in Developing Nations, 1975 to 2009." *American Sociological Review* 77(3):380–408.

Faust, Drew Gilpin. 2008. *This Republic of Suffering: Death and the American Civil War.* New York: Knopf.

Fernández Garcia, María Cristina. 2004. "Lynching in Guatemala: Legacy of War and Impunity." Fellow's Paper. Cambridge, MA: Weatherhead Centre for International Affairs, Harvard University.

Fogarty, Richard S., and David Killingray. 2015. "Demobilization in British and French Africa at the End of the First World War." *Journal of Contemporary History* 50(1):100–123.

Fox, Sean, and Kristian Hoelscher. 2012. "Political Order, Development and Social Violence." *Journal of Peace Research* 49(3):431–44.

Fregoso, Rosa-Linda, and Cynthia Beharano, eds. 2010. *Terrorizing Women: Feminicide in the Américas.* Durham, NC: Duke University Press.

Freud, Sigmund. 1957. "Thoughts for the Times on War and Death." In *The Standard Edition of the Complete Psychological Works of Sigmund Freud,* edited and translated by James Strachey. London: Hogarth. (Originally published 1915.)

Frommer, Benjamin. 2005. *National Cleansing: Retribution against Nazi Collaborators in Post-war Czechoslovakia.* Cambridge: Cambridge University Press.

Gartner, Rosemary. 1990. "The Victims of Homicide: A Temporal and Cross-National Comparison." *American Sociological Review* 55:92–106.

Ghobarah, Hazem Adam, Paul Huth, and Bruce Russett. 2003. "Civil Wars Kill and Maim People Long after the Shooting Stops." *American Political Science Review* 97(2):189–202.

Gilinskiy, Yakov, and Yakov Kostjukovsky. 2007. "From Thievish *Artel* to Criminal Corporation: The History of Organized Crime in Russia." In *Organised*

*Crime in Europe: Concepts, Patterns and Control Policies in the European Union and Beyond*, edited by Cyrille Fijnaut and Letizia Paoli. Norwell, MA: Springer.

Gilligan, Michael J., Benjamin J. Pasquale, and Cyrus Samii. 2014. "Civil War and Social Cohesion: Lab-in-the-Field Evidence from Nepal." *American Journal of Political Science* 58(3):604–19.

Gimbel, Cynthia, and Alan Booth. 1994. "Why Does Military Combat Experience Adversely Affect Marital Relations?" *Journal of Marriage and Family* 56 (3):691–703.

Gleditsch, Nils Petter, Peter Wallensteen, Mikael Eriksson, Margareta Sollenberg, and Håvard Strand. 2002. "Armed Conflict 1946–2001: A New Dataset." *Journal of Peace Research* 39(5):615–37.

Godoy, Angelina S. 2002. "Lynchings and the Democratisation of Terror in Post-war Guatemala: Implications for Human Rights." *Human Rights Quarterly* 24:640–61.

Grafman, J., K. Schwab, D. Warden, A. Pridgen, H. R. Brown, and A. M. Salazar. 1996. "Frontal Lobe Injuries, Violence, and Aggression: A Report of the Vietnam Head Injury Study." *Neurology* 46:1231–38.

Grandi, Francesca. 2013a. "New Incentives and Old Organizations: The Production of Violence after War." *Peace Economics, Peace Science and Public Policy* 19(3):309–19.

———. 2013b. "Why Do the Victors Kill the Vanquished? Explaining Political Violence in Post–World War II Italy." *Journal of Peace Research* 50(5):577–93.

Green, Penny, and Tony Ward. 2009. "The Transformation of Violence in Iraq." *British Journal of Criminology* 49:609–27.

Gvirsman, Shira Dvir, L. Rowell Huesmann, Eric F. Dubow, Simha F. Landau, Khalil Shikaki, and Paul Boxer. 2014. "The Effects of Mediated Exposure to Ethnic-Political Violence on Middle East Youths' Subsequent Post-traumatic Stress Symptoms and Aggressive Behavior." *Communications Research* 41(7): 961–90.

Haer, Roos, and Tobias Böhmelt. 2016. "Child Soldiers as Time Bombs? Adolescents' Participation in Rebel Groups and the Recurrence of Armed Conflict." *European Journal of International Relations* 22(2):408–36.

Hakeem, Michael. 1946. "Service in the Armed Forces and Criminality." *Journal of Criminal Law and Criminology* 37(2):120–31.

Hanawalt, Barbara A. 1979. *Crime and Conflict in English Communities, 1300–1348*. Cambridge, MA: Harvard University Press.

Handrahan, Lori. 2004. "Conflict, Gender, Ethnicity and Post-conflict Reconstruction." *Security Dialogue* 35(4):429–45.

Hay, Douglas. 1982. "War, Dearth and Theft in the Eighteenth Century: The Record of the English Courts." *Past and Present* 95:117–60.

Hecker, Tobias, Katharin Hermenau, Anna Maedl, Thomas Elbert, and Maggie Schauer. 2012. "Appetitive Aggression in Former Combatants—Derived from the Ongoing Conflict in DR Congo." *International Journal of Law and Psychiatry* 35:244–49.

Hecker, Tobias, Katharin Hermenau, Anna Maedl, Harald Hinkel, Maggie Schauer, and Thomas Elbert. 2013. "Does Perpetrating Violence Damage

Mental Health? Differences between Forcibly Recruited and Voluntary Combatants in DR Congo." *Journal of Traumatic Stress* 26(1):142–48.

Hiley-Young, Bruce, Dudley David Blake, Francis R. Abueg, Vitali Rozynko, and Fred D. Gusman. 1995. "Warzone Violence in Vietnam: An Examination of Premilitary, Military, and Postmilitary Factors in PTSD In-Patients." *Journal of Traumatic Stress* 8(1):125–41.

Höglund, Kristine. 2008. "Violence in War-to-Democracy Transitions." In *From War to Democracy: Dilemmas of Peacebuilding*, edited by Amanda K. Jarstad and Timothy D. Sisk. New York: Cambridge University Press.

Howarth, Kirsten. 2014. "Connecting the Dots: Liberal Peace and Post-conflict Violence and Crime." *Progress in Development Studies* 14(3):261–73.

Hughes, Melanie M. 2009. "Armed Conflict, International Linkages, and Women's Parliamentary Representation in Developing Nations." *Social Problems* 56(1):174–204.

Hughes, Melanie M., and Aili Mari Tripp. 2015. "Civil War and Trajectories of Change in Women's Political Representation in Africa, 1985–2010." *Social Forces* 93(4):1513–40.

Jamieson, Ruth. 1998. "A Criminology of War." In *The New European Criminology: Crime and Social Order in Europe*, edited by Vincenzo Ruggiero, Nigel South, and Ian Taylor. London: Routledge.

Jarman, Neil. 2004. "From War to Peace? Changing Patterns of Violence in Northern Ireland, 1990–2003." *Terrorism and Political Violence* 16(3):420–38.

Jones, Edgar, Nicola T. Fear, and Simon Wessely. 2007. "Shell Shock and Mild Traumatic Brain Injury: A Historical Review." *American Journal of Psychiatry* 164:1641–45.

Kamieński, Łukasz. 2016. *Shooting Up: A Short History of Drugs and War*. New York: Oxford University Press.

Kereteš, Gordana. 2006. "Children's Aggressive and Prosocial Behavior in Relation to War Exposure: Testing the Role of Perceived Parenting and Child's Gender." *International Journal of Behavioral Development* 30(3):227–39.

Kerig, Patricia K., and Cecilia Wainryb. 2013. "Introduction to the Special Issue, Part 1: New Research on Trauma, Psychopathology, and Resilience among Child Soldiers around the World." *Journal of Aggression, Maltreatment and Trauma* 22(7):685–97.

Klasen, Fiona, Gabriele Oettingen, Judith Daniels, Manuel Post, Catrin Hoyer, and Hubertus Adam. 2010. "Posttraumatic Resilience in Former Ugandan Child Soldiers." *Child Development* 81:1096–1113.

Klay, Phil. 2016. "Don't Confuse Veterans and Violence." *New York Times*, July 19. http://www.nytimes.com/2016/07/19/opinion/don't-confuse-veterans-and-violence.html.

Kleck, Gary. 1987. "America's Foreign Wars and the Legitimation of Domestic Violence." *Sociological Inquiry* 57(3):237–50.

Kleist, Karl. 1934. *Kriegverletzungen des Gehirns in ihrer Bedeutung für Himlokalisation und Hirnpathologie*. Leipzig: Barth.

Kohrt, Brandon A., Mark J. D. Jordans, Wietse A. Tol, Rebecca A. Speckman, Sujen M. Maharjan, Carol M. Worthman, and Ivan H. Komproe. 2008.

"Comparison of Mental Health between Former Child Soldiers and Children Never Conscripted by Armed Groups in Nepal." *Journal of the American Medical Association* 300:691–702.

Kramer, Alan. 1988. "'Law-Abiding Germans'? Social Disintegration, Crime and the Reimposition of Order in Post-war Western Germany, 1945–1949." In *The German Underworld: Deviants and Outcasts in German History*, edited by Richard J. Evans. London: Routledge.

Kurtenbach, Sabine. 2013. "The Happy Outcomes May Not Come at All: Post-war Violence in Central America." *Civil Wars* 15(1):105–22.

LaFree, Gary. 1998. *Losing Legitimacy: Street Crime and the Decline of Social Institutions*. Boulder, CO: Westview.

La Mattina, Giulia. 2014. "Civil Conflict, Sex Ratio and Intimate Partner Violence in Rwanda." Working Paper no. 175. Brighton: Households in Conflict Network, University of Sussex.

Landau, Simha F., Shira Dvir-Gvirsman, Rowell Huesmann, Eric F. Dubow, Paul Boxer, Jeremy Ginges, and Khalil Shikaki. 2010. "The Effects of Exposure to Violence on Aggressive Behavior: The Case of Arab and Jewish Children in Israel." In *Indirect and Direct Aggression*, edited by Karen Österman. Berlin: Peter Lang.

Lange, Katrin. 2007. "'Many a Lord Is Guilty, Indeed for Many a Poor Man's Dishonest Deed': Gangs of Robbers in Early Modern Germany." In *Organised Crime in Europe: Concepts, Patterns and Control Policies in the European Union and Beyond*, edited by Cyrille Fijnaut and Letizia Paoli. Norwell, MA: Springer.

Lappi-Seppälä, Tappio, and Martti Lehti. 2014. "Cross-Comparative Perspectives on Global Homicide Trends." In *Why Crime Rates Fall and Why They Don't*, edited by Michael Tonry. Vol. 43 of *Crime and Justice: A Review of Research*, edited by Michael Tonry. Chicago: University of Chicago Press.

Laub, John H., and Robert J. Sampson. 2003. *Shared Beginnings, Divergent Lives: Delinquent Boys to Age 70*. Cambridge, MA: Harvard University Press.

Lawson, Peter. 1986. "Property Crime and Hard Times in England, 1559–1624." *Law and History Review* 4(1):95–127.

Lawver, Timothy, Jeremy Jensen, and Randon Welton. 2010. "Serotonin Syndrome in the Deployed Setting." *Military Medicine* 175(12):950–52.

Le Billon, Philippe. 2000. "The Political Ecology of Transition in Cambodia, 1989–1999: War, Peace, and Forest Exploitation." *Development and Change* 31:785–805.

Lederman, Daniel, Norman Loayza, and Ana María Menéndez. 2002. "Violent Crime: Does Social Capital Matter?" *Economic Development and Cultural Change* 50(3):509–39.

Le Huérou, Anne, and Elisabeth Sieca-Kozlowski. 2012. "A 'Chechen Syndrome'? Russian Veterans of the Chechen War and the Transposition of War Violence to Society." In *War Veterans in Postwar Situations: Chechnya, Serbia, Turkey, Peru, and Côte d'Ivoire*, edited by Natalie Duclos. New York: Palgrave Macmillan.

Leloup, Pieter, Xavier Rousseaux, and Antoon Vrints. 2014. "Banditry in Occupied and Liberated Belgium, 1914–21: Social Practices and State Reactions." *Social History* 39(1):83–105.

Levy, Charles. 1988. "Agent Orange Exposure and Posttraumatic Stress Disorder." *Journal of Nervous and Mental Disease* 176(4):242–45.

Levy, Jack S., and T. Clifton Morgan. 1986. "The War-Weariness Hypothesis: An Empirical Test." *American Journal of Political Science* 30(1):26–49.

Liepmann, Moritz. 1930. *Krieg und Kriminalität in Deutschland*. Stuttgart: Deutsche Verlagsanstalt.

Lowe, Keith. 2012. *Savage Continent: Europe in the Aftermath of World War II*. New York: Viking.

Lupo, Salvatore. 2009. *History of the Mafia*. Translated by Antony Shugaar. New York: Columbia University Press.

Mac Ginty, Roger. 2010. "No War, No Peace: Why So Many Peace Processes Fail to Deliver Peace." *International Politics* 47(2):145–62.

Machiavelli, Niccoló. 2005. *The Prince*. Translated by Peter Bondanella. Oxford: Oxford University Press. (Originally published 1532 as *De Principatibus/Il principe*.)

Macksoud, Mona S., and J. Lawrence Aber. 1996. "The War Experiences and Psychosocial Development of Children in Lebanon." *Child Development* 67 (1):70–88.

MacManus, Deirdre, Kimberlie Dean, M. Al Bakir, A. C. Iversen, Lisa Hull, Tom Fahy, Simon Wessely, and Nicola T. Fear. 2012. "Violent Behaviour in UK Military Personnel Returning Home after Deployment." *Psychological Medicine* 42:1663–73.

MacManus, Deirdre, Kimberlie Dean, Margaret Jones, Roberto J. Rona, Neil Greenberg, Lisa Hull, Tom Fahy, Simon Wessely, and Nicola T. Fear. 2013. "Violent Offending by UK Military Personnel Deployed to Iraq and Afghanistan: A Data Linkage Cohort Study." *Lancet* 381:907–17.

Mannheim, Hermann. 1941*a*. "Crime in Wartime England." *Annals of the American Academy of Political and Social Science* 217:128–37.

———. 1941*b*. *War and Crime*. London: Watts.

———. 1955. *Group Problems in Crime and Punishment*. London: Routledge.

McMullin, Jaremey. 2004. "Reintegration of Combatants: Were the Right Lessons Learned in Mozambique?" *International Peacekeeping* 11(4):625–43.

McNeish, John-Alexander, and Oscar López Rivera. 2012. "The Multiple Forms of Violence in Post-war Guatemala." In *The Peace in Between: Post-war Violence and Peacebuilding*, edited by Astri Suhrke and Mats Berdal. Abingdon, UK: Routledge.

McWilliams, Monica, and Fionnuala Ní Aoláin. 2013. "'There Is a War Going On You Know': Addressing the Complexity of Violence against Women in Conflicted and Post Conflict Societies." *Transitional Justice Review* 1(2):4–44.

Meineck, Peter. 2016. "Combat Trauma and the Tragic Stage: Ancient Culture and Modern Catharsis?" In *Our Ancient Wars: Rethinking War through the*

*Classics*, edited by Victor Caston and Silke-Maria Weineck. Ann Arbor: University of Michigan Press.

Merridale, Catherine. 2001. *Night of Stone: Death and Memory in Twentieth Century Russia*. New York: Viking.

Miguel, Edward, Sebastián M. Saiegh, and Shanker Satyanath. 2011. "Civil War Exposure and Violence." *Economics and Politics* 23:59–73.

Moore, Thomas, Joseph Glenmullen, and Curt Furberg. 2010. "Prescription Drugs Associated with Reports of Violence towards Others." *PLoS One* 5 (12):e15337.

More, Sir Thomas. 1967. *Utopia*. In *The Essential Thomas More*, edited by James J. Greene and John P. Dolan. New York: New American Library. (Originally published 1516.)

Morenoff, Jeffrey D., Robert J. Sampson, and Stephen W. Raudenbush. 2001. "Neighborhood Inequality, Collective Efficacy, and the Spatial Dynamics of Urban Violence." *Criminology* 39(3):517–59.

Morton, Desmond. 1980. "'Kicking and Complaining': Demobilization Riots in the Canadian Expeditionary Forces, 1918–1919." *Canadian Historical Review* 61:334–60.

Mosse, George. 1990. *Fallen Soldiers: Reshaping the Memory of the World Wars*. Oxford: Oxford University Press.

Mueller-Bamouh, Veronika, Martina Ruf-Leuschner, Katalin Dohrmann, Maggie Schauer, and Thomas Elbert. 2016. "Are Experiences of Family and of Organized Violence Predictors of Aggression and Violent Behavior? A Study with Unaccompanied Refugee Minors." *European Journal of Psychotraumatology* 7:27856. DOI:10.3402/ejpt.v7.27856.

Muggah, Robert. 2006. "Emerging from the Shadow of War: A Critical Perspective on DDR and Weapons Reduction in the Post-conflict Period." *Contemporary Security Policy* 27(1):190–205.

Murray, Emma. 2016. "'The Veteran Offender': A Governmental Project in England and Wales." In *The Palgrave Handbook of Criminology and War*, edited by Sandra Walklate and Ross McGarry. Basingstoke, UK: Palgrave Macmillan.

Nandi, Corina, Anselm Crombach, Manasée Bambonye, Thomas Elbert, and Roland Weierstall. 2015. "Predictors of Posttraumatic Stress and Appetitive Aggression in Active Soldiers and Former Combatants." *European Journal of Psychotraumatology* 6:26553. DOI:10.3402/ejpt.v6.26553.

Nelson, Elizabeth. 2003. "Civilian Men and Domestic Violence in the Aftermath of the First World War." *Journal of Australian Studies* 27:97–108.

———. 2007. "Victims of War: The First World War, Returned Soldiers, and Understandings of Domestic Violence in Australia." *Journal of Women's History* 19(4):83–106.

*New York Times*. 2006. "Armies of Children." October 12. http://www.nytimes.com/2006/10/12/opinion/12thu3.html.

Ní Aoláin, Fionnuala, Naomi Cahn, and Dina Haynes. 2014. "A Gendered Reading of Security and Security Reform in Post-conflict Societies." In *Sexual Violence in Conflict and Post-conflict Societies: International Agendas and African*

*Contexts*, edited by Doris Buss, Joanne Lebert, Blair Rutherford, Donna Sharkey, and Obijiofor Aginam. New York: Routledge.

Ní Aoláin, Fionnuala, Dina Haynes, and Naomi Cahn. 2011. *On the Frontlines: Gender, War and the Post-conflict Process*. Oxford: Oxford University Press.

Nikolić-Ristanović, Vesna. 1996. "War and Violence against Women." In *The Gendered New World Order: Militarism, Development and the Environment*, edited by Jennifer Turpin and Lois Ann Lorentzen. New York: Routledge.

———. 1998. "War and Crime in the Former Yugoslavia." In *The New European Criminology: Crime and Social Order in Europe*, edited by Vincenzo Ruggiero, Nigel South, and Ian Taylor. London: Routledge.

Nordstrom, Carolyn. 1997. *A Different Kind of War Story*. Philadelphia: University of Pennsylvania Press.

———. 2004. *Shadows of War: Violence, Power, and International Profiteering in the Twenty-First Century*. Berkeley: University of California Press.

Nussio, Enzo, and Kimberly Howe. 2016. "When Protection Collapses: Post-demobilization Trajectories of Violence." *Terrorism and Political Violence* 28 (5):848–67.

Obert, Jonathan. 2014. "The Six-Shooter Marketplace: 19th-Century Gunfighting as Violence Expertise." *Studies in American Political Development* 28:49–79.

Odenwald, Michael, Birke Lingenfelder, Maggie Schauer, Frank Neuner, Brigitte Rockstroh, Harald Hinkel, and Thomas Elbert. 2007. "Screening for Posttraumatic Stress Disorder among Somali Ex-Combatants: A Validation Study." *Conflict and Health* 1:10. DOI:10.1186/1752-1505-1-10.

Oppenheimer, B. S., and M. A. Rothschild. 1918. "The Psychoneurotic Factor in the 'Irritable Heart' of Soldiers." *British Medical Journal* 13:29–31.

Orcutt, Holly K., Lynda A. King, and Daniel W. King. 2003. "Male-Perpetrated Violence among Vietnam Veteran Couples: Relationships with Veteran's Early Life Characteristics, Trauma History, and PTSD Symptomatology." *Journal of Traumatic Stress* 16(4):381–90.

Pankhurst, Donna. 2008. "Post-war Backlash Violence against Women: What Can Masculinity Explain?" In *Gendered Peace: Women's Struggles for Post-war Justice and Reconciliation*, edited by Donna Pankhurst. New York: Routledge.

Paris, Roland. 2010. "Saving Liberal Peacebuilding." *Review of International Studies* 36:337–65.

Peou, Sorpong. 2012. "Violence in Post-war Cambodia." In *The Peace in Between: Post-war Violence and Peacebuilding*, edited by Astri Suhrke and Mats Berdal. Abingdon, UK: Routledge.

Petrik, Norman, Angela M. Rosenberg, and Charles G. Watson. 1983. "Combat Experience and Youth: Influences on Reported Violence against Women." *Professional Psychology: Research and Practice* 14(6):895–99.

Pinker, Steven. 2011. *The Better Angels of Our Nature: Why Violence Has Declined*. New York: Penguin.

Pugh, Michael. 2005. "The Political Economy of Peacebuilding: A Critical Theory Perspective." *International Journal of Peace Studies* 10:23–42.

Qouta, Samir, Rajai-Leena Punamäki, and Eyad El Sarraj. 2008. "Does War Beget Child Aggression? Military Violence, Gender, Age, and Aggressive Behavior in Two Palestinian Samples." *Aggressive Behavior* 34(3):231–44.

Rehn, Elisabeth, and Ellen Johnson Sirleaf, eds. 2002. *Women War Peace: Progress of the World's Women*, vol. 1. New York: UNIFEM.

Rice, Andrew S. C. 2009. *The Teeth May Smile but the Heart Does Not Forget: Murder and Memory in Uganda*. New York: Metropolitan Books.

Richani, Nazih. 2007. "Systems of Violence and Their Political Economy in Post-conflict Situations." Unpublished manuscript, Department of Political Science, Dean University.

Richardson, Lewis F. 1960. *Arms and Insecurity: A Mathematical Study of the Causes and Origins of War*. Edited by Nicholas Rashevsky and Ernesto Trucco. Chicago: Quadrangle.

Rivera, Mauricio. 2016. "The Sources of Social Violence in Latin America: An Empirical Analysis of Homicide Rates, 1980–2010." *Journal of Peace Research* 53(1):84–99.

Rogers, Nicholas. 2012. *Mayhem: Post War Crime and Violence in Britain, 1748–1753*. New Haven, CT: Yale University Press.

Rosenbaum, Betty B. 1940. "Relationship between War and Crime in the United States." *Journal of Criminal Law and Criminology* 30:722–40.

Roth, Göran, Solvig Ekblad, and Helena Prochazka. 2009. "A Study of Aggression among Mass-Evacuated Kosovo Albanians." *Torture* 19(3):227–37.

Roth, Randolph. 2009. *American Homicide*. Cambridge, MA: Belknap.

Rousseaux, Xavier, Frederic Vesentini, and Antoon Vrints. 2009. "Violence and War: Measuring Homicide in Belgium (1900–1950)." In *Violence in Europe: Historical and Contemporary Perspectives*, edited by Sophie Body-Gendrot and Pieter Spierenburg. New York: Springer.

Russell, Wynne. 2007. "Sexual Violence against Men and Boys." *Forced Migration Review* 27:22–23.

Saile, Regina, Verena Ertl, Frank Neuner, and Claudia Catani. 2014. "Does War Contribute to Family Violence against Children? Findings from a Two-Generational Multi-informant Study in Northern Uganda." *Child Abuse and Neglect* 38(1):135–46.

Samset, Ingrid. 2012. "Sexual Violence: The Case of Eastern Congo." In *The Peace in Between: Post-war Violence and Peacebuilding*, edited by Astri Suhrke and Mats Berdal. Abingdon, UK: Routledge.

Sánchez, Fabio, Andrés Solimano, and Michel Formisano. 2005. "Conflict, Violence, and Crime in Colombia." In *Understanding Civil War: Europe, Central Asia, and Other Regions*, edited by Paul Collier and Nicholas Sambanis. Washington, DC: World Bank.

Savarese, Vincent W., Michael K. Suvak, Lynda A. King, and Daniel W. King. 2001. "Relationships among Alcohol Use, Hyperarousal, and Marital Abuse and Violence in Vietnam Veterans." *Journal of Traumatic Stress* 14(4):717–32.

Savolainen, Jukka. 2000. "Inequality, Welfare State, and Homicide: Further Support for the Institutional Anomie Theory." *Criminology* 38(4):1021–42.

Schafer, Jessica. 2007. *Soldiers at Peace: Veterans and Society after the Civil War in Mozambique*. New York: Palgrave Macmillan.

Schroder, William, and Ronald Dawe. 2007. *Soldier's Heart: Close-Up Today with PTSD in Vietnam Veterans*. Westport, CT: Praeger Security International.

Sellin, Thorsten. 1926. "Is Murder Increasing in Europe?" *Annals of the American Academy of Political and Social Science* 125(1):29–34.

Shair-Rosenfield, Sarah, and Reed M. Wood. 2017. "Governing Well after Civil War: How Improving Female Representation Prolongs Post-conflict Peace." *Journal of Politics* 79(3):995–1009.

Sharkey, Donna. 2014. "Through War to Peace: Sexual Violence and Adolescent Girls." In *Sexual Violence in Conflict and Post-conflict Societies: International Agendas and African Contexts*, edited by Doris Buss, Joanne Lebert, Blair Rutherford, Donna Sharkey, and Obijiofor Aginam. New York: Routledge.

Singer, J. David, and Melvin Small. 1972. *The Wages of War, 1816–1965: A Statistical Handbook*. New York: Wiley.

Sivakumaran, Sandy. 2007. "Sexual Violence against Men in Armed Conflict." *European Journal of International Law* 18(2):253–76.

Small, Melvin, and J. David Singer. 1982. *Resort to Arms: International and Civil War, 1816–1980*. Beverly Hills, CA: Sage.

Solangon, Sarah, and Preeti Patel. 2012. "Sexual Violence against Men in Countries Affected by Armed Conflict." *Conflict, Security, and Development* 12(4): 417–42.

Somasundaram, D. J., and S. Sivayokan. 1994. "War Trauma in a Civilian Population." *British Journal of Psychiatry* 165(4):524–27.

Starke, Wilhelm. 1884. *Verbrechen und Verbrecher in Preussen, 1854–1878*. Berlin: Enslin.

Steele, Jeanette. 2017. "Are Military Veterans More Likely for Shooting Sprees?" *San Diego Union-Tribune*, January 11. http://www.sandiegouniontribune.com/military/veterans/sd-me-veterans-violence-20170109-story.html.

Steenkamp, Christina. 2011. "In the Shadows of War and Peace: Making Sense of Violence after Peace Accords." *Conflict, Security and Development* 11(3):357–83.

———. 2014. *Violent Societies: Networks of Violence in Civil War and Peace*. New York: Springer.

Suhrke, Astri. 2012. "The Peace in Between." In *The Peace in Between: Post-war Violence and Peacebuilding*, edited by Astri Suhrke and Mats Berdal. Abingdon, UK: Routledge.

Suhrke, Astri, and Mats Berdal, eds. 2012. *The Peace in Between: Post-war Violence and Peacebuilding*. Abingdon, UK: Routledge.

Sumner, William Graham. 1906. *Folkways: A Study of the Sociological Importance of Usages, Manners, Customs, Mores, and Morals*. Boston: Ginn.

Sutherland, Edwin, and Donald Cressey. 1960. *Principles of Criminology*. Chicago: Lippincourt.

Taft, Casey T., Candice M. Monson, Claire L. Hebenstreit, Daniel W. King, and Lynda A. King. 2009. "Examining the Correlates of Aggression among Male and Female Vietnam Veterans." *Violence and Victims* 24(5):639–52.

Taft, Casey T., Anica P. Pless, Loretta J. Stalans, Karestan C. Koenen, Lynda A. King, and Daniel W. King. 2005. "Risk Factors for Partner Violence among a National Sample of Combat Veterans." *Journal of Consulting and Clinical Psychology* 73(1):151–59.

Taft, Casey T., Dawne S. Vogt, Amy D. Marshall, Jillian Panuzio, and Barbara L. Niles. 2007. "Aggression among Combat Veterans: Relationships with Combat Exposure and Symptoms of Posttraumatic Stress Disorder, Dysphoria, and Anxiety." *Journal of Traumatic Stress* 20(2):135–45.

Tallett, Frank. 1992. *War and Society in Early Modern Europe, 1495–1715*. London: Routledge.

Tarde, Gabriel. 1968. *Penal Philosophy*. Translated by Rapelje Howell. Montclair, NJ: Patterson Smith. (Originally published 1890 as *La philosophie pénale*.)

Tharp, Andra Teten, Michelle D. Sherman, Ursula Bowling, and Bradford J. Townsend. 2016*a*. "Intimate Partner Violence between Male Iraq and Afghanistan Veterans and Their Female Partners Who Seek Couples Therapy." *Journal of Interpersonal Violence* 31(6):1095–1115.

Tharp, Andra Teten, Michelle D. Sherman, Kristin Holland, Bradford Townsend, and Ursula Bowling. 2016*b*. "A Qualitative Study of Male Veterans' Violence Perpetration and Treatment Preferences." *Military Medicine* 181(8): 735–39.

Torres, M. Gabriela. 2008. "Social Justice amidst Guatemala's Post-conflict Violence." *Studies in Social Justice* 2(1):1–10.

Treadwell, James. 2016. "The Forces in the Firing Line? Social Policy and the 'Acceptable Face' of Violent Criminality." In *The Palgrave Handbook of Criminology and War*, edited by Sandra Walklate and Ross McGarry. London: Palgrave Macmillan.

Viterna, Jocelyn, and Kathleen Fallon. 2008. "Democratization, Women's Movements, and Gender-Equitable States: A Framework for Comparison." *American Sociological Review* 73:668–89.

von Hentig, Hans. 1947. *Crime: Causes and Conditions*. New York: McGraw-Hill.

Voogd, Jan. 2008. *Race, Riots, and Resistance: The Red Summer of 1919*. New York: Peter Lang.

Voors, Maarten, Eleanora Nillesen, Philip Verwimp, Erwin Bulte, Robert Lensink, and Daan van Soest. 2012. "Does Conflict Affect Preferences? Results from Field Experiments in Burundi." *American Economic Review* 102(2):941–64.

Wadham, Ben. 2016. "The Dark Side of Defence: Masculinities and Violence in the Military." In *The Palgrave Handbook of Criminology and War*, edited by Sandra Walklate and Ross McGarry. Basingstoke, UK: Palgrave Macmillan.

Walklate, Sandra, and Ross McGarry. 2016. "Murderousness in War: From My Lai to Marine A." In *Homicide, Gender and Responsibility*, edited by Kate Fitz-Gibbon and Sandra Walklate. London: Routledge.

Warner, Jessica, Gerhard Gmel, Kathryn Graham, and Bonnie Erickson. 2007. "A Time-Series Analysis of War and Levels of Interpersonal Violence in an English Military Town, 1700–1781." *Social Science History* 31(4):575–602.

Weierstall, Roland, and Thomas Elbert. 2011. "The Appetitive Aggression Scale—Development of an Instrument for the Assessment of Human's Attraction to Violence." *European Journal of Psychotraumatology* 2:8430. DOI:10 .3402/ejpt.v2i0.8430.

Wessells, Mike. 2006. *Child Soldiers: From Violence to Protection*. Cambridge, MA: Harvard University Press.

Wessely, Simon, Kenneth Craig Hyams, and Robert Bartholomew. 2001. "Psychological Implications of Chemical and Biological Weapons." *British Medical Journal* 323:878–79.

Willbach, Harry. 1948. "Recent Crimes and the Veterans." *Journal of Criminal Law and Criminology* 38(5):501–8.

Williams, Chad L. 2007. "Vanguards of the New Negro: African American Veterans and Post–World War I Racial Militancy." *Journal of African American History* 92:347–70.

Wing, Nick, and Matt Ferner. 2015. "Veterans Can Get All of These Prescription Drugs to Treat PTSD, but Not Weed." Huffington Post, June 23. http:// www.huffingtonpost.ca/entry/veterans-ptsd-marijuana-n-7506750.

Wood, Elizabeth. 2009. "Armed Groups and Sexual Violence: When Is Rape in Wartime Rare?" *Politics and Society* 37(1):131–62.

Wright, John Paul, David E. Carter, and Francis T. Cullen. 2005. "A Life-Course Analysis of Military Service in Vietnam." *Journal of Research in Crime and Delinquency* 42(1):55–83.

Yager, Joel. 1976. "Postcombat Violent Behavior in Psychiatrically Maladjusting Soldiers." *Archives of General Psychiatry* 33(11):1332–35.

Young, Allan. 1995. *The Harmony of Illusions: Inventing Post-traumatic Stress Disorder*. Princeton, NJ: Princeton University Press.

Ziemann, Benjamin. 2006. *War Experiences in Rural Germany, 1914–1923*. New York: Oxford University Press.

*John Braithwaite*

# Minimally Sufficient Deterrence

ABSTRACT

Dangers exist in both maximalist approaches to deterrence and minimalist ones. A minimal sufficiency strategy aims to avert these dangers. The objectives are to convince people that the webs of relationships within which they live mean that lawbreaking will ultimately lead to desistance and remorse and to persuading offenders that predatory crime is simply wrong. Alternative support and control strategies should be attempted until desistance finally occurs. Communities can be helped to understand that this is how minimally sufficient deterrence works. By relying on layered strategies, this approach takes deterrence theory onto the terrain of complexity theory. It integrates approaches based on social support and recovery capital, dynamic concentration of deterrence, restorative justice, shame and pride management, responsive regulation, responsivity, indirect reciprocity, and incapacitation. Deterrence fails when it rejects complexity in favor of simple theories such as rational choice.

Some criminologists are inclined to question why any role should be given to deterrent crime prevention strategies. The evidence for the power of deterrence in reducing crime is thin, after all (Nagin 2013; Chalfin and McCrary 2017; Tonry 2018). There are three reasons why deterrence should have a role. One is that a good meta-strategy for crime control achieves strength through the convergence of weaknesses: deterrence can help to motivate crime control strategies that are more effective than

Electronically published February 27, 2018

John Braithwaite is Distinguished Professor and founder of the Regulatory Institutions Network, Australian National University.

deterrence. Second, deterrence is a weak strategy that can be tried after various somewhat less weak strategies have failed, strengthening the efficacy of a complex approach tied together as a bricolage of strategies. Third, when deterrence of a specific offender fails, it might slightly strengthen general deterrence of other offenders. Sometimes punishment or the threat of punishment provokes defiant reactions that can make crime more likely, not less. For most values of relevant variables, defiance effects exceed deterrence, but there are some contexts in which specific deterrence exceeds defiance. For these reasons, I reject deterrence minimalism in favor of minimally sufficient deterrence.

Deterrence maximalism has even less appeal. Zero tolerance and other political slogans of deterrence maximalism are common, doubtless helpful in election campaigns, but are dismissed by scholars who understand the evidence. Deterrence is not the main game of crime control. Even so, it is reckless to fail to develop a coherent view of the constructive role deterrence must have in crime prevention. A transdisciplinary scientific consensus about the limits of deterrence is behind growing support for "less prison, more police, less crime" as a prescription grounded in preventive capacities of evidence-based policing (Durlauf and Nagin 2011; Travis, Western, and Redburn 2014). In light of the data on the limited effectiveness of deterrence and the cost of building prisons, it is imperative to advocate massive disinvestment from putting people in them.

Likewise, it is easy to dismiss maximizing the shame aimed at offenders, even though shame has a role in minimally sufficient deterrence. Some criminologists conclude that there is strong evidence that shame has power in crime control (Braithwaite 1989), but they do not advocate maximizing the shame directed at offenders. Persuasive evidence shows that this strategy leads to stigmatization, which makes crime worse (Ahmed et al. 2001, pp. 3–72).

Moreover, we know that healthy pride management may be as important as, or more important than, healthy shame management (Maruna 2001; Ahmed and Braithwaite 2011; Best 2017). Intentionally directing unhealthy shame at offenders may crowd healthy pride out. There is unhealthy shame that increases crime and healthy shame acknowledgment that helps prevent crime and repair harms. Likewise, there is unhealthy pride that fosters crime by vaunting superiority over others and humble pride in doing things well with others that is vital to crime prevention via pride in the identity of being a law-abiding citizen who cares about the suffering of others (Ahmed and Braithwaite 2011). Deterrence does best when it does not crowd out healthy shame acknowledgment and healthy pride in a law-abiding self. A virtue of minimally sufficient deterrence is that it minimizes that stigmatic crowding out that is inherent in deterrence maximalism.

Progressives who seek to minimize the quantum of fear or shame that criminal justice system processes invoke are also a danger. It is dangerous, for example, to conceive restorative justice as an abolitionist prescription that eliminates the need for punishment and deterrence. Restorative justice is a strategy that gives an opportunity to all the stakeholders in a crime to participate in a process that discusses who has been harmed or has needs, and what might be done to repair those harms and meet their needs (Zehr 2015). Because crime hurts, justice should heal. Restorative justice conceived as eliminating the need for deterrence is denial of the reality that if we gave criminal offenders the choice of either restorative justice processes in which they agree to repair the harm they caused or doing nothing and forgetting about it, most would opt to forget it. Offenders agree to participate in restorative justice because the alternative has deterrent elements. We see from this that a useful role for deterrence is that it motivates engagement with something that is more effective than deterrence: restorative justice and the rehabilitative and preventive measures for which restorative justice is a delivery vehicle. Indeed, wise integration of restorative justice, rehabilitation, and deterrence allows restorative justice to strengthen the preventive power of deterrence, in addition to allowing deterrence to strengthen restorative justice and rehabilitation. The ambition is to identify a good meta-strategy for crime control that achieves strengths from the convergence of weaknesses: in this example, weaknesses of both deterrence and restorative justice. Some restorative justice advocates are minimalists about shame (e.g., Maxwell and Morris 2002). A society in which rape and violence are minimally shameful will be a society with high rates of rape and violence (Braithwaite 1989, 1995). Hence, it is imperative to diagnose what a minimal sufficiency of the right kind of shame might mean.

Minimum deterrence and minimum shame are inferior to minimal sufficiency: just enough of the right kinds of deterrence and shame is needed. Deterrence and shaming are more effective when combined with a dynamic theory of social support. Communicating the shamefulness of predatory crime is more effective when combined with reintegration of offenders—reintegrative shaming. As with deterring crime, deterring warfare works better when armed fighters are simultaneously shown the costs of killing and shown a supportive peace dividend that benefits them, their family, and their community (Toft 2010; Braithwaite and D'Costa 2018, chap. 3). This is why there is strong evidence that armed peace-keepers prevent war when they do multidimensional peace building that supportively delivers peace dividends (Doyle and Sambanis 2006; Fortna 2008; Call 2012). It is also why simplistic strategies of deterrence maximalism by threatening foes with accelerating military investment can cause more war.

Criminological theory needs something better than cynicism driven by piling up empirical studies about limits of deterrence. Few citizens think deterrence has no role to play in the prevention of rape, theft, or corporate crime. In failing to develop a theory of deterrence that takes fear and shame seriously in social control, criminologists have handed the deterrence debate to maximalists.

This is sad because deterrence maximalists justify a greatly increased level of suffering for incarcerated people and their families. Maximalism increases crime by skewing government budgets to prisons that worsen the criminality of those sentenced to them (Nagin, Cullen, and Jonson 2009). Yet maximalists make more sense to the community than criminologists who say only that punishment deters little. One way of conceiving the imperative to take deterrence seriously, even if minimally, is that deterrence underwrites the greatest historical accomplishment of the justice system. Eisner (2003, p. 126) revealed sharply falling homicide rates between the sixteenth and seventeenth centuries across Europe, the period when some European states institutionalized courts to "discipline" violence. The capability of the courts in the eyes of citizens to deter violence was one reason they abandoned the private deterrence of blood feuds, thereby greatly reducing homicides (Pinker 2011).

A minimal sufficiency strategy of punishment can increase the power of deterrence theory in crime prevention substantially if its empirical claims are more strongly verified by future research and if it can win the political debate against maximalists. It can increase the power of deterrence with a policy that experiences release of the majority of prisoners even in the societies with the lowest imprisonment rates. Minimal sufficiency's claims are consistent with the rather limited existing evidence.

My aim here is to develop ideas toward a theory of minimally sufficient deterrence and to reflect on that existing evidence. To do that, I discuss seven interwoven principles of a crime prevention meta-strategy for minimally sufficient deterrence:

1. Escalate enforcement. Display intent to progressively escalate a responsive enforcement pyramid that involves progressive escalation of sanctions for wrongdoing and support for social responsibility.
2. Inexorability. Pursue inexorable consistency of detection of predatory crime. Communicate inexorable community commitment to stick with social support for those struggling with problems of lawbreaking until the problems are fixed.
3. Escalate social support. With repeated offending, increase social support. Even when there is escalation to a last resort of severe incapacitation, escalate social support further. Keep escalating social support until desistance is consolidated.
4. Sharpen the Sword of Damocles. Cultivate the perception that "Trouble hangs inexorably over my head; they want to support me to avert it."
5. Dynamic concentration of deterrence. Focus deterrence on lines that should never be crossed after an announcement date. Then progressively lift that line, raising our expectations of socially responsible citizens.
6. Community engagement. Engage the community with offenders in widening restorative conversations that educate in the shamefulness of criminal predation for the many who participate in the conversations. Avert stigmatization.
7. Modesty. Settle for the modest general deterrence delivered by this shamefulness and a minimal number of cases that escalate toward the peak of the enforcement pyramid.

In this essay, I first explain the idea of the responsive regulatory pyramid. It provides a scaffolding into which to insert all seven principles. Readers versed in the literature of restorative justice and responsive regulation may find much of the pyramid discussion familiar; I elaborate it for the benefit of others. I then explain the importance of inexorable response, then the theory of dynamic deterrence and defiance, and then how to constitute the shamefulness of the curriculum of crimes. I conclude with minimally sufficient general deterrence.

## I. The Regulatory Pyramid

The regulatory pyramid is a meta-strategy of regulation, a strategy for how to sequence strategies (Braithwaite 2008). It is relevant to regulating crime by organizations or individuals. Figure 1 is an example of a regulatory pyramid elaborated in the next section. The presumptive strategy (a presumption that can be overruled) is to start at the base of the pyramid and escalate slowly. This is a strategy for keeping the Sword of Damocles sharp by making it rare to reach the pointy end of the pyramid. I discuss the rationale for keeping the Sword of Damocles sharp

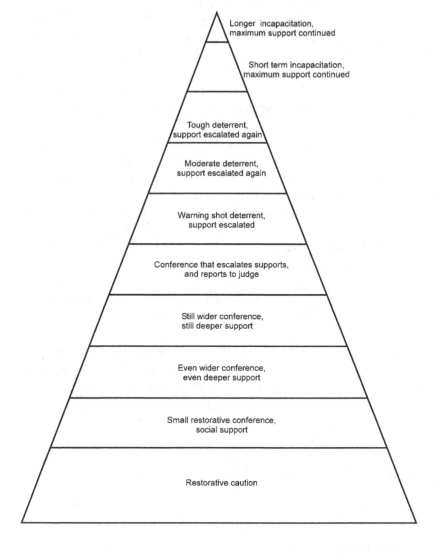

Longer incapacitation, maximum support continued

Short term incapacitation, maximum support continued

Tough deterrent, support escalated again

Moderate deterrent, support escalated again

Warning shot deterrent, support escalated

Conference that escalates supports, and reports to judge

Still wider conference, still deeper support

Even wider conference, even deeper support

Small restorative conference, social support

Restorative caution

FIG. 1.—Responsive pyramid model incorporating minimally sufficient deterrence

in a later section. Consistent with the limited evidence on what works with corporate crime enforcement (Schell-Busey et al. 2016), this is a strategy that provides a wide mix of regulatory options before measures are reached that risk blunting the Sword of Damocles. At the bottom of the pyramid are restorative strategies that provide support to offenders and victims, meet needs, and repair harms.

Responsive regulatory theory says that we should first look to the strengths of a lawbreaker and then seek to expand them. Mental health researchers led in showing that training in building on strengths improves quality of life and vocational and educational outcomes (Stanard 1999). When those outcomes are improved, recent econometric findings show more clearly than in the past that unemployment can be averted, that this reduces crime, and that wages for the poor can be increased, reducing crime by increasing the attractiveness of legitimate work compared to illegitimate work (Chalfin and McCrary 2017, pp. 33–35). This path to crime reduction is resource intensive, though less so than a massive prison system, and it is a benefit to the economy in contrast to the economic deadweight of many large prisons. The idea is to absorb weaknesses by expanding strengths. Put another way, regulators should not rush to law enforcement solutions before considering a range of restorative approaches that can be delivery vehicles for capacity building. As some regulated actors see their strengths expand to levels not previously conceived to be possible, regulators celebrate their innovation, publicize it, and support its extension. With corporate enforcement, research grants and prizes for rolling out new approaches that take internal compliance systems up through new ceilings for that industry offer an example. An example involving young black men in Minneapolis is use of celebration circles in which victims join with the offender's loved ones to celebrate the way an offender has repaired the harm, righted the wrong, and turned his life around (Braithwaite 2002, p. 103).

As we move up the pyramid through a first to a second to a third restorative conference, conference participants are likely to decide to escalate to increasingly punitive interventions. The policy idea is to persuade participants that they should also keep escalating to new ideas and resources for providing support for the offender. The philosophy of restorative justice is to empower stakeholders to take advice from experts but then to make their own decisions contextually attuned to the circumstances of their offender. This includes knowledge of the programs the community of care can persuade the offender to complete and the needs of his or her victim and other stakeholders in their conference. A problem with this is that it does lead to a bricolage of community responses rather than one that maps mechanically from "what works" criminology. This is a complex relational and community empowerment process in which the problem rather than a stigmatized individual is at the center of the circle. The content of the pyramid is not prescriptive. The use of terms such as "escalated support," between "wide" and "wider" support, and "escalated deterrence" without specifying escalation "to what specific measures" is intentional.

With complex phenomena, it is best not to follow the most evidence-based strategy, but the best meta-strategy. The research question of which strategy works best is trivial compared to the question of which meta-strategy works best. Rarely will the first strategy attempted work in a complex context that differs from the conditions of a controlled evaluation trial. A good meta-strategy will inform stakeholders of results from the "what works" literature and will presumptively try the most strongly supported strategy first and then the second most strongly supported strategy (after the first strategy fails). That presumption can be overridden in light of particular circumstances. Clinicians, by analogy, try one therapy after another for a patient, informed by their knowledge of the outcomes of randomized controlled trials and also their knowledge of particular cases, including what other medications patients are taking, their capabilities for surviving the side effects of a therapy, how strong their hearts are, and much more. As in restorative practice, clinicians can also decide what to recommend in order to catalyze community controls that will prevent spread of a contagion. In neither case does best practice involve a narrow focus on an individuated view of what works.

More detailed discussions of how to go about the process of deciding when and how to escalate up a responsive regulatory pyramid, and how to mobilize networked escalation as opposed to simple state escalation, can be found in Braithwaite, Makkai, and Braithwaite (2007) and Braithwaite (2008, 2011). Intervention in complex phenomena like criminal careers should follow a trajectory that first assumes answers are knowable and known and therefore apply evidence-based strategies from normal science (Braithwaite and D'Costa 2018, chap. 12). When that fails, assume the challenge is knowable but unknown (and work to acquire at least some contextual qualitative understanding of the knowable). Then if that repeatedly fails, assume one is dealing with a complex or chaotic phenomenon that is unknowable. In that situation of unknowability, do not surrender to analysis paralysis; keep probing with new forms of social support that come out of restorative conversations until a resonant response begins to produce positive change.

At the base of the responsive pyramid of sanctions are the most restorative, dialogue-based approaches we can craft for securing compliance with a just law. Of course, one reason for an approach that is deliberatively responsive to complexity is that a particular law, or its interpretation, may be of doubtful justice, in which case we can expect dialogue mainly to be about the justice of the law. If excessive force was used during arrest or if racism was in play, we can expect dialogue about whether it is the defendant or the police who have committed the greater crime. This is a good thing from a civic republican perspective, which provides a normative motivation for the theory (Braithwaite and Pettit 1990). As we move up the sanctions pyramid, increasingly demanding interventions are involved. The idea of the pyramid is that our presumption should always be to start at the base. Then escalate to somewhat punitive approaches only reluctantly and only when dialogue fails. Then escalate to even more punitive approaches only when more modest sanctions fail.

Strategic use of the pyramid requires the regulator to resist categorizing problems into minor matters that should be dealt with at the base of the pyramid, more serious ones that should be in the middle, and egregious crimes at the pyramid's peak. The presumptive preference, even for serious crimes, is to try dialogue first, overriding that presumption only if there are compelling reasons for doing so. There will be such reasons in exceptional cases: a violent first offender who vows to keep pursuing the victim to kill her may have to be locked up; a person who has never offended but attempts to blow herself up in a subway may be killed by police who get a clear shot. The 2005 incident in which British police shot an innocent Brazilian man in a subway who was suspected of terrorist intent illustrates the justification for the responsive regulatory imperative always to consider, however quickly, the viability of interventions at lower levels of the pyramid.

As we move up the pyramid in response to a failure to elicit restorative reform and repair, in most cases we eventually reach the point at which reform and repair are forthcoming, even if it is many years later. Whenever that point is reached, responsive regulation means that escalation is reversed; the regulator de-escalates down. The pyramid is firm yet forgiving in its demands for compliance. Reform must be rewarded just as recalcitrant refusal to reform is ultimately punished.

A dramatic transformation of criminal law jurisprudence will be necessary if evidence continues to mount supportive of responsive regulatory theory and we as a society are to reap the benefits of less crime (Braithwaite and Pettit 1990). The imperative to de-escalate deterrence responsively when an offender rehabilitates means that every year a reformed person remains in prison is needless suffering. It is a frittering away of society's scarce crime control resources.

If the empirical claims of responsive regulatory theory are right, this is also a missed opportunity to reduce crime by putting rewards for rejecting a life of crime alongside sanctions for embracing crime. In practical terms, what is needed when social support succeeds in helping a prisoner serving a long sentence turn his or her back on a life of crime is a return to the sentencing court for a hearing about the possibility of early release. The sentencing judge in such hearings should be obliged to take into account the views of victims who are willing to listen to the opinions of parole professionals, the offender, and the offender's family. From a responsive regulatory perspective, a criminal law that keeps people in prison until they have paid the proportionate penalty for their wrongdoing is a profound folly. It is an indefensible policy in terms of a dynamic theory of deterrence. It can make deterrence sense only under a passive deterrence theory, especially a maximalist one, the passive theory that minimally sufficient deterrence seeks to render obsolete.

The deterrent superiority of the active deterrence of the pyramid, as opposed to the passive deterrence of a fixed scale of consistently imposed penalties, is elaborated in Braithwaite (2002, pp. 73–136). Consistently proportionate punishment is justified by proponents of a just deserts theory of equal punishment for equal wrongs. Equal punishment for equal wrongs, however, is a danger to justice. It privileges punitive equality for offenders, while riding roughshod over the justice claims of future victims of crime who suffer because of an inferior crime prevention policy, of present victims who may not want equal justice for equal wrongs to apply in their case (e.g., who may prefer more compensation and less imprisonment), and of offenders' family members who suffer to variable degrees as a result of a breadwinner being in prison (Braithwaite 2002, 2003).

In any event, what kind of equality is expressed by a logic of equal punishment for equal wrongs when some offenders are lucky enough not to be raped or bashed in prison and others do suffer these horrors; when some are trapped in prison-induced contagions of drug addiction and others are not; when some acquire HIV, hepatitis, or tuberculosis in prison systems that are the best-known incubators of these contagions, and some do not? This is not to disagree that maximum sentences should be set on the basis of seriousness but to say that the right sentence is the minimally sufficient one.

Responsive regulation has had modest influence as a policy idea in the domains of business regulation and corporate crime enforcement because it formulated a way to reconcile the clear empirical evidence that sometimes sanctions work and sometimes they backfire—and likewise with social support. The evidence of this is just as clear with common crime; yet responsive regulation has had almost no influence on policing policies. This would not have surprised Edwin Sutherland ([1949] 1983), who 60 years ago first demonstrated propensities to tolerate forgiving approaches toward crime in the suites that are seldom evident toward crime in the streets.

Restorative justice provides stakeholders with professional advice on rehabilitation and prevention options they might choose. The community of care can then be mobilized to monitor and enforce compliance with whatever is undertaken. This is an approach informed by values that define not only a just legal order but also a caring civil society. These values are derived from the foundational republican value of freedom as nondomination (Braithwaite and Pettit 1990; Pettit 1997). Some who share these restorative values derive them from different foundations, including spiritual ones.

Ordering strategies in the pyramid is not just about putting less costly, less coercive, more respectful options lower down in order to save money and preserve freedom as nondomination. It is also that use of more dominating, less respectful forms of social control only after more dialogic forms have been tried first comes to be seen as more legitimate. When regulation is seen as more legitimate and more procedurally fair, compliance with law is more likely (Tyler 1990; Tyler and Huo 2002). Astute business regulators often set up this legitimacy explicitly (Dekker and Breakey 2016). During a restorative dialogue over an offense, the inspector will say there will be no penalty this time, but she hopes the manager understands that if she returns to find the company has slipped out of compliance again, she will have no choice but to refer it to the prosecutions unit. If and when the manager explicitly agrees that this is a reasonable approach, a future prosecution will likely be viewed as fair. Under this theory, therefore, privileging restorative justice at the base of the pyramid builds legitimacy and therefore prevents crime.

There is also a rational choice account of why the pyramid works. System capacity crises result in pretenses of consistent law enforcement when the reality is that punishment is spread thinly, weakly (Pontell 1978; Pontell, Black, and Geis 2014). Unfortunately, this problem will be worst when lawbreaking is worst; criminal justice is a sprinkler system that fails when the fire gets hot. Hardened offenders learn that the odds of serious punishment are low for any particular infraction. Tools like tax audits that are supposed to be about deterrence can backfire by teaching tax cheats how much they can get away with (Kinsey 1986).[1] The reluctance to escalate under the responsive pyramid model means that enforcement can be selective in a principled way. The display of the pyramid itself channels the rational actor down to the base of the pyramid. Noncompliance comes to be seen (accurately) as a slippery slope. In effect, the pyramid solves the system capacity problem by making punishment cheap. The pyramid says "unless you punish yourself for lawbreaking through an agreed action plan near the base of the pyramid, we will punish you more severely higher up the pyramid (and we stand ready to go as high as we have to)." So, it is cheaper for the rational actor to self-punish (as by agreeing to payouts to victims or community service). Some Asian criminal justice systems, such as that of Japan, work this way much of the time, even for serious crimes such as rape, aggravated assault, and murder that are frequently resolved through compensation and remorseful apology rather than through prison time, without such reparative leniency causing crime to spin out of control (Ahmed et al. 2001). Once the pyramid succeeds in creating a world in which most punishment is self-punishment, there is no longer a crisis of capacity to deliver punishment when it is needed. One of the messages the pyramid provides to corporate criminals is that "if you violate repeatedly without reform, it is going to be cheap for us to hurt you (because you are going to help us hurt you)" (Ayres and Braithwaite 1992, p. 44).

Paternoster and Simpson (1996) showed the limits of passive specific deterrence on intentions to commit corporate crime. When respondents held personal moral codes, these were more important for predicting compliance than were rational calculations of sanction threats (though the lat-

---

[1] On balance, however, Mazzolini, Pagani, and Santoro (2017) found that audits increased reported income by 8 percent on average, though audits that detected no extra tax liability reduced future reported income in the short term. See also Mendoza, Wielhouwer, and Kirchler (2017).

ter were important too). Appeals to business ethics (e.g., through restorative justice that exposes executives to consequences for victims of a corporate crime) therefore may be a better first strategy than sanction threats (Parker 2004). Best to succeed or fail with such ethical appeals first and then escalate to deterrence for the minority of contexts in which deterrence works better than ethical appeals. One of the psychological principles in play here is that when intrinsic motivation to comply with the law is intact, we do not want to crowd out intrinsic motivation with extrinsic threats (Ayres and Braithwaite 1992, pp. 49–50; Osterloh and Frey 2013; Frey 2017). Nine meta-analyses after responsive theory and behavioral economics picked up "crowding out" and "minimal sufficiency" from developmental psychology, there remains strong psychological evidence that crowding out does occur but also that intrinsic and extrinsic motivations both independently affect behavior (Cerasoli, Nicklin, and Ford 2014).

According to responsive regulatory theory, what we want is a legal system in which citizens learn that responsiveness is the way our legal institutions work. Once they see law as a responsive regulatory system, they know that there will be a chance to argue about unjust laws or unjust enforcement (as opposed to being forced into a lower court production line or a plea bargain). But they will also see that game playing to avoid legal obligations inexorably produces escalation. So does failure to listen to arguments about the harms their actions are doing and what redress is required. The forces of law are listening, fair, and therefore legitimate, but also ultimately are viewed as invincible.

A paradox of the pyramid is that to the extent that we can guarantee a commitment to escalate if steps are not taken to prevent the recurrence of lawbreaking, then escalation beyond the lower levels of the pyramid need rarely occur. This is the image of invincibility making self-regulation probable. Without locked-in commitment to escalation when reform fails to fix the problem, the system capacity crisis rebounds. A fundamental resource of responsive regulation is the belief of citizens in the inexorability of escalation if problems are not fixed.

Restorative justice works best with a specter of punishment threatening in the background but never threatened in the foreground. When punishment is thrust into the foreground even by implied threats, other-regarding deliberation is made difficult because the offender is pushed to deliberate in a self-regarding way—out of concern to protect him- or herself from punishment. This is not the way to engender empathy with the victim, internalization of the values of the law, and the values of restorative justice. The job of responsive regulators is to treat offenders as worthy of trust. When regulators do this, the law more often achieves its objectives (Braithwaite and Makkai 1994; Gangl, Hofmann, and Kirchler 2015; Haas et al. 2015). The ideal is to enculturate trust (in the foreground) while institutionalizing distrust (in the background) through deterrence as a last resort (Braithwaite 1998).

Testing theories about dynamic interventions layered in a pyramid is more complex than testing the effects of passive policies like heavier sentences because the effects of sequences of interventions must be tested. How can a regulatory pyramid be tested when it involves an entire suite of sequenced dialogic, then deterrent, and then incapacitative approaches? It has worked in raising an extra billion dollars in tax for each million spent on a program for multinational companies engaged in illegal profit shifting (to tax havens, e.g.; Braithwaite 2005, pp. 89–100). Evaluation in a tax compliance context requires first the creation of this whole pyramid of sequenced new policies for companies that have been paying no tax, and then observation of how much tax they pay after the new pyramid is put in place, as well as observing at what sequenced stage of the pyramid most tax payment starts to flow. The quality of information from the latter observations is instructive, yet low, because we do not know whether a compliance effect is the result of the last step up the pyramid or a combined effect of some subset of the whole sequence of escalations. A comparable evaluation challenge applies to problem-oriented policing as a meta-strategy. Randomizing some police patrols to problem-oriented policing shows that problem-oriented policing works as a meta-strategy (Braga 2002; Weisburd et al. 2010), but it gives feedback of limited quality on which initiatives addressing what problems produced the result. Even so, evaluating meta-strategies is more important work for criminology than evaluating single crime control strategies. How to think clearly about evidence in relation to dynamic theories of support and sanctions is the topic of a complementary paper (Braithwaite 2016).


II. Inexorability of Support and Sanctions

Inexorability has three elements:

- prioritizing increased consistency of detection above tougher punishment;

- always taking serious crimes seriously with a continuum of restorative responses to every detected serious crime; avoiding "do nothing" responses;
- escalating the seriousness of response to a second, third, and fourth offense; sticking with the problem until it goes away.


## A. Prioritize Detection

The inexorability piece of the theory builds on the evidence from the deterrence literature that perceived and actual severity of punishment are rarely good predictors of compliance with the law, while perceived and actual certainty of detection are often useful predictors (Blumstein 2011; Robinson 2011; Friesen 2012; Nagin 2013). One reason for this is that detection mobilizes not only formal punishment but also informal disapproval, which is a more powerful driver of compliance with the law (Braithwaite 1989). Theoretically, this is not just about an evolution of cooperation (Axelrod 1984), an evolution of compliance when noncompliance is visible to a punisher. The newer theoretical insight is that it is also about indirect reciprocity through fear of reputational loss even without repeated encounters with the same people (Berger 2011; Nowak 2012; Braithwaite and Hong 2015). Criminologists therefore tend to read the deterrence literature as showing that "detection deterrence" and "disapproval deterrence," both specific and general, are more powerful than deterrence by severe formal sentences. Minimally sufficient deterrence is based on this view that "detection deterrence," indirect reciprocity, and "disapproval deterrence" are indeed more powerful than deterrence by severe state punishment.


## B. Always Respond

Inexorability is absent in contemporary urban justice. Enforcement swamping and system capacity overload mean that young people picked up as minor first offenders learn that they do not receive significant punishments even if they are prosecuted. This is also likely to happen with their second, third, or fourth minor offenses during their teenage years. When the system does finally decide to hit youth offenders hard because someone decides they have "had enough chances," offenders wonder "why now?" Legitimacy is obviously a casualty of this policing strategy for muddling through system capacity crises. Tough punishment seems to repeat offenders to have unfairly come out of the blue, when they got away with worse in the past, when they see friends get away with even worse. Because this seems arbitrary, it has shallow legitimacy in their eyes. In the next section, I consider an alternative response approach to first, second, third, fourth, and fifth offenses.

## C. Escalate Responses

The trouble with inexorability is that it is hard to reconcile with minimal sufficiency of punishment. Punishing everyone detected seems like maximal net widening rather than minimally sufficient. The challenge of averting net widening is to craft a minimally sufficient response for a minor first offense. Police, teachers, or parents who observe children hitting each other do well to pause to insist that they stop fighting and say something nonstigmatizing like "You guys are better than that," and then walk on. This is a better way of taking violence seriously than looking the other way. It is more than "nattering" as one walks by without stopping the violence (Patterson and Bank 1989) but less than net widening, which creates some kind of recording of alleged wrongdoing.

Restorative theory can inform an inexorability that averts a perception of an arbitrary punishment lottery. The evidence is strong that restorative justice buttresses the legitimacy of the justice system (Tyler et al. 2007; Sherman 2014; Barnes et al. 2015; Miller and Hefner 2015). Prosecution is not the way to go with a first-offending child arrested for a petty offense. Nor is turning a blind eye. A restorative police caution with a degree of ritual seriousness is an option. Police can respond to a shopkeeper holding a child who has stolen something by ensuring the child returns stolen property and taking the shopkeeper's contact details, and then either taking the child home to ask parents or guardians what they intend to do or holding the child at the police station until parents arrive to take him home following a restorative caution. The restorative caution gives the child and parent space to come up with the suggestion that they will visit the shopkeeper together to apologize, perhaps even bake a cake or bring some flowers. Traditionalists see such idiosyncratic gestures of apology as strange elements to take seriously in criminal justice policy; yet that is the essence of trusting the community rather than the police with averting an offender's reaction that "nothing happened, so breaking the law is no big deal." Police tell the parents that they expect a text advising what has been done to apologize. The police say they may check that the shopkeeper is satisfied. In other words, most of the work of social disapproval is delegated away from the police. One reason for this as one approach to taking every crime seriously is the evidence that censure by families and closest friends is more likely to be a reintegrative form of shaming, while censure by criminal justice officials is more likely to be stigmatizing (Ahmed et al. 2001, pp. 157–76).

So, what to do with the teenager's second minor offense? The minimally sufficient deterrence suggestion is a restorative justice conference that the victim is invited to attend. The child's loved ones would be expected to sit in the circle for a serious family ritual of parents, grandparents, siblings, perhaps aunts, uncles, and a sports coach or a teacher trusted and nominated by the child. Communicating this expectation is important because a concern is to ensure that overburdened mothers do not shoulder all the burdens of social support. Wider circles of participation also enhance the effectiveness of restorative justice (Braithwaite 2002, pp. 50–51, 55, 74, 252–65).[2] Unlike a criminal trial that assembles people who can inflict maximum damage to those on the other side of the case, the restorative justice conference assembles people who can offer maximum support to their own side, be it the victim's or the offender's. At a meeting of two communities of care, communication of disapproval comes from those personally affected by the crime, but more importantly from those who most love the offender. Nathan Harris's evidence from restorative justice conferences is that only disapproval communicated by people the offender most loves is effective in inducing remorse (Harris 2001, pp. 157–76). People who are well liked but not loved are not potent at inducing remorse. Nor are the police.

While an informal police caution for a first offense is a minimalist response in terms of taking the crime seriously, a restorative justice conference for a second offense escalates to a longer family and community ritual with a trained facilitator and a wider circle of participation by people concerned about the child. Such a conference becomes a focused way of supporting children. Are they struggling in school? If so, what support can the conference mobilize? Are they struggling in their relationships? Are their friends leading them into trouble? Is there support from other friends who steer them clear of such trouble? If there are problems with

---

[2] This result is also evident in Wilson, Olaghere, and Kimbrell's (2017) meta-analysis finding that teen courts, impact panels, and reparative boards were ineffective forms of what some loosely call "restorative justice."

alcohol, drugs, or anger management, proactive support may be needed. In this world of social support, every child leans on a "youth support circle." This is a restoratively elaborated version of parent-teacher conferences in schools that meet every year with every child over 12, with their extended family, and with well-networked elders until the child is helped to get his or her first job or get into college (Braithwaite 2001). The youth support circle is designed to reduce stigmatization of crime by being universal; children who never do anything wrong have them. In that world of a better-funded, more communal, welfare state, this conference for a second offense has no extra cost because it would be integrated into routine youth support conferences for building human capital, affecting only the timing of a conference that might normally be annual.

What about a third criminal offense? A longer restorative conference with a wider circle of participants is needed, usually with a follow-up conference to celebrate completion of an agreement. That would be more onerous than the conference for the second offense. More importantly, the next conference would see an escalation of social support for the child compared to the first conference. A child welfare worker would attend. The expertise a trained social worker would bring would include knowledge of the range of options available in the area for rehabilitation of the young offender. The social worker should also have a knowledge of principles of risk-need-responsivity in evidence-based selection of rehabilitation options (Andrews and Bonta 1998, 2010), a sound knowledge of the "what works" literature of criminology, and a good clinical capacity for responsiveness to the complexities of the specific case. In a restorative justice conference, it is not the job of the expert to dictate to a family (Pennell and Burford 2000). Restorative justice works by delivering stronger implementation of conference agreements enforced by the parties themselves than courts can achieve with police enforcement. This was the biggest effect size in the Canadian Department of Justice meta-analysis of restorative justice by Latimer, Dowden, and Muise (2001). The effects of completion of restorative justice agreements were much stronger than the statistically significant effect of restorative justice on reduced reoffending compared to control group members.

We can reconcile these results by understanding that if a restorative justice conference and a court both send a child to a counterproductive program, restorative justice will do more damage. The child will be more likely to complete the counterproductive program when it was agreed to by the family and other conference stakeholders than when the same outcome is ordered by the court. Restorative justice does greater harm than court when it agrees on counterproductive measures and greater good than court when it agrees on effective measures. The reason is that restorative justice is a superior delivery vehicle for rehabilitation programs.

The idea is to strengthen this comparative advantage of restorative conferences by investing in experts who speak up when the family considers sending the child to a boot camp, experts who point out that the evidence for the effectiveness of boot camps is discouraging (Lipsey 2009; MacKenzie and Farrington 2015). It follows from this that a good way to reanalyze a meta-analysis such as that by Lipsey (2009) would be to assess whether the combination of highly effective interventions such as social cognitive programs with restorative justice as their delivery vehicle increases effect sizes. Put more provocatively, it is not useful to compare effect sizes for restorative justice with those for other programs because it is better to conceive of restorative justice as a way of delivering multiple strategies. It makes more sense to compare restorative justice with a court as an alternative delivery vehicle of diverse correctional options, as in Strang et al. (2013). The bigger insights might come from teasing out which specific combinations of programs and delivery vehicles have positive and negative synergies, as is done in the business regulation literature (Gunningham, Grabosky, and Sinclair 1998).

A conference for a fourth offense might allow the family to mobilize rehabilitative options from further afield or expensive options that are rationed. Critics might query why such an expansion of the quantum of social support would make a difference given that in Lipsey's (2009, p. 141) meta-analysis of youth justice programs, providing more hours of services surprisingly did not increase the effect sizes of interventions. Restorative justice programs were the big exception to this result; hours of restorative service provision strongly increased the already statistically significant effect size of restorative justice in reducing reoffending. Within the "restorative justice" category of programs, those that included a mediation component, as opposed to simple restitution, also had an effect size more than one-third higher (Lipsey 2009, p. 142).

A conference for a fourth offense might also send the conference option to court for approval (or modification) by a judge. A meta-analysis from seven British studies led by Joanna Shapland concluded that restorative justice conferences have benefits that average eight times their costs (Strang et al. 2013, pp. 44–46). This result is a reason we do not consider costly escalation to court until a fourth offense. Yet isn't escalation to something less cost-effective at any stage surely inept? Actually, there is a relevant complexity of the evidence that should leave us open to this. While the Strang et al. review found that court is clearly less effective in preventing crime than restorative justice, it also suggested that a combination of court and conference could be more effective than either separately. More data are needed to assess if this is robust. The quantitative transitional justice literature finds that war crime prosecutions, truth (and reconciliation) commissions, and amnesties all have limited or contextual explanatory power on their own. However, when all three are used together, that country can experience a strong reduction in human rights abuses, at least if the truth commission engagement with civil society is wide and deep and if amnesties are qualified rather than blanket (Olsen, Payne, and Reiter 2010; Dancy et al. 2013; see also Sikkink 2011, pp. 184–87). The combined cost of a restorative justice conference that then reports to court might also be less than the sum of its parts if the integration can be designed to streamline court processing. This is essentially how the most comprehensive youth justice conferencing program in the world operates in New Zealand (Johnstone 2013).

At a fourth conference, when a young person and a victim are on the precipice of deeper trouble, escalated interventionist expectations can be assumed by the community of care. For example, in a 2014 interview I was told of a teenager in an Irish Republican Army area of Belfast who had repeatedly assaulted his mother. The restorative conference was conducted by Community Restorative Justice Northern Ireland. One part of the community restorative justice agreement, which had many parts, was that four community members agreed to respond immediately to calls for help from the mother and participated in training on how they could respond. These were not civil servants living far away, arriving the next morning. They lived around the corner and committed to respond promptly 24 hours a day. This is a good example of how restorative justice can expand to a wider, more immediate, more proximate web of social control and social support, while still providing a softer web than court enforcement to protect the mother by locking up her child.

By this point in our inexorability narrative, deterrence maximalists will be aghast that we are at a fifth criminal offense with no formally punitive response presumed. The offender has had "five free hits": the police restorative caution, followed by three restorative justice conferences, and then a first court appearance, all "doing nothing" for punitive deterrence. Perhaps there will have been six if the first restorative caution was preceded by an informal warning on the run.

Contrary to maximalist fears, offenders do not perceive restorative justice conferences as "doing nothing," but as a grueling experience of meeting their victims in the presence of their loved ones (Umbreit and Coates 1992; Schiff 1999). Deterrence maximalists are wrong to see imprisonment as the only kind of perceptually tough response. Perceptually, the process is the punishment, as the title of Malcolm Feeley's (1979) book attests, especially when the process is designed with a ritual seriousness that is emotionally demanding.


### III. Dynamic Deterrence and Defiance

The Sword of Damocles is an ancient metaphor popularized by the Roman republican philosopher Cicero (1877, pp. 185–86). He based it on the story of Dionysius II, a Sicilian king of the fourth and fifth centuries BCE, who hung a sword attached by a horsehair above the head of a courtier called Damocles who envied the king. The ruler wanted to illustrate the insecurity of being king. Today, the Sword of Damocles generally refers to any ever-present peril hanging over the head of a person. The existence of an ever-present peril is an important element of minimally sufficient deterrence.

### A. Preserving the Sword

At the court appearance for a fifth offense in a criminal career, the court might signal that a sword hangs over the child or young adult. This is not best done as a threat. The power of the sword, according to Cicero, is not that it falls or is threatened; its power is that it hangs. The regulatory literature shows that the better signaling is for the judge to say at the outset of the court hearing for a fifth offense that its objective is to support the family and save them from having their child taken away. Perhaps only later than a fifth offense and only after an offense that is very serious would the judge ask whether the offender would think it reasonable that she be incarcerated to protect the community if she were to commit another offense of such seriousness.[3] The objective at that later trial is to open the

---

[3] Note the use of motivational interviewing techniques here, which are empirically established as techniques that are effective and that avert threat making (Rubak et al. 2005; Lundahl et al. 2010).

mind of the offender to the reasonableness of the community protecting itself with a custodial sentence. The idea at the next trial for the next serious offense would be to remind the offender that she herself in her last appearance said that a custodial sentence would be reasonable if an offense of this seriousness recurred. The judge would then concede the offender's point of view but mobilize social support for one last chance to stay in the community, while making it clear that next time she was likely to agree with the incapacitation recourse that the offender herself had concluded was reasonable in these circumstances.

At every stage, the minimally sufficient approach requires that the offender be led to see a new escalation of social support provided in response to a new transgression, but also a slippery slope toward a set of punitive options with life imprisonment at the peak of the pyramid. Of course, community service orders, fines, electronically monitored home detention, orders to a violent husband to transfer bank accounts to his wife so she has the financial capacity to leave him, and a diverse variety of other options that are found lower in the pyramid are available as alternatives to prison. The sheer diversity of community gifts of support conveys a message of care when it includes, for example, the Royal Society for the Protection of Cruelty to Animals program in Australia, which guarantees care to the pets of domestic violence victims who stay in abusive relationships to care for their pets or to the pets of offenders who are required to move out. The escalation of support as a life careens into deeper trouble is a way of increasing the legitimacy of more severe sanctions as a last resort when escalation to them does occur. It is also a strategy for combating the widespread perception of criminal offenders in many societies that the system lets you get away with it for years and then one day out of the blue locks you up. The proposal is inexorable both in escalating support and in the way it signals a move to escalating deterrence.

Why reserve court appearances until a fourth official detected offense? Why reserve serious sanctions for later still in a criminal career? One reason is the evidence from the Canberra randomized controlled trials of restorative justice led by Lawrence Sherman and Heather Strang. Offenders randomly assigned to restorative justice had greater fear of future criminal enforcement after a restorative justice experience than did offenders randomly assigned to criminal prosecution after their criminal trials (Braithwaite 2002, pp. 119–22). Offenders emerged from their restorative conferences more fearful that they would be rearrested if they offended again, more fearful of family and friends finding out, and more fearful of a future conference, compared to those assigned to court (Sherman and Strang 1997; Sherman et al. 1998). Minimally sufficient deterrence favors restorative justice for multiple early offenses in a criminal career because restorative justice sharpens the Sword of Damocles. Criminal trials blunt the sword hanging over the offender. After bringing down the courtroom sword, it loses mystique. The criminal trial in current judicial practice blunts the Sword of Damocles because in the majority of nonserious cases the offender is surprised at how easily she gets off as the court struggles with its system capacity overload.

The minimally sufficient deterrence idea is to hold the trial in reserve until it is time to take the case very seriously by projecting a clear trajectory of escalation to an ever bigger Sword of Damocles that is being averted by more and more support. Among other objectives, this support is intended to make that sharpening sword appear ever more just. Other kinds of criminological evidence support a Sword of Damocles effect (Sherman 1992, 2011), including Dunford's (1990) finding that a warrant for arrest deterred domestic violence substantially better than either actual arrest or nonarrest. The theoretical perspective of minimal sufficiency is that warrants for arrest have great attractions over actual arrest and that deferred prosecutions are more powerful tools than actual prosecutions. These are problem-solving tools that can enable support to play a larger role than sanctions. Concluding that deferred prosecutions are in principle powerful tools is not to deny that their widespread use in corporate criminal law has often approximated doing nothing in matters of a seriousness that called for doing quite a lot (Eisinger 2017).

## B. Dynamic Deterrence That Accounts for Defiance

Responsive regulatory theory argues that the passive deterrence thinking of the law and economics tradition, as in Gary Becker's (1993) Nobel Prize–winning work, has limited value. The reason is that real-world deterrence unfolds dynamically. Dynamic deterrence moves through sequences of threats; passive deterrence is static, involving levels of threat that are constant across time. International relations theorists have been more dynamically sophisticated than criminologists and economists of deterrence. They do not assume that, even though the United States has a bigger deterrent arsenal than the rest of the world's militaries, it works for the United States to say to another country "Do what we say or else!" There is evidence aplenty, from countries as close as Cuba, that threats are as likely to induce defiance as compliance. This is accepted even by conservative writers like Michael Rubin who oppose dialogue with "rogue states." Rubin (2014, p. 4) nevertheless conceived of Cuba, North Korea, Iran, Iraq, and Libya as "backlash states" that were "defiant." Former US Defense Secretary William Cohen tweaked this definition of rogue states to conceive of them as regimes "immune to traditional deterrence" (Rubin 2014, p. 4). While demands for compliance backed by passive deterrence work poorly in international affairs, when the United States dynamically escalates its deterrent power around a weaker country, as it did during the Cuban missile crisis, it can get a deterrent result (dismantled Cuban missiles). Of course, dynamic escalation of deterrence in international affairs is a dangerous game because little Cuba might mobilize powerful friends to dynamic escalation of their deterrent capabilities in response. Little Serbia did manage to dynamically escalate catastrophic deterrence by triggering the escalation to World War I after the assassination of Archduke Ferdinand by its citizens.

Psychologists of learning approach the way punishments work as dynamic learning sequences that are beyond the writ of static deterrence models. They demonstrated psychological reactance to threats (Brehm and Brehm 1981). Defiance is a more elegant term that Sherman (1992) deployed to describe this phenomenon.

A paradox of the pyramid is that by being able to escalate to tough responses at its peak, more of the regulatory action can be driven down to its deliberative base. Yet punishment, according to responsive regulatory theory, simultaneously increases deterrence and defiance. Figure 2 is a way of summarizing the implications of more than 50 experiments on defiance originally conducted by Brehm and Brehm (1981) and their colleagues, and many more since (e.g., Rains 2013). At low levels of punishment, defiance usually exceeds deterrence. Figure 2 expresses this as the resistance effect exceeding the capitulation effect at lower levels of coercion. The dashed line is the net compliance effect represented as a sum of the resistance score and the capitulation score. Only when punishment bites very deeply at the peak of the pyramid, resulting in many giving up on resistance, does the deterrence effect exceed the defiance effect.

Yet escalation only as far as the lower levels of the pyramid can elicit compliance when that first step up the ladder is seen as a signal of willingness to redeem the regulator's promise to keep climbing until the problem is fixed. Put another way, the first escalation becomes a wake-up call that convinces the offender that she or he is on a slippery slope. Social support

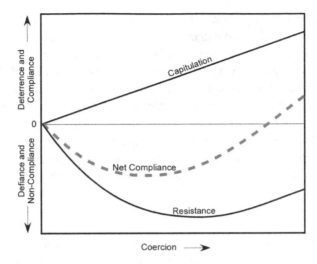

FIG. 2.—A theory of the effect of coercion on compliance as the net result of a capitulation effect and a defiant resistance effect. Source: Based loosely on experiments summarized by Brehm and Brehm (1981).

initiatives also help by signaling that paths off that slope are available. Perception of the dynamic inexorability of the pyramid does most deterrence work, not the passive general deterrent. Not only does the specific passive deterrent at low levels of the pyramid of sanctions fail to deter very effectively; it mostly engenders more defiance than deterrence.

Redundancy in the design of the pyramid also saves the day when defiance effects initially exceed deterrence effects. The redundancy idea is that all regulatory tools have deep dangers of counterproductivity. Therefore, one must deploy a mix of regulatory tools with heavy representation of dialogue and social support in the mix. The best way to deploy the mix is dynamically, so that, in sequence, the strengths of one tool have a chance to cover the weaknesses of another. For example, the pyramid in figure 1 is about the strengths of one form of restorative justice covering the weaknesses of other forms of restorative justice, the strengths of deterrence covering the weaknesses of restorative justice, the strengths of incapacitation covering the weaknesses of deterrence, and the strengths of strong social support covering the weaknesses of limp social support.

The risk of defiance exceeding deterrence is one reason that the peak of the pyramid should always be threatening in the background but not directly threatened in the foreground. Making threats increases defiance, turning the defiance curve in figure 2 more steeply downward. How then can police and judges be threatening in the background without making threats? One way is by being transparent for the first time that the pyramid is the new policy that precedes escalation. Law enforcers must be the change they want to see. They achieve this by communicating openly with society about the design policy of the pyramid. By inviting citizens to be partners in the democratic design of different regulatory pyramids for responding to different crime problems, citizens also come to learn about the inexorability of escalation until there is compliance with the law. The ideal is to communicate the inexorability of deterrence in this way rather than by making threats in specific cases.

## C. Dynamic Deterrence as a Remedy to Enforcement Swamping

A dependable, inexorable peak to the pyramid is a particular way of thinking about what Mark Kleiman (2009) calls dynamic concentration of deterrence, often called (in a misleadingly static way) focused deterrence.[4] For responsive regulation, the dynamic concentration of deterrence potency is at the rarely used peak of the pyramid. Kleiman, like David Kennedy (2009), reached a conclusion similar to responsive regulatory theory about the superiority of dynamic over passive deterrence through contemplating how to respond to enforcement swamping as a challenge for thinly resourced policing agencies.

Kleiman's dynamic concentration theory shows why abandoning random targeting in favor of a strategic concentration of targeting can work as long as monitoring works. In the simple case of scarce resources enabling targeting of only one of two regulated actors, the intuition that "concentrating on Al would allow Bob to run wild" is wrong. If Al is

---

[4] The danger of describing the theory behind innovations like Operation Ceasefire as "focused deterrence" is that it will be understood as a static policy of identifying the highest risk group for targeting. Even the principal authors of the strategy, who clearly understand its dynamic qualities, often describe a static deterrence targeting strategy, complemented by short breakouts into discussing its dynamic aspects (Kennedy, Kleiman, and Braga 2017). The most common mistake business regulators make concerning responsive regulation is to understand it as a static policy of triaging the highest risk groups for targeting with more deterrent strategies. The point of reframing deterrence is to push criminologists away from such static ways of thinking. Minimally sufficient deterrence commends restorative justice as an alternative to prison even in the highest-risk circumstances such as creeping genocide, actual genocide, or murders that risk further revenge killings (e.g., Braithwaite and Gohar 2014).

promised certain punishment, a rational Al will comply as long as compliance costs are less than penalties. "Then Bob, seeing that Al has complied, will himself comply; otherwise Bob knows that he would certainly be punished. So giving priority to Al actually increases pressure on Bob." In this we see the dynamic elements of the strategy. Kleiman (2009, p. 54) shows that this initial insight holds for a variety of conditions such as promising certain punishment of the second mover rather than the first and larger numbers of players. Dynamic concentration helps a little punishment go a long way.

Tax authorities have also learned how to respond to massive enforcement swamping when rich people, trusts, and companies follow their herds into illegal tax shelters. This is to announce that while the tax authority lacks the resources to enforce the law against all who stampede into shelters, they can prosecute the first risk taker to jump into a shelter after the date of their announcement of intent to attack particular shelters in the courts. This can be extremely effective in ending cascades of risky tax cheating by high-wealth individuals and corporations (Braithwaite 2005). Braithwaite (2012) discovered the same dynamic concentration in the wisdom of generals who face the biggest enforcement swamping challenge in the world today: small numbers of UN peacekeepers facing Africa's worst war in the Democratic Republic of Congo.

As usual, practitioners here were ahead of theory. Tax officials were ahead of us, as were those generals in Congo and that Texas ranger on the screen in our youth. The ranger faces a lynch mob with one bullet in his gun. He turns them away with the promise "the first to step forward dies." Kleiman (2009, pp. 49–67) elegantly theorizes why the dynamic concentration of deterrence by the Texas ranger works. A meta-analysis of 10 quasi-experimental and one randomized controlled trial of dynamic concentration found consistent effectiveness across studies and a medium-sized statistically significant crime reduction effect overall (Braga and Weisburd 2012, 2014; Weisburd, Farrington, and Gill 2017). The intuition that concentrating deterrence on Max will allow Mary to run wild turns out to be wrong in terms of rational choice theory (Kleiman 2009, pp. 49–67) and empirically wrong according to Braga, Apel, and Welsh (2013, p. 315), who found that with dynamically concentrated deterrence, "vicariously treated gangs were deterred by the treatment experiences of their rivals and allies." Dynamic focusing at the peak of a pyramid is just one way of concentrating limited enforcement resources that delivers dynamism to both specific and general deterrence.

## D. *Dynamically Raising the Bar Serious Offenders Must Jump*

Boston's Operation Ceasefire is criminology's *locus classicus* of the dynamic concentration of deterrence in showing how an inner-city justice system overwhelmed by the frequency of gang violence reduced homicide (Kennedy 2009). It was also "focused deterrence" in that it did not attempt to deter all crimes perpetrated by gang members, but only their gun crimes. My hypothesis is that the passively focused features of Operation Ceasefire may have some value, but its dynamic concentration of deterrence is more innovative and more germinal. It follows that a re-running and updating of the encouraging Braga and Weisburd (2012) meta-analysis are needed to compare those interventions that were simply focused and passive in their deterrence with those in which the intervention also delivered a dynamic concentration of deterrence. The dynamic concentration aspect of Operation Ceasefire involved the Texas ranger trope described above. Police sat down in meetings with gang leaders and gangs to let them know, in effect, that we know that you know that we do not have the capacity to go after all of you for all your sins. But we do have the capacity to go after all the offenses, and all the parole and probation breaches, of all the members of the next gang to use a firearm in a crime. This means that instead of concentrating deterrence on the worst offenders, deterrence was dynamically concentrated on the first offender to use a firearm after the announcement date. The theory of the intervention was that all gangs would self-regulate gun carrying and use to avoid being the first gang to be targeted or the second gang to be targeted after the first. The ethnographic side of the evidence on the formidable desistance of these gangs from gun use seems to support this hope (Kennedy 2009). For proportionality theorists, it is of course a weakness of the program that it diverts resources from prosecuting the most serious offenses to what might be minor parole violations after a gang uses guns.[5]

Operation Ceasefire was in tension with the minimally sufficient deterrence model in two ways, however. First, the approach was thin on restorative justice and social support as approaches that strengthen a deterrence strategy into which restorative justice and social support are integrated. There was certainly dialogue with gang members involved, and pathways out of the gang were discussed and even provided for some;

---

[5] This critique also applies to responsive regulation. It has been eloquently advanced by Karen Yeung (2004).

but from the perspective of minimally sufficient deterrence, it was too narrowly oriented to pulling levers to make deterrence more "swift and certain" for a strategically targeted subgroup. There are reasons to suspect that in some of these programs this swift and certain deterrence may have been communicated with Trumpian threats, which risk being counterproductive according to minimal sufficiency theory, defiance theory, and the theory of motivational interviewing.

There was insufficient attention in Operation Ceasefire to a dynamic approach to support. Under the minimally sufficient deterrence model, support peaks during the period in which desistance is setting in. I am inclined to read protests from the leaders of the innovation that this is not true as overstated and revisionist (Kennedy, Kleiman, and Braga 2017). That matters little. If moderately violent societies like the United States are to learn how to manage their hot spots better from experience with peacekeeping in extremely violent societies like Congo, we might be able to build a consensus for dynamic concentration of support to become more prominent than dynamic concentration of deterrence. This policy lesson has been better learned in international peacekeeping and peace building than in national policing to control organized violence (Braithwaite and D'Costa 2018, chap. 3). The lesson is that desistance should not only cause a lifting of punishment; the strategy should also maximally concentrate rewards at the moment of desistance. The rewards are not only tangible matters of vocational training and job placement, but also rituals of pride at celebration conferences in which loved ones eulogize peacemaking and rehearse redemption scripts (Maruna 2001).

Project HOPE is a drug court program in the focused deterrence tradition that initially seemed to have promising pyramidal features of escalated response targeted on hard cases. HOPE stood for Hawai'i Opportunity Probation with Enforcement. It has been adopted in dozens of US locations with Honest replacing Hawai'i, yet with mostly very limited investment in creating job or other "opportunities." Intervention escalated as drug users went off the rails. Yet it may be the program that ran off the rails; much of the rhetoric of its practitioners was maximalist, oriented to "swift and certain" deterrence. This happened when the evidence is not supportive of criminal justice swiftness, even though swiftness of parental response in child-rearing is important (Pratt and Turanovic 2018).

Hawken and Kleiman (2009) entitle their evaluation *Managing Drug Involved Probationers with Swift and Certain Sanctions: Evaluating Hawaii's*

*HOPE*. Duriez, Cullen, and Manchak (2014) raise the concern that the ideology driving the diffusion of Project HOPE has emphasized its "swift and certain" character, ignoring other positive features such as motivational interviewing training for officers in the program, something for which there is a strong evidence base (Rubak et al. 2005; Lundahl et al. 2010), which is why motivational interviewing has become central to responsive regulation (Braithwaite 2011). The literature reviews of HOPE can be characterized as somewhere between showing great promise and being discouraging (Lattimore et al. 2016).[6] As with Operation Ceasefire, they should be redone after some on-the-ground engagement with what each specific program actually does. They could be coded qualitatively or quantitatively according to four variables: how much deterrence is involved (HOPE's E: "Enforcement"), how much social support there is (HOPE's O: "Opportunity"), how dynamically concentrated the deterrence is, and how dynamically concentrated the support is. Meta-analyses might contribute more to science if they were more theoretically focused on what they evaluate and less focused on heterogeneous puzzles like HOPE that are in essence brands.

The second tension between minimally sufficient deterrence and Operation Ceasefire is that an approach that says your gang will be seriously targeted intensively only if it uses guns challenges the inexorability principle. In an enforcement swamping crisis, however, we must confront the reality that priorities must be set that start where it is most important to start. In Democratic Republic of Congo, that priority was mass rape atrocities in which hundreds of women and children were sometimes raped, murdered, or enslaved into mines (Braithwaite 2012). At least one peacekeeping commander was effective in reducing this seemingly impossible enforcement swamping crisis during the first decade of this century, according to my Congo fieldwork. He convinced assembled militant leaders that the next militant group to commit a mass rape atrocity would be the group on which peacekeepers would focus all their military capabilities to bring perpetrators to trial. In my Congo fieldwork trips early in this decade, I reproached the head of MONUSCO, the military com-

---

[6] Lattimore et al. (2016, p. 1103) describe the HOPE program they evaluated at four sites as a "program that emphasizes close monitoring; frequent drug testing; and swift, certain, and fair (SCF) sanctioning. It also reserves scarce treatment resources for those most in need." There is not much escalation of support in that description, nor any dynamic distinctiveness of the deterrence strategy to transcend the limits of static deterrence.

mander, the deputy commander, the general in charge of the relevant region, and the US ambassador for failure to implement this strategy against Colonel Cheka of Mai Mai Cheka, allegedly the worst perpetrator of mass rape atrocities, and some others like him. Within a year of the appearance of publications that discussed this (e.g., Braithwaite 2012), the United Nations announced a policy shift in the direction of dynamic concentration of deterrence, though this had nothing to do with the publications. The consensus of knowledgeable commentators is that this quickly improved the security of the people of Congo after 2014, particularly through the surrender of the M23 armed group that in 2012 captured Goma, a strategic city with a population of a million that is now liberated. In 2017 after almost 3 years of sustained military pressure to force surrender to face trial, Cheka turned himself in. That is no more than suggestive qualitative evidence for dynamic concentration of deterrence from the least likely case (Eckstein 1975) of probably the world's most extreme and persistent enforcement swamping crisis in recent decades.

Gun violence was obviously a good target for Operation Ceasefire. It produced a wonderful result in reducing shootings and homicide by more than 30 percent, a result that continued to be supported in more recent work on dynamic concentration of deterrence on US gang violence (Braga, Apel, and Welsh 2013; Kennedy, Kleiman, and Braga 2017). The strategy, however, fails the inexorability test of minimally sufficient deterrence because inexorability happens only for the particular offense in focus (usually gun crime). Prioritizing of greatest harm is desirable and might not deeply threaten inexorability as long as there is a strategy to move on to clean up one kind of gang crime after another, to move down to the B-list of gang harms and then a C-list after the A-list of gun homicide harms has been tamed.[7] Then a strategy like Operation Ceasefire perhaps in the long run could pass the inexorability test; likewise with enforcement swamping crises with tax shelters that the United States and Australia have faced in recent decades. Australia learned that it is possible gradually to raise the bar on tax compliance obligations. This is achieved by targeting the 10 worst tax compliers each year, a different 10 each year because last year's terrible 10 are no longer so terrible this year:

---

[7] At times, practitioners speak of A-lists and B-lists in static terms, by e.g. arguing that police go after an A-list of the most serious offenders for automatic prosecution, putting only the B-list into an Operation Ceasefire or a deferred prosecution program.

When the judgment is made that there is a culture of tax cheating in a particular market segment, the industry norm revealed in the multivariate analysis is still used to target those furthest below the norm for audit and other compliance tools. But more of them can be targeted than in other industries. And when they are caught out by the audit, the bar they are required to reach before they are released from targeted surveillance can be raised a little higher than the industry norm. As a result of the worst 10 compliers in the industry moving from way below the old norm to above it, the norm of course is moved upwards. Then in the next year, a new set of the worst 10 in the industry is moved up above that higher norm. This raises the bar again. We can in this way keep raising the bar with problem industries until they are paying their fair share. (Braithwaite 2005, p. 160)

Stampedes of the wealthy into tax shelter booms do end, as they did in Australia in the late 1970s and again around 2000 (Braithwaite 2005). Cascades of open-air drug markets taking over the great cities, even the stairs of the New York Public Library, also end, and that contributed to the downward cascade of homicide in Manhattan (Zimring 2011). Consider a brief list of accomplishments in reversing catastrophic cascades. The ozone hole was substantially closed even though it seemed unstoppable until the Montreal Protocol started to reverse the cascade into chemicals that were widening it (Kuttippurath and Nair 2017). Resources were provided to developing countries to comply with the Montreal Protocol after 1987, and there were diplomatic shots across their bows as well, particularly by US embassies (Braithwaite and Drahos 2000, pp. 261–67). Perhaps too late, perhaps not, today we see at least the beginnings of reverse cascades from coal to solar. President Kennedy predicted a cascade of 15–25 nuclear powers by the 1970s; yet there are still only the United States, Russia, China, the United Kingdom, France, Israel, India, Pakistan, and North Korea thanks to civilizing forces in international civil society that won a 2017 Nobel Peace Prize and dogged regulatory inspection in places like Iraq under the nuclear nonproliferation regime (Braithwaite and Drahos 2000, p. 318). Interminable civil wars in the places where the worst wars have cascaded for longest, such as Democratic Republic of Congo, will also one day reverse to cascades of peace.

The trend in regulatory theory is to conceive ever greater sophistication in risk assessment and risk management as the main game of how best to cope with the seemingly impossible challenges of regulatory enforcement swamping (Black and Baldwin 2010). Though this is not totally wrong, I suspect we learn most from worst cases like Cambodia after its multiple cascades of genocidal violence beyond the 1970s. In the 1990s, particularly since 1998, downward cascades of violence began to spread in Cambodia that Broadhurst, Bouhours, and Bouhours (2015, 2018) described as a dynamic "civilizing process" (Elias 1978; Pinker 2011). Broadhurst and his colleagues document that local police and UN peacekeepers did useful things to help trigger the reverse cascades. As they show with Cambodia, as a least likely case (Eckstein 1975), it is not so much that police were geniuses of risk analysis. Rather they did something that Malcolm Sparrow (2000) simply describes as pick some important problems and fix them.

Cambodia was more a matter of return to long-run momentum toward civilizing processes that citizens crave and governments pursue when they seek legitimacy from citizens and with the international community. This was combined with police and peacekeepers helping out with an A-list of violence problems that they helped clean up, eventually moving on to B- and C-lists. A-list criminality included robbery, homicide, and kidnapping, with cattle theft being high on the B-list because this can be financially devastating in rural areas. Local police became quite popular according to Broadhurst and his colleagues and gradually moved away from putting bullets in the heads of desperados and toward peacetime policing.

We can learn from local priests in Rwanda who acted like Texas rangers without even a single bullet in the midst of Rwanda's cascade of genocide. The priests stood their ground, stopping the genocide from spreading to their community through their emotional dominance in insisting that their church would not stand for this in their village (Klusemann 2012). Other priests who tried this were hacked down. Together, long-run civilizing processes helped by dynamic concentrations of sanctions and support and gradually raising the bar on what kinds of violence are intolerable eventually can pacify even a Cambodia or a Rwanda or close an ozone hole. This can be done without filling prisons.[8] Or so I hypothesize.

---

[8] Rwanda did fill its prisons with 126,000 charged with participation in its 1995 genocide. Many were children who were raped in prison and died from HIV-AIDS. Many others were innocents forced to participate after seeing their family members hacked to death for refusing. Defendants were executed on the judgments of second-year law students. In the end, that tiny, poor society did not have the capacity to deliver justice to 126,000 for such serious crimes. Most were released to face traditional *gacaca*, which some of the time was somewhat restorative in approach (Clark 2010).

IV. Conversations across the Curriculum of Crimes

Restorative justice principles are useful to a minimally sufficient deterrence strategy because defiance (Sherman 1992, 2011) is a critical risk. Defiance is reduced when communities of care do most of the work. Nathan Harris found that perceived informal disapproval of those most loved inside restorative justice conferences, not of criminal justice actors, does the work of persuading offenders that their crime is shameful, persuading them to remorse and repair of the harm to victims and to their own family (Harris 2001, pp. 157–76). In restorative justice, there is no need for anyone to invoke the concept of shame or for anyone directly to shame offenders. Loved ones discussing how concerned they are about the consequences of the crime, the suffering of victims, and what the family can do to help repair the harm is the way to elicit remorse without defiance. Motivational interviewing of these loved ones can draw this out.

Conversely, there is evidence that stigmatization (as opposed to reintegrative shaming) increases crime in criminal justice processes (Ahmed et al. 2001; Braithwaite, Ahmed, and Braithwaite 2006; Tyler et al. 2007) and in business regulation (Makkai and Braithwaite 1994; Harris 2017). Stigmatized offenders are treated as bad people who have done bad things, while reintegratively shamed offenders are treated as essentially good people who have done a bad thing. Stigmatized offenders are cast out from the community of the law-abiding without paying attention to reintegration rituals that might have drawn them back into the law-abiding community. Aversion of stigmatization is critical to an effective package of minimally sufficient deterrence.

The theory of reintegrative shaming argues that shame is important to crime control and to problem solving (Leach and Cidam 2015; Spruit et al. 2016). Societies in which rape is not shameful will have a lot of rape. Societies in which feminist politics communicates the shamefulness of rape and domestic violence can enjoy steeply reduced rates of these crimes, as Pinker's (2011, pp. 196–201) analyses of declining rates of rape and domestic violence and growing shamefulness of these crimes in certain Western societies suggest. Broadhurst, Bouhours, and Bouhours (2015, pp. 310–13) likewise diagnose repeated surveys in Myanmar since 1996 to show declining domestic violence, growing disapproval of wife beating, and growing public awareness campaigns about why it is wrong. Feminist politics is just one kind of engagement around the shamefulness of certain crimes.

One of the virtues of deliberative forms of justice such as restorative justice is that they increase the active participation of citizens in their democracy through the judicial branch of governance, through children's participation in antibullying programs in schools, and through involvement of environmental activists and fishermen in the regulation of environmental crimes. Restorative justice therefore has a role to play in educating citizens in the curriculum of crimes and why they are shameful, through their participation in restorative conversations about the crimes of their classmates, their neighbors, their family members, and themselves.

Existing criminal justice institutions by contrast are overly professionalized. One consequence is they provide no space for democratic deliberation with the young about why crimes that affect people are wrong and what should be done about them. Democratic citizens can sit in the public gallery for criminal trials, but few do; and if they try to participate in the conversation about the rights and wrongs of the matter from the gallery, they are silenced.

Penal populism that increases punitiveness is certainly a risk within contemporary criminal law jurisprudence (Lacey 2008). Advocacy for minimally sufficient deterrence, however, is advocacy of quite a radical transformation of these dysfunctional institutions. Ordinary people are more punitive than the courts when they read accounts of cases and sentences in the media. When they read about the rich complexity of the same case as the judge hears it, they recommend sentences similar to those of the judge. The more information they have, the less punitive they are (Doob and Roberts 1983, 1988). When citizens have the chance to engage directly with offenders and the complexity of their circumstances in a restorative conference, their vengefulness reduces even further (Strang et al. 2013, pp. 40–42), which explains why restorative justice conferences produce less punitive outcomes on average than does traditional criminal justice processing (Braithwaite 2002, pp. 146–48).

In sum, the restorative justice component of minimally sufficient deterrence calms defiance, helps educate offenders and the entire community to the shamefulness of crime and to the curriculum of crimes, while laying foundations for minimal sufficiency of punishment that can defeat penal populism's maximalist politics. A utopian world can be imagined in which each year 1 percent of the population took responsibility for an offense in a restorative justice conference conducted by the criminal justice system, a school, a university, or a workplace. If 10 supporters of victims or offenders attended each conference, conversations about the curriculum of crimes would ripple across 10 percent of the population each year. Because human beings are story-telling animals, we learn the shamefulness of the curriculum of crimes through participating in, and retelling, stories of which we are a part. This retelling can do most of the work of constituting the curriculum of crimes, especially when newer crimes such as profit shifting by multinational corporations begin to become transparent. Consciences are formed by operation of "the criminal law as a moral eye-opener" (Andenaes 1974, pp. 116–17), especially when shamefulness is suppressed through a politics of domination with crimes such as torture and sexual and gender-based violence.

## V. Minimal Sufficiency of General Deterrence

The preceding section was partly about the general deterrence that arises from citizens talking with one another about why something like rape or torture is wrong. Reintegrative shaming theory advances the idea that general deterrence by means of the internalization of shame (anticipated self-shaming rather than shame sanctions) combined with a path out of shame (Leach and Cidam 2015; Spruit et al. 2016) is more important than deterrence by sentences handed down by courts (Ahmed et al. 2001). It is also about the restorative justice political strategy for community support for a less punitive justice system. Satisfaction with the justice, with the respect for victim rights, and with the effectiveness of restorative justice in crime prevention is high (normally over 80 percent) for citizens who sit in on restorative justice conferences (Braithwaite 2002, pp. 45–71; Wilson, Olaghere, and Kimbrell 2017). Part of the practical politics of driving punishment down to minimally sufficient deterrence is convincing politicians who see restorative justice as a soft option to sit in on a conference and chat afterward with the participants. This is important because democratic politics is the key constraint on whether and how judges or police can use minimally sufficient deterrence.

The literature on the consequences of police strikes (Andenaes 1974) has long persuaded criminologists that crime spikes when deterrence is taken off the table. The contention of minimally sufficient deterrence is that courts will have little to do in delivering minimally sufficient general deterrence if citizens are empowered conversationally about the shamefulness of the curriculum of crimes (Braithwaite 1989, pp. 77–79). Courts have to ensure through some form of incapacitation that the community is protected from modest numbers of people who are a severe danger to the community. The hypothesis is that minimally sufficient deterrence will be provided by general deterrence resulting from incapacitation cases, combined with others in which repeated failures of social support and moderate deterrents escalate to severe deterrents toward the peak of a pyramid.

This hypothesis has not been empirically tested, but it is consistent with the evidence that, as long as deterrence does not fall to zero, increasing average prison terms does not have much effect in reducing crime (Nagin 2013; Chalfin and McCrary 2017). It seems unlikely that a society would face crime risks from insufficient passive general deterrence if it takes seriously shame management and education about the curriculum of crimes and if it puts into place a credible peak as a last resort in its pyramid of dynamic deterrence. We cannot completely do without passive general deterrence, but a minimally sufficient quantum of it delivered by the model I propose here may be enough to achieve the limited work general deterrence can do.

My proposals can be accomplished only incrementally; learning through monitoring is important to reveal any explosion of crime driven by a deficit in passive general deterrence (Braithwaite and Pettit 1990, pp. 140–55; Dorf and Sabel 1998). If and when empirical evidence suggested this was happening, incremental movement could be halted and adjusted to bolster passive general deterrence. My prediction, however, is that as societies such as the United States and Russia with imprisonment rates over 600 per 100,000 reduce their passive general deterrence toward that of societies such as India, Indonesia, and Japan with imprisonment rates in the 30s to 40s, passive deterrence deficits will not cause crime waves. This is suggested by cross-national comparisons of crime that show that low incarceration societies, many in Asia, often have low crime rates.

## VI. Conclusion

Inexorability is a core principle of minimally sufficient deterrence: pursue inexorable consistency of detection and disapproval of predatory crime. This implies fusing the debate on dynamic concentration of deterrence with the debate about less prison and more and better police.

Indeed, the move away from the nihilism about policing prevalent at the time of the Kansas City Preventive Patrol Experiment is a light on the hill for criminologists (Nagin, Solow, and Lum 2015). So is the move away from nihilism about rehabilitation that was prevalent at the time of "Nothing Works" (Lipton, Martinson, and Wilks 1975). Policing and rehabilitation are useless only if they are unresponsively deployed. For example, evidence-based refinement of responsivity of rehabilitation can improve the menu of options in the pyramid of support in figure 1 (Andrews and Bonta 1998, 2010; Manchak and Cullen 2015). Developmentalists have convincingly shown that social support is important to crime prevention long before the first offense occurs (Cullen 1994). This is a vital piece for any integrated theory of crime prevention. My arguments here on minimally sufficient deterrence are, however, limited to an integrated strategy of deterrence. Deterrence is far from the most important element of a sophisticated strategy to protect citizens from crime.

I have introduced suggestive evidence that an inexorably supportive firm hand might help in preventing crime, in preventing the collapse of welfare states that struggle to deter corporate tax evasion, and in addressing many other challenges of crime control.[9] The white-collar crime piece of this is important because, as Sutherland ([1949] 1983) instructed, any theory of crime that provides an account of crimes of the powerless but not of crimes of the powerful is troubling, indeed profoundly misleading. It might be credible as a theory of something more specific than crime. Moreover, the dominance of theories in criminology that fail this test means criminology buttresses oppression when it normalizes prisons that hold tiny proportions of wealthy white criminals.

The evidence adduced in support of minimally sufficient deterrence is no more than suggestive. It is common for criminological theories to have something going for them while being wrong in most contexts. Until minimally sufficient deterrence is subjected to an array of different kinds of empirical investigations, this may be as true of it as it is of theories of passive deterrence that currently dominate thinking. I have attempted to show that minimally sufficient deterrence has promise as a strategy for moving from passive to dynamic deterrence because it starts

[9] For a more developed analysis of the empirical evidence for and against restorative justice and responsive regulation, see Braithwaite (2016) and more recent meta-analyses by Wong et al. (2016), Bouffard, Cooper, and Bergseth (2017), and Wilson, Olaghere, and Kimbrell (2017), all of which show significant, usually moderate, effects of restorative justice in reducing reoffending.

from what we already know about deterrence and defiance, and because it integrates insights from other relational theories that each enjoy a body of empirical support. These are theories of social support (Cullen 1994), responsivity (Andrews and Bonta 1998, 2010), responsive regulation (Braithwaite 2008), sharpening the Sword of Damocles (Dunford 1990; Sherman 1992, 2011), dynamic concentration of deterrence (Kleiman 2009), and shame and pride management (Ahmed et al. 2001) combined with indirect reciprocity (Berger 2011; Nowak 2012). I have attempted to explore the imperative, grounded in complexity theory, for abandoning applied social science that tests specific parsimonious theories in favor of applying meta-theories, theories about how to organize multiple theories, and meta-strategies, strategies about how to sequence many strategies.

While minimally sufficient deterrence is based on what we know about deterrence and defiance, that knowledge base has wide gaps of unknown knowables and unknowables that are complex or chaotic (Braithwaite and D'Costa 2018, chap. 12). The future gap-filling research agenda can be framed under the seven policy principles of minimally sufficient deterrence:

1.  Escalate enforcement. Display intent to progressively escalate a responsive enforcement pyramid that involves progressive escalation of sanctions for wrongdoing and support for social responsibility.

This has been the heartland research priority of Valerie Braithwaite's and my research group since 1980 (e.g., see more than a hundred empirical evaluations of the application of responsive regulation to tax compliance by the Centre for Tax System Integrity: http://ctsi.org.au/; more broadly, see http://johnbraithwaite.com/responsive-regulation/).

2.  Inexorability. Pursue inexorable consistency of detection of predatory crime. Communicate inexorable community commitment to stick with social support for those struggling with problems of lawbreaking until the problems are fixed.

Critical research contributions here bring together the established agenda of measuring the effects of perceived certainty of detection with perceptions that my supporters will deliver me unconditional support, sticking with my problems until they are fixed. While increasing consistency of detection will increase deterrence, having police be everywhere at all times risks undermining legitimacy, motivating defiance. Lawrence Sherman has coined the idea of a sweet spot of intensity of just enough deterrence through police presence at hot spots. Gibson, Slothower, and Sherman (2017) found such an optimal sweet spot of minimally sufficient patrol in Merseyside, UK. Though it is well established that intensive patrol at hot spots can reduce crime (Braga, Papachristos, and Hureau 2014), Gibson and her colleagues are the first to explore the possibility of reducing the intensity of hot-spot patrol without increasing crime, perhaps even reducing it somewhat through optimizing that sweet spot. This work opens a path to understanding cost-effective, minimally sufficient patrol.

3. Escalate social support. With repeated offending, increase social support. Even when there is escalation to a last resort of severe incapacitation, escalate social support further. Keep escalating social support until desistance is consolidated.

Perhaps the most critical research needed here is macrosociological and macroeconomic work on strategies for sustaining a more credible welfare state. It may be feasible to be politically effective in struggling for return to improving the condition of the welfare state.

4. Sharpen the Sword of Damocles. Cultivate the perception that "Trouble hangs inexorably over my head; they want to support me to avert it."

Here the "less prison" research agenda shows the kind of work that illuminates Sword of Damocles possibilities (Sherman 2011). This is illustrated through Slothower et al.'s (2017) West Midlands Police experiment, Offender Management by Turning Point (Deferred Prosecution with a Plan). Random assignment to deferred prosecution combined with social support substantially reduced crime harm, reduced the cost of the justice system, and increased victim satisfaction with outcomes, when compared with prosecuted cases.

5. Dynamic concentration of deterrence. Focus deterrence on lines that should never be crossed after an announcement date. Then

progressively lift that line, raising our expectations of socially re-sponsible citizens.

Research in this tradition led by David Kennedy and Mark Kleiman has not been linked to evidence-based learning on restorative justice and responsive business regulation, nor to dynamic concentration expe-rience of international peacekeepers regulating war zones and negotiat-ing gang surrenders into peace zones. A more interdisciplinary research imagination is required to see the complex of strategies, including esca-lated social support and reconciliation, within which to embed dynamic concentration of deterrence to increase its effectiveness. Future research must distinguish static focused deterrence effects from dynamic concen-tration effects.

6.  Community engagement. Engage the community with offenders in widening restorative conversations that educate in the shame-fulness of criminal predation for the many who participate in the conversations. Avert stigmatization.

The research required here includes the intersection of work on com-munity engagement with crime control (e.g., Sampson, Raudenbush, and Earls 1997; Pratt and Cullen 2005; Odgers et al. 2009) and research on the Connectedness, Hope, Identity, Meaning, and Empowerment (CHIME) conclusion by Leamy et al. (2011) in their review of the "re-covery capital" research tradition (Best 2017). The CHIME conclusion is that connectedness, hope, identity, meaning, and empowerment are needed for capacity for recovery from problems such as drug addiction, alcoholism, suicide attempts, and arrests. It is important to integrate the best psychological and criminological research on pride and shame dy-namics and on shame acknowledgment as offenders renarrate their lives (Leach and Cidam 2015; Spruit et al. 2016).

7.  Modesty. Settle for the modest general deterrence delivered by this shamefulness and a minimal number of cases that escalate to-ward the peak of the enforcement pyramid.

This is the "decrementalist" research strategy recommended by Braith-waite and Pettit (1990) on republican theory and criminal justice. It means evaluation research on how low imprisonment can go without crime beginning to increase. When we have no choice but to lock up extremely dangerous people, we can be justifiably pessimistic that this will deter those specific people when released. Yet others seeing that imprisonment does sometimes happen may deliver a modest quantum of general deterrence of the rest of the population. Braithwaite and Pettit's (1990) decrementalist research agenda went nowhere in the 28 years since it was proposed. No countries have pursued progressive reductions of imprisonment rates until empirical evidence emerged that serious crime problems were the result. This is a measure of how wide the gap is in every country between minimally sufficient deterrence and criminal justice policy.

REFERENCES

Ahmed, Eliza, and John Braithwaite. 2011. "Shame, Pride and Workplace Bullying." In *Emotions, Crime and Justice*, edited by Susanne Karstedt, Ian Loader, and Heather Strang. Oxford: Hart.
Ahmed, Eliza, Nathan Harris, John Braithwaite, and Valerie Braithwaite. 2001. *Shame Management through Reintegration*. Cambridge: Cambridge University Press.
Andenaes, Johannes. 1974. *Punishment and Deterrence*. Ann Arbor: University of Michigan Press.
Andrews, Donald A., and James Bonta. 1998. *The Psychology of Criminal Conduct*. 2nd ed. Cincinnati: Anderson.
———. 2010. "Rehabilitating Criminal Justice Policy and Practice." *Psychology, Public Policy, and Law* 16(1):39–55.
Axelrod, Robert M. 1984. *The Evolution of Cooperation*. New York: Basic Books.
Ayres, Ian, and John Braithwaite. 1992. *Responsive Regulation: Transcending the Deregulation Debate*. New York: Oxford University Press.
Barnes, Geoffrey C., Jordan M. Hyatt, Caroline M. Angel, Heather Strang, and Lawrence W. Sherman. 2015. "Are Restorative Justice Conferences More Fair than Criminal Courts? Comparing Levels of Observed Procedural Justice in the Reintegrative Shaming Experiments (RISE)." *Criminal Justice Policy Review* 26(2):103–30.
Becker, Gary S. 1993. "Nobel Lecture: The Economic Way of Looking at Behavior." *Journal of Political Economy* 101(3):385–409.
Berger, Ulrich. 2011. "Learning to Cooperate via Indirect Reciprocity." *Games and Economic Behavior* 72(1):30–37.
Best, David. 2017. "Developing Strengths-Based Recovery Systems through Community Connections." *Addiction* 112(5):759–61.

Black, Julia, and Robert Baldwin. 2010. "Really Responsive Risk-Based Regulation." *Law and Policy* 32(2):181–213.

Blumstein, Alfred. 2011. "Approaches to Reducing Both Imprisonment and Crime." *Criminology and Public Policy* 10(1):93–102.

Bouffard, Jeff, Maisha Cooper, and Kathleen Bergseth. 2017. "The Effectiveness of Various Restorative Justice Interventions on Recidivism Outcomes among Juvenile Offenders." *Youth Violence and Juvenile Justice* 15(4):465–80.

Braga, Anthony A. 2002. *Problem-Oriented Policing and Crime Prevention*. Monsey, NY: Criminal Justice Press.

Braga, Anthony A., Robert Apel, and Brandon C. Welsh. 2013. "The Spillover Effects of Focused Deterrence on Gang Violence." *Evaluation Review* 37(3–4):314–42.

Braga, Anthony A., Andrew V. Papachristos, and David M. Hureau. 2014. "The Effects of Hot Spots Policing on Crime: An Updated Systematic Review and Meta-Analysis." *Justice Quarterly* 31(4):633–63.

Braga, Anthony A., and David L. Weisburd. 2012. "The Effects of Focused Deterrence Strategies on Crime: A Systematic Review and Meta-Analysis of the Empirical Evidence." *Journal of Research in Crime and Delinquency* 49(3):323–58.

———. 2014. "Must We Settle for Less Rigorous Evaluations in Large Area-Based Crime Prevention Programs? Lessons from a Campbell Review of Focused Deterrence." *Journal of Experimental Criminology* 10(4):573–97.

Braithwaite, John. 1989. *Crime, Shame, and Reintegration*. Cambridge: Cambridge University Press.

———. 1995. "Inequality and Republican Criminology." In *Crime and Inequality*, edited by John Hagan and Ruth D. Peterson. Palo Alto, CA: Stanford University Press.

———. 1998. "Institutionalizing Distrust, Enculturating Trust." In *Trust and Governance*, edited by Valerie Braithwaite and Margaret Levi. New York: Russell Sage Foundation.

———. 2001. "Youth Development Circles." *Oxford Review of Education* 27(2):239–52.

———. 2002. *Restorative Justice and Responsive Regulation*. New York and Sydney: Oxford University Press and Federation Press.

———. 2003. "Principles of Restorative Justice." In *Restorative Justice and Criminal Justice: Competing or Reconcilable Paradigms?* edited by Andrew von Hirsch, Julian V. Roberts, Anthony Bottoms, Kent Roach, and Mara Schiff. Oxford: Hart.

———. 2005. *Markets in Vice, Markets in Virtue*. Sydney and New York: Federation Press and Oxford University Press.

———. 2008. *Regulatory Capitalism: How It Works, Ideas for Making It Work Better*. Cheltenham, UK: Elgar.

———. 2011. "The Essence of Responsive Regulation." *University of British Columbia Law Review* 44:475–520.

———. 2012. "Cascades of Violence and a Global Criminology of Place." *Australian and New Zealand Journal of Criminology* 45:299–315.

————. 2016. "Restorative Justice and Responsive Regulation: The Question of Evidence." RegNet Working Paper no. 51. Canberra: Australian National University, School of Regulation and Global Governance.

Braithwaite, John, Eliza Ahmed, and Valerie Braithwaite. 2006. "Shame, Restorative Justice and Crime." In *Taking Stock: The Status of Criminological Theory*, edited by Francis T. Cullen, John Paul Wright, and Kristie R. Blevins. New Brunswick, NJ: Transaction.

Braithwaite, John, and Bina D'Costa. 2018. *Cascades of Violence*. Canberra: ANU Press.

Braithwaite, John, and Peter Drahos. 2000. *Global Business Regulation*. Cambridge: Cambridge University Press.

Braithwaite, John, and Ali Gohar. 2014. "Restorative Justice, Policing, and Insurgency: Learning from Pakistan." *Law and Society Review* 48(3):531–61.

Braithwaite, John, and Seung-Hun Hong. 2015. "The Iteration Deficit in Responsive Regulation: Are Regulatory Ambassadors an Answer?" *Regulation and Governance* 9(1):16–29.

Braithwaite, John, and Toni Makkai. 1994. "Trust and Compliance." *Policing and Society* 4(1):1–12.

Braithwaite, John, Toni Makkai, and Valerie Braithwaite. 2007. *Regulating Aged Care: Ritualism and the New Pyramid*. Cheltenham, UK: Elgar.

Braithwaite, John, and Philip Pettit. 1990. *Not Just Deserts: A Theory of Criminal Justice*. Oxford: Oxford University Press.

Brehm, Sharon S., and Jack W. Brehm. 1981. *Psychological Reactance: A Theory of Freedom and Control*. New York: Academic Press.

Broadhurst, Roderic, Thierry Bouhours, and Brigitte Bouhours. 2015. *Violence and the Civilising Process in Cambodia*. Cambridge: Cambridge University Press.

————. 2018. "Violence and Elias's Historical Sociology: The Case of Cambodia." *British Journal of Criminology*, forthcoming.

Call, Charles T. 2012. *Why Peace Fails: The Causes and Prevention of Civil War Recurrence*. Washington, DC: Georgetown University Press.

Cerasoli, Christopher P., Jessica M. Nicklin, and Michael T. Ford. 2014. "Intrinsic Motivation and Extrinsic Incentives Jointly Predict Performance: A 40-Year Meta-Analysis." *Psychological Bulletin* 140(4):980–1008.

Chalfin, Aaron, and Justin McCrary. 2017. "Criminal Deterrence: A Review of the Literature." *Journal of Economic Literature* 55(1):5–48.

Cicero, Marcus Tullius. 1877. *Tusculan Disputations*. Translated by C. D. Yonge. New York: Harper & Brothers.

Clark, Phil. 2010. *The Gacaca Courts, Post-genocide Justice and Reconciliation in Rwanda: Justice without Lawyers*. Cambridge: Cambridge University Press.

Cullen, Francis T. 1994. "Social Support as an Organizing Concept for Criminology." *Justice Quarterly* 11(4):527–59.

Dancy, Geoff, Bridget Marchesi, Tricia Olsen, Leigh Payne, Andrew Reiter, and Kathryn Sikkink. 2013. "Stopping State Agents of Violence or Promoting Political Compromise? The Powerful Role of Transitional Justice Mechanisms." Paper presented at the American Political Science Association annual meeting, Chicago.

Dekker, Sidney W. A., and Hugh Breakey. 2016. "'Just Culture': Improving Safety by Achieving Substantive, Procedural and Restorative Justice." *Safety Science* 85:187–93.

Doob, Anthony, and Julian V. Roberts. 1983. *Sentencing: An Analysis of the Public's View of Sentencing*. Ottawa: Department of Justice, Canada.

———. 1988. "Public Attitudes towards Sentencing in Canada." In *Public Attitudes to Sentencing*, edited by Nigel Walker and Mike Hough. Aldershot, UK: Gower.

Dorf, Michael C., and Charles F. Sabel. 1998. "A Constitution of Democratic Experimentalism." *Columbia Law Review* 98(2):267–473.

Doyle, Michael W., and Nicholas Sambanis. 2006. *Making War and Building Peace: United Nations Peace Operations*. Princeton, NJ: Princeton University Press.

Dunford, Franklin W. 1990. "System-Initiated Warrants for Suspects of Misdemeanor Domestic Assault: A Pilot Study." *Justice Quarterly* 7(4):631–53.

Duriez, Stephanie A., Francis T. Cullen, and Sarah M. Manchak. 2014. "Is Project HOPE Creating a False Sense of Hope: A Case Study in Correctional Popularity." *Federal Probation* 78:57–70.

Durlauf, Steven N., and Daniel S. Nagin. 2011. "Overview of 'Imprisonment and Crime: Can Both Be Reduced?'" *Criminology and Public Policy* 10(1):9–12.

Eckstein, Harry. 1975. "Case Study and Theory in Political Science." In *Handbook of Political Science*, vol. 7, edited by Fred I. Greenstein and Nelson W. Polsby. Reading, MA: Addison-Wesley.

Eisinger, Jesse. 2017. *The Chickenshit Club: Why the Justice Department Fails to Prosecute Executives*. New York: Simon & Schuster.

Eisner, Manuel. 2003. "Long-Term Historical Trends in Violent Crime." In *Crime and Justice: A Review of Research*, vol. 30, edited by Michael Tonry. Chicago: University of Chicago Press.

Elias, Norbert. 1978. *The Civilizing Process*. 2 vols. Oxford: Oxford University Press.

Feeley, Malcolm M. 1979. *The Process Is the Punishment: Handling Cases in a Lower Criminal Court*. New York: Sage.

Fortna, Virginia Page. 2008. *Does Peacekeeping Work: Shaping Belligerents' Choices after Civil War*. Princeton, NJ: Princeton University Press.

Frey, Bruno. 2017. "Policy Consequences of Pay-for-Performance and Crowding-Out." *Journal of Behavioral Economics for Policy* 1(1):55–59.

Friesen, Lana. 2012. "Certainty of Punishment versus Severity of Punishment: An Experimental Investigation." *Southern Economic Journal* 79(2):399–421.

Gangl, Katharina, Eva Hofmann, and Erich Kirchler. 2015. "Tax Authorities' Interaction with Taxpayers: A Conception of Compliance in Social Dilemmas by Power and Trust." *New Ideas in Psychology* 37:13–23.

Gibson, Christopher, Molly Slothower, and Lawrence W. Sherman. 2017. "A Cost-Effectiveness Comparison of Two Patrol Strategies." *Cambridge Journal of Evidence-Based Policing* 1(4):225–43.

Gunningham, Neil, Peter Grabosky, and Darren Sinclair. 1998. *Smart Regulation*. Oxford: Oxford University Press.

Haas, Nicole E., Maarten Van Craen, Wesley G. Skogan, and Diego M. Fleitas. 2015. "Explaining Officer Compliance: The Importance of Procedural Justice and Trust inside a Police Organization." *Criminology and Criminal Justice* 15 (4):442–63.

Harris, Nathan. 2001. "Shaming and Shame: Regulating Drink-Driving." In *Shame Management through Reintegration*, edited by Eliza Ahmed, Nathan Harris, John Braithwaite, and Valerie Braithwaite. Cambridge: Cambridge University Press.

———. 2017. "Shame in Regulatory Settings." In *Regulatory Theory: Foundations and Applications*, edited by Peter Drahos. Canberra: ANU Press.

Hawken, Angela, and Mark Kleiman. 2009. *Managing Drug Involved Probationers with Swift and Certain Sanctions: Evaluating Hawaii's HOPE*. Washington, DC: National Institute of Justice.

Johnstone, Gerry. 2013. *Restorative Justice: Ideas, Values, Debates*. London: Routledge.

Kennedy, David M. 2009. *Deterrence and Crime Prevention: Reconsidering the Prospect of Sanction*. New York: Routledge.

Kennedy, David M., Mark A. R. Kleiman, and Anthony A. Braga. 2017. "Beyond Deterrence." In *Handbook of Crime Prevention and Community Safety*, 2nd ed., edited by Nick Tilley and Aiden Sidebottom. London: Routledge.

Kinsey, Karyl A. 1986. "Theories and Models of Tax Cheating." *Criminal Justice Abstracts* 18:402–20.

Kleiman, Mark. 2009. *When Brute Force Fails: How to Have Less Crime and Less Punishment*. Princeton, NJ: Princeton University Press.

Klusemann, Stefan. 2012. "Massacres as Process: A Micro-sociological Theory of Internal Patterns of Mass Atrocities." *European Journal of Criminology* 9 (5):468–80.

Kuttippurath, Jayanarayanan, and Prijitha J. Nair. 2017. "The Signs of Antarctic Ozone Hole Recovery." *Scientific Reports* 7(1). DOI:10.1038/s41598-017-00722-7.

Lacey, Nicola. 2008. *The Prisoners' Dilemma: Political Economy and Punishment in Contemporary Democracies*. Cambridge: Cambridge University Press.

Latimer, Jeff, Craig Dowden, and Danielle Muise. 2001. *The Effectiveness of Restorative Justice Practices: A Meta-Analysis*. Ottawa: Department of Justice, Canada.

Lattimore, Pamela K., Doris Layton MacKenzie, Gary Zajac, Debbie Dawes, Elaine Arsenault, and Stephen Tueller. 2016. "Outcome Findings from the HOPE Demonstration Field Experiment." *Criminology and Public Policy* 15 (4):1103–41.

Leach, Colin Wayne, and Atilla Cidam. 2015. "When Is Shame Linked to Constructive Approach Orientation? A Meta-Analysis." *Journal of Personality and Social Psychology* 109(6):983–1002.

Leamy, Mary, Victoria Bird, Clair Le Boutillier, Julie Williams, and Mike Slade. 2011. "Conceptual Framework for Personal Recovery in Mental Health: Systematic Review and Narrative Synthesis." *British Journal of Psychiatry* 199 (6):445–52.

Lipsey, Mark W. 2009. "The Primary Factors That Characterize Effective Interventions with Juvenile Offenders: A Meta-Analytic Overview." *Victims and Offenders* 4(2):124–47.

Lipton, Douglas S., Robert Martinson, and Judith Wilks. 1975. *The Effectiveness of Correctional Treatment: A Survey of Treatment Evaluation Studies.* New York: Praeger.

Lundahl, Brad W., Chelsea Kunz, Cynthia Brownell, Derrik Tollefson, and Brian L. Burke. 2010. "A Meta-Analysis of Motivational Interviewing: Twenty-Five Years of Empirical Studies." *Research on Social Work Practice* 20(2):137–60.

MacKenzie, Doris L., and David P. Farrington. 2015. "Preventing Future Offending of Delinquents and Offenders: What Have We Learned from Experiments and Meta-Analyses?" *Journal of Experimental Criminology* 11(4):565–95.

Makkai, Toni, and John Braithwaite. 1994. "Reintegrative Shaming and Compliance with Regulatory Standards." *Criminology* 32(3):361–85.

Manchak, Sarah M., and Francis T. Cullen. 2015. "Intervening Effectively with Juvenile Offenders: Answers from Meta-Analysis." In *The Development of Criminal and Antisocial Behavior*, edited by Julien Morizot and Lila Kazemian. New York: Springer.

Maruna, Shadd. 2001. *Making Good: How Ex-Convicts Reform and Rebuild Their Lives.* Washington, DC: American Psychological Association.

Maxwell, Gabrielle, and Allison Morris. 2002. "The Role of Shame, Guilt, and Remorse in Restorative Justice Processes for Young People." In *Restorative Justice: Theoretical Foundations*, edited by Elmar G. M. Weitekamp and Hans-Jürgen Kerner. Cullompton, Devon, UK: Willan.

Mazzolini, Gabriele, Laura Pagani, and Alessandro Santoro. 2017. "The Deterrence Effect of Real-World Operational Tax Audits." Working Paper no. 359. Milan: University of Milan Bicocca, Department of Economics, Management, and Statistics. Available at Social Science Research Network.

Mendoza, Juan P., Jacco L. Wielhouwer, and Erich Kirchler. 2017. "The Backfiring Effect of Auditing on Tax Compliance." *Journal of Economic Psychology* 62:284–94.

Miller, Susan L., and M. Kristen Hefner. 2015. "Procedural Justice for Victims and Offenders? Exploring Restorative Justice Processes in Australia and the US." *Justice Quarterly* 32(1):142–67.

Nagin, Daniel S. 2013. "Deterrence in the Twenty-First Century." In *Crime and Justice in America, 1975–2025*, edited by Michael Tonry. Vol. 42 of *Crime and Justice: A Review of Research*, edited by Michael Tonry. Chicago: University of Chicago Press.

Nagin, Daniel S., Francis T. Cullen, and Cheryl Lero Jonson. 2009. "Imprisonment and Reoffending." In *Crime and Justice: A Review of Research*, vol. 38, edited by Michael Tonry. Chicago: University of Chicago Press.

Nagin, Daniel S., Robert M. Solow, and Cynthia Lum. 2015. "Deterrence, Criminal Opportunities, and Police." *Criminology* 53(1):74–100.

Nowak, Martin A. 2012. "Evolving Cooperation." *Journal of Theoretical Biology* 299:1–8.

Odgers, Candice L., Terrie E. Moffitt, Laura M. Tach, Robert J. Sampson, Alan Taylor, Charlotte L. Matthews, and Avshalom Caspi. 2009. "The Protective Effects of Neighborhood Collective Efficacy on British Children Growing Up in Deprivation: A Developmental Analysis." *Developmental Psychology* 45 (4):942–57.

Olsen, Tricia D., Leigh A. Payne, and Andrew Reiter. 2010. *Transitional Justice in the Balance: Comparing Processes, Weighing Efficacy.* Washington, DC: US Institute of Peace.

Osterloh, Margit, and Buno S. Frey. 2013. "Motivation Governance." In *Handbook of Economic Organization*, edited by Anna Grandori. Cheltenham, UK: Elgar.

Parker, Christine. 2004. "Restorative Justice in Business Regulation? The Australian Competition and Consumer Commission's Use of Enforceable Undertakings." *Modern Law Review* 67(2):209–46.

Paternoster, Raymond, and Sally Simpson. 1996. "Sanction Threats and Appeals to Morality: Testing a Rational Choice Model of Corporate Crime." *Law and Society Review* 30(3):549–83.

Patterson, Gerald R., and Lew Bank. 1989. "Some Amplifying Mechanisms for Pathologic Processes in Families." In *Systems and Development: The Minnesota Symposia on Child Psychology*. Hillsdale, NJ: Erlbaum.

Pennell, Joan, and Gale Burford. 2000. "Family Group Decision Making: Protecting Children and Women." *Child Welfare* 79(2):131–58.

Pettit, Philip. 1997. *Republicanism.* Oxford: Oxford University Press.

Pinker, Jonathan. 2011. *The Better Angels of Our Nature.* New York: Penguin.

Pontell, Henry N. 1978. "Deterrence: Theory versus Practice." *Criminology* 16 (1):3–22.

Pontell, Henry N., William K. Black, and Gilbert Geis. 2014. "Too Big to Fail, Too Powerful to Ail? On the Absence of Criminal Prosecutions after the 2008 Financial Meltdown." *Crime, Law, and Social Change* 61(1):1–13.

Pratt, Travis C., and Francis T. Cullen. 2005. "Assessing Macro-Level Predictors and Theories of Crime: A Meta-Analysis." In *Crime and Justice: A Review of Research*, vol. 32, edited by Michael Tonry. Chicago: University of Chicago Press.

Pratt, Travis C., and Jillian J. Turanovic. 2018. "Celerity and Deterrence." In *Deterrence, Choice, and Crime: Contemporary Perspectives*, edited by Daniel S. Nagin, Francis T. Cullen, and Cheryl Lero Jonson. New York: Routledge, forthcoming.

Rains, Stephen A. 2013. "The Nature of Psychological Reactance Revisited: A Meta-Analytic Review." *Human Communication Research* 39(1):47–73.

Robinson, Laurie O. 2011. "Exploring Certainty and Severity." *Criminology and Public Policy* 10(1):85–92.

Rubak, Sune, Annelli Sandbæk, Torsten Lauritzen, and Bo Christensen. 2005. "Motivational Interviewing: A Systematic Review and Meta-Analysis." *British Journal of General Practice* 5(513):305–12.

Rubin, Michael. 2014. *Dancing with the Devil: The Perils of Engaging Rogue Regimes.* New York: Encounter.

Sampson, Robert J., Stephen W. Raudenbush, and Felton Earls. 1997. "Neighborhoods and Violent Crime: A Multilevel Study of Collective Efficacy." *Science* 277(5328):918–24.

Schell-Busey, Natalie, Sally S. Simpson, Melissa Rorie, and Mariel Alper. 2016. "What Works? A Systematic Review of Corporate Crime Deterrence." *Criminology and Public Policy* 15(2):387–416.

Schiff, Mara F. 1999. "The Impact of Restorative Interventions on Juvenile Offenders." In *Restorative Juvenile Justice*, edited by Lode Walgrave and Gordon Bazemore. Monsey, NY: Criminal Justice Press.

Sherman, Lawrence W. 1992. *Policing Domestic Violence*. New York: Free Press.

———. 2011. "Offender Desistance Policing: Less Prison and More Evidence of Rehabilitating Offenders." In *Antisocial Behavior and Crime: Contributions of Developmental and Evaluation Research to Prevention and Intervention*, edited by Thomas Bliesener, Andreas Beelmann, and Mark Stemmler. Cambridge, MA: Hogrefe.

———. 2014. "Experiments in Criminal Sanctions: Labeling, Defiance, and Restorative Justice." In *Labeling Theory: Empirical Tests*, edited by David P. Farrington and Joseph Murray. New Brunswick, NJ: Transaction.

Sherman, Lawrence W., and Heather Strang. 1997. "Restorative Justice and Deterring Crime." RISE Working Paper no. 4. Canberra: Australian National University, Law Program, Research School of Social Sciences.

Sherman, Lawrence W., Heather Strang, Gregory C. Barnes, John Braithwaite, Nova Inkpen, and M. M. Teh. 1998. *Experiments in Restorative Policing: A Progress Report*. Canberra: Australian National University, Law Program, Research School of Social Sciences.

Sikkink, Kathryn. 2011. *The Justice Cascade: How Human Rights Prosecutions Are Changing World Politics*. New York: Norton.

Slothower, Molly, Peter Neyroud, Jamie Hobday, Lawrence Sherman, Barak Ariel, Eleanor Neyroud, and Geoffrey Barnes. 2017. *The Turning Point Project 2-Year Outcomes*. Report to Chief Officers. Birmingham, UK: West Midlands Police.

Sparrow, Malcolm K. 2000. *The Regulatory Craft*. Washington, DC: Brookings Institution.

Spruit, Anouk, Frans Schalkwijk, Eveline Van Vugt, and Geert Jan Stams. 2016. "The Relation between Self-Conscious Emotions and Delinquency: A Meta-Analysis." *Aggression and Violent Behavior* 28:12–20.

Stanard, Rebecca Powell. 1999. "The Effect of Training in a Strengths Model of Case Management on Client Outcomes in a Community Mental Health Center." *Community Mental Health Journal* 35(2):169–79.

Strang, Heather, Lawrence W. Sherman, Evan Mayo-Wilson, Daniel Woods, and Ariel Barak. 2013. *Restorative Justice Conferencing (RJC) Using Face-to-Face Meetings of Offenders and Victims: Effects on Offender Recidivism and Victim Satisfaction; a Systematic Review*. Oslo: Campbell Collaboration.

Sutherland, Edwin. 1983. *White-Collar Crime: The Uncut Version*. New Haven, CT: Yale University Press. (Originally published 1949.)

Toft, Monica Duffy. 2010. *Securing the Peace: The Durable Settlement of Civil Wars*. Princeton, NJ: Princeton University Press.

Tonry, Michael. 2018. "An Honest Politician's Guide to Deterrence." In *Deterrence, Choice, and Crime: Contemporary Perspectives*, edited by Daniel S. Nagin, Francis T. Cullen, and Cheryl Lero Jonson. New York: Routledge, forthcoming.

Travis, Jeremy, Bruce Western, and F. Stevens Redburn, eds. 2014. *The Growth of Incarceration in the United States: Exploring Causes and Consequences*. Washington, DC: National Academies Press.

Tyler, Tom R. 1990. *Why People Obey the Law*. New Haven, CT: Yale University Press.

Tyler, Tom R., and Yuen J. Huo. 2002. *Trust in the Law: Encouraging Public Cooperation with the Police and Courts*. New York: Russell Sage Foundation.

Tyler, Tom R., Lawrence Sherman, Heather Strang, Geoffrey C. Barnes, and Daniel Woods. 2007. "Reintegrative Shaming, Procedural Justice, and Recidivism: The Engagement of Offenders' Psychological Mechanisms in the Canberra RISE Drinking-and-Driving Experiment." *Law and Society Review* 41(3):553–86.

Umbreit, Mark, and Robert Coates. 1992. *Victim-Offender Mediation: An Analysis of Programs in Four States of the US*. Minneapolis: Citizens Council Mediation Services.

Weisburd, David, David P. Farrington, and Charlotte Gill. 2017. "What Works in Crime Prevention and Rehabilitation." *Criminology and Public Policy* 16 (2):415–49.

Weisburd, David, Cody W. Telep, Joshua C. Hinkle, and John E. Eck. 2010. "Is Problem-Oriented Policing Effective in Reducing Crime and Disorder? Findings from a Campbell Systematic Review." *Criminology and Public Policy* 9(1):139–72.

Wilson, David B., Ajima Olaghere, and Catherine S. Kimbrell. 2017. *Effectiveness of Restorative Justice Principles in Juvenile Justice: A Meta-Analysis*. Washington, DC: US Department of Justice, Office of Juvenile Justice and Delinquency Prevention.

Wong, Jennifer S., Jessica Bouchard, Jason Gravel, Martin Bouchard, and Carlo Morselli. 2016. "Can At-Risk Youth Be Diverted from Crime? A Meta-Analysis of Restorative Diversion Programs." *Criminal Justice and Behavior* 43(10):1310–29.

Yeung, Karen. 2004. *Securing Compliance*. Oxford: Oxford University Press.

Zehr, Howard. 2015. *The Little Book of Restorative Justice*. New York: Skyhorse Publishing.

Zimring, Franklin E. 2011. *The City That Became Safe: New York's Lessons for Urban Crime and Its Control*. New York: Oxford University Press.

*Michael Tonry*

# Punishment and Human Dignity: Sentencing Principles for Twenty-First-Century America

ABSTRACT

A new conception of justice in punishment is needed that is premised on respect for offenders' human dignity. It needs to acknowledge retributive and
utilitarian values and incorporate independently important values of fairness
and equal treatment. Punishment principles, policies, and practices lined up
nicely in mid-twentieth-century America. Utilitarian principles implied a
primary goal of crime prevention through rehabilitation and avoidance of
unnecessary suffering by offenders. Judges and parole boards were empowered
to tailor decisions to fit offenders' circumstances and interests. Corrections
officials sought to address rehabilitative needs and facilitate achievement of
successful, law-abiding lives. The system often did not work as it should, but its
ideals, aspirations, and aims were clear. In our time, there are no commonly
shared principles; sentencing laws and practices are unprecedentedly rigid and
severe; judges and parole boards often lack authority to make sensible or just
decisions; corrections officials are expected simultaneously to act as police
officers, actuaries, and social workers; and injustice is ubiquitous.

There is no commonly accepted normative framework in the United States
for thinking or talking about punishment. This is unique among western
European and English-speaking countries. In Scandinavian countries, al-

Electronically published March 9, 2018
    Michael Tonry is professor of law and public policy, University of Minnesota.

119

most all philosophers, lawyers, and judges, and most policy makers, agree that the severity of punishments should be proportioned to the seriousness of crimes, that comparable offenders should be treated as equally as is humanly possible, and that offenders should not be avoidably damaged by what happens to them. In German-speaking, Benelux, and southern European countries, proportionality is widely agreed to be the primary consideration but counterbalanced by reluctance to harm people by imprisoning them and by aspirations to facilitate offenders' achievement of satisfying, law-abiding lives. In other English-speaking countries, proportionality and equality receive relatively less emphasis than in western Europe but considerably more than in the United States. Utilitarian considerations of deterrence, incapacitation, and moral education loom comparatively large, but constrained by widely shared concerns that offenders be treated fairly and not be punished unduly severely.[1]

Please don't misunderstand. The preceding paragraph is not meant to suggest that other Western countries' systems deliver perfect justice or achieve the fairness, consistency, and equal treatment to which they aspire. Human institutions never work like that no matter how hard people try. The descriptions nonetheless accurately depict common aspirations to treat offenders justly and empathetically, to honor the biblical injunction to do unto others as you would have them do unto you.

In all of those other countries, legal institutions, processes, and rules aim to assure that offenders are treated justly, consistently, and humanely or, as the late American philosopher Ronald Dworkin (1977) put it, as equals and with concern and respect for their interests. As protection against foreseeable pressures toward injustice, decisions affecting individuals are insulated from influence by politicians or public opinion: judges and prosecutors are career civil servants. There are tight limits on maximum sentences. When, rarely, laws prescribe particular or minimum sentences for specific crimes, judges have discretion to impose lesser ones.

The United States is an outlier in all these matters. Only in America are judges and prosecutors elected[2] and are public opinion, media attention, or political considerations widely believed to be germane to their

---

[1] Sources for assertions about other countries' legal systems in this paragraph and in the next few can be found in Tonry (2012, 2016*b*).

[2] Except in nonpartisan elections in a handful of Swiss cantons.

work. Only here has the sentencing authority of judges, who are ethically obligated to do justice in individual cases, been subordinated to powers of prosecutors and legislators who have political, career advancement, and other self-interested objectives in mind. To them, concern and respect for offenders' interests are seldom centrally important. Often—as when mandatory minimum sentence, truth-in-sentencing, three-strikes, and life without parole laws apply—they are entirely absent. Only in the United States are prison sentences often measured in decades and lifetimes. Only in the United States is meaningful review of sentences in individual cases largely unavailable.[3]

Those stark contrasts are recent. They date from the 1970s and 1980s. Before that, the American approach was different from those of other countries but principled and coherent. Every jurisdiction had an indeterminate sentencing system in which treatment of offenders was to be individualized in every case and at every stage. There was wide support for rehabilitation as the primary goal; for judges, parole boards, and prison officials to take account of individuals' circumstances and interests in making decisions about them; and for imposition of the least restrictive appropriate sentence. Retribution per se was not a goal. Retribution is "the unstudied belief of most men," observed Jerome Michael and Herbert Wechsler (1940, pp. 7, 11), two of the twentieth century's most influential criminal lawyers, but that, like any other ignoble intuition, should be ignored. "No legal provision can be justified merely because it calls for the punishment of the morally guilty by penalties proportioned to their guilt," they continued, "or criticized merely because it fails to do so."

"Rehabilitation," observed Wechsler, later the primary draftsman of the *Model Penal Code* (American Law Institute 1962), "is in itself a social value of importance, a value, it is well to note, that is and ought to be the prime goal" (1961, p. 468). Under the code, judges in every case could

---

[3] This is mostly because the US Supreme Court since the 1970s has emasculated constitutional standards for review of disproportionately severe punishments under the Eighth Amendment's prohibition of cruel and unusual punishments. In *Harmelin v. Michigan*, 501 U.S. 957, 1001 (1991), in which the defendant, a first offender convicted of cocaine possession, was sentenced to life without parole, Justice Kennedy observed, "The Eighth Amendment does not require strict proportionality between crime and sentence. Rather, it forbids only extreme sentences that are 'grossly disproportionate' to the crime." The Court laid foundations earlier. In *Rummel v. Estelle*, 445 U.S. 263, 274 (1980), upholding a sentence of life without parole for theft of $120.75, the Court observed that the proportionality principle "would . . . come into play in the extreme example . . . if a legislature made overtime parking a felony punishable by life imprisonment."

impose any lawful sentence from unsupervised probation to the maximum authorized by law. There were no mandatory minimum sentences and no probation ineligibility laws. Parole boards could release prisoners any time after they became eligible. The code created presumptions against the use of imprisonment in every case, including homicides, and in favor of parole release. Prison officials could grant time off for good behavior.

The *Model Penal Code* was not merely an academic exercise. It was commissioned and approved by the American Law Institute, a law reform organization composed mostly of lawyers in large law firms and state and federal judges (Tonry 2004, chap. 7). The drafting committee contained many more judges, prosecutors, defense lawyers, and corrections officials than professors. Nearly half of the code was drafted under the direction of Paul C. Tappan, a career parole official.

Politicians and public officials were on board. This can be seen in a series of contemporaneous initiatives. In 1963, the Advisory Committee of Judges proposed the Model Sentencing Act. In 1967, the President's Commission on Law Enforcement and Administration of Justice led by US Attorney General Nicholas Katzenbach issued its report, *The Challenge of Crime in a Free Society*. In 1971, the National Commission on Reform of Federal Criminal Laws chaired by California Governor Edmund Brown released a *Proposed Federal Criminal Code*. In 1973, the National Advisory Commission on Criminal Justice Standards and Goals, appointed by President Richard M. Nixon and chaired by Republican Delaware Governor Russell Peterson, issued its report. All four documents, like the *Model Penal Code*, supported indeterminate sentencing and sought to improve it.

That consensus soon collapsed. In the cultural climate of the 1970s, when the prisoners' rights, civil rights, and due process movements were strongest, individualized decision making was widely believed to be unfair, to result in unjust disparities, and to produce arbitrary, capricious, and racially biased results (Blumstein et al. 1983). Emphases on individual rights, exemplified by the writings of John Rawls (1971), Robert Nozick (1974), and Ronald Dworkin (1977), helped shape an intellectual climate that emphasized fairness, consistency, and equal treatment.

All of those developments fit more comfortably with retributive than with utilitarian values. Marvin Frankel (1973), a prominent federal judge, described American sentencing as "lawless" and offered then-radical proposals to improve it. Influential books by Norval Morris (1974) and

Andreas von Hirsch (1976) promoted "limiting retributive" and "just deserts" theories calling for the fairness, evenhandedness, and consistency that indeterminate sentencing was said to lack.[4]

A large and sophisticated theoretical literature on retribution emerged but quickly became entirely disconnected from punishment policies and practices. It appeared in the 1970s as if fairer, more just sentencing systems would be widely adopted to replace indeterminate sentencing, but that happened only in a few places, and only for a few years. Criminal justice policy instead became highly politicized, legislatures enacted laws of historically unprecedented severity and rigidity, few people seemed to care much about the new laws' effects on individual offenders, and imprisonment rates began a three-decade increase (Tonry 2016a, chap. 2). It is impossible to develop principled retributive justifications for lengthy prison terms for sellers of a few grams of drugs, minimum 25-year or life sentences for routine property crimes, or life without parole for almost anything or anyone. Proportionality between offense seriousness and punishment severity is an element of all retributive conceptions of punitive justice. Minor drug sales, thefts, and assaults are in everyone's minds less serious than rapes and serious violence but often are punished more severely.

As things now stand, there is no generally accepted American jurisprudence of punishment. Mandatory minimum sentence, three-strikes, and life without parole laws, indefensible by any normative theory, coexist with a few state sentencing guidelines systems loosely based on retributive premises and a majority of state systems with hodge-podges of features of determinate and indeterminate sentencing. A plethora of drug and other problem-solving courts, restorative justice initiatives, prisoner reentry programs, and reinvigorated treatment programs fit comfortably within the utilitarian values of indeterminate sentencing.

The lack of a widely agreed jurisprudence is not merely untidy, a matter that should be of concern only to ivory tower intellectuals. It has huge and morally troubling consequences. Individuals charged with drug or violent offenses subject to lengthy mandatory minimum prison sentences, for example, almost always serve those sentences if they are prosecuted and

---

[4] Von Hirsch, named Andreas when he was born in Germany, used the anglicized Andrew when he lived in the United States and England. Since returning to Germany, he has resumed use of Andreas, including in scholarly writing. Sources are listed under the name in which they were originally published.

124     Michael Tonry

convicted. However, if prosecutors or judges divert them to drug courts, mental health programs, or elsewhere, they may avoid conviction, imprisonment, or both. For cases not subject to mandatories, prosecutors and judges possess unfettered discretion.[5] The luck of the draw, not normative ideas about justice, determines whether people wind up in prison for years, in community treatment programs, or diverted from the criminal justice system.

Retributive theories remain in vogue in law schools and philosophy departments but do not provide adequate guidance for thinking about justice in the real world. Theorists focus mostly on blameworthiness and moral communication, and incidentally on crime prevention, even though punishment implicates a wider range of important values and interests including fairness and equal treatment. Difficult problems, the English political theorist Isaiah Berlin observed, almost always encompass competing normative principles: "The world that we encounter in ordinary experience is one in which we are faced with choices between ends equally ultimate, and claims equally absolute, the realization of some of which must inevitably involve the sacrifice of others" (2002, pp. 213–14).

Abortion is one example. Some people believe fetuses are human beings, human life is sacred, and abortion is morally wrong and should be prohibited. Others believe women are entitled to control their bodies, pregnancy is quintessentially a private matter, and state interference is morally wrong and should be eschewed. Public policy must favor one set of beliefs over the other or compromise both.

Child protection offers a less polarized example. Most people believe in a principle of family autonomy: parents should be allowed to decide what kinds of lives they and their children live; this implies a strong presumption against state interference. Minimization of harm to children implies a presumption in favor of state action whenever risks exist. Probably everyone believes that family autonomy should be respected and that children should be protected. Both goals cannot be simultaneously maximized. Any imaginable policy choice involves trade-offs: greater autonomy means heightened risks; reduced risks mean less autonomy.

[5] Meaningful appellate sentence review is unavailable in most states. The US Supreme Court in *Bordenkircher v. Hayes*, 434 U.S. 357 (1978), held that discretionary charging decisions by prosecutors are seldom reviewable by courts, and many of the 90–95 percent of defendants who plead guilty are required as a condition to waive their rights to appeal (King and O'Neill 2005).

The way forward concerning punishment becomes clearer when we recognize that it implicates multiple, competing values, including not only deserved punishment and crime prevention but also fairness and equal treatment. A comprehensive jurisprudence of just punishment for twenty-first-century America would thus incorporate four propositions:

- *Justice as Fairness*: Processes for responding to crimes should be publicly known, implemented in good faith, and applied evenhandedly (Rawls 1958).
- *Justice as Equal Treatment*: Defendants and offenders should be treated as equals; their interests should be accorded concern and respect when decisions affecting them are made (Dworkin 1977).
- *Justice as Proportionality*: Offenders should never be punished more severely than can be justified by their blameworthiness in relation to the severity of punishments justly imposed on others for the same and different offenses (Morris 1974).
- *Justice as Parsimony*: Offenders should never be punished more severely than can be justified by appropriate, valid, normative purposes (Tonry 1994).

Those four propositions describe what people accused or convicted of crimes would want for themselves or their loved ones. They describe minimum, interacting requirements of a just system of punishment. Together they provide answers to problems that traditional punishment theories by themselves cannot resolve. Respect for human dignity does not appear as a separate proposition. It encompasses all four propositions.

Human dignity is often dismissed as a nebulous, primarily rhetorical concept (Macklin 2003; cf. Waldron 2014). The reason is partly that neither the term nor the concept plays an independent, substantive role in American law (Steiker 2014) and partly that the term appears prominently in the preambles to international human rights documents such as the 1948 UN Universal Declaration of Human Rights but in their texts is given no concrete work to do (Waldron 2012).

These critiques have merit when human dignity is used rhetorically, but not when it is used concretely, as I show in Section II, in relation to sentencing and other individualized decisions affecting individuals. Torture denies human dignity to its victims. So does solitary confinement in a supermax prison. So does requiring people to live in squalid, inhuman conditions. So does denial to individuals of the possibility ever to live a satisfying life. So does making decisions about individuals' lives and futures without taking account of their circumstances and interests. None of those practices is practically necessary or morally justifiable. Conceptual and procedural tools exist to acknowledge human dignity in relation to punishment and sentencing. The preceding four propositions about justice in punishment encapsulate them.

The idea that punishment implicates values and interests other than moral blameworthiness, crime prevention, and moral education is not new. Immanuel Kant and Jeremy Bentham, the pioneers of retributive and utilitarian punishment theories, recognized two centuries ago that extrinsic considerations sometimes limit or forbid punishments that could otherwise be justified.[6] I don't endorse the propositions they offer but quote them to illustrate that even single-minded theorists recognize that punishment implicates values other than retribution and crime prevention.

In this essay, I explain why retributive theories that dominate contemporary scholarly writing cannot adequately elucidate what a just punishment system should look like. I discuss utilitarian and other nonretributive theories only briefly and incidentally. They attract little contemporary support; most people who think or write about these subjects are retributivists of one sort or another. I begin in the first section with a brief primer on punishment philosophy for readers who may not be familiar with retributive punishment theories, ideas, and concepts.[7] I then canvass a series of fundamental dilemmas courts face on which retributive theories cast little light. These include how to assess blameworthiness, practical problems in administration of the criminal law, and the multiple offense paradox that punishments per offense usually decrease when offenses are sentenced simultaneously but increase when they are sentenced successively (Tonry 2017).

---

[6] Kant ([1797] 2011, p. 34) observed that sometimes the sovereign "will want to avoid adversely affecting the feelings of the people" and some penalty other than the uniquely deserved one may be imposed. Bentham ([1789] 1970, p. 164) wrote that otherwise appropriate punishments should not be imposed when too many people would have to be punished, making the aggregate punishment too great; when punishment would cause the loss of the offender's "extraordinary value" to the community; when community opinion is strongly that the offense or offender should not be punished, or punished so much; and when relations with foreign powers would be undermined.

[7] The primer focuses on basic concepts and uncontroversial distinctions. Readers familiar with punishment philosophy may want to skim or skip subsection I.A.

In the second section, I elaborate on the normative framework set out above. Proportionality, a retributive touchstone, is a core component. It provides tools for comparing punishments for different offenses and different offenders. It and Benthamite parsimony set intelligible limits on punishments that may justly be imposed. So, however, independently, do fairness and equality.

## I. The Limited Reach of Retributivism

Few would disagree that authoritative, normative expression of censure for wrongdoing is the, or a, core function of criminal convictions and punishments imposed by judges. Big disagreements emerge, however, when the focus shifts from judges to offenders. To decide how much censure one offender deserves relative to deserved censures of others, convincing ways to assess blameworthiness and to determine just punishments are needed. Large conceptual disagreements and practical impediments stand in the way. Before I discuss them, I first provide a brief introduction to punishment theory.

### A. A Punishment Primer

Three main strands of punishment theory—retributivism, utilitarianism, and positivism—emerged over the last two centuries. Retributive theories, first developed in some detail in Germany by Kant ([1797] 1965) and Georg Wilhelm Friedrich Hegel ([1821] 1991), called for imposition of punishments apportioned to the seriousness of crimes. Kant famously observed: "What kind and what degree of punishment does public legal justice adopt as its principle and standard? None other than the principle of equality.... Accordingly, any undeserved evil that you afflict on someone else among the people is one that you [deserve].... Only the law of retribution (*jus talionis*) can determine exactly the kind and degree of punishment" ([1797] 2011, p. 32).[8] Retributive ideas, usually less dogmatic than Kant's, have been continuously influential in continental Europe though not in the United States (Pifferi 2012, 2016). In the United States they gained support in the 1960s and 1970s and remain

---

[8] Hegel expressed the same view: "The universal feeling of peoples and individuals towards crime is, and always has been, that it deserves to be punished, and that *what the criminal has done should be done to him*" (Hegel [1821] 2011, p. 46; my emphasis)

influential today. There are many different kinds of retributive theory, but they share the view that moral blameworthiness is an important consideration in determining just punishments.

Utilitarian theory is usually dated from the publication in 1764 of Cesare Beccaria's *Dei delitti e delle pene* (*On Crimes and Punishments*; 2007). He urged that punishments be scaled to the seriousness of crimes and used to deter offenders and others from wrongdoing. Bentham ([1789] 1970, [1830] 2008), the archetypal utilitarian theorist, developed deterrent ideas in far greater detail. Bentham's proposals were based on ideas he shared with Beccaria, combined with a model of rational human beings who engage in calculation of pains and pleasures. The pains of punishment should always exceed the envisioned pleasures to be gained from crime.

The object of the criminal law for Bentham was to "augment the total happiness of the community" and "to exclude, as far as may be, every thing that tends to subtract from that happiness: in other words, to exclude mischief" (1970, p. 158). Crime is a form of mischief. To prevent crime through deterrence, Bentham offered detailed prescriptions. Punishments should be severer for more serious crimes to encourage offenders to commit lesser ones, should be increased if the probability of apprehension is low so the deterrent message will not be diluted, should be incrementally scaled to each detail of a contemplated offense so offenders have incentives to stop partway, and should be lower for attempted than for completed offenses to provide incentive to desist. Critically, however, despite his view that the idea of abstract human rights is "nonsense upon stilts" (Bentham 2002, pp. 317–401; Schofield 2003), everyone's happiness—including that of offenders—counts: "But all punishment is mischief: all punishment in itself is evil. Upon the principle of utility, if it ought at all to be admitted, it ought only to be admitted in as far as it promises to exclude some greater evil" (Bentham 1970, p. 158). Bentham's ideas shaped prevailing ways of thinking in English-speaking countries and provided the impetus to indeterminate sentencing as it emerged and endured in the United States. They remain central in other English-speaking countries.

In our time, the word "consequentialism" is often substituted for utilitarianism.[9] This, however, is based on a misconception that utilitarians

---

[9] In our time, the only well-developed nonutilitarian punishment theory that might also fall under the consequentialist heading is John Braithwaite and Philip Pettit's "republican theory" (1990, 2001). It differs from classic utilitarianism in that it seeks to maximize not

are interested only in deterrence. Bentham did, it is true, emphasize deterrent considerations. However, he also wrote about rehabilitation, incapacitation, and moral education, as did others who preceded him.[10] His overriding aim was to minimize the harms that result from crime, both to victims and to offenders.

In earlier times, including in the United States, many American intellectuals could be described as "positivists" (e.g., Glueck 1928; Pifferi 2016). Positivism is most famously associated with the Italian criminal lawyer Enrico Ferri (1906, 1921). Ferri, like many others of his time, was a determinist and believed that crime resulted primarily from social, economic, and psychological forces affecting offenders. The only valid purpose of the criminal law, he wrote, is the prevention of crime. Accordingly, the likelihood of reoffending should be the primary consideration. All prison sentences should be indeterminate, potentially for life, including for people convicted of minor offenses. Prisoners should be imprisoned only if they are dangerous. They should be released when they cease to be dangerous but held indefinitely if their dangerousness does not abate. Reverberations of positivism echoed through the mid-twentieth century (e.g., Wootton 1959, 1963; Ancel 1965; Menninger 1966), but it has largely disappeared in theoretical writing. Similar views are inarticulately present in the implicit logic behind contemporary prison sentences measured in decades and lifetimes and enactment of three-strikes, career criminal, sexual predator, and life without parole laws.

Only retributivist theories are much discussed in our time or, for that reason, in the rest of this essay. Their details vary; the implications vary

---

happiness or, synonymously, utility, but "dominion." Dominion is the human capacity to live an unconstrained life of one's choosing, limited by the obligation to respect others' rights to dominion over their own lives. Crimes violate victims' dominion. The theory has been discussed mostly in relation to restorative justice concerning which it calls for a decrementalist strategy of reduction in the use of punishment. Braithwaite (2018, p. 110), however, plaintively noted, "Braithwaite and Pettit's (1990) decrementalist research agenda went nowhere in the 28 years since it was proposed." Republican theory in relation to punishment has not provoked much writing by others, so I do not pursue it further here.

[10] William Blackstone, in his *Commentaries on the Laws of England*, e.g., earlier wrote that the end of punishment is not "atonement or expiation," but "a precaution against future offenses of the same kind. This is effected three ways: either by the amendment of the offender himself; ... or by deterring others ...; or, lastly, by depriving the party injuring of the power to do future mischief [by execution, permanent confinement, slavery, or exile]" ([1769] 1979, p. 13). Bentham (1970, p. 158, n. a) offers a similar list of crime prevention mechanisms.

less.[11] Retributivist ideas began to revive in the 1950s in writings by Norval Morris (1953), John Rawls (1955), and H. L. A. Hart (1959), who argued in different ways that preventive goals should be combined with retributive limits.

Many kinds of primarily retributive theories emerged. In the first generation, Herbert Morris (1966), Jeffrie Murphy (1973), and Andreas von Hirsch (1976) argued that people in a democratic society benefit from public order and security, including others' law-abidingness, are reciprocally obligated in return to accept the burdens and responsibilities of citizenship, and should be punished if they do not. The next generation, exemplified by Joel Feinberg (1970), Herbert Morris (1981), Jean Hampton (1984), and Antony Duff (2001), in different ways emphasized moral communication with offenders, victims, and the larger community about the wrongfulness of crime. Related censure theories offered by Duff (1986) and von Hirsch (1994) focused more narrowly on authoritative denunciation of wrongdoing. A third generation, harking back to Kant and Hegel, portrayed punishment as a morally necessary consequence of culpable wrongdoing (Robinson 1987; Moore 1993).

The lines that separate different kinds of retributive theory blur. Some, especially communicative theories, are difficult to distinguish from utilitarian ones. Most deal only with justification of punishment as an institution and do not explicitly address questions pertinent to individual offenders, particularly how much they should be punished.[12] Discussions of whether the state may justly punish offenders, and why, are intellectually interesting but not especially helpful to policy makers, prosecutors, and judges.

Retributivists of every stripe believe that offenders' blameworthiness is fundamental in some way to justifying punishment. They differ on what

[11] Many efforts have been made to describe and taxonomize varieties of retributivism. Classic ones include Hart (1968, postscript), Cottingham (1979), Mackie (1982), and Walker (1991). I provide a recent accounting (Tonry 2011).

[12] For example: "One question is: What might justify the state's creation of legal institutions of punishment? This is what we call the 'justification' question. The second question is: Once the state has determined someone's liability for a crime, how much and what kind of punishment should the state mete out in response? This is the 'sentencing' question. *That a retributivist theorist gives a retributive (or, specifically, communicative) answer to the justification question does not require her to offer a precise answer for each sentencing question. . . . A retributive conception of proportionality need not have much in the way of precision to say about the particular details of punishment's implementation*" (Markel 2010, pp. 950–51; emphasis added).

way. Because some basic retributivist concepts and distinctions arise in subsequent parts of this essay, I highlight several.

1. *Positive and Negative Retributivism.* Positive retributivism is a sword that cuts deservedly deeply and precisely. Negative retributivism is a shield that protects against undeservedly severe punishments.

Positive retributivists believe that deserved punishments must be imposed. Kant and Hegel are often portrayed as positive retributivists. Remember Kant's "principle of equality" and *jus talionis*? Paul Robinson (1987, 2008) and von Hirsch (1994, 2017) offer similar arguments.

Negative retributivists, to the contrary, believe that offenders' blameworthiness in relation to particular crimes sets upper limits on deserved punishments that may but need not be imposed. If good reasons exist for a lesser punishment, or no punishment at all, that is what should be done.

"Limiting retributivism," a form of negative retributivism associated with Norval Morris (1974), warrants separate mention primarily because it has been particularly influential (Frase 2013). The *Model Penal Code: Sentencing,* for example, explicitly adopts it as a normative premise (American Law Institute 2017, sec. 3.102[2]).

2. *Mixed Theories.* "Mixed theories" encompass combinations of retributive ideas with instrumental ideas about preventive effects of sanctions, the significance of contextual considerations, or special circumstances of individual cases. All negative retributivist theories, including limiting retributivism, are mixed theories.[13]

Use of the term mixed theory dates from Hart's *Punishment and Responsibility* (1968), a seminal work, in which he summarized his primarily utilitarian personal beliefs but noted that widely held views about deserved punishment need also to be taken into account. Hart and Norval Morris (1974), essentially utilitarians, believed widely shared intuitions about equality and proportionality in punishment to be important. They feared that the criminal law would lose legitimacy in citizens' eyes, and thus effectiveness, if it departed too much from prevailing community sentiments. Few people today espouse unqualified retributive views (e.g., Moore 1993). Nearly all modern writers offer mixed theories.

3. *Censure and Hard Treatment.* Many contemporary retributivists regard punishment as a form of moral communication (e.g., von Hirsch

[13] Braithwaite and Pettit's republican theory (1990, 2001) is better thought of as a form of negative retributivism than as a utilitarian or consequentialist theory. They are adamant that the offender's moral culpability sets an absolute, proportionate upper limit on punishment severity and equally adamant that retributive considerations are otherwise irrelevant.

2017). They generally feel obliged, however, to explain why communication of censure for wrongdoing is not the end of the matter: "You have sinned; go forth and sin no more." Most punishments for crime, however, involve intrusive, burdensome, or otherwise unpleasant elements. Many writers as a result partition punishment into censure and "hard treatment" and try separately to justify hard treatment. Most efforts are nonretributive (von Hirsch 2017: "prudential reasons to obey the law") or unconvincing (H. Morris 1981; Duff 2001: offenders themselves would wish it so).

4. *Ordinal and Cardinal Desert.* This distinction, first proposed by von Hirsch (1992), addresses the problem of knowing what specific punishment a particular offender deserves. God may know, but human beings have widely different intuitions. The solution, von Hirsch proposed, is to distinguish between punishment that is in some sense absolutely deserved, which he called cardinal desert, and punishment that is deserved for particular crimes relative to those deserved for other crimes. This he called ordinal desert. Ordinal desert can be coherently calculated by creating scales of offense seriousness and specifying appropriate punishments for the most and least serious offenses. Once that's done, a punishment scale can be created that parallels the offense seriousness scale.[14] The absolutely deserved punishment for robbery may be unknowable, but everyone would agree that the relatively deserved punishment for simple robbery, all else being equal, should normally be less than for aggravated robbery and more than for theft.

These concepts and terms recur throughout the rest of this essay. I use and refer to them because they are in common usage. As a practical matter, however, the problems and solutions I discuss are common to all retributive theories, whether positive or negative, and all mixed theories.

## B. Conceptual Impediments

Retributive and mixed theories that link deserved punishments to the seriousness of the crimes of which people are convicted cannot by them-

---

[14] Hegel recognized that prevailing ideas about severity of deserved punishment change over time: "With the progress of education, however, attitudes toward crime become more lenient, and punishments today are not nearly so harsh as they were a hundred years ago. It is not the crimes or punishments themselves which change, but the relation between the two" (2011, p. 42).

selves resolve two inescapable problems: the multiple offense paradox and assessment of blameworthiness.

1. *The Multiple Offense Paradox.* The emerging if exiguous literature on punishment for multiple crimes exposes a paradox that retributive theories, whether positive ones that specify punishments that must be imposed or negative ones that set upper limits, cannot adequately address or explain. Punishments of people convicted of multiple crimes are often discounted if sentences are imposed at one time (a "bulk discount") but enhanced if imposed at different times (a "recidivist premium"; Reitz 2010). This is perverse. Exactly the same sets of crimes can be handled either way—in one omnibus prosecution or in a series—depending on how prosecutors choose to proceed or on the happenstance of when offenses come to light. This is a serious problem because it arises in a majority of cases. Most convicted offenders are concurrently convicted of multiple offenses, have been previously convicted, or both.

*a. The Recidivist Premium.* Some writers, including George Fletcher (1978), Richard Singer (1979), and Mirko Bagaric (2010), reject the recidivist premium in principle. Their logic is that punishing repeat offenders more severely because of their prior convictions is double counting. The increment of additional punishment for the new crime is in effect additional punishment for earlier ones. The constitutional doctrine of double jeopardy forbids the state to try someone twice for the same crime. By extension, the state should not punish someone twice for the same crime.

The few efforts that have been made by retributivists to justify the recidivist premium are unpersuasive. I am not alone in my skepticism. Richard Lippke (2016, p. 17) surveyed the arguments and similarly concluded, "Like others, I find the arguments given on behalf of recidivist premiums unconvincing."

One unconvincing argument is that repeat offenders who commit new offenses are more blameworthy than first offenders because previous convictions impose special obligations not to offend again (Lee 2010). Everyone, however, has a civic responsibility not to commit crimes. It is hard to explain why the responsibility to obey the law is greater for the previously convicted. It cannot be because greater knowledge or self-control can reasonably be imputed to them. Most repeat offenders no doubt know that behavior they contemplate is unlawful, but so do most first offenders. Members of both groups sometimes commit offenses under extreme social, economic, or circumstantial pressures, or influenced

by deviant subcultural norms, that make law-abidingness especially difficult. This might or might not make individuals less blameworthy, but it
offers no basis for differentiating between first-time and repeat offenders.

Other unconvincing arguments supporting the recidivist premium assert that repeat offending is evidence of bad character or constitutes disrespect or defiance of the court, the criminal law, or the state (Bennett
2010; Lee 2017). If any of these considerations were taken seriously, it
would require that specific increments of punishment be attributed to
character flaws or traits. Punishments for a subsequent crime could be
deconstructed into the conventional $X$ months that would be imposed
for a first robbery and an increment of $Y$ months, for example, for bad
character. Defiance, disrespectfulness, and bad character, however, are
not criminal offenses. They might be punishable in China, but not in a
liberal democratic state.

Von Hirsch (1986, 2017) has argued that punishments should be
discounted for first offenses, and possibly one or a few more. This is a different kind of argument than those justifying the recidivist premium even
though the result, punishing repeat offenders more severely than first
offenders, is the same. It is based on the premise that first and early
offenses may have resulted from extraordinary circumstances or otherwise have been "out of character" and thus warrant less-than-deserved
punishment. This is a contingent characterological claim about first offenders: they may, on average, be more responsible people than recidivists are and should be given the benefit of the doubt. There may be
good policy reasons to give first offenders benefits of doubts, and this often happens (Braithwaite 2018), but justifying them as reflections of hypothesized good or bad character is as troubling here as elsewhere. Von
Hirsch in any case, once the first or early offender discount is exhausted,
would not allow increased punishments on account of former offenses.

Contrary to any argument that can be made for the recidivist premium, an empirically grounded argument can be made that prior convictions should mitigate rather than aggravate punishments for subsequent
crimes. Collateral social and legal effects of convictions make it foreseeably more difficult for former offenders than for nonoffenders to live law-
abiding lives (Ashworth and Wasik 2017). Research showing that imprisonment makes people more, not less, likely to commit subsequent offenses
confirms this (e.g., Nagin, Cullen, and Jonson 2009).

*b. The Bulk Discount.* No one rejects the bulk discount in principle,
with the tentative exception of Jesper Ryberg (2017), who canvasses pos-

sible arguments for it and finds none he judges to be persuasive.[15] Lippke (2011) offers the most extensive analysis to date of what a jurisprudence of bulk discounts, taken seriously, might look like and shows that it would be immensely complex and not generally justifiable.

Policy justifications have been offered. One is that no punishment should be so "crushing" that it deprives a person of a large fraction of his or her remaining life (Jareborg 1998; Ashworth and Wasik 2017) or a high proportion of the prime years of life (Bottoms 1998). A second is that bulk discounts can be justified as extensions of mercy based on judges' holistic assessments of offenders' lives and blameworthiness (Bottoms 2017). These propositions, however, are ad hoc, unimbedded in broader general theories, and ungeneralizable. The policy they try to justify is no doubt desirable, lest individuals suffer extreme punishments based on the fortuity that they have been charged with more rather than fewer offenses, but it cannot be justified in terms of retributive theories.

There is convincing empirical evidence that majorities of the public, judges, and offenders approve of both the bulk discount and the recidivist premium (Roberts 2008; Roberts and De Keijser 2017). Some argue that those broadly shared intuitions justify the paradox either because democratic values require acknowledgment of and deference to widely shared beliefs or because failure to do so will undermine the legitimacy of law and the legal process in citizens' minds (Roberts 2011; Ryberg and Roberts 2014). Common intuitions, however, by themselves cannot offer a principled justification for anything. Widely shared intuitions, for example, about racial, gender, ethnic, and sexual preference differences, or in our time about the moral worthiness of immigrants, are often empirically indefensible and normatively repellent.

*c. Empirical Reality.*  No one has satisfactorily offered principled justification for why punitive punches should be pulled when people are sentenced for multiple offenses but swung harder when they have previously been convicted. This is not a small failure. These issues arise in a large majority of criminal cases. The typical defendant is not a first-timer charged with a single offense but a recidivist offender charged with multiple offenses.

Table 1 presents 2009 American data, the most recent available when this was written, on multiple current charges of felony defendants in the

---

[15] Ryberg (2001) was a decade ahead of the game, canvassing multiple offense issues in detail long before others began writing about them.

TABLE 1

Multiple Charges, by Most Serious Felony,
75 Largest US Counties, 2009

| Most Serious Charge | No Other Charge (%) | Other Charges (%) |
|---|---|---|
| All felonies | 45 | 55 |
| Violence | 37 | 63 |
| Murder | 39 | 61 |
| Rape | 32 | 68 |
| Robbery | 39 | 61 |
| Property | 47 | 53 |
| Motor vehicle theft | 48 | 52 |
| Burglary | 33 | 67 |
| Drugs | 46 | 54 |

SOURCE.—Reaves (2013), table 2.

state courts of the 75 most populous counties. Fifty-five percent of all felony defendants' cases involved multiple charges, including 61–68 percent of violent crimes and 53 percent of property crimes (Reaves 2013).[16]

Table 2 presents data on prior convictions. Overall, 60 percent of felony defendants had at least one prior conviction; 43 percent had prior felony convictions, 30 percent had two or more prior felony convictions, and 11 percent had more than four. For specific offenses, 48 percent of murder defendants had prior convictions as did 53 percent of all violent crime defendants, 56 percent of property crime defendants, and 66 percent of drug defendants.

The first-time defendant with a clean record is not a mythological beast, but he or she is far from the norm. The multiple offender paradox exposes the inadequacy of traditional or any imaginable retributive theories by themselves. The challenges it poses are equally insurmountable for positive versions of retributive theory that would specify precise punishments in individual cases, for negative versions that specify upper limits, or for mixed theories. Theories of punishment that cannot coher-

---

[16] The American experience is paralleled elsewhere. Anthony Doob in private communication reported that Statistics Canada data for 2014 show that nationally 60 percent of convictions involved more than one offense, ranging from 55 percent in Quebec to 72 percent in the Yukon. Roberts and de Keijser (2017, p. 1) write of England and Wales, "In England and Wales, the Sentencing Council has estimated that approximately 40 percent of sentencing decisions involved multiple crimes." Good national data are unavailable in either country about the percentage of convicted offenders who have previously been convicted.

TABLE 2

Prior Convictions, by Most Serious Felony,
75 Largest US Counties, 2009

| Most Serious Charge | No Prior Convictions (%) | Misdemeanor Convictions Only (%) | One Felony Only (%) | Two to Four Felonies (%) | Four-Plus Felonies (%) |
|---|---|---|---|---|---|
| All felonies | 40 | 17 | 13 | 19 | 11 |
| Violence | 47 | 16 | 13 | 16 | 8 |
| Murder | 52 | 9 | 13 | 14 | 13 |
| Rape | 49 | 15 | 14 | 12 | 10 |
| Robbery | 48 | 13 | 13 | 17 | 9 |
| Property | 44 | 16 | 11 | 16 | 13 |
| Motor vehicle theft | 38 | 14 | 11 | 20 | 17 |
| Burglary | 39 | 17 | 13 | 18 | 13 |
| Drugs | 34 | 16 | 13 | 22 | 15 |

SOURCE.—Reaves (2013), table 7.

ently explain how half to two-thirds of people convicted of crime should be punished are fundamentally incomplete.

2. *Blameworthiness.* Most retributive theories assume that assessments of blameworthiness can be made more or less objectively, on the basis of the offense of conviction perhaps modified by circumstances such as weapon use, gratuitous violence, or a victim's special vulnerability that seem inextricably related to moral assessment of the seriousness of the crime. Serious arguments have been made, however, that decisions about punishment should incorporate subjective assessments of the offender's blameworthiness and of the foreseeable effects of contemplated punishments on him or her as a unique individual.

Assessments of blameworthiness are difficult and contested. Nothing inherent in any retributive theory entails a particular approach. Assessments and resulting punishments might be based, objectively, solely on the seriousness of the crimes of which individuals are convicted or, subjectively, on crimes' distinctive features and the social, psychological, economic, and situational circumstances causally related to their commission (von Hirsch 1976; Tonry 2014). Criminal law in English-speaking countries takes no account of motives, caring only about the classic *mens rea* categories of intention, knowledge, recklessness, and negligence, and allows only limited space for defenses of duress, necessity, immaturity, emotional distress, and mental disability and usually none at all for harms resulting from imperfect self-defense and other honest but unreasonable mistakes.[17] If the substantive criminal law does not take account of these and other complexities of human lives, decisions about punishment can incorporate what Hart (1968) approvingly called informal mitigation. Nigel Walker (1991) proposed that, if retributivists take moral blameworthiness seriously, assessments should be subjective. That, he observed, is how the Recording Angel would do it.

A similar question can be asked about the effects of punishments on individuals. Adam Kolber (2009) and others have proposed that judges making punishment decisions take account of their foreseeable subjective effects on individuals.[18] Otherwise, the suffering caused by seemingly generic punishments will be radically different. Claustrophobic and mentally ill people, for example, will be affected by close confinement substantially differently than are people who are not similarly afflicted. Confinement of people with dependent children will have substantially different direct and collateral effects than does confinement of the childless. Imprisonment may mean very different things to a young gang leader, a flamboyantly gay man, an employed middle-aged parent, and someone who is seriously ill. To ignore such things in relation to comparably culpable people, however culpability is measured, is to accept huge differences in the pains imposed on them.

Walker, Hart, and Kolber make much the better arguments. Systems of punishment that ignore fundamental differences in offenders' subjective blameworthiness, or radical differences in the effects on them of ostensibly generic punishments, cannot be reasonably described as just.

---

[17] In common law countries but typically not in continental European civil law countries, affirmative defenses such as self-defense are not available to defendants who honestly but unreasonably believe their actions to be justifiable. Imperfect self-defense cases, e.g., involve defendants who genuinely believe themselves to be threatened by serious bodily harm or death when they were not and when reasonable persons would have known they were not.

[18] Kolber revived ideas at least two centuries old. Bentham (1970, chap. VI) was adamant that punishments must be adjusted to offenders' "sensibilities." Kant (1965, p. 101) called for attention to be paid "to the special sensibilities of the upper classes" so that the privileged will be punished equivalently to the poor. His most vivid example is of a "man of a higher class" who would be condemned to "solitary and painful confinement" for an offense for which a "social inferior" would be called on only to apologize "because by this means, in addition to the discomfort suffered, the pride of the offender will be painfully affected, and thus his humiliation will compensate for the offense as like for like."

## C. Practical Impediments

The practical impediments are no less confounding. These problems are most acute in the United States, where 90–95 percent of convictions in almost all jurisdictions result from guilty pleas, most emerging from diverse forms of plea negotiation. Practices vary widely. In many charge bargains, some among multiple charges of similar offenses are dismissed. Even in a world of bulk discounts, this reduces sentences. In other charge bargains, defendants are allowed to plead guilty to less serious charges (e.g., theft or sexual assault); more serious ones (e.g., robbery or rape) are dismissed. Conviction numbers and labels thus become fundamentally misleading. In sentence bargaining, defendants plead guilty to the offenses charged, but in exchange for an agreed sentence. In fact bargaining, prosecutors agree not to allege facts that if proven would result in a mandatory minimum sentence, trigger policies that prescribe aggravated penalties, or offend idiosyncratic judicial sensibilities that lawyers believe make harsher penalties more likely. Patterns of plea negotiation often vary substantially between counties within a state: charge dismissals in some, charge reductions in some, and sentence agreements in others. People convicted of the same nominal crime will often have engaged in very different behaviors. Many different kinds of acts reflecting diverse degrees of objective blameworthiness are hidden behind the names of the offenses of which people are convicted. Finally, a "trial tax" almost always results in harsher sentences for defendants convicted at trial than they would have received otherwise (Kim 2015).

These problems are not uniquely American. Plea bargaining in England and Wales is less ornate than in the United States but results in as much as a one-third reduction in sentence for defendants who plead guilty early (Ashworth 2015). From the defendant's perspective, the English trial tax can be 50 percent. This is considerably higher than is conventional in the United States.

Retributive punishment theories cannot in their own terms provide much guidance for thinking about the handling of particular cases. Blameworthiness, the core concept, is difficult to define in theory and harder to characterize in practice. That does not, of course, make blameworthiness unimportant, but it can provide at best a partial account of how a principled system of punishment should operate. Like the shadows flickering on the walls of Plato's cave, it provides impressions of what a just system might look like, but no more than that.

The problems with real-world application of retributive punishment theories are fundamental. They are also ironic; the retributivist revival was a reaction to real-world problems. It occurred neither in a vacuum nor from turbulence in university philosophy departments but in response to perceptions of stark injustices (Matravers 2011). By emphasizing blameworthiness as a primary consideration, and a limit on the discretions of officials, it aimed to right wrongs.

What is needed is a conceptual account of punishment that can address real-world problems in principled ways. The following section suggests how one can be developed.

## II. Just Punishment

Questions about justice in punishment cannot be answered by invocation only of retributive and utilitarian theories. They are "monist," which implies, asserted Berlin (2002), the false view that moral questions have single correct answers and that all those answers dovetail within a single, coherent moral system. In the introduction, I quoted and illustrated Berlin's famous assertion about value pluralism and the inevitability of conflicts between implications of equally important first principles.

Punishment is a realm in which value pluralism is unavoidable. Since the times of Bentham and Kant, conflict between the implications of preventive utilitarian and blame-imputing retributive premises have been evident, leading to zero-sum-game arguments and the emergence of mixed theories. Values other than those associated with retributivism and utilitarianism, however, also need to be taken into account. Before making that case, two preliminary matters warrant redundant mention.

First, as many people believe about abortion, perhaps the best solution to value conflict about punishment is simply to choose between polar approaches. This is not a real option. No one subscribes in our time to unconstrained utilitarianism. Almost no one subscribes to positive retributivism, the view that people must be punished in a particular amount that is proportionate to the seriousness of their crime, no less and no more. Most people subscribe to forms of negative retributivism or other mixed theories. These positions by definition encompass nonretributive values.

Second, if no single "pure" normative framework is imaginable, perhaps the best approach is simply to adopt a mixed theory approach that directs judges to take retributive and utilitarian elements into account as appears warranted. As Section I made clear, that won't work. No form of retributivism by itself, or combined only with instrumental crime prevention considerations, can resolve the multiple offense paradox, adequately specify criteria for assessing blameworthiness, or take account of practical administrative issues. In any case, directing judges simply to choose governing punishment purposes case by case would recreate the problems, and dangers, of unconstrained discretion that indeterminate sentencing presented and the retributivist revival sought to address.

A just punishment system would be pluralist and take account of competing normative claims. It would in retributive terms take account of offenders' blameworthiness. It would in Bentham's terms be parsimonious, imposing no unjustifiable human suffering. It would in Dworkin's terms treat offenders with equal concern and respect, allowing each to be assessed according to appropriate criteria in his or her individual circumstances and situation. It would in Rawls's terms be fair, using procedures and standards that are transparent, consistent, and evenhandedly applied.

Fairness, equality, proportionality, and parsimony can all be subsumed within a broader concept of respect for human dignity. The term "human dignity" has, however, wrongly, a bad name in some intellectual circles: largely because of particular contexts, and ways, in which it is used and because it is often used polemically to express strong opposition to something the speaker abhors. Harvard psychologist Steven Pinker (2008, p. 28), for example, wrote that "the problem is that 'dignity' is a squishy, subjective notion, hardly up to the heavyweight moral demands assigned to it." The context was his frustration that religious members of the second President Bush's Council on Bioethics decried abortion, birth control, and fetal tissue research as violations of human dignity, which he found troubling and dogmatic. Pinker's reaction, however, was overblown. He should have objected not to the words "human dignity" but to their use as conversation-stopping "polar words." Thurman Arnold (1937) long ago showed that epithets such as communist and fascist, or in our time racist, sexist, and homophobic, stop discussions entirely or shift their focus from whatever is under consideration to whether the adjectives are being unfairly used. Opposing fetal tissue research as a violation of human dignity is a polemical parallel to use of pro-life and pro-choice to label positions on abortion, emotionally satisfying to advocates but not conducive to dispassionate discussion or problem solving.

Lawyers are troubled by the term's absence from American constitutional law. Harvard law professor Carol Steiker observed that "dignity remains largely a constitutional cipher, lacking a home in any specific amendment of the Bill of Rights or a substantial or well-theorized role in American constitutional jurisprudence" (2014, p. 20). She argued that the concept may be better used to express a general social value than to characterize an individual right and has "collective" value in explaining why practices such as shaming, extreme punishments, and some mandatory sentencing laws are objectionable. Her context is American constitutional law at the end of a 40-year period in which conservative US Supreme Court justices have systematically impoverished legal understanding of individual rights generally, especially concerning the criminal justice system. "Human dignity," however, is no more amorphous than "privacy," "due process," "equal protection," and "cruel and unusual," terms with which American courts and lawyers have dealt for two centuries. That courts have not yet developed a jurisprudence of human dignity does not mean that they cannot or should not.[19]

Philosophers have not until recently begun to develop robust understandings of human dignity, but that is changing (e.g., Darwell 2006, 2013; Waldron 2012). Meir Dan-Cohen argued that all of the substantive criminal law, a much broader subject than punishment, should be reconceptualized to replace its traditional emphasis on the "harm principle" with "what may be called the *dignity principle:* the view that the main goal of the criminal law is to defend the unique moral worth of every human being" (2002, p. 150; emphasis in original).

Jeremy Waldron in "What Do the Philosophers Have against Dignity?" (2014) surveyed writing by philosophers troubled by the term's historic associations with social rank and religiosity. As his title implies, he was unconvinced that the concept is inherently too vague to be useful and offered a platform, free of those associations, on which he and others might build: "To respect someone you have to pay attention to them and their situation. . . . As a foundational idea, human dignity might ascribe to each person a very high rank, associated with the sanctity of her body, her control of herself, the demands she can make on others, and her determination of her own destiny, values and capacities" (pp. 10, 15).

---

[19] Law reviews abound in articles considering the possibilities (e.g., Rao 2008). Henry (2011) identified five emerging legal applications of dignity concepts—concerning institutional status, equality, liberty, personal integrity, and collective virtue.

Waldron's insistence that attention be paid to people and their situation—"morality requires us to do this anyway" (p. 15)—is not very different from Dworkin's (1977) insistence that people be treated as equals and that their situations and circumstances be considered with concern and respect when decisions are made affecting their interests. That is how a just punishment system should deal with people convicted of crimes. This is what Steiker (2014, p. 34) seems to mean when she observed that "respecting the individuality of offenders in sentencing implicates both collective and individual dignity interests." The US Supreme Court in *Woodson v. North Carolina*, 428 U.S. 280, 288 and 304 (1976), acknowledged, though only concerning capital punishment, that "individualizing sentencing determinations generally reflects simply enlightened policy" and that not doing so would be to treat "all persons convicted of a designated offense not as uniquely individual human beings but as members of a faceless, undifferentiated mass." That is self-evidently right, making the Supreme Court's Eighth Amendment jurisprudence of disproportionately severe punishment other than capital punishment a moral anomaly (see n. 3).

Human dignity provides a framework for thinking about punishment for crime. As on many other issues concerning punishment, Kant and Bentham understood this better than many contemporary writers do. Kant, a positive retributivist in the terms used in this essay, argued that convicted murderers should be executed even in a dissolving island society in which all inhabitants would soon embark on ships to live in other places. However, he observed, the murderer should be treated with respect: "But the death of the criminal must be kept entirely free of any maltreatment that would make an abomination of the humanity residing in the person suffering it" (2011, p. 33).

Bentham insisted that all punishment is "evil" and justifiable only when its benefits exceed the detriments experienced by the offender. In making that determination, he further insisted that punishments be individualized to take account of the offender's "sensibilities," those personal characteristics that might make the experience of punishment worse for a particular individual than for others. His notion of what this encompassed was exhaustive.[20] His Rule 6 on the distribution of punishment thus provided:

---

[20] "Of Circumstances Influencing Sensibility.... It may be of use to sum up all the circumstances which can be found to influence the effect of *any* exciting cause.... They seem to be as follows: 1. Health. 2. Strength. 3. Hardiness. 4. Bodily imperfection. 5. Quantity

It is further to be observed, that owing to the different manners and degrees in which persons under different circumstances are affected by the same exciting cause, a punishment which is the same in name will not always either really produce, or even so much as appear to others to produce, in two different persons the same degree of pain: therefore, *That the quantity actually inflicted on each individual offender may correspond to the quantity intended for similar offenders in general, the several circumstances influencing sensibility ought always to be taken into account.* (Bentham 1970, p. 169; emphasis in original)

Taken together, Kant's and Bentham's views, not unlike Dworkin's, require that offenders be treated with concern and respect and treated in ways that accord with their dignity as individual human beings.

Proportionality, parsimony, equality, and fairness are values that characterize a punishment system that respects human dignity. Determining just punishments in individual cases is intrinsically difficult. Nuanced differences between defendants and suspects, and among offenses, lead practitioners to want to handle seemingly similar offenses in different ways. Issues of social and racial injustice are salient in every courtroom. Whether social and economic disadvantage should provide a defense to criminal charges or an appropriate basis for systematic mitigation of punishment is one. Whether evidence of social, racial, ethnic, or religious bias in the operation of criminal justice systems should be taken into account at sentencing is another. A third is that all purposeful infliction of pain including state punishment is an undesirable thing to do, as Bentham believed, and should always lead to imposition of the least restrictive appropriate punishment, or none at all if proportionality concerns do not otherwise require.

English philosopher Matt Matravers (2011, p. 37) explained why retributive principles by themselves are insufficient justifications for punishment. He observed that "the issue is not one of reconciling [punish-

---

and quality of knowledge. 6. Strength of intellectual powers. 7. Firmness of mind. 8. Steadiness of mind. 9. Bent of inclination. 10. Moral sensibility. 11. Moral biases. 12. Religious sensibility. 13. Religious biases. 14. Sympathetic sensibility. 15. Sympathetic biases. 16. Antipathetic sensibility. 17. Antipathetic biases. 18. Insanity. 19. Habitual occupations. 20. Pecuniary circumstances. 21. Connexions in the way of sympathy. 22. Connexions in the way of antipathy. 23. Radical frame of body. 24. Radical frame of mind. 25. Sex. 26. Age. 27. Rank. 28. Education. 29. Climate. 30. Lineage. 31. Government. 32. Religious profession" (Bentham 1970, p. 52).

ment] practices to desert . . . but rather it is one of thinking about the requirements of liberal justice as a whole." Thought of in that way, it is clear—as the multiple offense paradox and myriad subjective differences between seemingly comparable cases demonstrate—that values other than blameworthiness and crime prevention should be taken into account.

Incorporation of fairness and equal treatment values into a comprehensive jurisprudence of punishment raises three major matters.[21] First, these additional values are not simply side constraints on the pursuit of retributive or utilitarian aims. Dworkin (1977) long ago wrote of "rights as trumps." Fairness and equal treatment need to be recognized as trumps on punishments that might otherwise be justly imposed.

Retributive or utilitarian reasoning may sometimes appear to justify punishments that other values forbid. Retributivists, for example, often argue that the logic of utilitarianism justifies punishment of innocent people if that will minimize human suffering. The classic example is the wrongful conviction and punishment in the American South of an innocent black man charged with rape of a white woman when the judge believes doing so will avert race riots or lynchings (McCloskey 1965). Critics point out that retributivism implies breathtakingly severe punishments and is irreconcilable with the bulk discount: if 3 months is a just punishment for one drug sale or shoplifting conviction, then 300 months should be right for 100 (Ryberg 2017).

When such issues arise, the retributive or utilitarian punishment logic must give way: knowing convictions or punishments of innocent people and imprisonment of people for 25 years for minor offenses are irreconcilable with respect for human dignity. The moral deficiencies inherent in knowing conviction of the innocent are self-evident. Imposition of 25-year prison terms for trifling crimes, no matter how many, warrants elaboration. It violates fairness values. Prosecutors possess enormous discretion and seldom charge or insist on guilty pleas to enormous numbers of equivalent crimes. It denies equal treatment by implying that trifling crimes in any number warrant more censure than individual instances of serious sexual or other violence or large property offenses. It also

---

[21] "Equal treatment" here and below is used not literally to mean identical or the same treatment but as shorthand for Dworkin's "treatment as an equal" with concern and respect. This means that individuals' personal circumstances and characteristics need to be taken sensitively into account when considering how general rules should be applied.

denies equal treatment by ignoring the underlying psychological or situational reasons why people commit large numbers of minor crimes. More importantly, it implies that the offender's interest in living an autonomous life is unimportant, even though 25 years is more than half of a human being's best years and lengthy imprisonment fundamentally handicaps ex-prisoners' prospects for a good life.

Other countries' legal systems take human dignity seriously in relation to punishment (Whitman 2016). The German constitution declares dignity to be a fundamental principle that governs all applications of law (Whitman 2004). The German Constitutional Court, for example, has forbidden many prison practices that are commonplace in the United States as violations of human dignity. It declared life without parole sentences unconstitutional in part because they are incompatible with human dignity: no human being should be denied the possibility of hope for a better future life (*lebenslange Freiheitsstrafe*, 21 June 1977, 45 BverfGE 187). Similar ideas underlie the shorter maximum prison sentences—often 12 or 14 years for any offense or set of offenses other than murder, and much shorter for most offenses—authorized in continental European than in Anglo-Saxon legal systems (van Zyl Smit and Snacken 2009). They also underlie the ad hoc rationalizations—"crushing sentences," depriving an individual of too large a portion of his or her remaining life, mercy—that are offered in other countries to explain the bulk discounts received by people convicted of multiple offenses (Jareborg 1998 [Sweden]; Ashworth and Wasik 2017 [England and Wales]; Bottoms 2017 [Australia]).

Second, the multiple values the practice of punishment implicates are not simply alternatives from which judges should choose; all set independent limits. American criminal codes usually provide that the purposes of the criminal law, punishment, or sentencing include at least imposition of deserved punishment, deterrence, incapacitation, and rehabilitation. Those lists serve as buffets from which judges may choose and provide no criteria for making the choices. Matravers (forthcoming) proposes something like a buffet when he calls for a "plural" rather than a "mixed" account of punishment in which censure and deterrence are independent governing principles: "The results may well be counter-intuitive (one might end up threatening more severe hard treatment for less serious, but harder to detect, crimes than for more serious, more easily detected, crimes)," he observes, but "it is not inconsistent so long as censure and deterrence are independent."

This is not very different from Henry M. Hart's (1958, p. 401) classic refutation of the *Model Penal Code*'s primarily rehabilitative purposes.[22] He observed that deterrence, rehabilitation, incapacitation, norm reinforcement, satisfaction of the "community's sense of just retribution," and "even socialized vengeance" all have roles to play and that judges and parole boards must take account of them case by case as they are pertinent. Note, however, a fundamental contextual difference. Matravers wrote at a time when retributivism was widely seen as relevant, including by him, as a principled justification for punishment. When Hart wrote 60 years earlier, indeterminate sentencing and utilitarian approaches were unchallenged. Retribution to him was germane not as a general guiding principle but only sometimes, usually in connection with sensational cases, as acknowledgment of public opinion.

Matravers's example of serious crimes punished less severely than lesser ones and Hart's elaboration illustrate and underlay the core problems of indeterminate sentencing that retributive theorists in the 1970s sought to address and remedy. Punishing lesser crimes more harshly than greater ones defies common morality and undermines basic social norms. Conferring authority on individual judges to choose among and apply irreconcilable purposes assures outcomes often based more on judicial idiosyncrasies, personalities, and ideologies than on differences between offenses and offenders. Broad discretions are especially vulnerable to influence by invidious considerations including racial and class bias, negative stereotypes, and unconscious bias.

Third, a comprehensive jurisprudence of just punishment that respects human dignity would require subjective assessments of blameworthiness. David Luban (2007, pp. 70–72) observed that subjectivity lies at the heart of human dignity and that "having human dignity means having a story of one's own. . . . Human beings have ontological heft because each of us is an 'I', and I have ontological heft. For others to treat me as though I have none fundamentally denigrates my status in the world. It amounts to a form of humiliation that violates my human dignity."

William James in *The Varieties of Religious Experience* (1902) offers a similar, more general, metaphorical observation about the need to take

---

[22] Both Matravers and Hart explicitly refer to the purposes of the criminal law rather than of punishment but appear to subsume punishment's within the criminal law's purposes. H. L. A. Hart (1968), by contrast, distinguishes between the—for him, preventive—purposes of the criminal law and other possible purposes of punishment.

individuals seriously: "Any object that is infinitely important to us and awakens our devotion feels to us also as if it must be *sui generis* and unique. Probably a crab would be filled with a sense of outrage if it could hear us classify it without ado or apology as a crustacean, and thus dispose of it. 'I am no such thing,' it would say; 'I am MYSELF, MYSELF alone'" (p. 3).

Plutarch (1957, p. 355) observed of boys playing by a stream on a summer day, "Though boys throw stones at frogs in sport, yet the frogs do not die in sport but in earnest." The frog's perspective, Luban's subjective perspective, cannot be justly ignored. A just sentencing system must harness the tension between the requirement of fairness that there be general standards that apply to all and the requirement of justice that all ethically important grounds for distinguishing between individuals be taken into account.

In the introduction, I described a comprehensive jurisprudence of just punishment consisting of principles of fairness, equality, proportionality, and parsimony. Blameworthiness and censure play central roles. No sentencing system could be said to be just unless it set rigid upper limits, keyed to blameworthiness, on the severity of punishment and unless values of fairness, equal treatment, and parsimony are respected.

Human dignity underlies the case for fairness, which largely concerns process; the case for parsimony, which requires avoidance of gratuitous harm; and the case for treatment as an equal, which requires consideration of an offender's circumstances and situation. This proposed jurisprudence of just punishment allows judges to make individualized assessments of blameworthiness and insists that gratuitous harm not be done. It recognizes the complexity and myriad differing circumstances of human lives. It cannot resolve fundamental issues of social and racial injustice but empowers judges to make individualized assessments of offenders' particular circumstances and blameworthiness within the constraints set by the other principles.

The proposed jurisprudence provides solutions to the multiple offense paradox. The bulk discount is morally necessary. Without it, punishments would be so severe that they would be incompatible with human dignity and so mechanical that they would fail to treat offenders and their interests with equal concern and respect. Every human being has but one life to live, lives it within particular circumstances, and makes countless mistakes. To ignore that is to ignore that we are human.

The recidivist premium to the contrary is morally unjustifiable. If the potential aggregate severity of sentences for multiple current convictions calls for imposition of something much less, for "mercy," the burdens of recidivist premiums call at least as loudly. Depriving individuals of a large part of their remaining lives is as wrong when it is done piecemeal as when it is done at one time. Other objections to the recidivist premium are familiar ones. Imposition of increments of additional punishment because of earlier convictions is double counting, effectively punishing offenders a second time for their prior offenses. Punishing a subsequent offense more severely than a first offender is punished for the same offense breaks the link between blameworthiness and deserved punishment.

The proposed jurisprudence of just punishment provides a firm foundation for operation of the parsimony principle. Lippke (2017) has argued that "parsimony" is redundant, an empty concept, because both retributive and utilitarian theories explicitly reject punishment more severe than is theoretically justifiable. Parsimony is better understood, however, as deriving not from punishment principles but from respect for human dignity. Bentham was adamant: "All punishment is mischief: all punishment in itself is evil. . . . If it ought at all to be admitted, it ought only to be admitted in as far as it promises to exclude some greater evil" (1970, p. 158).

Bentham's view was imbedded within utilitarianism. It is better viewed as coming from outside as Braithwaite and Pettit (1990, 2001) do when they describe "dominion," the capacity to live a life of one's choosing, as the value most at stake in thinking about both crime and punishment.

The requirement that all people be treated with equal concern and respect can help address the problem of "just deserts in an unjust society" (von Hirsch 1976; Tonry 2014). Punishments of people living fundamentally disadvantaged lives, or who are powerfully affected by mental disabilities or acute problems of drug dependence, should be determined in terms of the choices and possibilities available to them and not on the false premise that the hard realities of their lives are different than they are, or do not matter.

There is one important problem, however, that the proposed jurisprudence cannot meaningfully address: determination of ordinally deserved punishments or of the anchoring points of penalty scales that are necessary for any system of ordinally proportionate punishments to work

(Lacey and Pickard 2015). Those judgments depend on cultural attitudes toward crime, criminals, and punishment severity that vary widely and that no mechanical or theoretical fix can resolve. Palpable differences exist between countries in such matters: think only of contrasts between the United States and Scandinavia or between England and Switzerland. Achieving acceptance of ideas about ordinal proportionality and the moral necessity of interoffense comparisons in punishment is a more easily achievable goal and constitutes steps in the right direction.

The issues discussed in the preceding paragraphs require much fuller exploration and elaboration than is possible here. The important thing to recognize, however, is that they raise problems that retributive punishment theories now in use cannot adequately address by themselves but that a normative framework incorporating fundamental principles of fairness, equality, proportionality, and parsimony could.

Moving toward a comprehensive jurisprudence of just punishment will require partial abandonment or substantial amplification of most retributive and mixed theories of punishment. This change may not be as unlikely as some may believe. It will require a paradigm shift, which Thomas Kuhn (1962) demonstrated seldom happens in the physical sciences until prevailing ways of thinking change sufficiently to absorb unfamiliar, seemingly heretical ideas. However, that is what happened when retributive punishment theories replaced utilitarian ones in the minds of most policy makers, philosophers, and academic lawyers in the 1960s and 1970s. The American law professor Albert Alschuler (1978, p. 552) bewilderedly described the then-recent sea change in attitudes toward the rehabilitative presuppositions of indeterminate sentencing: "That I and many other academics adhered in large part to this reformative viewpoint only a decade or so ago seems almost incredible to most of us today." Nozick (1981, pp. 2–3) explained how such things happen:

> When a philosopher sees that premises he accepts logically imply a conclusion he has rejected until now, he faces a choice: he may accept this conclusion or reject one of the previously accepted premises.... His choice will depend on which is greater, the degree of his commitment to the various premises or the degree of his commitment to denying the conclusion. It is implausible that these are independent of how strongly he wants certain things to be true. The various means of control over conclusions explain why so few philosophers publish ones that (continue to) upset them.

It is time for proponents of retributive and mixed theories to adopt and argue for new "premisses."

REFERENCES

Advisory Council of Judges, National Council on Crime and Delinquency. 1963. *Model Sentencing Act*. Hackensack, NJ: National Council on Crime and Delinquency.

Alschuler, Albert. 1978. "Sentencing Reform and Prosecutorial Power." *University of Pennsylvania Law Review* 126:550–77.

American Law Institute. 1962. *Model Penal Code*. Proposed Official Draft. Philadelphia: American Law Institute.

———. 2017. *Model Penal Code: Sentencing*. Philadelphia: American Law Institute.

Ancel, Marc. 1965. *Social Defence: A Modern Approach to Criminal Problems*. London: Routledge & Kegan Paul.

Arnold, Thurman. 1937. *The Folklore of Capitalism*. New Haven, CT: Yale University Press.

Ashworth, Andrew. 2015. *Sentencing and Criminal Justice*. 5th ed. Cambridge: Cambridge University Press.

Ashworth, Andrew, and Martin Wasik. 2017. "Sentencing the Multiple Offender: In Search of a 'Just and Proportionate' Total Sentence." In *More than One Crime: Sentencing the Multiple Offender*, edited by Jesper Ryberg, Julian V. Roberts, and Jan W. de Keijser. New York: Oxford University Press.

Bagaric, Mirko. 2010. "Double Punishment and Punishing Character: The Unfairness of Prior Convictions." *Criminal Justice Ethics* 19:10–28.

Beccaria, Cesare. 2007. *On Crimes and Punishments, and Other Writings*. Translated by Aaron Thomas and Jeremy Parzen. Toronto: University of Toronto Press. (Originally published 1764.)

Bennett, C. 2010. "'More to Apologise For': Can We Find a Basis for the Recidivist Premium in a Communicative Theory of Punishment?" In *Previous Convictions at Sentencing: Theoretical and Applied Perspectives*, edited by J. V. Roberts and A. von Hirsch. Oxford: Hart.

Bentham, Jeremy. 1970. *An Introduction to the Principles of Morals and Legislation*. Edited by J. H. Burns and H. L. A. Hart. Oxford: Clarendon. (Originally published 1789.)

———. 2002. "Nonsense Upon Stilts, or Pandora's Box Opened, or the French Declaration of Rights Prefixed to the Constitution of 1791 Laid Open and Exposed." In *The Collected Works of Jeremy Bentham. Rights, Representation, and Reform: Nonsense Upon Stilts and Other Writings on the French Revolution*, edited by Philip Schofield, Catherine Pease-Watkin, and Cyprian Blamires. Oxford: Oxford University Press.

———. 2008. *The Rationale of Punishment*. Amherst, NY: Kessinger. (Originally published 1830.)

Berlin, Isaiah. 2002. *Liberty*. Edited by Henry Hardy. Oxford: Oxford University Press.

Blackstone, William. 1979. *Commentaries on the Laws of England*. Chicago: University of Chicago Press. (Originally published 1769.)

Blumstein, Alfred, Jacqueline Cohen, Susan E. Martin, and Michael Tonry, eds. 1983. *Research on Sentencing: The Search for Reform*. Washington, DC: National Academy Press.

Bottoms, Anthony E. 1998. "Five Puzzles in von Hirsch's Theory of Punishment." In *Fundamentals of Sentencing Theory*, edited by Andrew Ashworth and Martin Wasik. Oxford: Oxford University Press.

———. 2017. "Exploring an Institutionalist and Post-Desert Theoretical Approach to Multiple Offence Sentencing." In *More than One Crime: Sentencing the Multiple Offender*, edited by Jesper Ryberg, Julian V. Roberts, and Jan W. de Keijser. New York: Oxford University Press.

Braithwaite, John. 2018. "Minimally Sufficient Deterrence." In *Crime and Justice: A Review of Research*, vol. 47, edited by Michael Tonry. Chicago: University of Chicago Press.

Braithwaite, John, and Philip Pettit. 1990. *Not Just Deserts: A Republican Theory of Criminal Justice*. New York: Oxford University Press.

———. 2001. "Republicanism and Restorative Justice: An Explanatory and Normative Connection." In *Restorative Justice: Philosophy to Practice*, edited by John Braithwaite and Heather Strang. Burlington, VT: Ashgate.

Cottingham, J. G. 1979. "Varieties of Retributivism." *Philosophical Quarterly* 29:238–46.

Dan-Cohen, Meir. 2002. *Harmful Thoughts: Essays on Law, Self, and Morality*. Princeton, NJ: Princeton University Press.

Darwall, Stephen. 2006. *The Second-Person Standpoint: Morality, Respect, and Accountability*. Cambridge, MA: Harvard University Press.

———. 2013. *Morality, Authority, and Law: Essays in Second-Personal Ethics I*. New York: Oxford University Press.

Duff, R. Antony. 1986. *Trials and Punishments*. Cambridge: Cambridge University Press.

———. 2001. *Punishment, Communication, and Community*. New York: Oxford University Press.

Dworkin, Ronald. 1977. *Taking Rights Seriously*. Cambridge, MA: Harvard University Press.

Feinberg, Joel. 1970. *Doing and Deserving*. Princeton, NJ: Princeton University Press.

Ferri, Enrico. 1906. *The Positive School of Criminology*. Translated by Ernest Untermann. Chicago: C. H. Kerr.

———. 1921. *Relazione sul Progetto Preliminare di Codice Penale Italiano*. Milan: L'Universelle.

Fletcher, George. 1978. *Rethinking Criminal Law*. Boston: Little, Brown.

Frankel, Marvin. 1973. *Criminal Sentences: Law without Order*. New York: Hill & Wang.

Frase, Richard S. 2013. *Just Sentencing: Principles and Procedures for a Workable System*. New York: Oxford University Press.

Glueck, Sheldon. 1928. "Principles of a Rational Penal Code." *Harvard Law Review* 41(4):453–82.

Hampton, Jean. 1984. "The Moral Education Theory of Punishment." *Philosophy and Public Affairs* 13(3):208–38.

Hart, H. L. A. 1959. "Prolegomenon to the Principles of Punishment." *Proceedings of the Aristotelian Society*, n.s., 60:1–26.

———. 1968. *Punishment and Responsibility: Essays in the Philosophy of Law*. Oxford: Oxford University Press.

Hart, Henry M. 1958. "The Aims of the Criminal Law." *Law and Contemporary Problems* 23:401–42.

Hegel, G. W. F. 1991. "Wrong [Das Unrecht]." In *Elements of the Philosophy of Right*, edited by Allen W. Wood; translated by H. B. Nisbet. Cambridge: Cambridge University Press. (Originally published 1821.)

———. 2011. "Wrong [Das Unrecht]." In *Why Punish? How Much?* edited by Michael Tonry. New York: Oxford University Press. (Originally published 1821.)

Henry, Leslie Meltzer. 2011. "The Jurisprudence of Dignity." *University of Pennsylvania Law Review* 160:169–233.

James, William. 1902. *The Varieties of Religious Experience*. New York: Longmans, Green.

Jareborg, Nils. 1998. "Why Bulk Discounts in Sentencing?" In *Fundamentals of Sentencing Theory: Essays in Honour of Andrew von Hirsch*, edited by Andrew Ashworth and Martin Wasik. Oxford: Oxford University Press.

Kant, Immanuel. 1965. "The Penal Law and the Law of Pardon." In *The Metaphysical Elements of Justice*, translated by John Ladd. Indianapolis: Liberal Arts Press/Bobbs-Merrill. (Originally published 1797.)

———. 2011. "The Penal Law and the Law of Pardon." In *Why Punish? How Much?* edited by Michael Tonry. New York: Oxford University Press. (Originally published 1797.)

Kim, Andrew Chongseh. 2015. "Underestimating the Trial Penalty: An Empirical Analysis of the Federal Trial Penalty and Critique of the Abrams Study." *Mississippi Law Journal* 84(5):1195–1255.

King, Nancy J., and Michael E. O'Neill. 2005. "Appeal Waivers and the Future of Sentencing Policy." *Duke Law Journal* 55(2):209–61.

Kolber, Adam. 2009. "The Subjective Experience of Punishment." *Columbia Law Review* 109:182–236.

Kuhn, Thomas. 1962. *The Structure of Scientific Revolutions*. Chicago: University of Chicago Press.

Lacey, Nicola, and Hanna Pickard. 2015. "The Chimera of Proportionality: Institutionalising Limits on Punishment in Contemporary Social and Political Systems." *Modern Law Review* 78(2):216–40.

Lee, Y. 2010. "Repeat Offenders and the Question of Desert." In *Previous Convictions at Sentencing: Theoretical and Applied Perspectives*, edited by Julian V. Roberts and Andrew von Hirsch. Oxford: Hart.

———. 2017. "Retributivism and Totality—Can Bulk Discounts for Multiple Offending Fit the Crime?" In *More than One Crime: Sentencing the Multiple Offender*, edited by Jesper Ryberg, Julian V. Roberts, and Jan W. de Keijser. New York: Oxford University Press.

Lippke, Richard L. 2011. "Retributive Sentencing, Multiple Offenders, and Bulk Discounts." In *Retributivism: Essays on Theory and Policy*, edited by M. D. White. New York: Oxford University Press.

———. 2016. "The Ethics of Recidivist Premiums." In *The Routledge Handbook of Criminal Justice Ethics*, edited by Jonathan Jacobs and Jonathan Jackson. Abingdon, UK: Routledge.

———. 2017. "Parsimony and the Sentencing of Multiple Offenders." In *More than One Crime: Sentencing the Multiple Offender*, edited by Jesper Ryberg, Julian V. Roberts, and Jan W. de Keijser. New York: Oxford University Press.

Luban, David. 2007. *Legal Ethics and Human Dignity*. Cambridge: Cambridge University Press.

Mackie, John L. 1982. "Morality and the Retributive Emotions." *Criminal Justice Ethics* 1(1):3–10.

Macklin, Ruth. 2003. "Dignity Is a Useless Concept: It Means No More than Respect for Persons or Their Autonomy." *British Medical Journal* 327(December):1419–20.

Markel, Dan. 2010. "Bentham on Stilts: The Bare Relevance of Subjectivity to Retributive Justice." *California Law Review* 98:907–87.

Matravers, Matt. 2011. "Is Twenty-First Century Punishment Post-Desert?" In *Retributivism Has a Past: Has It a Future?* edited by Michael Tonry. New York: Oxford University Press.

———. Forthcoming. "Rootless Desert and Unanchored Censure." In *Penal Censure: Engagements Within and Beyond Desert Theory*, edited by Antje du Bois-Pedain and Anthony E. Bottoms. London: Hart/Bloomsbury.

McCloskey, H. J. 1965. "A Non-utilitarian Approach to Punishment." *Inquiry: An Interdisciplinary Journal of Philosophy* 8(1–4):249–63.

Menninger, Karl. 1966. *The Crime of Punishment*. New York: Viking.

Michael, Jerome, and Herbert Wechsler. 1940. *Criminal Law and Its Administration*. Chicago: Foundation.

Moore, Michael S. 1993. "Justifying Retributivism." *Israeli Law Review* 27:15–36.

Morris, Herbert. 1966. "Persons and Punishment." *Monist* 52:475–501.

———. 1981. "A Paternalist Theory of Punishment." *American Philosophical Quarterly* 18:263–71.

Morris, Norval. 1953. "Sentencing Convicted Criminals." *Australian Law Review* 27:186–208.

———. 1974. *The Future of Imprisonment*. Chicago: University of Chicago Press.

Murphy, Jeffrie. 1973. "Marxism and Retribution." *Philosophy and Public Affairs* 2:217–43.

Nagin, Daniel S., Francis T. Cullen, and Cheryl Lero Jonson. 2009. "Imprisonment and Reoffending." In *Crime and Justice: A Review of Research*, vol. 38, edited by Michael Tonry. Chicago: University of Chicago Press.

National Advisory Commission on Criminal Justice Standards and Goals. 1973. *A National Strategy to Reduce Crime*. Washington, DC: US Government Printing Office.

National Commission on Reform of Federal Criminal Laws. 1971. *Report: Proposed Federal Criminal Code*. Washington, DC: US Government Printing Office.

Nozick, Robert. 1974. *Anarchy, State, and Utopia*. Cambridge, MA: Harvard University Press.

———. 1981. *Philosophical Explanations*. Cambridge, MA: Harvard University Press.

Pifferi, Michele. 2012. "Individualization of Punishment and the Rule of Law: Reshaping Legality in the United States and Europe between the 19th and the 20th Century." *American Journal of Legal History* 52(3):325–76.

———. 2016. *Reinventing Punishment: A Comparative History of Criminology and Penology in the 19th and 20th Century*. Oxford: Oxford University Press.

Pinker, Steven. 2008. "The Stupidity of Dignity." *New Republic*, May 27.

Plutarch. 1957. "Whether Land or Sea Animals Are Cleverer." In *Moralia*, vol. 12, translated by Harold Cherniss. Cambridge, MA: Harvard University Press.

President's Commission on Law Enforcement and Administration of Justice. 1967. *The Challenge of Crime in a Free Society*. Washington, DC: US Government Printing Office.

Rao, Neomi. 2008. "On the Use and Abuse of Dignity in Constitutional Law." *Columbia Journal of European Law* 14:201–56.

Rawls, John. 1955. "Two Concepts of Rules." *Philosophical Review* 64(1):3–32.

———. 1958. "Justice as Fairness." *Philosophical Review* 67(2):164–94.

———. 1971. *A Theory of Justice*. Cambridge, MA: Harvard University Press.

Reaves, Brian A. 2013. *Felony Defendants in Large Urban Counties, 2009—Statistical Tables*. Washington, DC: US Department of Justice, Bureau of Justice Statistics.

Reitz, Kevin. 2010. "The Illusion of Proportionality: Desert and Repeat Offenders." In *Previous Convictions at Sentencing: Theoretical and Applied Perspectives*, edited by Julian V. Roberts and Andrew von Hirsch. Oxford: Hart.

Roberts, Julian V. 2008. *Punishing Persistent Offenders: Exploring Community and Offender Perspectives*. Oxford: Oxford University Press.

———. 2011. "The Future of State Punishment: The Role of Public Opinion in Sentencing." In *Retributivism Has a Past: Has It a Future?* edited by Michael Tonry. Oxford: Oxford University Press.

Roberts, Julian V., and Jan W. de Keijser. 2017. "Sentencing the Multiple Offender: Setting the Stage." In *Sentencing Multiple Crimes*, edited by Jesper Ryberg, Julian V. Roberts, and Jan W. de Keijser. Oxford: Oxford University Press.

Robinson, Paul H. 1987. "Hybrid Principles for the Distribution of Criminal Sanctions." *Northwestern University Law Review* 82:19–42.

———. 2008. *Distributive Principles of the Criminal Law: Who Should Be Punished How Much?* New York. Oxford University Press.

156     Michael Tonry

Ryberg, Jesper. 2001. "Recidivism, Multiple Offending, and Legal Justice." *Danish Yearbook of Philosophy* 36:69–94.
———. 2017. "Retributivism, Multiple Offending, and Overall Proportionality." In *More than One Crime: Sentencing the Multiple Offender*, edited by Jesper Ryberg, Julian V. Roberts, and Jan W. de Keijser. New York: Oxford University Press.
Ryberg, Jesper, and Julian V. Roberts, eds. 2014. *Popular Punishment: On the Normative Significance of Public Opinion.* Oxford: Oxford University Press.
Schofield, Philip. 2003. "Jeremy Bentham's 'Nonsense Upon Stilts.'" *Utilitas* 15 (1):1–26.
Singer, Richard G. 1979. *Just Deserts: Sentencing Based on Equality and Desert.* Lexington, MA: Ballinger.
Steiker, Carol S. 2014. "'To See Justice in a Grain of Sand': Dignity and Indignity in American Criminal Justice." In *The Punitive Imagination—Law, Justice, and Responsibility*, edited by Austin Sarat. Tuscaloosa: University of Alabama Press.
Tonry, Michael. 1994. "Proportionality, Parsimony, and Interchangeability of Punishments." In *Penal Theory and Penal Practice*, edited by R. A. Duff, S. E. Marshall, R. E. Dobash, and R. P. Dobash. Manchester: Manchester University Press.
———. 2004. *Thinking about Crime: Sense and Sensibility in American Penal Culture.* New York: Oxford University Press.
———, ed. 2011. *Why Punish? How Much?* New York: Oxford University Press.
———, ed. 2012. *Prosecutors and Politics: A Comparative Perspective.* Vol. 41 of *Crime and Justice: A Review of Research*, edited by Michael Tonry. Chicago: University of Chicago Press.
———. 2014. "Can Deserts Be Just in an Unjust World?" In *Liberal Criminal Theory: Essays for Andreas von Hirsch*, edited by A. P. Simester, Ulfrid Neumann, and Antje du Bois-Pedain. Oxford: Hart.
———. 2016a. *Sentencing Fragments.* New York: Oxford University Press.
———, ed. 2016b. *Sentencing Policies and Practices in Western Countries: Comparative and Cross-National Perspectives.* Vol. 45 of *Crime and Justice: A Review of Research*, edited by Michael Tonry. Chicago: University of Chicago Press.
———. 2017. "Solving the Multiple Offense Paradox." In *More than One Crime: Sentencing the Multiple Offender*, edited by Jesper Ryberg, Julian V. Roberts, and Jan W. de Keijser. Oxford: Oxford University Press.
United Nations. 1948. *Universal Declaration of Human Rights.* Geneva: United Nations.
van Zyl Smit, Dirk, and Sonja Snacken. 2009. *Principles of European Prison Law and Policy: Penology and Human Rights.* Oxford: Oxford University Press.
von Hirsch, Andreas. 2017. *Deserved Criminal Sentences: An Overview.* Oxford: Hart.
von Hirsch, Andrew. 1976. *Doing Justice: The Choice of Punishments.* New York: Hill & Wang.
———. 1986. *Past or Future Crimes: Deservedness and Dangerousness in the Sentencing of Criminals.* Manchester: Manchester University Press.

―――. 1992. "Proportionality in the Philosophy of Punishment." In *Crime and Justice: A Review of Research*, vol. 16, edited by Michael Tonry. Chicago: University of Chicago Press.

―――. 1994. *Censure and Sanctions*. Oxford: Oxford University Press.

Waldron, Jeremy. 2012. *Dignity, Rank, and Rights*. New York: Oxford University Press.

―――. 2014. "What Do the Philosophers Have against Dignity?" Working Paper 14-59, Public Law and Legal Theory Research Series. New York: New York University Law School.

Walker, Nigel. 1991. *Why Punish?* Oxford: Oxford University Press.

Wechsler, Herbert. 1961. "Sentencing, Correction, and the Model Penal Code." *University of Pennsylvania Law Review* 109(4):465–93.

Whitman, James. 2004. "The Two Western Cultures of Privacy: Dignity versus Liberty." *Yale Law Journal* 113:1151–1221.

―――. 2016. "Presumption of Innocence or Presumption of Mercy? Weighing Two Western Modes of Justice." *Texas Law Review* 94:933–93.

Wootton, Barbara. 1959. *Social Science and Social Pathology*. London: Allen & Unwin.

―――. 1963. *Crime and the Criminal Law*. London: Stevens.

*Stefan Harrendorf*

# Prospects, Problems, and Pitfalls in Comparative Analyses of Criminal Justice Data

ABSTRACT

Official crime and criminal justice data are influenced by different substantive
(e.g., victims' reporting rates), legal (e.g., offense definitions), and statistical (e.g.,
counting rules) factors. This complicates international comparison. The UN
Crime Trends Survey, Eurostat's crime statistics, and the European Sourcebook
of Crime and Criminal Justice Statistics try to enhance comparability and document remaining differences. The UN survey and Eurostat rely on the International Classification of Crimes for Statistical Purposes, which has potential but
is not yet satisfactorily applied. The European Sourcebook provides the most
detailed and best-verified data among the three. Even standardized data need
to be compared with extreme caution. Crime levels are not a valid measure of
crime in different countries, with the possible exception of completed intentional
homicide. Total crime rates depend mainly on the internationally differing
quality of police work. Comparisons of crime trends are less problematic but
depend on the offenses under comparison being not defined too differently.
Indicators expressed as ratios of different system-based values have increased
comparability. Owing to immense differences in crime rates and criminal justice
variables, mean crime rates for the world or Europe cannot be calculated.
Country clusters need to be built very carefully.

International comparison of crime and criminal justice data is complex,
almost impossible. Direct comparisons of national statistics on crime and

Electronically published March 9, 2018
Stefan Harrendorf is professor of criminology, criminal law, criminal procedure, and
comparative criminal law and justice, University of Greifswald, Germany. He is grateful
to Michael Tonry for comments on an earlier draft.

159

criminal justice are unreliable not only because of language barriers and translation problems but more importantly because concepts and categories used in national statistics are not created to facilitate international comparisons but to meet information needs of criminal justice agencies, other administrative bodies, and politicians.

National statistics necessarily mirror the criminal law and criminal procedure in a given country. They cannot record behavior that is not considered criminal in a particular country. What is recorded as "theft" or "robbery" depends on how theft or robbery is defined in the criminal law and varies significantly between countries. Selection and definition processes in case processing also vary significantly, depending on the provisions of criminal procedure and criminal law and on practices that have developed around them (Wade 2006; Jehle, Smit, and Zila 2008). International or cross-national analyses cannot be credibly based on simple comparisons of national data. They need to use data from international surveys such as the European Sourcebook of Crime and Criminal Justice Statistics, the United Nations Crime Trends Survey, Eurostat data, and the Council of Europe's SPACE data on imprisonment and community penalties.

The surveys try to enhance comparability of data in various ways including by standardizing offense definitions. They are based on secondary analyses of data originally collected for administrative purposes by national statistical systems. The surveys can never achieve perfect data comparability (with perplexing consequences for European criminal justice policy; de Bondt 2014). They can, however, carefully document differences and use various adjustments to enhance comparability. Huge amounts of metadata are collected in addition to statistical data (e.g., Aebi et al. 2014).

Researchers often make use of official national data for comparative analyses based on very general ceteris paribus assumptions, which are neither critically tested nor very convincing. For example, with regard to Cavadino and Dignan's (2006) study on relations between political economy and imprisonment rates, David Nelken observed,

> Cavadino and Dignan, like most of those comparing a large range of incarceration rates, spend little time on persuading us that crime rates are really the same in all the countries they are comparing. But it is this, the assumption that crime levels are "constant" in the places being compared, that sets the puzzle they are trying to solve. How can

some societies live with high crime rates without concomitant expansion of the prison realm? If countries with higher prison rates were actually dealing with higher threats from crime, this would not be news, and we could hardly say that we were fairly comparing levels of punitiveness. (Rather, we would be showing how neo-liberalism increases both crime and punishment.) On the other hand, it is strange that the good things about more inclusive welfare-oriented or egalitarian social-democratic societies do not also reduce the level, or severity, of crimes being committed, rather than only shaping the response to them. And since our ideal is presumably to live in places that have both low levels of punishment and low crime, it is a pity that this inconvenient point is passed over so quickly. (2010, p. 61)

See also Pakes (2015, p. 6). Indeed, studies show that there is at least some relationship between crime rates and incarceration rates, although it is restricted to the more serious crimes, especially, but not necessarily only, to completed homicide (for homicide: Lappi-Seppälä 2011; Lappi-Seppälä and Lehti 2014; Harrendorf 2017b; for other severe offenses in western Europe: Aebi, Linde, and Delgrande 2015).

There are innumerable other examples of careless use of official criminal justice data for testing comparative hypotheses (e.g., Churchill and Laryea [2017] on relations between ethnic diversity and crime; further examples below). As a general rule, one needs to keep in mind that data from different countries depend on different substantive, legal, and statistical factors, making meaningful comparisons very difficult (von Hofer 2000). For example, legal offense definitions differ significantly (Harrendorf 2012), as do statistical recording rules (e.g., whether offenses are recorded when first coming to police attention [input], only after verified [output], or at some intermediate point: Aebi 2008, 2010) and victim reporting rates (van Dijk, van Kesteren, and Smit 2007). The problems multiply concerning the total number of recorded criminal offenses; this is a black box with unknowable contents. The borderline between criminal and noncriminal behavior is drawn differently in different countries, leading to large overall total crime rate differences (Harrendorf 2011). Another confounding difficulty is the connection between overall crime rates and the quality of police work (Harrendorf 2017a), a subject I discuss below.

It is thus unwise simply to use national official data for offense categories such as burglary, robbery, homicide, or total crime to test hypotheses about the relationship between crimes and other variables usually correlated with criminal behavior (as, e.g., in Rosenfeld and Messner [2009] or Buonanno, Drago, and Galbiati [2014]). As long as it is not clear that what is recorded as "burglary" is everywhere the same (which it is not; Tonry and Farrington 2005; Aebi et al. 2014, pp. 370–73, 390–92), we cannot use the data as a comparable measure. National crime data are fundamentally incomparable in many respects. Of course, it is possible to compare oranges with apples, as both are fruit. But we should know that the level of comparison is fruit only and not mistake apples for oranges.

Additional problems arise in relation to country clustering. In Rosenfeld and Messner (2009) and Buonanno, Drago, and Galbiati (2014), data from selected European countries are combined to form a country cluster called "EU" or "Europe." The cluster in Rosenfeld and Messner (2009) consists of Denmark, France, Germany, Greece, Hungary, Ireland, Italy, the Netherlands, and Portugal. That in Buonanno, Drago, and Galbiati (2014) consists of Austria, France, Germany, Italy, the Netherlands, Spain, and the United Kingdom. In Europe, however, official crime rates per 100,000 population differ enormously between countries, without obvious relationship to the true incidence of crime, and depending on nationally distinctive legal, statistical, and case processing factors. For example, total crime levels in Europe in 2010 ranged between 476 per 100,000 population in Armenia and 14,671 in Sweden, a 30-fold difference (Aebi et al. 2014). Variation coefficients (standard deviations divided by the mean) are extremely high, and the mean of country results cannot be validly interpreted to represent all the different countries (Harrendorf 2012). It cannot measure "EU" or "European" crime levels.

Country clustering is a complex but feasible task, as some studies such as Smit, Marshall, and van Gammeren (2008) show. It needs, however, to be done in more sophisticated ways than just by taking a convenience sample of EU countries and using their combined values as a proxy for the EU or Europe.

Von Hofer (2000) sought to raise awareness of the vast methodological problems involved in international comparisons, but to my knowledge no publication has as yet provided a comprehensive overview of prospects, problems, and pitfalls associated with this type of work. That is my aim. In Section I, I briefly discuss reasons why one would want to compare crime and criminal justice data internationally. In Section II, I address the main data collection initiatives in Europe and worldwide, including the European Sourcebook of Criminal Justice Statistics, the United Nations Crime Trends Survey, and Eurostat's data collection. I discuss the advantages and weaknesses of each and show possible ways to improve data quality and comparability. Since both the United Nations and Eurostat data collection rely on the recently developed International Classification of Crimes for Statistical Purposes for their offense definitions, I also discuss this classification system and show how users can assess data quality of these surveys (UNODC 2015). Section III explains what can and cannot be done with comparative crime and criminal justice data concerning analyses of crime levels and trends. Credible comparisons of crime levels are difficult to achieve. It is preferable to compare ratios that are completely system-based, that is, that consist of a numerator and a denominator both taken from official statistics (e.g., relative growth rates, ratios of convictions to suspects). Official data are a good source for learning about differences in criminal justice systems including, for example, case attrition, punitiveness, and police, prosecution, and court practices; however, official data should be used with extreme caution when the focus is on comparisons of crime problems in different countries. Section IV sums up and suggests how comparative projects using crime and criminal justice data should be planned and conducted.

## I. Why Compare?

"Why Compare?" is the title of the first chapter of David Nelken's important *Comparative Criminal Justice* (2010). The simplest reason is pure scientific interest and curiosity. Comparative work may add to the knowledge base of fundamental research. Criminal justice system differences and commonalities may as well be analyzed with policy questions in mind, for example, to assess use of alternative sanctions available in other systems to decide whether they should be adopted at home. One might seek ways to reduce the prison population by comparative analyses of punitiveness and its determinants, or one might look for functional equivalents in different countries for dealing with dangerous offenders. The aim may also be to identify shared principles and structures to gain deeper understanding of what is and should be going on in different criminal justice systems (Nelken 2010; Ebbe 2013; Pakes 2015; Tonry 2015).

Comparison of crime and criminal justice data, as a special aspect or variant of comparative research, is not necessarily an end in itself, but will often be motivated by policy concerns. De Bondt (2014) has shown how heavily EU criminal justice policy depends on comparative data on offenses and legal instruments that are subject to harmonization. She has also shown that existing data fall utterly short of this aim.

Comparative studies may also provide additional insights into what national statistics actually mean. If, for example, comparative research shows that the recorded rate of total criminal offenses per 100,000 population in a given country is strongly dependent on the quality of police work, and not on the "reality" of crime, this is important information for a proper understanding of national crime rates (Harrendorf 2017*a*).

The goal of comparative studies might be to learn more about crime in international perspective (Heiskanen 2010; Aebi and Linde 2012). It might also be to learn more about criminal justice system reactions to crime or more generally about the work and functions of the different actors in the system (Blumstein, Tonry, and van Ness 2005; Smit, van Dijk, and Decae 2012). Both aims are important, yet I try to show why national crime and criminal justice system statistics are not the best place to look for comparative data on crime problems, but are an excellent starting point for efforts to delve into the differences between systems.

## II. How to Compare?

Comparison of crime rates and criminal justice processes in different countries is inherently difficult. Statistical systems exist to meet operational and information needs of criminal justice practitioners and agencies, not the data needs of national or comparative researchers. Statistical systems differ between countries as do criminal codes and criminal justice system processes. Definitions of specific offenses vary from place to place as do lines of demarcation between wrongful behaviors treated as crimes and others handled with administrative penalties or not at all. In this section, I discuss existing efforts to create international data systems that can be used for comparative purposes.

### A. Problems of International Comparison

Crime and criminal justice data are strongly dependent on national legal, statistical, and substantive characteristics that negatively affect comparability and cannot be fully controlled for, even with the aid of international surveys (Hofer 2000; Aebi 2008, 2010; Harrendorf 2012).

*Statistical factors* encompass the influence of different statistical practices, such as the use of input, intermediate, or output police crime recording practices. In input systems, cases are recorded when they are reported to the police. In output systems, cases are recorded only after investigations have been completed. Intermediate systems fall in between. Inevitably, information about the case is more detailed and more reliable in output systems. The operational definition of the crime the police use can change between when a case is reported and when it is solved. In output systems, cases in which the offender remained unknown or for which there was insufficient evidence may not be counted, leading to lower rates of recorded crime (Aebi 2008, 2010). Yet that is not necessarily so. In many countries, the police do not have legal authority to drop cases for legal or factual reasons (Elsner, Smit, and Zila 2008). Even cases involving unknown offenders may be referred to the prosecutor (Aebi et al. 2014, pp. 139–40).

Other rules influencing comparability involve counting of multiple or serial offenses or offenders. Imagine a series of 20 burglaries committed between 2013 and 2016 by an individual that were reported to the police in 2016 and for which investigations were completed in 2017. In some countries, this series of events would be recorded as one burglary, in others as 20 (Aebi et al. 2014, pp. 102–3). To complicate matters further, the recording might refer to the year in which the investigation was completed, the year in which the crimes were reported, or the different years in which they were committed.

*Legal factors* encompass national differences in criminal law and procedure. From a criminal law perspective, theft is not *Diebstahl* is not *кража* is not *varkaus* is not *kradzież*, although each of these words is simply a translation of the others. Offense definitions vary significantly between countries (Harrendorf 2012; Aebi et al. 2014, pp. 369–403), thereby further reducing comparability. For example, the Anglo-American concept of burglary does not exist in most continental European systems (Tonry and Farrington 2005, p. 3; Harrendorf 2012, p. 42). In some legal systems, subtypes of aggravated theft may be more or less—though never exactly—functionally equivalent.

Problems multiply with efforts to compare the total number of criminal offenses. The borderline between criminal behavior and deviant but noncriminal behavior is different in each system. Some countries exclude minor traffic offenses from criminal law coverage and crime statistics. Others exclude certain minor property offenses or minor bodily injuries (Harrendorf 2012; Aebi et al. 2014).

The rules of criminal procedure also vary. One fundamental contrast is between countries with criminal justice systems governed by the "expediency principle," which authorizes police, prosecutors, and judges to make decisions in individual cases for prudential reasons, and countries governed by the "legality principle" in which they do not have that authority. For example, in expediency principle countries such as the Netherlands and the United States, the police, the prosecution service, and the courts have authority to drop cases because of established policies, lack of a public interest in proceeding further, or the suspect's fulfillment of specified conditions. Yet, as a reaction to increasing caseloads while criminal justice funding and staff levels remained the same or were even reduced, even countries that traditionally adhere to the legality principle (like Germany) have usually added important exceptions from this principle to their Codes of Criminal Procedure. This introduces a kind of expediency principle for some crimes, especially petty offenses. This results in final dispositions without formal convictions, thereby increasing attrition between police and conviction statistics. The extent to which these powers are available differs substantially between countries (Wade 2006; Elsner, Smit, and Zila 2008; Jehle, Smit, and Zila 2008).

Finally, *substantive* factors refer to operational, organizational, and behavioral differences unrelated to legal or statistical rules. The propensity of victims to report an offense to the police is one important factor. Another is the willingness of the police to record and investigate reported offenses. This depends in part on the amount of corruption in a given system. From a global perspective, police corruption is an important problem. According to Transparency International (2013, p. 11), 31 percent of respondents worldwide admit that they or someone from their household bribed a police officer in the preceding year. This is the highest rate among all institutions covered. Police were considered the second-most-corrupt institution, just after political parties (p. 16).

Table 1 summarizes factors that affect official crime statistics. A methodologically sound comparative study would need to control for them, eliminate their influence to the extent possible, and thoroughly disclose the remaining comparability problems. Cross-national comparisons based on unmodified data on recorded offenses with the same translated name (e.g., "theft") are not credible.

## TABLE 1

### Substantive, Legal, and Statistical Factors Influencing Comparability

| Substantive | Legal | Statistical |
| --- | --- | --- |
| "True" crime levels (including the "dark figure") | Offense definitions | Time of recording (input, output, or intermediate) |
| "True" crime structure (including the "dark figure") | Content and scope of the criminal law | Counting rules for multiple current offenses |
| Reporting by victims | Legality or expediency principle | Counting rules for serial offenses |
| Control activities by the police | Diversion, procedural decriminalization | Counting rules for multiperson offenses |
| Police willingness to record offenses | Plea bargaining; other agreed dispositions | Counting rules for persons suspected of multiple offenses |
| Clearance efforts | Structure of criminal procedure | Counting rules for multiple sanctions |
| | Age of criminal responsibility | Minimum age for inclusion in statistics |
| | Sentencing laws and implementation | Prison population counting rules |

The best way to get high-quality comparative data would be to collect them in different countries using identical methods, such as by relying on case files of the courts or prosecution services. This is what Lovett and Kelly (2009) did in their study of attrition in reported rape cases across Europe. This at least eliminates the statistical factors, although legal and substantive factors remain relevant. However, for financial reasons and owing to time restrictions, it is seldom possible to collect comparative data that way. In that case, international surveys provide the next-best sources of information.

The international surveys try to take account of legal and statistical influences. Data are collected by means of a questionnaire, trying to standardize respondents' replies, thereby increasing comparability, and thoroughly documenting remaining differences (Aebi et al. 2014, pp. 17–21). Controlling for substantive factors would be desirable, too, but that is much more difficult. In theory, some of those factors also can be addressed, for example, by taking account of victim reporting rates from victimization surveys. This is not, however, yet part of the regular methodology of any international survey.

Full data comparability cannot be achieved and inherent limitations of secondary data analysis cannot be overcome. Data are obtained from very different legal and juridical contexts, produced in criminal justice systems that vary substantially in quality and efficiency, and recorded according to differing statistical rules.

## B. *A Brief Inventory*

Before I discuss methodological details, a brief inventory of international surveys now available may be useful. Because my focus is on crime and criminal justice, I do not discuss surveys of victims, such as the International Crime Victim Survey (van Dijk, van Kesteren, and Smit 2007), or of offenders, such as the International Self-Report Delinquency Study (Junger-Tas et al. 2010). Table 2 provides information on the major international surveys and their coverage.

The oldest international crime survey, which began in 1950, was conducted by Interpol and based on police statistics. It was discontinued in 2006 because of serious quality issues (Interpol 2006; Rubin et al. 2008; Barberet 2009). The oldest ongoing survey is the United Nations Crime Trends Survey (hereafter, the UN Survey; https://data.unodc.org/), covering data since 1970 (Lewis 2012) and carried out by the UN Office on Drugs and Crime (UNODC). It is the only data collection with worldwide scope covering all stages of the criminal justice process (police, prosecution, courts, and prisons). Much of the data, especially concerning prosecution and courts, are not very detailed. The UN Survey long had problems with high nonresponse rates, especially from developing countries, leading to predominant coverage of countries from North America and Europe (Rubin et al. 2008; Alvazzi del Frate 2010). Response rates have recently increased, especially from Latin America, but coverage remains poor for Africa and some Asian regions (UN Economic and Social Council 2016, p. 33).

The UNODC also collects data on drug use, prices, seizures, and related subjects by means of its Annual Reports Questionnaire and the Individual Drug Seizure Reports (see the UNODC website). The annual reports also ask about persons brought into formal contact with the justice system in connection with drug-related offenses; comparable questions were removed from the UN Survey, probably to avoid double collection. Results on drug offenses are included in the World Drug Report (e.g., UNODC 2016*b*, pp. 101–2). Another data source for worldwide data, concerning only prisons, is the World Prison Brief, a database compiled by the Institute for Criminal Policy Research at Birkbeck University in London (Lewis 2012).[1] It is based primarily on data provided by national prison departments.

The "official" data collection in Europe is carried out by Eurostat for the European Union member states, European Free Trade Association countries, candidate countries, and potential candidate countries. Data are available from 2005 onward (Eurostat 2017*b*, p. 3). In 2014 Eurostat joined forces with the UNODC in collecting the data for those countries, relying on the UN Survey questionnaire, with supplements of relevance for European Union policy (pp. 4, 9–10). The scope of data collection is thus quite similar to that of the UN Survey with the same limitations, including meager coverage of prosecution and courts.

The most complete data collection initiative for Europe is the European Sourcebook of Crime and Criminal Justice Statistics (hereafter the European Sourcebook), which was patterned on the American Sourcebook of Criminal Justice Statistics (Killias 1995). It was started in 1993 under the auspices of the Council of Europe. After production of a draft model (Council of Europe 1995) and a first regular edition, covering 1990–95 (Council of Europe 1999), the project was continued by an experts group without further Council of Europe funding. Data collection for the fourth edition covering 2003–7 (Aebi et al. 2010) and the fifth covering 2007–11 (Aebi et al. 2014) paralleled European Union projects on specific topics (Jehle and Harrendorf 2010; Heiskanen et al. 2014).

Since 2011, the Euopean Sourcebook has been organized as an association under German law (*eingetragener Verein*), that is, as a legal entity somewhat separate from the current composition of the experts group in charge of questionnaire development and data collection, collation, and validation. The European Sourcebook, like the UN Survey and Eurostat data collections, covers all criminal justice stages from police investigation through execution of sentences. It is the most comprehensive international survey in the number of variables on which data are collected and in the level of detail. It is wider in geographical coverage than the Eurostat survey but narrower than the UN Survey. Data are collected for all member states of the Council of Europe except for microstates.[2]

---

[1] The database is available at http://www.prisonstudies.org/world-prison-brief-data. The institute's site is at http://icpr.org.uk/.

[2] For the fifth edition, data collection was also extended to Kosovo (UN/R 1244/99). Microstates are defined here as states with a population below 100,000. These are Andorra, Liechtenstein, Monaco, and San Marino.

TABLE 2

International Crime and Criminal Justice Surveys

| Name | Regional Scope | Thematical Focus | Agency, Funding | Latest Date Published Data Available |
|---|---|---|---|---|
| International Crime Victim Survey/European Survey on Crime and Safety | World (selected countries); Europe | Victimization; fear of crime; punitiveness; satisfaction with police | Research group, differing sponsors (e.g., EU, Dutch, and UK governments) | 2004/5 (plus methodological pilot study 2010 in some countries) |
| International Self-Report Delinquency Study | World (selected countries); Europe | Juvenile delinquency and victimization | Research group, differing sponsors (e.g., EU) | 2012–17 (differing by country) |
| Interpol International Crime Statistics | World | Official crime data (police) | Interpol | 2004 (discontinued) |
| UN Survey of Crime Trends and Operations of Criminal Justice Systems | World | Official crime and criminal justice data (police, prosecution, courts, prisons) | UN Office on Drugs and Crime | 2015 |
| World Drug Report (Annual Reports Questionnaire and Individual Drug Seizure Reports) | World | Drug-related data (use, supply, crime, seizures) | UN Office on Drugs and Crime | 2015 |
| World Prison Brief | World | Prison data | Institute for Criminal Policy Research, Birkbeck, University of London | 2017 (differing by country) |

170

| Source | Coverage | Data content | Provider | Year |
|---|---|---|---|---|
| Eurostat Crime and Criminal Justice Statistics | Europe (EU member states, EFTA countries, candidate countries, and potential candidate countries) | Official crime and criminal justice data (police, prosecution, courts, prisons) | Eurostat (EU statistical office) | 2015 |
| European Sourcebook of Crime and Criminal Justice Statistics | Europe (Council of Europe member states except microstates) | Official crime and criminal justice data (police, prosecution, courts, prisons, probation agencies) | Research group, differing sponsors (e.g., EU, Dutch, Swiss, and UK governments, Council of Europe) | 2011 |
| Annual Penal Statistics of the Council of Europe (SPACE I + II) | Europe (Council of Europe member states) | Prison data (SPACE I), probation data (SPACE II) | University of Lausanne (funded by the Council of Europe) | 2015 |
| European Judicial Systems: Efficiency and Quality of Justice | Europe (Council of Europe member states) | Prosecution and court data | European Commission for the Efficiency of Justice, Council of Europe | 2014 |
| Statistical Bulletin of the European Monitoring Centre for Drugs and Drug Addiction | Europe (EU member states, candidate countries, Norway) | Drug-related data (use, supply, crime, seizures) | European Monitoring Centre for Drugs and Drug Addiction, EU | 2015 |

Full coverage has never been achieved but has come quite close. Thirty-nine countries were covered in the fifth edition. Because the United Kingdom includes distinct criminal justice systems for England and Wales, Scotland, and Northern Ireland, each is covered separately (Aebi et al. 2014, p. 9). The UN Survey and Eurostat do the same.

There are a few other multinational data collections in Europe. These include the annual SPACE (Statistiques Pénales Annuelles du Conseil de l'Europe; http://www.coe.int/en/web/prison/space) reports on correctional populations. SPACE is overseen and funded by the Council of Europe. Data on incarceration and prisons have been collected since 1983 (SPACE I; e.g., Aebi, Tiago, and Burkhardt 2017) and on noncustodial sanctions and measures since 1992 (SPACE II; e.g., Aebi and Chopin 2016). SPACE II collects data on the execution of community sanctions and measures under the supervision or care of probation agencies (Jehle and Harrendorf 2014).

In addition, a Council of Europe program develops reports on "European Judicial Systems: Efficiency and Quality of Justice." These are regularly prepared by the European Commission for the Efficiency of Justice (e.g., 2016). It evaluates the quality and efficiency of European court systems including the work of prosecution agencies.

A final regular data report is the Statistical Bulletin of the European Monitoring Centre for Drugs and Drug Addiction (e.g., 2017). The focus is comparable to that of the UN World Drug Report (UNODC 2016*b*). Hence, the only crime and criminal justice data collected pertain to drug offenses, legal responses to them, and seizures; the overall focus is on drug use, supply, health consequences, and treatment. Finally, regarding reconviction data, there is no regular comparative survey, but pilot work has been done (Wartna and Nijssen 2006; Wartna et al. 2014).

In the methodological discussions that follow, I focus only on the three general surveys: the UN Survey, Eurostat, and the European Sourcebook. Since Eurostat and the UN basically use the same methodology and questionnaire, comparisons are between two different approaches.

## C. General Methodology

In order to standardize national replies as much as possible, surveys not only collect absolute numbers of different crimes or sanctions imposed but rely on metadata concerning definitions of offenses, prosecutorial case disposition methods, sanctions and measures, and data recording rules. Ideally, the questionnaires used for data collection are well designed and take account of knowledge from earlier comparative studies and the knowledge of each expert involved concerning his or her national system.

1. *Standard Definitions.*   Standard offense definitions are used, which means that national data must be adjusted to fit the definitions. The European Sourcebook augments the standard definition with lists of foreseeable variations and provides clear rules to include or exclude them. Table 3 sets out intentional homicide from the fifth edition questionnaire as an example. Respondents are informed that they should follow the rules as closely as possible and adapt the data they report accordingly. In Germany, for example, assault leading to death (i.e., intentional assault that unintentionally, but negligently, causes the death of the victim) is a distinct offense that is separately recorded in national statistics; according to German law, it would not be considered intentional homicide. Yet to be consistent with Anglo-American concepts of homicide, which often consider such cases as intentional killings, the standard definition requires respondents to add cases of assault leading to death to the officially recorded cases of intentional homicide. This is what is done when Germany replies to the questionnaire.

TABLE 3

Standard Definition of Intentional Homicide, European Sourcebook

| Intentional Homicide: Standard Definition: Intentional Killing of a Person | | | | |
|---|---|---|---|---|
| | Indicate if Included in or Excluded From: | | | |
| | Police Statistics | | Conviction Statistics | |
| | Incl. | Excl. | Incl. | Excl. |
| Include the following: | | | | |
| • assault leading to death | | | | |
| • euthanasia | | | | |
| • infanticide | | | | |
| • attempts | | | | |
| Exclude the following: | | | | |
| • assistance with suicide | | | | |
| • abortion | | | | |
| • negligent killing | | | | |

SOURCE.—Fifth edition questionnaire of European Sourcebook (Aebi et al. 2012, p. 10).

It is, of course, not always possible to adapt national data to fit the standard definitions and to follow all of the inclusion and exclusion rules. Respondents are accordingly asked to indicate whether they were able to follow the rules, as table 3 illustrates. The system of standard definitions has a prescriptive purpose—to achieve maximum standardization—but also aims to document remaining differences. Conformity with the inclusion and exclusion rules is reported separately for police and conviction statistics. Usually, it is much easier to adhere to the standard definition on the police level than on the conviction level, as conviction statistics depend more strongly on legal offense categories. For some offenses, especially theft of a motor vehicle, burglary, and domestic burglary, this results in a large proportion of countries being completely unable to provide conviction data, typically because these categories do not exist as separate criminal code offenses and are also not separately identifiable in statistics (Harrendorf 2012, pp. 39, 42).

Eurostat and the UN Survey until recently also used quite similar standard definitions but did not have sophisticated systems for identifying variations. The surveys simply asked "Was this definition applied in your country?" and provided space for comments. Most respondents tick "yes" or "no" but provide no comments.

More recently, the UNODC and Eurostat switched to another classification model, the International Classification of Crimes for Statistical Purposes (ICCS). The idea was to create an event-based classification system that did not rely on criminal law definitions in order to enhance comparability (UNODC 2015, p. 8). The classification system is comprehensive and aims at classifying all possible criminal acts. The earlier systems of standard definitions were selective, focusing only on specific crimes and the total number of offenses.

Apart from this criterion of exhaustiveness, the ICCS includes additional criteria of mutual exclusivity of classifications and statistical feasibility, that is, the capacity in principle of identifying these acts in national statistics (UNODC 2015, pp. 12–13). The classification is hierarchical, involving one top level and up to three further sublevels of increasing detail. The 11 level 1 categories are set out below:

- acts leading to death or intending to cause death,
- acts leading to harm or intending to cause harm to the person,
- injurious acts of a sexual nature,
- acts against property involving violence or threat against a person,

- acts against property only,
- acts involving controlled psychoactive substances or other drugs,
- acts involving fraud, deception, or corruption,
- acts against public order, authority, and provisions of the state,
- acts against public safety and state security,
- acts against the natural environment, and, finally,
- other criminal acts not elsewhere classified.

For the level 2 category of intentional homicide, for example, the ICCS gives this standard definition: "Unlawful death inflicted upon a person with the intent to cause death or serious injury" (UNODC 2015, p. 33).

Like the European Sourcebook approach, the ICCS provides inclusions and exclusions for each offense, but they are often more detailed. For intentional homicide:

Inclusions: Murder; honour killing; serious assault leading to death; death as a result of terrorist activities; dowry-related killings; femicide; infanticide; voluntary manslaughter; extrajudicial killings; killings caused by excessive use of force by law enforcement/state officials.

Exclusions: Death due to legal interventions; justifiable homicide in self-defence; attempted intentional homicide (0102); homicide without the element of intent is non-intentional homicide (0103); non-negligent or involuntary manslaughter (01031); assisting suicide or instigating suicide (0104); illegal feticide (0106); euthanasia (0105).

The codes in the exclusion lists refer to other offense categories of the ICCS. They result from implementation of the two principles of mutual exclusivity and exhaustiveness. The inclusion and exclusion lists are elaborated in a large number of footnotes, providing standard definitions for many of the items mentioned in the lists (like "murder" or "honour killing"). The classification system, finally, requires recording of several disaggregation variables, concerning the event, the victim, the perpetrator, and some further descriptive data (UNODC 2015, p. 21).[3] The document explaining and presenting the classification system is 130 pages long.

---

[3] The variables for events are as follows: attempted/completed; type of weapon used; situational context; geographic location; date and time; type of location; motive; cybercrime related; reported by. For the victim: sex; age; age status (minor/adult); victim-perpetrator relationship; citizenship; legal status (natural/legal person); intoxication status; economic sector of business victim. For the perpetrator: sex; age; age status (minor/adult); victim-perpetrator relationship; citizenship; legal status (natural/legal person); intoxication status; economic activity status; recidivist status. For further descriptive data: threats included;

The ICCS is very ambitious. However, everything depends on how it is used in practice. It is not meant to be a legal classification system; it is not a model penal code for all countries in the world. Hence, the ICCS cannot alter national legal factors influencing data comparability. Even an "event-based" classification system does not change dependency of national statistics on national criminal law. Of course, the influence of such factors can be reduced if countries comply with the classification system. But that is also true of the standard definition system used by the European Sourcebook, which uses classifications as much event-based as the ICCS.

Perhaps the UN and the European Union will have the influence and power in coming years to persuade more and more countries to use the ICCS categories in national statistical systems. This would be an important improvement. It is, however, not realistic to expect that any country with an existing statistical system will ever completely switch to the ICCS. That would render all existing national data incomparable with new data. Apart from that, statistics would largely lose their connection to national laws. This would be very helpful for international comparisons but would create serious problems in the national contexts in which the data are primarily used.

National statistical offices could parallel code their national data according to the ICCS, that is, use the national and the international classifications in parallel. This would mean substantial additional work for practitioners and statistical systems. It is more realistic to expect that national statistical offices will often cross-code data for the ICCS from national categories (Jehle 2012*b*, p. 138). This is not different from the current approach for the European Sourcebook.

In practice, both UNODC and Eurostat (which uses the UNODC questionnaires plus some additional modules; Eurostat 2017*b*, pp. 4, 9) continue to employ a simplistic system for collection of metadata. As before, they inform respondents about the required definitions. Regarding compliance, they ask "Do data comply with this definition (yes/no)?" again with the possibility to provide comments (UNODC 2016*a*). Most respondents are not interested in providing lengthy textual explanations; the added value of the ICCS, as now used, is almost certainly minimal. What is the use of a sophisticated classification system if there is no prac-

---

aiding/abetting included; accessory/accomplice included; conspiracy/planning/preparation included; incitement to commit crime included.

tical way to monitor compliance? The European Sourcebook system is—
as of now—superior in practice, but the ICCS has great potential.

Standard definitions are needed both for offenses and for other variables that are subject to variation because of legal and statistical factors. A comparative study, for example, recently showed that the concept of a "cleared case" in police statistics differs significantly between countries (Brå 2015). This could be the first, initial suspicion, as in Germany, or it could require a suspicion so strong that it justifies an indictment or an equivalent decision by the prosecuting authority as in Sweden. The number of cleared cases is not recorded in any existing international survey, but the same problems arise concerning the definition of the "suspect"; clearance in general means that a suspect has been identified. No survey yet provides such a definition.

For other concepts, such as "conviction," both the European Sourcebook and the UN Survey feature standard definitions. In the European Sourcebook, definitions are structured similarly to offense definitions and are accompanied by lists of ambiguous cases with clear instructions about inclusion and exclusion. Respondents are asked for each rule whether they followed it. The fifth edition questionnaire provides that "conviction means that the person was found guilty, according to the law, of having committed an offence and therefore has a criminal record." Inclusions are "court convictions; sanctions imposed by the prosecutor (or by the court, but on application of the prosecutor and without a formal court hearing) that lead to a formal verdict and count as a conviction (e.g. penal order, *Strafbefehl*); convictions of minors in regular criminal proceedings . . .; convictions of minors in juvenile criminal proceedings." Exclusions are "sanctions imposed by the prosecutor that do not lead to a formal verdict and do not count as a conviction (e.g. conditional disposals); sanctions/measures imposed by the police; sanctions/measures imposed by other state bodies; reactions on criminal or deviant behaviour of minors imposed in family court or youth welfare proceedings" (Aebi et al. 2012, p. 69).

The UN Survey definition is as follows: "'Persons Convicted' means persons found guilty by any legal body authorized to pronounce a conviction under national criminal law, whether or not the conviction was later upheld. The total number of persons convicted should also include persons convicted of serious special law offences but exclude persons convicted of minor road traffic offences, misdemeanours and other petty offences" (UNODC 2016a). The UN Survey definition thus also involves inclusions and exclusions, but compliance is verified only by asking about it and providing opportunity to give comments. This lack of information about compliance with definitions is a fundamental problem for both the UN Survey and Eurostat because they mainly use the same questionnaire. As with offense definitions, this is a crucial weakness.

2. *Rules of Statistical Recording.* Another system is used for rules relating to the statistical counting of offenses, offenders, convictions, and other factors. In some cases, a preferential counting unit is given. For example, concerning prosecution statistics, the European Sourcebook questionnaire states, "The counting unit required here is the case (in the sense of proceedings relating to one person only) dealt with by prosecuting authorities" (Aebi et al. 2012, p. 50). Afterward, respondents can choose which counting unit they actually used (case, proceedings, person, other). In many other cases, no preferential method for counting cases is specified. For example, the European Sourcebook questionnaire simply documents how multiple offenses by the same offender, or single offenses committed by multiple offenders, are counted (as one case or as multiple cases). Regarding statistical differences, this documentary method (without additional standardization) is used not only in the Euopean Sourcebook but also in UN and Eurostat data collections because it is assumed that such statistical rules cannot be changed afterward.

While this is true for aggregate statistical databases, even for these traditional national statistics, different counting rules may already be applied. For example, national statistics might include data on the input of cases, on pending cases, and on the output of cases at the police level. If international surveys now simply ask about the stage of investigation the data refer to, without providing information about the preferred stage, they miss an important opportunity for further standardization. Since increasing numbers of national statistical systems are based on an electronic database that contains all individual recorded cases, with the option to aggregate statistics as needed, possibilities for later adaptations of data to comply with counting rules have now even increased.

Another reason not to standardize statistical counting rules might be that it would seem arbitrary to choose one preferred recording method among several in use. Yet this is not true: The preferred method can be identified easily by using two simple rules. First, if one of several possible rules of statistical recording provides better data quality, that rule is to be preferred. Second, if there is no superior rule, the statistical rule that is most commonly applied should be used.

For police data, output statistics in principle deliver better-quality data, since police then have more information on which to base classifications. Some cases, however, that appear in input statistics may not appear in output statistics, especially in countries where cases for which an offender was not found or which were evidentially insufficient are not recorded in the output (Aebi 2008, p. 208). Intermediate systems are the most problematic, because it will be unclear how far the police have advanced in investigating a crime. In such statistics this will be subject to variation (Aebi 2008, p. 208).

The ICCS takes no account of statistical recording practices, for example, concerning counting of multiple offenses or offenders. The reason is that the ICCS is a crime classification system, not a full model for a statistical recording system. However, this seriously reduces the potential of the ICCS to produce truly comparable data in the future.

There are no other international approaches aiming at standardizing counting rules. The UN *Manual for the Development of a System of Criminal Justice Statistics* acknowledges that different counting units make it difficult to compare national crime and criminal justice statistics but does not prescribe standardization (UN Statistics Division 2003, p. 19).

3. *Respondents.* A crucial question is who completes the questionnaires. In all international data collections, usually one questionnaire is sent to each country.[4] For the UN Survey and Eurostat, the questionnaires go through official channels and the respondents are state employees working in national statistical offices, the police, the prison administration, and other government agencies.

The European Sourcebook, because it is an independent research enterprise, can be more flexible. Many respondents are researchers at universities or other research institutions. The main selection criterion is expertise concerning the national criminal justice system. The contact persons are referred to as national correspondents. This capacity to choose the best-qualified national correspondent leads to improved data quality. Unfortunately, it is not always possible to find a national correspondent in every country. This is especially a problem for countries in which criminology is not well developed in universities. In these coun-

---

[4] In some cases, there might also be more questionnaires per country, as for the United Kingdom, which—because of the different criminal justice systems—receives three questionnaires, one for England and Wales, one for Scotland, and one for Northern Ireland.

tries, all depends on the willingness of national statistical offices to co-operate. Problems finding a qualified correspondent for the European Sourcebook are intensified at least for some countries because it has not been possible so far to remunerate correspondents, even though the work involved is substantial.

4. *Presentation of Data.* Data from international surveys are presented as rates per 100,000 population, or as percentages of a larger total (e.g., the percentage of women among offenders registered on the police level). Yet it is of almost equal importance that the raw data (the absolute values and all metadata) are made publicly available, in order to allow users to better assess the quality of the data and for more precise computation of indices, change rates, and the like. This is especially important for the European Sourcebook, in which rates per 100,000 population are truncated and presented without decimals or with only one decimal. All three data collections make the absolute values for the collected data available. For the UN Survey and the European Sourcebook, all metadata are readily accessible. For Eurostat, the individual metadata are also available on the internet, but finding them is somewhat difficult.[5]

## D. Quality Assessment

Complex data collections like these need sophisticated and thorough data validation routines. In principle, three different types of checks can, and should, be carried out: consistency, trends, and other sources checks (Harrendorf and Smit 2010, pp. 146–47).

*Consistency* (or internal validity) checks aim at internal consistency. Some of the reported data are interrelated; therefore, some general rules can be fixed. For example, all subcategories within a breakdown need to be smaller than the total (e.g., the number of female offenders needs to be smaller than the total number). Where a total is broken down completely into subcategories, these subcategories should usually sum to 100 percent, yet this is not necessarily the case. Imagine a breakdown by sanction type: in many countries, a principal sanction rule is applied for the total (i.e., only the most severe sanction is counted), but it is not always also applied for the subcategories. In such a country, the subcat-

[5] See https://data.unodc.org/ for the UN Crime Trends Survey, http://ec.europa.eu/eurostat/web/crime/database/ for Eurostat, and https://wp.unil.ch/europeansourcebook/data-base/ for the European Sourcebook. The direct link to the Eurostat national metadata is http://ec.europa.eu/eurostat/cache/metadata/Annexes/crim_esms_an2.pdf.

egories would add up to more than 100 percent if some offenders receive multiple sanctions in a single court decision.

Criminal procedure can be envisioned as a process of case selection and definition during which cases are successively filtered out. This is often visualized as a funnel (e.g., Cole and Smith 2011, p. 14; Jehle 2015, p. 9). A conceptualization more consistent with the process is a picture of a series of gateways and gatekeepers (Harrendorf 2017a). Attrition is a natural occurrence and happens at and between different stages of the process, for example, within the police level between input and output, between the police and prosecution, within the prosecution level between input and output, and between the prosecution and the court (Harrendorf, Jehle, and Smit 2014).

Numbers can be expected to decrease during the process, with the number of offenses recorded at the police level being larger than the number of suspects found, the number of suspects larger than the number of persons indicted, that number larger than the number of persons convicted, and that number larger than the number of persons sent to prison. This can also be used for internal consistency checks, yet once again some deviations are possible. For example, the number of suspects can be larger than the number of recorded offenses if the following three criteria are cumulatively fulfilled: for a given offense clearance rates are high, the offense is at least sometimes committed by multiple offenders, and counting rules treat offenses by multiple offenders as one offense but register each suspect separately. The same effect can occur for offenses with high clearance rates if offenses are registered on an input basis and suspects are registered only later when they are identified. In such a system, an offense might be recorded in 2014 but the suspect not be identified until 2015. Because of this time lag, offender ratios (suspects per 100 registered offenses) above 100 percent are possible. Homicide data often show offender ratios above 100 percent (Harrendorf 2017a).[6]

Internal validity checks can also identify implausible outliers outside the acceptable range. Because of the large variation in international data, this is, however, restricted to extreme cases.

*Trend* checks look at time series for a certain variable and look for odd "jumps" in the magnitude of a variable. When this occurs between survey

---

[6] For further examples of consistency checks, see Harrendorf and Smit (2010, pp. 146–47).

waves, this may indicate a change in the way a category was cross-coded from the national system or a different handling of the inclusion and exclusion rules of offense definitions. Or there might be changes in criminal or procedural law or in the rules of statistical recording. Of course, even large changes could result from substantive factors such as changes in priorities or efficiency of police work or in the true incidence of crime.

Finally, *other sources* checks compare results with values a country reported to another international survey for a similar variable. Data on the prison population reported to the European Sourcebook could, for example, be compared to UN Survey data, SPACE I data, and World Prison Brief data. Trend and other sources checks can show huge differences between data reported for one survey wave or to one source and another survey wave or source because of, among other things, a different understanding or handling of standard offense definitions. Malby (2010a, p. 57) gives an excellent example concerning huge differences in the trend for drug trafficking and the total number of drug offenses in Germany according to several international surveys.

For the fifth edition of the European Sourcebook, internal consistency, trends, and other sources checks were programmed in SPSS, with an Excel output file per country listing all inconsistencies found. These then need explanation or correction. A validation system is used in which different members of the experts group act as regional coordinators for groups of countries. Each regional coordinator is in charge of data validation for his or her countries. The validation file helps here, as the regional coordinator can decide which inconsistencies can already be explained by the existing metadata (e.g., a major change in criminal law) or by other factors, and which need to be reported back to the national correspondent. The correspondent will then receive a list of inconsistencies that need correction or explanation. A second validation system, based on responsibilities for specific chapters of the sourcebook (police, prosecution, courts, corrections, offense definitions), leads to further improvement of quality control.

Eurostat also reports that it applies consistency, trend, and other sources checks and resolves inconsistencies together with the national contacts, either by correction of the value or by explanation (Eurostat 2017a, p. 27). Since the UN Survey and Eurostat share the data collected, this automatically leads to a validation of UN data for these countries. To what extent UN data for other countries are validated is not clear. Yet it can be expected that—differently from earlier years (cf. Harrendorf

2013*b*)—at least some validation is carried out. Some internal, unpublished reports show that there have been some efforts to validate UN data at least since 2009/10 (Harrendorf 2010). On the basis of the available information, the Europe Sourcebook group applies the strictest validation procedures.

Harrendorf (2012, 2013*b*) showed that there is an additional possibility for data validation, relying on variation coefficients of reported data. There is huge variation in reported international data even for Europe in total levels of registered crimes per 100,000 population and in other variables. Therefore, it is not easy to say when a value is totally outside the acceptable range. Harrendorf found out that there is an almost perfect linear relationship between the means of offense, suspect, and conviction rates for different offenses in the European Sourcebook and UN Survey data and the respective standard deviations. On the basis of this assumption, exceptionally high variation coefficients for particular offenses or years indicate a problem with data quality or comparability. Harrendorf (2013*b*) was able to confirm that variation coefficients for unvalidated data were, in principle, higher than for validated data. This allows use of variation coefficients as an additional validation tool on a summary (not country-specific) level. Exceptionally high variation coefficients hint at a data problem and indicate that a closer look at the data is necessary.

As long as international surveys publish all their raw data (absolute values and all metadata), these checks can also be carried out after publication (e.g., Harrendorf and Smit 2010, pp. 146–47). Users of international surveys should take a critical look at data before using them comparatively, keeping in mind the quality indicators discussed. If a time series has odd and sudden increases or decreases between adjacent years, it is necessary to find out why. If the data look strange, they should not be trusted! Identified errors should be corrected, for example, by replacing the data with data from another international survey for an (almost) identical variable. For time series, interpolation might also be an option. There may, however, be a plausible explanation for odd values, so the metadata should be examined before discarding a value.

## E. Shortcomings and Possible Improvements

Even the best methodology cannot eliminate all negative effects on data comparability of legal and statistical differences between countries.

The influences of substantive factors are not even taken into account by current surveys. There is also no useful information available on the relative intensity of the effects of different legal, statistical, and substantive factors on data collected in different countries. It is doubtful that this information will ever be obtained. Thus, it is impossible to use statistical weighting to adjust for substantive, legal, and statistical differences between countries (Aebi 2008, p. 217).

The UN Survey and Eurostat do not have a system to record deviations from standard definitions and their inclusions and exclusions. This could easily be changed and would substantially improve data quality and comparability. The European Sourcebook system, in which correspondents are asked to provide explicit information about inclusions and exclusions, could serve as a model. Apart from that, legal factors, especially offense definitions, are addressed adequately in all three surveys. More troubling is how statistical recording rules are handled. Here, it would be useful to switch to prescribed or at least preferred counting rules combined with precise questions regarding compliance with them.

Finally, international surveys should begin systematically to collect and collate data on substantive factors that influence data comparability. This is of immense importance, as the 30-fold difference between official total crime rates in Sweden and Armenia demonstrates; it cannot be explained by legal and statistical differences. Substantive factors such as differing rates of victim reporting or police quality and efficiency are even more influential; likewise for other variables. Some essential data, such as the prevalence and incidence of victimization, reporting rates, and citizen satisfaction with police work, can be taken from victimization surveys. The European Sourcebook has incorporated some data from international and, in the fifth edition (Aebi et al. 2014), national victimization surveys. This approach needs to be made more systematic and focused on key substantive factors.

While, in principle, the proposed changes should improve comparability of national data in international surveys, they pose formidable management challenges (Harrendorf 2012). Data quality is now strongly dependent on how thoroughly national correspondents complete questionnaires and how much effort they invest in enhancing data comparability by adhering to standard definitions and rules. Doing so increases workloads as respondents may need to combine data from several national statistical categories to conform to standard definitions. However, because of time restrictions or methodological misunderstandings, correspondents sometimes make mistakes or fail to follow rules. Some use more or less unmodified data from national statistics, although modifications were necessary and possible. Others misunderstand definitions or inclusion and exclusion rules. Such omissions, misunderstandings, and errors cannot always be identified.

It is therefore important for project managers to stay in close contact with national correspondents while questionnaires are being completed and validated. This is why the European Sourcebook uses regional coordinators with responsibility for only a few countries. It is also why conferences of all national correspondents held during the data collection phase have proven important.

### III. Making Sense of Comparative Data
Crime and criminal justice data are produced by criminal justice practitioners and measure the quality and quantity of their work. The data do not measure the reality of crime, the true number of acts, or omissions that violate criminal laws in a given country. There is no constant or knowable relationship between crimes that are committed and crimes that come to the attention of criminal justice system agencies. This is a problem for any national research study but presents greater difficulties for comparative studies because of national differences in legal, statistical, and substantive factors. And just as the ratio between committed crimes and those that come to the attention of the police varies from year to year and between offenses, it also varies between countries.

### A. Rate Comparisons
That Sweden in 2010 had the highest European crime rate per 100,000 population does not mean that Sweden is the most dangerous country in Europe. There may be many other explanations. First, the criminal law may be used extensively, defining petty wrongs or administrative violations as criminal that are handled administratively or not at all in other countries. Second, statistical counting rules may inflate crime rates. Police use of input rather than output statistics tends to produce higher crime levels (Aebi 2008, 2010). Crime rates also increase if a principal offense rule is not used—recording each of several simultaneous offenses separately, for example, robbery and murder committed in the same event—rather than only the most serious. Likewise, separately recording each of a series of similar offenses inflates crime rates. Sweden

does all of these things (Brå 2015, pp. 9–11). High crime rates may also be based on substantive factors such as a higher victim reporting rate or greater likelihood that the police record crimes (von Hofer 2000).

For these reasons, it is often advised not to make direct comparisons of rates per 100,000 but to use trend comparisons (Aebi et al. 2014, p. 21; Eurostat 2017b, p. 36). This is, however, not the full picture. It is important to find out what internationally varying crime levels mean in order to understand when direct comparison is feasible and when it is not. There is, for example, evidence that total crime rates are mainly a function of the quality of police work (Harrendorf 2017a). The better the police performance, the higher the crime rate. This is shown in figure 1.

There is an almost perfect linear relationship in figure 1 between police performance in a country and the total number of recorded offenses; the correlation coefficient is 0.80 ($R^2 = 0.65$).[7] Diverse factors explain this relationship. When the police are known or seen to perform well, more incidents are reported and more cases are recorded because of proactive police activities. Low levels of corruption mean that suspects cannot often avoid recording and subsequent prosecution in exchange for money or other favors. The strong correlation suggests that legal or statistical factors are secondary (for further details, see Harrendorf [2017a]). Similar results occur for minor offenses. The correlation coefficient for the relation between the Police Performance Index (PPI)[8] and the theft rate per 100,000 population in 2010 was also 0.80.

For severe offenses, there is no clear relation between crime rates and the PPI. The correlation coefficient for robbery is 0.16, for the total of attempted and completed homicides −0.09, and for attempted homicide

[7] Albania and Sweden were excluded as outliers. Albanian reports of total offenses to the European Sourcebook seem to include only cleared cases. For Sweden the number of total recorded offenses is artificially high, partly because of statistical counting rules (Brå 2015).

[8] The PPI (Pare 2014) is based on five variables (reporting of crimes by victims, satisfaction with the police reaction, general satisfaction with police work, businesses' view of police trustworthiness with respect to law enforcement, and victimization by corruption). Four of these variables were taken from the International Crime Victims Survey for 2004/5 (van Dijk, van Kesteren, and Smit 2007) and one (businesses' trust) from the World Economic Forum survey (Porter et al. 2004). The index is largely consistent with one proposed by van Dijk (2008) but replaces the homicide clearance rate with the corruption measure, which is an improvement since there is significant variation in the definition of what "clearance" means (Pare 2014; Brå 2015). The PPI was used unmodified even though the index uses data from 2003 and 2004. This assumes that there were no significant changes in police performance between these years; this is confirmed by the correlation coefficient for the PPI with crime data for 2004 being similar to that for 2010.

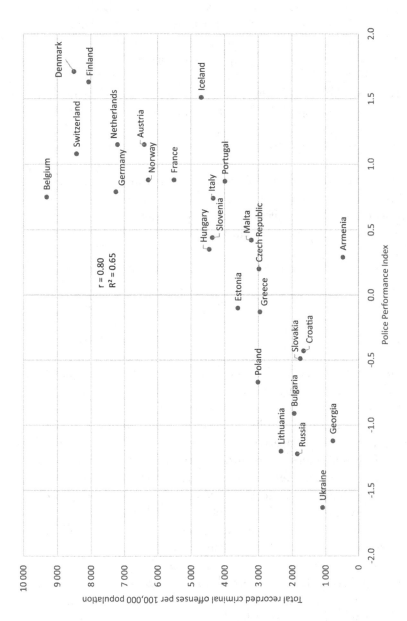

Fig. 1.—Police performance and total crime per 100,000 population, 2010. Source: raw data for the fifth edition European Sourcebook (Aebi et al. 2014); Police Performance Index (PPI; Pare 2014). Albania and Sweden are excluded as outliers.

0.11. For completed homicide, there is a negative correlation ($r =$ $-0.64$); see figure 2. A similar result was found in a worldwide analysis on the connection between police performance and completed homicide rates in 77 countries ($r = -0.72$; Pare 2014, p. 264).

Pare identified several possible explanations for the negative connection between the PPI and the homicide rate, concluding that all have some relevance, but that the strength of the effects of each is unclear (Pare 2014; see Harrendorf 2017*a*). These are the explanations offered:

- higher clearance and conviction ratios that may operate as deterrents,
- different controls of problem behaviors and crimes that may escalate into homicide (e.g., excessive drinking, burglary),
- strict enforcement of firearm and weapon laws,
- successful interventions against violent hot spots and criminal gangs,
- different measures to pacify conflicts, separate conflict parties, and to protect victims,
- use of force, bound by the principle of proportionality; deadly force as *ultima ratio*, and
- providing alternatives to revenge, vigilantism, and vendettas.

In addition, different levels of legitimacy and procedural justice may directly affect citizens' willingness to abide by the law (Tyler 2006).

These correlations between police performance and crime rates have implications for data comparability. For the total of crime and for minor offenses, rates can be compared but are mainly an indirect measure of police performance, more or less unrelated to the reality of crime. That rates for most severe crimes are not correlated with the PPI does not mean that these rates are totally unrelated to police performance. It can, however, be expected that other variables, especially the incidence of a given crime, have greater influence on crime rates for severe offenses. This hypothesis is supported by the strong negative correlation between police performance and completed homicide rates. The above-mentioned plausible explanations for such a correlation all imply an increase of the true amount of homicide in a society, and not only of cases recorded by the police. There is no plausible mechanism by which weak police performance would only increase police recording of completed homicides.

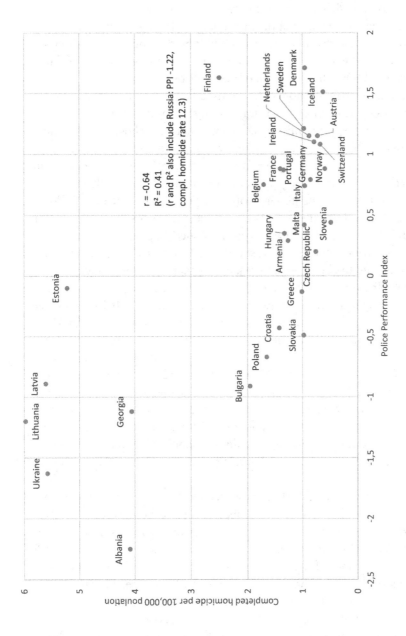

Fig. 2.—Police performance and completed homicide rates per 100,000 population, 2010. Source: raw data for the fifth edition European Sourcebook (Aebi et al. 2014), supplemented by World Health Organization causes of death statistics; **PPI** (Pare 2014).

Crime levels for serious offenses (except homicide) therefore need to be compared with extreme caution, as they are not a valid measure either of police performance or of the incidence of offenses. This supports the widespread view that completed homicide is the only offense category for which police data may come close to the true picture of crime (Malby 2010*b*; UNODC 2014). Yet there may still be some doubts.

Clearance rates for homicide are usually high, but identification of deaths resulting from homicide is not straightforward. Problems exist especially with respect to missing bodies and persons whose circumstances are unknowable, and with clinical differentiation between natural and unnatural deaths. Concerning the latter, there can be severe problems in cases that do not intuitively appear to be violent deaths, such as poisonings, especially if the victim was ill or old (Mätzler and Wirth 2016). Problems also arise from the systems used to certify deaths. In Germany, for example, death certificates are typically issued by nonspecialized, often family, doctors. They often invest little time in the exercise and, in order not to irritate the bereaved and risk losing them as future patients, often do not adhere to the rules (such as undressing the body and checking it fully for any signs of unnatural death; Rückert 2000; Arbeitsgruppe der AOLG 2011). Partly as a result (and also because of insufficient funding), postmortems are seldom ordered: only in 2 percent of all registered deaths (Stang 2015), compared with, for example, 17 percent examined by coroners in England and Wales (Ministry of Justice 2016). Thus in Germany it is estimated that only one in three homicides is recorded as such, leading to a very large undercount (Brinkmann et al. 1997). More postmortems would reduce the number of unidentified homicides. National differences in postmortem rates will substantially influence comparability of homicide rates. Efforts made to find missing persons are also subject to international variation.

Finally, in dysfunctional criminal justice systems, offenders may get away with murder by bribing a police officer or because no one dares or even wishes to report the murder to the police. Low postmortem rates and lack of efforts to find missing persons can also serve as indices for weak performance of the criminal justice system. In a dysfunctional system, more homicides should go unnoticed by the police. That the correlation between the PPI and the rate of completed homicides is negative could mean, however, that more homicides are recorded in dysfunctional systems. This could be explained by the hypothesis of a higher incidence of homicides. Together, these two inconsistent hypotheses lead to the expectation that the number of recorded cases will increase in a dysfunctional system, but also that many cases go unnoticed. High official homicide rates thus may imply a high level of undetected offenses and low homicide rates a low one.

The UN Survey and Eurostat collect few data on suspects or convictions for specific offenses. The European Sourcebook by contrast provides a detailed breakdown of data by offense type for police-recorded offenses, suspects, and convicted persons. In principle, it is even more questionable to compare these latter rates, since data on suspects in countries with input statistics are recorded later in the process than offense data. Data on convicted persons are necessarily recorded later than police data. Conviction data are more strongly influenced by attrition processes than data on suspects, and data on suspects are subject to additional attrition compared with data on police-recorded offenses. Since attrition processes differ significantly between countries, depending on the architecture of the criminal justice system and criminal procedure rules and practices, comparability is further reduced for variables relating to later stages of the process (Wade 2006; Jehle, Smit, and Zila 2008).

For cases that are not filtered out, however, offense classification will increase in precision, as the initial suspicion that a particular offense was committed increases to certainty beyond reasonable doubt. Depending on the research question being asked, conviction data or data on suspects are thus not necessarily inferior to offense data (Aebi and Linde 2012).

The concerns discussed above concerning rate comparisons also apply to conviction rates and suspects. However, another option for rate comparisons becomes available when combining data on offenses, suspects, and convicted persons. Attrition processes can be compared on the basis of the relation of these rates to each other in different countries (Jehle 2012*a*; Harrendorf 2017*a*).

Incarceration rates are compared at least as often as police-recorded completed homicide rates are. The level of incarceration is often taken as a direct measure of punitiveness (Hinds 2005; Cavadino and Dignan 2006). Differences in crime rates for serious offenses are seldom taken into account, even though they might at least partly explain differences in use of imprisonment (for homicide: Lappi-Seppälä 2008, 2011; Harrendorf 2017*b*; for other serious offenses: Aebi, Linde, and Delgrande 2015). Incarceration rates are, however, negatively correlated to the PPI (Harrendorf 2017*b*). This is shown in figure 3.

The negative correlation coefficient of $-0.69$ is similar in magnitude to the coefficient for the relationship between the PPI and completed homicides. The (positive) correlation between the completed homicides

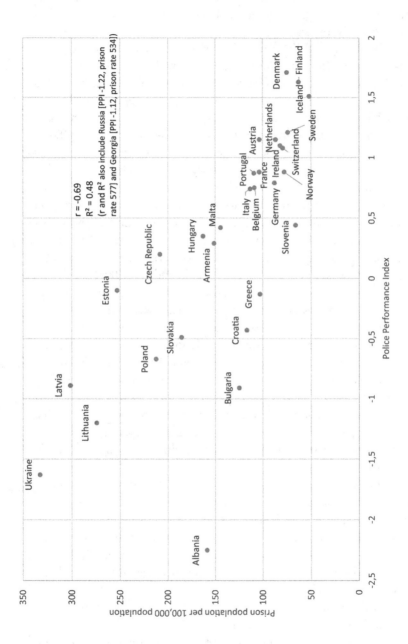

Fig. 3.—Police performance and prisoners per 100,000 population, September 1, 2010. Source: raw data for the fifth edition European Sourcebook (Aebi et al. 2014); PPI (Pare 2014); for some countries, a different reference date within 2010 was used.

rate and incarceration rates is a bit stronger (0.85; Harrendorf 2017*b*). The reason might be that there is a direct effect of a high number of homicides on incarceration: Where many homicides occur, more people are imprisoned for longer periods. The negative correlation of both rates with the PPI suggests an additional plausible explanation: a high imprisonment rate, like low total crime rates and high homicide rates, may indicate a dysfunctional criminal justice system. Countries with dysfunctional systems are probably more prone to punitive responses to crime. Harsh punishments might be necessary to defend the legal order. By contrast, systems that are seen to be just, fair, and trustworthy can be more self-confident and restrict punishment to a minimum (Lappi-Seppälä 2008; Harrendorf 2017*b*; also see Hegel 1821, sec. 218).

## B. Trend Comparisons

Rate comparisons are possible but need to be carefully made. Interpretation of differences found is never straightforward, and only police-recorded completed homicide rates can serve as a plausible proxy for real-world crime levels. Warnings about rate comparisons between countries are appropriate (Aebi et al. 2014, p. 21; Eurostat 2017*b*, p. 36). Trend comparisons have the advantage that the values being compared are change rates relative to a reference year. They are not directly influenced by legal or statistical differences between countries (except when there are major changes in criminal procedure or in recording rules during the period under study). Yet for a meaningful comparison of trends it is still necessary to know that there are no fundamental differences in offense definitions and recording practices. It is also necessary to understand that change rates are influenced by different substantive factors. An increase or decrease in a crime rate is not necessarily due to a change in the incidence of the offense in society. It might, for example, be due to changes in the willingness of victims to report. Thus even seemingly identical trends in different countries may have different substantive causes. It is impossible to explain developments in crime rates without taking into account other sources of information such as victimization surveys.

Some elementary data comparability is a prerequisite for trend comparisons, making it important which offenses are compared. The European Sourcebook provides standard offense definitions together with inclusion and exclusion rules. It also asks correspondents to indicate whether these rules have been followed. These answers can be used to estimate the overall comparability of data for offense categories. Offenses with definitions that are consistent in all respects in many countries should, in principle, have higher comparability than offenses for which many correspondents had to deviate from the definitions and rules. If a country was unable even to report data for a certain offense, this may also indicate a serious problem with the offense definition. For example, the offense may not be separately identifiable (Harrendorf 2012).

Figures 4 and 5 show the overall conformity with offense definitions at the police level for the fifth edition of the European Sourcebook. The percentage of countries completely unable to report data is generally low, but there are many offense definitions that could not be followed for the majority of countries. Sexual assault, robbery, theft, domestic burglary, and money laundering are the only offenses with conformity rates of 50 percent or higher.[9]

Other meaningful comparisons are possible, for example, by evaluating the answers about applicability of the different inclusion and exclusion rules in detail (Harrendorf 2012). Space limitations preclude pursuit of that topic in this essay.

[9] The standard definition of sexual assault is "sexual contact with a person against her/his will or with a person who cannot validly consent to sexual acts. Include the following: any sexual acts committed with violence or threat of violence, any sexual acts committed with abuse of authority or undue pressure, any sexual acts committed against a helpless person, any sexual acts committed against a marital partner against her/his will, acts considered as rape, acts considered as physical sexual abuse of a child, attempts. Exclude the following: any verbal or any other form of non-physical molestation, pornography" (Aebi et al. 2014, pp. 383–84). Compared to the fourth edition European Sourcebook (Aebi et al. 2010), the offense definition for sexual assault was changed, as conformity rates and data availability for the earlier definition were poor (cf. Harrendorf 2012). Obviously, the change of the definition increased comparability. The standard definition of robbery is "stealing from a person with force or threat of force. Include the following: muggings (bag-snatchings), theft immediately followed by force or threat of force used to keep hold of the stolen goods, attempts. Exclude the following: pick-pocketing, extortion, blackmailing" (Aebi et al. 2014, pp. 387–88). The standard definition of theft is "depriving a person or organization of property with the intent to keep it. Include the following: minor (e.g. small value) theft, burglary, theft of motor vehicles, attempts. Exclude the following: embezzlement (including theft by employees), robbery, receiving/handling stolen goods" (p. 388). The standard definition of domestic burglary is "gaining access to closed private premises (e.g. by use of force against an object) with the objective to steal goods. Include the following: theft from an attic or basement in a multi-dwelling building, theft from a secondary residence (even if unoccupied), attempts. Exclude the following: theft from a factory, shop, office, etc., theft from a detached garage, shed, barn or stable, theft from a fenced meadow/compound" (p. 392). The standard definition of money laundering is "specific financial transactions to conceal the identity, source, and/or destination of money or non-monetary property deriving from criminal activities. Include the following: receiving and handling illegally obtained (but not stolen) non-monetary property, attempts. Exclude the following: receiving/handling stolen property, violations of the 'know-your-customer' rule (i.e. negligence in identification of customer's identity or origin of funds)" (p. 395).

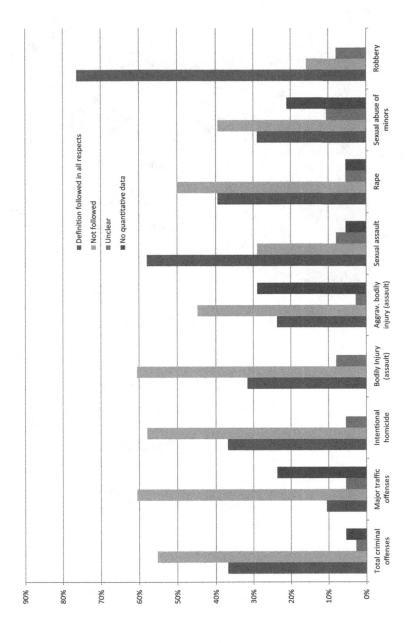

FIG. 4.—Overall conformity with offense definitions, police level, part I. Source: raw data for the fifth edition European Sourcebook (Aebi et al. 2014).

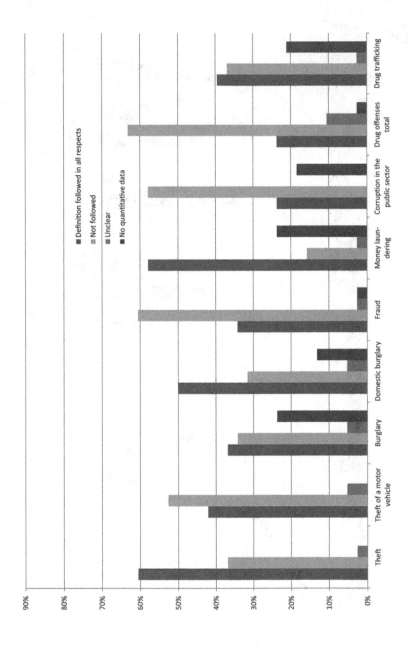

Fig. 5.—Overall conformity with offense definitions, police level, part II. Source: raw data for the fifth edition European Sourebook (Aebi et al. 2014).

However, some limitations of assessments of comparability based on overall conformity rates need to be mentioned. First, overall conformity rates are sensitive to the number of items on the inclusion and exclusion lists. The probability that a country cannot follow a definition in all respects increases with the number of items. The high conformity rate for robbery is likely also due to its short list of inclusions and exclusions compared with, for example, fraud.[10]

Second, some rules are more important for comparability than others because they affect larger proportions of offenses or offenders. Data comparability for theft, for example, is affected more by exclusion of minor thefts than by inclusion of robbery.

Homicide is an offense with low conformity rates but probably has good international comparability. Some other offenses have high conformity in definitions but still lack comparability, for example, because of strong influence of substantive factors. Money laundering is such an offense, as the exceptionally high variation coefficients show (Harrendorf 2012). High conformity is, however, at least an indicator of increased comparability. Trend comparisons are therefore especially likely to be valid for theft, robbery, sexual assault, and homicide and at the police level also for domestic burglary.[11]

The total of criminal offenses for most purposes is not reliable for international comparison. First, it is a black box with unknown content with respect to the offenses covered, mainly because borderlines between criminal and other forms of deviant behavior are drawn differently in each country (Harrendorf 2011). The total rate is mainly a measure of the quality of police work (this is also for the theft rate). Yet the trend for total criminal offenses is important for international comparison, as it shows the overall workload of the system. This cannot be shown by any of the specific offenses. That the total rate mainly measures the quality of police work also does not rule out comparison, but offers cautions about the meaning of varying trends and rates.

---

[10] Standard definition (Aebi et al. 2014, p. 393): "deceiving someone or taking advantage of someone's error with the intent to unlawfully gain financial benefits, thereby causing the deceived person to enter any operation that will be damaging to his/her or a third person's financial interests. Include the following: attempts. Exclude the following: receiving/handling stolen property, forgery of documents, passports etc., tax and customs offences, subsidy fraud, fraud involving welfare payments, money laundering, forgery of money/payment instruments, consuming goods or services, breaching of trust/embezzlement."

[11] On a convictions level, many countries are unable to report data, since domestic burglary is not a criminal law concept in their country (cf. Aebi et al. 2014, p. 373).

## C. Building and Comparing System-Based Indicators

Trends can thus be compared more easily than rates because the influence of legal and statistical differences is minimized. Another way to improve comparability is to build indicators as ratios of two different, system-based variables. By doing so, influences of different legal and substantive factors such as offense definitions or reporting rates are controlled for, assuming that the influence of these factors is the same for the numerator and denominator variables. The same is true for statistical factors such as different counting rules. Counting rules can, however, be controlled effectively only if both the numerator and denominator variables stem from the same statistics or from different statistics that apply the same methodology. In practice, different national statistical systems often have different counting rules.

System-based indicators are therefore a good approximation for major system-based differences, for example, attrition processes or punitiveness (Jehle 2012a; Smit, van Eijk, and Decae 2012; Harrendorf 2013b; Harrendorf, Jehle, and Smit 2014). Attrition, for example, can be measured by comparing ratios such as the offender ratio (suspects per 100 recorded offenses) and the conviction ratio (convicted persons per 100 suspects). For punitiveness, several possible system-based measures are superior to a simple comparison of incarceration rates. One such possibility is a ratio using the total number of prisoners or of convicted prisoners as the numerator and the total number of convictions as the denominator (cf. Harrendorf 2017b, pp. 145–51; also see Lappi-Seppälä [2008, pp. 327–28], relating the numbers of prisoners to the number of police-recorded crimes). Since the prison stock mainly depends on the number and length of unsuspended prison sentences issued by the courts, this is a plausible indicator of relative harshness (Smit 2009; Smit, van Eijk, and Decae 2012; Harrendorf 2013a). Of course such an indicator is still highly correlated with the imprisonment rate itself (Lappi-Seppälä 2008, pp. 327–28). Results discussed above in Section III.A also showed that incarceration rates can at least be seen as a proxy for punitiveness and—together with low total crime rates and high homicide rates—are an indicator for a dysfunctional criminal justice system.

## D. Country Clustering

The immense differences in the rates for crime and criminal justice variables also complicate the development and comparative interpretation of country clusters. Variation coefficients are a measure of relative variation, as they are a ratio calculated by dividing the standard deviation by the mean. Variation coefficients are often higher than 100 percent (Harrendorf 2012, 2013*b*). Thus, the mean does not represent the individual country results. Even if data for all countries in the world were available, neither the population-weighted nor the unweighted mean would provide a meaningful world representation. This is also true for Eurostat or European Sourcebook data with respect to Europe. Only arbitrary results would be produced if means were generated for a convenience sample of countries located on the same continent. For each sample of countries chosen, the mean would be very different from that for any other sample. I criticized that approach in the introduction.

Country clustering is useful only for groups of countries in which the legal architecture and practices are comparable. Smit, Marshall, and van Gammeren (2008) illustrate an innovative empirical approach to country clustering. By use of Categorical Principal Components Analysis, they identified groups of countries that resemble each other in their rates for different variables, but also taking into account some geographical, political, and cultural characteristics. They concluded that it is feasible and sensible to cluster European countries into four large groups: East, Central, North/West, and South. They summarized rules to determine the exact positioning of countries:

> First, all countries that used to be Soviet states are placed in the category "East."
> Secondly, all "countries in transition," that is, all countries that used to be in the sphere of influence of the Soviet Union before the 1990s, are placed in the category "Central." The former Yugoslavian countries are not in this category.[12]
> The remainder of the countries are divided into two categories "North/West" and "South" on geographical grounds only. With "South" meaning south of the Pyrenees and the Alps. The USA and Canada are placed in the category "North/West." (2008, p. 186)

Of course, this approach to country clustering is only an example. There are other sensible possibilities. Most important is that country clusters

---

[12] The countries from former Yugoslavia are placed in the "South" category. On substantive reasons not to put these countries into the "Central" category, with respect to the criminal justice policy of former Yugoslavia, see Flander and Meško (2016).

need to be construed on the basis of a clear theoretical concept. Such a concept can be derived from differences and similarities of criminal justice systems or rely on a typology of political economies (cf. Cavadino and Dignan 2006).

## IV. Planning and Carrying Out a Meaningful Comparative Study

I have tried to provide an overview of the prospects, problems, and pitfalls of comparative studies. Achieving data comparability is difficult, almost impossible. Data are strongly influenced by different substantive, legal, and statistical factors, which make it impossible simply to use unmodified data from different national statistic systems. Usually, it is necessary to rely on international surveys for more or less comparable data. These surveys try to increase comparability by adapting data to specific standards and thoroughly documenting remaining differences. Data from the UN Survey, the Eurostat data collection, and the European Sourcebook have distinct advantages and disadvantages.

I tried to explain what can, and cannot or should not, be done with international crime and criminal justice system data. In comparing national data from international surveys, it is important to follow certain rules. The main ones are summarized below.

1.  Do not use comparative crime and criminal justice data if the research question can be answered by relying on data from international victim or offender surveys. International comparability for these surveys is better.
2.  Do not use comparative crime and criminal justice data to investigate the true incidence of crime in different countries; international victim or offender surveys are better for this. However, as an exception, it may be feasible to compare levels and trends for completed homicide in different countries and use them as indicators.
3.  Comparisons of rates for crime and criminal justice variables between countries should be made extremely cautiously. This does not rule them out, but the interpretation of differences found may be complex.
4.  Crime rates are based on the work of actors involved in the criminal justice process and are necessarily influenced by the quality

and efficiency of their work. Some rates, like the total of criminal offenses, can be seen as a proxy for qualitative police performance.

5. Trend comparisons are more reliable than rate comparisons, as the influence of legal and statistical factors is reduced. They should be preferred, if possible.

6. Comparability can be improved by controlling for the influence of distorting factors by using indicators calculated as ratios of two different variables.

7. Punitiveness in international comparisons should not be measured only by incarceration rates. Other indicators, such as the ratio between the size of the prison population on a given date and the number of convictions that year, are also instructive.

8. Country clustering is a suspect task, since data variations between countries are huge. Mean crime rates for the world or even for Europe cannot be credibly calculated. Country clusters are potentially feasible only for countries for which data are highly similar.

9. The best way to obtain comparable data for different countries is to conduct a multicountry study using an identical methodology, for example, by relying on case files of the courts or prosecution services.

10. If you have to rely on secondary analysis of statistical data, never use national data unmodified in comparative projects. Use data from international surveys.

11. Choose the survey that best provides the variables you need and that fits the regional scope of your study.

12. For European studies, the European Sourcebook is preferable to using Eurostat or UN Survey data because it much more fully documents differences in offense definitions and recording practices and has a better validation process.

13. If data look strange, do not trust them! Look critically at data before using them and check for internal consistency, inexplicable increases or decreases in trends, and differing values for the same or comparable variables from other surveys.

14. Try to correct wrong or suspect data by replacing them with data for an (almost) identical variable from another international survey.

15. Remember in comparing offense-related cross-national data that data for some offenses are much more reliable and comparable than for others.

16. When drawing from the European Sourcebook, data for theft, robbery, sexual assault, and homicide, and at the police level also for domestic burglary, are relatively comparable.

REFERENCES

Aebi, Marcelo F. 2008. "Measuring the Influence of Statistical Counting Rules on Cross-National Differences in Recorded Crime." In *Crime and Criminal Justice Systems in Europe and North America, 1995–2004*, edited by Kauko Aromaa and Markku Heiskanen. Helsinki: Helsinki United Nations Institute.
———. 2010. "Methodological Issues in the Comparison of Police-Recorded Crime Rates." In *International Handbook of Criminology*, edited by Shlomo Giora Shoham, Paul Knepper, and Martin Kett. Boca Raton, FL: CRC Press.
Aebi, Marcelo F., Galma Akdeniz, Gordon Barclay, Claudia Campistol, Stefano Caneppele, Beata Gruszczyńska, et al. 2012. *European Sourcebook of Crime and Criminal Justice Statistics.* Questionnaire Covering the Years 2007–2011. Lausanne: University of Lausanne.
———. 2014. *European Sourcebook of Crime and Criminal Justice Statistics—2014.* 5th ed. Helsinki: Helsinki United Nations Institute.
Aebi, Marcelo F., Bruno Aubusson de Cavarlay, Gordon Barclay, Beata Gruszczyńska, Stefan Harrendorf, Markku Heiskanen, et al. 2010. *European Sourcebook of Crime and Criminal Justice Statistics—2010.* 4th ed. Den Haag: Boom.
Aebi, Marcelo F., and Julien Chopin. 2016. *Council of Europe Annual Penal Statistics. SPACE II Survey 2015: Persons Serving Non-custodial Sanctions and Measures in 2015.* Strasbourg: Council of Europe.
Aebi, Marcelo F., and Antonia Linde. 2012. "Conviction Statistics as an Indicator of Crime Trends in Europe from 1990 to 2006." *European Journal on Criminal Policy and Research* 18(1):103–44.
Aebi, Marcelo F., Antonia Linde, and Natalia Delgrande. 2015. "Is There a Relationship between Imprisonment and Crime in Western Europe?" *European Journal on Criminal Policy and Research* 21:425–46.
Aebi, Marcelo F., Mélanie M. Tiago, and Christine Burkhardt. 2017. *Council of Europe Annual Penal Statistics. SPACE I—Prison Populations: Survey 2015.* Updated April 25. Strasbourg: Council of Europe.
Alvazzi del Frate, Anna. 2010. "Crime and Criminal Justice Statistics Challenges." In *International Statistics on Crime and Justice*, edited by Stefan Harrendorf, Markku Heiskanen, and Steven Malby. Helsinki: Helsinki United Nations Institute.
Arbeitsgruppe der AOLG. 2011. *Verbesserung der Qualität der äußeren Leichenschau.* Berlin: Arbeitsgruppe der AOLG.
Barberet, Rosemary. 2009. "The Legacy of INTERPOL Crime Data to Cross-National Criminology." *International Journal of Comparative and Applied Criminal Justice* 33(2):193–210.

Blumstein, Alfred, Michael Tonry, and Ashley Van Ness. 2005. "Cross-National Measures of Punitiveness." In *Crime and Punishment in Western Countries, 1980–1999*, edited by Michael Tonry and David P. Farrington. Vol. 33 of *Crime and Justice: A Review of Research*, edited by Michael Tonry. Chicago: University of Chicago Press.

Brå (Brottsförebyggande rådet). 2015. *The Clearance Rate in Sweden and in Other Countries*. Stockholm: Brå.

Brinkmann, Bernd, S. Banaschak, H. Bratzke, U. Cremer, G. Drese, C. Erfurt, et al. 1997. "Fehlleistungen bei der Leichenschau in der Bundesrepublik Deutschland: Ergebnisse einer multizentrischen Studie." *Archiv für Kriminologie* 199:1–12, 65–74.

Buonanno, Paolo, Francesco Drago, and Roberto Galbiati. 2014. "How Much Should We Trust Crime Statistics? A Comparison between UE and US." LIEPP Working Paper no. 19. Paris: Sciences Po.

Cavadino, Michael, and James Dignan. 2006. "Penal Policy and Political Economy." *Criminology and Criminal Justice* 6(4):435–56.

Churchill, Sefa Awaworyi, and Emmanuel Laryea. 2017. "Crime and Ethnic Diversity: Cross-Country Evidence." *Crime and Delinquency*. Online First, September 23.

Cole, George F., and Christopher E. Smith. 2011. *Criminal Justice in America*. 6th ed. Belmont, MA: Wadsworth.

Council of Europe. 1995. *European Sourcebook of Crime and Criminal Justice Statistics*. Draft model. Strasbourg: Council of Europe.

———. 1999. *European Sourcebook of Crime and Criminal Justice Statistics*. Strasbourg: Council of Europe.

de Bondt, Wendy. 2014. "Evidence Based EU Criminal Policy Making: In Search of Matching Data." *European Journal on Criminal Policy and Research* 20(1):23–49.

Ebbe, Obi N. I. 2013. "The Purpose of Comparative and International Criminal Justice Systems." In *Comparative and International Criminal Justice Systems: Policing, Judiciary, and Corrections*. 3rd ed. Boca Raton, FL: CRC Press.

Elsner, Beatrix, Paul Smit, and Josef Zila. 2008. "Police Case-Ending Possibilities within Criminal Investigations." *European Journal on Criminal Policy and Research* 14(2–3):191–201.

European Commission for the Efficiency of Justice. 2016. *European Judicial Systems: Efficiency and Quality of Justice*. CEPEJ Studies no. 23. Strasbourg: Council of Europe.

European Monitoring Centre for Drugs and Drug Addiction. 2017. *Statistical Bulletin 2017*. Lisbon: EMCDDA. http://www.emcdda.europa.eu/data/stats2017_en.

Eurostat. 2017a. *Crime and Criminal Justice Statistics*. Summary Quality Report on the 2016 Data Collection. Luxembourg: Eurostat.

———. 2017b. *Crime and Criminal Justice Statistics: Methodological Guide for Users*. 2017 Version. Luxembourg: Eurostat.

Flander, Benjamin, and Gorazd Meško. 2016. "Penal and Prison Policy on the Sunny Side of the Alps: The Swan Song of Slovenian Exceptionalism?" *European Journal on Criminal Policy and Research* 22:565–91.

Harrendorf, Stefan. 2010. *A Validation of Selected 10th and 11th CTS Variables as a Pretest for a General Automated Validation of the Crime Trends Survey Results.* Final report to the UN Office on Drugs and Crime. Göttingen: University of Göttingen.

———. 2011. "How to Measure Punitiveness in Global Perspective: What Can Be Learned from International Survey Data?" In *Punitivity: International Developments*, vol. 1, *Punitiveness: A Global Phenomenon?* edited by Helmut Kury and Evelyn Shea. Bochum, Germany: Brockmeyer.

———. 2012. "Offence Definitions in the European Sourcebook of Crime and Criminal Justice Statistics and Their Influence on Data Quality and Comparability." *European Journal on Criminal Policy and Research* 18(1):23–53.

———. 2013*a*. "Methodische Überlegungen zu Möglichkeiten und Grenzen vergleichender Punitivitätsmessung auf der Grundlage internationaler Kriminalitätssurveys." In *Täter-Taten-Opfer: Grundlagenfragen und aktuelle Probleme der Kriminalität*, edited by Dieter Dölling and Jörg-Martin Jehle. Mönchengladbach, Germany: Forum Verlag Godesberg.

———. 2013*b*. "Towards Comparable International Crime and Criminal Justice Statistics: Where Do We Stand? What Can We Expect?" In *Criminology, Criminal Policy and Criminal Law in an International Perspective: Essays in Honour of Martin Killias on the Occasion of His 65th Birthday*, edited by André Kuhn, Christian Schwarzenegger, Pierre Margot, Andreas Donatsch, Marcelo F. Aebi, and Daniel Jositsch. Zürich: Stämpfli.

———. 2017*a*. "Attrition in and Performance of Criminal Justice Systems in Europe: A Comparative Approach." *European Journal on Criminal Policy and Research*. Online First, September 7.

———. 2017*b*. "Justizieller Umgang mit kriminellem Verhalten im internationalen Vergleich: Was kann 'Comparative Criminal Justice' leisten?" *Rechtswissenschaft* 8(2):113–52.

Harrendorf, Stefan, Jörg-Martin Jehle, and Paul Smit. 2014. "Attrition." In *Recording Community Sanctions and Measures and Assessing Attrition: A Methodological Study on Comparative Data in Europe*, edited by Markku Heiskanen, Marcelo F. Aebi, Willem van der Brugge, and Jörg-Martin Jehle. Helsinki: Helsinki United Nations Institute.

Harrendorf, Stefan, and Paul Smit. 2010. "Attributes of Criminal Justice Systems: Resources, Performance, and Punitivity." In *International Statistics on Crime and Justice*, edited by Stefan Harrendorf, Markku Heiskanen, and Steven Malby. Helsinki: Helsinki United Nations Institute.

Hegel, Georg W. F. 1821. *Grundlinien der Philosophie des Rechts*. Berlin: Nicolai.

Heiskanen, Markku. 2010. "Trends in Police-Recorded Crime." In *International Statistics on Crime and Justice*, edited by Stefan Harrendorf, Markku Heiskanen, and Steven Malby. Helsinki: Helsinki United Nations Institute.

Heiskanen, Markku, Marcelo F. Aebi, Willem van der Brugge, and Jörg-Martin Jehl, eds. 2014. *Recording Community Sanctions and Measures and Assessing Attrition: A Methodological Study on Comparative Data in Europe*. Helsinki: Helsinki United Nations Institute.

Hinds, Lynette R. 2005. "Crime Control in Western Countries, 1970 to 2000." In *The New Punitiveness: Trends, Theories, Perspectives*, edited by John Pratt, David Brown, Mark Brown, Simon Hallsworth, and Wayne Morrison. Cullompton, Devon, UK: Willan.

Interpol General Assembly. 2006. *Resolution AG-2006-RES-19: Proposal to Discontinue the Production of Crime Statistics*. Rio de Janeiro: Interpol.

Jehle, Jörg-Martin. 2012*a*. "Attrition and Conviction Rates of Sexual Offences in Europe." *European Journal on Criminal Policy and Research* 18(1):145–61.

———. 2012*b*. "How to Improve the International Comparability of Crime Statistics." In *New Types of Crime: Proceedings of the International Seminar Held in Connection with HEUNI's Thirtieth Anniversary 20 October 2011*. Helsinki: Helsinki United Nations Institute.

———. 2015. *Criminal Justice in Germany: Facts and Figures*. 6th ed. Mönchengladbach, Germany: Forum Verlag Godesberg.

Jehle, Jörg-Martin, and Stefan Harrendorf, eds. 2010. *Defining and Registering Criminal Offences and Measures: Standards for a European Comparison*. Göttingen, Germany: Universitätsverlag Göttingen.

———. 2014. "How to Record Data on Community Sanctions and Measures and the Work of Probation Agencies across Europe: The Approach of the European Sourcebook." In *Organized Crime, Corruption, and Crime Prevention: Essays in Honor of Ernesto U. Savona*, edited by Stefano Caneppele and Francesco Calderoni. New York: Springer.

Jehle, Jörg-Martin, Paul Smit, and Josef Zila. 2008. "The Public Prosecutor as Key-Player: Prosecutorial Case-Ending Decisions." *European Journal on Criminal Policy and Research* 14(2–3):161–79.

Junger-Tas, Josine, Ineke Haen Marshall, Dirk Enzmann, Martin Killias, Majone Steketee, and Beata Gruszczyńska, eds. 2010. *Juvenile Delinquency in Europe and Beyond: Results of the Second International Self-Report Delinquency Study*. New York: Springer.

Killias, Martin. 1995. "The European Sourcebook of Crime and Criminal Justice Statistics." *European Journal on Criminal Policy and Research* 3(4):108–17.

Lappi-Seppälä, Tapio. 2008. "Trust, Welfare, and Political Culture: Explaining Differences in National Penal Policies." In *Crime and Justice: A Review of Research*, vol. 37, edited by Michael Tonry. Chicago: University of Chicago Press.

———. 2011. "Explaining Imprisonment in Europe." *European Journal of Criminology* 8:303–28.

Lappi-Seppälä, Tapio, and Martti Lehti. 2014. "Cross-Comparative Perspectives on Global Homicide Trends." In *Why Crime Rates Fall and Why They Don't*, edited by Michael Tonry. Vol. 43 of *Crime and Justice: A Review of Research*, edited by Michael Tonry. Chicago: University of Chicago Press.

Lewis, Chris G. 2012. "Crime and Justice Statistics Collected by International Agencies." *European Journal on Criminal Policy and Research* 18(1):5–21.

Lovett, Jo, and Liz Kelly. 2009. *Different Systems, Similar Outcomes? Tracking Attrition in Reported Rape Cases across Europe*. London: Child and Woman Abuse Studies Unit, London Metropolitan University.

Malby, Steven. 2010*a*. "Drug Crime." In *International Statistics on Crime and Justice*, edited by Stefan Harrendorf, Markku Heiskanen, and Steven Malby. Helsinki: Helsinki United Nations Institute.

———. 2010*b*. "Homicide." In *International Statistics on Crime and Justice*, edited by Stefan Harrendorf, Markku Heiskanen, and Steven Malby. Helsinki: Helsinki United Nations Institute.

Mätzler, Armin, and Ingo Wirth. 2016. *Todesermittlung: Grundlagen und Fälle*. 5th ed. Heidelberg: C. F. Müller.

Ministry of Justice, England and Wales. 2016. *Coroners Statistics Annual 2015*. London: Ministry of Justice.

Nelken, David. 2010. *Comparative Criminal Justice: Making Sense of Difference*. London: Sage.

Pakes, Francis. 2015. *Comparative Criminal Justice*. 3rd ed. Abingdon, UK: Routledge.

Pare, Paul-Philippe. 2014. "Indicators of Police Performance and Their Relationships with Homicide Rates across 77 Nations." *International Criminal Justice Review* 24(3):254–70.

Porter, Michael E., Klaus Schwab, Xavier Sala-i-Martin, and Augusto Lopez-Claros. 2004. *The Global Competitiveness Report, 2003–2004*. New York: Oxford University Press.

Rosenfeld, Richard, and Steven F. Messner. 2009. "The Crime Drop in Comparative Perspective: The Impact of the Economy and Imprisonment on American and European Burglary Rates." *British Journal of Sociology* 60(3): 445–71.

Rubin, Marilyn M., Richard Culp, Peter Mameli, and Michael Walker. 2008. "Using Cross-National Studies to Illuminate the Crime Problem: One Less Data Source Left Standing." *Journal of Contemporary Criminal Justice* 24(1): 50–68.

Rückert, Sabine. 2000. *Tote haben keine Lobby: Die Dunkelziffer der vertuschten Morde*. Hamburg: Hoffmann & Campe.

Smit, Paul. 2009. "Nederland in internationaal perspectief." In *Criminaliteit en Rechtshandhaving 2008*, edited by Sandra N. Kalidien and A. Th. J. Eggen. Den Haag: Boom.

Smit, Paul, Ineke Haen Marshall, and Mirjam van Gammeren. 2008. "An Empirical Approach to Country Clustering." In *Crime and Criminal Justice Systems in Europe and North America, 1995–2004*, edited by Kauko Aromaa and Markku Heiskanen. Helsinki: Helsinki United Nations Institute.

Smit, Paul, Anneke van Eijk, and Rob Decae. 2012. "Trends in the Reaction on Crime in Criminal Justice Systems in Europe in 1990–2007: A Comparison of Four European Regions." *European Journal on Criminal Policy and Research* 18 (1):55–82.

Stang, Michael. 2015. *Rechtsmedizin: Defizite bei Leichenschau und Obduktion*. http://www.deutschlandfunk.de/rechtsmedizin-defizite-bei-leichenschau-und-obduktion.676.de.html?dram:article_id=338753.

Tonry, Michael. 2015. "Is Cross-National and Comparative Research on the Criminal Justice System Useful?" *European Journal of Criminology* 12(4):505–16.

Tonry, Michael, and David P. Farrington. 2005. "Punishment and Crime across Space and Time." In *Crime and Punishment in Western Countries, 1980–1999*, edited by Michael Tonry and David P. Farrington. Vol. 33 of *Crime and Justice: A Review of Research*, edited by Michael Tonry. Chicago: University of Chicago Press.

Transparency International. 2013. *Global Corruption Barometer 2013*. Berlin: Transparency International.

Tyler, Tom R. 2006. *Why People Obey the Law*. Princeton, NJ: Princeton University Press.

UN Economic and Social Council. 2015. *Annual Report Questionnaire*. Part 4: *Extent and Patterns of and Trends in Drug Crop Cultivation and Drug Manufacture and Trafficking*. Vienna: UN Economic and Social Council.

———. 2016. *World Crime Trends and Emerging Issues and Responses in the Field of Crime Prevention and Criminal Justice: Note by the Secretariat*. E/CN.15/2016/10. Commission on Crime Prevention and Criminal Justice, 25th session, May 23–27. Vienna: UN Economic and Social Council.

UNODC (UN Office on Drugs and Crime). 2014. *Global Study on Homicide 2013: Trends, Contexts, Data*. Vienna: UNODC.

———. 2015. *International Classification of Crimes for Statistical Purposes*. Vienna: UNODC.

———. 2016a. *United Nations Survey of Crime Trends and Operations of Criminal Justice Systems (UN-CTS)—2016*. Vienna: UNODC.

———. 2016b. *World Drug Report 2016*. Vienna: UNODC.

UN Statistics Division. 2003. *Manual for the Development of a System of Criminal Justice Statistics*. ST/ESA/STAT/SER.F/89. New York: UN Statistics Division.

van Dijk, Jan. 2008. *The World of Crime*. Thousand Oaks, CA: Sage.

van Dijk, Jan, John van Kesteren, and Paul Smit. 2007. *Criminal Victimisation in International Perspective: Key Findings from the 2004–2005 ICVS and EU ICS*. Den Haag: Boom.

von Hofer, Hanns. 2000. "Crime Statistics as Constructs: The Case of Swedish Rape Statistics." *European Journal on Criminal Policy and Research* 8(1):77–89.

Wade, Marianne. 2006. "The Power to Decide: Prosecutorial Control, Diversion and Punishment in European Criminal Justice Systems Today." In *Coping with Overloaded Criminal Justice Systems: The Rise of Prosecutorial Power across Europe*, edited by Jörg-Martin Jehle and Marianne Wade. Berlin: Springer.

Wartna, Bouke S. J., Ian Knowles, Ian Morton, Susan M. Alma, and Nikolaj Tollenaar. 2014. "Comparison of Reoffending Rates across Countries: An International Pilot Study." In *National Reconviction Statistics and Studies in Europe*, edited by Hans-Jörg Albrecht and Jörg-Martin Jehle. Göttingen, Germany: Universitätsverlag Göttingen.

Wartna, Bouke S. J., and L. T. J. Nijssen. 2006. *National Studies on Recidivism: An Inventory of Large-Scale Recidivism Research in 33 European Countries*. WODC Studies on Recidivism. Fact Sheet 2006-11. Den Haag: Research and Documentation Center, Netherlands Ministry of Justice.

*Rhys Hester, Richard S. Frase, Julian V. Roberts,*
*and Kelly Lyn Mitchell*

# Prior Record Enhancements at Sentencing: Unsettled Justifications and Unsettling Consequences

ABSTRACT

The consequences of a person's prior crimes remain after the debt to society is
paid and the sentence is discharged. While the practice of using prior
convictions to enhance the severity of sentence imposed is universal, prior
record enhancements (PREs) play a particularly important role in US sentencing, and especially in guidelines jurisdictions. In grid-based guidelines,
criminal history constitutes one of the two dimensions of the grid. The
enhancements are hard to justify. Retributive theories generally reject the use
of robust, cumulative record-based enhancements. Research into recidivism
suggests that the preventive benefits of PREs have been overstated. The
public support the consideration of prior convictions at sentencing, but there
is convincing evidence that people are less punitive in their views than are
many US guideline schemes. PREs exacerbate racial disparities in prison
admissions and populations, result in significant additional prison costs, undermine offense-based proportionality, and disrupt prison resource prioritization.

The consequences of a person's past crimes remain long after the debt to
society has been paid and the sentence discharged. Prior convictions af-

Electronically published March 5, 2018
Rhys Hester is deputy director, Pennsylvania Commission on Sentencing, and associate
research professor of sociology and criminology, Pennsylvania State University. Richard
S. Frase is Benjamin N. Burger Professor of Criminal Law, University of Minnesota Law

209

fect one's life for decades by impairing job prospects, limiting eligibility for social programs and benefits, and imposing social stigma. Individuals pay for their crimes once and then pay over and over again. Nowhere is the impact of prior convictions more direct or more palpable than at sentencing for a new offense. People with histories of prior crimes are sent to prison more often and for longer, practices we refer to as prior record enhancements (PREs).[1] Sometimes offenders are punished for the past under three-strikes, habitual offender, and career criminal laws that mandate starkly harsher punishments for repeat offenders. In other instances this increased punishment for past actions occurs because sentencing guidelines systems weight criminal history heavily.

Prior record enhancements are not unique to the United States, although like current punishment practices generally, the extent of additional punishment from PREs in the United States is exceptional. In other countries, prior convictions normally carry only a modest enhancement relative to the punishment imposed on first offenders (e.g., Roberts and Pina-Sánchez 2014, 2015). In countries without formal guidelines (most jurisdictions) it is hard to determine how much weight prior convictions carry at sentencing or which dimensions of criminal history are influential. Most jurisdictions (including New Zealand, Canada, and Australia) leave the interpretation of an offender's record, and the weight it should carry, to the discretion of trial courts (see Roberts 2008). This is also true in US states without guidelines, which constitute slightly more than half of US jurisdictions. As with nonguidelines nations, it is difficult to gauge the magnitude of PREs in US nonguidelines states because of a lack of data. There are, however, some indications that PREs are more pronounced under guidelines, at least in terms of multiplying prison sentence lengths (as opposed to their effect on in-out decisions; Hester 2017).

In many US states, sentencing guidelines provide detailed rules regulating the ways prior convictions should be counted, as well as the specific weight they should have on sentence outcomes; judicial discretion is curbed in the interests of promoting greater consistency across cases. The quest for uniformity and consistency led to mechanical quantification of many of the factors important to sentencing, such as the circumstances

School. Julian V. Roberts is professor of criminology, University of Oxford. Kelly Lyn Mitchell is executive director, Robina Institute of Criminal Law and Criminal Justice.

[1] We interchangeably use the term "criminal history enhancements."

of the crime and characteristics of the offender, including his or her prior record. Guidelines create rules for scoring this information; the majority of guidelines jurisdictions use a sentencing matrix or grid to recommend a sentence based on the severity of the current offense and the offender's prior record. Offenders with the highest criminal history scores receive prison recommendations that are often many times greater than the sentences recommended for first-time offenders convicted of the same offense. On average, across all guidelines systems, record-based prison length enhancements produce a sixfold increase in punishment, although there is considerable variation among the systems (Frase and Hester, forthcoming *b*). At the high end, some state grids impose over a 10-fold average increase. For some offense categories the multiplier is an astounding 30.[2] When the multiplier is that high, only 3 percent of individuals' current sentence can be considered punishment for the crime they are being convicted of; 97 percent is allocated for prior behavior for which they have already been convicted and sentenced and for which they have already satisfied their debt to society.

Despite the universal nature of record-based sentencing enhancements and the significant effects they have on sentencing outcomes, the subject attracted little attention from scholars until relatively recently.[3] For many observers, PREs may seem like an uncontroversial element of contemporary sentencing, as unproblematic as increasing the severity of punishment to reflect the seriousness of the current crime. But on closer inspection enhancements raise important and unsettling issues.

There is no uniform concept of "criminal history" or "prior record," and jurisdictions vary widely in the factors they mechanically incorporate in prior record scores. A "prior record" can mean a plethora of different things: A person with a single, 30-year-old misdemeanor; an individual

---

[2] This example comes from seriousness level III of the Washington guidelines. Offenders with an offender score of 0 are recommended for 2 months' incarceration while offenders in the highest offender score category of 9+ are recommended for 59.5 months— just short of 5 years. These are main-grid average multipliers; on some specialized grids and offense levels, the high-low ratios are even higher (e.g., on level VII of the Maryland property crimes grid, the multiplier is 96).

[3] For a recent survey of all US guidelines systems employing some sort of criminal history score, see Frase et al. (2015). This survey is part of a major research project at the University of Minnesota's Robina Institute of Criminal Law and Criminal Justice (http://robinainstitute.umn.edu/areas-expertise/criminal-history-enhancements). Several other recent works have examined the rationales for PREs (see, e.g., Roberts and von Hirsch 2010; Tamburrini and Ryberg 2012).

with a few drug and property felonies; a person with a string of robbery and attempted murder convictions; and an individual with scores of burglary and theft crimes over the course of decades—all have "a record." Second, intuition aside, articulating the justifications for PREs—on both retributive and risk-based grounds—proves a more difficult task than many people might imagine. As we discuss in detail below, retributive sentencing theorists have failed to agree on a justification for PRE policies that garners widespread endorsement (Roberts and von Hirsch 2010). And while consequentialist theories posit that sanctions might rehabilitate, deter, or incapacitate, the empirical literature suggests that more severe sanctions are ineffective in reducing crime (Nagin 2013). Third, PRE practices have significant unintended consequences: exacerbating race disparities, confounding offense-based proportionality, and disrupting prison resource prioritization. As a result, prison populations are full of older, less violent offenders who are more likely to be persons of color—all at great cost and little benefit to the public.

A generation ago, *Crime and Justice* published the first review of the research and practice of prior record enhancements, with a focus on US systems (Roberts 1997*b*). In this essay we revisit these important issues, drawing on a resurgence of writing and research. Over the past two decades, retributive theorists have revisited the relevance of prior convictions. Several early retributive writers took the position that prior convictions do not affect the seriousness of the crime or the offender's culpability and therefore have no place in the sentencing equation (e.g., Fletcher 1978; Singer 1979). But von Hirsch (1976) set forth a retributive argument for enhancing punishment on the basis of prior record; his view, that culpability increased along with the number of prior convictions, influenced the earliest sentencing guidelines commissions in states such as Minnesota and Washington (Parent 1988; Boerner and Lieb 2001). A recent wave of scholarship has reopened the debate. Von Hirsch subsequently amended his earlier view and now endorses a more limited role for enhancing sentences on retributive grounds (von Hirsch 2010). Others continue to struggle to articulate retributivist justifications (see, e.g., Roberts 2008; Lee 2009, 2010; Frase 2010, 2013).

The empirical literature on the relationship between prior and future offending has grown significantly in recent years, yielding many new insights. The link between past and future crime could justify PREs on utilitarian, preventive grounds. Here, too, received wisdom has evolved.

It is likely that some priors, and some dimensions of criminal history, have more predictive power than others (Frase 2015*a*). An important line of research has documented the declining significance of prior convictions for the purposes of predicting future crime: after a number of years, the predictive power of a criminal conviction declines (e.g., Kurleycheck, Brame, and Bushway 2006, 2007; Blumstein and Nakamura 2009; cf. Bushway, Nieuwbeerta, and Blokland 2011). Analyses have also questioned the complacent assumption that repeat offenders always represent a higher risk of reoffending, and research has led to a more nuanced evaluation of which dimensions of an offender's criminal history score predict reoffending most reliably. This research has had modest influence on sentencing commissions. For example, the US Sentencing Commission removed its "recency premium," which had imposed additional punishment when the priors were committed in a relatively short period prior to the current offense, because it contributed little to the predictive accuracy of the criminal history score (US Sentencing Commission 2010). Mostly, though, state commissions have made little effort to examine or evaluate their PRE policies.

Furthermore, even if a criminal history score successfully predicts a higher likelihood of future offending, the question of the appropriate enhancement is far from settled. What utilitarian purpose is served by doubling, tripling, or imposing a sixfold increase in prison time on an individual who is actuarially more likely (though not certain) to reoffend in the future? The most obvious answers are that increasing the penalty should specifically deter the person being punished and should reduce crime through incapacitation. We address these issues for the first time in the context of PREs, drawing on a growing body of literature that finds no specific deterrent effect of longer prison terms and that frequently reports modest effects in the opposite direction: that prison tends to increase, not reduce, a person's likelihood of reoffending. We also discuss serious problems in justifying PREs across the board on the basis of incapacitation. Lower-level, nonviolent offenders have higher rates of recidivism; since prison is such an expensive endeavor, it is doubtful that the costs of additional years in prison are worth the benefits in preventing low-level property, drug, and public order offenses through incapacitation.

As a consequence of new public opinion research, we are now better placed to understand social reaction to prior record enhancements. One barrier to revising criminal history enhancements has long been public support for the practice (Roberts 2008). We are learning that public support may be less robust than was previously thought and founded on unrealistic expectations of the preventive efficacy of PREs. Finally, research has exposed a number of adverse, unintended consequences of PREs. They have a clearly disproportionate impact on racial minorities. Frase (2009) has demonstrated that most of the racial disparity introduced at the sentencing phase in Minnesota arises as a result of the criminal history axis of the Minnesota grid. Similar effects exist in other guidelines states (Frase and Hester 2015). This disproportionate impact is but one unintended consequence of PREs and serves as a salutary reminder that apparently race-neutral sentencing practices can have very different effects on certain profiles of offenders (Tonry 2011).

Here is how this essay is organized. In Section I we provide an overview of PREs, how they are defined and used, and how scores differ across jurisdictions. We also discuss the considerable variation in the levels of additional punishment imposed for a prior record. In Section II we review the literature on the justifications of punishment in the context of PREs. Despite the intuitive appeal of PREs, the articulation of a convincing retributive-based account of the punishment enhancements has proven elusive. While some severity premium may be appropriate on desert grounds, retributive theory also imposes a limitation on the degree of prior record enhancement in a way that is not currently recognized by most sentencing guidelines jurisdictions. We further conclude, on the best current evidence, that PREs as presently conceived cannot be justified on consequentialist grounds of rehabilitation or deterrence. Across-the-board, nonselective incapacitation is also a poor fit. In Section III, we turn to the adverse impacts of PREs, which include exacerbating racial disparities, undermining offense-based proportionality, confounding prison use priorities, and imposing severe financial impacts on the strained prison system. Section IV concludes with suggestions for future research and a brief sketch of a model approach to PREs. We identify troubling components that should not be included in criminal history scores, suggest upper limits on the effect that prior record should have on sentence lengths, describe several appropriate first-offender mitigation rules, and propose that judges should have express authority to depart from recommended sentences in light of case-specific prior record circumstances. If guidelines systems were to adopt these provisions, jurisdictions could substantially reduce costs and reshape their sentencing systems to be fairer, more proportional, and more efficient—all without detriment to public safety.

## I. Use of Prior Record Enhancements

An offender's criminal history is frequently considered an important factor for sentencing in both determinate and indeterminate sentencing systems, and criminal history has been built into every sentencing guidelines scheme as one key dimension (Roberts 1997a; Frase et al. 2015; Tonry 2016). For jurisdictions that use a sentencing grid, criminal history represents one axis on the grid while offense severity forms the other, and the presumptive sentence lies at the intersection of the two. For guidelines jurisdictions that do not use a grid, criminal history is usually computed on a worksheet, and the resulting points, when added to points relating to offense severity, determine the recommended sentence.

The universal use of prior record in guidelines masks great diversity. Variation exists on the dimensions included in the score, in how items are weighted, and on the magnitude of increased punishment based on higher criminal history scores. Prior record is universally used, but how it is used is far from universal.

### A. Scoring Criminal History

Criminal history scores are composed of multiple elements that vary from jurisdiction to jurisdiction. Criminal history almost always includes some accounting of prior felonies and misdemeanors, but these offenses are not simply tallied pursuant to a universally agreed-on formula. In most jurisdictions, felony points are added on the basis of severity level or offense classification, with different point weights assigned to different classifications. For example, in Arkansas possible point values are .25, .5, or 1; in Minnesota .5, 1, 1.5, 2, or 3; in North Carolina 1, 2, 4, 6, 9, or 10; under the Florida worksheet system, point values range from .2 to 29 (Hester 2015). Misdemeanors likewise are assigned points, almost always valued lower than felonies, and often several misdemeanors are required to garner one criminal history point. Some jurisdictions incorporate "patterning" rules under which similar priors are given even greater weight (Wright 2002; Roberts 2015b).

Prior record scores often include factors such as current custody status (whether the offender was under some type of supervision or incarceration when the offense was committed) or prior probation violations (Roberts 1997*b*). Some jurisdictions broadly define prior offenses so that when multiple current offenses are sentenced, each is included in the criminal history on the next offense to be sentenced (Frase 2015*c*). In contrast, a few jurisdictions incorporate decay or gap rules that wash out or eliminate prior offenses from the criminal history score if they are very old or if the individual was crime-free for a specified number of years (Mitchell 2015).

Almost all states include juvenile adjudications in criminal history scores, although for other purposes courts are increasingly being influenced by research demonstrating the different cognitive functioning of adolescents (Monahan, Skeem, and Lowenkamp 2017). North Carolina is the only state that does not include juvenile adjudications in the prior record score, but juveniles are processed in adult court once they reach age 16 (N.C. Gen. Stat. Ann. § 7B-1604 [2016]). In some jurisdictions juvenile priors are underweighted or points are capped so that they do not weigh as heavily as adult convictions. Important court decisions have declared juveniles to be less culpable on the basis of the research that shows, for instance, that parts of the brain in the frontal lobe associated with regulating aggression, long-range planning, abstract thinking, and perhaps even moral judgment are not fully formed until adulthood (*Roper v. Simmons*, 543 U.S. 551 [2005]; *Graham v. Florida*, 560 U.S. 48 [2010]; *Miller v. Alabama*, 567 U.S. 460 [2012]). Whether the cognitive research cited in the *Roper-Graham-Miller* line of cases will influence how guidelines deal with prior juvenile offenses remains an open question. The moral justification for enhancing punishment on the basis of acts committed as a juvenile may be on more tenuous grounds than for PREs imposed for adult convictions. Moreover, juvenile proceedings generally have fewer procedural safeguards (no right to a jury trial, limited presence and effectiveness of counsel) and are designed for a different purpose (rehabilitation) than adult proceedings. Juvenile adjudications may thus not be as reliable or factually accurate as adult convictions (see, generally, Feld [2003]). However, individuals who begin offending at an early age tend to have longer criminal careers and to commit more offenses on average than individuals who begin offending later in their lives (Farrington 2012). Thus, age at onset may be highly relevant to the risk and public safety calculus, thereby justifying the inclusion of some recognition of the juvenile record in the criminal history score.

These criminal history scoring rules operate behind the scenes: in the texts of statutes or guidelines, on case worksheets, and in case management software. They are not apparent from a given grid, which simply refers to an aggregate score or category. As a result, these various scoring, weighting, limitation, exclusion, and inclusion rules are out of public view and likely get taken for granted. The point we stress is that not all criminal history scores are the same. Jurisdictions include many factors that can inflate scores—guidelines policy decisions that translate into substantial increases in the punishment imposed.

## B. Magnitude of Criminal History Enhancements

Separate from how scores are calculated is the issue of how enhancements based on those scores are implemented. We refer to this as the "magnitude" of prior record enhancement. The magnitude of a PRE is the amount of additional punishment imposed at sentencing solely attributable to criminal history. Enhancement magnitude affects both dispositions (when a person receives a prison sentence rather than probation) and durations (when a person receives a longer prison term). To illustrate, consider figure 1, which shows two rows of the Minnesota standard grid.

The numbers in the grid cells represent the recommended punishment in months. At some levels, as represented by severity level 7, the grid addresses both the prison disposition decision and sentence duration. The three shaded cells on the far left side of row 7 indicate a recommendation of a stayed prison sentence, meaning the guidelines recom-

| OFFENSE SEVERITY LEVEL (Illustrative offenses) | | Criminal History Score | | | | | | |
|---|---|---|---|---|---|---|---|---|
| | | 0 | 1 | 2 | 3 | 4 | 5 | 6 or more |
| Aggravated robbery, 1st degree; burglary, 1st degree (with weapon or assault) | 8 | 48 41-57 | 58 50-69 | 68 58-81 | 78 67-93 | 88 75-105 | 98 84-117 | 108 92-129 |
| Felony DWI; financial exploitation of a vulnerable adult | 7 | 36 | 42 | 48 | 54 46-64 | 60 51-72 | 66 57-79 | 72 62-84 |

FIG. 1.—Excerpt from the Minnesota Sentencing Guidelines grid. Source: Minnesota Sentencing Guidelines Commission (2017, p. 79).

mend probation; the durations shown in these cells of 36, 42, or 48 months indicate the prison sentence that should be imposed if the offender does not successfully complete probation. For severity level 7, an offender with a criminal history score of 2 would receive probation and a suspended 48-month prison sentence while an offender with a criminal history score of 3 would receive a 54-month executed prison sentence. In a metaphorical sense, the difference in outcomes is night and day. In a literal sense, the difference is 1,620 nights and days in prison rather than on probation, all because of a single additional criminal history point.

For higher rows on the grid (e.g., severity level 8), all convicted offenders are recommended for executed prison sentences, regardless of criminal history. At all offense severity levels, higher criminal history scores receive longer recommended prison terms. An individual guilty of a level 8 offense who has a criminal history score of 6 or more is recommended for 108 months, which is 2.25 times longer than the 48 months recommended for a criminal history score of 0 ($108/48 = 2.25$). We refer to this durational measure as the "multiplier" and use it to quantify how much more prison time is imposed because of prior record. We average the multipliers for all of the severity levels on a grid to produce an overall multiplier figure for the grid as a whole.

Using this method, we compared 12 US grid-based guidelines systems and found a remarkable degree of variation in overall enhancement multipliers, which ranged from 1.7 to 14.4 with an average across all of the systems of 6.4 (Frase and Hester 2015). Figure 2 provides a bar chart with the results of this 12-jurisdiction comparison. In Washington, DC, offenders in the highest criminal history category have recommended prison terms 70 percent longer than offenders in the lowest history category, while in Kansas the high-history recommendation is 1,340 percent longer. The average multiplier of 6.4, for all 12 systems, represents a 540 percent increase from lowest to highest.

One can also look at these multipliers in terms of months and years in prison. The average multiplier of 6.4 means that, if a first offender is recommended for a particular crime to 18 months in prison, the high-history offender attracts a recommended sentence of 115 months for the same offense. The additional 97 months is attributable to the second offender's prior record—offenses for which he has already been found guilty, been sentenced, and satisfied his debt to society. Yet those past satisfied debts account for 84 percent of his total sentence.

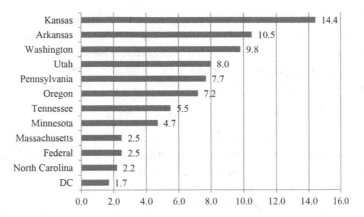

Fig. 2.—Criminal history enhancements, 12 jurisdictions. Calculations are based on published grids as of 2012. For jurisdictions with multiple grids, only the primary grid is reported. Source: Frase and Hester (2015).

Given this diversity of magnitudes, we question whether PREs can be justified as currently conceived and implemented in these 12 jurisdictions. If PREs can be supported on retributive grounds, surely some jurisdictions are fundamentally under- or overpunishing offenders with prior records. Similarly, if PREs are justified on utilitarian harm-prevention grounds, the vast magnitude of the ranges suggests that some jurisdictions must be under- or overpunishing in the name of risk reduction. But invoking an appropriate limit on PREs assumes that the imposition of a prior record enhancement is indeed justifiable. Despite the widespread intuitive appeal of PREs, convincingly articulating a justification for their imposition is a challenge.

In addition to the guidelines criminal history enhancements discussed above, it is important to keep in mind that prior convictions can also enhance sentence severity—often with an even greater magnitude—through policies such as three-strikes and habitual offender laws. For example, in three-strikes jurisdictions, offenders convicted of specified offenses can receive sentences as severe as 25 years to life, or life without parole, when they have the requisite prior felony record (see, e.g., *Ewing v. California*, 538 U.S. 11 [2003]). In many places the present and past felonies have to be serious violent offenses, but other places include drug offenses and nonviolent felonies. Habitual offender laws work in a similar way, though they usually target a specific category of repeat offending (e.g., burglaries).

Regardless of the mechanism—whether a three-strikes statute, habitual offender law, or guidelines criminal history score—the decision to enhance a penalty on the basis of past convictions must be supported by one or more accepted purposes of punishment. Such justification is often weak or entirely lacking.

## II. Questioning the Justifications

In this section we examine the justifications for criminal history enhancements. We first review attempts to justify enhancements using retributive punishment theory. We then turn to consequentialist theories and discuss how, even if a guidelines system's criminal history score is empirically validated as predictive of reoffending, the resulting increases in punishment must be tied to reductions in offending. We review the literature in this area and show that committal to prison and longer prison terms do not rehabilitate and do not seem to deter (specifically or generally). Worse, the prison experience may actually make some offenders more likely to reoffend than they would have been without a prison term. For some offenses such as drug trafficking, incapacitation does not reduce crime because of replacement effects. For other offenses, incapacitation may reduce crime but at significant cost and, often, with declining crime control benefits due to offender aging. In short, an across-the-board policy to enhance punishment for recidivists at all offending levels cannot be justified on either retributive or consequentialist grounds.

### A. The Unsettled Retributive Justifications

A retributive rationale for prior record enhancements is commonly assumed or asserted by sentencing commissions, judges, and other policy makers (Roberts 2015*a*), but the specific reasons for this rationale are rarely expounded. In this section we review the work of sentencing philosophers whose ideas have been widely divergent. Writers who accept a retributive justification for prior record enhancements disagree about whether and to what extent prior record can be viewed as an aggravating factor, or whether it should be only a mitigating factor for offenders with little or no criminal record. Some writers maintain that there is no convincing retributive justification at all.

Most desert theorists agree that a person's desert, or moral blameworthiness, depends on two basic factors (von Hirsch 1993, pp. 29–33). First is the seriousness of the harms that person has caused or risked by his criminal acts (offense factors). Second is the person's individual culpability in committing those acts (offender factors), as measured by such things as his or her degree of culpable intent (*mens rea*); good or bad motives; situational pressures; mental or emotional conditions that may diminish the offender's capacity to obey the law; and, for multi-offender crimes, that offender's greater or lesser role in the crime. Most desert-based theories have assumed that prior record enhancements must be justified by variations in the second (offender culpability) factor, though a few writers have suggested a harm-based retributive rationale.

Any retributive prior record enhancement theory must establish that prior convictions make the offender more blameworthy, in terms of increased offender culpability or increased offense harm, for the current offense. An offender with many prior convictions may very well be more blameworthy in an overall sense, but he cannot now be given more punishment for his prior crimes because he has already been punished for those; added punishment for these priors would be inconsistent with the values that underlie constitutional double jeopardy principles. The task for the retributive theorist is to articulate why an individual's past convictions, for which he has already been punished and satisfied his debt, now make that individual more culpable for the current offense.

1. *Reduced Culpability of Offenders with Little or No Prior Record.* Most of the retributive theories we discuss regard prior record as an aggravator: culpability increases with the number of past convictions. However, we first discuss theories that view the issue from the opposite angle: theories of mitigation that propose that offenders with few or no prior convictions deserve less punishment than would otherwise attach to a crime of this nature. Rather than aggravating for the recidivist, these theories mitigate for the novice. There are two basic varieties of this theory. One grants mitigation only to first offenders; the other grants a steadily declining degree of mitigation as offenders acquire more prior convictions, until at some point no mitigation applies (the latter version is sometimes referred to as progressive loss of mitigation; von Hirsch 2010). The basic distinction is whether a person gets a second chance or instead perhaps a third, fourth, or fifth chance, with the punishment increasing each time up until the point the offender receives the fully deserved punishment with no mitigation.

Both versions of this theory argue that first offenders can plausibly claim that their offense was out of character and that society should be less willing to fully convert its condemnation of the offender's criminal act into condemnation of the actor (von Hirsch 1985; Wasik and von Hirsch 1994; Ashworth 2005; Roberts 2010). Von Hirsch (1985, pp. 83–85) argues that, given human frailty, some sympathy and understanding are due to an offender's first "lapse" (although this argument seems more like an appeal to mercy than a claim of reduced culpability). Some writers would continue to permit mitigation for a third offense, or even a fourth, although the rationale for mitigation becomes strained at that point (Roberts 2010).

Each version of mitigation theory has advantages and disadvantages. Broader versions are more congruent with actual law and practice, which often call for a continuing escalation of penalties for each additional prior conviction. But, as noted above, such theories are unconvincing when applied to an offender with several prior convictions. The desert grounds for granting leniency to first offenders seem more convincing, and such leniency enjoys widespread acceptance among scholars (e.g., O'Neill, Maxfield, and Harer 2004). But an approach that considered only prior record when sentencing first offenders may confront strong opposition from practitioners and policy makers because it would invalidate much of current sentencing law and practice. Both kinds of reduced-desert theory have been criticized as inappropriate when sentencing serious crimes or crimes that involve extensive planning (Roberts 2012).

However, reduced-desert theories have one very important advantage over "aggravation" rationales, all of which posit enhanced culpability for second and subsequent crimes. The reduced-desert approach has a clear upper limit, based on desert factors associated with the current offense, whereas the logic of enhanced-desert theories seems to permit an open-ended escalation of sanction severity (von Hirsch 2010). The idea that the current offense should set an upper limit on sanction severity finds support in sentencing guidelines systems, all of which recognize an offense-based "cap" beyond which criminal history no longer raises the guidelines recommended sentence. For example, under the Minnesota guidelines the criminal history point score is capped at "6 or more" (see fig. 1). Thus, while an offender could potentially accumulate 10, 20, or more criminal history points, the PRE enhancement ceases after 6. Consider again the example offered in the introduction in which 97 percent of an offender's sentence is attributable not to the current criminal act but to prior record: at some point, an ever-increasing criminal history enhancement leads to absurdity. The next five sections examine "aggravation" theories, positing that repeat offenders become increasingly blameworthy with each additional prior conviction.

2. *Bad Character.* Character theories of enhanced punishment for repeat offenders seem to be based on the idea that such offenders have shown themselves to be more and more wicked and indifferent to the rights of others with each additional crime (Lee 2009, 2010). But punishing bad character violates the fundamental principle that people are punished for what they have done (and with what intent), not for who or what they are (Bagaric 2000; Tonry 2010). Indeed, punishment simply for one's status (e.g., being an addict) is unconstitutional (*Robinson v. California*, 370 U.S. 660 [1962]).

There are also practical problems in applying this approach: how much more blameworthy does the offender become with each additional crime, and is there any upper limit to penalty enhancements? Character theories can eventually lead to the conclusion that the offender is such an outlaw that he has forfeited any right to have his punishment limited by retributive, human rights, or other deontological principles. Such an open-ended forfeiture concept may indeed be the core rationale of three-strikes and repeat and career offender statutes, which almost all retributive scholars oppose.

3. *Heightened Notice and Defiance.* Two other aggravated-blame theories—notice and defiance—posit enhanced culpability for offenders who, after receiving formal condemnation of their prior criminal acts, ignore society's explicit warning and commit further crime in open defiance of these warnings and the law (Lee 2009). Both types of theory appear to assume that the current offense was committed after conviction and sentence for the prior crime; notice theory may also assume substantial similarity between the prior and the current offense. The offender was previously warned: "don't commit this crime." However, criminal record enhancement rules are often much broader in each of these respects. Thus, many sentencing guidelines systems count as "priors" convictions that were entered after the current offense was committed (Frase 2015*b*). And almost all courts consider prior convictions even if they were for very different kinds of crimes (although similar priors sometimes receive extra weight; Roberts 2015*b*). Notice theory also seems inapplicable to very serious crimes such as murder and armed robbery, as to which moral values and legal prohibitions are not seriously in doubt. And the theory provides no clear rationale to impose

further enhancement of punishment severity for a third, fourth, or fifth offense.

As for defiance theories, there is considerable doubt that such a rationale is acceptable in a legal system in which people are punished for their acts, not their thoughts and attitudes (von Hirsch 1985, pp. 79–80). One possible answer to this criticism might invoke an expressive theory (e.g., Hampton 1984) according to which offenders are punished to repudiate their false moral claim to act without regard to the rights of others or of society; arguably, such false claims grow more offensive with each additional crime. As we discuss below, a version of this rationale for enhancement can also be supported under a consequentialist, "denunciation" theory. But under either type of defiance theory it is entirely unclear how much enhancement is allowed, and with what limits.

4. *Omission Theories.*   This theory is elaborated in detail by Youngjae Lee (2009, 2010) and has also been advocated by other writers (MacPherson 2002; Bennett 2010, 2012; Dagger 2012). It argues that a repeat offender's culpability is enhanced because he has failed to take appropriate action to control his criminal tendencies in light of his earlier crime, conviction, and punishment. Lee's theory seems to assume that, because of the prior convictions, the offender is or ought to be aware of his or her heightened risk of offending. From this actual or constructive awareness Lee derives a heightened duty on the parts of offenders to rearrange their lives in ways that ensure they will avoid further criminality. Christopher Bennett (2010) restates Lee's theory in terms of a communicative theory; on this view, punishment symbolizes how sorry an offender ought to feel and, therefore, how strong an obligation he or she has not to offend again.

Compared to some of the desert theories previously discussed, this theory has the potential to better explain rules that steadily escalate sentence severity as the number of prior convictions increases: the duty of the offender to control his criminal tendencies becomes steadily more important and obvious. This theory also offers a workable formula for determining how much to enhance the repeat offender's sentence and when to discontinue further enhancement for additional prior convictions: since the theory blames offenders for failing to address their manifest risk of reoffending and since risking harm is less culpable than actually causing harm, the added penalty for the former should not exceed the penalty for the latter (Lee 2010, p. 67). In practical terms, this translates into a rule of thumb that prior record, no matter how extensive, should never account for more than half of the total sentence. Stated differently, offenders with the longest records should not receive penalties more than twice as severe as penalties given to first offenders who commit the same offense (Frase 2013, p. 185).

However, omission theory suffers from some of the defects of aggravation theories discussed above: it seems to apply mainly to offenders whose past and current crimes are similar, or at least caused by the same risk factors, and it seems to explain only prior record enhancements involving a conviction entered before the current offense was committed. In addition, such a theory might require courts to engage in difficult assessments of the extent to which the offender tried but was unable to control his criminal tendencies. More fundamentally, the theory does not convincingly explain why convicted offenders should be deemed to have a higher duty than anyone else to avoid committing crimes. Finally, the theory violates the general principle that liability for an omission is exceptional in the criminal laws of the United States and other common law countries and can exist only where a duty to perform the required act has previously been clearly established by statute, case law, or other means (Tonry 2010).

5. *Reserved-Desert Theory.*   Other writers have suggested an enhancement rationale based on the idea that, if the offender did not receive all of his deserved punishment in one or more prior sentencings, the unimposed "reserved" severity is available to enhance his punishment for the current crime (Morris 1982, p. 185; Roberts 1997*b*, pp. 353–54; 2008, p. 226). However, this theory finds no support in traditional recidivist enhancements, which have never been scaled or limited by a reserved-desert concept. Offenders receive prior record enhancements without regard to the degree of leniency given them in prior cases (Davis 1985, p. 41). Moreover, the theory yields perverse results; it would dictate that offenders who were so culpable that they were fully punished in prior sentencings cannot receive any recidivist premium. This theory would also be quite difficult to put into effect and, for both practical and legal reasons, could operate only prospectively (Frase 2010). Courts would have to begin making express findings of full desert and reserved desert at each sentencing; until this became routine, a later court would have no way of knowing how much desert was reserved in prior sentencings. Such findings would also be needed to avoid double jeopardy issues in order to make clear that later sentence enhancements are not additional punishment for prior crimes; added punishment would be deemed to have

already been imposed, but suspended, for the earlier crimes. And until the new system was fully in place, "old system" convictions lacking any express finding of reserved desert might have to be ignored.

6. *Greater-Harm Theory.* Most desert theorists seem to assume that variations in the actual or threatened harm caused by a new offense do not explain or justify prior record enhancements; the harm to the victim of the current offense, burglary, for example, is deemed to be the same regardless of the offender's prior conviction record (Roberts 2010). But some writers have suggested that an offender's prior record of crime may affect how we view his most recent criminal acts (Durham 1987; Frase 2010; Tamburrini 2012). The repeat offender's current burglary is perhaps more disturbing, to both the victim and society, in light of—and in proportion to—his prior crimes. We may conclude that this offender poses a heightened threat to all of us, and heightened to a degree roughly proportional to his prior record. This conclusion makes us fearful and reduces our level of trust in others; it also forces victims and public officials to take extra precautions against this offender, which may be expensive or inconvenient. These are real harms associated with the current offense, foreseeably caused by the offender's past and current crimes.

One problem in applying this theory is that the supposed greater harms associated with a recidivist's crime may be too speculative to permit a proportionately scaled sentence enhancement. Another problem is the theory's potential to justify a limitless escalation of sentence severity: our feelings of fear and distrust, and the extra precautions that victims and officials feel compelled to take, could continue and accelerate with increases in the offender's prior record, eventually yielding a penalty far in excess of the seriousness of the actual crime being sentenced. The greater-harm theory does not provide any practical formula for deciding how much to enhance for each additional prior offense and when to stop adding enhancements.

7. *Rejection of Any Retributive Rationale.* A number of writers have argued that an offender's prior conviction record is unrelated to his desert and should have no bearing on the severity of his current sentence (Fletcher 1978; Singer 1979; Davis 1985; Duff 2001; Tonry 2010; Dagger 2012; Bagaric 2014). Another group of writers have argued that many offenders with extensive conviction records are actually less culpable than offenders with fewer priors, since the former suffer from psychological, social, or economic handicaps that make it much more difficult for them to obey the law, even after being repeatedly punished

(Corlett 2012; Petersen 2012; Lippke 2015). Indeed, many of these handicaps are due to unjust societal conditions, and some are the predictable result of prior punishments imposed on the offender. In short, these writers conclude that desert is unaffected (or may even be mitigated) by prior convictions.

The view that desert is not increased by prior convictions has much to commend it given the problems with desert-based enhancement theories. But when combined with a strict view of desert, this approach seems to rule out any consideration of prior record in determining sentence severity, even as a basis to mitigate penalties for first offenders. This view is thus likely to be ignored by sentencing policy makers and practitioners and might even discredit desert theory so much as to lead them to ignore desert principles entirely (Frase 2010, 2013).

8. *Intuition and Public Opinion.*   Finally, we address the apparent intuition among the public that prior crimes make a person more blameworthy.[4] As Tonry (2004, p. 117) notes, "Many people have an intuition that offenders who have previously been convicted of a crime should be dealt with more harshly." Research in this area has generated important insights into community attitudes, but there are also a number of unanswered questions. It seems that the public supports prior record enhancements within limits, but the reasons for the support are an unknown mix of intuition, retribution, and perceived crime control benefits. Consequently, the fundamental takeaways are that the public supports prior record enhancements but also supports limiting them to an extent not reflected in most guidelines systems.

Studies across the United States and other nations including Canada, the United Kingdom, Australia, Japan, and Russia have found that the public would impose harsher sentences when the offender has prior convictions (e.g., Knight 1965; Doob and Roberts 1983; Mande and English 1989; Sanders and Hamilton 1992; Doble 1995; Applegate et al. 1996; Mattinson and Mirrlees-Black 2000; Tufts and Roberts 2002; for a review of the research, see Roberts [2008, chap. 8]).[5] This finding

---

[4] When asked about important sentencing factors, respondents in Britain, Canada, Australia, Belgium, and the United States all place previous convictions high on the list of factors, usually just behind the seriousness of the crime (e.g., Doob and Roberts 1983; Indermaur 1990; Roberts and Hough 2011).

[5] The basic finding that people support prior record enhancements needs to be seen in context. Research in several countries has shown that people overestimate criminal recidivism rates and underestimate the proportion of offenders who appear for sentencing for

alone establishes that the "flat rate" desert model, which excludes prior crimes, is inconsistent with public opinion but fails to resolve the question of whether the public endorses the progressive loss of mitigation model or an aggravation theory, or is using prior record as a proxy for consequentialist, risk-based reasons.

A sample of respondents in the United Kingdom were randomly assigned to read one of three descriptions of a case in which the offender had no, two, or five previous convictions and then impose a sentence (Roberts 2008). The results were consistent with an aggravation theory, but the premiums did not increase in a linear fashion. The clearest distinctions emerged between the first and the second scenarios. Respondents sentencing the first offender assigned, on average, a sentence of 28.6 months, compared to 40.9 months for the offender with two priors. Thus sentence lengths increased by almost half for two prior convictions. However, the increase between the second and third scenarios was only 12 percent (from 40.95 to 46.22 months). That the magnitude of the recidivist premium is far more modest at higher levels of criminal history suggests that the public is sensitive to the threat to conviction offense proportionality if sentences escalate indefinitely to reflect the number of prior crimes. The public would appear to favor a modified version of aggravation in which sentence severity rises to reflect the number of prior convictions but is subject to proportional limits. The importance of proportionality emerges from a number of other studies. The results can also be interpreted as consistent with a progressive loss of mitigation argument.

Several surveys have found that as the recidivist premium results in increasingly disproportionate punishments, public support declines. Subjects in research by Finkel et al. (1996) were asked to sentence a number of cases, some of which involved first offenders, others recidivists. Responses suggested that people sentenced according to a proportionality-based logic that assigned some limited role to the offender's previous convictions. The researchers concluded that "past priors matter and are taken into account in a punishment calculus: Participants did not limit their punishment to the last [i.e., instant] offense when they knew there

---

the first time (Roberts and White 1986; Stalans and Diamond 1990; Redondo, Luque, and Funes 1996; Roberts 1996). Support for these enhancements also likely reflects an unjustified faith in the effectiveness of individual deterrence and a lack of awareness of the costs associated with robust prior record sentencing enhancements.

were six priors, but neither did they dramatically, geometrically, or exponentially escalate their punishments because of priors. What we did find is that they sentence in an additive way, with retribution and proportionalism in mind, but refraining from excess" (pp. 481–82).[6]

In a more recent study we investigated two key questions relating to prior record enhancements using a national US-based sample (Hester et al. 2017). We examined whether there should be "look-back" limits on prior crimes and whether criminal history scores should include juvenile priors. Public responses related to both research questions suggested that most guidelines are more punitive and less forgiving than the general public.

Respondents were asked whether they would favor a new law that would prevent judges from considering "old offenses" for the purposes of sentencing for a current crime. Sixty-five percent of respondents supported the policy while 35 percent preferred to count all offenses, regardless of their age. Respondents who were in favor of a temporal limit were asked a follow-up question of how long they thought a prior conviction should remain relevant for the purposes of enhancing subsequent sentences, with potential responses of 5, 10, 15, and 20 years. Almost one-quarter of the subsample chose 5 years with a further 53 percent selecting 10 years. Look-back limits vary considerably across the United States, but this pattern of responses is more forgiving than current guideline systems. These responses demonstrate clear public support for look-back limits on prior crimes.

We also asked respondents to sentence hypothetical cases. For instance, we asked respondents to sentence an offender and, using a within-subjects design, asked them how changing aspects of the prior record would change their sentence recommendations. This vignette involved a current conviction for possession of stolen property; the respondents first sentenced the offender on the basis of information that he was a first-time offender and then received follow-up questions asking how their sentence would change if he had a prior auto theft conviction 1 year earlier. The question was repeated two more times with the age of the prior auto theft changing to 9 and then 14 years. Fifty-six percent of respondents would have increased the sentence for the 1-year-old prior,

<hr/>

[6] See also Applegate et al. (1996) for research showing the limits on public support for recidivist statutes.

but that fell significantly to 21 percent and then 13 percent when the respondents were asked to assume the prior was 9 and 14 years old. The public was less punitive as the age of the prior offense increased. Again, this suggests that the guidelines approach that assigns the same weight to all priors is inconsistent with, and more punitive than, public opinion.

In addition, we asked respondents about limitations on juvenile crimes. Seventy-one percent were in favor of a policy that would restrict the use of sentencing enhancements for prior offenses committed while a juvenile and 29 percent against. Taken together these findings suggest that current guidelines in many states are inconsistent with public attitudes: they count prior crimes that the public would disregard, and they assign full weight to previous convictions that the public would discount.

Overall, the public opinion research suggests that the public overestimates both recidivism rates and the effectiveness of deterrent sentencing strategies and underestimates the influence of environmental causes of crime (Roberts and White 1986; Redondo and Funes 1996). Public sentencing preferences become more punitive when the offender has prior convictions. There are limits, however; the public are sensitive to proportionality in sentencing, and they oppose the more robust enhancements. The public support the use of look-back limits and restricting the inclusion of juvenile priors. They also enhance punishment based on older prior crimes less than for recent crimes. In all these respects, most guidelines show some inconsistencies with public attitudes.

We recognize that proposals for drastic changes to PRE practices may be met with strident opposition based in large part on the strong intuition associated with their use. Both scholars and policy makers must think carefully about the proper counsel to take from intuition. As Tonry (2010, pp. 108–9) observes, in the not-so-distant past, common intuitions supported the right of husbands to discipline wives, the treatment of homosexuality as a mental disorder, and the belief "that the sky would fall if black people had equal access to public accommodation." The better approach would be to treat intuition as a philosophical proposition or an implicit hypothesis. We should then be able to offer logical proofs that bear out the proposition for retributive rationales, or engage in empirical hypothesis tests, where appropriate, for consequentialist positions.

9. *Summary.* Of all the desert-based theories, the grant of leniency to first offenders offers the most persuasive arguments and has the broadest support, at least when the current crime is not very serious. In exceptional

cases these arguments may also support leniency for an offender with a single prior conviction. In our view, developed more fully below, sentence enhancements for repeat offenders should be limited because desert is increased only modestly, if at all, as the number of prior convictions increases. Desert principles also require such enhancements to be reduced or eliminated if the offender has manifestly taken steps to try to address the causes of his or her criminality. And because desert principles give predominant weight to the goal of making punishment severity proportional to the seriousness of the conviction offense, recidivist enhancements must be "capped," as is done in almost all sentencing guidelines systems; at some point, additional prior convictions should not further increase sentence severity.[7]

Indeed, we would go further than most guidelines systems in this respect in order to reduce the number of cases in which repeat offenders receive penalties more severe than offenders convicted of more serious crimes. Our position is designed to be consistent with the view that retributive principles define just punishment, within a fairly narrow minimum-to-maximum range. Of course, if one adopts a more flexible, "limiting retributive" model (see, e.g., Morris 1974; Morris and Tonry 1990; Frase 2013; American Law Institute 2017), first offenders and repeat offenders may be subject to a broader range of deserved penalties. But even under that model, prior record enhancements must be much more limited than they are now to maintain offense-based sentence proportionality.

## B.  Consequentialist Justifications

Apart from retributive rationales, it is possible that consequentialist (or utilitarian) theories of punishment justify the imposition of PREs. Punishment in the name of rehabilitation, specific deterrence, general deter-

---

[7] Of course, the benefit of PRE "caps" depends on how they are structured; statutory maximums also provide a kind of offense-based severity cap, yet these maximums are often so high (because they are based on the worst-imaginable case) and so haphazard (because they are enacted at different times) that they do little to promote sentencing proportionality. In most guidelines systems, however, recommended sentence ranges for offenders in the highest criminal history category fall short of applicable statutory maximums, and they fall well below those in systems with low or moderate PRE multipliers (highest-history vs. lowest-history sentence severity). Granted, some systems have very high multipliers; but many of those multipliers would be even higher if PREs were not capped. Finally, in most guidelines systems the capped highest-history ranges are not haphazard; they are scaled in at least rough proportion to offense severity ranking under the guidelines.

rence, incapacitation, and denunciation all share the same goal of reducing offending—of either the person being punished or other would-be offenders. If a punishment strategy systematically fails to reduce the harm from crime from one of these or similar mechanisms, then the punishment is gratuitous and cannot be justified on consequentialist grounds. Assuming that a given criminal history score distinguishes among different levels of recidivism risk,[8] the question is then, How does the additional punishment imposed because of prior record reduce crime or harm?

1. *Prison Does Not Rehabilitate.*   Sentencing offenders to prison in and of itself, of course, does nothing to rehabilitate them, although some programs administered in prison may do so. As currently designed, PRE policies are simply unrelated to rehabilitation since criminal history increases punitiveness, and any assignment to programming occurs separately. In some instances, the offender might be sentenced to a treatment program consistent with guidelines recommendations, but such decisions are not triggered by PREs; if anything, having a prior offense (or a certain type of prior offense) is more likely to make the offender ineligible for treatment programs.

2. *Longer Prison Terms Do Not Deter.*   There is very little research on the deterrent effects of PRE-based marginal increases in punishment severity. However, studies of non-PRE increases in punishment are instructive. Nagin, Cullen, and Jonson (2009) conducted a comprehensive review of 73 empirical studies that examined whether the experience of punishment served to deter future offending. They concluded that while the "scientific jury is still out . . . the great majority of studies point to a

---

[8] This assumption warrants investigation. Criminal history scores may not account for different levels of risk of reoffending among groups based on their prior records (e.g., are offenders with a criminal history score of 4 more likely to reoffend than those with a criminal history score of 3?). For the most part, criminal history scores were developed in an ad hoc, "back-of-the-envelope," fashion (Tonry 2010). The one exception is the federal system, which based its criminal history score on two validated risk assessment instruments (US Sentencing Commission 2004; Frase et al. 2015). For other jurisdictions, since scores were not developed through empirical analysis, whether the cutoffs that divide categories of offenders represent differences in the likelihood of reoffending is anybody's guess: empirical validation of the score is the only way to assess predictive validity. Given the diverse practices in what factors are included and how they are weighted, it seems likely that not all criminal history scores are created equally for purposes of prediction. This research gap needs attention. Surely the highest-history offenders will be more likely to recidivate than first offenders, but whether each step up in prior record score (1 to 2, 2 to 3, etc.) represents distinctions among classes of offenders is a more dubious proposition; since those distinctions directly translate to more punishment, jurisdictions should undertake the task to validate their scores.

null or criminogenic effect of the prison experience on subsequent offending" (p. 178).[9] Nagin, Cullen, and Jonson discuss several reasons why the experience of prison may not serve as an effective deterrent. Under an economic model that explains behavior as the product of cost-benefit analyses, the prison experience may not be so unpleasant as to alter subsequent behavior. Offenders may also engage in a version of the "gambler's fallacy," believing that since they were previously caught and punished it is highly unlikely they would be so unlucky as to get caught and punished again. In addition, if a person's decision-making is not guided by a cost-benefit analysis, but by emotions or other mechanisms instead (see Katz 1988), then the negative effects of the prison experience would be irrelevant to future unlawful behavior. Whatever the mechanics, neither receiving a prison sentence rather than a nonprison sentence nor getting a longer sentence rather than a shorter one appears to reduce the reoffending of the person punished. What is worse, the prison experience may make individuals more likely to reoffend than they would otherwise have been with a nonprison (or shorter prison) sentence (Nagin, Cullen, and Jonson 2009; Travis, Western, and Redburn 2014).

Similarly, increased punishment does not appear to have a general deterrent effect. Several recent reviews of studies covering a range of methodological approaches come to this same conclusion (Durlauf and Nagin 2009; Nagin 2013; Travis, Western, and Redburn 2014; Frase and Roberts, forthcoming). As Nagin (2013) observes, there is especially little evidence that increasing already long prison sentences yields any general deterrent effects, which leads him to question three-strikes statutes, life without the possibility of parole sentences, and other long mandatory sentencing policies. We would add PRE policies to this list: they mechanically make sentences longer without any evidence that they make the public safer. Ultimately, Durlauf and Nagin (2009, p. 81) conclude, "The key empirical conclusion . . . is that there is relatively little reliable evidence of variation in the severity of punishment . . . having a substantial deterrent effect." Accordingly, to the extent that sentencing guidelines impose increasing sanctions on the basis of higher prior records,

---

[9] Subsequent studies on the specific deterrent effects of punishment continue to support these conclusions (Meade et al. 2013; Nagin and Snodgrass 2013; Cochran, Mears, and Bales 2014; Mitchell et al. 2016).

for reasons of deterrence, they do so without support of empirical evidence. Perhaps there are contexts within the criminal law in which the interactions of population type, punishment type, and dosage converge for beneficial deterrent effect. But these potential micro-specifications aside, the takeaway from the current state of the research is that enhancing punishment—through PREs or by other means—does not enhance deterrence.

3. *The Costs of Incapacitation Mostly Outweigh the Benefits.* By definition, longer prison terms resulting from PREs incapacitate individuals for longer. Undoubtedly, some crime is averted on this basis. But attempting to justify linear, incremental prior record enhancements for all but the most serious and high-rate offenders stretches incapacitation theory beyond the bounds of its logic.

It is questionable whether the evidence supports incapacitation as a crime reduction policy at all—even in a highly selective form—because of the difficulty in establishing any larger effects on crime rates. Research findings that attempt to measure the crime control effects of incapacitation vary. The National Academy of Sciences panel on mass incarceration (Travis, Western, and Redburn 2014) concluded that the preponderance is that increasing the size of prison populations does lead to less crime. But at some point the marginal effect flattens out: after the quintupling of the prison population over the past half century, US jurisdictions are probably past that point of diminishing returns.

At the very least, it is difficult to assess any current crime control value of incarceration. Studies usually frame results as elasticities, meaning they estimate the percentage of crime reduction for every 1 percent increase in the imprisonment rate. Elasticity estimates vary by study, from as high as $-.69$ or $-.93$ to as low as $-.06$ (Abrams 2013; Travis, Western, and Redburn 2014). An elasticity of $-1$ would indicate a 1 percent decrease in crime for every 1 percent increase in imprisonment; an elasticity of $-.2$ would indicate a decrease of 0.2 percent in crime for every increase of 1 percent in prison—or, by extrapolation, a 1 percent decrease in crime for every 5 percent increase in imprisonment. As the National Academy review discusses, simulation studies suggest an elasticity range of $-.1$ to $-.3$ while econometric studies range from findings of no difference to $-.4$. If, for example, the true effect were $-.2$ (the midpoint of both of those ranges), that would mean a 5 percent increase in the prison population would be required to achieve a corresponding 1 percent decline in the crime rate. However, as the National Academy of

Sciences recently reported, "we cannot arrive at a precise estimate, or even a range of estimates, of the magnitude of the effect of incarceration on crime rates" (Travis, Western, and Redburn 2014, p. 141).

The academy panel reviewed several reasons why incapacitation appears to have a modest (and potentially null) effect on crime. First, for some crimes, we should expect no crime savings through incapacitation due to replacement effects (Piquero and Blumstein 2007). When one individual is imprisoned for drug distribution, another simply steps up to fill the market vacuum. Second, many crimes involve co-offending—especially among young offenders. If a criminal act is a group effort, removing one group member will not necessarily result in any crime savings. Third, as the scale of incarceration increases, the crime prevention returns of incapacitation diminish because the highest-rate offenders will already have been skimmed off (Travis, Western, and Redburn 2014).

Incapacitation is also an overly broad mechanism in that it captures some lower-rate offenders for whom the costs of societal removal fail to match the benefits and holds many once violent or high-rate offenders for far too long, well past the ages when they would have naturally desisted from crime. For most, the frequency of criminal behavior peaks in the teens and early 20s and declines steadily thereafter (Hirschi and Gottfredson 1983; Sampson and Laub 1995; Piquero, Farrington, and Blumstein 2007). By the time offenders reach their 40s and 50s, their rates of offending will have substantially declined and most will have desisted entirely, or soon will. Even the small subset of "chronic," "career," or "life course persistent" offenders display this pattern and eventually desist, albeit more slowly (Sampson and Laub 1995; US Sentencing Commission 2004, p. 28). Moreover, many guidelines PRE rules largely or entirely ignore recent gaps or declines in offending. Yet the emerging "redemption" literature shows that, on average, once an offender goes approximately 7 years without an arrest, his or her likelihood of being subsequently rearrested is roughly the same as that of the population that has never been arrested (Kurlycheck, Brame, and Bushway 2006, 2007; Blumstein and Nakamura 2009; but see Bushway, Nieuwbeerta, and Blokland 2011).

For all of these reasons, incapacitation is a poor theoretical justification for prior record enhancements, at least when they are mechanically and incrementally applied to all repeat offenders. The logic of incapacitation, which may or may not hold up for high-rate recidivists, simply does not extend to broad-based PRE policies. For the vast majority of offenders—

those convicted of low- and medium-severity offenses—attempts to justify PREs through incapacitation are misplaced. Imposing a 30-year sentence on all first-time misdemeanants would also prevent some future criminal activity, but with absurd consequences to individual offenders, their families, and communities, and the criminal justice infrastructure as well. Any differences between such a policy and the use of PREs to incapacitate offenders at every level of a guidelines regime are differences in degree, not in kind. Incapacitation fails to provide a convincing rationalization for existing PREs; the magnitude and frequency of these enhancements are vastly greater than needed to achieve legitimate incapacitation goals in a cost-effective manner.

4. *Any Crime Control Benefits of Denunciation Are Uncertain.* Many writers have argued that punishment prevents crime through processes quite different from those examined above, processes that depend on internalized values rather than fear of punishment, physical restraint, or addressing criminogenic factors. This theory is most often called denunciation, but it has also been referred to as moral education, positive general prevention, or the communicative, educative, or expressive function of punishment (Ewing 1929; Hart 1958; Andenaes 1966; Feinberg 1970; Greenawalt 2001; Robinson 2008). The theory posits that criminal penalties serve to reinforce important social norms of law-abiding behavior and relative crime seriousness: punishment conveys the wrongfulness of the crime and also the degree of wrong and harm relative to other crimes and offenders. These norms guide and restrain behavior even when the chances of detection, conviction, and serious punishment are slight.[10]

Although denunciation theory has traditionally focused entirely on the seriousness of the offender's conviction offense, a version of this theory might provide a further crime control rationale for criminal history enhancements. The question becomes, What norms are being rein-

---

[10] Denunciation theory has also been justified on nonconsequentialist grounds—as something that is the right thing to do even if it has no demonstrable beneficial effects (von Hirsch 1976, 1985, 1993; Duff 1986, 2001; Kleinig 1998; Markel 2009). Whether consequentialist or not, most versions of the theory see it as a positive goal and justification for punishment. But under both the original and the recently revised *Model Penal Code* sentencing provisions, this concept is viewed as a negative, limiting principle. See American Law Institute (1962), sec. 7.01(1)(c); (2017), sec. 6.06(2) (a sentence of incarceration may be imposed when a lesser penalty would "depreciate the seriousness" of the offender's crime).

forced when we punish recidivists more severely? The most plausible recidivist-denunciation theory would seem to be that we need to counter the destructive messages that repeat offenders are sending. Such offenders, by their disregard for the censure and penalties imposed at the time of their prior sentences, risk lowering respect for the law and the courts, undercutting the positive expressive functions of conviction and sentencing.

However, there are several problems with extending denunciation theory in this way. Part of the appeal of denunciation is its tacit reassurance that if an offender shows disrespect for the law through repeated offending, the legal system will answer in kind by elevating punishment. A counter to that implicit need to elevate punishment is for society simply to accept the transaction: if we set an appropriate punishment range for an offense and a particular offender chooses to reoffend and receive that punishment, the law has done its job and no further escalation is needed. The offender will get the appropriate and deserved punishment each time. Because he is being punished, the public will not perceive an erosion in respect for the rule of law, and accordingly there is no need for escalated punishment. In addition, this extended denunciation could undercut traditional denunciation by reducing the proportionality of the punishment of the current crime. We could end up contradicting the positive expressive value of punishment by imposing longer sentences for less serious offenses due to PREs. In any case, the crime control effects of denunciation are diffuse and long-term, which makes those effects difficult if not impossible to measure with any precision (or to separate from crime control benefits produced by other mechanisms). In short, denunciation theory does not provide a convincing crime control rationale for recidivist enhancements.

5. *Summary.* Despite the intuitive appeal of PRE policies, it is difficult to justify them on retributive grounds except perhaps to justify mitigation for first offenders. There is certainly no cohesive, prevailing retributive theory of aggravation that would justify the linear increases in PREs found in guidelines systems. Nor does rehabilitation or deterrence provide strong justification for these increases. The best current evidence suggests that, if anything, offenders become more likely to recidivate when exposed to more severe sanctions, not less. Some view incapacitation as a compelling policy when used selectively for a small subpopulation of violent and high-rate offenders, but incapacitation does

not justify increasing the punishment of all repeat offenders in the manner effected by PREs.


### III.  Adverse Consequences

While the intended crime-reduction effects of PREs are not realized or achievable, a number of undesirable unintended consequences carry widespread impacts. PREs exacerbate racial disparities, confound offense-based proportionality, undermine prison-resource prioritization, and compound issues related to fiscal strains on the prison system and taxpayers. We explore each of these in turn.


### A.  Racial Disproportionality

Criminal history enhancements contribute significantly to racial disproportionality in prison populations. Prior research, from both guidelines and nonguidelines jurisdictions, has found consistent racial differences in prior record (Frase 2009; Frase and Hester, forthcoming a). And prior record, in turn, has consistently been found to exert a strong effect on sentencing severity (Weidner, Frase, and Schultz 2005; Wang et al. 2013; Ulmer, Painter-Davis, and Tinik 2016). First, PREs cause higher proportions of black offenders to be sentenced to prison rather than a community sentence (Frase 2009; Frase and Hester, forthcoming a). Second, criminal history affects decisions such as sentence length and the likelihood of receiving a favorable departure from a guidelines recommendation (Frase 2009). All told, the combined effects of prison commitment and sentence length decisions work to the substantial disadvantage of black offenders. Research from Minnesota, for example, shows that the percentage of black individuals receiving an executed prison term is almost 50 percent greater than the percentage for white individuals, and well over half of this racial difference is due to black individuals having higher criminal history scores (the remainder is due to differences in offense severity and eligibility for mandatory prison terms; Frase and Hester, forthcoming a). The average length of executed prison sentences for black Minnesota offenders is about 20 percent longer than the average for white offenders. The average prison months imposed on black offenders in Minnesota for 2012–14 was 73 percent greater than the average for white offenders (16.7 vs. 9.7, respectively). About half of the racial differences in executed prison durations and prison months were due to black individuals having higher criminal history scores.

## B. *Undermining Offense-Based Proportionality*

Sentencing proportionality is an important goal of almost all guidelines reforms; that is, more serious crimes should receive more severe sanctions. Offense-based proportionality is particularly important under a retributive theory of punishment, but it also has crime control value (Frase 2013). Penalties that increase with crime seriousness send valuable standard-setting and norm-reinforcing messages about the relative gravity of different crimes. Under guidelines, sentence severity depends primarily on two factors: the severity of the conviction offense and the magnitude of the offender's criminal history score. Accordingly, the greater the magnitude of criminal history enhancements, the less the sentence depends on the severity of the offense being sentenced, lowering the proportionality of punishment for that offense.

Frase and Hester (forthcoming *b*) examine levels of proportionality on guidelines grids using a method that measures how much criminal history enhancements undercut offense proportionality through overlapping sentencing ranges, that is, when low-level offenses carry more severe punishment than higher-severity offenses because of criminal history enhancements. For example, in Minnesota the highest-history offenders convicted at severity level 1 on the main grid (e.g., fleeing a police officer) have a recommended executed prison sentence of 19 months, which is more severe than the recommended 18-month suspended sentence specified for lowest-history offenders convicted at severity level 5 (e.g., residential burglary), four levels higher on the grid. Of the Minnesota main grid's 77 total cells, only 23 percent are what Frase and Hester define as "fully proportionate," meaning that the recommended sentences for offenders convicted in those cells are more severe than all recommended sentences at lower offense severity levels on the grid and are also less severe than all recommended sentences at higher levels on the grid. Notably, most of these fully proportionate cells are at the top of the Minnesota grid, where few offenders are sentenced (because most offenders are convicted of lower-severity crimes). In 2014, only 2 percent of Minnesota offenders sentenced on that grid were convicted in a cell with a fully proportionate prison duration as defined above.

## C. *Undermining Prison-Use Priorities*

Many jurisdictions give higher priority to incarceration of offenders convicted of violent crimes and use community-based options to sanction nonviolent offenders.[11] But nonviolent offenders often have high recidivism rates (Langan and Levin 2002), so they tend to accumulate higher criminal history scores. PREs thus greatly increase the number of nonviolent offenders who receive recommended prison sentences, while also increasing the lengths of their prison terms, undermining the violent crimes priority policy.

To demonstrate the effect of criminal history on prison commit recommendations, it is useful to focus on offenders in what we refer to as "zone 2" of a guidelines grid; these are offenders convicted of low- or medium-severity crimes who are recommended for a prison sentence only because their criminal history score pushed them across the grid (Frase and Hester 2015). Frase and Hester (forthcoming *b*) report that in Minnesota, North Carolina, and Washington in 2014, at least two-thirds of the zone 2 offenders were sentenced for a non–person offense. Moreover, even many of the "person" crimes were not particularly violent. For example, 80 percent of Minnesota main-grid zone 2 person offenders convicted in 2014 were ranked at severity level 4 or lower on that grid (out of 11 levels) and were not charged with having a dangerous weapon. Yet most of these offenders were sent to prison because of their prior record status.

Targeting high-risk offenders for imprisonment is another commonly endorsed sentencing priority (Frase 2015*a*; Roberts 2015*a*), although, as we discussed above, it is easy to exaggerate the crime-preventive benefits of such a policy. Criminal history enhancements might help achieve this goal if prior record closely approximated an offender's recidivism risk and if the additional punishment imposed were effective in counteracting that higher risk. But many offenders with higher criminal history scores are already well past their peak offending years or will pass that peak before they finish serving a prison term. These aging offenders become increasingly costly to support in prison (Fellner and Vinck 2012). High-magnitude criminal history enhancements thus are likely to contribute to an aged, low-risk, high-cost inmate population; sending many older offenders to prison results in a mismatch between criminal history enhancement and efficient risk management. At the same time PREs overpredict risk for some younger offenders, further increasing the num-

---

[11] See, e.g., Minnesota Sentencing Guidelines Commission (1984, pp. v, 97); Delaware Sentencing Accountability Commission (2015, p. 22; goal of "incapacitation of the violence-prone offender"); Kansas Sentencing Commission (2009, p. 2; goal of "promoting public safety by incarcerating violent offenders").

bers of low-risk offenders sent to or kept in prison. This occurs because these enhancements are imposed according to a formula that disregards the lower risk level of some offenders.

Finally, it is important to clarify what risk is being examined. Presumably, the greatest public and policy maker concerns would be over violent, sexual, and other traumatizing and physically harmful offenses (Gottfredson and Gottfredson 1990; Vigorita 2003). But recidivism analysis almost always examines offending in much broader terms, often defining recidivism as rearrest (regardless of whether a conviction follows) for any nontraffic offense. Thus, many offenders who are designated as "high-risk" are likely to commit only additional drug crimes, low-level property crimes, or public order offenses; they are not likely to commit crimes that involve violence or traumatizing victimization. The public and policy makers would do well to consider carefully whether sound policy demands that these likely low-level recidivists be imprisoned at a cost of tens of thousands of dollars per inmate per year.

## D. Fiscal Impacts

Because PREs increase the number of individuals going to prison and the lengths of their prison terms, they come with a substantial fiscal cost. Frase and Hester (forthcoming *b*) estimated the costs attributable to PREs in Kansas, Minnesota, and North Carolina for 2014. They found a wide range of the bed needs imposed in 2014 that were attributable to the zone 2 offenders (high-history, low and medium offense severity). In Kansas, 36 percent of all prison commits came from zone 2; in Minnesota it was 51 percent and in North Carolina 18 percent. The corresponding bed needs attributable to zone 2 were 20 percent for Kansas, 36 percent for Minnesota, and 13 percent for North Carolina.[12] Frase and Hester estimate the fiscal impacts in 2014 were $28 million for Kansas, $160 million for Minnesota, and $131 million for North Carolina. These are prison beds occupied by medium- to low-severity offenders who are recommended to prison only because of their prior convictions.

Frase and Hester also examined the fiscal costs in Minnesota that flow from the other problematic criminal history effects noted above: race

---

[12] The percentage of bed needs from zone 2 should be lower than the percentage of total prison commitments from zone 2 because, by definition, zone 2 does not include the highest-severity offenders who receive the longest prison terms, often measured in decades.

disproportionality, confounded prison bed prioritization, and the age-crime issue. They estimated that racial overrepresentation due to criminal history amounts to $25 million per year in prison operation costs, that over $90 million per year is allocated for zone 2 non–person offenders, and that almost $50 million per year is spent on zone 2 offenders who were 40 or older at sentencing.

In many guidelines jurisdictions, governments are allocating tens of millions of dollars per year to imprison aging low-risk offenders; these "investments" are yielding greater racial disparities. For many readers, moral and ethical concerns will be paramount to fiscal considerations, particularly concerning an issue like racial disparity. Nevertheless, given the salience of fiscal responsibility for some policy makers, it is worth emphasizing both the underlying adverse outcomes and the concomitant steep price tag. There may be justifiable reasons for imposing PREs, though we have struggled to find a convincing retributive or consequentialist rationale that would even remotely support the linear, multiplicative, aggravation-style PRE policies currently in place. Since the moral and financial consequences are so weighty, any such justifications for PREs should be carefully examined and convincingly articulated.

## IV. Conclusion

Offenders pay again and again for their prior crimes, and so do their families, their communities, and the general public. There are many serious collateral consequences of criminal convictions, but paying again for past crimes is especially pronounced in the United States. The "recidivist premium" exists in almost all modern sentencing regimes, but it is particularly strong—or, at least, much more visible—in American state and federal jurisdictions that have implemented sentencing guidelines. Almost all of these guidelines regimes incorporate criminal history scoring formulas that greatly increase the recommended and imposed penalties for offenders with prior convictions.

The high cost and adverse effects of prior record sentence enhancements might be tolerable if they served important punishment purposes, but all of the potential justifications for these enhancements are weak. Despite repeated and diverse scholarly effort, the retributive justification—that a repeat offender's latest crime is more blameworthy because of his prior convictions—is unpersuasive except perhaps as a basis to mitigate sentences for some first offenders. The crime control rationale—that a repeat offender poses a higher risk of further crime, thus justifying more severe punishment—is unproven and, in many respects, implausible. Almost no American guidelines system has empirically validated the risk-predictive accuracy of its criminal history score and score components (and the formulas and components vary widely across guidelines systems; Frase et al. 2015). Moreover, even if a particular formula predicts risk fairly accurately, with limited under- and overprediction, the more severe penalties imposed under these formulas are not likely to have cost-effective crime-reducing effects. Longer prison terms do not rehabilitate or specifically deter most offenders, and they make many of them more crime-prone. The general deterrent claims of longer terms seem particularly implausible given what we know about the marginal deterrent effects of higher penalties.

Prisons sometimes prevent crime by mere incapacitation, but routine prior record enhancements seem guaranteed to overpredict risk for many offenders (especially older offenders) while underpredicting risk for others. Although opinion research consistently shows public support for giving higher penalties to repeat offenders, popular views are largely intuitive and not based on particular punishment goals and rationales. New research does show, however, that the public endorses limits on the magnitude of these enhancements, on the use of very old convictions, and on the counting of offenses committed when the offender was a juvenile. In each of those respects, the public would place greater limits on prior record enhancements than are found in many guidelines systems.

Much is still unknown about these important sentencing policy issues, and we need further research in one or more guidelines systems on the following topics:

- How well does the criminal history score and each score component predict future crime, especially serious and violent crime, and how do nonscore factors (e.g., current offense, offender age) affect prediction accuracy?
- What are the crime control benefits of the more severe sentences imposed because of prior record?
- What are the fiscal costs and adverse impacts (racial disparate impact, offense disproportionality, increased numbers of nonviolent and aging inmates) of prior record enhancements?
- Which components of each system's prior record formula have major racial impacts, and do those components have strong justification?

- To what extent is public support for prior record enhancements based on assumptions of higher levels of desert, higher risk, or other specific rationales?

Reform cannot wait until all of these questions are answered. On the basis of current knowledge, here is how we would design a model system of prior record enhancement under sentencing guidelines:

1. Criminal history scores should include only components with the strongest normative and empirical justifications. Many existing formulas include troubling components, including juvenile court adjudications; adult misdemeanor convictions; adult convictions from many years earlier (many systems have no look-back limits at all or have limits that formally or in practice do not exclude convictions entered many decades earlier); custody status points (which double-count the prior conviction and, in case of release revocation, triple-count the current offense; this should just be a factor judges may consider, particularly on the question of "disposition" noted below); heavy weighting of prior crimes according to severity (there is little evidence tying prior severity to future risk); and "patterning" enhancements for offenders previously convicted of the same crime (this is sometimes a valid factor for courts to consider, but temporal and other variations do not support routine, formulaic enhancement).

2. Recommended custody-duration enhancements should not increase at a steady or uniform rate as the criminal history score rises. Retributive and risk-based rationales justify a substantial difference in penalty severity, between first offenders and low-history repeat offenders (e.g., history score of 1); however, the pace of enhancement should be much more modest as offender scores continue to rise.[13]

3. To limit the costs and other adverse effects of prior record enhancements and, in particular, to maintain proportionality be-

---

[13] Rather than having straight linear increases in prison length by criminal history score, as current guidelines do, PREs should follow a two-stage or bent-line approach that roughly resembles the shape of a hockey stick held with the blade pointing down (Frase and Roberts, forthcoming). For low-history offenders the PRE should reflect the first-offender discount, meaning that PRE would rise sharply at first (the blade end of the stick). Subsequently, PREs should follow a modest line with little slope.

tween sentence severity and conviction offense seriousness, the recommended duration for highest-history offenders should not be more than two times greater than the recommended sentence for no-history (or lowest-history) offenders. This "doubling" limit ensures that an offender's prior record never counts more than his current crime.[14]

4. Offense proportionality should be promoted by providing that the ranges of recommended (typical-case) sentences for adjoining offense severity levels do not overlap: high-history offenders should not be recommended for prison terms that are more severe than recommended terms for low-history offenders committing more serious crimes (excluding first offenders, to accommodate the mitigations we propose above).

5. Additional mitigation for first offenders should be expressly authorized. First-offender mitigation has the strongest retributive rationale and also a strong crime control basis: these offenders deserve a second chance, and most of them will not be seen again in criminal court. At least one guidelines system expressly recognizes the special status of these offenders (Boerner and Lieb [2001, pp. 84–86], discussing Washington's first-offender "waiver" provision). Finally, the public strongly supports mitigation for first offenders (Hester et al. 2017).

6. Judges should have authority to adjust the sentence upon a finding that the offender's criminal history score does not accurately reflect the risk of serious recidivism; judges already have authority to depart based on atypical offense facts, and the same should be true for offender-related factors.

7. A particularly strong basis to mitigate sentences, even for offenders with a number of prior convictions, would exist in which the court finds that, notwithstanding his most recent crime, the offender has made substantial efforts to address the causes of his offending. Such mitigation should almost always be recognized if the current offense is not very serious and was preceded by a substantial crime-

---

[14] Tonry (2017) has recently suggested the premium should never be over 1.5. Although selecting a maximum premium is somewhat arbitrary, we offer an upper limit of 2.0, which, to us, has an inherent, natural appeal: however much the past counts, surely it should not count more than the present criminal act. And 2.0 is the upper bound; in most cases, it should count much less.

free period since the offender's last conviction. Another strong case for discretionary (or even presumptive) mitigation would be for older offenders, especially those whose recent crimes are declining in frequency or seriousness. One of the most serious defects of current prior record enhancement formulas is that they ignore the well-documented lower risk of aging offenders.

In most existing guidelines systems, adoption of the model provisions above would substantially reduce the costs and adverse impacts of prior record enhancements. The result would be a sentencing system that is fairer, more proportional, and more efficient but no less effective in controlling crime.

While our primary focus in this essay has been on prior record enhancements under sentencing guidelines, in almost every instance our arguments carry the same or greater force for other types of record-based enhancements such as three-strikes and repeat-offender statutes. These enhancements often involve additional imprisonment for decades or for life; yet their relationship to valid punishment purposes, whether retributive or consequentialist, is as dubious, if not more so, than the justifications for substantial guidelines PREs. Likewise, the undesirable consequences of three-strikes and repeat-offender laws are as serious as or more serious than the consequences we have examined in this essay. All substantial prior record enhancements worsen racial disparities, reduce the proportionality of punishment relative to the crime being sentenced, and increase the size and cost of prison populations. When such enhancements, whether under guidelines or repeat-offender statutes, are applied to aging and other low-risk offenders or to those convicted of nonviolent crimes, they also undermine prison resource priorities.

Like the larger problems of mass incarceration and mass supervision, prior record enhancements have been overused and underevaluated. All of these policies need to be reexamined and substantially cut back to levels that are more fair and more cost-effective.

REFERENCES

Abrams, David S. 2013. "The Imprisoner's Dilemma: A Cost-Benefit Approach to Incarceration." *Iowa Law Review* 98:905–69.
American Law Institute. 1962. *Model Penal Code*. Proposed official draft. Philadelphia: American Law Institute.

————. 2017. *Model Penal Code: Sentencing*. Tentative Draft no. 5. Philadelphia: American Law Institute.

Andenaes, Johannes. 1966. "The General Preventative Effects of Punishment." *University of Pennsylvania Law Review* 114:949–83.

Applegate, Brandon K., Francis T. Cullen, Michael G. Turner, and Jody L. Sundt. 1996. "Assessing Public Support for 3-Strikes and You're Out Laws: Global versus Specific Attitudes." *Crime and Delinquency* 42:517–34.

Ashworth, Andrew J. 2005. *Sentencing and Criminal Justice*. Cambridge: Cambridge University Press.

Bagaric, Mirko. 2000. "Double Punishment and Punishing Character: The Unfairness of Prior Convictions." *Criminal Justice Ethics* 19:10–28.

————. 2014. "The Punishment Should Fit the Crime—Not the Prior Convictions of the Person That Committed the Crime: An Argument for Less Impact Being Accorded to Previous Convictions in Sentencing." *San Diego Law Review* 51:343–418.

Bennett, Chris. 2010. "More to Apologize For." In *Previous Convictions at Sentencing: Theoretical and Applied Perspectives*, edited by Julian V. Roberts and Andrew von Hirsch. Oxford: Hart.

————. 2012. "Do Multiple and Repeat Offenders Pose a Problem for Retributive Sentencing Theory?" In *Recidivist Punishments: The Philosopher's View*, edited by Claudio Tamburrini and Jesper Ryberg. New York: Lexington.

Blumstein, Alfred, and Kiminori Nakamura. 2009. "Redemption in the Presence of Widespread Criminal Background Checks." *Criminology* 47:327–59.

Boerner, David, and Roxanne Lieb. 2001. "Sentencing Reform in the Other Washington." In *Crime and Justice: A Review of Research*, vol. 28, edited by Michael Tonry. Chicago: University of Chicago Press.

Bushway, Shawn D., Paul Nieuwbeerta, and Arjan Blokland. 2011. "The Predictive Value of Criminal Background Checks: Do Age and Criminal History Affect Time to Redemption?" *Criminology* 49(1):27–60.

Cochran, Joshua C., Daniel P. Mears, and William D. Bales. 2014. "Assessing the Effectiveness of Correctional Sanctions." *Journal of Quantitative Criminology* 30(2):317–47.

Corlett, J. Angelo. 2012. "Retributivism and Recidivism." In *Recidivist Punishments: The Philosopher's View*, edited by Claudio Tamburrini and Jesper Ryberg. New York: Lexington.

Dagger, Richard. 2012. "Playing Fair with Recidivists." In *Recidivist Punishments: The Philosopher's View*, edited by Claudio Tamburrini and Jesper Ryberg. New York: Lexington.

Davis, Michael. 1985. "Just Deserts for Recidivists." *Criminal Justice Ethics* 4:29–50.

Delaware Sentencing Accountability Commission. 2015. *Delaware Sentencing Accountability Commission Benchbook*. http://courts.delaware.gov/Superior/pdf/benchbook_2015.pdf.

Doble, John. 1995. *Crime and Corrections: The Views of the People of Oklahoma*. Englewood Cliffs, NJ: Doble Research Associates.

Doob, Anthony, and Julian V. Roberts. 1983. *Sentencing: An Analysis of the Public's View*. Ottawa: Department of Justice Canada.

Duff, R. Antony. 1986. *Trials and Punishments*. Cambridge: Cambridge University Press.

———. 2001. *Punishment, Communication, and Community*. Oxford: Oxford University Press.

Durham, Alexis. 1987. "Justice in Sentencing: The Role of Prior Record of Criminal Involvement." *Journal of Criminal Law and Criminology* 78:614–43.

Durlauf, Steven F., and Daniel S. Nagin. 2009. "The Deterrent Effect of Imprisonment." In *Controlling Crime: Strategies and Tradeoffs*, edited by Philip J. Cook, Jens Ludwig, and Justin McCrary. Chicago: University of Chicago Press.

Ewing, Alfred C. 1929. *The Morality of Punishment*. London: Kegan Paul, Trench Trubner.

Farrington, David P. 2012. "Childhood Risk Factors for Young Adult Offending: Onset and Persistence." In *Young Adult Offenders: Lost in Transition?* edited by Friedrich Lösel, Anthony Bottoms, and David P. Farrington. London: Routledge.

Feinberg, Joel. 1970. *Doing and Deserving: Essays in the Theory of Responsibility*. Princeton, NJ: Princeton University Press.

Feld, Barry C. 2003. "The Constitutional Tension between Apprendi and McKeiver: Sentence Enhancements Based on Delinquency Convictions and the Quality of Justice in Juvenile Courts." *Wake Forest Law Review* 38:1111–1224.

Fellner, Jamie, and Patrick Vinck. 2012. *Old behind Bars: The Aging Prison Population in the United States*. New York: Human Rights Watch.

Finkel, Norman J., Stephen T. Maloney, Monique Z. Valbuena, and Jennifer Groscup. 1996. "Recidivism, Proportionalism, and Individualized Punishment." *American Behavioral Scientist* 39:474–87.

Fletcher, George. 1978. *Rethinking Criminal Law*. Boston: Little, Brown.

Frase, Richard S. 2009. "What Explains Persistent Racial Disproportionality in Minnesota's Prison and Jail Populations?" In *Crime and Justice: A Review of Research*, vol. 38, edited by Michael Tonry. Chicago: University of Chicago Press.

———. 2010. "Prior-Conviction Sentencing Enhancements: Rationales and Limits Based on Retributive and Utilitarian Proportionality Principles and Social Equality Goals." In *Previous Convictions at Sentencing: Theoretical and Applied Perspectives*, edited by Julian V. Roberts and Andrew von Hirsch. Oxford: Hart.

———. 2013. *Just Sentencing: Principles and Procedures for a Workable System*. New York: Oxford University Press.

———. 2015a. "The Relationship between Criminal History and Recidivism Risk." In *Criminal History Enhancements Sourcebook*, edited by Richard S. Frase, Julian V. Roberts, Rhys Hester, and Kelly Lyn Mitchell. Minneapolis: Robina Institute of Criminal Law and Criminal Justice.

———. 2015b. "Timing of Current and Prior Crimes: What Counts as a 'Prior' Conviction?" In *Criminal History Enhancements Sourcebook*, edited by Richard S. Frase, Julian V. Roberts, Rhys Hester, and Kelly Lyn Mitchell. Minneapolis: Robina Institute of Criminal Law and Criminal Justice.

———. 2015*c*. "The Treatment of Multiple Current Offenses." In *Criminal History Enhancements Sourcebook*, edited by Richard S. Frase, Julian V. Roberts, Rhys Hester, and Kelly Lyn Mitchell. Minneapolis: Robina Institute of Criminal Law and Criminal Justice.

Frase, Richard S., and Rhys Hester. 2015. "Criminal History Enhancements as a Cause of Minority Over-representation." In *Criminal History Enhancements Sourcebook*, edited by Richard S. Frase, Julian V. Roberts, Rhys Hester, and Kelly Lyn Mitchell. Minneapolis: Robina Institute of Criminal Law and Criminal Justice.

———. Forthcoming *a*. "Disproportionate Impact on Minority Offenders." In *Criminal History Enhancements*, edited by Richard S. Frase and Julian V. Roberts. New York: Oxford University Press.

———. Forthcoming *b*. "Magnitude of Criminal History Impacts on Sentence Severity." In *Criminal History Enhancements*, edited by Richard S. Frase and Julian V. Roberts. New York: Oxford University Press.

Frase, Richard, and Julian V. Roberts, eds. Forthcoming. *Criminal History Enhancements*. New York: Oxford University Press.

Frase, Richard S., Julian V. Roberts, Rhys Hester, and Kelly Lyn Mitchell, eds. 2015. *Criminal History Enhancements Sourcebook*. Minneapolis: Robina Institute of Criminal Law and Criminal Justice.

Gottfredson, Stephen D., and Don M. Gottfredson. 1990. *Classification, Prediction and Criminal Justice Policy*. Final report to the National Institute of Justice. Washington, DC: US Department of Justice, National Institute of Justice.

Greenawalt, Kent. 2001. "Punishment." In *Encyclopedia of Crime and Justice*, vol. 3, 2nd ed., edited by Joshua Dressler. New York: Macmillan.

Hampton, Jean. 1984. "The Moral Education Theory of Punishment." *Philosophy and Public Affairs* 13:208–38.

Hart, Henry M. 1958. "The Aims of the Criminal Law." *Law and Contemporary Problems* 23:401–41.

Hester, Rhys. 2015. "Prior Offense Weighting and Special Eligibility Rules for High Criminal History Categories." In *Criminal History Enhancements Sourcebook*, edited by Richard S. Frase, Julian V. Roberts, Rhys Hester, and Kelly Lyn Mitchell. Minneapolis: Robina Institute of Criminal Law and Criminal Justice.

———. 2017. "Punishing for the Past (Sometimes): Perspectives on Criminal History Enhancements from Non-guidelines Judges." Working paper, Pennsylvania State University.

Hester, Rhys, Julian V. Roberts, Richard S. Frase, and Kelly Mitchell. 2017. "A Measure of Tolerance: Public Attitudes on Sentencing Enhancements for Old and Juvenile Prior Records." *Corrections: Policy, Practice, and Research*. https://doi.org/10.1080/23774657.2017.1343105.

Hirschi, Travis, and Michael Gottfredson. 1983. "Age and the Explanation of Crime." *American Journal of Sociology* 89(3):552–84.

Indermaur, David. 1990. *Crime Seriousness and Sentencing: A Comparison of Court Practice and the Perceptions of a Sample of the Public and Judges*. Mount Lawley, Australia: Western Australian College of Advanced Education.

Kansas Sentencing Commission. 2009. *Kansas Sentencing Proportionality Recommendations: Report on Proposed Improvements and Modifications to Kansas Sentencing Laws.* http://www.accesskansas.org/ksc/2009proportionality/Proportionality_Report_Updated_1-24-09.pdf.

Katz, Jack. 1988. *Seductions of Crime: Moral and Sensual Attractions in Doing Evil.* New York: Basic Books.

Kleinig, John. 1998. "The Hardness of Hard Treatment." In *Fundamentals of Sentencing Theory: Essays in Honour of Andrew von Hirsch,* edited by Andrew J. Ashworth and Martin Wasik. Oxford: Clarendon.

Knight, Douglas W. 1965. "Punishment Selection as a Function of Biographical Information." *Journal of Criminal Law, Criminology, and Police Science* 56:325–27.

Kurlycheck, Megan C., Robert Brame, and Shawn D. Bushway. 2006. "Scarlet Letters and Recidivism: Does an Old Criminal Record Predict Future Offending?" *Criminology and Public Policy* 5:483–503.

———. 2007. "Enduring Risk? Old Criminal Records and Predictions of Future Criminal Involvement." *Crime and Delinquency* 53(1):64–83.

Langan, Patrick A., and David J. Levin. 2002. "Recidivism of Prisoners Released in 1994." Washington, DC: US Department of Justice, Bureau of Justice Statistics.

Lee, Youngjae. 2009. "Recidivism as Omission: A Relational Account." *Texas Law Review* 87:571–622.

———. 2010. "Repeat Offenders and the Question of Desert." In *Previous Convictions at Sentencing: Theoretical and Applied Perspectives,* edited by Julian V. Roberts and Andrew von Hirsch. Oxford: Hart.

Lippke, Richard. 2015. "The Ethics of Recidivist Premiums." In *The Routledge Handbook of Criminal Justice Ethics,* edited by Jonathan Jacobs and Jonathan Jackson. New York: Routledge.

MacPherson, Darcy. 2002. "The Relevance of Prior Record in the Criminal Law: A Response to the Theory of Professor von Hirsch." *Queen's Law Journal* 28:177–219.

Mande, Mary, and Kim English. 1989. *The Effect of Public Opinion on Correctional Policy: A Comparison of Opinions and Practices.* Denver: Colorado Department of Public Safety, Division of Criminal Justice.

Markel, Dan. 2009. "Executing Retributivism: Panetti and the Future of the Eighth Amendment." *Northwestern University Law Review* 103:1163–1222.

Mattinson, Joanna, and Catriona Mirrlees-Black. 2000. *Attitudes to Crime and Criminal Justice: Findings from the 1998 British Crime Survey.* London: Home Office.

Meade, Benjamin, Benjamin Steiner, Matthew Makarios, and Lawrence Travis. 2013. "Estimating a Dose-Response Relationship between Time Served in Prison and Recidivism." *Journal of Research in Crime and Delinquency* 50(4):525–50.

Minnesota Sentencing Guidelines Commission. 1984. *The Impact of the Minnesota Sentencing Guidelines: Three Year Evaluation.* St. Paul: Minnesota Sentencing Guidelines Commission.

———. 2017. *Minnesota Sentencing Guidelines and Commentary.* http://mn.gov/msgc-stat/documents/2017Guidelines/2017Guidelines.pdf.

Mitchell, Kelly L. 2015. "Decay and Gap Policies." In *Criminal History Enhancements Sourcebook*, edited by Richard S. Frase, Julian V. Roberts, Rhys Hester, and Kelly Lyn Mitchell. Minneapolis: Robina Institute of Criminal Law and Criminal Justice.

Mitchell, Ojmarrh, Joshua C. Cochran, David P. Mears, and William D. Bales. 2016. "Examining Prison Effects on Recidivism: A Regression Discontinuity Approach." *Justice Quarterly* 34(4):571–96.

Monahan, John, Jennifer L. Skeem, and Christopher T. Lowenkamp. 2017. "Age, Risk Assessment, and Sanctioning: Overestimating the Old, Underestimating the Young." *Law and Human Behavior* 41(2):191–201.

Morris, Norval. 1974. *The Future of Imprisonment*. Chicago: University of Chicago Press.

———. 1982. *Madness and the Criminal Law*. Chicago: University of Chicago Press.

Morris, Norval, and Michael Tonry. 1990. *Between Prison and Probation: Intermediate Punishments in a Rational Sentencing System*. New York: Oxford University Press.

Nagin, Daniel S. 2013. "Deterrence in the Twenty-First Century." In *Crime and Justice in America, 1975–2025*, edited by Michael Tonry. Vol. 42 of *Crime and Justice: A Review of Research*, edited by Michael Tonry. Chicago: University of Chicago Press.

Nagin, Daniel S., Francis T. Cullen, and Cheryl Lero Jonson. 2009. "Imprisonment and Reoffending." In *Crime and Justice: A Review of Research*, vol. 38, edited by Michael Tonry. Chicago: University of Chicago Press.

Nagin, Daniel S., and G. Matthew Snodgrass. 2013. "The Effect of Incarceration on Re-offending: Evidence from a Natural Experiment in Pennsylvania." *Journal of Quantitative Criminology* 29(4):601–42.

O'Neill, Michael Edmund, Linda Drazag Maxfield, and Miles D. Harer. 2004. "Past as Prologue: Reconciling Recidivism and Culpability." *Fordham Law Review* 73:245–95.

Parent, Dale G. 1988. *Structuring Criminal Sentences: The Evolution of Minnesota's Sentencing Guidelines*. Stoneham, MA: Butterworth.

Petersen, Thomas S. 2012. "Less for Recidivists? Why Retributivists Have a Reason to Punish Repeat Offenders Less Harshly than First-Time Offenders." In *Recidivist Punishments: The Philosopher's View*, edited by Claudio Tamburrini and Jesper Ryberg. New York: Lexington.

Piquero, Alex R., and Alfred Blumstein. 2007. "Does Incapacitation Reduce Crime?" *Journal of Quantitative Criminology* 23(4):267–85.

Piquero, Alex R., David P. Farrington, and Alfred Blumstein. 2007. *Key Issues in Criminal Career Research: New Analyses of the Cambridge Study in Delinquent Development*. Cambridge: Cambridge University Press.

Redondo, S., E. Luque, and J. Funes. 1996. "Social Beliefs about Recidivism in Crime." In *Psychology, Law, and Criminal Justice*, edited by Graham Davies, Sally Lloyd-Bostock, Mary McMurran, and C. Wilson. New York: de Gruyter.

Roberts, Julian V. 1996. "Public Opinion, Criminal Record and the Sentencing Process." *American Behavioral Scientist* 39:488–99.

————. 1997a. "Refining the Role of Criminal Record in the Federal Sentencing Guidelines: Few Lessons from the States." *Federal Sentencing Reporter* 9:213–15.

————. 1997b. "The Role of Criminal Record in the Sentencing Process." In *Crime and Justice: A Review of Research*, vol. 22, edited by Michael Tonry. Chicago: University of Chicago Press.

————. 2008. *Punishing Persistent Offenders*. Oxford: Oxford University Press.

————. 2010. "First Offender Sentencing Discounts: Exploring the Justifications." In *Previous Convictions at Sentencing: Theoretical and Applied Perspectives*, edited by Julian V. Roberts and Andrew von Hirsch. Oxford: Hart.

————. 2012. "Past and Present Crimes: The Role of Previous Convictions at Sentencing." In *Recidivist Punishments: The Philosopher's View*, edited by Claudio Tamburrini and Jesper Ryberg. New York: Lexington.

————. 2015a. "Justifying Criminal History Enhancements at Sentencing." In *Criminal History Enhancements Sourcebook*, edited by Richard S. Frase, Julian V. Roberts, Rhys Hester, and Kelly Lyn Mitchell. Minneapolis: Robina Institute of Criminal Law and Criminal Justice.

————. 2015b. "Severity Premium for Similar Prior Offending: Patterning Rules." In *Criminal History Enhancements Sourcebook*, edited by Richard S. Frase, Julian V. Roberts, Rhys Hester, and Kelly Lyn Mitchell. Minneapolis: Robina Institute of Criminal Law and Criminal Justice.

Roberts, Julian V., and Michael Hough. 2011. "Custody or Community? Exploring the Boundaries of Public Punitiveness in England and Wales." *Criminology and Criminal Justice* 11:185–202.

Roberts, Julian V., and Jose Pina-Sánchez. 2014. "Previous Convictions at Sentencing: Exploring Empirical Trends in the Crown Court." *Criminal Law Review* 8:575–88.

————. 2015. "Paying for the Past: The Role of Previous Convictions at Sentencing in the Crown Court." In *Exploring Sentencing Practice in England and Wales* edited by Julian V. Roberts. London: Palgrave Macmillan.

Roberts, Julian V., and Andrew von Hirsch. 2010. *Previous Convictions at Sentencing*. Oxford: Hart.

Roberts, Julian V., and Nicholas R. White. 1986. "Public Estimates of Recidivism Rates: Consequences of a Criminal Stereotype." *Canadian Journal of Criminology* 28:229–41.

Robinson, Paul H. 2008. *Distributive Principles of Criminal Law: Who Should Be Punished? How Much?* New York: Oxford University Press.

Sampson, Robert J., and John H. Laub. 1995. *Crime in the Making: Pathways and Turning Points through Life*. Cambridge, MA: Harvard University Press.

Sanders, Joseph, and V. Lee Hamilton. 1992. "Legal Cultures and Punishment Repertoires in Japan, Russia, and the United States." *Law and Society Review* 26:117–40.

Singer, Richard. 1979. *Just Deserts: Sentencing Based on Equality and Desert*. Cambridge, MA: Ballinger.

Stalans, Loretta, and Shari Diamond. 1990. "Formation and Change in Lay Evaluations of Criminal Sentencing: Misrepresentation and Discontent." *Law and Human Behavior* 14:199–214.

Tamburrini, Claudio. 2012. "What's Wrong with Recidivist Punishments?" In *Recidivist Punishments: The Philosopher's View*, edited by Claudio Tamburrini and Jesper Ryberg. New York: Lexington.

Tamburrini, Claudio, and Jesper Ryberg, eds. 2012. *Recidivist Punishments: The Philosopher's View*. New York Lexington.

Tonry, Michael. 2004. *Punishment and Politics*. Cullompton, Devon, UK: Willan.

———. 2010. "The Questionable Relevance of Previous Convictions to Punishments for Later Crimes." In *Previous Convictions at Sentencing: Theoretical and Applied Perspectives*, edited by Julian V. Roberts and Andrew von Hirsch. Oxford: Hart.

———. 2011. *Punishing Race*. New York: Oxford University Press.

———. 2016. *Sentencing Fragments: Penal Reform in America, 1975–2025*. New York: Oxford University Press.

———. 2017. "Making American Sentencing Just, Humane, and Effective." In *Reinventing American Criminal Justice*, edited by Michael Tonry and Daniel S. Nagin. Vol. 46 of *Crime and Justice: A Review of Research*, edited by Michael Tonry. Chicago: University of Chicago Press.

Travis, Jeremy, Bruce Western, and Steve Redburn. 2014. *The Growth of Incarceration in the United States: Exploring Causes and Consequences*. Committee on the Causes and Consequences of High Rates of Incarceration. Washington, DC: National Academies Press.

Tufts, Jennifer, and Julian V. Roberts. 2002. "Sentencing Juvenile Offenders: Public Preferences and Judicial Practice." *Criminal Justice Policy Review* 13:46–64.

Ulmer, Jeffery T., Noah Painter-Davis, and Leigh Tinik. 2016. "Disproportionate Imprisonment of Black and Hispanic Males: Sentencing Discretion, Processing Outcomes, and Policy Structures." *Justice Quarterly* 33(4):642–81.

US Sentencing Commission. 2004. *Release 1: Measuring Recidivism: The Criminal History Computation of the Federal Sentencing Guidelines*. http://www.ussc.gov /Research/Research_Publications/Recidivism/200405_Recidivism_Criminal _History.pdf.

———. 2010. *Computation of "Recency" Criminal History Points under USSG §4A1.1(e)*. http://www.ussc.gov/Research/Research_Publications/2010/20100818 _Recency_Report.pdf.

Vigorita, Michael S. 2003. "Judicial Risk Assessment: The Impact of Risk, Stakes, and Jurisdiction." *Criminal Justice Policy Review* 14(3):361–76.

von Hirsch, Andrew. 1976. *Doing Justice*. Boston: Northeastern University Press.

———. 1985. *Past or Future Crimes? Deservedness and Dangerousness in the Sentencing of Criminals*. New Brunswick, NJ: Rutgers University Press.

———. 1993. *Censure and Sanctions*. Oxford: Clarendon.

———. 2010. "Proportionality and the Progressive Loss of Mitigation: Some Further Reflections." In *Previous Convictions at Sentencing: Theoretical and Applied Perspectives*, edited by Julian V. Roberts and Andrew von Hirsch. Oxford: Hart.

Wang, Xia, Daniel P. Mears, Cassia Spohn, and Lisa Dario. 2013. "Assessing the Differential Effects of Race and Ethnicity on Sentence Outcomes under Different Sentencing Systems." *Crime and Delinquency* 59(1):87–114.

Wasik, Martin, and Andrew von Hirsch. 1994. "Section 29 Revised: Previous Convictions in Sentencing." *Criminal Law Review* (June):409–18.
Weidner, Robert R., Richard S. Frase, and Jennifer S. Schultz. 2005. "The Impact of Contextual Factors on the Decision to Imprison in Large Urban Jurisdictions: A Multi-level Analysis." *Crime and Delinquency* 51:400–424.
Wright, Ronald E. 2002. "Counting the Cost of Sentencing in North Carolina, 1980–2000." In *Crime and Justice: A Review of Research*, vol. 29, edited by Michael Tonry. Chicago: University of Chicago Press.

*Joseph Murray, Yulia Shenderovich, Frances Gardner, Christopher Mikton, James H. Derzon, Jianghong Liu, and Manuel Eisner*

# Risk Factors for Antisocial Behavior in Low- and Middle-Income Countries: A Systematic Review of Longitudinal Studies

ABSTRACT

Violent crime is a major cause of social instability, injury, and death in low- and middle-income countries. Longitudinal studies in high-income countries have provided important evidence on developmental precursors of violence and other antisocial behaviors. However, there may be unique influences or different risk factor effects in other social settings. Extensive searches in seven languages and screening of over 60,000 references identified 39 longitudinal studies of antisocial behavior in low- and middle-income countries. Many risk factors have roughly the same average effects as when studied in high-income countries. Stability of aggression over a 3-year period is almost identical across low- and middle-income countries and high-income countries. Dimensions of comorbid psychopathology such as low self-control, hyperactivity, and sensation seeking are associated with antisocial behavior in low- and middle-income countries, but some early physical health factors have consistently weak or null effects.

Electronically published March 26, 2018
Joseph Murray is professor, Postgraduate Program in Epidemiology, Federal University of Pelotas, Brazil. Yulia Shenderovich is a doctoral candidate, Institute of Criminology, Cambridge University. Frances Gardner is professor of child and family psychology, De-

Although 80 percent of the world's population live in low- and middle-income countries (LMICs), most behavioral research has been conducted in "WEIRD" populations—Western, Educated, Industrialized, and Democratic societies (Henrich, Heine, and Norenzayan 2010). This raises fundamental questions about the generalizability of current scientific knowledge and its utility for practice and policy across all human societies. In this essay, we review evidence on risk factors for antisocial behavior in LMICs and consider whether results from high-income countries (HICs) apply similarly in LMICs.

Violence is a major cause of social instability, injury, mental health problems, and death in many LMICs (Bowman et al. 2008; Matzopoulos et al. 2008). For example, in Latin America and the Caribbean, interpersonal violence was the leading cause of death among 15–49-year-olds in 2013 (Institute for Health Metrics and Evaluation 2016). Violence is a complex, multifactorial behavior, often preceded by childhood conduct disorders, which also carry many adverse consequences through the life course. Prospective longitudinal studies provide the strongest evidence about predictors of violence, conduct disorders, and other antisocial behaviors, but major reviews of the literature have focused almost exclusively on HICs. Because risk processes for antisocial behavior may not be universal, identifying robust predictors of antisocial behavior in LMICs is a priority to develop effective interventions for most of the world.

Different types of antisocial behavior have different geographic patterns. Homicide, the most serious form of interpersonal violence, shows enormous variation across both time and space. In western Europe, homi-

partment of Social Policy and Intervention, Oxford University. Christopher Mikton is lecturer, Department of Health and Social Sciences, University of the West of England. James Derzon is senior research public health analyst, Center for Advanced Methods Development, Research Triangle Institute. Jianghong Liu is associate professor of nursing and public health, School of Nursing and Perelman School of Medicine, University of Pennsylvania. Manuel Eisner is professor of comparative and developmental criminology, Institute of Criminology, Cambridge University. We thank Tomas Allen and Isla Kuhn for vital help in developing the search strategy and Antonia Concha Errazuriz, Bruno Dalponte, Dong Yiqun, Franziska Mager, Lana Ghuneim, Lana Yoo, Lídia Maria de Oliveira Morais, Maria Paula Godoy, Simón Escoffier Martínez, Sze Long Mui, Yan Zhang, Zehang Chen, Li Jiawei, Ma Li, Li Tianqing, Wei Junfan, and Zheng Anqing for searches, screening, and translation in languages other than English. We are especially grateful to Adrian Raine, Christiane Duarte, Jie Chen and Jianxin Zhang, Mark Boyes, Phillip Davidson, and Edwin Wijngaarden, who provided additional data from and information about their studies. This work was funded by grants to Joseph Murray from the Wellcome Trust (089963/Z/09/Z) and the Bernard van Leer Foundation (222-2014-010).

cide rates declined from about 25 homicides per 100,000 people per year in the Middle Ages to about 1.0 per year in the early twenty-first century (Eisner 2014). Currently, the highest rates of homicide are found in LMICs in the Americas and in sub-Saharan Africa, with rates comparable to those in Europe many centuries ago. In 2013, there were 23.6 homicides per 100,000 people in Latin America and the Caribbean and 20.3 in southern sub-Saharan Africa (Institute for Health Metrics and Evaluation 2016). Rates of nonfatal violence are considerably harder to compare across countries, but self-report surveys suggest levels of assault are nearly three times higher in LMICs than in HICs (Wolf, Gray, and Fazel 2014). In contrast to these striking geographic variations in violence, rates of childhood conduct disorder (about 3.6 percent) and oppositional defiant disorder (2.1 percent) appear to be fairly constant around the globe (Canino et al. 2010; Polanczyk et al. 2015). This geographic variability in violence and similarity in rates of childhood disruptive disorders are puzzling given the strong stability of antisocial behavior in individuals through time, at least within HICs (Olweus 1979). Possibly, varying levels of stability in antisocial behavior across LMICs could help explain these patterns.

Developmental and life course theories of antisocial behavior highlight the influence of individual and environmental processes involved in self-control, moral reasoning, social bonding, and social learning from early life through adulthood (Farrington 2005b; Eisner and Malti 2015). Prospective longitudinal studies provide the most important evidence on the natural history of antisocial behavior and the interplay of multiple risk and protective factors through the life course and across different ecological levels (Farrington 2013). Evidence from major longitudinal studies has been synthesized in several prior narrative and meta-analytic reviews (Lipsey and Derzon 1998; Rutter, Giller, and Hagell 1998; Hawkins et al. 2000; Derzon 2010; Murray and Farrington 2010; Farrington 2013, 2015b; Tanner-Smith, Wilson, and Lipsey 2013; Eisner and Malti 2015). Key risk factors identified include individual factors such as impulsivity, low IQ, and low school achievement; parenting factors such as poor supervision, punitive or erratic discipline, cold attitude, and child physical abuse; other parent and family characteristics, such as parental conflict, disrupted families, antisocial parents, large family size, and low family income; antisocial peers, high delinquency rate schools, and high-crime neighborhoods. Results are not always consistent across studies, complex interactions still need to be clarified, and the identification of causes, as opposed to mere statistical associations, remains a major challenge for research, but increasing progress is being made (Jaffee, Strait, and Odgers 2012).

Despite the advances made in longitudinal research on antisocial behavior, prior reviews of this evidence focus almost exclusively on studies in western Europe, North America, and Australasia. For example, David Farrington (2015*b*) recently reviewed 30 key longitudinal studies in criminology, and all but one were conducted in high-income countries, possibly because of the strong criteria used to select studies for inclusion in the review—studies with at least 300 participants, personal interviews, and follow-ups of at least 5 years. In other areas of behavioral science, WEIRD populations are considered "among the least representative populations one could find for generalizing about humans" (Henrich, Heine, and Norenzayan 2010, p. 61). Why prior reviews have not included more LMIC studies is not entirely clear. It is possible that relevant longitudinal studies are lacking in LMICs, that prior reviews did not aim to cover LMICs, or that standard reviewing methods (e.g., searching only in English) do not locate studies in LMICs. We imagine that most scholars assume that good longitudinal studies are lacking in LMICs.

It should be noted that some longitudinal surveys in HICs selected participants from socioeconomically disadvantaged populations, for example, the working-class sample living in inner London recruited in the classic Cambridge Study in Delinquent Development (Piquero, Farrington, and Blumstein 2007; Farrington, Piquero, and Jennings 2013) and the inner-city black youths included in the Philadelphia cohort of the Collaborative Perinatal Project (Denno 1990; Tibbetts and Piquero 1999). However, it would of course be a mistake to simply extrapolate results from these populations to people living in LMICs, with different levels of poverty and inequality and sociocultural conditions.

Given the focus of prior reviews on longitudinal studies in HICs, we aim here to synthesize the available evidence on risk factors for antisocial behavior in LMICs and consider whether findings are comparable across settings. We bring together findings from a surprisingly large number of longitudinal studies in LMICs, identified through extensive searches in seven languages. In the first section of the essay, we introduce theoretical perspectives on why risk factors for antisocial behavior could vary across the globe and define key terms used in the subsequent review of the empirical evidence. Section II describes the types of community-based, longitudinal studies that we searched for in LMICs, how we searched for them, and the approach we used to review their findings. Section III describes the 39 longitudinal studies we identified in LMICs and synthesizes their findings, organized in an ecological model of individual-level factors, early health factors, child rearing processes, maltreatment and other adversities, family characteristics, and wider social influences. Although these studies have produced an enormous collection of results, for most risk factors we examine, only a small handful of individual surveys in LMICs provide relevant evidence. We quantitatively pool the results wherever possible using meta-analysis and summarize all study findings in the text to provide a single, comprehensive resource that details existing findings on risk factors in LMICs. Section IV discusses broad theoretical and research implications.

Table 1 gives an overview of the results from our meta-analyses of LMIC studies, where similar constructs were available in prior reviews of studies from HICs. With few exceptions, average bivariate associations were very similar between LMICs and HICs. These similar findings across vastly different sociocultural contexts point toward global similarity in risk factors for antisocial behavior. However, there are two important caveats to this conclusion. First, because the associations represent bivariate correlations, one cannot draw conclusions about the similarity of causal processes. Second, these average associations mask considerable variability in results across different LMIC studies, which could represent context-specific influences of risk factors on antisocial behavior, as well as methodological variation between studies. Half of the meta-analyses of LMIC studies had at least moderate heterogeneity in the results.

Although it is difficult to draw broad conclusions about overall replicability of risk factors based on the current LMIC evidence, and for some risk factors only a very small number of studies were available, the following key empirical findings emerged. First, past behavior was the strongest predictor of future antisocial behavior in LMICs, and associations were very similar to those found previously in HIC studies. Second, other relatively strong bivariate predictors of antisocial behavior in LMICs included hyperactivity and sensation seeking, low social competence, authoritarian parenting, and maternal smoking in pregnancy. Third, for these and other risk factors in LMICs, associations with antisocial behavior were generally similar in size, or slightly smaller than those in HICs, although some associations, such as having a large family and low maternal education, were considerably weaker in LMICs than in HICs. Fourth, there was little specificity in the type of antisocial behavior predicted by

## TABLE 1
### Comparison of Average Risk Factor Associations for Antisocial Behavior in Low- and Middle-Income Countries (LMICs) and High-Income Countries (HICs)

| Risk Factor | Strength of Association in LMICs: This Review | Strength of Association in HICs: Prior Reviews |
|---|---|---|
| Individual-level risk factors: | | |
| Prior aggression | Large for aggression | Large for aggression[1] |
| Prior conduct problems | Large for conduct problems | Large for conduct problems[2] |
| Hyperactivity | Medium for violence | Medium for violence[3] |
| Poor educational performance | Negligible for crime | Small for crime[4] |
| Drug use | Negligible for intimate partner violence | Small for violence[3] |
| | Large for violence | Large for violence[3] |
| Early life health risk factors: | | |
| Low birth weight | Negligible for conduct problems | Negligible for conduct problems[5] |
| Premature birth | Negligible for conduct problems | Negligible for conduct problems[5] |
| Child rearing practices: | | |
| Maternal authoritarian parenting | Medium for conduct problems & aggression | Medium for conduct problems[2] |
| Maternal warmth | Small for conduct problems & aggression | Medium for conduct problems[2] |
| Maternal authoritative parenting | Medium for conduct problems & aggression | Medium for conduct problems[2] |
| Family sociodemographic factors: | | |
| Poor family during childhood | Small for conduct problems | Medium for conduct problems[2] |
| | Small for violence | Small for violence[3] |
| Low maternal education | Small for conduct problems | Large for conduct problems[2] |
| Young mother at birth | Small for conduct problems | Small for conduct problems[2] |
| | Small for violence | Negligible for violence[2] |
| Many siblings | Negligible for violence | Medium for violence[2] |

NOTE.—Associations are bivariate correlations. The strength of association is described as follows (see Sec. II): negligible, $d < 0.10$; small, $d = 0.10$; medium, $d = 0.25$; large, $d = 0.50$. References for prior reviews in HICs: [1]Olweus (1979); [2]Derzon (2010); [3]Lipsey and Derzon (1998); [4]Tanner-Smith, Wilson, and Lipsey (2013); [5]Aarnoudse-Moens et al. (2009). For some risk factors in the current review, described later in the essay, no prior, comparable review was located for studies in HICs.

risk factors in LMICs, but associations tended to be stronger for child conduct problems and aggression, compared with youth crime or violence. This may be due to a longer time span between the risk factors and young adult outcomes of crime and violence. Fifth, there was good evidence that some of the early health factors studied, such as low birth weight, were not associated with antisocial behavior. Finally, there was substantial heterogeneity in the results for many risk factors investigated in LMICs; however, it is not currently possible to determine if this reflects variations in methodology between studies or substantive differences across social contexts.

We conclude that, although individual studies have provided important local evidence in a number of LMICs, and some broad patterns of findings are discernible, the bigger picture concerning replicability of findings across context is unclear, given the limited evidence available on each risk factor and methodological differences between existing studies in LMICs. It would therefore be premature to conclude whether the etiology of antisocial behavior reflects universal human phenomena or a mix of universal and context-contingent factors. We outline our hopes for a new generation of global coordinated research projects, using common methods and measures, to provide robust evidence on the degree of universality versus specificity of different risk processes involved in antisocial behavior across the life course.

## I. Theories, Aims, and Definitions

In this section, we review theoretical perspectives on why risk factors might influence antisocial behavior differently across social contexts and specify our aims and definitions.

### A. Why Might Risk Factors for Antisocial Behavior Not Be Universal?

It is possible that risk factors previously identified in HICs reflect universal patterns of human behavior and that similar empirical patterns will obtain consistently across all societies. Some existing studies have compared risk factors between different HICs and found very similar associations, for example, between Pittsburgh, Pennsylvania, and London, England (Farrington and Loeber 1999; see also Farrington 2015a). However, given the great diversity in social contexts across LMICs, there are several reasons why risk and protective factors might not replicate so consistently elsewhere. First, even within HICs, numerous surveys suggest that the effects of individual-level and family-level risk factors can depend on community context; that is, there are interaction effects between risk factors across ecological levels. For example, in the Pittsburgh Youth Study, boys' impulsivity level was positively associated with crime for males living in poor neighborhoods but posed reduced risk for those in better-off neighborhoods (Lynam et al. 2000). Many studies show that parental supervision has stronger effects on child antisocial behavior in high-risk social settings than in less deprived contexts (Schonberg and Shaw 2007). Therefore, looking across the globe to consider populations in radically different socioeconomic and cultural circumstances in LMICs, there may be systematic variability in risk factor associations according to geographic location.

Schonberg and Shaw (2007) discuss two theories why individual and family-level risk factors will probably have stronger effects on child behavior in more deprived social settings. First is the idea that risk factor effects increase when they co-occur: that cumulative risk exposure has multiplicative effects (Appleyard et al. 2005). This "synergistic model" also predicts that risk factors are more likely to co-occur in deprived social settings. Therefore, a single risk factor in a deprived context is likely to have stronger effects on child antisocial behavior than in less deprived settings. A second and related theory also predicts stronger risk factor effects in contexts of adversity but emphasizes the interaction between "vulnerability factors" and "provoking agents" (Schonberg and Shaw 2007). According to this perspective, individual vulnerability factors (such as genetic disposition) result in antisocial behavior only if provoking agents in the environment are also present. For example, adoption studies have shown that increased genetic risk for antisocial behavior, indicated by biological parents having a criminal record, predicts antisocial behavior only when adopting families also present some form of environmental risk (Raine 2002*b*). Hence, individual-level risk factors should have larger effects in disadvantaged environments that trigger those dispositions.

A contrasting theoretical perspective predicts that individual-level risk factors will have weaker associations with antisocial behavior in high-risk environments because strong social forces override individual-level influences in these settings. Raine (2013) calls this the "social push" hypothesis. Accordingly, biological risk factors should have their strongest influence on antisocial behavior in relatively benign social environments and, by contrast, be overridden in contexts of high social adversity. Raine describes a range of findings on biological factors such as resting heart rate and skin-conductance reactivity, showing that effects are stronger in less disadvantaged social contexts.

Rutter (1999) points to other, more general, considerations about how social contexts can influence risk factor effects. He particularly emphasizes the issue of what a risk factor means socially, pointing to several ways this could influence its effects on behavior. For example, the marked changes in social views concerning childbearing out of wedlock through the twentieth century imply different consequences for mothers and children, with far greater effect in the 1930s, when unmarried mothers were viewed with serious social disapproval, than in later decades. The relative distribution of a risk factor across the population is another facet of social meaning that could alter a risk factor's effects. Specifically, a risk factor's influence might depend on a person's relative social standing rather than an absolute effect. A clear example is the advantage that educational attainment buys in the job market: large population increases in educational attainment have altered the minimum qualification level required to obtain skilled jobs (Rutter 1999). Thinking cross-sectionally, risk factor effects could also vary between countries because of different distributions of risk factors between populations. For example, varying levels of income inequality might mean that low family income has different associations with antisocial behavior across different countries. Rutter terms this a "comparative social context effect" because it reflects the importance of a person's social standing in relation to others.

In summary, from four theoretical perspectives, different broad empirical predictions may be made about patterns of risk factor effects in LMICs. First, according to a universalist view, risk factor associations should be consistent both in and across LMICs compared with HICs. Second, individual- and family-level risk factors would be expected to have stronger effects in LMICs than in HICs, according to a "multiplicative effects" model, because of the higher likelihood of exposure to additional social disadvantage in LMICs. Third, according to the "social push" perspective, individual-level risk factors should have weaker effects in LMICs than in HICs because greater social disadvantage in LMICs overrides individual-level influences. According to both the "multiplicative effects" model and the "social push" model, variation in risk factor associations would also be expected across LMICs, given their many sociocultural differences. Fourth, if social meanings of risk factors influence their effects, one would also expect heterogeneity in effects, both across LMICs and between LMICs and HICs.

## B. Aims

Longitudinal evidence from LMICs is important to test the universality of current developmental and life course theories, identify any context-specific influences on antisocial behavior, and deliver effective interventions in areas of the world most affected by violence. Longitudinal research in LMICs is also important because some risk factors do not occur commonly in HICs. For example, prospective evidence on the link between early childhood malnutrition and antisocial behavior was first described in the Mauritius Child Development Study (Liu et al. 2004). Also, causal inference can be strengthened from research in LMICs if the patterning of underlying confounding factors is different from that in HICs (Batty et al. 2007; Ebrahim et al. 2013). For example, a recent Brazilian study of breast feeding provided plausible evidence of causal effects on intelligence because breast feeding was not strongly socially patterned in that setting, although breast feeding is highly associated with maternal education and income in many HICs (Victora et al. 2015). Considering the importance of synthesizing evidence on predictors of antisocial behavior in LMICs, we have four aims:

1. To identify and characterize existing longitudinal studies of antisocial behavior in LMICs.
2. To synthesize findings in LMICs on longitudinal predictors of child conduct problems and aggression and youth crime and violence.
3. To compare average risk factor associations in LMICs with previous findings from HICs.
4. To examine the consistency of results across LMICs to provide evidence about the possible universality or cross-country or cultural specificity of predictors.

## C. Definitions

"Low- and middle-income countries" (LMICs) are defined as countries with a low- or middle-income status according to the World Bank; they are also sometimes referred to as developing countries. Because a country's income status can change from year to year, we defined LMICs as countries classified as low- or middle-income during more than half of the years 1987–2012 for which World Bank classifications were available. By this definition, 164 countries were identified as LMICs. Although categorizing countries as low- and middle-income is internationally recognized, the terms hide great disparity within and across countries. For example, about 75 percent of the world's poor live in middle-income countries such as China, India, and Brazil (Sumner 2011). Despite enormous sociocultural heterogeneity across low- and middle-income countries, most have elevated rates of absolute poverty, income inequality, and violence, placing families, communities, and youths at greater risk (Knerr, Gardner, and Cluver 2013).

"Conduct problems" refer to antisocial behaviors in childhood and adolescence that are symptomatic of oppositional defiant disorder and conduct disorders (American Psychiatric Association 2013). We acknowledge that LMICs are spread across a wide range of cultures, and there is not a consensus about the universality of psychiatric disorders, given the lack of biological markers and gold standards for validation (Canino and Alegria 2008). However, in our review, nearly all studies examined conduct problem symptoms, rather than diagnoses, using instruments such as Achenbach's System of Empirically Based Assessment (e.g., the "externalizing" subscale of the Child Behavior Checklist; Achenbach and Rescorla 2000) or the Strengths and Difficulties Questionnaire ("conduct problems" subscale; Goodman 1997), which ask respondents about child behaviors such as temper tantrums, stealing, lying, and fighting. These instruments have shown good psychometric properties across a range of cultures and settings (Achenbach, Rescorla, and Ivanova 2012; Rescorla et al. 2012).

"Aggression" refers to behaviors intended to cause physical or psychological harm to others. We examine risk factors for child and adolescent aggression separately from general conduct problems because of the large literature on aggression as a specific type of conduct problem, with different developmental patterns, subtypes, and potentially different prognoses and risk factors (Eisner and Malti 2015). Measures such as the aggression subscale on the Child Behavior Checklist (Achenbach and Rescorla 2000) are commonly used to assess the extent of children's aggressive behaviors.

"Violence" is defined by the World Health Organization (2002, p. 5) as "the intentional use of physical force or power, threatened or actual . . . that either results in or has a high likelihood of resulting in injury, death, psychological harm, maldevelopment, or deprivation." We review studies of interpersonal physical violence by youths (10–29 years old) committed both within families, or with intimate partners, and in the community. We exclude studies of suicidal behaviors or other forms of self-directed violence. Violence can be measured using self-reports or reports by other knowledgeable people (such as parents or teachers) or by collecting official records (e.g., police or court records). We also review findings on risk factors for youth crime that includes nonviolent offending, for two reasons. First, nonviolent offending is one manifestation of conduct disorder, and second, violent and nonviolent criminal behaviors are highly associated (Farrington 1998).

"Antisocial behavior" refers to a wide variety of behaviors that violate societal norms or laws (Rutter, Giller, and Hagell 1998), including the various behaviors we examine—child aggression and conduct problems and youth violence and crime. Given the strong correlations between these behaviors, some researchers consider them manifestations of the same underlying individual potential for antisocial conduct (Farrington 1991, 2005*a*).

We generally use the terms "childhood" to refer to ages under 10, "adolescence" to ages 10–17, and "young adulthood" to ages 18–29, with "youth" referring to ages 10–29, following the World Health Organization's (2015) definition of youth violence. However, sometimes we had to use other distinctions made in the literature regarding specific studies or types of variables.

We review "longitudinal predictors," which are variables associated with and preceding conduct problems or violence. Longitudinal predictors that increase the risk for adverse outcomes are called "risk factors." Although most predictors we consider are risk factors, some variables lower the risk of an adverse outcome and are called "protective factors." Direct protective factors predict a lower probability of antisocial behavior across the whole population, whereas buffering protective factors predict a low probability of antisocial behavior specifically among at-risk groups (Lösel and Farrington 2012). A distinction might also be drawn between "explanatory" and "nonexplanatory" risk factors; explanatory ones clearly measure a construct different from the outcome behavior, and nonexplanatory ones could be measuring the same underlying construct as the outcome (Farrington, Gaffney, and Ttofi 2017). For example, drug and alcohol abuse could be measuring the same underlying construct (such as a broad externalizing behavior syndrome; Patrick et al. 2015) as offending. Maybe peer delinquency is also measuring the same underlying construct as delinquency, because of co-offending.

Prospective longitudinal studies are the gold standard for investigating risk and protective factors because they can establish clear temporal order and avoid bias that can arise in retrospective studies (Kraemer, Lowe, and Kupfer 2005). We consider only prospectively measured predictors of antisocial behavior in longitudinal studies. Hence, we do not include findings on correlates measured at the same time as antisocial behavior. Also, we do not review effects of prevention programs unless they yield insight into the effects of naturally occurring risk factors. We focus on modifiable risk factors that can change during the life course, and therefore might be targets for interventions, rather than static risk factors such as a person's sex or race.

Critically, predictors are not necessarily causal. A risk factor might predict conduct problems or violence merely because it is associated with other causes (confounders), not because it itself influences the behavior. Therefore, although longitudinal predictors meet two criteria for causation (precedence and association), many do not meet a third criterion—that no confounding variable explains the association. Identifying which predictors are causes and which are merely markers of other causes is a major challenge for research, requiring use of experimental or quasi-experimental studies and genetically sensitive research designs to help rule out alternative explanations (Rutter et al. 2001; Shadish, Cook, and Campbell 2002; Rutter 2003; Kraemer, Lowe, and Kupfer 2005; Murray, Farrington, and Eisner 2009; Jaffee, Strait, and Odgers 2012; Eisner and Malti 2015). Most findings we summarize do not permit strong causal inference, but we highlight studies that used stronger methods to improve causal inference, such as negative controls, experiments that target specific risk factors, cross-cohort comparisons, and twin studies (Richmond et al. 2014). Analysis of within-individual change through time has also been recommended as a way to improve causal inference in longitudinal studies (Farrington 1988; Murray, Farrington, and Eisner 2009).

## II. Methods
Systematic reviews use thorough and explicit search methods, with preset eligibility criteria to locate all available evidence on a research topic, and ideally use quantitative analyses to synthesize the results from primary studies. In this section we detail the systematic review methods used to search for longitudinal studies in low- and middle-income countries, eligibility criteria, and our approach to synthesizing the results on risk factors for antisocial behavior.

## A. Search Strategy

We conducted an extensive search for all available evidence on correlates and predictors of childhood conduct problems, aggression, and youth crime and violence in LMICs in multiple languages. Full details of the search and screening methods and the review protocol are described in a separate article (Shenderovich et al. 2016). In summary, we first developed a broad and sensitive search strategy for multiple electronic databases. The search strategy combined terms for low- and middle-income countries, including names of all individual LMICs and relevant regions; children and youths; and relevant outcomes, including antisocial behavior, conduct problems and disorders, externalizing, aggression, bullying, crime, violence, gang membership, and so forth. We searched the following databases in August–September 2013 without restriction on study years or languages: PsycINFO, MEDLINE, EMBASE, CINAHL, EconLit, Criminal Justice Abstracts, Russian Academy of Sciences Bibliographies, Sociological Abstracts and Social Services Abstracts, Applied Social Sciences Index and Abstracts, International Bibliography of the Social Sciences, ERIC, Web of Science, National Criminal Justice Reference Service Abstracts Database, CENTRAL, JOLIS, World Bank, Open Grey, Global Health Library, and Google Scholar.

To complement the English language searches, we used translated search terms in six other languages to search Google Scholar and 12 regional databases: Index Medicus, King Saud University Repository, and YU-DSpace Repository in Arabic; CNKI, Wanfang Data, and Cqvip in Chinese; Index Medicus Afro, Revue de Médicine tropicale, Agence Universitaire de la Francophonie, and Refdoc in French; Elibrary.ru and Panteleimon in Russian; and LILACS and SciELO in Spanish and Portuguese. A further search for grey literature was conducted by entering the keywords into general internet search engines, including Google and Baidu, and contacting over 200 researchers in the field to locate unpublished studies. Jim Derzon (2010) also searched his large database of longitudinal studies to locate any other possibly eligible studies.

## B. Eligibility Criteria and Screening

The review protocol was prepared with preset inclusion criteria. Inclusion criteria specified the population, outcome measures, and several methodological quality criteria for drawing conclusions about risk factors (Murray, Farrington, and Eisner 2009; Jolliffe et al. 2012). Only prospective longitudinal studies were included in this essay, although cross-sectional and retrospective studies will be examined in other publications. To be eligible, studies must have met all the following criteria:

1. The study was conducted in an LMIC.
2. The study included at least 100 participants.
3. The study reported at least one test of association between a potential predictor of childhood conduct problems or aggression, youth violence, or crime.
4. Conduct problems and aggression were measured between birth and age 18, and youth crime and violence were measured between ages 10 and 29.
5. Child conduct problems and aggression were measured using standardized instruments such as the Child Behavior Checklist or instruments with enough detail to determine that items concerning other behaviors, such as hyperactivity, were not included in the outcome.
6. Measures of violence and crime were based on self-reports, criminal records, or other reports.
7. The risk factor and the outcome were measured at the level of an individual. For example, studies of group-level correlates of neighborhood crime rates were not included. Ecological research was beyond our scope.
8. Participants must have been recruited using random or stratified probability sampling or sampling of an entire population of children or youths in the community.
9. If participants were recruited at schools or other institutions, such as maternity hospitals in birth cohort studies, participants must have been recruited from at least two such institutions to increase generalizability of the findings.
10. Only prospective longitudinal studies were eligible.

We excluded cross-sectional and retrospective studies and excluded several longitudinal studies if they reported only correlates measured at the same time as the behavioral outcome (Jackson 2001; Botcheva, Feldman, and Liederman 2002; Velásquez et al. 2002; Friday et al. 2003, 2005; Taylor et al. 2004; Samms-Vaughan, Jackson, and Ashley 2005; Reyes et al. 2008; Zhou et al. 2012). Experimental studies that evaluated interventions that changed potential risk or protective factors for conduct problems, aggression, crime, or violence were included, as experimental studies can help identify causal effects of modifiable exposures.

All 44,318 titles and abstracts in English were screened for potentially relevant studies by Yulia Shenderovich, with Joseph Murray supervising decisions in cases of doubt. Non-English searches and screening of 17,290 titles and abstracts were conducted by six graduate students—four native speakers and two students fluent in the relevant languages. For all references referring to potentially eligible studies, 1,437 full texts were retrieved and screened. A team of 17 people translated all potentially eligible texts reported in languages other than English. All studies meeting the eligibility criteria, whether published or unpublished, conducted at any time up until the searches were completed were eligible. Two authors verified that all studies included met all eligibility criteria. Figure 1 shows a PRISMA flow diagram for the search and screening process.

## C. Synthesis of Findings

We followed prior reviews (Hawkins et al. 1998; Rutter, Giller, and Hagell 1998; Hill 2002; Farrington and Welsh 2007; Murray and Farrington 2010; Tanner-Smith, Wilson, and Lipsey 2013) and grouped risk factors according to a bioecological model (Bronfenbrenner and Morris 2007) in the following categories: individual factors; perinatal and early childhood health factors; child rearing factors; maltreatment and other adverse life events; family characteristics; peer factors; school factors, community factors, and cultural influences. Findings are reported in relation to the age at which children were exposed to each risk factor and age at outcome measurement, and separately for females and males, wherever original results were stratified by sex.

Meta-analyses were used to synthesize multiple findings from different studies for the same risk factor–outcome association. Evidence was also narratively reviewed to characterize the evidence included in the meta-analyses and to discuss additional findings that were ineligible for meta-analysis. Meta-analyses were conducted using random-effects models (using metan in Stata 12.1), given expected heterogeneity of results across different samples. Prior meta-analyses of predictors of antisocial behavior have generally synthesized only bivariate associations from primary studies (Hawkins et al. 1998; Lipsey and Derzon 1998; Derzon 2010; Tanner-Smith, Wilson, and Lipsey 2013). Most of the meta-analyses we undertook also synthesize only bivariate associations. However, if multiple studies applied similar methods to calculate covariate-adjusted associations, we also meta-analyzed those results, separately, to consider the strength of risk factor associations independent of possible confounding

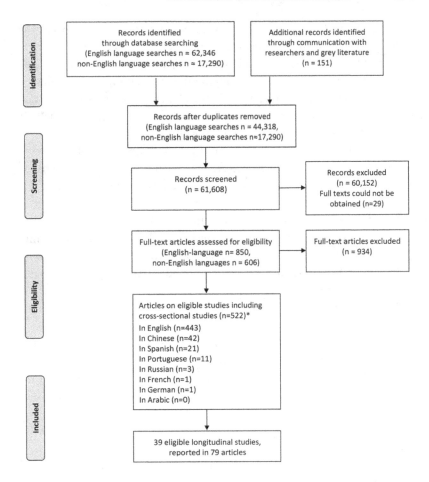

Fig. 1.—PRISMA flow diagram of review search and screening process. * Three studies were reclassified as eligible since Shenderovich et al. (2016).

variables. Studies that adjusted for potentially mediating mechanisms (variables on the causal pathway between the predictor and outcome) were not included in meta-analyses (Victora et al. 1997). Adjusting for mediating variables will downwardly bias estimates of risk factor effects.

All studies meeting the eligibility criteria were included in the narrative review, but only studies with an effect size and standard error were included in meta-analyses. For this reason and because we judged some studies too different in their designs and analyses to warrant quantitative pooling of results, some meta-analyses contain fewer studies than the corresponding narrative reviews. Specifically, all findings were included in meta-analyses, unless: multiple studies were not available for the same risk factor–outcome association, mediating mechanisms were adjusted for in the analysis, it was not possible to calculate an effect size for a particular study, or multiple studies used such different designs and analyses that we judged meta-analysis was inappropriate.

Despite these restrictions, many studies had multiple results that were eligible for meta-analyses. To ensure that each meta-analysis was based on independent results, the following procedures were followed:

1. Separate meta-analyses were conducted for each predictor.
2. Separate meta-analyses were conducted for each outcome of child conduct problems and aggression and youth violence and crime.
3. Separate meta-analyses were conducted for bivariate and covariate-adjusted results.
4. Males and females were treated as separate samples where results were stratified by sex.
5. Where there were still multiple results from a single study, the outcome assessed longest after the predictor was used.
6. Where there were still multiple results from a single study, they were averaged, and the average effect size was used in meta-analysis.

Meta-analyses were used first to estimate average associations in LMIC studies. These findings were also compared with results from comparable reviews of longitudinal studies in HICs, to consider the robustness of findings between HICs and LMICs. However, average results in LMICs may obscure important heterogeneity in risk factor effects, for example, between different regions. For most risk factors, it was not possible to test whether results from LMICs varied systematically by region (or by other possible moderators, such as methodological characteristics of the studies), because meta-analyses included too few studies for this type of moderator analysis. However, for the variable that had the largest number of effect sizes (prior conduct problems and aggression), we grouped relevant results according to world region (World Health Organization [WHO] regions of Africa, Americas, Europe, and Western Pacific region) and tested whether these regions or other study characteristics moderated effect sizes in meta-analysis.

In the narrative review, we report effect sizes as they were presented in individual studies in their original form, for example, as odds ratios (OR) or risk ratios (RR) for dichotomous associations and correlations ($r$) or standardized regression coefficients for associations with continuous outcomes. Unless stated otherwise, results are based on bivariate tests of associations between predictors and outcomes. Meta-analytic results are reported using the standardized mean difference ($d$), representing the difference in the behavioral outcome (in standard deviation units) between individuals exposed to a risk factor and individuals not exposed. The same type of effect size ($d$) was used to report meta-analyses of associations adjusted for confounding variables. Sometimes, the terms small, medium, and large are used to describe the magnitude of an effect size, often following Jacob Cohen's (1988) suggestions. However, existing conventions about what constitutes small, medium, and large, including those of Cohen, are not empirically grounded and ignore the context of the research (Hill et al. 2008). To describe the size of risk factor associations, we used empirical benchmarks based on all 96 effect sizes coded for the meta-analyses. First, we rank-ordered the 96 (absolute) effect sizes, ranging from 0.0 to 5.5, and then divided them into quartiles. The quartiles were then used to define minimum values for small ($d = 0.10$), medium ($d = 0.25$), and large ($d = 0.50$) associations. Equivalent cutoffs for ORs are approximately 1.2, 1.6, and 2.5, respectively. This internal approach—defining the magnitude of effect sizes relative to other findings on the same theme—is similar to that used by Lipsey and Wilson (1993) in their meta-analysis of psychosocial interventions. We also report the $I^2$ statistic for meta-analytic results, which shows the proportion of the total variance in effect sizes that is beyond chance. As a rough rule of thumb, $I^2 = 0$ percent suggests no heterogeneity, $I^2 = 25$ percent suggests low heterogeneity, $I^2 = 50$ percent suggests moderate heterogeneity, and $I^2 = 75$ percent suggests high heterogeneity (Higgins et al. 2003).

### III. Empirical Findings

This section synthesizes results from 39 longitudinal studies of child conduct problems, aggression, and youth violence and crime in 18 low- and middle-income countries. Section A describes the studies, and Sections B–J present their results grouped according to a bioecological categorization of risk factors. Section K compares meta-analytic results with meta-analytic results from previous reviews of studies of risk factors in high-income countries.

## A. *Description of the Studies*

Of the 39 studies eligible, 12 were conducted in China, six in Brazil, five in South Africa (one of which also included a sample in Tanzania), two in the Czech Republic, two in Jamaica, and one in each of Barbados, Belarus, Chile, Colombia, Croatia, Guatemala, Mauritius, the Philippines, Poland, Puerto Rico, Russia, the Seychelles, and former Yugoslavia. Levels of serious violence in these countries range widely. Compared to the global average of six homicides per 100,000 people per year, homicide rates were lower in Chile, China, Croatia, the Czech Republic, Mauritius, and Poland in 2013; higher (up to 15 per 100,000) in Barbados, Belarus, the Philippines, and the Seychelles; and very high (over 15 per 100,000) in Brazil, Colombia, Guatemala, Jamaica, Russia, and South Africa (Institute for Health Metrics and Evaluation 2016). Looking at development levels in terms of the Human Development Index, indicating longevity, education, and income levels, most included countries ($n = 15/18$) had a high level of development in 2014 (UN Development Programme 2015). Two (Poland and Czech Republic) were classified as very highly developed, 13 were highly developed, and three (Guatemala, Philippines, and South Africa) were considered as having a medium level of development. No country had a low level of human development. Two countries (Puerto Rico and former Yugoslavia) lacked data on homicide and human development.

Table 2 summarizes the characteristics of the 39 studies. The study numbers shown in table 2 are used throughout this essay to refer to individual study results (e.g., #1 refers to the Barbados Nutrition Study). Twenty-nine of the studies focused on childhood conduct problems or aggression, five focused on youth violence or crime, and another five examined both childhood conduct problems or aggression and youth violence or crime. Twelve studies were based on birth cohorts, one study sampled children using health care registers, 18 recruited children in preschools or schools, four were based on household samples, and four used a matched risk–control group design, in which children exposed to a risk factor were matched with a control group and both groups were prospectively followed until outcome assessment. Ten studies assessed participants only during childhood (up to age 9), 22 assessed participants during adolescence (between ages 10 and 19), and seven followed

## TABLE 2
### Longitudinal Studies of Child and Youth Antisocial Behavior in Low- and Middle-Income Countries

| Study # | Location | Study Name (Papers in Review) | Sample Type | Baseline Characteristics | Age at Follow-Ups | Data Sources | Outcomes in Review |
|---|---|---|---|---|---|---|---|
| 1 | Barbados: National | Barbados Nutrition Study (Galler and Ramsey 1989; Galler et al. 2011; Galler et al. 2012) | Matched risk and control groups | 129 children with malnutrition (*marasmus*) in first year of life in 1967–72, and 129 children without malnutrition (recruited at ages 5–11) matched on sex, age, handedness, and neighborhood | 5–11, 9–15, 11–17 years | Parents, self-report, teachers, medical exams | Conduct problems |
| 2 | Belarus: Minsk city, Minsk region, Brest, Mogilev, Gomel, Vitebsk, Grodno | Promotion of Breastfeeding Intervention Trial (Kramer et al. 2008) | Birth cohort | 17,046 healthy breast-fed infants weighing at least 2,500 g, born in 1996–97, included in a cluster randomized trial of an intervention that substantially increased the duration children were breast-fed | 1, 2, 3, 6, 9 months; 1, 6, 11 years | Parents, teachers, medical assessments | Conduct problems |
| 3 | Brazil: Pelotas | 1982 Pelotas Birth Cohort Study (Caicedo et al. 2010) | Birth cohort | 5,914 children born in hospitals in city of Pelotas in 1982 | 1, 3, 13, 14, 18, 19, 23, 25, 30 years; criminal records to age 30 | Parents, self-report, medical exams, criminal records | Violence |

TABLE 2 (*Continued*)

| Study # | Location | Study Name (Papers in Review) | Sample Type | Baseline Characteristics | Age at Follow-Ups | Data Sources | Outcomes in Review |
|---|---|---|---|---|---|---|---|
| 4 | Brazil: Pelotas (compared with British study) | 1993 Pelotas Birth Cohort Study (Anselmi et al. 2008; Brion et al. 2010; Anselmi et al. 2012; Kieling et al. 2013; Murray, Maughan, et al. 2015; Murray, Menezes, et al. 2015) | Birth cohort | 5,249 children born in hospitals in city of Pelotas in 1993 | 1, 3, and 6 months; 1 and 4 years (subsample); 11, 15, and 18 years (full sample); criminal records to age 18 | Parents, self-report, medical exams, criminal records | Conduct problems, crime, violence |
| 5 | Brazil: Pelotas | 2004 Pelotas Birth Cohort Study (Matijasevich et al. 2014; Petresco et al. 2014)[a] | Birth cohort | 4,231 children born in hospitals in city of Pelotas in 2004 | 3 months; 1, 2, 4, and 6 years | Parents, self-report, medical exams | Conduct problems |
| 6 | Brazil: Pernambuco State | ENSUZI (Emond et al. 2006) | Matched risk and control groups | 202 low-birth-weight infants and 212 non-low-birth-weight infants from low-income families born in maternity centers in 1993, matched on sex (39% male) and time of birth; included in trial of zinc treatment | 8 years | Parents, teachers, medical exams | Conduct problems |

276

| | | | | | | | |
|---|---|---|---|---|---|---|---|
| 7 | Brazil: São Gonçalo | São Gonçalo 2005 Study[b] (de Assis et al. 2013) | School sample | 500 children in 1st elementary grade (age 7 years) randomly sampled in 54 public schools in 2005 | 8 and 10 years | Parents | Conduct problems |
| 8 | Brazil: São Luís | The 1997/98 São Luís Cohort (Rodriguez et al. 2011) | Birth cohort | 2,443 singleton births randomly sampled in city of São Luis in 1997–98 | 8 years (subsample) | Parents | Conduct problems |
| 9 | Chile: Santiago | Santiago 1992/93 Study[b] (de la Barra, Toledo, and Rodriguez 2003, 2005) | School sample | 1,279 1st graders (age 6 years) from seven schools in three districts of West Santiago in 1992/93 | 11 years | Teachers and parents | Aggression, conduct problems |
| 10 | China: Beijing | Beijing 2000 Study[b] (Zhou et al. 2008; Tao, Zhou, and Wang 2010; Zhou, Main, and Wang 2010; Chen et al. 2011) | School sample | 425 children aged 6–9 in 1st and 2nd grades in two elementary schools in Beijing in 2000 | 10–13 years | Parents, self-report, peers, teachers | Conduct problems |
| 11 | China: Beijing | Beijing 2002 Study[b] (Chen et al. 2012) | School sample | 1,162 3rd-grade children (age 9 years) in nine elementary schools in Beijing in 2002 | 10, 11, and 12 years | Teachers, self-report, and peers | Aggression |
| 12 | China: Beijing | Beijing 2004 Study[b] (Zhang 2013) | Preschool sample | 115 children age 2 years in three nursery schools in Beijing in 2004 | 3 and 4 years | Parents | Conduct problems |

TABLE 2 (*Continued*)

| Study # | Location | Study Name (Papers in Review) | Sample Type | Baseline Characteristics | Age at Follow-Ups | Data Sources | Outcomes in Review |
|---|---|---|---|---|---|---|---|
| 13 | China: Beijing | Beijing Twin Study (Hou et al. 2013) | School sample | 1,387 pairs of twins age 10–18 years in 620 schools in Beijing in 2008–9 | 12–20 years | Parents and self-report | Conduct problems |
| 14 | China: Beijing | Beijing-Daxing Study[b] (Zhu, Yan, and Li 2011) | Health care system sample | 122 children age 2–3 years in the Daxing District of Beijing registered in the health care management system | 4–5 years | Parents | Conduct problems |
| 15 | China: Beijing and Shanghai | Beijing-Shanghai 1994–95 Study[b] (Chen et al. 2002; Wang et al. 2006) | Birth cohort | 216 children age 2 years randomly selected from local birth registration offices in Beijing and Shanghai in 1994–95 | 4 years | Direct observation, parents | Aggression |
| 16 | China: Jinan | Jinan 2000 Study[b] (Zhang et al. 2003) | Preschool sample | 217 children mean age 3 years in four preschools in Jinan city, Shandong in 2000 | 4, 4.5 years | Direct observation | Aggression |
| 17 | China: Jinan | Jinan Study[b] (Chen 2011; Chen 2012) | School sample | 1,618 children age 9 years and 2,164 children age 11 years in 11 primary schools in Jinan city, Shandong | 10, 11, 12, 13, 14 years | Parents, self-report, peers | Aggression |

278

| | | | | | | |
|---|---|---|---|---|---|---|
| 18 | China: Jintan | China Jintan Child Cohort Study (Liu et al. 2014) | Preschool sample | 1,656 children age 3–5 years in four preschools in Jintan city in 2004–5 | 6 years | Parents, teachers, medical exams | Aggression, conduct problems |
| 19 | China: Nanjing | Nanjing Survey (Tseng et al. 2000) | Preschool sample | 697 children age 3–6 years in urban and rural areas of Nanjing city in 1984–85 | 7–10, 9–12, and 13–16 years | Parents | Conduct problems |
| 20 | China: Shanghai | Shanghai Longitudinal Project (Chen, Rubin, and Li 1997; Chen et al. 1999) | School sample | 480 children in 2nd and 4th grades (mean ages 7 and 10) in two schools in Shanghai city in 1990 | 11 years (younger children) 14 years (older children) | Parents, teachers, peers | Aggression, conduct problems |
| 21 | China: Shanghai | Shanghai 1994 Study[b] (Chen et al. 2000; Chen, He, and Li 2004) | School sample | 540 children in 6th grade (mean age 11 years) in four schools in Shanghai city in 1994 | 13 years | Parents, self-report, teachers, peers, school records | Aggression, conduct problems |
| 22 | Colombia: Bogotá, Medellin, and Barranquilla | Colombia 1995/96 Study (Brook et al. 2003; Brook, Brook, and Whiteman 2007) | Household sample | 2,837 adolescents age 12–17 living with biological mothers randomly sampled in Bogotá, Medellin, and Barranquilla cities in 1995/96 | 14–19 years | Parents, self-report | Delinquency, violence |
| 23 | Croatia: Zagreb | Children in War (Rabotegsaric, Zuzul, and Kerestes 1994) | Preschool sample | 686 children on average age 5 years in eight preschools in Zagreb city in 1991 | 6 years | Preschool teachers | Aggression |

TABLE 2 (*Continued*)

| Study # | Location | Study Name (Papers in Review) | Sample Type | Baseline Characteristics | Age at Follow-Ups | Data Sources | Outcomes in Review |
|---|---|---|---|---|---|---|---|
| 24 | Czech Republic: Prague | Prague Study (Dytrych, Matějček, and Schüller 1988; Kubička et al. 1995) | Matched risk and control groups | 220 children whose mothers applied for and were denied abortion during pregnancy in 1961–63, matched with 220 children in the same school classes in 1970, in Prague | 9, 14–16, 21–23, 27–31, 32–35 | Parents, self-report, teachers, criminal, medical, and other official records | Crime |
| 25 | Czech Republic: Brno | European Longitudinal Study of Pregnancy and Childhood (ELSPAC) (Kukla, Hruba, and Tyrlik 2008) | Birth cohort | 7,589 children with expected dates of delivery March 1991–June 1992 in Brno city or with expected delivery April 1991–June 1992 in Znojmo rural district | 8, 11, and 13 years | Parents, self-report, teachers, medical exams | Aggression, conduct problems |
| 26 | Guatemala: Guatemala City | Guatemala 2006 Study[b] (DiGirolamo et al. 2010) | School sample | 750 children aged 6–11 years in five public schools in a poor community in Guatemala city, included in trial of a zinc supplement in 2006 | 6.5–11.5 years | Parents, self-reports, medical exams | Aggression, conduct problems |

| | Location | Study | Design | Sample | Ages | Measures | Outcomes |
|---|---|---|---|---|---|---|---|
| 27 | Jamaica: Kingston | Jamaica 1986 Study[b] (Chang et al. 2002; Walker, Chang, et al. 2007) | Matched risk and control groups | 129 children with stunting aged 9–24 months in poor neighborhoods and 84 nonstunted children matched on age, sex, and neighborhood, in Kingston in 1986–87, included in a trial of a diet supplement and home visit intervention of 2-year duration | 7–8, 11–12, 17–18 years | Parents, self-report, psychological assessment | Conduct problems, antisocial behavior |
| 28 | Mauritius: Vacoas and Quatre Bornes | Mauritius Child Health Project (Clark 1982; Venables 1989; Raine, Venables, and Mednick 1997; Raine et al. 1998; Raine et al. 2002; Liu et al. 2004; Liu et al. 2009; Gao et al. 2010a; Gao et al. 2010b; Gao et al. 2013) | Birth cohort | 1,795 children born in Vacoas and Quatre Bornes towns in 1969–70, recruited at age 3 using vaccination records, with 100 participants given a nutritional, educational, and physical exercise program | 4, 5, and 6 years (subsample); 8, 11, 17, 23, 28, and 35 years (full sample) | Parents, self-report, medical exams, hospital records, criminal records | Aggression, antisocial behavior, crime, violence |
| 29 | Philippines: Cebu | Cebu Longitudinal Health and Nutrition Survey (Fehringer and Hindin 2009) | Birth cohort | 3,080 children born in Cebu between May 1983 and April 1984 | 1, 2, 8, 11, 15, 18, 21, 23 years | Parents, self-report, medical exams | Intimate partner violence |

## TABLE 2 (*Continued*)

| Study # | Location | Study Name (Papers in Review) | Sample Type | Baseline Characteristics | Age at Follow-Ups | Data Sources | Outcomes in Review |
|---|---|---|---|---|---|---|---|
| 30 | Poland: Warsaw (compared with studies in Australia, Finland, Germany, Israel, Netherlands, US) | Poland 1979 Study[b] (Frączek 1986; Groebel 1988) | School sample | 260 children in 1st and 3rd grades (ages 7 and 9 years) in two schools in Warsaw in 1979 | 7, 8, 9 years (younger children); 9, 10, 11 years (older children) | Parents, self-reports, peer nominations | Aggression |
| 31 | Puerto Rico: Standard Metropolitan Areas in Puerto Rico (compared with study in US) | Boricua Youth Study (Bird et al. 2007; Duarte et al. 2008; Maldonado-Molina et al. 2009; Jennings et al. 2010) | Household sample | 1,353 children mean age 9 years (range 5–13) randomly sampled in standard metropolitan areas of San Juan and Caguas cities in 2000 (matched with 1,414 Puerto Rican children living in the Bronx, NY) | 10, 11 years (on average) | Parents, self-report | Conduct problems/ disorders, delinquency |
| 32 | Russia: Voronezh | Voronezh 1995 Study[b] (Leavitt et al. 2013; Nelson et al. 2014) | Preschool sample | 212 children age 3–6 years in three nursery schools in Voronezh city in 1995 | 13–16 years | Parents, self-report, teachers, peers | Aggression |

282

| # | Location | Study | Sample type | Description | Ages | Data source | Outcome |
|---|---|---|---|---|---|---|---|
| 33 | Seychelles | Seychelles Child Development Cohort (Myers et al. 2000; Davidson et al. 2011) | Birth cohort | 779 children born in the Seychelles (about 50% of all live births) in 1989 | 6, 19, and 29 months; 5.5, 9, 10.5, 17, 19, 22, and 24 years | Parents, self-report, medical exams | Conduct problems |
| 34 | South Africa: Cape Town | Cape Area Panel Study (Seekings and Thaler 2011; Thaler 2011) | Household sample | 4,752 youths age 14–22 years randomly selected in metropolitan Cape Town in 2002 | 15–23 and 16–24 years (subsamples); 17–25, 18–26, and 20–29 years | Self-report | Violence |
| 35 | South Africa: Cape Town and Mankweng; Tanzania: Dar es Salaam | SATZ (Wubs et al. 2013) | School sample | 7,274 children age 10–18 years in Cape Town and Makweng (South Africa) and Dar es Salaam (Tanzania) in 2004; included in a trial of school-based HIV prevention programs | 10.5–18.5, 11–19 years (two follow-ups at half year intervals) | Self-report | Intimate partner violence |
| 36 | South Africa: greater Johannesburg area | Birth to Twenty (Barbarin, Richter, and DeWet 2001; Sabet et al. 2009) | Birth cohort | 3,275 children born in Soweto-Johannesburg during 7 weeks in 1990 | 6 months; 1, 2, 3–4, 5, 7–8, 9–10, 11–12, 13, 14, 15 years | Parents, medical exams | Aggression, conduct problems |
| 37 | South Africa: Western Cape and Mpumalanga provinces | Young Carers South Africa (Boyes et al. 2014; Waller, Gardner, and Cluver 2014) | Household sample | 3,515 children age 10–17 living in the Western Cape and Mpumalanga in 2009–11 | 11–18 years | Self-report | Conduct problems |

TABLE 2 (*Continued*)

| Study # | Location | Study Name (Papers in Review) | Sample Type | Baseline Characteristics | Age at Follow-Ups | Data Sources | Outcomes in Review |
|---|---|---|---|---|---|---|---|
| 38 | South Africa: National | South Africa 1974 Study[b] (Botha and Mels 1990) | School sample | 2,476 white children age 9–12 years in school grades 3–5 across South Africa in 1974 | 12–15, 14–17, 16–19 | Self-report and teachers | Aggression |
| 39 | Yugoslavia (Kosovo): K. Mitrovica and Pristina | Yugoslavia Prospective Study of Environmental Lead Exposure (Wasserman et al. 1998; Factor-Litvak et al. 1999; Wasserman et al. 2001) | Birth cohort | 706 children (stratified on lead levels in blood) whose mothers were recruited midpregnancy in K. Mitrovica (next to a lead smelter) and Pristina (relatively unexposed to lead), Yugoslavia in 1985–1986 | 6 months; 1, 2, 3, 4, 5, 6, 7 years | Parents and self-report | Aggression, conduct problems |

[a] Results in Matijasevich et al. (2014) are based on analyses pooling the entire 2004 Pelotas Birth Cohort Study and a subsample of the 1993 Pelotas Birth Cohort Study.

[b] Name assigned to study in this review (not official study name).

participants into young adulthood (20+). The studies used a mixture of participants' self-reports, direct observations, parent reports, teacher reports, peer reports, medical exams, and official records to assess behavior and possible risk and protective factors. Three studies (#4, #30, #31) made direct comparisons of results with matched samples in high-income countries. Six studies involved evaluations of interventions, including zinc supplement interventions in Brazil and Guatemala (#6, #26), a diet supplement and home visits by health workers in Jamaica (#27), a nutritional and environmental enrichment program in Mauritius (#28), an HIV prevention program in South Africa and Tanzania (#35), and a breast-feeding promotion program in Belarus (#2).

In total, 96 effect sizes were extracted for use in meta-analyses. Table 3 shows that studies in Brazil and China contributed the majority of effect sizes to the meta-analyses. The most common results were for individual-level predictors and conduct problem outcomes. Most effect sizes were smaller than 0.50, and the vast majority (88 out of 95) represent bivariate associations.

## B. Individual-Level Characteristics

Longitudinal studies in HICs have identified numerous individual characteristics that are associated with antisocial behavior, including biological factors such as low resting heart rate, and psychological factors including temperament, hyperactivity, low IQ, poor social skills, and positive attitudes toward delinquency (Hinshaw 1992; Rutter, Giller, and Hagell 1998; Hill 2002; Farrington and Welsh 2007; Murray and Farrington 2010). Of course, not all risk factors consistently replicate across studies, but one of the strongest and most replicable predictors of future antisocial behavior is prior antisocial behavior (Lipsey and Derzon 1998). We first review evidence for such continuity in antisocial behavior in LMICs before considering evidence on other individual biological and psychological factors. Table 4 shows the meta-analytic results for individual-level factors, and findings from individual studies are summarized below.

1. *Continuity in Antisocial Behavior through Time.* In a classic review, Dan Olweus (1979) found that the continuity in an individual's aggressive behavior through time was about as strong as continuity in intelligence. Across 16 samples in the United States, England, and Sweden, the (disattenuated) correlation coefficient for the continuity in aggression was 0.68, with an average time interval between measures of 5.8 years

# TABLE 3
## Study Results Included in Meta-Analyses

|  | Number of Effect Sizes |
|---|---|
| Type of risk factor: |  |
| Individual | 32 |
| Early health | 23 |
| Parenting | 14 |
| Family | 27 |
| Behavioral outcome: |  |
| Aggression | 20 |
| Conduct problems | 50 |
| Violence | 24 |
| Crime | 2 |
| Participant sex: |  |
| Females only | 14 |
| Males only | 19 |
| Females and males | 63 |
| Effect size ($d$): |  |
| $<-0.50$ | 3 |
| $-0.50$ to $0.20$ | 7 |
| $-0.20$ to $0.00$ | 13 |
| $0.01$ to $0.20$ | 31 |
| $0.21$ to $0.50$ | 19 |
| $0.51$ to $0.80$ | 8 |
| $0.81$ to $1.00$ | 5 |
| $>1.00$ | 10 |
| Bivariate/adjusted effect size: |  |
| Bivariate | 89 |
| Adjusted | 7 |
| Country of study: |  |
| Barbados | 2 |
| Brazil | 41 |
| Chile | 2 |
| China | 27 |
| Croatia | 1 |
| Czech Republic | 1 |
| Jamaica | 3 |
| Mauritius | 3 |
| Philippines | 1 |
| Poland | 1 |
| Puerto Rico | 1 |
| Russia | 5 |
| South Africa | 6 |
| Yugoslavia | 2 |

## TABLE 4

### Meta-Analytic Results for Associations between Individual Factors and Child Conduct Problems and Youth Violence

| Predictor | Behavioral Outcome | Number of Studies | Studies Included (#) | Type of Association | Effect Size $d$ | 95% CI | $p^a$ | Heterogeneity $I^2$ | $p^b$ |
|---|---|---|---|---|---|---|---|---|---|
| Prior aggression | Aggression | 9 | (4, 11, 10, 13, 16, 20, 21, 27, 30) | Bivariate | 1.6 | (.9 to 3.3) | <.001 | 99.3% | <.001 |
| Prior conduct problems | Conduct problems | 9 | (4, 9, 10, 12, 13, 14, 28, 31, 37) | Bivariate | .9 | (.6 to 2.1) | <.001 | 97.1% | <.001 |
|  | Crime | 2 | (4, 28) | Bivariate | .12 | (−.20 to .44) | .437 | 76% | .041 |
|  | Violence | 2 | (4, 22) | Bivariate | .34 | (.13 to .56) | .018 | 83% | .015 |
| Hyperactivity | Conduct problems | 2 | (9, 10) | Bivariate | .51 | (.34 to .69) | <.001 | 0% | .590 |
|  | Crime | 2 | (4, 28) | Bivariate | .04 | (−.40 to .47) | .867 | 87% | .006 |
| Poor educational performance | Aggression | 2 | (10, 21) | Bivariate | .00 | (−.53 to .52) | .993 | 93% | <.001 |
|  | Intimate partner violence | 2 | (28, 34) | Bivariate | .05 | (−.17 to .28) | .650 | 78% | .032 |
| Drug use | Violence | 2 | (23, 34) | Bivariate | .69 | (.46 to .92) | <.001 | 51% | .154 |
| Sociability | Conduct problems | 2 | (20, 21) | Bivariate | −.03 | (−.20 to .14) | .701 | 0% | .335 |
| Social competence | Conduct problems | 2 | (10, 21) | Bivariate | −.43 | (−.58 to −.28) | <.001 | 0% | .735 |

NOTE.—# = study ID number shown in table 2; $p^a$ = $p$-value for $d$ effect size; $p^b$ = $p$-value for a $\chi^2$ test for heterogeneity. Random-effects models.

(Olweus 1979). In our review of LMICs, nine studies assessed the continuity of aggression, and nine studies assessed the continuity of conduct problems, using the same informants on both occasions.[1] To compare the extent of continuity in aggression and conduct problems in these studies with previous findings from HICs, we used the same procedure as Olweus and calculated disattenuated correlation coefficients.[2] We combined results for both sexes, as there were few studies with separate results for males and females. The average time interval between assessments was 3.0 years (range 1.0–8.0 years) for aggression and 2.8 years (range 0.8–8.0 years) for conduct problems.

Pooling results from nine LMIC studies in meta-analysis, the average disattenuated correlation coefficient for continuity in aggression was 0.75 (95% confidence interval [CI] = 0.40 to 0.91, $p < 0.001$). To compare this with results from Olweus's review, we estimated the correlation coefficient in Olweus's review for the same time interval (3 years).[3] Results were almost identical: the disattenuated correlation was 0.73 for studies with a 3-year interval in Olweus's review. Considering the continuity in conduct problems in LMICs, pooling results from nine studies, the average disattenuated correlation coefficient was 0.49 (95% CI = 0.36 to 0.61, $p < 0.001$).

There was significant ( $p < 0.001$ ) heterogeneity in the results for both continuity in aggression and conduct problems in LMICs. Figure 2 shows the extent of continuity in aggression and conduct problems according to the time interval between measures, with no clear pattern in

---

[1] Studies included were Frączek (1986), Botha and Mels (1990), Chen, Rubin, and Li (1997), Raine, Venables, and Mednick (1997), Zhang et al. (2003), Chen, He, and Li (2004), de la Barra, Toledo, and Rodríguez (2005), Anselmi et al. (2008), Duarte et al. (2008), Zhou, Main, and Wang (2010), Zhu, Yan, and Li (2011), Chen et al. (2012), Hou et al. (2013), and Zhang (2013).

[2] Attenuation refers to the systematic reduction in continuity coefficients caused by measurement error. Disattenuated correlation coefficients are estimated using the following equation:

$$r_d = r_{xy}/\sqrt{(r_{xx} \times r_{yy})},$$

where $r_d$ is the disattenuated correlation coefficient, $r_{xy}$ is the observed correlation between $x$ and $y$, and $r_{xx}$ and $r_{yy}$ are the reliability coefficients for $x$ and $y$. Following Olweus (1979), if incomplete data were available on reliability coefficients, values were estimated from similar studies, using higher values wherever appropriate, because using low-reliability coefficients can artificially inflate estimates of the disattenuated correlation.

[3] This was calculated from the regression model estimated by Olweus: $y = 0.78 - (0.18 \times x)$, where $y$ is the disattenuated correlation coefficient and $x$ is the interval between measures in years (in this case 3.0).

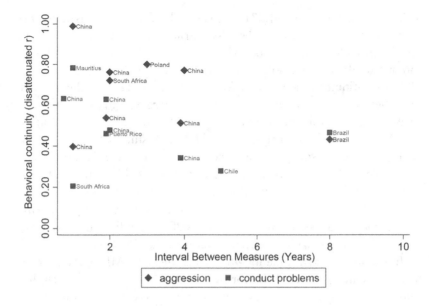

Fig. 2.—Continuity in aggression and conduct problems through time in LMICs, according to the time interval between measures.

the results. In meta-regression, we also tested whether the extent of continuity was related to children's age at first assessment, the time interval between measures, the Human Development Index score of the country of study, the country homicide rate, and the WHO region of the study. No variable was significantly related to continuity in aggression or continuity in conduct problems (all $p > 0.05$). To compare with other meta-analytic results in this review, the results for continuity in aggression and conduct problems were converted into a $d$-type effect size and are shown in table 4.[4]

Three studies in LMICs found a small amount of continuity evident between childhood conduct problems and later violence or crime. Among 11-year-olds in Pelotas, Brazil, conduct problems predicted self-reported violence at age 18 (RR = 1.4 for males and 1.9 for females; #4: Murray, Menezes, et al. 2015). The corresponding increased risk for nonviolent

---

[4] These meta-analyses were conducted on the basis of uncorrected correlation coefficients, rather than disattenuated ones, to increase comparability with other results in the review. For other risk factors, reliability information was not available to calculate disattenuated associations.

crime was 1.7 for males and 2.7 for females. This continuity was quite similar to that found in a matched study in Britain (Murray, Menezes, et al. 2015). In Colombia, boys' behavior problems at school at ages 12–17 predicted self-reported violence 2 years later ($r = 0.22$; #22: Brook et al. 2001). Continuity in violent behavior itself from ages 12–17 to 2 years later was slightly stronger ($r = 0.37$). However, there was no association between conduct problems measured at age 11 and crime at age 23 ($d = -0.08$ in follow-back analyses) in a Mauritius study (#28: Gao et al. 2013). Pooling results for the association between conduct problems and violence for males in two of these studies (#4, #22), the effect size was medium ($d = 0.34$, table 4) with significant heterogeneity between the two. Pooling results for the association between conduct problems and crime for males in two studies (#4, #28), the effect size was small ($d = 0.12$, table 4) with significant heterogeneity.

In summary, across nine longitudinal studies in LMICs, the average continuity in aggressive behavior over 3 years was very similar to that found previously in HICs. However, there was less continuity in conduct problems than aggression in LMICs, and the association between conduct problems in childhood and crime and violence in young adulthood was weak. There was marked heterogeneity in the extent of continuity in antisocial behavior in LMIC studies, but this was not explained by differences in participant age, length of follow-up period, or other study characteristics.

2. *Biological Factors.*  Biological factors that have been related to the development of antisocial behavior in HIC settings include genetic influences, characteristics of brain structure and functioning, features of the autonomic nervous system, and hormonal influences (see, e.g., Rutter, Giller, and Hagell 1998; Raine 2013; DeLisi and Vaughn 2015). An interesting question is whether biological factors have similar effects across LMIC settings, or whether biological influences are attenuated in contexts in which social adversity is greater, as suggested by the social push hypothesis (Raine 2013). Only one longitudinal study in an LMIC examined a genetic influence on antisocial behavior: in a test of the interaction between the genetic polymorphism encoding the monoamine oxidase A (MAOA) enzyme and child maltreatment, originally reported by Caspi et al. (2002) for males in New Zealand. In Pelotas, Brazil, there was no evidence of a main effect of the same MAOA genetic variant on boys' conduct problems at age 15 or of an interaction between the MAOA variant and maltreatment in predicting conduct problems (#4: Kieling et al. 2013).

The Mauritius Child Health Project (#28) provides unique evidence on the association between several biological variables and antisocial behavior. Children who were taller ($d = 0.30$), weighed more ($d = 0.25$), and had greater body "bulk" ($d = 0.25$) at age 3 were more likely to be aggressive at age 11, but they were not more likely to show nonaggressive conduct problems (Raine et al. 1998). Presumably, these associations reflect physical ability to dominate in a fight, which would explain why there was no association with nonaggressive behaviors. Biological measures of electrodermal activity (e.g., skin concordance during an auditory paradigm) were also used as indicators of child fear conditioning and emotionality and tested in relation to antisocial behavior. Electrodermal measures of emotionality at age 3 were associated with teacher ratings of child aggression at age 9 for males, but not for females (Clark 1982). Electrodermal measures of fear conditioning at age 3 also predicted officially recorded crime up to age 23 (Gao et al. 2010$a$). Furthermore, children with persistently low fear conditioning between ages 3 and 8 had more aggressive ($d = 0.57$) and nonaggressive conduct problems ($d = 0.52$) at age 8 (Gao et al. 2010$b$). In relation to autonomic functioning, low resting heart rate when children were age 3 predicted aggressive behavior (RR $= 2.1$) at age 11, but not nonaggressive conduct problems, after adjustment for other biological and psychological covariates (Raine et al. 1997). In the only test of brain functioning and antisocial behavior in an LMIC study, individuals in the Mauritius study with criminal records at age 23 were compared with controls on measures of P3 amplitude at age 11, a particular brain response during a cognitive task that reflects attentional processing capacity. Criminal offenders had lower P3 amplitude compared with controls ($d = 0.32$), and this association persisted even after adjusting for antisocial behavior and hyperactivity at age 11 and alcoholism at age 23 (Gao et al. 2013).

In summary, only two longitudinal studies provide evidence on biological risk factors for antisocial behavior in LMICs. The lack of a gene-environment interaction in the Brazilian study could reflect a predominance of social factors causing conduct problems in that context, measurement differences across studies, or a more generic replication problem in gene-by-environment research (Duncan and Keller 2011; but see Byrd and Manuck [2014] for positive meta-analytic results on the maltreatment-by-MAOA finding). In Mauritius, a small LMIC country with relatively low levels of serious violence (UN Office on Drugs and Crime 2013), numerous childhood biological indicators (larger body size, low resting heart rate, low skin conductance, autonomic fear conditioning, and P3 amplitude) were associated with later conduct problems, particularly aggression, and some measures also predicted increased risk of crime in early adulthood. These investigations in Mauritius are unique within the LMIC studies reviewed here, and many are novel worldwide.

3. *Early Child Temperament.* Although research in HICs has highlighted the importance of children's early temperament for the development of antisocial behavior (White et al. 1990; Caspi et al. 1995), results on this topic from four studies in Brazil, China, and Mauritius were mixed. In Pelotas, Brazil, no aspect of temperament or psychosocial functioning (withdrawn, somatic complaints, anxious/depressed, social problems, thought problems) at age 4 predicted conduct problems at age 12, adjusting for baseline conduct problems and family socioeconomic status (#4: Anselmi et al. 2008). It is possible that these null findings arose because of "overcontrol," that is, the adjustment of baseline conduct problems, which might themselves have been affected by early temperament. In a study in Beijing and Shanghai, children's affective behaviors with their mothers were assessed at age 2, but these were not associated with aggression at age 4 (#15: Wang et al. 2006). However, in a second study in Beijing, both child internalizing problems ($r = 0.28$) and social competence ($r = -0.35$) at age 2 predicted conduct problems 1 year later (#12: Zhang 2013). In Mauritius, having a sensation-seeking temperament at age 3 predicted aggressive, but not nonaggressive, conduct problems at age 11, adjusting for covariates including height, weight, and body size (#28: Raine et al. 1998), but fearlessness at age 3 was not predictive. As previously discussed, early biological measures that tap into constructs of emotionality and poor fear conditioning were also associated with aggression at age 8 in the Mauritius study (#28) and with crime up to age 23.

In summary, two studies in China and Mauritius found associations between several early temperament characteristics (stimulation seeking, poor social competence, emotionality, and poor fear conditioning) and later antisocial behavior, but further research is needed to clarify the effects, given that two other studies reported null findings.

4. *Hyperactivity and Attention Deficit.* Hyperactivity is one of the most robust risk factors for conduct problems and crime found across longitudinal studies in HICs, with numerous related concepts also predicting antisocial behavior, including attention deficit, restlessness, clumsiness, low

self-control, impulsiveness, and risk taking (Rutter, Giller, and Hagell 1998; Pratt et al. 2002; Jolliffe and Farrington 2008; Murray and Farrington 2010). Results from two studies in Chile and China were consistent with this literature. In Chile, hyperactivity at age 6 predicted conduct problems (OR = 2.2) at age 11 (#9: de la Barra, Toledo, and Rodríguez 2005), and among 6–9-year-olds in Beijing, higher effortful control (the reverse of impulsiveness) predicted less aggression and fewer conduct problems at ages 10–13 ($r = -0.26$ for both outcomes, averaging across parent, teacher, and child reports; #10: Zhou, Main, and Wang 2010). Pooling results from these two studies (#9, #10), there was an overall moderate bivariate association between hyperactivity and conduct problems ($d = 0.51$, table 4). However, in Pelotas, Brazil, hyperactivity at age 4 did not significantly predict conduct problems at age 12, independently of baseline conduct problems and socioeconomic status (#4: Anselmi et al. 2008). Again, it is possible that the total effects of hyperactivity were underestimated because baseline conduct problems were adjusted for in the analysis (no bivariate results were available to include in meta-analysis).

Considering hyperactivity measured after early childhood, three LMIC studies assessed associations with violence and crime in LMICs. Meta-analyzing results from two studies (#4, #28), the average bivariate association was almost zero ($d = 0.04$, table 4), but there was considerable heterogeneity. Specifically, in Mauritius, there was no significant association between hyperactivity at age 11 and crime at age 23 (#28: Gao et al. 2013). However, in Pelotas, Brazil, hyperactivity at age 11 predicted violence at age 18 (RR = 1.8 females, 1.3 males), although results for nonviolent crime were weaker and nonsignificant (RR = 1.3 females, 1.2 males), adjusting for child conduct problems and perinatal and family factors (#4: Murray, Menezes, et al. 2015). Comparing associations with a matched British study, the effects of hyperactivity on violent and nonviolent crime in Pelotas were similar between sites (Murray, Menezes, et al. 2015). In a third study that examined trajectories of delinquency (and could not be included in the meta-analysis), sensation-seeking among 5–13-year-olds in Puerto Rico predicted delinquent behavior over a 2-year period for both girls and boys, adjusting for various other individual, family, and social factors. Compared with Puerto Rican children living in New York, associations were similar between the two sites, even though the shape of the trajectories differed (#31: Maldonado-Molina et al. 2009; Jennings et al. 2010).

In summary, studies in LMICs generally show positive associations between hyperactivity, conduct problems, and violence but weak associations with youth crime.

5. *Internalizing Problems.* Internalizing problems are characterized by symptoms of anxiety and depression and are related to other concepts such as sensitivity, shyness, and poor self-concept. In six studies in LMICs, there were only null or weak associations between measures of internalizing problems and antisocial behavior. The studies are summarized below but were too heterogeneous in their designs and analyses to pool in meta-analyses. Three studies of internalizing problems and antisocial behavior were conducted in China, all showing weak or null associations. In the first, in Beijing, there was no significant association between child depressive symptoms and aggressive behavior over four waves of assessment between ages 9 and 12 (#11: Chen et al. 2012). This was a rather special study because repeated waves of data were used to account for continuity in behavior when estimating the associations. In a second study, in Shanghai, shyness at mean age 11 was only weakly associated with lower aggression 2 years later ($r = -0.10$), and there was no significant association between low self-worth and aggression (#21: Chen, He, and Li 2004). In another Shanghai study, neither shyness/sensitivity nor poor self-perception at ages 7 and 10 was significantly associated with conduct problems 4 years later (#20: Chen et al. 1999).

Additional weak or null associations concerning internalizing problems were found in Chile and Colombia. In Santiago, Chile, neither "social contact" nor "emotional maturity" among 6-year-olds significantly predicted conduct problems at age 11 (#9: de la Barra, Toledo, and Rodríguez 2003, 2005). Greater "sensitivity" among 12–17-year-old Colombian males was only weakly associated ($r = -0.06$) with lower levels of violence 2 years later (#22: Brook, Brook, and Whiteman 2007). However, in Puerto Rico, children's self-esteem at ages 5–13 predicted trajectories of delinquency over the following 2 years (#31: Maldonado-Molina et al. 2009). Higher self-esteem was observed among children whose delinquency remained persistently low compared with children who had initially high then declining rates of delinquency. Interestingly, a rather different pattern emerged among Puerto Rican children living in New York, where self-esteem was highest among children who had persistently elevated levels of delinquency over the 3-year study period (Maldonado-Molina et al. 2009).

To summarize, existing evidence in LMICs generally suggests weak or no associations between internalizing problems or related concepts and conduct problems.

6. *Intelligence and Educational Performance.* Low intelligence and poor educational attainment are well-replicated predictors of antisocial behavior in HICs (Hinshaw 1992; Rutter, Giller, and Hagell 1998; Farrington and Welsh 2007; Murray and Farrington 2010). Three studies in LMICs also found that low intelligence predicted various forms of antisocial behavior, but associations were robust after adjustment for confounding factors in only two studies. Meta-analyses were not conducted because of the different outcomes assessed across the studies. In Mauritius, low spatial intelligence, but not verbal intelligence, at age 3 predicted persistent antisocial behavior between ages 8 and 17, adjusting for social adversity, hyperactivity, and reading ability (#28: Raine et al. 2002). Also, in the Seychelles, children with lower intelligence scores at age 11 had more conduct problems at 17, adjusting for children's mercury exposure, maternal IQ, and socioeconomic position (#33: Davidson et al. 2011). Among Polish children aged 7 and 9, lower intelligence did not predict aggression over a 2-year period, adjusting for baseline aggression, violent television viewing, and sociodemographic factors (#30: Frączek 1986).

Regarding school performance, two Chinese studies found only weak effects on antisocial behavior, and their pooled bivariate association was zero ($d = 0.00$, table 4). In Beijing, lower school grades at ages 6–9 had a weak association with conduct problems ($r = 0.16$) but were also associated with less aggression ($r = -0.13$) at ages 10–13, averaging across parent, teacher, and child reports (#10: Zhou, Main, and Wang 2010). In Shanghai, children with lower participation and competence in school activities at mean age 11 had slightly higher aggression scores ($r = 0.13$) 2 years later (#21: Chen, He, and Li 2004).

Two studies in the Philippines (#29) and South Africa (#34) also showed null or weak associations between lower educational achievement and violence, and their pooled bivariate association was almost zero ($d = 0.04$, table 4), with significant heterogeneity between their results. The first study, in the Philippines, found that completing fewer school years by age 18 was not significantly associated with perpetrating intimate partner violence 3 years later, either in bivariate analysis or in adjusting for family of origin characteristics and other individual and household factors (#29: Fehringer and Hindin 2009). Among South African males, those with low educational attainment at ages 18–26 were at increased risk (OR = 1.4) for self-reported perpetration of family or intimate partner violence 3 years later (#34: Thaler 2011). However, in this study, there was no association with violence against strangers, adjusting for childhood background factors and youth unemployment (Seekings and Thaler 2011).

In summary, there are few studies concerning intelligence and school performance and the development of antisocial behavior in LMICs. Existing studies in China, Mauritius, Poland, South Africa, and the Philippines show weak and inconsistent associations.

7. *Drug and Alcohol Use.* Drug and alcohol use might contribute to antisocial behavior in several ways, including through physiological changes that increase disinhibited behavior, disruption of family and social bonds, involvement in theft to purchase drugs, and increasing contact with organized violent groups involved in drug trafficking (Goldstein 1985; Rutter, Giller, and Hagell 1998; Atkinson et al. 2009). Substance use problems could also be an indicator of a broad externalizing behavior syndrome, underpinned by a common construct of behavioral disinhibition (Patrick et al. 2015) and as such represent a marker rather than an explanatory cause of other antisocial behaviors. Although drug use is generally less common in LMICs than in HICs, it is associated with greater risk of mortality in LMICs than in HICs (Medina-Mora and Gibbs 2013).

Only three longitudinal studies have investigated drug or alcohol use as possible risk factors for antisocial behavior in LMICs: one found no association with conduct problems, and two showed associations with violence and delinquency. Two studies (#22, #34) that could be meta-analyzed showed a large-sized average bivariate association between drug use and violence ($d = 0.69$, table 4). In the first study, conducted in Colombia, marijuana use by 12–17-year-old males was associated with four times the odds of participation in delinquency 2 years later (#22: Brook et al. 2003), and lifetime drug use was associated ($r = 0.36$) with increased levels of violence (Brook, Brook, and Whiteman 2007). In the second study, South African males aged 14–22 who reported drug taking or drinking multiple times over a 4-year period were at increased risk for perpetrating family or intimate partner violence 7 years later (OR = 2.6 for drugs; OR = 1.5 for drinking; #34: Thaler 2011). Heavy drinking across multiple waves was also associated with increased risk (OR = 1.7) of violence against strangers, adjusting for drinking and drug taking in the participant's childhood home and neighborhood poverty in childhood (#34: Seekings and Thaler 2011). However, in another South African study (not in the meta-analysis because only adjusted results were available), a combined measure of alcohol and drug use at ages 10–17 was only weakly associated with conduct problems 1 year later ($\beta = 0.04$), adjusting for baseline measures of conduct problems, poverty, sociodemographics, and violence exposure (#37: Waller, Gardner, and Cluver 2014). The adjustment for baseline conduct problems in this study might have caused an underestimation of the total effect of drug and alcohol use on conduct problems.

In summary, two studies in LMICs show associations between drug use and later antisocial behavior, but it is not clear which mechanisms are involved or whether these represent causal effects. Future research should test possible competing mechanisms and incorporate tests of whether drug use predicts antisocial behavior only because they both form a broader syndrome of externalizing behavior.

8. *Other, Less Studied, Individual Factors.* Numerous other individual factors have been found to relate to the development of antisocial behavior in HICs but have not been extensively investigated in LMICs. Here, we summarize findings from the few studies in LMICs that examined antisocial behavior in relation to social competence, locus of control, attitudes toward deviance, and religiosity. One would expect that attitudes favorable to antisocial behavior would strongly predict antisocial behavior itself. Indeed, in Puerto Rico, 5–13-year-old children with positive attitudes to delinquency were most likely to have a high but declining rate of delinquency, adjusting for several other individual, family, and social factors (#31: Maldonado-Molina et al. 2009; Jennings et al. 2010). Similar effects were observed in a matched sample of Puerto Rican youths in New York (Maldonado-Molina et al. 2009; Jennings et al. 2010). However, in Colombia, a tolerant attitude toward "deviance" at ages 12–17 predicted ($r = 0.17$) violent behavior 2 years later only weakly (#22: Brook, Brook, and Whiteman 2007).

Two studies in Shanghai (#20, #21) showed no association between children's sociability and later conduct problems (Chen et al. 1999, 2000). The pooled bivariate association in these studies was almost zero ($d = -0.03$, table 4). However, prosocial behavior at age 11 predicted fewer conduct problems 2 years later ($r = -0.22$) in one of the studies (#21: Chen et al. 2000), and social competence at ages 6–9 also predicted fewer conduct problems 4 years later in another study in Beijing (average $r = -0.20$; #10: Tao, Zhou, and Wang 2010; Chen et al. 2011). The pooled bivariate association between social competence/prosocial behavior and conduct problems in these two studies (#10, #21) was medium and negative ($d = -0.43$, table 4).

The psychological trait of having an "external locus of control" was investigated as a possible predictor of delinquency in San Juan, Puerto Rico (#31). External locus of control means perceiving your life as mainly influenced by uncontrollable, external forces. Children aged 5–13 with a higher external locus of control were more likely to show high but declining trajectories of delinquency over a 2-year period (#31: Maldonado-Molina et al. 2009), in contrast to a matched sample in the Bronx, New York, where external locus of control did not associate with any particular delinquency trajectory.

Religiosity has been theorized to be protective against antisocial behavior (Baier and Wright 2001). However, a study in the Philippines found no association between frequent church attendance at age 18 and risk of perpetration of intimate partner violence 3 years later, in either bivariate or multivariate analyses (both RR = 1.0), adjusting for family of origin characteristics including intergenerational violence and other individual and household factors (#29: Fehringer and Hindin 2009).

In summary, a small number of LMIC studies suggest antisocial behavior might have a small association with low levels of social competence, having an external locus of control, and having attitudes favorable to delinquency. The limited evidence available in LMICs suggests no association between antisocial behavior and sociability or religiosity.

## C. Prenatal and Early Health Influences

It is estimated that over 200 million children in LMICs do not reach their developmental potential by age 5 because of nutritional deficiencies, exposure to toxins, violence, poverty, and other health and social problems early in life (Grantham-McGregor et al. 2007; Walker, Wachs, et al. 2007). Some longitudinal research in HICs suggests that early health risks affect children's neurological development and thereby increase vulnerability to environmental stresses causing antisocial behavior (Moffitt 1993; Raine 2002a; Brennan, Grekin, and Mednick 2003; Liu 2011). This line of research has led to the development of prevention programs from pregnancy onward to enhance children's development and reduce risk of adverse outcomes, including antisocial behavior (Tremblay and Japel 2003). Eleven longitudinal studies in LMICs examined pregnancy and perinatal factors as possible influences on child conduct problems and youth violence, in Brazil, the Czech Republic, Mauritius, South Africa, and former

Yugoslavia. Meta-analytic results are shown in table 5, with results from individual studies summarized below.

1. *Prenatal and Birth Factors.* Unplanned pregnancy was examined as a possible risk factor for children's antisocial behavior in Pelotas, Brazil (#4: Murray, Maughan, et al. 2015). However, it was only weakly associated with offspring conduct problems at age 11 (females RR = 1.3; males RR = 1.2) and violence at age 18 (females RR = 1.5; males RR = 1.2). The very different, and less common, event of an unwanted pregnancy was the focus of a long-term prospective investigation in the Czech Republic. Children of mothers who, unsuccessfully, applied for an abortion were compared with matched control children in the same school classes and assessed in adulthood. Children from unwanted pregnancies were more likely than control children (OR = 2.2) to have a criminal record by ages 22–24 (#24: Dytrych, Matějček, and Schüller 1988), but there was almost no difference (OR = 1.2) in the probability of having a criminal record at age 30 (Kubička et al. 1995), suggesting an attenuation of long-term risk associated with unwanted pregnancies.

Maternal smoking in pregnancy was examined as a predictor of child conduct problems in four studies in Brazil, the Czech Republic, and former Yugoslavia. Meta-analysis of these studies revealed a medium-sized average bivariate association (d = 0.36, across #4, #25, #39) and reduced covariate-adjusted association (d = 0.26, across #4, #5, #39; table 5). In Pelotas, Brazil, maternal smoking in pregnancy was associated with children's conduct problems at age 4 (OR = 1.4), adjusting for paternal smoking, parental education, family income, and social class (#4: Brion et al. 2010). That children's conduct problems were associated with maternal but not paternal smoking increased the plausibility of biological effects of tobacco exposure in utero (Brion et al. 2010). In contrast to many HICs, maternal smoking in pregnancy was not strongly socially patterned in Pelotas, Brazil, helping to rule out explanations based on family income or social class. Associations with conduct problems persisted in follow-ups of the same cohort at ages 11 and 15 (#4: Anselmi et al. 2012; Murray, Maughan, et al. 2015). In another study in Pelotas, Brazil, maternal smoking in pregnancy was associated with higher levels of children's conduct problems at age 4 (d = 0.25), adjusting for a range of sociodemographic factors, maternal psychopathology, and childbirth characteristics (#5: Matijasevich et al. 2014). Also, in former Yugoslavia, maternal smoking in pregnancy predicted conduct problems at ages 4–5, adjusting for age, sex, ethnicity, lead exposure, birth weight, maternal education, and

TABLE 5

Meta-Analytic Results for Associations between Early Life Health Factors and Child Conduct Problems and Youth Violence

| Predictor | Behavioral Outcome | Number of Studies | Studies Included (#) | Type of Association | Effect Size $d$ | 95% CI | $p^a$ | Heterogeneity | |
| --- | --- | --- | --- | --- | --- | --- | --- | --- | --- |
| | | | | | | | | $I^2$ | $p^b$ |
| Maternal smoking in pregnancy | Conduct problems | 3 | (4, 25, 39) | Bivariate | .36 | (.30 to .42) | <.001 | 0% | .600 |
| | | 3 | (4, 5, 39) | Adjusted | .26 | (.20 to .32) | <.001 | 0% | .461 |
| | Violence | 2 | (3, 4) | Bivariate | .13 | (.00 to .26) | .055 | 45% | .180 |
| Low birth weight | Conduct problems | 3 | (6, 8, 36) | Bivariate | .01 | (−.12 to .14) | .857 | 0% | .908 |
| | | 2 | (5, 36) | Adjusted | .02 | (−.07 to .11) | .679 | 0% | .324 |
| Premature birth | Conduct problems | 4 | (4, 5, 8) | Bivariate | .04 | (−.03 to .10) | .283 | 0% | .942 |
| Malnutrition | Conduct problems | 3 | (1, 26, 28) | Bivariate | .35 | (.01 to .69) | .044 | 82% | .004 |
| | Conduct problems | 2 | (1, 27) | Adjusted | .35 | (.07 to .73) | .013 | 0% | .822 |

NOTE.—# = study ID number shown in table 2; $p^a$ = $p$-value for $d$ effect size; $p^b$ = $p$-value for a $\chi^2$ test for heterogeneity. Random-effects models.

parental warmth toward the child (#39: Wasserman et al. 2001). Moreover, maternal smoking in pregnancy predicted conduct problems at age 8 (e.g., OR = 1.7 for "provokes fights") in the Czech Republic, although associations weakened by age 13 (#25: Kukla, Hruba, and Tyrlik 2008).

Only two studies in LMICs investigated whether maternal smoking in pregnancy predicted youth violence, both in Pelotas, Brazil. Their pooled bivariate results yielded a small and nonsignificant association ($d = 0.13$, table 5). In a cohort of children born in 1982, there was no association between maternal smoking in pregnancy and conviction for violence up to age 25, either in bivariate analyses or in adjusting for sociodemographic factors (adjusted RR = 1.1 for males, 0.8 for females; #3: Caicedo et al. 2010). However, in a later cohort, born in 1993, maternal smoking in pregnancy predicted self-reported violence at age 18 for females (RR = 1.7), but not for males (RR = 1.1; #4: Murray, Maughan, et al. 2015).

Maternal alcohol use in pregnancy, urinary infection in pregnancy, and intrauterine growth restriction were also examined as predictors of conduct problems and violence in the 1993 cohort in Pelotas, Brazil (#4: Murray, Maughan, et al. 2015). Conduct problems at age 11 were moderately associated with maternal alcohol use in pregnancy (males only, RR = 1.5) and urinary infection in pregnancy (females only, RR = 1.3), but not intrauterine growth restriction for either sex. The only variable associated with violence at age 18 was maternal alcohol use in pregnancy (males only, RR = 1.5). These findings were compared with those from a matched study in Britain; several risk factor associations were weaker in Pelotas than in the British study, especially for males (Murray, Maughan, et al. 2015).

Mercury exposure in utero was investigated as another toxin that might affect children's neurodevelopment and later antisocial behavior in a study in the Seychelles (#33). However, there was no association between mercury exposure and children's aggressive or conduct problem behaviors at ages 5 and 17 (Myers et al. 2000; Davidson et al. 2011).

Complications at birth (such as breech birth, use of forceps during delivery, caesarean delivery, or difficulty with breathing) were weakly associated with conduct problems at age 11 in Mauritius, and this relationship was partly mediated by low IQ (#28: Liu et al. 2009). However, in Pelotas, Brazil, birth complications did not predict violent crime up to age 25, adjusting for sociodemographic factors and maternal smoking in pregnancy (RR = 1.1 for males and 1.2 for females; #3: Caicedo et al. 2010).

Six studies, in Brazil, South Africa, the Seychelles, and former Yugoslavia, convincingly show that there is no association between low birth weight and children's conduct problems. Individually, each reported no association (#5, #6, #8, #33, #36, #39; Myers et al. 2000; Wasserman et al. 2001; Emond et al. 2006; Sabet et al. 2009; Rodriguez et al. 2011; Matijasevich et al. 2014). Pooling effect sizes for low birth weight (<2,500 grams) reported in three studies (#6, #8, #36), the average association with conduct problems was almost zero ($d = 0.01$, table 5). Covariate-adjusted results were also nonsignificant in five studies (Myers et al. 2000; Wasserman et al. 2001; Sabet et al. 2009; Rodriguez et al. 2011; Matijasevich et al. 2014) and almost zero ($d = 0.02$, table 5) in meta-analysis of two studies for which effect sizes could be computed (#5, #36). Birth weight was also unrelated to violent crime in the 1982 Pelotas study, both before and after adjusting for sociodemographic factors (adjusted RR = 1.3 for males; #3: Caicedo et al. 2010). Similarly, premature birth did not predict child conduct problems in all three Brazilian studies that tested the association (#4, #5, #8: Rodriguez et al. 2011; Matijasevich et al. 2014; Murray, Maughan, et al. 2015). The pooled bivariate association in these three studies was almost zero ($d = 0.04$, table 5), and one covariate-adjusted result was nonsignificant (#8: Rodriguez et al. 2011).

In summary, the perinatal factor most consistently associated with child conduct problems in LMIC studies is maternal smoking in pregnancy. Although the evidence is limited, it points toward a possible biological effect of this risk factor, given that maternal smoking but not paternal smoking was predictive in one study, and some results showed associations even after adjustment for covariates. However, similar results have previously been reported in HICs (for a review and meta-analysis, see Wakschlag et al. [2002]; Pratt, McGloin, and Fearn [2006]), only to be questioned by null findings in studies with stronger research designs, including twin studies and sibling comparisons (Maughan et al. 2004; D'Onofrio et al. 2008; Jaffee, Strait, and Odgers 2012). Hence, it is difficult to know whether the associations observed in studies in LMICs really reflect causal effects. Several studies consistently showed that low birth weight and preterm birth were not associated with children's conduct problems, which is consistent with a prior meta-analysis of very low birth weight and prematurity in HICs (Aarnoudse-Moens et al. 2009). Limited evidence on associations between unplanned pregnancy, unwanted pregnancy, alcohol use in pregnancy, intrauterine growth restriction, and birth complications also suggested zero or only weak associations with conduct problems and violence. These various null and weak findings in LMIC studies are important to consider, given prominent theories predicting adverse influences of early health risks on antisocial behavior via effects on neurological functioning (Raine 2002*a*, 2013; Eryigit Madzwamuse et al. 2015). However, these studies tended to examine health risks in isolation. Studies in HICs show that prenatal and perinatal health risks are influential when considered in interaction with subsequent adverse social environments (Piquero and Tibbetts 1999; Tibbetts and Piquero 1999; Raine 2002*b*), as predicted by some developmental theories (Moffitt 1993). Future research should test for such interactions in LMIC studies.

2. *Early Life Health Influences.* Malnutrition in the first years of life and early exposure to toxins, such as lead, have been hypothesized to increase risk for antisocial behavior via effects on neurological processes related to behavior control (Raine 2002*a*; Liu 2011). Seven studies examined health factors including malnutrition and exposure to toxins in early childhood as possible risk factors for later antisocial behavior in Barbados, Brazil, China, Guatemala, Jamaica, Mauritius, and former Yugoslavia. Three studies had mixed findings on the effects of malnutrition (see studies #1, #27, #28). Their pooled bivariate association between early malnutrition and later conduct problems was medium ($d = 0.35$, table 5), with high heterogeneity in the results. Pooling covariate-adjusted results available in two studies (#1, #27) produced a similar association ($d = 0.35$, table 5) without heterogeneity. Their individual findings were as follows. In Barbados (#1), children with malnutrition in their first year of life were at increased risk for self-reported conduct problems at ages 11–17 ($\beta = 0.19$), adjusting for living conditions in the home (Galler et al. 2012), but malnutrition did not independently predict parent-rated aggression or teacher-rated conduct problems at 9–17 (Galler and Ramsey 1989; Galler et al. 2011). In Jamaica (#27), children with stunting at ages 9–24 months were at increased risk for parent-reported conduct problems at ages 11–12 and oppositional behavior at age 17, but not teacher-reported conduct problems at ages 11–12 or self-reported antisocial behavior at age 17 (Chang et al. 2002; Walker, Chang, et al. 2007). In the same study, there was no significant difference in oppositional-antisocial behavior by stunting status, adjusting for both housing conditions and witnessing violence (#27: Walker, Chang, et al. 2007). In Mauritius, malnutrition at age 3 predicted aggression at 8 and conduct disorder at 17, but there was no association with aggression or delinquency at age 11 or 17 (#28: Liu et al. 2004).

It has been suggested that breast feeding may reduce risk for antisocial behavior because of its positive effects on mother-child bonding and nutrients in breast milk that contribute to neuronal development (Anderson, Johnstone, and Remley 1999; Fergusson and Woodward 1999; Caicedo et al. 2010). Little evidence is available on this topic in high-income countries. However, a strong test of the hypothesis was conducted in Belarus, in a large cluster-randomized trial evaluating effects of breast feeding promotion by pediatric health workers in selected hospitals. Breast feeding duration was substantially increased in the experimental group, and this was found to improve infant health up to age 1 (#2: Kramer et al. 2001). However, at age 6, the experimental and control groups had identical levels of conduct problems, as rated by both parents ($d = 0.0$) and teachers ($d = 0.0$), indicating no protective effect of breast feeding on child conduct problems (#2: Kramer et al. 2008). Null results for breast feeding were also reported in relation to violence in Pelotas, Brazil, where longer breast feeding duration did not predict differential risk for violent conviction up to age 25 (#3: Caicedo et al. 2010). The relative lack of socioeconomic patterning in rates of breast feeding in the Pelotas context helped rule out confounding in this study.

Lead ingestion has been hypothesized to influence child development and antisocial behavior via its effects on cognition and brain functioning. Many ecological studies suggest an association between environmental lead levels and criminal behavior (Nevin 2007; Mielke and Zahran 2012). Neurological research shows effects of lead exposure on brain development (Wright et al. 2008), and a longitudinal study in the United States found an association between pre- and postnatal lead exposure and adult crime (Cecil et al. 2008). However, longitudinal data from LMICs have not supported the lead–antisocial behavior hypothesis. In former Yugoslavia, five out of six measures of blood lead levels taken up to age 2.5 were not associated with child aggression at age 3 (#39: Wasserman et al. 1998; Factor-Litvak et al. 1999). In the same study, children's average lead exposure during early childhood was not associated with aggression at ages 4–5 in bivariate analyses, although it was associated ($B = 0.32$) with the delinquency subscale of the Child Behavior Checklist after adjusting for sociodemographics, early health factors, and maternal warmth and responsiveness (Wasserman et al. 2001). In a Chinese study, children's blood lead levels at age 3 did not significantly predict aggressive or oppositional defiant behavior at age 5, adjusting for sociodemographic factors and child IQ (#18: Liu et al. 2014).

In Guatemala, the effects of a zinc supplementation intervention on the mental health of school children aged 6–11 were investigated in a randomized control trial (#26: DiGirolamo et al. 2010). Although the intervention successfully increased zinc levels ($d = 0.29$), among treated children there was no evidence that increases in zinc changed child aggressive behavior or conduct problems.

In summary, although there is some evidence for a small association between malnutrition and child conduct problems, existing evidence in LMICs does not suggest a strong influence of early childhood health factors on the development of conduct problems or violence. Individual studies of zinc and lead exposure indicated no effect on antisocial behavior. Two LMIC studies on breast feeding, including one randomized control trial, are particularly unusual in the literature and provide strong evidence that breast feeding is not a direct protective factor for antisocial behavior.

### D. Child Rearing Processes

Child rearing processes play a fundamental role in several major theories of the development of antisocial behavior (Moffitt 1993; Patterson 1995; Farrington 2005b). However, the effects of any given parenting practice may depend partly on cultural norms and the meanings given to those behaviors (Lansford et al. 2005). For example, it has been suggested that tougher parenting styles may predict better adjustment for children in high-risk communities but worse adjustment for children in low-risk environments (Cummings, Davies, and Campbell 2000). There is considerable variability across LMICs in the extent of use of harsh discipline, including physical punishment, and its cultural acceptability (Lansford and Deater-Deckard 2012; UN Children's Fund 2014); hence it may be expected that parenting practices would have heterogeneous effects on child behavior across different cultural contexts.

1. *Harsh, Coercive, and Rejecting Parenting.* Parental harsh and inconsistent discipline is considered an important risk factor contributing to escalating difficulties in parent-child interactions and the onset and persistence of behavior problems (Rothbaum and Weisz 1994; Patterson 1995; Smith and Stern 1997; McCord 1998; Farrington 2002; Gershoff 2002). For example, a meta-analysis of 88 studies showed that corporal punishment was associated with increased child aggression ($d = 0.36$) and adult crime and antisocial behavior ($d = 0.42$; Gershoff 2002). Moreover, although familial confounding and child effects (child behavior

causing harsh parenting) are relevant, quasi-experimental studies and randomized experiments are consistent with the view that harsh parenting is a causal risk factor for antisocial behavior (Jaffee, Strait, and Odgers 2012).

Longitudinal evidence on associations between harsh parenting and child antisocial behavior in LMICs comes from China, Russia, Brazil, Poland, Puerto Rico, South Africa, and Colombia. Findings from individual studies are summarized below, and meta-analytic results are shown in table 6. It is important to note that associations between parenting and child adjustment tend to be highest when assessments of both variables are based on parental reports (Collishaw et al. 2009). Nearly all studies in LMICs used parental reports to assess parenting practices; therefore, we pay particular attention to whether or not child behavior was also assessed by parents or by other informants.

"Authoritarian parenting" refers to a general style of parenting involving coercion, harsh punishment, and withdrawal of affection and has been linked to the development of antisocial behavior in various studies in HICs (Baumrind 1966; Farrington 2002; Hoeve et al. 2009). In LMICs, two studies, in China (#10) and Russia (#32), reported weak associations between maternal authoritarian parenting and child conduct problems. In the Chinese study, authoritarian parenting when children were 6–9 years old weakly predicted ($r = 0.14$) child conduct problems reported by parents, teachers, and children themselves 3 years later, adjusting for other parental characteristics and child conduct problems at baseline (Zhou et al. 2008; see also Tao, Zhou, and Wang 2010; #10: Chen et al. 2011). In the Russian study, maternal authoritarian parenting in the preschool years predicted self-rated adolescent physical aggression for girls ($\beta = 0.34$) and relational aggression for boys ($\beta = 0.35$), adjusting for other parenting factors and preschool child aggression (#32: Nelson et al. 2014). However, in the same study, maternal authoritarian parenting did not significantly predict relational aggression for girls or physical aggression for boys; and paternal authoritarian parenting was not associated with any child outcome. The pooled bivariate association between maternal authoritarian parenting and child behavior problems in these studies was medium-sized and significant ($d = 0.38$, table 6).

Other studies of authoritarian parenting were not meta-analyzed because they examined only specific subdomains of authoritarian parenting, but nearly all reported positive associations with child behavior problems. Three such studies were conducted in Beijing. The first (#14) found that

## TABLE 6
### Meta-Analytic Results for Associations between Child Rearing Factors and Child Conduct Problems

| Predictor | Behavioral Outcome | Number of Studies | Studies Included (#) | Type of Association | Effect Size $d$ | 95% CI | $p^a$ | Heterogeneity $I^2$ | Heterogeneity $p^b$ |
|---|---|---|---|---|---|---|---|---|---|
| Maternal authoritarian parenting | Conduct problems and aggression | 2 | (10, 32) | Bivariate | .38 | (.21 to .58) | <.001 | 0% | .853 |
| Maternal warmth | Conduct problems and aggression | 3 | (12, 10, 15, 20) | Bivariate | −.12 | (−.32 to .07) | .224 | 37% | .189 |
| Maternal authoritative parenting | Conduct problems and aggression | 3 | (11, 15, 32) | Bivariate | −.26 | (−.62 to .10) | .162 | 66% | .018 |
| Paternal authoritative parenting | Aggression | 2 | (15, 32) | Bivariate | −.25 | (−.51 to .0) | .053 | 0% | .387 |

NOTE.—# = study ID number shown in table 2; $p^a$ = $p$-value for $d$ effect size; $p^b$ = $p$-value for a $\chi^2$ test for heterogeneity. Random-effects models.

parental rejecting behaviors of 2-year-olds predicted parent-rated conduct problems ($\beta$ = 0.25) when children were aged 4, adjusting for baseline child conduct problems (Zhu et al. 2011). A second study of 2-year-olds in Beijing (#15) found that parental power assertion and harsh parenting when children were aged 2 predicted observer-rated child aggression at age 4 ($\beta$ = 0.16), adjusting for other parenting factors and child non-compliance at baseline (Chen et al. 2002). In a third Beijing study (#10), punitive parental reactions to children's negative emotions, when they were aged 6–9, also weakly correlated with children's conduct problems 3 years later ($\beta$ = 0.07), adjusting for baseline child behavior and family socioeconomic position (Tao, Zhou, and Wang 2010).

Studies in Brazil and Poland also showed positive associations between specific aspects of authoritarian parenting and antisocial behavior. In São Gonçalo, Brazil, parental verbal aggression when children were aged 7 predicted increased parent-rated conduct problems over the next 3 years ($d$ = 0.30), adjusting for baseline sociodemographic factors and various types of home and community violence (#7: de Assis et al. 2013). In Poland (#30), parenting characterized as rejecting of children at ages 7 and 9 was associated with child aggression over the next 3 years in both parent and self-reports ($\beta$ = 0.32 for boys and 0.30 for girls), adjusting for other parenting variables, sociodemographics, and violent television viewing (Frączek 1986). Parental "punishment" (presumably referring to harsh punishment) also predicted girls' ($\beta$ = 0.20) peer-rated aggressive behavior, but there was no significant association for boys (#30: Frączek 1986). More equivocal results were reported from a Russian study (#32) that examined parental "psychological control" of preschool children as a possible predictor of adolescent self-reported aggression. For boys, there was no significant association, adjusting for other parenting factors and early child aggression (Nelson et al. 2014). For girls, paternal psychological control predicted more relational and physical aggression ($\beta$ = 0.40 and 0.36, respectively), but maternal psychological control predicted less physical aggression ($\beta$ = −0.26) and was not associated with relational aggression.

Hou et al. (2013) conducted a rare genetically sensitive study of the effects of hostile parenting on children in Beijing, China (#13). Differences in parents' treatment of monozygotic twins were examined in relation to subsequent twin differences in conduct problems, assessed by parent and self-reports. Twins exposed to more parental hostility than their twin sibling at ages 10–18 did not show more conduct problems 2 years later. By contrast, initial twin differences in conduct problems did predict later parental hostility. This suggested that, rather than parental hostility causing increases in conduct problems, the reverse was true: child conduct problems elicited higher levels of parental hostility in adolescence.

Two studies that examined indicators of harsh parenting in relation to delinquent or violent behavior in LMICs had different findings. In Colombia, strict parental discipline reported by adolescents at ages 12–17 was not associated with self-reported violent behavior 2 years later (#22: Brook, Brook, and Whiteman 2007). In Puerto Rico, parental coercive discipline reported by children aged 5–13 was highest among those with a high rate of delinquency that quite rapidly declined over the next 2 years (#31: Maldonado-Molina et al. 2009).

As would be expected, parent-child conflict was associated with antisocial behavior in the two studies that examined this issue in LMICs. Among 2-year-old Chinese children, mother-child conflict predicted mother-reported child conduct problems ($r = 0.37$) 9 months later (#12: Zhang 2013). In Colombia, adolescent-reported conflict with parents at ages 12–17 was weakly associated with self-reported violent behavior ($r = 0.14$) 2 years later (#22: Brook, Brook, and Whiteman 2007). Given that the studies analyzed different outcomes, they were not meta-analyzed.

In summary, studies of authoritarian parenting styles and specific aspects of harsh parenting generally show associations with child antisocial behavior in LMICs, although not all findings were positive. Notably, all studies relied on questionnaires to assess parents' attitudes and behaviors, and all but two relied on parental reports. More sensitive observational measures may reveal different patterns. A particular problem with interpreting associations found in these studies is that harsh parenting practices can arise in response to child misbehavior (possible reverse causation), and genetic influences might produce spurious associations between parental and child behaviors (Jaffee, Strait, and Odgers 2012), as suggested by one genetically sensitive study conducted in China (Hou et al. 2013). Causal inference should be strengthened in future research in LMICs by conducting more observational studies that examine within-individual change in both parenting and child behavior through time, employing genetically sensitive research designs, and also by conducting randomized trials of parenting programs designed to reduce child behavior problems, and testing whether intervention effects are mediated by reductions in harsh parenting practices (Rutter et al. 2001). Such studies have been conducted in HICs (Forehand et al. 2014), but not to our knowledge as part of randomized trials in LMICs (Knerr, Gardner, and Cluver 2013).

2. *Authoritative and Warm Parenting.* In contrast to harsh and reject-ing parenting behaviors, an "authoritative" parenting style, combining warmth and limit setting guided by explanations, is theorized to reduce child problem behavior (Larzelere, Morris, and Harrist 2013). However, findings on this issue were mixed in three studies in LMICs, producing a medium-sized, nonsignificant association in meta-analysis. Individual studies included in the meta-analysis were conducted in Russia and China. Among Russian preschool children, authoritative parenting predicted lower levels of self-reported physical aggression for boys ($\beta = -0.29$ mothers; $\beta = -0.39$ fathers), but not for girls, adjusting for other parent-ing factors (#32: Nelson et al. 2014). Considering relational aggression as an outcome in the same study, only paternal authoritative parenting was predictive, and only for boys ($\beta = -0.39$; #32: Nelson et al. 2014). Among 6–9-year-old children in Beijing, authoritative parenting predicted slightly fewer ($r = -0.12$) child conduct problems 3 years later, assessed by par-ents, teachers, and children themselves, adjusting for other parental characteristics and child conduct problems at baseline (Zhou et al. 2008; see also Tao, Zhou, and Wang 2010; #10: Chen et al. 2011). In another Beijing study, maternal "inductive parenting" (a concept similar to author-itative parenting), when children were aged 2, predicted less observer-rated aggression for girls ($r = -0.45$), but not for boys; paternal inductive parenting was not associated with child aggression (#15: Chen et al. 2002). In a meta-analysis of these three studies (#10, #15, #32), the bivariate asso-ciation between maternal authoritative parenting and child conduct prob-lems and aggression was medium but nonsignificant ($d = -0.26$, table 6), with significant heterogeneity. Meta-analysis of the two studies (#15, #32) that examined the bivariate association between paternal authoritative par-enting and child aggression was of similar magnitude ($d = -0.25$, table 6).

We conducted a separate meta-analysis of bivariate results from four Chinese studies that examined related subdimensions of authoritative parenting: parental warmth, closeness, acceptance, and responsiveness. Among 2-year-olds in Beijing, paternal warmth ($r = -0.21$), but not ma-ternal warmth, predicted less observer-rated child aggression at age 4 (#15: Chen et al. 2002). In another sample of 2-year-old children in Beijing, mother-child closeness predicted fewer ($r = -0.28$) conduct problems reported by mothers at ages 3–4 (#12: Zhang 2013). A third Beijing study found no significant association between parental supportiveness in re-sponse to child negative emotions among 6–9-year-olds and child conduct problems 3 years later (#10: Tao, Zhou, and Wang 2010). However, in a Shanghai study, maternal acceptance (warmth, enjoyment, and less rejection) toward 7- and 10-year-old children predicted less ($\beta = -0.14$) child aggressive and disruptive behavior 4 years later, as reported by peers (#20: Chen et al. 1999). Pooling results across these studies (#12, #10, #15, #20) produced a small bivariate association between maternal "warmth" and child behavior problems ($d = -0.12$) that was not significant (table 6).

Three other studies in Poland, former Yugoslavia, and Puerto Rico examined specific aspects of authoritative parenting in multivariate models and had mixed results. Among 7- and 9-year-old Polish children, parental "nurturance" predicted lower peer-rated aggressive behavior ($\beta = -0.19$) for girls over a 3-year period, adjusting for sociodemographics, other parenting variables, and child violent television viewing, but there was no significant association for boys (#30: Frączek 1986). In former Yugoslavia, observer ratings of parental warmth and responsiveness with 3-year-old children predicted reduced maternal-reported conduct problems, but not aggression, when children were aged 4–5, adjusting for perinatal and demographic factors (#39: Wasserman et al. 2001). In Puerto Rico, levels of family and social support toward children aged 9, on average, did not significantly predict self-reported delinquency over the next 2 years, as was also found in a matched sample in New York (#31: Maldonado-Molina et al. 2009).

In the genetically sensitive twin study in Beijing (#13), Hou et al. (2013) examined differences in levels of parental warmth between monozygotic twins as a predictor of twin differences in conduct problems, assessed using both parent and self-reports. The results were null: twin differences in maternal and paternal warmth at ages 10–18 did not associate with levels of conduct problems 2 years later.

Authoritative parenting might be contrasted with overly permissive parenting in which children are not given clear limits about behavior. In Voronezh in Russia, "overly permissive" parenting during children's preschool years was examined as a possible predictor of adolescent self-rated relational or physical aggression, adjusting for other parenting factors and child aggression in preschool (#32: Nelson et al. 2014). For boys, there was no significant association. For girls, high permissiveness by fathers predicted more physical aggression ($\beta = 0.45$); however, high permissiveness by mothers predicted less physical aggression ($\beta = -0.23$), and there were no significant associations with relational aggression.

Among Colombian males, those who reported fewer parental rules at ages 12–17 had marginally higher levels of self-reported violence 2 years later ($r = 0.08$; #22: Brook, Brook, and Whiteman 2007).

In summary, although several studies in LMICs found that authoritative parenting was associated with less child antisocial behavior, results were not consistent, and few studies adjusted for other child and family factors when estimating these effects. As with research on harsh parenting, future studies about the effects of authoritative parenting should use observational measures and strengthen causal inference by analyzing within-individual change, using genetically sensitive designs, and integrating findings from observational studies with those from randomized trials of parenting programs.

### E. Maltreatment and Other Adverse Life Events

Stressful life experiences including maltreatment predict a range of adverse health and behavioral outcomes. The effects of multiple stressful events have been highlighted as of particular importance for children's development (Anda et al. 2005). Stress can affect neurocognitive and endocrine systems, children's relationships, and learning processes that are implicated in the development of antisocial behavior (Susman 2006). Recent estimates suggest that more than half of children (ages 2–17) worldwide experienced violence during a 1-year period (Hillis et al. 2016). Across 25 LMICs, it was estimated that between 20 and 50 percent of 13–15-year-old children were physically attacked in the previous 12 months (UN Children's Fund 2014). In this section, we review evidence from LMICs on the effects of maltreatment and other adverse life events on antisocial behavior. The studies summarized below were considered too heterogeneous in their designs and analyses to pool in meta-analyses.

Surprisingly, the three longitudinal studies in LMICs that examined effects of maltreatment on antisocial behavior all found weak or null associations. In São Gonçalo, Brazil, severe parental physical violence against children, reported by parents when children were aged 7, was not significantly associated with child conduct problems over the following 3 years, adjusting for baseline sociodemographic factors and other home and community violence (#7: de Assis et al. 2013). In South Africa, physical, emotional, and sexual maltreatment reported by adolescents aged 10–17 was only weakly associated ($\beta = 0.04$) with conduct problems 1 year later, adjusting for baseline levels of child behavior, poverty, and other forms of home and community violence (#37: Waller, Gardner, and Cluver 2014). In another South African study, male youths aged 14–22 who reported having been physically abused as a child were not at increased risk of perpetrating family or intimate partner violence 7 years later (#34: Thaler 2011).

These same three studies in Brazil and South Africa, and a fourth in the Philippines, also reported weak or null effects of other forms of family violence on antisocial behavior. In São Gonçalo, Brazil, physical violence between grandparents when children were aged 7 was weakly associated ($d = 0.32$) with conduct problems over the next 3 years, adjusting for baseline sociodemographic factors and other types of home and community violence (#7: de Assis et al. 2013); physical violence between parents was not significantly predictive. In South Africa, exposure to family physical and emotional violence at ages 10–17 was not associated ($\beta = 0.01$) with conduct problems 1 year later, adjusting for baseline poverty level, child behavior, maltreatment, and community violence (#37: Waller, Gardner, and Cluver 2014). Also in South Africa, intimate partner violence suffered by mothers until children were age 5 was weakly associated with child aggression ($r = 0.13$), but not with oppositional behavior at age 5 (#36: Barbarin, Richter, and DeWet 2001). In Cebu, the Philippines, recall of interparental violence at age 18 was not associated with perpetrating intimate partner violence 3 years later, in either bivariate or multivariate analyses, adjusting for other family of origin characteristics and current individual and household factors (#29: Fehringer and Hindin 2009).

War-related trauma increases children's risk for mental health problems such as post-traumatic stress disorder (Thabet and Vostanis 1999). A study conducted in Croatia (#23) was the only longitudinal study in an LMIC to compare child antisocial behavior according to differences in exposure to war. The study included 208 children in Zagreb assessed at age 5 in 1991, before the war in Yugoslavia started, who were then followed up at age 6, during the war (#23: Rabotegsaric, Zuzul, and Kerestes 1994). Comparing the same children before and during the war, no change in aggression was observed. Also, there was no difference in levels of aggression between children during the war and a control group of the same age prior to the war. However, the extent of exposure to wartime traumatic events was not assessed in this study, which is an important moderator of the effects of war on other mental health outcomes such as post-traumatic stress disorder (Pine, Costello, and Masten 2005).

Four studies in LMICs examined other forms of stressful life events, such as death of a family member, permanent house moves, and experiences of discrimination, in relation to child antisocial behavior. In Pelotas, Brazil, a composite measure of stressful life events up to age 11 predicted conduct problems at age 15 ($d = 0.39$, comparing children who experienced multiple stressful events versus no events; #4: Anselmi et al. 2012). In Colombia, experiences of discrimination at ages 12–17 were not associated ($r = 0.01$) with violent behavior 2 years later (#22: Brook, Brook, and Whiteman 2007). In Puerto Rico, stressful life events at mean age 9 were most common among children who then showed high but rapidly declining delinquency rates, followed by children who showed low but stable rates of delinquency over a 2-year period (#31: Maldonado-Molina et al. 2009). In a matched sample of Puerto Rican children in New York, stressful life events were most common among children with a high and increasing rate of offending.

Some of these findings on effects of stressful life events in LMICs are at odds with comparable findings in HICs. Perhaps the most striking difference concerns the effects of child maltreatment. A meta-analysis of the effects of experiencing violence on antisocial behavior in HICs revealed an overall association of $d = 0.55$ but found a reduced effect ($d = 0.31$) among prospective studies, many of which involved child maltreatment (Wilson, Stover, and Berkowitz 2009). Quite similar associations were found for violence experienced in the home ($d = 0.34$) and in the community ($d = 0.24$). In their review of studies with genetically sensitive research designs, Jaffee et al. (2012) concluded that maltreatment does have causal effects on children's antisocial behavior, with genetic factors explaining only a very small amount of the association. The null and weak findings on the effects of witnessing violence between other family members were largely in keeping with findings of Wilson et al. (2009, p. 773), who concluded that "the overall relationship between witnessing violence and juvenile delinquency was negligible ($d = .15$)."

In summary, associations between child conduct problems and experiences of violence in the home, including maltreatment, were weak or inconsistent in LMIC studies, and associations with other stressful life events were also generally weak. However, the true consequences of these experiences on young people's behavior may be obscured in these studies because many adjusted for possible mediating mechanisms, including child behavior measured at the same time as the exposure variable, which could downwardly bias the results. Further research is required on the influence of stressful life events on children in LMICs, particularly experiences of violence, with careful treatment of confounders and mediators used in analyses. Other severe traumas experienced by many children in LMICs, such as female genital mutilation, being orphaned by AIDS, traumas associated with child labor, and wartime traumas, are very important areas for future research (Benjet et al. 2009).

*F. Family Characteristics*

Family influences play a central role in developmental theories of antisocial behavior (Farrington 1994) and represent a key focus for preventive intervention (Farrington and Welsh 2003). The earlier section on child rearing processes highlighted the importance of parenting practices such as discipline methods, supervision, and affection. In this section, we consider associations between antisocial behavior outcomes and parental mental health and behavior, family socioeconomic factors, and family demographics. Jim Derzon's (2010) meta-analysis of longitudinal studies in HICs confirmed the following significant correlations between family factors and crime: family stress, $r = 0.214$; parent antisocial behavior, $r = 0.150$; broken home, $r = 0.095$; separated from parents, $r = 0.083$; low family socioeconomic status, $r = 0.129$; large family size, $r = 0.110$; young parent(s), $r = 0.079$; and urban housing, $r = 0.133$.

1. *Parental Mental Health and Behavior.* Parental care of children may be compromised if parents themselves experience stress and mental health problems (Cummings, Davies, and Campbell 2000; Keenan and Shaw 2003). This is potentially a major issue in LMICs where rates of maternal mental disorders are estimated to be significantly higher than in HICs (Affonso et al. 2000; Walker, Wachs, et al. 2007). Higher rates of mental disorders among poor populations in LMICs are driven by experiences of anxiety associated with economic insecurity, hopelessness regarding future opportunities, rapid social changes, and risks of violence and physical ill health (Patel and Kleinman 2003). However, only two studies prospectively examined maternal mental health as a possible risk factor for children's conduct problems in LMICs. Both were in Pelotas, Brazil, and both were consistent with the literature in HICs in showing higher rates of child behavior problems among children whose mothers had mental health problems. In the first study, children whose mothers screened positive for mental health problems when children were aged 11 had raised levels of conduct problems at age 15 ($d = 0.54$; #4: Anselmi et al.

2012). In a second study, maternal psychiatric problems when children were 3 months old predicted conduct problems, rule breaking, and aggressive behaviors at age 4, adjusting for a range of sociodemographic factors and children's characteristics at birth (#5: Matijasevich et al. 2014).

Chen et al. (2011) proposed that Eastern and Western cultures have different values about emotion expression, and as such, parental expression of emotion might have different effects on children in China compared with Western countries, where most previous research on this topic had been conducted. In a study in Beijing, they examined associations between three types of parental emotion expression in the family (negative dominant expression, positive expression, and negative submissive expression) when children were 6–9 years old and tested for associations with children's conduct problems 3 years later (#10: Chen et al. 2011). Adjusting for family socioeconomic status, parenting styles, and child conduct problems at baseline, only parental expression of negative dominant emotion predicted ($\beta = 0.25$) later child conduct problems.

The intergenerational transmission of antisocial behavior is a major theme in the international literature, with both genetic and environmental mechanisms implicated in the transmission (Rhee and Waldman 2002; Thornberry et al. 2003; Farrington, Coid, and Murray 2009; Murray, Farrington, and Sekol 2012). No longitudinal study in an LMIC tested the link between parental crime and child antisocial behavior. However, among 12–17-year-olds in Colombia, illicit drug use by parents and siblings was weakly associated with youth violence 2 years later ($r = 0.07$ for mothers, $r = 0.18$ for fathers, $r = 0.16$ for siblings; #22: Brook, Brook, and Whiteman 2007). Problematic parental drug use can undermine household stability and child care (Barnard and McKeganey 2004), which could affect antisocial behavior. In South Africa, 14–22-year-olds who reported that drugs or alcohol were used in their childhood home were more likely (OR $= 1.7$) to self-report violence against strangers 7 years later, adjusting for education, unemployment, childhood poverty, and family structure (#34: Seekings and Thaler 2011). In the Philippines, parental alcohol use (not necessarily problematic use) when children were aged 10 was not significantly associated with perpetration of partner violence at age 21 (#29: Fehringer and Hindin 2009).

In summary, the evidence on the influence of parental mental health and behavior on child and youth antisocial behavior is extremely sparse in LMICs. The few existing studies, in Brazil, Colombia, South Africa, and the Philippines, show positive associations between parental mental health problems and child conduct problems, and parental illicit drug use and youth violence, although no study used a genetically informative design to disentangle potential environmental effects from genetic influences. A single study in China suggests a particular role of parental negative dominant expressivity as a potential predictor of child conduct problems.

2. *Family Poverty, Parental Education, and Employment.* Poverty and low socioeconomic status can influence child development through proximal influences in the home, such as undernutrition or overcrowding, and through more distal mechanisms such as reduced educational opportunities (Wachs 1999; Walker et al. 2011). Quasi-experimental studies in HICs suggest causal effects of family poverty on antisocial behavior (Jaffee, Strait, and Odgers 2012). Therefore, children from impoverished backgrounds in LMICs may be at increased risk for conduct problems or violence. Meta-analytic results on this topic are shown in table 7, with findings from individual studies summarized below.

Six studies in LMICs examined associations between poverty and child conduct problems. The three studies (#4, #5, #37) that were included in a meta-analysis were conducted in Brazil and South Africa. The pooled bivariate association between poverty and conduct problems was small ($d = 0.12$, table 7), with high heterogeneity in the results. In Pelotas, Brazil, low family income at birth was associated with child conduct problems at age 11 for boys (RR = 1.3) and girls (RR = 1.5; #4: Murray, Maughan, et al. 2015). Also, children whose families remained poor or became poor between birth and age 11 had more conduct problems at age 15 ($\beta = 0.61$, comparing persistently low versus persistently high family income groups), adjusting for other sociodemographic factors (#4: Anselmi et al. 2012). These effects were partly explained by stressful life events and maternal mental health problems associated with poverty (Anselmi et al. 2012). In a second study in Pelotas, lower family wealth at birth was also associated with oppositional behavior and conduct disorder at age 6 (RR = 5.0, comparing bottom and top income quintiles); however, this association was mainly a function of the highest income group having a particularly low risk of disorder compared to all other groups (#5: Petresco et al. 2014). In South Africa, family poverty at ages 10–17 was not associated with conduct problems 1 year later (#37: Waller, Gardner, and Cluver 2014). Three other studies that lacked sufficient information for inclusion in the meta-analysis were conducted in Brazil and Poland and had similarly weak or null results. In São Luís, Brazil, children in low-income families at birth were not at increased risk of conduct problems

## TABLE 7

Meta-Analytic Results on Family Sociodemographic Factors in Relation to Child Conduct Problems and Youth Violence

| Predictor | Behavioral Outcome | Number of Studies | Studies Included (#) | Type of Association | Effect Size $d$ | 95% CI | $p^a$ | Heterogeneity $I^2$ | $p^b$ |
|---|---|---|---|---|---|---|---|---|---|
| Poor family during childhood | Conduct problems | 3 | (4, 5, 37) | Bivariate | .12 | (.03 to .21) | .012 | 82% | .001 |
| | Violence | 2 | (3, 4) | Bivariate | .18 | (.07 to .30) | .001 | 0% | .658 |
| Low maternal education | Conduct problems | 3 | (4, 8, 12) | Bivariate | .15 | (−.02 to .32) | .088 | 57% | .099 |
| Young mother at birth | Conduct problems | 2 | (4, 8) | Bivariate | .20 | (−.03 to .42) | .087 | 83% | .015 |
| | Violence | 2 | (3, 4) | Bivariate | .21 | (.01 to .41) | .045 | 60% | .059 |
| Single mother at birth | Conduct problems | 2 | (4, 8) | Bivariate | .17 | (.09 to .25) | <.001 | 0% | .424 |
| | Violence | 2 | (3, 4) | Bivariate | .01 | (−.13 to .15) | .853 | 0% | .793 |
| Many siblings | Violence | 2 | (3, 4) | Bivariate | .06 | (−.06 to .19) | .324 | 0% | .598 |

NOTE.—# = study ID number shown in table 2; $p^a$ = $p$-value for $d$ effect size; $p^b$ = $p$-value for a $\chi^2$ test for heterogeneity. Random-effects models.

at ages 7–9, compared to children in medium-income families, although there was some increased risk comparing children in middle-income families to those in high-income families (RR = 1.3; #8: Rodriguez et al. 2011). In São Gonçalo, Brazil, 7-year-old children in poor families did not have significantly increased rates of conduct problems over the next 3 years, adjusting for other sociodemographic factors and experiences of violence (#7: de Assis et al. 2013). Among Polish children aged 7 and 9, parental income was not significantly associated with children's aggressive behavior over the next 3 years, adjusting for baseline aggression, IQ, and sociodemographic factors (#30: Frączek 1986).

Considering family poverty as a predictor of violence, results from two of the Pelotas cohorts in Brazil were pooled in a meta-analysis. In the first study, children whose family income was below the minimum wage at birth in 1982 had a higher risk for conviction for violence up to age 25 (males OR = 2.3, females OR = 1.4), compared to all other children (#3: Caicedo et al. 2010). However, in the later 1993 Pelotas Birth Cohort Study, low family income at birth was not significantly associated with self-reported violence at age 18 for males (RR = 1.2) or females (RR = 1.4; #4: Murray, Maughan, et al. 2015); also effect sizes were smaller in this Brazilian study than in a matched British birth cohort (Murray, Maughan, et al. 2015). Combining results from these two cohorts, the association between family poverty and violence was weak ($d = 0.18$, table 7).

In three other studies in Puerto Rico, the Philippines, and South Africa, associations between family poverty and general delinquency and intimate partner violence were all null. In Puerto Rico, family welfare receipt among 5–13-year-old children did not predict trajectories of delinquency over the next 2 years, as was also found in a matched sample in New York (#31: Maldonado-Molina et al. 2009). Among 10-year-olds in the Philippines, neither household income nor wealth predicted perpetration of partner violence at age 21 (#29: Fehringer and Hindin 2009). In South Africa, males aged 14–22 who reported having been poor as a child were not at significantly higher risk of self-reported perpetration of family or intimate partner violence 7 years later (#34: Thaler 2011).

Low parental education was investigated as a predictor of antisocial behavior in eight studies in Brazil, China, the Philippines, Poland, and former Yugoslavia. Pooling bivariate results that were available in three of the studies in Brazil and China (#4, #8, #12), the association between low maternal education at birth and child conduct problems was weak ($d = 0.15$, table 7) and nonsignificant, with moderate heterogeneity in the results. Five other studies (#5, #7, #8, #29, #37) also reported nonsignificant covariate-adjusted associations between parental education and child conduct problems and aggression (Frączek 1986; Wasserman et al. 2001; Rodriguez et al. 2011; de Assis et al. 2013; Matijasevich et al. 2014). These could not be meta-analyzed given differences in the multivariate analyses used.

Related concepts of family socioeconomic status and parental IQ were investigated in two studies. In Beijing (#10), a combined measure of low parental education and low family income when children were aged 6–9 was positively associated with child conduct problems 4 years later ($\beta =$ 0.16), adjusting for parenting styles and child behavior at baseline (see also Tao, Zhou, and Wang 2010; Chen et al. 2011). In a study in the Seychelles (#33), family socioeconomic position at age 9 was unassociated with conduct problems at age 17, but maternal IQ at age 10 was negatively predictive, adjusting for the child's own IQ and mercury exposure (Davidson et al. 2011).

Two studies that examined the association between low parental education and youth violence had weak and null findings. In Pelotas, Brazil, low maternal education at birth was associated with self-reported violence at age 18 for females (RR = 1.4) but not for males (RR = 1.1; #4: Murray, Maughan, et al. 2015). These results were similar to those found in a matched British study (Murray, Maughan, et al. 2015). In the Philippines, maternal education, indicated by the number of years of schooling, was not associated with perpetration of partner violence at age 21, either before or after adjusting for other parental sociodemographics and domestic violence in the childhood home (RR = 0.96 for both estimates; #29: Fehringer and Hindin 2009).

Parental employment status was not associated with child conduct problems or aggression in three studies in Brazil and Poland. In Pelotas, Brazil, children born to parents who had a "proletariat" occupation were not more likely than children of "bourgeois" parents to show conduct problems at age 4 (#4: Brion et al. 2010). Also, in São Gonçalo, Brazil, having unemployed parents at age 7 did not significantly predict child conduct problems over the following 3 years, adjusting for other family sociodemographics and experiences of violence (#7: de Assis et al. 2013). In Poland, paternal occupational status when children were aged 7 and 9 was not significantly associated with child aggressive behavior over the next 3 years, adjusting for baseline aggression, IQ, violent television viewing, and other sociodemographics (#30: Frączek 1986).

Thaler (2011) found significant associations between South African men's own poverty and unemployment at ages 17–25 and perpetration of family or intimate partner violence 4 years later (#34); odds ratios were 2.0 for being very poor and 1.8 for unemployment.

In summary, existing LMICs studies reveal only weak associations between childhood poverty, parental education, and employment with future antisocial behavior. Some LMIC studies included mediating mechanisms in adjusted analyses, meaning that the overall effects of socioeconomic factors might have been underestimated in those studies. However, bivariate associations also tended to be weak or null, suggesting that these family background factors are not important influences on the development of conduct problems or violence in these studies. These findings on poverty in the family of origin and its impact on antisocial behavior are not markedly different from those reported in HICs. In a meta-analysis of predictors for youth crime and violence, based on 41 prospective studies in HICs, Tanner-Smith et al. (2013) found that correlations between socioeconomic status and later crime and violence were weak ($r < 0.20$) or nonsignificant, regardless of the age at which the predictor was measured (childhood, early adolescence, or later adolescence) and of the age at which the outcome was measured (early adolescence, late adolescence, or early adulthood). An examination of studies using designs that allow stronger causal inferences concluded that poverty and family income do have a causal role in antisocial behavior (Jaffee, Strait, and Odgers 2012), but it did not provide a pooled effect size estimate that could be compared to our findings. The only LMIC study that investigated the influence of poverty and unemployment in young adulthood (as opposed to poverty and unemployment in the family of origin) found a positive association with family and partner violence in South Africa.

3. *Parental Age, Marital Status, and Family Size.* Sociodemographic factors that have been associated with antisocial behavior in HICs include being born to a teenage parent, living in a single-parent household, and having a large family (Hawkins et al. 1998; Jaffee, Strait, and Odgers 2001; Derzon 2010; Murray and Farrington 2010). There is also some evidence for causal effects of young motherhood and divorce on children's antisocial behavior (Jaffee, Strait, and Odgers 2012). Results from two Brazilian studies (#4, #8) on the association between low maternal age at birth (<20 years) and child conduct problems were combined in a meta-analysis. In Pelotas (#4), having a young mother at birth was associated with child conduct problems at both age 11 (RR = 1.3 for males,

1.5 for females; Murray, Maughan, et al. 2015) and age 15 ($d = 0.30$; Anselmi et al. 2012). However, in São Luís, lower maternal age at birth was not associated with child conduct problems (#8: Rodriguez et al. 2011). The meta-analysis of these two studies (#4, #8) produced a weak and nonsignificant association between low maternal age at birth and child conduct problems ($d = 0.20$, table 7), with significant heterogeneity in the results. Additional evidence on this topic comes from a later study in Pelotas, which did find an association between lower maternal age and child conduct problems at age 4, adjusting for other sociodemographic factors, maternal psychiatric disorder, and childbirth characteristics (#5: Matijasevich et al. 2014). However, in São Gonçalo, Brazil, lower parental age was not associated with child conduct problems over the next 3 years, adjusting for other sociodemographic factors and experiences of violence (#7: de Assis et al. 2013). Moreover, in the Seychelles, maternal age was not associated with child conduct problems at age 5 (Myers et al. 2000).

Considering risk for violence, in the 1982 cohort in Pelotas, Brazil, having a young mother at birth (<20 years) predicted conviction for violence up to age 25 for females, adjusting for other sociodemographic factors and maternal smoking in pregnancy (bivariate RR = 3.8, adjusted RR = 2.9); however, there was no significant association for males (#3: Caicedo et al. 2010). In the later 1993 Pelotas cohort, having a young mother at birth (<20 years) was not associated with self-reported violence at age 18 for males or females (#4: Murray, Maughan, et al. 2015). Pooling the bivariate results from these two studies, having a young mother at birth (<20 years) was weakly associated with youth violence ($d = 0.21$, table 7). In the Philippines, maternal age was not associated with perpetration of intimate partner violence at age 21, either in bivariate analyses or in multivariate analyses adjusting for other family factors in childhood (#29: Fehringer and Hindin 2009).

Three Brazilian studies (#4, #5, #8) examined the association between parental marital status and child conduct problems; their pooled bivariate association was almost zero ($d = 0.01$, table 7). In the 1993 Pelotas cohort, having a single mother at birth was associated with child conduct problems both at age 11 (RR = 1.2 for males; RR = 1.4 for females; #4: Murray, Maughan, et al. 2015) and at age 15 ($d = 0.19$; #4: Anselmi et al. 2012). In the later 2004 Pelotas cohort, having a single mother at birth was also associated with child conduct problems at age 4, adjusting for other sociodemographic factors, maternal psychiatric disorder, and childbirth characteristics (#5: Matijasevich et al. 2014). However, in São

Luís, Brazil, having a single mother at birth was not significantly associated with child conduct problems (#8: Rodriguez et al. 2011). Considering violence as an outcome, there was no association with having a single mother at birth in the two older (1982 and 1993) Pelotas cohorts (#3: Caicedo et al. 2010; #4: Murray, Maughan, et al. 2015).

Three studies examined whether large family size was associated with child conduct problems. Two of the studies in Pelotas, Brazil, reported weak and null associations. In the 1993 cohort, having three or more siblings at birth was weakly associated with conduct problems at age 11 (RR = 1.2 for both males and females; #4: Murray, Maughan, et al. 2015). In the 2004 cohort, maternal parity at birth was not associated with child conduct problems at age 4, adjusting for other sociodemographic factors, maternal psychiatric disorder, and childbirth characteristics (#5: Matijasevich et al. 2014). In China, the single-child policy represents a unique setting to investigate family size and child behavior. A study in Nanjing compared 3–6-year-olds with and without siblings on 116 different behaviors assessed four times over a 10-year period. For boys, only four conduct behaviors were significantly more frequent when siblings were present (#19: Tseng et al. 2000). For girls with siblings, only temper tantrums were more frequent than for girls without siblings. The very large number of tests conducted in this study (116 each for boys and girls) suggests that these may well be chance findings.

Youth violence was investigated in relation to family size in the two Pelotas studies of children born in 1982 and 1993. In the 1982 cohort, violent conviction up to age 25 was assessed in relation to how many younger and older siblings children had had at age 4. For males, having any younger siblings predicted increased risk of violence (RR = 1.9), adjusting for family sociodemographics, mother smoking in pregnancy, and childbirth characteristics, but there was no significant association with having older siblings and no significant association for females (#3: Caicedo et al. 2010). In the 1993 cohort, there was no significant association between having three or more older siblings at birth and risk of self-reported violence at age 18 (#4: Murray, Maughan, et al. 2015). Combining these two studies in meta-analysis, the association between having multiple older siblings (two or more in the 1982 cohort, three or more in the 1993 cohort) and youth violence was almost zero ($d = 0.06$, table 7).

In summary, existing evidence suggests only weak associations between some family sociodemographic factors in the development of conduct problems and violence in LMICs. Notably, nearly all studies to date have been conducted in Brazil. The associations between having a young mother at birth and conduct problems and violence were small. The association between having a single mother at birth and conduct problems was small, and there was no association with violence. There was a negligible association between having a large family and conduct problems, and no association with violence.

4. *Other, Less Studied, Family Factors.* In the Philippines, parental joint decision making and maternal church attendance measured when children were aged 10 were not associated with perpetration of partner violence at age 21, adjusting for sociodemographic factors, intergenerational violence, and other youth characteristics (#29: Fehringer and Hindin 2009).

In former Yugoslavia, living in an apartment (compared to in a house or on a farm) in the perinatal period was not significantly associated with child aggression at age 3, adjusting for sociodemographic factors and an assessment of the child's home learning environment (#39: Wasserman et al. 1998).

## G. Peer Characteristics

Adolescence is a period of heightened social sensitivity when peers exert strong influence on risk-taking behaviors (Blakemore and Mills 2014). Two types of peer influence have been studied extensively in relation to antisocial behavior: reinforcement or modeling of antisocial behavior by antisocial peers and possible protective effects of having a supportive friendship network (Jaffee, Strait, and Odgers 2012; Eisner and Malti 2015). It is important to emphasize that spurious associations between peer characteristics and child antisocial behavior can arise in two main ways. First, antisocial children may seek companionship with peers showing similar antisocial tendencies; second, children's own aggressive behaviors may cause particular peer responses, such as social rejection (Jaffee, Strait, and Odgers 2012). Hence, the issue of social causation versus social selection is particularly difficult to disentangle concerning peer effects. Studies of peer influences on antisocial behavior in LMICs were considered too heterogeneous in their designs and analyses to pool results in meta-analyses, but individual study results are summarized below.

Four studies in China, Colombia, Puerto Rico, and South Africa examined the influence of antisocial peers on antisocial behavior. A genetically sensitive study in Beijing is particularly interesting because it tested whether twin differences in antisocial peers at ages 10–18 predicted twin differences in conduct problems 2 years later (#13: Hou et al. 2013). The results did not support the social causation hypothesis: initial differences between twins in peer antisocial behavior did not predict later differences in conduct problems, adjusting for baseline parental warmth/hostility and child conduct problems. In Colombia (#22), 12–17-year-olds whose peers were involved in delinquency and drug use were at increased risk for violent behavior 2 years later ($r = 0.22$ and $0.27$, respectively; Brook, Brook, and Whiteman 2007). However, associations were nonsignificant when adjusted for individual characteristics and violent behavior measured at baseline. Among 5–13-year-olds in Puerto Rico, differences in peer delinquency levels predicted children's own delinquency over the following 3 years (#31: Maldonado-Molina et al. 2009). Specifically, peer delinquency was highest among children whose own delinquency showed an initially high but declining trajectory. Interestingly, in a matched sample in New York, peer delinquency was also highest among children who had declining delinquency rates rather than those who had high and increasing rates of delinquency (Maldonado-Molina et al. 2009). In South Africa, 14–22-year-olds who had many friends using drugs were at increased risk for perpetration of family and intimate partner violence 7 years later ($OR = 1.5$), but having many friends drinking alcohol was not associated with this outcome (#34: Thaler 2011).

Peer popularity and peer rejection were investigated in three studies in China and Puerto Rico, and each found a significant association with antisocial behavior. In Beijing, there were bidirectional relationships, with aggressive behaviors increasing risk for subsequent social rejection, and social rejection also contributing to later aggression, over a 4-year period from age 9 (#11: Chen et al. 2012). In Shanghai, greater popularity at mean age 11 was associated with less aggression 2 years later ($r = -0.24$; #21: Chen, He, and Li 2004). In Puerto Rico, peer relations at 5–13 differed only slightly according to children's trajectories of delinquency over the next 2 years, with positive peer relations being highest among nonoffenders (#31: Maldonado-Molina et al. 2009). There was no significant association in a matched sample in New York (Maldonado-Molina et al. 2009).

Three studies in LMICs suggest a weak association between both bullying and peer victimization and antisocial behavior. In São Gonçalo, Brazil, violent victimization at school among 7-year-olds was very weakly associated with conduct problems in the next 3 years ($d = 0.15$), adjusting for baseline sociodemographic factors and other types of home and community violence (#7: de Assis et al. 2013). In Jinan, China, victimization

by peers and child aggression were assessed annually for 4 years among
children aged 9 and 11 years at baseline. Physical victimization by peers
was weakly associated with physical aggression ($\beta = 0.05$), and relational
victimization by peers was weakly associated with relational aggression
($\beta = 0.05$), but only in the last years of the study, not before transitioning
from primary to middle school (#17: Chen 2012). In South Africa, experiencing any bullying at ages 10–17 was only weakly associated with conduct
problems 1 year later ($d = 0.16$), but experiencing four or more types
of bullying was strongly associated ($d = 0.58$) and remained significant
adjusting for child demographics, family poverty, and residence location
(#37: Boyes et al. 2014).

In summary, nine studies in LMICs suggest that antisocial behavior is
positively associated with both peer victimization and having antisocial
peers, and it is inversely associated with both peer popularity and positive peer relations. The relatively weak association found between peer
victimization and antisocial behavior is broadly consistent with a 2012
meta-analysis that found that bullying victimization predicted violence
with an odds ratio of 1.43 (equivalent to a small effect size of $d = 0.19$;
Ttofi, Farrington, and Lösel 2012). Regarding the influence of antisocial
peers, limited evidence from LMICs suggests that reverse causation is
important, with one genetically sensitive study finding no effect of peer
antisocial behavior on later conduct problems and another study showing
bidirectional effects between aggression and social rejection.

## H. School Environment

In HICs, it is well established that there are large differences in rates of
antisocial behavior between different schools (Rutter, Giller, and Hagell
1998). Children with antisocial behaviors disproportionately attend high–
delinquency rate schools that have high levels of distrust between teachers
and students, low commitment to the school by students, and unclear and
inconsistently enforced rules (Graham 1988). However, what is less clear
is to what extent such differences reflect school influences related to their
organization, climate, and practices or different intakes of children into
schools (Rutter et al. 1979; Rutter, Giller, and Hagell 1998). Only one
study in an LMIC examined the influence of school environment on youth
antisocial behavior. In Puerto Rico (#31), the school environment was
assessed at ages 5–13 by asking children about factors such as the number of substitute teachers they had had in the previous year. School envi-

ronments were much more negative among children with high initial delinquency rates, which then declined over a 2-year period, and among children with moderate and stable delinquency rates, compared to children with a nonoffending trajectory (respectively, $d = 1.1$ and $0.6$; #31: Maldonado-Molina et al. 2009). Negative school environment also distinguished children's delinquency trajectories after adjusting for a range of individual, family, peer, and social factors. And negative school environment was also found to be important for delinquency trajectories in a matched sample in New York: children with a high and increasing rate of delinquency had the most negative school environments (Maldonado-Molina et al. 2009).

In summary, a single LMIC longitudinal study conducted in Puerto Rico found large effects of school environment on children's delinquent development. However, much more research is needed on this important topic, particularly using experimental and quasi-experimental designs to test causal mechanisms (Rutter, Giller, and Hagell 1998).

*I. Community Influences*

A long history of research in HICs has established that offenders tend disproportionately to live in inner-city areas characterized by physical deterioration, neighborhood disorganization, and high residential mobility (Shaw and McKay 1969). However, it is difficult to determine to what extent the areas themselves influence antisocial behavior and to what extent people with antisocial behavior tend to live in deprived areas, for example, because of family poverty or public housing allocation policies.

Few LMIC studies examined associations between neighborhood characteristics and antisocial behavior, and they were too heterogeneous to pool in a meta-analysis. Considering the influence of neighborhood crime rates, Brook et al. (2007) investigated whether drug availability, neighborhood risk, and danger on the street predicted youth violent behavior 2 years later among 12–17-year-old Colombians (#22). Only community drug availability was significantly associated with perpetrating violence ($r = 0.11$). In South Africa, community violence and political violence near children's homes were assessed from children's birth to age 5. Community violence was associated with child aggression ($r = 0.13$), but not oppositional behavior at age 5 (#36: Barbarin et al. 2001); political violence was not associated with aggressive or oppositional behavior.

The only study to examine neighborhood poverty was a South African survey of 14–22-year-old males. Youths who had grown up in poor neighborhoods were at increased risk (OR = 1.7) for perpetrating family or intimate partner violence 7 years later (#34: Thaler 2011). However, in separate analysis of the same study, there was no association between childhood neighborhood poverty and perpetrating violence against strangers (#34: Seekings and Thaler 2011).

Violent victimization in the community was inconsistently associated with conduct problems in three studies in LMICs. In São Gonçalo, Brazil, violent victimization in the community at age 7 was not significantly associated with conduct problems over the next 3 years, adjusting for baseline sociodemographic factors and other types of home and school violence (#7: de Assis et al. 2013). In South Africa, witnessing or being a victim of serious violence in the community at ages 10–17 was only weakly associated ($\beta = 0.07$) with conduct problems 1 year later, adjusting for baseline child behavior, poverty, and violence in the home (#37: Waller, Gardner, and Cluver 2014). Also in South Africa, violent victimization of a family member between children's birth and age 5 was weakly associated with oppositional behaviors ($r = 0.07$), but not aggression at age 5 (#36: Barbarin et al. 2001).

Two studies in LMICs found positive associations between violent victimization and perpetration of violence or delinquency. In Colombia, violent victimization at ages 12–17 was associated ($r = 0.31$) with violent behavior 2 years later (#22: Brook, Brook, and Whiteman 2007). In Puerto Rico, exposure to violence at mean age 9 was highest among children who had high but rapidly declining delinquency rates over the next 2 years, followed by children who had low but stable rates of delinquency (#31: Maldonado-Molina et al. 2009). In a matched sample of Puerto Rican children living in New York, exposure to violence was highest among children with a high and increasing rate of offending—a delinquency trajectory that did not exist in the sample living in Puerto Rico (Maldonado-Molina et al. 2009).

In summary, limited evidence suggests small associations between antisocial behavior and community poverty, drug availability, and violence in Colombia and South Africa. Individual studies report associations between violent victimization and later violence, but evidence was inconsistent regarding the association between victimization and conduct problems.

*J. Cultural and Media Influences*

The influence of media violence on children and youths is an important theme in the international literature (Rutter, Giller, and Hagell 1998; Huesmann et al. 2003; Bushman and Huesmann 2006). Its effects on children were studied in Poland as part of a large international project on this topic (Huesmann and Eron 1986). At baseline, Polish children aged 7–9 were interviewed about their favorite television programs, which were then coded by research staff for violent content. Preference for violent television programs was associated with child aggression over a 3-year period ($r = 0.14$ for both boys and girls), independently of baseline levels of aggression (#30: Frączek 1986; Groebel 1988) and also independently of child IQ, parenting factors, and parental social class. Associations between violent television viewing and aggression in matched samples in HICs were for boys and girls, respectively, $r = 0.15$ and $0.14$ in the United States; $r = 0.08$ and $0.00$ in Australia; $r = 0.21$ and $0.65$ in Finland; and $r = 0.29$ and $0.52$ in Israel, adjusting for baseline aggression (Groebel 1988). Hence, associations varied considerably between countries, and the small correlations in Poland were most similar to those in the United States. In Colombia, 12–17-year-old males who reported a preference for violent television also reported more violent behavior ($r = 0.14$) 2 years later (#22: Brook, Brook, and Whiteman 2007). Of course, this association could reflect proviolent attitudes causing a preference for both violent television and violent behavior.

Cultural beliefs about masculinity and sexual entitlement may facilitate perpetration of intimate partner violence (Santana et al. 2006; Jewkes et al. 2011). Believing in male sexual entitlement was investigated as a possible risk factor for perpetrating intimate partner violence in a study in three towns in South Africa and Tanzania (#35: Wubs et al. 2013). Adjusting for baseline violence at ages 10–18, adolescents who believed in male sexual entitlement were more likely to perpetrate intimate partner violence 6 months later in all three study sites (OR = 1.3 in Cape Town; OR = 1.6 in Mankweng; OR = 1.8 in Dar es Salaam), although the association persisted to a 1-year follow-up only in Cape Town (OR = 1.3).

A unique investigation of the effects of "acculturation" and "cultural stress" was conducted in San Juan, Puerto Rico, and in a matched sample of Puerto Rican families in New York. When children were aged 5–13, children and parents were assessed for levels of "acculturation" (meaning how much they used English and were integrated into US cultural norms) and "cultural stress" (meaning how much distress they experienced from pressure to adapt to US cultural norms). Children's conduct problems were predicted only by parental acculturation and cultural stress ($r = 0.15$ and $0.13$, respectively), and only in the San Juan sample, not in the matched New York sample (#31: Duarte et al. 2008). However, children's delinquency rates did vary according to their own levels of acculturation in San Juan: children who showed initially high and then declining levels of delinquency over 2 years had higher levels of acculturation than children in the nonoffending group and children in the stable but moderate delinquency group (#31: Maldonado-Molina et al. 2009; Jennings et al. 2010); this difference was not observed in the matched New York sample.

In summary, there are few longitudinal studies on the influence of cultural and media influences on antisocial behavior in LMICs. Small associations were observed between television violence and antisocial behavior. A single study in South Africa found short-term associations between beliefs about male sexual entitlement and intimate partner violence. One study found a weak association between the degree of family integration into US culture and the development of antisocial behavior among Puerto Rican children.

## K. Relative Strength of Predictors and Comparison of Results with Those of High-Income Countries

In this section, we consider the relative size of risk factor associations estimated in the meta-analyses of studies in LMICs and how those results compare with findings from existing similar meta-analyses of longitudinal studies in HICs. To compare like with like, we examine bivariate associations from the current review while recognizing that these are less informative regarding causal inference. We used findings from prior meta-analyses that examined a wide range of risk factors in HICs (Lipsey and Derzon 1998; Derzon 2010; Tanner-Smith, Wilson, and Lipsey 2013), as well as searching for additional meta-analyses of individual risk factors in bibliographic databases and David Farrington's recent systematic review of reviews (Farrington, Gaffney, and Ttofti 2017). Additional meta-analyses of bivariate associations based on longitudinal studies from HICs were located only for aggression (Olweus 1979) and very low birth weight/prematurity (Aarnoudse-Moens et al. 2009). Note that in the latter review, the cutoff for very low birth weight (<1,500 grams) was lower than that for low birth weight (<2,500 grams) in our review.

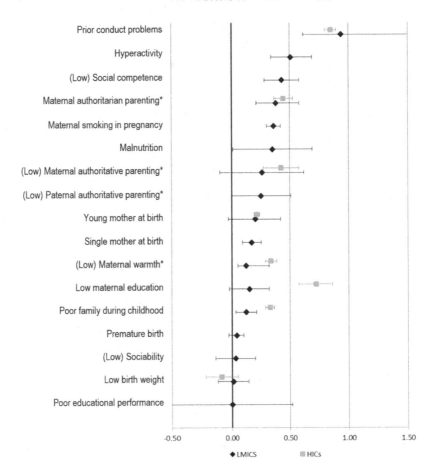

Fig. 3.—Longitudinal predictors of child conduct problems: average bivariate associations (*d* and 95 percent confidence interval). * Results refer to aggression or conduct problems with aggression.

Figures 3 and 4 show the pooled bivariate associations between risk factors and child conduct problems and youth violence in LMICs, ordered by size. Consistent with evidence from HICs (Lipsey and Derzon 1998; Tanner-Smith, Wilson, and Lipsey 2013), the strongest associations in LMICs relate to prior measures of antisocial behavior: prior conduct problems predicting later conduct problems and drug use and conduct problems predicting violence. The next-strongest predictors of conduct problems in LMICs were hyperactivity, low social competence, maternal

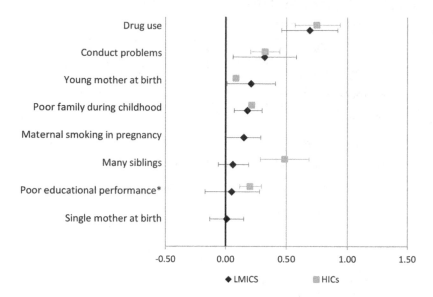

FIG. 4.—Longitudinal predictors of youth violence: average bivariate associations ($d$ and 95 percent confidence interval). * Results for LMICs refer to intimate partner violence.

authoritarian parenting, maternal smoking in pregnancy, and malnutrition, with associations ranging from $d = 0.35$ to $0.51$. For violence, the next-strongest risk factors, after prior antisocial behavior, were having a young mother at birth, family poverty during childhood, and maternal smoking in pregnancy, but the strength of these associations was small ($d = 0.15$ to $0.21$). Associations for comparable constructs assessed in HICs (also shown in figs. 3 and 4) were generally similar or slightly stronger compared with those from LMICs. In fact, the only significant and large differences were for low maternal education and having a poor family, associated more strongly with conduct problems in HICs (both $p < 0.001$), and having many siblings, which was also more strongly associated with violence in HICs ($p < 0.001$).

## IV. Discussion

We identified 39 longitudinal studies of child and youth antisocial behavior in low- and middle-income countries. This is a remarkable number of studies, given that prior reviews have been based almost exclusively on surveys in WEIRD populations in HICs. Studies in LMICs variously examined the roles of individual factors, child rearing processes, adverse childhood experiences, family characteristics, and peer, school, community, and cultural factors in the development of antisocial behavior, although for a number of risk factors, evidence in LMICs was sparse. Below, we discuss key theoretical issues related to the findings, focusing on the following general themes: global replicability of risk factors, the stability of antisocial behavior through time, paradoxical cross-country rates of conduct disorder and serious violence, early childhood as a possible sensitive period, the role of parenting factors, and some striking null findings that emerged in the review.

## A. Global Risk Factors for Antisocial Behavior?

This review of risk factors for antisocial behavior in LMIC countries was motivated, in part, by a fundamental question of criminology: Do theories of offending and antisocial behavior have universal validity across all human societies? Or are there differences between societies, not only in the prevalence of causal mechanisms but also in their effects?

Many developmental and life course theories in criminology were developed in the 1990s. They responded to an increasing set of regularities, based on a growing number of longitudinal studies in HICs, that required explanation. Prominent theories developed in this period include, for example, Terrie Moffitt's (1993) dual taxonomy of offending behavior, Thornberry and Krohn's (Thornberry et al. 1994; Thornberry and Krohn 2005) interactional theory of antisocial behavior, Sampson and Laub's (1993) age-graded informal control theory, and Farrington's (2003) integrated cognitive antisocial potential theory; others are described by Farrington (2005*b*).

Few if any of these life course and developmental theories in criminology specify the range of societies and contexts that they apply to. An exception is Moffitt's dual taxonomy in that the adolescence-limited group is believed to reflect underlying tensions associated with the transition from childhood to adulthood that are specific to modern societies. In contrast, most theories implicitly assume that the causal mechanisms involved in the stability and change of antisocial behavior apply to all societies, at all times, in all places.

The present review has brought together a previously unknown wealth of regularities and evidence on risk factors in LMICs. In the broadest sense, findings on the patterning of risk factors are consistent with what has been found in HICs. Measures of underlying psychological propensity show the highest associations with antisocial behavior over time, proximal risk factors tend to be more consistently associated, and distal risk factors generally have weak associations with behavioral outcomes. This first set of findings points to generalizability of results across the globe.

While important, these regularities provide limited insight into whether the life course theories developed in criminology have universal validity, let alone which theory is more suited to explain the empirical regularities. The reason is that, although average risk factor associations were generally similar between LMICs and HICs, heterogeneity was common between individual studies in LMICs. We emphasize that this could be primarily an artifact of different methodologies applied across surveys; however, it is also possible that it reflects true differences in risk factor effects between geographic locations and cultural groups in LMICs.

This systematic review consists of 39 studies from five continents: 13 studies were conducted in Asia, eight in South America, seven in Africa, seven in Europe, and four in North America, which entail diverse economic conditions, societies, and cultures. As discussed by Schonberg and Shaw (2007), variations in socioeconomic surroundings may alter the effects of individual- and family-level risk factors because of multiplicative effects of risk factors when they accumulate. Also, societies differ along other, broader, cultural dimensions that could also alter proximal mechanisms in the development of antisocial behavior. Major cultural dimensions identified in cross-national studies include individualism-collectivism, uncertainty avoidance, masculinity-femininity, power distance, long- and short-term orientation, and indulgence-restraint (Hofstede and Hofstede 2001); traditionalist values versus secular-rational values, survival values versus self-expression values (Inglehart, Basanez, and Moreno 1998); and tight versus loose cultures (Gelfand et al. 2011). As well as influencing the prevalence rates of risk factors, such as particular parenting practices (Lansford et al. 2005; Bornstein 2012), these sociocultural dimensions could interact with proximal processes to produce different risk factor effects (Lansford 2010).

Cultural factors relating to discipline, moral development, and tolerance of deviance may be particularly relevant in influencing individual- and family-level risk factors for antisocial behavior. For example, Rutter (1999) argued that the link between a risk factor and an outcome may depend on whether either variable denotes an "illegitimate" behavior within a cultural context. We examined various constructs whose normative connotations vary across settings. These include, for example, parental corporal punishment, school bullying, gender-based violence against women, parental separation, breast feeding, and premarital sex. Unfortunately, however, the small number of studies in LMICs for each specific variable, and the lack of information about normative expectations in each study context, make it impossible to say whether normative context or other macro-level variables do moderate associations between putative risk factors and outcomes. For the same reason, it is not possible to conclude whether current evidence better supports the hypothesis of "multiplicative effects" of risk factors (stronger effects in contexts of social disadvantage) or the "social push" hypothesis (weaker effects of biological risk factors in disadvantaged environments).

We highlight three main methodological influences that could also give rise to the heterogeneity observed in results across LMICs: assessment instruments, sources of information, and variables adjusted for in analyses. First, when studies use different instruments to assess the same variable, results could differ because of different validity or reliability levels of each instrument. Even when the same instrument is used across studies, variance in item functioning may mean that results differ because of a lack of adequate cross-cultural adaptation of instruments. Second, variations in the informants used to collect data, on both risk factors and outcomes, could cause variations in the findings. For example, parental reports and child self-reports of maltreatment exposure are likely to have very different validity, and both were used in different studies. Third, heterogeneity in effects may also result from different confounding variables adjusted for in each study. Even when considering only bivariate associations, different "confounding structures" across social settings—the degree of social patterning of risk factors—could give rise to different associations.

Therefore, while the amount of evidence on risk factors for antisocial behavior in LMICs is far greater than we had expected before embarking on this work and includes some intriguing individual results, the broad findings, comparing both across and between LMICs and HICs, do not resolve the fundamental issue of the universal validity of causal mechanisms for antisocial behavior. As we discuss below, this should motivate new studies across LMICs, particularly new cross-cultural collaborative research projects, using similar methodologies to test for context effects on risk factor associations.

## B. *Stability of Aggression in LMICs*

In LMIC studies, the average continuity in aggressive behavior when measured with the same informant over a 3-year period was high (adjusted $r = 0.75$) and almost identical to the extent of continuity found in studies in HICs (Olweus 1979). However, there was also considerable variation in LMIC results that was not explained by differences in child age, the time lag between assessments of aggression, or several country-level characteristics, such as homicide rates or development levels. More recent evidence from HICs also demonstrates considerable heterogeneity in the stability of various types of antisocial behavior (Derzon 2001). This heterogeneity might relate to methodological issues, such as different instruments used, or it might be explained by the causal mechanisms underlying the stability of aggression. Olweus (1979) suggested that stability of aggression is caused by relatively constant individual characteristics or motivational systems. Current theories suggest that these tendencies are due to time-invariant genetic influences, neurocognitive impairments incurred in the first years of life, and stable personality characteristics, such as psychopathy or callous-unemotional traits (van Goozen et al. 2007; Frick and White 2008). It is hard to see how such time-constant factors could explain variation in the stability of aggression between contexts. However, "state-dependent" theories might offer more explanation. State-dependent theories propose that stability in aggression is primarily caused by continuity in the social environment. Continuity in social bonds, social learning processes, strains, and negative life events are cited as important causes (Eisner and Malti 2015). Importantly, changes in those same processes could also cause changes in the degree of stability in aggression. Therefore, according to theories of state dependency, different degrees of continuity in social conditions between LMICs could account for different levels of stability in aggression. Future research should test the different possible social mechanisms involved.

## C. *The Prevalence Paradox: International Rates of Conduct Problems and Serious Violence*

Several studies in LMICs demonstrated some continuity in conduct problems through time and an association between conduct problems and later violence. This general continuity in antisocial behavior produces an apparent paradox, considering the fairly constant rates of conduct disorder found around the globe (Canino et al. 2010) in contrast to the enormous cross-country variability in levels of serious violence, with rates of homicide ranging from about one per 100,000 persons in the United Kingdom to about 90 in Honduras (UN Office on Drugs and Crime 2013). How can these contrasting geographic patterns for conduct disorder and violence occur alongside continuity in antisocial behavior, including from conduct problems to violence? Why might countries with higher levels of violence not also have higher levels of child conduct disorder? One possible explanation concerns the aforementioned heterogeneity in levels of stability in antisocial behavior. For example, there might be stronger continuity of antisocial behavior in countries that have higher rates of violence. However, we found no evidence to support this hypothesis: the stability of aggression did not vary systematically with national homicide rates.

A second possible explanation for the puzzling differences in geographic patterns of conduct disorder and violence, alongside individual-level stability in antisocial behavior, concerns the specific subtypes of antisocial behavior being considered. Behavioral stability was strongest for aggression, but it was weaker for conduct problems and weaker still for continuity between childhood conduct problems and youth crime or violence (see also Derzon [2001] and Burt [2012] for similar findings in HICs). Hence, we believe that the quite constant rates of conduct disorders observed across geographic regions are compatible with varying levels of violence, simply because continuity from conduct problems to violence is not strong: childhood conduct problems are far from deterministic of future violence. It should also be considered that although rates of conduct disorder appear similar across cultures (Canino et al. 2010), rates of child behavior problems, as measured by the Child Behavior Checklist, show modest cross-national variability (Rescorla et al. 2012). Therefore, it is also possible that rates of serious violence do covary with levels of child behavior problems measured as symptom scores, but we are not aware of studies that have tested this hypothesis.

## D. Early Childhood as a Sensitive Period of Development

The first 1,000 days of life are considered a critical window of opportunity to set children on a path of healthy development by ensuring adequate nutrition, cognitive stimulation, and safe and caring environments (Engle et al. 2007). Early health problems have been hypothesized to influence child behavior via effects on the developing brain, with possible risk factors including prenatal and postnatal malnutrition, tobacco and alcohol use in pregnancy, birth complications, brain injury, and exposure to toxins (Liu 2011). However, in the current review, birth cohort studies in LMICs showed mostly weak or zero effects of several early health factors on antisocial behavior. For instance, one of the most consistent findings was the absence of an association between low birth weight and antisocial behavior—replicated across six studies and producing a pooled effect size of zero. Weak or null findings were also found for premature birth, birth complications, lead and mercury exposure, breast feeding, and zinc consumption. Results for the association between malnutrition and antisocial behavior were mixed, and although several studies reported positive associations between maternal smoking in pregnancy and antisocial behavior, the causal status of these findings is unclear, given the lack of genetically sensitive research designs in LMIC studies. More robust studies of maternal smoking in pregnancy have revealed null or weak effects on antisocial behavior in HICs (Jaffee, Strait, and Odgers 2012). Hence, the general conclusion must be that the evidence to date generally shows weak or no influence of early life health factors in the development of antisocial behavior in LMICs.

Weak effects of early health factors have also been reported in several longitudinal studies in HICs. For example, low birth weight was not an independent predictor of conduct problems or crime in a British birth cohort (Murray et al. 2010). However, the consistent null results in LMIC studies are striking, especially given that many LMICs have relatively poor neonatal health care provision (Lawn, Cousens, and Zupan 2005). The null and weak findings in LMICs may have implications for developmental theories that hypothesize particularly strong effects of early health factors in the context of high social risk, for example, Moffitt's (1993) theory of life course persistent antisocial behavior. However, to test such developmental theories adequately, future LMIC studies need to use repeated measures to distinguish trajectories of antisocial behavior according to age of onset and persistence through the life course. Also needed are studies of possible interactions between early health variables and social risk factors within LMIC settings, which are proposed as key processes in causing early onset and persistent antisocial behavior (Moffitt 1993).

## E. Parenting Influences

Weak and null findings on early health factors do not imply that early childhood is not a sensitive period, as other types of early influences might be more important for the development of antisocial behavior.

In particular, several LMIC studies found associations between parenting practices measured in preschool years and subsequent conduct problems. Authoritarian parenting practices, such as coercive discipline, were positively associated with child antisocial behavior, whereas authoritative parenting practices, combining warmth and clear limit setting, predicted fewer behavior problems. However, these results were not all consistent, effect sizes were generally modest, and studies lacked more sophisticated designs for ruling out reciprocal causation and for disentangling the effects of parental behavior from other confounding variables.

Overall, the findings are at least moderately consistent with the notion that parenting practices are predictive of conduct problems and violence in LMICs, just as they are in HICs. It should be noted that effect sizes are modest in HICs, around $r = 0.2$ (Hoeve et al. 2009), as well as in our review. In particular, our findings are important in showing that in countries such as China, where authoritarian parenting values are thought to be more normative than in the West (Chao 1994), such parenting styles nevertheless are still associated with higher levels of conduct problems, just as they are in "Western" countries, including in the studies we examined in Poland and Russia. Similarly, positive, "authoritative" styles of parenting tended to be associated with lower levels of child conduct problems, just as they are in HICs, albeit with more inconsistent findings across LMIC studies.

Although there is a lack of clear-cut evidence for the causal role of parenting in the LMIC studies, confidence in the causal role of parenting as an intervention strategy comes from extensive evidence from randomized trials, both in the field and in lab conditions in HICs (Piquero et al. 2009, 2016; Leijten et al. 2015). Although the majority of parenting field trials are in HICs, an increasing number have been conducted in LMICs (Mejia, Calam, and Sanders 2012; Knerr, Gardner, and Cluver 2013; Leijten et al. 2016), and most of these trials show improvements in positive parenting and in child problem behavior, in a range of age groups from toddlerhood through teenage years. Furthermore, findings from systematic reviews of interventions are broadly consistent with our risk factor findings, suggesting that cultural variation in parenting need not necessarily be a barrier to transporting such programs across countries, cultures, and service contexts. Thus, effect sizes were equivalent for parenting interventions developed within a particular country, compared to those imported from abroad (Leijten et al. 2016). A second review suggested that effectiveness of parenting interventions when transported from one country to another was not dependent on the degree of similarity between countries in cultural values or child and family policy regimes (Gardner, Montgomery, and Knerr 2015).

### F. Striking Null Findings in LMICs

Early health factors had only weak associations with antisocial behavior in LMICs. Perhaps more surprisingly, several other potential risk factors also failed to have positive associations with antisocial behavior. For example, poor educational performance, maltreatment, large family size, low maternal education, and family poverty had notably weak or null associations. However, it would be wrong to assume that evidence in HICs provides a completely different, consistent set of positive results. With respect to some risk factors, null results in LMIC studies may reflect inconsistent evidence in the global literature. For example, the failed replication of an MAOA-abuse interaction in predicting conduct problems in a Brazilian study (Kieling et al. 2013) may reflect generally inconsistent results rather than anything specific about the Brazilian context (Duncan and Keller 2011).

However, some of our null findings were surprising, particularly those concerning the lack of effects of maltreatment on conduct problems or violence; albeit only three studies examined this topic, and so only tentative conclusions are warranted. There are several possible explanations for the differences between generally positive findings in HICs and the null findings from LMICs with regard to the association between child maltreatment and later antisocial behavior. First, there may be true differences. One possible explanation might be that harsh physical punishment and child maltreatment are more widespread and considered more normative in LMICs. This might lead more children to believe that harsh punishment is used as part of a planned strategy that is in their best interests, which might reduce some of its adverse effects (Lansford 2010; Vittrup and Holden 2010). Second, it is possible that the larger effects found in HICs (see, e.g., Wilson, Stover, and Berkowitz [2009] for the most comparable results in HICs) are due to the longer time periods between measures of exposure and outcome in studies in HICs and possible "sleeper effects"—whereby effects that are weak or undetectable at first strengthen and become measurable later. The time lags in the eight prospective studies in HICs included in the review by Wilson et al. (2009) range between 3 and 24 years, with many in the region of 10 years. The equivalent time lags in the three studies in our review were 3 years (de Assis et al. 2013), 1 year (Waller, Gardner, and Cluver 2014), and 7 years

(Thaler 2011)—a mean of 3.7. There is some evidence for "sleeper effects" in relation to corporal punishment and harsh parenting (Tanner-Smith, Wilson, and Lipsey 2013; Coley, Kull, and Carrano 2014), child sexual abuse (Putnam 2003; Smith, Ireland, and Thornberry 2005; Trickett, Noll, and Putnam 2011), and exposure to intimate partner violence (Vu et al. 2016). Third, it is also possible that differences are due to methodological factors, such as differences in types of child maltreatment considered as predictors (physical, sexual, psychological, neglect) or sources of reports (self-report, parental reports, administrative records).

## G. Strengths and Limitations

We are not aware of any prior review that has synthesized, narratively or meta-analytically, evidence on longitudinal predictors of antisocial behavior across LMICs. This review, we believe, has several important strengths, including the enormous search efforts that went into locating studies in LMICs in multiple languages, the large number of eligible studies retrieved, meta-analytic synthesis of many risk factors, and comparisons made with findings from HICs. However, there are also important reasons to treat our findings with caution.

Importantly, almost none of the primary studies used methods that allow for strong causal inference. Apart from a few studies that used randomized trials to target specific risk factors or a single study that used twins to eliminate genetic confounding, nearly all studies relied on regression-based models to adjust for a limited number of possible confounding factors. An increasing range of advanced study designs and analytic methods can help improve causal inference about risk factors (Jaffee, Strait, and Odgers 2012), but these have been rarely used in studies in LMICs. In the context of regression-based studies, it was often unclear whether the covariates that were included in multivariate models really represented confounding factors that should be controlled for when estimating causal effects, or whether they actually measured mediating mechanisms on the causal pathway between the risk factor and behavioral outcome. Adjusting for mediating mechanisms can bias estimates of risk factor total effects downward (Schisterman, Cole, and Platt 2009), and considerable care is needed in selecting variables for inclusion in multivariate models in future research. A related point is that researchers sometimes included earlier measures of the outcome variable in multivariate models. By doing this, the coefficient for the risk factor will represent its association with change in the outcome through time, which may not be the objective of the study. These considerations raise doubts about how to interpret some individual study findings. However, our meta-analyses excluded such studies when calculating pooled effect sizes. Most prior meta-analyses of risk factors in HICs (Hawkins et al. 1998; Lipsey and Derzon 1998; Derzon 2010; Tanner-Smith, Wilson, and Lipsey 2013) have synthesized only bivariate associations, and our meta-analyses also mostly synthesized only bivariate associations, although we were able to pool some covariate-adjusted effect sizes.

As in HICs, the longitudinal studies in LMICs used many different sampling methods, follow-up periods, informants, and measures. Hence, heterogeneity in results seems as likely to reflect methodological variations as possible true differences in effects of predictors across different LMIC contexts. Unfortunately, relatively few primary studies were available for each risk factor considered; hence, it was rarely possible to investigate the population characteristics or study features that might explain any observed heterogeneity.

Although we included studies from 14 different LMICs, the vast majority came from Brazil and China, two powerful countries in their respective regions, but with vastly different cultures and sociopolitical structures. Such large, medium-income countries also dominate in other areas of research in LMICs; for example, a systematic review on predictors of physical activity in LMICs found most evidence in Brazil and China (Sallis et al. 2016). Notably, apart from studies in three countries (China, the Philippines, and South Africa), there was no other evidence available from Asia or Africa. Also, although violence is a critical issue affecting many LMICs, of the 39 studies reviewed here, only seven provided data on predictors of violence. Therefore, the evidence base is particularly weak for drawing conclusions about predictors of violence, despite the major impact that it has on many LMICs.

A further limitation in the evidence we reviewed concerns the high likelihood of reporting and publication bias in observational studies, which may explain some of the heterogeneity and failure to replicate across studies, in both HICs and LMICs. Outcome reporting bias has been well documented in randomized control trials (Smyth et al. 2011), and it is likely to be a greater source of bias in observational studies, where prespecified protocols are rarer than for trials, analytic strategies are more varied, and data may be available for many investigators to mine. Where weak associations were found in individual studies, these might be accounted for by methodological limitations, in terms of low-quality measures or high rates of attrition, for example. However, some weak and null findings were replicated across multiple studies with different methodologies, increasing confidence that those variables really were not associated with antisocial behavior.

### H. Implications for Research

Some key issues confronting LMIC populations have not received adequate research attention in relation to the development of antisocial behavior. Experiences of civil conflict and migration are major issues that require study in LMICs. Other severe traumas commonly experienced in LMICs, such as female genital mutilation, being orphaned by AIDS, and stresses associated with child labor, are important areas for future research. Research with a resilience framework would be particularly valuable to consider ways in which individuals may cope with such traumas in LMIC contexts. Another research priority is to develop understanding of how macro-level influences that are known to covary with violence, such as illegitimate state institutions and national levels of income-inequality (Nivette 2011; Nivette and Eisner 2013), interact with individual development to cause antisocial behavior in LMICs. New studies should increase construct and internal validity by using multiple informants, well-validated and culturally adapted measures, and appropriate designs to increase understanding of causal mechanisms, such as sibling and twin studies, natural experiments, and analytic approaches such as propensity scores, analysis of within-individual change, and instrumental variables.

As new studies are conducted and additional results become available from more diverse settings across LMICs, it will become possible to assess the robustness of the current findings and identify causes of heterogeneity between study results. Understanding of the processes involved in the development of conduct problems, aggression, and delinquency across different cultures could be substantially enhanced from comparative longitudinal studies. These would be studies that are based on comparable sampling strategies, measurement tools, and analytic approaches in two or more populations with different cultural, economic, or social characteristics. Such studies would allow research to rule out many of the possible methodological reasons for heterogeneity between studies and provide a much better basis for understanding the extent to which there is cross-cultural variation in mechanisms leading to antisocial behavior. David Farrington (2001) laid out a program for comparative cross-national longitudinal surveys in Europe, which would investigate to what extent criminal careers, risk factors, and intervention effects are the same across participating countries. He recommends correlating the strength of risk factor associations across sites (see, e.g., Farrington et al. 2015). Even more ambitiously, a similar research program could be advanced across LMICs. An existing consortium of birth cohort studies in Brazil, Guatemala, India, the Philippines, and South Africa coordinates research on health, nutrition, and human capital in those settings (Richter et al. 2012). New projects could compare influences on the development of antisocial behavior and violence across LMICs.

A series of measures could help to improve comparability of developmental risk factor research across LMICs and human societies more generally. First, it seems important that studies conducted in different cultures use comparable and cross-culturally validated instruments to measure core constructs such as parenting, self-control, or aggression. Organizations such as the UNICEF Office of Research or the World Health Organization can help to promote good practice through recommendations. Second, developmental studies should be encouraged to publish research protocols similar to protocols for experimental studies. This would help to improve understanding of which putative risk factors were measured in a study and to what extent published results are based on fishing expeditions or on hypothesis-driven deductive reasoning.

Future syntheses of research on antisocial behavior should take a global view. Given the striking restriction of previous reviews to literature from HICs, we aimed to synthesize the existing evidence in LMICs. However, future reviews could encompass all world regions, increasing both the statistical power for quantitative syntheses of results and the potential to examine methodological and substantive factors that explain heterogeneity in findings around the globe.

## V. Conclusion

A large body of longitudinal research on antisocial behavior from LMICs has been excluded from most reviews on this topic. The most robust findings that emerge from these studies are that conduct problems tend to persist; dimensions of comorbid psychopathology such as low self-control, hyperactivity, and sensation seeking are also associated with antisocial behavior; many risk factors appear to have roughly the same average effects as when studied in HICs; and some early health factors have weak or null effects. The time is ripe for a new generation of collaborative research, with carefully coordinated methods, to identify global and context-specific mechanisms involved in the development of antisocial behaviors.

## REFERENCES

Aarnoudse-Moens, C. S. H., N. Weisglas-Kuperus, J. B. van Goudoever, and J. Oosterlaan. 2009. "Meta-Analysis of Neurobehavioral Outcomes in Very Preterm and/or Very Low Birth Weight Children." *Pediatrics* 124(2):717–28.

Achenbach, T. M., and L. A. Rescorla. 2000. *Manual for the Aseba School-Age Forms and Profiles*. Burlington: Research Center for Children, Youth, and Families, University of Vermont.

Achenbach, T. M., L. A. Rescorla, and M. Y. Ivanova. 2012. "International Epidemiology of Child and Adolescent Psychopathology I: Diagnoses, Dimensions, and Conceptual Issues." *Journal of the American Academy of Child and Adolescent Psychiatry* 51(12):1261–72.

Affonso, D. D., A. K. De, J. A. Horowitz, and L. J. Mayberry. 2000. "An International Study Exploring Levels of Postpartum Depressive Symptomatology." *Journal of Psychosomatic Research* 49(3):207–16.

American Psychiatric Association. 2013. *Diagnostic and Statistical Manual of Mental Disorders*. 5th ed. Washington, DC: American Psychiatric Association.

Anda, R. F., V. J. Felitti, J. D. Bremner, J. D. Walker, C. Whitfield, B. D. Perry, S. R. Dube, and W. H. Giles. 2005. "The Enduring Effects of Abuse and Related Adverse Experiences in Childhood." *European Archives of Psychiatry and Clinical Neuroscience* 256(3):174–86.

Anderson, J. W., B. M. Johnstone, and D. T. Remley. 1999. "Breast-Feeding and Cognitive Development: A Meta-Analysis." *American Journal of Clinical Nutrition* 70(4):525–35.

Anselmi, L., F. C. Barros, M. L. M. Teodoro, C. A. Piccinini, A. M. B. Menezes, C. L. Araujo, and L. A. Rohde. 2008. "Continuity of Behavioral and Emotional Problems from Pre-school Years to Pre-adolescence in a Developing Country." *Journal of Child Psychology and Psychiatry* 49(5):499–507.

Anselmi, L., A. M. B. Menezes, P. C. Hallal, F. Wehrmeister, H. Gonçalves, F. C. Barros, J. Murray, and L. A. Rohde. 2012. "Socioeconomic Changes and Adolescent Psychopathology in a Brazilian Birth Cohort Study." *Journal of Adolescent Health* 51(6):S5–S10.

Appleyard, K., B. Egeland, M. H. M. van Dulman, and L. A. Sroufe. 2005. "When More Is Not Better: The Role of Cumulative Risk in Child Behavior Outcomes." *Journal of Child Psychology and Psychiatry* 46(3):235–45.

Atkinson, A., Z. Anderson, K. Hughes, M. A. Bellis, H. Sumnall, and Q. Syed. 2009. *Interpersonal Violence and Illicit Drugs*. Liverpool: Centre for Public Health, Liverpool John Moores University.

Baier, C. J., and B. R. E. Wright. 2001. "'If You Love Me, Keep My Commandments': A Meta-Analysis of the Effect of Religion on Crime." *Journal of Research in Crime and Delinquency* 38(1):3–21.

Barbarin, O. A., L. Richter, and T. DeWet. 2001. "Exposure to Violence, Coping Resources, and Psychological Adjustment of South African Children." *American Journal of Orthopsychiatry* 71(1):16–25.

Barnard, M., and N. McKeganey. 2004. "The Impact of Parental Problem Drug Use on Children: What Is the Problem and What Can Be Done to Help?" *Addiction* 99(5): 552–59.

Batty, G. D., J. G. Alves, J. Correia, and D. A. Lawlor. 2007. "Examining Life-Course Influences on Chronic Disease: The Importance of Birth Cohort Studies from Low- and Middle-Income Countries; an Overview." *Brazilian Journal of Medical and Biological Research* 40(9):1277–86.

Baumrind, D. 1966. "Effects of Authoritative Parental Control on Child Behavior." *Child Development* 37(4):887–907.

Benjet, C., G. Borges, M. E. Medina-Mora, J. Zambranom, and S. Aguilar-Gaxiola. 2009. "Youth Mental Health in a Populous City of the Developing World: Results from the Mexican Adolescent Mental Health Survey." *Journal of Child Psychology and Psychiatry* 50(4):386–95.

Bird, H. R, P. E. Shrout, M. Davies, G. Canino, C. S. Duarte, S. A. Shen, and R. Loeber. 2007. "Longitudinal Development of Antisocial Behaviors in Young and Early Adolescent Puerto Rican Children at Two Sites." *Journal of the American Academy of Child and Adolescent Psychiatry* 46(1):5–14.

Blakemore, S.-J., and K. L. Mills. 2014. "Is Adolescence a Sensitive Period for Sociocultural Processing?" *Annual Review of Psychology* 65:187–207.

Bornstein, M. H. 2012. "Cultural Approaches to Parenting." *Parenting* 12(2–3):212–21.

Botcheva, L. B., S. S. Feldman, and P. H. Liederman. 2002. "Can Stability in School Processes Offset the Negative Effects of Sociopolitical Upheaval on Adolescents' Adaptation?" *Youth and Society* 34(1):55–88.

Botha, M. P., and G. Mels. 1990. "Stability of Aggression among Adolescents over Time: A South African Study." *Aggressive Behavior* 16(6):361–80.

Bowman, B., R. Matzopoulos, A. Butchart, and J. A. Mercy. 2008. "The Impact of Violence on Development in Low- to Middle-Income Countries." *International Journal of Injury Control and Safety Promotion* 15(4):209–19.

Boyes, M. E., L. Bowes, L. D. Cluver, C. L. Ward, and N. A. Badcock. 2014. "Bullying Victimisation, Internalising Symptoms, and Conduct Problems in South African Children and Adolescents: A Longitudinal Investigation." *Journal of Abnormal Child Psychology* 42(8):1313–24.

Brennan, P. A., E. R. Grekin, and S. A. Mednick. 2003. "Prenatal and Perinatal Influences on Conduct Disorder and Serious Delinquency." In *Causes of Conduct Disorder and Juvenile Delinquency*, edited by B. B. Lahey, T. E. Moffitt, and A. Caspi. New York: Guilford.

Brion, M.-J., C. Victora, A. Matijasevich, B. Horta, L. Anselmi, C. Steer, A. M. B. Menezes, D. A. Lawlor, and G. Davey Smith. 2010. "Maternal Smoking and

Child Psychological Problems: Disentangling Causal and Noncausal Effects." *Pediatrics* 126(1):e57–65.

Bronfenbrenner, U., and P. A. Morris. 2007. "The Bioecological Model of Human Development." In *Handbook of Child Psychology*, edited by R. M. Lerner. Hoboken, NJ: Wiley.

Brook, J. S., D. W. Brook, M. De La Rosa, M. Whiteman, E. Johnson, and I. Montoya. 2001. "Adolescent Illegal Drug Use: The Impact of Personality, Family, and Environmental Factors." *Journal of Behavioral Medicine* 24(2):183–203.

Brook, J. S., D. W. Brook, Z. Rosen, and C. R. Rabbitt. 2003. "Earlier Marijuana Use and Later Problem Behavior in Colombian Youths." *Journal of the American Academy of Child and Adolescent Psychiatry* 42(4):485–92.

Brook, J. S., D. W. Brook, and M. Whiteman. 2007. "Growing Up in a Violent Society: Longitudinal Predictors of Violence in Colombian Adolescents." *American Journal of Community Psychology* 40(1–2):82–95.

Burt, S. A. 2012. "How Do We Optimally Conceptualize the Heterogeneity within Antisocial Behavior? An Argument for Aggressive versus Non-aggressive Behavioral Dimensions." *Clinical Psychology Review* 32(4):263–79.

Bushman, B. J., and L. Huesmann. 2006. "Short-Term and Long-Term Effects of Violent Media on Aggression in Children and Adults." *Archives of Pediatrics and Adolescent Medicine* 160(4):348–52.

Byrd, A. L., and S. B. Manuck. 2014. "MAOA, Childhood Maltreatment, and Antisocial Behavior: Meta-Analysis of a Gene-Environment Interaction." *Biological Psychiatry* 75(1):9–17.

Caicedo, B., H. Gonçalves, D. A. González, and C. G. Victora. 2010. "Violent Delinquency in a Brazilian Birth Cohort: The Roles of Breast Feeding, Early Poverty and Demographic Factors." *Paediatric and Perinatal Epidemiology* 24 (1):12–23.

Canino, G., and M. Alegria. 2008. "Psychiatric Diagnosis: Is It Universal or Relative to Culture?" *Journal of Child Psychology and Psychiatry* 49(3):237–50.

Canino, G., G. Polanczyk, J. Bauermeister, L. Rohde, and P. Frick. 2010. "Does the Prevalence of CD and ODD Vary across Cultures?" *Social Psychiatry and Psychiatric Epidemiology* 45(7):695–704.

Caspi, A., B. Henry, R. O. McGee, T. E. Moffitt, and P. A. Silva. 1995. "Temperamental Origins of Child and Adolescent Behavior Problems: From Age Three to Age Fifteen." *Child Development* 66(1):55–68.

Caspi, A., J. McClay, T. E. Moffitt, J. Mill, J. Martin, I. W. Craig, A. Taylor, and R. Poulton. 2002. "Role of Genotype in the Cycle of Violence in Maltreated Children." *Science* 297(2):851–54.

Cecil, K. M., C. J. Brubaker, C. M. Adler, K. N. Dietrich, M. Altaye, J. C. Egelhoff, et al. 2008. "Decreased Brain Volume in Adults with Childhood Lead Exposure." *PLOS Medicine* 5(5):e112.

Chang, S. M., S. P. Walker, S. Grantham-McGregor, and C. A. Powell. 2002. "Early Childhood Stunting and Later Behaviour and School Achievement." *Journal of Child Psychology and Psychiatry* 43(6):775–83.

348     Joseph Murray et al.

Chao, R. K. 1994. "Beyond Parental Control and Authoritarian Parenting Style: Understanding Chinese Parenting through the Cultural Notion of Training." *Child Development* 65(4):1111–19.

Chen, L. 2012. "青少年早期的同伴侵害_发展轨迹_相关因素及性别差异_陈亮" [Children's peer victimization: Development, relevant elements, and gender difference]." Thesis, Shandong Normal University, Jinan, Shangdong, China.

Chen, S., Q. Zhou, N. Eisenberg, C. Valiente, and Y. Wang. 2011. "Parental Expressivity and Parenting Styles in Chinese Families: Prospective and Unique Relations to Children's Psychological Adjustment." *Parenting* 11(4):288–307.

Chen, X., Y. He, and D. Li. 2004. "Self-Perceptions of Social Competence and Self-Worth in Chinese Children: Relations with Social and School Performance." *Social Development* 13(4):570–89.

Chen, X., X. Huang, L. Wang, and L. Chang. 2012. "Aggression, Peer Relationships, and Depression in Chinese Children: A Multiwave Longitudinal Study." *Journal of Child Psychology and Psychiatry and Allied Disciplines* 53(12):1233–41.

Chen, X., D. Li, Z.-Y. Li, B.-S. Li, and M. Liu. 2000. "Sociable and Prosocial Dimensions of Social Competence in Chinese Children: Common and Unique Contributions to Social, Academic, and Psychological Adjustment." *Developmental Psychology* 36(3):302–14.

Chen, X., K. H. Rubin, and B.-S. Li. 1997. "Maternal Acceptance and Social and School Adjustment in Chinese Children: A Four-Year Longitudinal Study." *Merrill-Palmer Quarterly* 43(4):663–81.

Chen, X., K. H. Rubin, B.-S. Li, and D. Li. 1999. "Adolescent Outcomes of Social Functioning in Chinese Children." *International Journal of Behavioral Development* 23(1):199–223.

Chen, X., L. Wang, H. Chen, and M. Liu. 2002. "Noncompliance and Child-Rearing Attitudes as Predictors of Aggressive Behaviour: A Longitudinal Study in Chinese Children." *International Journal of Behavioral Development* 26(3):225–33.

Clark, F. A. 1982. "Relationship of Electrodermal Activity in 3-Year-Olds to Their Levels of Aggression at Age 9: A Study of a Physiologic Substrate of Temperament." PhD diss., University of Southern California.

Cohen, J. 1988. *Statistical Power Analysis for the Behavioral Sciences*. 2nd ed. Hillsdale, NJ: Erlbaum.

Coley, R. L., M. A. Kull, and J. Carrano. 2014. "Parental Endorsement of Spanking and Children's Internalizing and Externalizing Problems in African American and Hispanic Families." *Journal of Family Psychology* 28(1):22–31.

Collishaw, S., R. Goodman, T. Ford, S. Rabe-Hesketh, and A. Pickles. 2009. "How Far Are Associations between Child, Family and Community Factors and Child Psychopathology Informant-Specific and Informant-General?" *Journal of Child Psychology and Psychiatry* 50(5):571–80.

Cummings, E. M., P. T. Davies, and S. B. Campbell. 2000. *Developmental Psychopathology and Family Process: Theory, Research, and Clinical Implications*. New York: Guilford.

Davidson, P. W., D. A. Cory-Slechta, S. W. Thurston, L.-S. Huang, C. F. Shamlaye, D. Gunzler, et al. 2011. "Fish Consumption and Prenatal Methylmercury Exposure: Cognitive and Behavioral Outcomes in the Main Cohort at 17 Years from the Seychelles Child Development Study." *Neurotoxicology* 32 (6):711–17.

de Assis, S. G., R. d. V. C. de Oliveira, T. de Oliveira Pires, J. Q. Avanci, and R. P. Pesce. 2013. "Family, School and Community Violence and Problem Behavior in Childhood: Results from a Longitudinal Study in Brazil." *Paediatrics Today* 9(1):36–48.

de la Barra, F., V. Toledo, and J. Rodríguez. 2003. "Estudio de salud mental en dos cohortes de niños escolares de Santiago Occidente. III: Predictores tempranos de problemas conductuales y cognitivos" [Mental health study in two cohorts of schoolchildren from West Santiago. III: Early predictors of behavioral and cognitive problems]. *Revista Chilena de Neuro-Psiquiatria* 41(1):65–74.

———. 2005. "Prediction of Behavioral Problems in Chilean Schoolchildren." *Child Psychiatry and Human Development* 35(3):227–43.

DeLisi, M., and M. G. Vaughn, eds. 2015. *The Routledge International Handbook of Biosocial Criminology*. Abingdon, UK: Routledge.

Denno, D. W. 1990. *Biology and Violence: From Birth to Adulthood*. Cambridge: Cambridge University Press.

Derzon, J. H. 2001. "Antisocial Behavior and the Prediction of Violence: A Meta-Analysis." *Psychology in the Schools* 38(2):93–106.

———. 2010. "The Correspondence of Family Features with Problem, Aggressive, Criminal, and Violent Behavior: A Meta-Analysis." *Journal of Experimental Criminology* 6(3):263–92.

DiGirolamo, A. M., M. Ramirez-Zea, M. Wang, R. Flores-Ayala, R. Martorell, L. M. Neufeld, et al. 2010. "Randomized Trial of the Effect of Zinc Supplementation on the Mental Health of School-Age Children in Guatemala." *American Journal of Clinical Nutrition* 92(5):1241–50.

D'Onofrio, B. M., C. A. Van Hulle, I. D. Waldman, J. L. Rodgers, K. P. Harden, P. J. Rathouz, and B. B. Lahey. 2008. "Smoking during Pregnancy and Offspring Externalizing Problems: An Exploration of Genetic and Environmental Confounds." *Development and Psychopathology* 20(1):139–64.

Duarte, C. S., H. R. Bird, P. E. Shrout, P. Wu, R. Lewis-Fernandez, S. Shen, and G. Canino. 2008. "Culture and Psychiatric Symptoms in Puerto Rican Children: Longitudinal Results from One Ethnic Group in Two Contexts." *Journal of Child Psychology and Psychiatry* 49(5):563–72.

Duncan, L. E., and M. C. Keller. 2011. "A Critical Review of the First 10 Years of Candidate Gene-by-Environment Interaction Research in Psychiatry." *American Journal of Psychiatry* 168(10):1041–49.

Dytrych, Z., Z. Matějček, and V. Schüller. 1988. "The Prague Cohort: Adolescence and Early Adulthood." In *Born Unwanted: Developmental Effects of Denied Abortion*, edited by Henry P. David, Zdeněk Dytrych, Zdeněk Matějček, and Vratislav Schüller. New York: Springer.

Ebrahim, S., N. Pearce, L. Smeeth, J. P. Casas, S. Jaffar, and P. Piot. 2013. "Tackling Non-communicable Diseases in Low- and Middle-Income Countries: Is the Evidence from High-Income Countries All We Need?" *PLoS Medical* 10(1):e1001377.

Eisner, M. 2014. "From Swords to Words: Does Macro-Level Change in Self-Control Predict Long-Term Variation in Levels of Homicide?" In *Why Crime Rates Fall and Why They Don't*, edited by Michael Tonry. Vol. 43 of *Crime and Justice: A Review of Research*, edited by Michael Tonry. Chicago: University of Chicago Press.

Eisner, M., and T. Malti. 2015. "The Development of Aggressive Behavior and Violence." In *Handbook of Child Psychology and Developmental Science*, vol. 3, *Social, Emotional and Personality Development*, edited by M. E. Lamb. New York: Wiley.

Emond, A. M., P. I. C. Lira, M. C. Lima, S. M. Grantham-McGregor, and A. Ashworth. 2006. "Development and Behaviour of Low-Birthweight Term Infants at 8 Years in Northeast Brazil: A Longitudinal Study." *Acta Paediatrica, International Journal of Paediatrics* 95(10):1249–57.

Engle, P. L., L. C. H. Fernald, H. Alderman, J. Behrman, C. O'Gara, A. Yousafzai, et al. 2007. "Strategies for Reducing Inequalities and Improving Developmental Outcomes for Young Children in Low-Income and Middle-Income Countries." *Lancet* 378(9799):1339–53.

Eryigit Madzwamuse, S., N. Baumann, J. Jaekel, P. Bartmann, and D. Wolke. 2015. "Neuro-Cognitive Performance of Very Preterm or Very Low Birth Weight Adults at 26 Years." *Journal of Child Psychology and Psychiatry* 56(8): 857–64.

Factor-Litvak, P., G. Wasserman, J. K. Kline, and J. Graziano. 1999. "The Yugoslavia Prospective Study of Environmental Lead Exposure." *Environmental Health Perspectives* 107(1):9–15.

Farrington, D. P. 1988. "Studying Changes within Individuals: The Causes of Offending." In *Studies of Psychosocial Risk: The Power of Longitudinal Data*, edited by M. Rutter. Cambridge: Cambridge University Press.

———. 1991. "Antisocial Personality from Childhood to Adulthood." *Psychologist* 4(9):389–94.

———. 1994. "The Influence of the Family on Delinquent Development." In *Crime and the Family*, edited by C. Henricson. London: Family Policy Studies Centre.

———. 1998. "Predictors, Causes, and Correlates of Male Youth Violence." In *Youth Violence*, edited by Michael Tonry and Mark H. Moore. Vol. 24 of *Crime and Justice: A Review of Research*, edited by Michael Tonry. Chicago: University of Chicago Press.

———. 2001. "The Need for a Coordinated Program of Cross-National Comparative Longitudinal Research." In *Psychology and Law in a Changing World: New Trends in Theory, Research and Practice*, edited by G. B. Traverso and L. Bagnoli. London: Routledge.

———. 2002. "Families and Crime." In *Crime: Public Policies for Crime Control*, edited by J. Q. Wilson and J. Petersilia. Oakland, CA: Institute for Contemporary Studies Press.

———. 2003. "Developmental and Life-Course Criminology: Key Theoretical and Empirical Issues. The 2002 Sutherland Award Address." *Criminology* 41: 221–55.

———. 2005*a*. "Childhood Origins of Antisocial Behavior." *Clinical Psychology and Psychotherapy* 12(3):177–90.

———, ed. 2005*b*. *Integrated Developmental and Life-Course Theories of Offending.* Vol. 14. New Brunswick, NJ: Transaction.

———. 2013. "Longitudinal and Experimental Research in Criminology." In *Crime and Justice in America, 1975–2025*, edited by Michael Tonry. Vol. 42 of *Crime and Justice: A Review of Research*, edited by Michael Tonry. Chicago: University of Chicago Press.

———. 2015*a*. "Cross-National Comparative Research on Criminal Careers, Risk Factors, Crime and Punishment." *European Journal of Criminology* 12(4):386–99.

———. 2015*b*. "Prospective Longitudinal Research on the Development of Offending." *Australian and New Zealand Journal of Criminology* 48(3):314–35.

Farrington, D. P., J. W. Coid, and J. Murray. 2009. "Family Factors in the Intergenerational Transmission of Offending." *Criminal Behaviour and Mental Health* 19(2):109–24.

Farrington, D. P., H. Gaffney, and M. M. Ttofi. 2017. "Systematic Reviews of Explanatory Risk Factors for Violence, Offending, and Delinquency." *Aggression and Violent Behavior* 33(suppl. C):24–36.

Farrington, D. P., and R. Loeber. 1999. "Transatlantic Replicability of Risk Factors in the Development of Delinquency." In *Historical and Geographical Influences on Psychopathology*, edited by P. Cohen, C. Slomkowski, and L. N. Robins. Mahwah, NJ: Erlbaum.

Farrington, D. P., A. R. Piquero, and W. G. Jennings. 2013. *Offending from Childhood to Late Middle Age: Recent Results from the Cambridge Study in Delinquent Development.* New York: Springer Science & Business Media.

Farrington, D. P., M. M. Ttofi, R. V. Crago, and J. W. Coid. 2015. "Intergenerational Similarities in Risk Factors for Offending." *Journal of Developmental and Life-Course Criminology* 1(1):48–62.

Farrington, D. P., and B. C. Welsh. 2003. "Family-Based Prevention of Offending: A Meta-Analysis." *Australian and New Zealand Journal of Criminology* 36(2):127–51

———. 2007. *Saving Children from a Life of Crime: Early Risk Factors and Effective Interventions.* Oxford: Oxford University Press.

Fehringer, J. A., and M. J. Hindin. 2009. "Like Parent, Like Child: Intergenerational Transmission of Partner Violence in Cebu, the Philippines." *Journal of Adolescent Health* 44(4):363–71.

Fergusson, D. M., and L. J. Woodward. 1999. "Breast Feeding and Later Psychosocial Adjustment." *Paediatric and Perinatal Epidemiology* 13(2):144–57.

Forehand, R., N. Lafko, J. Parent, and K. B. Burt. 2014. "Is Parenting the Mediator of Change in Behavioral Parent Training for Externalizing Problems of Youth?" *Clinical Psychology Review* 34(8):608–19.

Frączek, A. 1986. "Sociocultural Environment, Television Viewing, and the Development of Aggression among Children in Poland." In *Television and the Aggressive Child: A Cross-National Comparison*, edited by L. R. Huesmann and L. D. Eron. Oxford: Routledge.

Frick, P. J., and S. F. White. 2008. "Research Review: The Importance of Callous-Unemotional Traits for Developmental Models of Aggressive and Antisocial Behavior." *Journal of Child Psychology and Psychiatry* 49(4):359–75.

Friday, P. C., X. Ren, E. Weitekamp, H.-J. Kerner, and T. Taylor. 2005. "A Chinese Birth Cohort: Theoretical Implications." *Journal of Research in Crime and Delinquency* 42(2):123–46.

Friday, P. C., X. Ren, E. Weitekamp, and K. U. Leuven. 2003. *Delinquency in a Chinese Birth Cohort, Final Report.* Washington, DC: US Department of Justice.

Galler, J. R., C. P. Bryce, D. P. Waber, R. S. Hock, R. Harrison, G. D. Eaglesfield, and G. Fitzmaurice. 2012. "Infant Malnutrition Predicts Conduct Problems in Adolescents." *Nutritional Neuroscience* 15(4):186–92.

Galler, J. R., C. P. Bryce, D. P. Waber, G. Medford, G. D. Eaglesfield, and G. Fitzmaurice. 2011. "Early Malnutrition Predicts Parent Reports of Externalizing Behaviors at Ages 9–17." *Nutritional Neuroscience* 14(4):138–44.

Galler, J. R., and F. Ramsey. 1989. "A Follow-Up Study of the Influence of Early Malnutrition on Development: Behavior at Home and at School." *Journal of the American Academy of Child and Adolescent Psychiatry* 28(2): 254–61.

Gao, Y., A. Raine, P. H. Venables, M. E. Dawson, and S. A. Mednick. 2010a. "Association of Poor Childhood Fear Conditioning and Adult Crime." *American Journal of Psychiatry* 167(1):56–60.

———. 2010b. "Reduced Electrodermal Fear Conditioning from Ages 3 to 8 Years Is Associated with Aggressive Behavior at Age 8 Years." *Journal of Child Psychology and Psychiatry* 51(5):550–58.

Gao, Y., A. Raine, P. H. Venables, and S. A. Mednick. 2013. "The Association between P3 Amplitude at Age 11 and Criminal Offending at Age 23." *Journal of Clinical Child and Adolescent Psychology* 42(1):120–30.

Gardner, F., P. Montgomery, and W. Knerr. 2015. "Transporting Evidence-Based Parenting Programs for Child Problem Behavior (Age 3–10) between Countries: Systematic Review and Meta-Analysis." *Journal of Clinical Child and Adolescent Psychology* 45(6):749–62.

Gelfand, M. J., J. L. Raver, L. Nishii, L. M. Leslie, J. Lun, B. C. Lim, et al. 2011. "Differences between Tight and Loose Cultures: A 33-Nation Study." *Science* 332(6033):1100–1104.

Gershoff, E. T. 2002. "Corporal Punishment by Parents and Associated Child Behaviors and Experiences: A Meta-Analytic and Theoretical Review." *Psychological Bulletin* 128(4):539–79.

Goldstein, P. J. 1985. "The Drugs/Violence Nexus: A Tripartite Conceptual Framework." *Journal of Drug Issues* 15(4):493–506.

Goodman, R. 1997. "The Strengths and Difficulties Questionnaire: A Research Note." *Journal of Child Psychology and Psychiatry* 38(5):581–86.

Graham, J. 1988. *Schools, Disruptive Behaviour and Delinquency.* London: Her Majesty's Stationery Office.

Grantham-McGregor, S., Y. B. Cheung, S. Cueto, P. Glewwe, L. Richter, and B. Strupp. 2007. "Developmental Potential in the First 5 Years for Children in Developing Countries." *Lancet* 369(9555):60–70.

Groebel, J. 1988. "Sozialisation Durch Fernsehgewalt: Ergebnisse Einer Kulturvergleichenden Studie" [Socialisation through television violence: Results from a culturally comparative study]. *Publizistik* 33:468–80.

Hawkins, J. D., T. I. Herrenkohl, D. P. Farrington, D. Brewer, R. F. Catalano, and T. W. Harachi. 1998. "A Review of Predictors of Youth Violence." In *Serious and Violent Juvenile Offenders: Risk Factors and Successful Interventions*, edited by D. P. Farrington and R. Loeber. Thousand Oaks, CA: Sage.

Hawkins, J. D., T. I. Herrenkohl, D. P. Farrington, D. Brewer, R. F. Catalano, T. W. Harachi, and L. Cothern. 2000. *Predictors of Youth Violence*. Washington, DC: Office of Juvenile Justice and Delinquency Prevention, US Department of Justice.

Henrich, J., S. J. Heine, and A. Norenzayan. 2010. "The Weirdest People in the World?" *Behavioral and Brain Sciences* 33(2–3):61–83.

Higgins, J. P. T., S. G. Thompson, J. J. Deeks, and D. G. Altman. 2003. "Measuring Inconsistency in Meta-Analyses." *British Medical Journal* 327(7414): 557–60.

Hill, C. J., H. S. Bloom, A. R. Black, and M. W. Lipsey. 2008. "Empirical Benchmarks for Interpreting Effect Sizes in Research." *Child Development Perspectives* 2(3):172–77.

Hill, J. 2002. "Biological, Psychological and Social Processes in the Conduct Disorders." *Journal of Child Psychology and Psychiatry* 43(1):133–64.

Hillis, S., J. Mercy, A. Amobi, and H. Kress. 2016. "Global Prevalence of Past-Year Violence against Children: A Systematic Review and Minimum Estimates." *Pediatrics* 137(3):1–13.

Hinshaw, S. P. 1992. "Externalizing Behavior Problems and Academic Underachievement in Childhood and Adolescence: Causal Relationships and Underlying Mechanisms." *Psychological Bulletin* 111(1):127–55.

Hoeve, M., J. Dubas, V. Eichelsheim, P. van der Laan, W. Smeenk, and J. Gerris. 2009. "The Relationship between Parenting and Delinquency: A Meta-Analysis." *Journal of Abnormal Child Psychology* 37(6):749–75.

Hofstede, G. H., and G. Hofstede. 2001. *Culture's Consequences: Comparing Values, Behaviors, Institutions and Organizations across Nations*. Thousand Oaks, CA: Sage.

Hou, J., Z. Chen, M. N. Natsuaki, X. Li, X. Yang, J. Zhang, and J. Zhang. 2013. "A Longitudinal Investigation of the Associations among Parenting, Deviant Peer Affiliation, and Externalizing Behaviors: A Monozygotic Twin Differences Design." *Twin Research and Human Genetics* 16(3):698–706.

Huesmann, L. R., and L. D. Eron, eds. 1986. *Television and the Aggressive Child: A Cross-National Comparison*. Oxford: Routledge.

Huesmann, L. R., J. Moise-Titus, C.-L. Podolski, and L. D. Eron. 2003. "Longitudinal Relations between Children's Exposure to TV Violence and Their Aggressive and Violent Behavior in Young Adulthood: 1977–1992." *Developmental Psychology* 39(2):201–21.

Inglehart, R. F., M. Basanez, and A. Moreno. 1998. *Human Values and Beliefs*. Ann Arbor: University of Michigan Press.

Institute for Health Metrics and Evaluation. 2016. *Global Burden of Disease Study 2013: Results by Location, Cause, and Risk Factor*. Seattle: Institute for Health Metrics and Evaluation. http://www.healthdata.org/gbd/data.

Jackson, M. 2001. *Improving Behaviour in Jamaican Children: A Model for Intervention Based on Epidemiological Analysis*. Kingston, Jamaica: Department of Community Health and Psychiatry, University of the West Indies.

Jaffee, S., A. Caspi, T. E. Moffitt, J. Belsky, and P. Silva. 2001. "Why Are Children Born to Teen Mothers at Risk for Adverse Outcomes in Young Adulthood? Results from a 20-Year Longitudinal Study." *Development and Psychopathology* 13:377–97.

Jaffee, S. R., L. B. Strait, and C. L. Odgers. 2012. "From Correlates to Causes: Can Quasi-Experimental Studies and Statistical Innovations Bring Us Closer to Identifying the Causes of Antisocial Behavior?" *Psychological Bulletin* 138 (2):272–95.

Jennings, W. G., M. M. Maldonado-Molina, A. R. Piquero, C. L. Odgers, H. Bird, and G. Canino. 2010. "Sex Differences in Trajectories of Offending among Puerto Rican Youth." *Crime and Delinquency* 56(3):327–57.

Jewkes, R., Y. Sikweyiya, R. Morrell, and K. Dunkle. 2011. "Gender Inequitable Masculinity and Sexual Entitlement in Rape Perpetration South Africa: Findings of a Cross-Sectional Study." *PLoS ONE* 6(12):e29590.

Jolliffe, D., and D. P. Farrington. 2008. "A Systematic Review of the Relationship between Childhood Impulsiveness and Later Violence." In *Personality, Personality Disorder, and Risk of Violence*, edited by M. McMurran and R. C. Howard. London: Wiley.

Jolliffe, D., J. Murray, D. P. Farrington, and C. Vannick. 2012. "Testing the Cambridge Quality Checklists on a Review of Disrupted Families and Crime." *Criminal Behaviour and Mental Health* 22(5):303–14.

Keenan, K., and D. S. Shaw. 2003. "Starting at the Beginning: Exploring the Etiology of Antisocial Behavior in the First Years of Life." In *Causes of Conduct Disorder and Juvenile Delinquency*. New York: Guilford.

Kieling, C., M. H. Hutz, J. P. Genro, G. V. Polanczyk, L. Anselmi, S. Camey, et al. 2013. "Gene-Environment Interaction in Externalizing Problems among Adolescents: Evidence from the Pelotas 1993 Birth Cohort Study." *Journal of Child Psychology and Psychiatry* 54(3):298–304.

Knerr, W., F. Gardner, and L. Cluver. 2013. "Improving Positive Parenting Skills and Reducing Harsh and Abusive Parenting in Low- and Middle-Income Countries: A Systematic Review." *Prevention Science* 14(4):1–12.

Kraemer, H. C., K. K. Lowe, and D. J. Kupfer. 2005. *To Your Health: How to Understand What Research Tells Us about Risk*. New York: Oxford University Press.

Kramer, M. S., B. Chalmers, E. D. Hodnett, Z. Sevkovskaya, I. Dzikovich, S. Shapiro, et al. 2001. "Promotion of Breastfeeding Intervention Trial (Probit): A Randomized Trial in the Republic of Belarus." *Journal of the American Medical Association* 285(4):413–20.

Kramer, M. S., E. Fombonne, S. Igumnov, I. Vanilovich, L. Matush, E. Mironova, et al. 2008. "Effects of Prolonged and Exclusive Breastfeeding on Child

Behavior and Maternal Adjustment: Evidence from a Large, Randomized Trial." *Pediatrics* 121(3):e435–40.

Kubička, L., Z. Matějček, H. P. David, Z. Dytrych, W. B. Miller, and Z. Roth. 1995. "Children from Unwanted Pregnancies in Prague, Czech Republic Revisited at Age Thirty." *Acta Psychiatrica Scandinavica* 91(6):361–69.

Kukla, L., D. Hruba, and M. Tyrlik. 2008. "Maternal Smoking during Pregnancy, Behavioral Problems and School Performances of Their School-Aged Children." *Central European Journal of Public Health* 16(2):71–76.

Lansford, J. E. 2010. "The Special Problem of Cultural Differences in Effects of Corporal Punishment." *Law and Contemporary Problems* 73(2):89–106.

Lansford, J. E., L. Chang, K. A. Dodge, P. S. Malone, P. Oburu, K. Palmérus, et al. 2005. "Physical Discipline and Children's Adjustment: Cultural Normativeness as a Moderator." *Child Development* 76(6):1234–46.

Lansford, J. E., and K. Deater-Deckard. 2012. "Childrearing Discipline and Violence in Developing Countries." *Child Development* 83(1):62–75.

Larzelere, R. E., A. S. E. Morris, and A. W. Harrist. 2013. *Authoritative Parenting: Synthesizing Nurturance and Discipline for Optimal Child Development.* Washington, DC: American Psychological Association.

Lawn, J. E., S. Cousens, and J. Zupan. 2005. "4 Million Neonatal Deaths: When? Where? Why?" *Lancet* 365(9462):891–900.

Leavitt, C. E., D. A. Nelson, S. M. Coyne, and C. H. Hart. 2013. "Adolescent Disclosure and Concealment: Longitudinal and Concurrent Associations with Aggression." *Aggressive Behavior* 39(5):335–45.

Leijten, P., T. J. Dishion, S. Thomaes, M. A. J. Raaijmakers, B. Orobio de Castro, and W. Matthys. 2015. "Bringing Parenting Interventions Back to the Future: How Randomized Microtrials May Benefit Parenting Intervention Efficacy." *Clinical Psychology: Science and Practice* 22(1):47–57.

Leijten, P., G. J. Melendez-Torres, W. Knerr, and F. Gardner. 2016. "Transported versus Homegrown Parenting Interventions for Reducing Disruptive Child Behavior: A Multilevel Meta-Regression Study." *Journal of the American Academy of Child and Adolescent Psychiatry* 55(7):610–17.

Lipsey, M. W., and J. H. Derzon. 1998. "Predictors of Violent or Serious Delinquency in Adolescence and Early Adulthood: A Synthesis of Longitudinal Research." In *Serious and Violent Juvenile Offenders: Risk Factors and Successful Interventions*, edited by D. P. Farrington and R. Loeber. Thousand Oaks, CA: Sage.

Lipsey, M. W., and D. B. Wilson. 1993. "The Efficacy of Psychological, Educational, and Behavioral Treatment: Confirmation from Meta-Analysis." *American Psychologist* 48(12):1181–1209.

Liu, J. 2011. "Early Health Risk Factors for Violence: Conceptualization, Evidence, and Implications." *Aggression and Violent Behavior* 16(1):63–73.

Liu, J., X. Liu, W. Wang, L. McCauley, J. Pinto-Martin, Y. Wang, L. Li, C. Yan, and W. J. Rogan. 2014. "Blood Lead Levels and Children's Behavioral and Emotional Problems: A Cohort Study." *Journal of the American Medical Association Pediatrics* 168(8):737–45.

Liu, J., A. Raine, P. H. Venables, and S. A. Mednick. 2004. "Malnutrition at Age 3 Years and Externalizing Behavior Problems at Ages 8, 11, and 17 Years." *American Journal of Psychiatry* 161(11):2005–13.

Liu, J. H., A. Raine, A. Wuerker, P. H. Venables, and S. Mednick. 2009. "The Association of Birth Complications and Externalizing Behavior in Early Adolescents: Direct and Mediating Effects." *Journal of Research on Adolescence* 19 (1):93–111.

Lösel, F., and D. P. Farrington. 2012. "Direct Protective and Buffering Protective Factors in the Development of Youth Violence." *American Journal of Preventive Medicine* 43(2):S8–S23.

Lynam, D. R., A. Caspi, T. E. Moffitt, P. O. H. Wikstrom, R. Loeber, and S. Novak. 2000. "The Interaction between Impulsivity and Neighborhood Context on Offending: The Effects of Impulsivity Are Stronger in Poorer Neighborhoods." *Journal of Abnormal Psychology* 109(4):563–74.

Maldonado-Molina, M. M., A. R. Piquero, W. G. Jennings, H. Bird, and G. Canino. 2009. "Trajectories of Delinquency among Puerto Rican Children and Adolescents at Two Sites." *Journal of Research in Crime and Delinquency* 46(2):144–81.

Matijasevich, A., E. Murray, A. Stein, L. Anselmi, A. M. Menezes, I. S. Santos, et al. 2014. "Increase in Child Behavior Problems among Urban Brazilian 4-Year Olds: 1993 and 2004 Pelotas Birth Cohorts." *Journal of Child Psychology and Psychiatry* 55(10):1125–34.

Matzopoulos, R., B. Bowman, A. Butchart, and J. A. Mercy. 2008. "The Impact of Violence on Health in Low- to Middle-Income Countries." *International Journal of Injury Control and Safety Promotion* 15(4):177–87.

Maughan, B., A. Taylor, A. Caspi, and T. E. Moffitt. 2004. "Prenatal Smoking and Early Childhood Conduct Problems: Testing Genetic and Environmental Explanations of the Association." *American Journal of Psychiatry* 61(8):836–43.

McCord, J., ed. 1998. *Coercion and Punishment in Long-Term Perspectives.* Cambridge: Cambridge University Press.

Medina-Mora, M. E., and S. E. Gibbs. 2013. "Implications of Science for Illicit Drug Use Policies for Adolescents in Low- and Middle-Income Countries." *Journal of Adolescent Health* 52(2):S33–S35.

Mejia, A., R. Calam, and M. R. Sanders. 2012. "A Review of Parenting Programs in Developing Countries: Opportunities and Challenges for Preventing Emotional and Behavioral Difficulties in Children." *Clinical Child and Family Psychology Review* 15(2):163–75.

Mielke, H. W., and S. Zahran. 2012. "The Urban Rise and Fall of Air Lead (Pb) and the Latent Surge and Retreat of Societal Violence." *Environment International* 43(suppl. C):48–55.

Moffitt, T. E. 1993. "Adolescence-Limited and Life-Course-Persistent Antisocial Behavior: A Developmental Taxonomy." *Psychological Review* 100(4):674–701.

Murray, J., and D. P. Farrington. 2010. "Risk Factors for Conduct Disorder and Delinquency: Key Findings from Longitudinal Studies." *Canadian Journal of Psychiatry* 55(10):633–42.

Murray, J., D. P. Farrington, and M. P. Eisner. 2009. "Drawing Conclusions about Causes from Systematic Reviews of Risk Factors: The Cambridge Quality Checklists." *Journal of Experimental Criminology* 5(1):1–23.

Murray, J., D. P. Farrington, and I. Sekol. 2012. "Children's Antisocial Behavior, Mental Health, Drug Use, and Educational Performance after Parental Incarceration: A Systematic Review and Meta-Analysis." *Psychological Bulletin* 138(2):175–210.

Murray, J., B. Irving, D. P. Farrington, I. Colman, and C. A. J. Bloxsom. 2010. "Very Early Predictors of Conduct Problems and Crime: Results from a National Cohort Study." *Journal of Child Psychology and Psychiatry* 51(11):1198–1207.

Murray, J., B. Maughan, A. M. B. Menezes, M. Hickman, J. MacLeod, A. Matijasevich, et al. 2015. "Perinatal and Sociodemographic Factors at Birth Predicting Conduct Problems and Violence to Age 18 years: Comparison of Brazilian and British Birth Cohorts." *Journal of Child Psychology and Psychiatry* 56(8):835–932.

Murray, J., A. M. B. Menezes, M. Hickman, B. Maughan, E. Gallo, A. Matijasevich, et al. 2015. "Childhood Behaviour Problems Predict Crime and Violence in Late Adolescence: Brazilian and British Birth Cohort Studies." *Social Psychiatry and Psychiatric Epidemiology* 50(4):579–89.

Myers, G. J., P. W. Davidson, D. Palumbo, C. Shamlaye, C. Cox, E. Cernichiari, and T. W. Clarkson. 2000. "Secondary Analysis from the Seychelles Child Development Study: The Child Behavior Checklist." *Environmental Research* 84(1):12–19.

Nelson, D. A., S. M. Coyne, S. M. Swanson, C. H. Hart, and J. A. Olsen. 2014. "Parenting, Relational Aggression, and Borderline Personality Features: Associations over Time in a Russian Longitudinal Sample." *Development and Psychopathology* 26(special issue 3):773–87.

Nevin, R. 2007. "Understanding International Crime Trends: The Legacy of Preschool Lead Exposure." *Environmental Research* 104(3):315–36.

Nivette, A. E. 2011. "Cross-National Predictors of Crime: A Meta-Analysis." *Homicide Studies* 15(2):103–31.

Nivette, A. E., and M. Eisner. 2013. "Do Legitimate Polities Have Fewer Homicides? A Cross-National Analysis." *Homicide Studies* 17(1):3–26.

Olweus, D. 1979. "Stability of Aggressive Reaction Patterns in Males: A Review." *Psychological Bulletin* 86(4):852–75.

Patel, V., and A. Kleinman. 2003. "Poverty and Common Mental Disorders in Developing Countries." *Bulletin of the World Health Organization* 81:609–15.

Patrick, C. J., J. Foell, N. C. Venables, and D. A. Worthy. 2015. "Substance Use Disorders as Externalizing Outcomes." In *The Oxford Handbook of Externalizing Spectrum Disorders*, edited by T. P. Beauchaine and S. P. Hinshaw. Oxford: Oxford University Press.

Patterson, G. R. 1995. "Coercion as a Basis for Early Age of Onset for Arrest." In *Coercion and Punishment in Long-Term Perspectives*, edited by J. McCord. Cambridge: Cambridge University Press.

Petresco, S., L. Anselmi, I. Santos, A. D. Barros, B. Fleitlich-Bilyk, F. Barros, and A. Matijasevich. 2014. "Prevalence and Comorbidity of Psychiatric Disorders among 6-Year-Old Children: 2004 Pelotas Birth Cohort." *Social Psychiatry and Psychiatric Epidemiology* 49(6):975–83.

Pine, D. S., J. Costello, and A. Masten. 2005. "Trauma, Proximity, and Developmental Psychopathology: The Effects of War and Terrorism on Children." *Neuropsychopharmacology* 30(10):1781–92.

Piquero, A. R., D. P. Farrington, and A. Blumstein. 2007. *Key Issues in Criminal Career Research: New Analyses of the Cambridge Study in Delinquent Development.* Cambridge: Cambridge University Press.

Piquero, A. R., D. P. Farrington, B. C. Welsh, R. Tremblay, and W. G. Jennings. 2009. "Effects of Early Family/Parent Training Programs on Antisocial Behavior and Delinquency." *Journal of Experimental Criminology* 5(2):83–120.

Piquero, A. R., W. G. Jennings, B. Diamond, D. P. Farrington, R. E. Tremblay, B. C. Welsh, and J. M. R. Gonzalez. 2016. "A Meta-Analysis Update on the Effects of Early Family/Parent Training Programs on Antisocial Behavior and Delinquency." *Journal of Experimental Criminology* 12(2):229–48.

Piquero, A. R., and S. Tibbetts. 1999. "The Impact of Pre/Perinatal Disturbances and Disadvantaged Familial Environment in Predicting Criminal Offending." *Studies on Crime and Crime Prevention* 8(1):42–70.

Polanczyk, G. V., G. A. Salum, L. S. Sugaya, A. Caye, and L. A. Rohde. 2015. "Annual Research Review: A Meta-Analysis of the Worldwide Prevalence of Mental Disorders in Children and Adolescents." *Journal of Child Psychology and Psychiatry* 56(3):345–65.

Pratt, T. C., F. T. Cullen, K. R. Blevins, L. Daigle, and J. D. Unnever. 2002. "The Relationship of Attention Deficit Hyperactivity Disorder to Crime and Delinquency: A Meta-Analysis." *International Journal of Police Science and Management* 4(4):344–60.

Pratt, T. C., J. M. McGloin, and N. E. Fearn. 2006. "Maternal Cigarette Smoking during Pregnancy and Criminal/Deviant Behavior: A Meta-Analysis." *International Journal of Offender Therapy and Comparative Criminology* 50(6):672–90.

Putnam, F. W. 2003. "Ten-Year Research Update Review: Child Sexual Abuse." *Journal of the American Academy of Child and Adolescent Psychiatry* 42(3):269–78.

Rabotegsaric, Z., M. Zuzul, and G. Kerestes. 1994. "War and Children's Aggressive and Prosocial Behavior." *European Journal of Personality* 8(3):201–12.

Raine, A. 2002a. "Annotation: The Role of Prefrontal Deficits, Low Autonomic Arousal, and Early Health Factors in the Development of Antisocial and Aggressive Behavior in Children." *Journal of Child Psychology and Psychiatry* 43 (4):417–34.

———. 2002b. "Biosocial Studies of Antisocial and Violent Behavior in Children and Adults: A Review." *Journal of Abnormal Child Psychology* 30(4):311–26.

———. 2013. *The Anatomy of Violence: The Biological Roots of Crime.* London: Penguin.

Raine, A., C. Reynolds, P. H. Venables, S. A. Mednick, and D. P. Farrington. 1998. "Fearlessness, Stimulation-Seeking, and Large Body Size at Age 3 Years as Early Predispositions to Childhood Aggression at Age 11 Years." *Archives of General Psychiatry* 55(8):745–51.

Raine, A., P. H. Venables, and S. A. Mednick. 1997. "Low Resting Heart Rate at Age 3 Years Predisposes to Aggression at Age 11 Years: Evidence from the Mauritius Child Health Project." *Journal of the American Academy of Child and Adolescent Psychiatry* 36(10):1457–64.

Raine, A., P. S. Yaralian, C. Reynolds, P. H. Venables, and S. A. Mednick. 2002. "Spatial but Not Verbal Cognitive Deficits at Age 3 Years in Persistently Antisocial Individuals." *Development and Psychopathology* 14(1):25–44.

Rescorla, L., M. Y. Ivanova, T. M. Achenbach, I. Begovac, M. Chahed, M. B. Drugli, et al. 2012. "International Epidemiology of Child and Adolescent Psychopathology II: Integration and Applications of Dimensional Findings from 44 Societies." *Journal of the American Academy of Child and Adolescent Psychiatry* 51(12):1273–83.

Reyes, J. C., R. R. Robles, H. M. Colón, J. Negrón, T. D. Matos, J. Calderón, and O. M. Pérez. 2008. "Neighborhood Disorganization, Substance Use, and Violence among Adolescents in Puerto Rico." *Journal of Interpersonal Violence* 23(11):1499–1512.

Rhee, S. H., and I. D. Waldman. 2002. "Genetic and Environmental Influences on Antisocial Behavior: A Meta-Analysis of Twin and Adoption Studies." *Psychological Bulletin* 128(3):490–529.

Richmond, R. C., A. Al-Amin, G. Davey Smith, and C. L. Relton. 2014. "Approaches for Drawing Causal Inferences from Epidemiological Birth Cohorts: A Review." *Early Human Development* 90(11):769–80.

Richter, L. M., C. G. Victora, P. C. Hallal, L. S. Adair, S. K. Bhargava, C. H. Fall, et al. 2012. "Cohort Profile: The Consortium of Health-Orientated Research in Transitioning Societies." *International Journal of Epidemiology* 41 (3):621–26.

Rodriguez, J. D. M., A. A. M. da Silva, H. Bettiol, M. A. Barbieri, and R. J. Rona. 2011. "The Impact of Perinatal and Socioeconomic Factors on Mental Health Problems of Children from a Poor Brazilian City: A Longitudinal Study." *Social Psychiatry and Psychiatric Epidemiology* 46(5):381–91.

Rothbaum, F., and J. R. Weisz. 1994. "Parental Caregiving and Child Externalizing Behavior in Nonclinical Samples: A Meta-Analysis." *Psychological Bulletin* 116(1):55–74.

Rutter, M. 1999. "Social Context: Meanings, Measures and Mechanisms." *European Review* 7(1):139–49.

———. 2003. "Crucial Paths from Risk Indicator to Causal Mechanism." In *Causes of Conduct Disorder and Juvenile Delinquency*, edited by B. B. Lahey, T. E. Moffitt, and A. Caspi. New York: Guilford.

Rutter, M., H. Giller, and A. Hagell. 1998. *Antisocial Behavior by Young People.* Cambridge: Cambridge University Press.

Rutter, M., B. Maughan, P. Mortimer, and J. Ouston. 1979. *Fifteen Thousand Hours: Secondary Schools and Their Effects on Children.* Cambridge, MA: Harvard University Press.

Rutter, M., A. Pickles, R. Murray, and L. Eaves. 2001. "Testing Hypotheses on Specific Environmental Causal Effects on Behavior." *Psychological Bulletin* 127 (3):291–324.

Sabet, F., L. M. Richter, P. G. Ramchandani, A. Stein, M. A. Quigley, and S. A. Norris. 2009. "Low Birthweight and Subsequent Emotional and Behavioural Outcomes in 12-Year-Old Children in Soweto, South Africa: Findings from Birth to Twenty." *International Journal of Epidemiology* 38(4):944–54.

Sallis, J. F., F. Bull, R. Guthold, G. W. Heath, S. Inoue, P. Kelly, et al. 2016. "Progress in Physical Activity over the Olympic Quadrennium." *Lancet* 388 (10051):1325–36.

Samms-Vaughan, M., M. Jackson, and D. Ashley. 2005. "Urban Jamaican Children's Exposure to Community Violence." *West Indian Medical Journal* 54 (1):14–21.

Sampson, R. J., and J. H. Laub. 1993. *Crime in the Making: Pathways and Turning Points through Life.* Cambridge, MA: Harvard University Press.

Santana, M. C., A. Raj, M. R. Decker, A. La Marche, and J. G. Silverman. 2006. "Masculine Gender Roles Associated with Increased Sexual Risk and Intimate Partner Violence Perpetration among Young Adult Men." *Journal of Urban Health* 83(4):575–85.

Schisterman, E. F., S. R. Cole, and R. W. Platt. 2009. "Overadjustment Bias and Unnecessary Adjustment in Epidemiologic Studies." *Epidemiology* 20(4): 488–95.

Schonberg, M. A., and D. S. Shaw. 2007. "Do the Predictors of Child Conduct Problems Vary by High- and Low-Levels of Socioeconomic and Neighborhood Risk?" *Clinical Child and Family Psychology Review* 10(2):101–36.

Seekings, J., and K. M. Thaler. 2011. "Socio-economic Conditions, Young Men and Violence in Cape Town." CSSR Working Paper no. 285. Cape Town: Centre for Social Science Research, University of Cape Town.

Shadish, W. R., T. D. Cook, and D. T. Campbell. 2002. *Experimental and Quasi-Experimental Designs for Generalized Causal Inference.* Boston: Houghton Mifflin.

Shaw, C. R., and H. D. McKay. 1969. *Juvenile Delinquency and Urban Areas.* Chicago: University of Chicago Press.

Shenderovich, Y., M. Eisner, C. Mikton, F. Gardner, J. Liu, and J. Murray. 2016. "Methods for Conducting Systematic Reviews of Risk Factors in Low- and Middle-Income Countries." *BMC Medical Research Methodology* 16:32.

Smith, C. A., T. O. Ireland, and T. P. Thornberry. 2005. "Adolescent Maltreatment and Its Impact on Young Adult Antisocial Behavior." *Child Abuse and Neglect* 29(10):1099–119.

Smith, C. A., and S. B. Stern. 1997. "Delinquency and Antisocial Behavior: A Review of Family Processes and Intervention Research." *Social Service Review* 71(3): 382–420.

Smyth, R. M. D., J. J. Kirkham, A. Jacoby, D. G. Altman, C. Gamble, and P. R. Williamson. 2011. "Frequency and Reasons for Outcome Reporting Bias in Clinical Trials: Interviews with Trialists." *British Medical Journal* 342:c7153.

Sumner, A. 2011. *The New Bottom Billion: What If Most of the World's Poor Live in Middle-Income Countries?* London: Center for Global Development.

Susman, E. J. 2006. "Psychobiology of Persistent Antisocial Behavior: Stress, Early Vulnerabilities and the Attenuation Hypothesis." *Neuroscience and Biobehavioral Reviews* 30(3):376–89.

Tanner-Smith, E. E., S. J. Wilson, and M. Lipsey. 2013. "Risk Factors and Crime "In *The Oxford Handbook of Criminological Theory*, edited by F. T. Cullen and P. Wilcox. Oxford: Oxford University Press.

Tao, A., Q. Zhou, and Y. Wang. 2010. "Parental Reactions to Children's Negative Emotions: Prospective Relations to Chinese Children's Psychological Adjustment." *Journal of Family Psychology* 24(2):135–44.

Taylor, T. J., P. C. Friday, X. Ren, E. G. M. Weitekamp, and H. J. Kerner. 2004. "Risk and Protective Factors Related to Offending: Results from a Chinese Cohort Study." *Australian and New Zealand Journal of Criminology* 37:13–31.

Thabet, A. A. M., and P. Vostanis. 1999. "Post-traumatic Stress Reactions in Children of War." *Journal of Child Psychology and Psychiatry and Allied Disciplines* 40(3):385–91.

Thaler, K. 2011. "Drivers of Male Perpetration of Family and Intimate Partner Violence in Cape Town." CSSR Working Paper no. 289. Cape Town: Centre for Social Science Research, University of Cape Town.

Thornberry, T. P., A. Freeman-Gallant, A. J. Lizotte, M. D. Krohn, and C. A. Smith. 2003. "Linked Lives: The Intergenerational Transmission of Antisocial Behavior." *Journal of Abnormal Child Psychology* 31(2):171–84.

Thornberry, T. P., and M. D. Krohn. 2005. "Applying Interactional Theory to the Explanation of Continuity and Change in Antisocial Behavior." *Integrated Developmental and Life-Course Theories of Offending* 14:183–209.

Thornberry, T. P., A. J. Lizotte, M. D. Krohn, M. Farnworth, and S. J. Jang. 1994. "Delinquent Peers, Beliefs, and Delinquent-Behavior: A Longitudinal Test of Interactional Theory." *Criminology* 32(1):47–83.

Tibbetts, S. G., and A. R. Piquero. 1999. "The Influence of Gender, Low Birth Weight, and Disadvantaged Environment in Predicting Early Onset of Offending: A Test of Moffitt's Interactional Hypothesis." *Criminology* 37(4): 843–77.

Tremblay, R. E., and C. Japel. 2003. "Prevention during Pregnancy, Infancy and the Preschool Years." In *Early Prevention of Adult Antisocial Behaviour*, edited by D. P. Farrington and J. Coid. Cambridge: Cambridge University Press.

Trickett, P. K., J. G. Noll, and F. W. Putnam. 2011. "The Impact of Sexual Abuse on Female Development: Lessons from a Multigenerational, Longitudinal Research Study." *Development and Psychopathology* 23(2):453–76.

Tseng, W.-S., K.-T. Tao, J. Hsu, J.-H. Qiu, B. Li, and D. Goebert. 2000. "Longitudinal Analysis of Development among Single and Nonsingle Children in Nanjing, China: Ten-Year Follow-Up Study." *Journal of Nervous and Mental Disease* 188(10):701–7.

Ttofi, M. M., D. P. Farrington, and F. Lösel. 2012. "School Bullying as a Predictor of Violence Later in Life: A Systematic Review and Meta-Analysis of Prospective Longitudinal Studies." *Aggression and Violent Behavior* 17(5):405–18.

UN Children's Fund. 2014. *Hidden in Plain Sight: A Statistical Analysis of Violence against Children*. New York: UNICEF.

UN Development Programme. 2015. *Human Development Report 2015*. New York: UN Development Programme.

UN Office on Drugs and Crime. 2013. *Global Study on Homicide 2013: Trends, Contexts, Data*. Vienna: UN Office on Drugs and Crime.

van Goozen, S. H. M., G. Fairchild, H. Snoek, and G. T. Harold. 2007. "The Evidence for a Neurobiological Model of Childhood Antisocial Behavior." *Psychological Bulletin* 133(1):149–82.

Velásquez, H., F. P. Cabrera, S. M. Chainé, A. C. Caso-López, and N. B. Torres. 2002. "Factores de riesgo, factores protectores y generalización del comportamiento agresivo en una muestra de niños en edad escolar" [Risk factors, protective factors, and prevalence of aggressive behavior in a sample of school children]. *Salud Mental* 25(3):27–40.

Venables, P. H. 1989. "The Emanuel Miller Memorial Lecture 1987: Childhood Markers for Adult Disorders." *Journal of Child Psychology and Psychiatry* 30(3):347–64.

Victora, C. G., B. L. Horta, C. L. de Mola, L. Quevedo, R. T. Pinheiro, D. P. Gigante, H. Gonçalves, and F. C. Barros. 2015. "Association between Breastfeeding and Intelligence, Educational Attainment, and Income at 30 Years of Age: A Prospective Birth Cohort Study from Brazil." *Lancet Global Health* 3(4): e199–205.

Victora, C. G., S. R. Huttly, S. C. Fuchs, and M. T. Olinto. 1997. "The Role of Conceptual Frameworks in Epidemiological Analysis: A Hierarchical Approach." *International Journal of Epidemiology* 26(1):224–27.

Vittrup, B., and G. W. Holden. 2010. "Children's Assessments of Corporal Punishment and Other Disciplinary Practices: The Role of Age, Race, Sex, and Exposure to Spanking." *Journal of Applied Developmental Psychology* 31(3):211–20.

Vu, N. L., E. N. Jouriles, R. McDonald, and D. Rosenfield. 2016. "Children's Exposure to Intimate Partner Violence: A Meta-Analysis of Longitudinal Associations with Child Adjustment Problems." *Clinical Psychology Review* 46:25–33.

Wachs, T. D. 1999. *Necessary but Not Sufficient: The Respective Roles of Single and Multiple Influences on Individual Development*. Washington, DC: American Psychological Association.

Wakschlag, L. S., K. E. Pickett, E. Cook, N. L. Benowitz, and B. L. Leventhal. 2002. "Maternal Smoking during Pregnancy and Severe Antisocial Behavior in Offspring: A Review." *American Journal of Public Health* 92(6):966–74.

Walker, S. P., S. M. Chang, C. A. Powell, E. Simonoff, and S. M. Grantham-McGregor. 2007. "Early Childhood Stunting Is Associated with Poor Psychological Functioning in Late Adolescence and Effects Are Reduced by Psychosocial Stimulation." *Journal of Nutrition* 137(11):2464–69.

Walker, S. P., T. D. Wachs, S. Grantham-McGregor, M. M. Black, C. A. Nelson, S. L. Huffman, et al. 2011. "Inequality in Early Childhood: Risk and Protective Factors for Early Child Development." *Lancet* 378(9799):1325–38.

Walker, S. P., T. D. Wachs, J. Meeks Gardner, B. Lozoff, G. A. Wasserman, E. Pollitt, and J. A. Carter. 2007. "Child Development: Risk Factors for Adverse Outcomes in Developing Countries." *Lancet* 369(9556):145–57.

Waller, R., F. Gardner, and L. Cluver. 2014. "Shared and Unique Predictors of Antisocial and Substance Use Behavior among a Nationally Representative Sample of South African Youth." *Aggression and Violent Behavior* 19(6):629–36.

Wang, L., X. Chen, H. Chen, L. Cui, and M. Li. 2006. "Affect and Maternal Parenting as Predictors of Adaptive and Maladaptive Behaviors in Chinese Children." *International Journal of Behavioral Development* 30(2):158–66.

Wasserman, G. A., X. Liu, D. S. Pine, and J. H. Graziano. 2001. "Contribution of Maternal Smoking during Pregnancy and Lead Exposure to Early Child Behavior Problems." *Neurotoxicology and Teratology* 23(1):13–21.

Wasserman, G. A., B. Staghezza-Jaramillo, P. Shrout, D. Popovac, and J. Graziano. 1998. "The Effect of Lead Exposure on Behavior Problems in Preschool Children." *American Journal of Public Health* 88(3):481–86.

White, J. L., T. E. Moffitt, F. Earls, L. Robins, and P. A. Silva. 1990. "How Early Can We Tell? Predictors of Childhood Conduct Disorder and Adolescent Delinquency." *Criminology* 28(4):507–33.

Wilson, H. W., C. S. Stover, and S. J. Berkowitz. 2009. "Research Review: The Relationship between Childhood Violence Exposure and Juvenile Antisocial Behavior: A Meta-Analytic Review." *Journal of Child Psychology and Psychiatry* 50(7):769–79.

Wolf, A., R. Gray, and S. Fazel. 2014. "Violence as a Public Health Problem: An Ecological Study of 169 Countries." *Social Science and Medicine* 104:220–27.

World Health Organization. 2002. *World Report on Violence and Health*. Geneva: World Health Organization.

———. 2015. *Preventing Youth Violence: An Overview of the Evidence*. Geneva: World Health Organization.

Wright, J. P., K. N. Dietrich, M. D. Ris, R. W. Hornung, S. D. Wessel, B. P. Lanphear, M. Ho, and M. N. Rae. 2008. "Association of Prenatal and Childhood Blood Lead Concentrations with Criminal Arrests in Early Adulthood." *PLOS Medicine* 5(5):e101.

Wubs, A. G., L. E. Aaro, C. Mathews, H. E. Onya, and J. Mbwambo. 2013. "Associations between Attitudes toward Violence and Intimate Partner Violence in South Africa and Tanzania." *Violence and Victims* 28(2):324–40.

Zhang, W., L. Ji, X. Gong, Q. Zhang, and W. Yiwen. 2003. "A Longitudinal Study on the Development of 3- to 4-Year-Old Children's Aggressive Behavior." *Psychological Science* 26(1):49–52.

Zhang, X. 2013. "The Longitudinal Interplay of Psychopathology and Social Competence during Chinese Children's Transition to Preschool." *Infant and Child Development* 22(2):198–215.

Zhou, Q., A. Main, and Y. Wang. 2010. "The Relations of Temperamental Effortful Control and Anger/Frustration to Chinese Children's Academic Achievement and Social Adjustment: A Longitudinal Study." *Journal of Educational Psychology* 102(1):180–96.

Zhou, Q., Y. Wang, X. Deng, N. Eisenberg, S. A. Wolchik, and J. Y. Tein. 2008. "Relations of Parenting and Temperament to Chinese Children's Experience of Negative Life Events, Coping Efficacy, and Externalizing Problems." *Child Development* 79(3):493–513.

Zhou, Z. H., H. Y. Xiong, R. Jia, G. Y. Yang, T. Y. Guo, Z. Y. Meng, G. Y. Huang, and Y. Zhang. 2012. "The Risk Behaviors and Mental Health of De- tained Adolescents: A Controlled, Prospective Longitudinal Study." *PLoS ONE* 7(5):e37199.

Zhu, X. N., S. J. Yan, and D. Y. Li. 2011. "北京大兴区农村父母养育方式与2~4 岁儿童行为问题" [Parents' child rearing attitude and children's behavioral problems at 2–3 and 4–5 years old in Daxing District of Beijing]. 中国儿童 保健杂志 [Chinese journal of child health care] 3(19):262–64.

*Craig Haney*

# The Psychological Effects of Solitary Confinement: A Systematic Critique

ABSTRACT

Research findings on the psychological effects of solitary confinement have been strikingly consistent since the early nineteenth century. Studies have identified a wide range of frequently occurring adverse psychological reactions that commonly affect prisoners in isolation units. The prevalence of psychological distress is extremely high. Nonetheless, use of solitary confinement in the United States vastly increased in recent decades. Advocates defend its use, often citing two recent studies to support claims that isolation has no significant adverse psychological effects, including even on mentally ill people. Those studies, however, are fundamentally flawed, their results are not credible, and they should be disregarded. Critically and comprehensively analyzing the numerous flaws that compromise this recent scholarship underscores the distinction between methodological form and substance, the danger of privileging quantitative data irrespective of their quality, and the importance of considering the fraught nature of the prison context in which research results are actually generated. Solitary confinement has well-documented adverse effects. Its use should be eliminated entirely for some groups of prisoners and greatly reduced for others.

Doing prison research, Alison Liebling has long reminded us, is deeply emotional and intellectually challenging, with different methodological approaches "competing for epistemological prominence—often from different sides of the prison wall" (1999, p. 148). It takes place in "an in-

Electronically published March 9, 2018
   Craig Haney is Distinguished Professor of Psychology, University of California, Santa Cruz.

tense, risk-laden, emotionally fraught environment" (p. 163) and within a closed environment in which prison administrators tightly control access to data and most prisoners manifest an entirely legitimate and understandable skepticism toward data gatherers.

This helps explain why, in Liebling's words, "the pains of imprisonment are tragically underestimated by conventional methodological approaches to prison life" (p. 165). The more these conventional approaches encourage us to conceive of prisons as more or less traditional research settings and prisoners as mere specimens to be "objectively assessed," the less likely we are to gain useful insights into prison life or accurately represent the experience of those living inside.

These cautions are doubly applicable to research on solitary confinement.[1] It involves involuntary isolation of prisoners nearly around the clock in sparse cells located in remote or inaccessible units. Solitary confinement denies prisoners any meaningful social contact and access to positive environmental stimulation.

These prisons within prisons are nearly impenetrable to outside researchers (or anyone else). Prison officials tightly control access to solitary confinement units and to the prisoners inside them. They typically rebuff attempts by researchers to observe conditions and practices, let alone to carefully assess their potentially harmful effects. Prisoners in solitary confinement tend to be even more self-protective than other prisoners are (as part of their accommodation to harsh and frequently abusive conditions) and reluctant to have their "measure" taken by persons whom they have no reason to trust. They generally subscribe strongly to prisoner norms against displaying or acknowledging vulnerabilities that could be interpreted as weakness. The inapt pejorative designation of them as collectively "the worst of the worst" does not inspire confidence in or candor toward outsiders, and certainly not toward anyone remotely associated with the prison administration.

These realities pose a host of methodological challenges for anyone interested in understanding the nature and effects of prison isolation. This is in part why studies of the effects of solitary confinement on prisoners

---

[1] I use "solitary confinement" to refer to forms of prison isolation in which prisoners are housed involuntarily in their cells for upward of 23 hours per day and denied the opportunity to engage in normal and meaningful social interaction and congregate activities, including correctional programming. The term subsumes a range of prison nomenclature including "administrative segregation," "security housing units," "high security," and "close management," among others.

have rarely, if ever, approximated experimental research designs (including quasi- or natural experimental designs).

Solitary confinement units not only are largely impenetrable to outsiders but also, of course, are subject to legal and ethical restrictions that preclude random assignment of prisoners into them. The rigid prison rules and operating procedures that govern these places can easily frustrate the use of the kind of meticulous controls over conditions and participants that are needed to carry out anything remotely resembling an experiment. The distinctiveness of solitary confinement units and the nonnegotiable staff mandates under which they operate make it difficult, if not impossible, to implement rigorous conventional research designs (e.g., representative samples, control groups, repeated measures). Efforts to conduct randomized or truly controlled studies inevitably face significant risks that the data collected will be so confounded by inevitable methodological compromises as to be uninterpretable and, therefore, meaningless.

Nonetheless, scholars and researchers know a great deal about the negative effects of solitary confinement. We have firsthand or autobiographical accounts by former prisoners (e.g., Burney 1961) and staff members (e.g., Rundle 1973; Slater 1986); ethnographic, interview, and observational research (e.g., Benjamin and Lux 1975; Toch 1975; Hilliard 1976; Jackson 1983; Rhodes 2004; Reiter 2016); and cross-sectional studies that assess prisoners' psychological reactions at particular times (e.g., Grassian 1983; Brodsky and Scogin 1988; Haney 2003).

Much of the important research is qualitative, but there is a substantial amount of it and the findings are robust. They can also be "triangulated," that is, studied through a range of methods and in settings sometimes similar but not necessarily identical to solitary confinement (e.g., Turner, Cardinal, and Burton 2017). Numerous literature reviews have noted that scientists from diverse disciplinary backgrounds, working independently and across several continents, and over many decades, have reached almost identical conclusions about the negative effects of isolation in general and solitary confinement in particular (e.g., Haney and Lynch 1997; Haney 2003; Grassian 2006; Smith 2006; Arrigo and Bullock 2008). Those robust findings are also theoretically coherent. That is, they are consistent with and explained by a rapidly growing literature on the importance of meaningful social contact for maintenance of mental and physical health.

Largely because of the robustness and theoretical underpinnings of the data, numerous scientific and professional organizations have reached a broad consensus about the damaging effects of solitary confinement. Several years ago, for example, a National Academies of Science committee reviewed the existing research and concluded that solitary confinement can precipitate such "serious psychological change" in prisoners that the practice "is best minimized" (National Research Council 2014, p. 201). The American Psychological Association (2016, p. 1), the world's largest professional association of psychologists, asserted that "solitary confinement is associated with severe harm to physical and mental health among both youth and adults, including: increased risk of self-mutilation, and suicidal ideation; greater anxiety, depression, sleep disturbance, paranoia, and aggression; exacerbation of the onset of pre-existing mental illness and trauma symptoms; [and] increased risk of cardiovascular problems."

Similarly, the National Commission on Correctional Health Care (2016), a highly respected organization of correctional medical and mental health professionals, promulgated a series of "principles" with respect to solitary confinement. They are intended to guide the ethical conduct of its members, including that placement in solitary confinement for longer than 15 days represents "cruel, inhumane, and degrading treatment" that is "harmful to an individual's health" (p. 260) and that "health care staff must advocate" to remove persons from solitary confinement whenever "their medical or mental health deteriorates" (p. 261).

Summarizing this growing consensus, a joint 2016 statement of the Association of State Correctional Administrators (the largest professional association of American prison administrators) and Yale Law School's Liman Public Interest Program observed that demands for change in use of solitary confinement are being made around the world. More specifically,

> Commitments to reform and efforts to limit or abolish the use of isolating confinement come from stakeholders and actors in and out of government. Documentation of the harms of isolation, coupled with its costs and the dearth of evidence suggesting that it enhances security, has prompted prison directors, legislatures, executive branch officials, and advocacy groups to try to limit reliance on restricted housing. Instead of being cast as the solution to a problem, restricted housing has come to be understood by many as a problem in need of a solution. (Association of State Correctional Administrators and the Arthur Liman Public Interest Program 2016, p. 15)

Even more recently, the director of the Colorado Department of Corrections, Rick Raemisch, announced that Colorado has ended use of long-term solitary confinement, so that even prisoners "who commit serious violations like assault will now spend at most 15 days in solitary" (2017, p. A25). This development in Colorado is especially notable, for reasons that become clear in the pages that follow.

Against this backdrop, in 2009 and 2010 word began to circulate among prison researchers and policy makers that a new, supposedly unassailable scientific study—the "Colorado study"—had produced results that contravened many decades of empirical findings on the harmful effects of prison isolation. Lovell and Toch (2011, p. 3) characterized a number of its findings as "flabbergasting," and indeed they were. Among the most startling were that a year-long stay in solitary confinement resulted in no "significant decline in psychological well-being over time"; that on most measures, including cognitive performance, "there was improved functioning over time"; and most remarkably that many more mentally ill prisoners benefited from isolation than were damaged by it (O'Keefe et al. 2010, pp. 54, 78). The Colorado researchers thus reported data indicating that solitary confinement made prisoners feel and think better, especially if they were mentally ill.

In fact, however, the Colorado study was riddled with serious methodological problems that limited its value and made the meaning of the results impossible to decipher. Notwithstanding its authors' frank, albeit at times opaque and oblique, acknowledgments of some of its fundamental weaknesses, defenders of solitary confinement have seized on it. It has become a last bastion of resistance against a widespread and growing consensus that use of solitary confinement should be eliminated or drastically limited.

The Colorado study's influence has been amplified by an equally flawed meta-analysis that relied very heavily on it and significantly mischaracterized the prior literature on the effects of isolated confinement (Morgan et al. 2016). Of course, the influence of a fundamentally flawed study can grow if it and the data it produced are included in literature reviews that overlook glaring weaknesses. This risk is greater in meta-analytic than in narrative literature reviews that focus on decontextualized "effect sizes" irrespective of methodological shortcomings of individual studies. Unlike narrative reviews, meta-analyses include only quantitative outcomes or effects. This elevates the importance of numerical outcomes and often scants nuanced assessments of data quality. This is particularly a problem for prison research, an enterprise that is fraught with emotional and methodological challenges, in which aspects of the institutional context or setting can fundamentally alter the nature of the research and the meaning of its results. That is precisely what happened in the Morgan et al. (2016) meta-analysis.

In the following pages, I first discuss the scientific basis for the broad consensus that solitary confinement has substantial negative psychological effects on prisoners. I then discuss the Colorado study and the Morgan et al. (2016) meta-analysis based largely on it. Both are textbook examples of how things can go terribly wrong when researchers fail to take account of the unique nature of the prison environment, the special emotional and methodological challenges of prison research in general, and the contingent and unpredictable conditions and practices that affect solitary confinement units in particular.


## I. Solitary Confinement Research and Practice

Documentation of the damaging nature and psychological effects of solitary confinement has a very long history, dating at least to the early nineteenth century, when solitary confinement was the modal form of imprisonment. The notion that prisoners could be reformed—made "penitent"—by time spent in isolation dominated American correctional thinking and practice and eventually spread throughout Europe. Yet the practice was recognized as a dangerous failure not long after its inception. Haney and Lynch (1997), Toch (2003), Grassian (2006), and Smith (2006) reviewed much of the early historical literature. Reports on solitary confinement at Pentonville Prison in England described "twenty times more cases of mental disease than in any other prison in the country" (Hibbert 1963, p. 160). Accounts of solitary confinement in the Netherlands documented "again and again, reports of insanity, suicide, and the complete alienation of prisoners from social life" (Franke 1992, p. 128). Newspaper reports from Philadelphia observed that prisoners in solitary confinement at the Walnut Street Jail "beg, with the greatest earnestness, that they may be hanged out of their misery" (Masur 1989, p. 83). Charles Dickens concluded that a prisoner kept in that "melancholy house" was like "a man buried alive . . . dead to everything but torturing anxieties and horrible despair" (Dickens 1842, p. 116). A similar regime in Auburn, New York, was described as "a hopeless failure that led to a marked prevalence of sickness and insanity on the part of convicts in solitary confinement" (Barnes 1921, p. 53). Stuart Grassian (2006, pp. 342–43) reported that "between 1854 and 1909, thirty-seven articles appeared in German scientific journals on the subject of psychotic disturbances among prisoners." The "most consistent factor" accounting for prison psychoses, "reported in over half the total literature, was solitary confinement."

Systematic early studies of solitary confinement in the United States used what is now seen as a somewhat outmoded theoretical framework, focusing narrowly on sensory rather than social deprivation (e.g., Scott and Gendreau 1969; Gendreau et al. 1972). Even so, the authors of one early study concluded that "excessive deprivation of liberty, here defined as near complete confinement to the cell, results in deep emotional disturbances" (Cormier and Williams 1966, p. 484). In a review of the sensory deprivation literature, Haney and Lynch (1997) noted that "the dissimilarities between conditions created in these studies and those in solitary confinement or punitive segregation in correctional institutions are obvious." They also observed that, nonetheless, the early research did "emphasize the importance of sensory stimulation in human experience and the dramatic effects that can be produced when such stimulation is significantly curtailed" (p. 502).

More recent research focuses on the psychological damage that results from social deprivation. Hans Toch's large-scale psychological study of prisoners in crisis in New York State correctional facilities included important observations about the effects of isolation. After conducting numerous in-depth interviews, Toch (1975, p. 54) concluded that "isolation panic" was a serious problem in solitary confinement. The symptoms Toch described included rage, panic, loss of control and breakdowns, psychological regression, and build-ups of physiological and psychic tension that led to incidents of self-mutilation. He noted that isolation panic could occur under other conditions of confinement but that it was "most sharply prevalent in segregation." Moreover, it marked an important dichotomy for prisoners: the "distinction between imprisonment, which is tolerable, and isolation, which is not."

Empirical studies have identified a wide range of frequently occurring adverse psychological reactions to solitary confinement.[2] These include

---

[2] For reviews of the literature documenting these adverse reactions, see Haney and Lynch (1997), Haney (2003), Cloyes et al. (2006), Grassian (2006), Smith (2006), and Arrigo and Bullock (2008).

stress-related reactions (such as decreased appetite, trembling hands, sweating palms, heart palpitations, and a sense of impending emotional breakdown); sleep disturbances (including nightmares and sleeplessness); heightened levels of anxiety and panic; irritability, aggression, and rage; paranoia, ruminations, and violent fantasies; cognitive dysfunction, hypersensitivity to stimuli, and hallucinations; loss of emotional control, mood swings, lethargy, flattened affect, and depression; increased suicidality and instances of self-harm; and, finally, paradoxical tendencies to further social withdrawal.

The prevalence of psychological distress, at least as suffered in certain solitary confinement settings, appears to be extremely high. A study conducted at the Security Housing Unit (SHU) at Pelican Bay State Prison in California (Haney 1993; Reiter 2016), an especially severe solitary confinement facility, is illustrative. Structured interviews were used to assess a randomly selected, representative sample of 100 prisoners to determine the prevalence of symptoms of psychological stress, trauma, and isolation-related psychopathology (Haney 2003). The interviews included demographic questions, brief social and institutional histories, and systematic assessments of 25 items, based in part on the Omnibus Stress Index (Jones 1976) and on other instruments similar to those used in Brodsky and Scogin (1988). Every symptom of psychological stress and trauma but one (fainting) was experienced by more than half of the assessed prisoners; many were reported by two-thirds or more and some by nearly everyone. Well over half of the prisoners reported distress-related symptoms—headaches, trembling, sweaty palms, and heart palpitations.

High numbers of the Pelican Bay SHU prisoners also reported suffering from isolation-related symptoms of pathology. Nearly all reported ruminations or intrusive thoughts, oversensitivity to external stimuli, irrational anger and irritability, difficulties with attention and often with memory, and a tendency to withdraw socially. Almost as many reported symptoms indicative of mood or emotional disorders: concerns over emotional flatness or losing the ability to feel, swings in emotional response, and feelings of depression or sadness that did not go away. Finally, sizable minorities reported symptoms that are typically associated only with more extreme forms of psychopathology—hallucinations, perceptual distortions, and thoughts of suicide.

Social withdrawal, a common reaction to solitary, is related to a broader set of social pathologies that prisoners often experience as they attempt to adapt to an environment devoid of normal, meaningful social contact. In order to exist and function in solitary confinement, where day-to-day life lacks meaningful interaction and closeness with others, prisoners have little choice but to adapt in ways that are asocial and, ultimately, psychologically harmful.

A large international literature has reached similar conclusions on the adverse psychological effects of solitary confinement. Solitary confinement not only is a common form of mistreatment to which prisoners of war have been subjected and been adversely affected (e.g., Hinkle and Wolff 1956) but also is associated with "higher levels of later life disability" among returnees (Hunt et al. 2008, p. 616). It is frequently used as a component of torture (e.g., Foster, Davis, and Sandler 1987; Nowak 2006; Reyes 2007). Solitary confinement has been studied in more traditional international criminal justice contexts as well. For example, Barte (1989, p. 52) concluded that solitary confinement in French prisons had such "psychopathogenic" effects that prisoners placed there for extended periods could become schizophrenic, making the practice unjustifiable, counterproductive, and "a denial of the bonds that unite humankind."

Koch (1986, pp. 124–25) studied "acute isolation syndrome" among detainees in Denmark that occurred after only a few days in isolation and included "problems of concentration, restlessness, failure of memory, sleeping problems and impaired sense of time and ability to follow the rhythm of day and night." If isolation persisted for a few weeks or more, it could lead to "chronic isolation syndrome," including intensified difficulties with memory and concentration, "inexplicable fatigue," a "distinct emotional liability" that included fits of rage, hallucinations, and the "extremely common" belief among prisoners that "they have gone or are going mad."

Volkart, Dittrich, et al. (1983) studied penal isolation in Switzerland. They concluded that, compared with prisoners in normal confinement, those in solitary displayed considerably more psychopathological symptoms, including heightened feelings of anxiety, emotional hypersensitivity, ideas of persecution, and thought disorders (see also Waligora 1974; Volkart, Rothenfluh, et al. 1983; Bauer et al. 1993).

The major reviews of the literature reach the same conclusions as the seminal studies. Haney and Lynch (1997, pp. 530, 537) noted that "distinctive patterns of negative effects have emerged clearly, consistently, and unequivocally from personal accounts, descriptive studies, and systematic research on solitary and punitive segregation." The "psychologically destructive treatment" to which prisoners are exposed in solitary confinement is so severe that it likely "would not be countenanced for any other group in our society."

Grassian's extensive survey of solitary confinement research concluded that "the restriction of environmental stimulation and social isolation associated with confinement in solitary are strikingly toxic to mental functioning, including, in some prisoners, a stuporous condition associated with perceptual and cognitive impairment and affective disturbances" (2006, p. 354).

That same year, Smith's comprehensive review concluded that "the vast majority" of studies on the effects of solitary confinement "document significant negative health effects" (2006, p. 456). He observed that "research on effects of solitary confinement has produced a massive body of data documenting serious adverse health effects" (p. 475) including "anger, hatred, bitterness, boredom, stress, loss of the sense of reality, suicidal thoughts, trouble sleeping, impaired concentration, confusion, depression, and hallucinations" (p. 488).

Similarly, Arrigo and Bullock (2008) concluded that "nearly all investigators acknowledge that long-term segregation, mistreatment by correctional staff, and preexisting psychological vulnerability are all apt to result in negative mental health consequences for convicts" and that "the extreme isolation and harsh conditions of confinement in [solitary confinement] typically exacerbate the symptoms of mental illness" (p. 632).

There is an important, theoretically coherent framework that helps explain the consistency of these conclusions. A burgeoning literature in social psychology and related disciplines shows that solitary confinement is a potentially harmful form of sensory deprivation but also, and more destructively, exposes prisoners to pathological levels of social deprivation. Numerous studies have established the critical psychological significance of social contact, connectedness, and belonging (e.g., Fiorillo and Sabatini 2011; Hafner et al. 2011; Cacioppo and Cacioppo 2012). Meaningful social interactions and social connectedness can have a positive effect on people's physical and mental health in settings outside of prison and, conversely, social isolation in general can undermine health and psychological well-being. Thus, it makes sound psychological sense that exposure to especially severe forms of material, sensory, and social deprivation harms prisoners' mental health.

Indeed, researchers have concluded that human brains are "wired to connect" to others (Lieberman 2013). Thwarting the need to establish and maintain connections to others undermines psychological well-being and increases physical morbidity and mortality. Because "social connection is crucial to human development, health, and survival," experts have called for it to be recognized as a national public health priority (Holt-Lunstad, Robles, and Sbarra 2017, p. 527). The involuntary, coercive, hostile, and demeaning aspects of solitary confinement are likely to exacerbate the negative effects of social isolation that have repeatedly been documented in more benign contexts.

Given these long-standing and theoretically informed findings, a study purporting to show that psychological effects of solitary confinement range from harmless to beneficial would normally not be taken seriously. Sometimes, however, the appearance of seemingly objective scientific findings provides legitimacy to doubtful conclusions, especially when they support contested policy or political agendas. That is precisely what happened in the case of the Colorado study. Its authors described it as a scientific advance over all previous studies, and some commentators prematurely lauded its methodological rigor. It appeared on the surface to be an ambitious and well-designed longitudinal study, with appropriate comparison groups and a host of dependent variables that were to be examined. Data were collected through the repeated administration of instruments said to be validated, and an unusually large number of prisoners were to be assessed over a 1-year period.

The reality was very different. The project could not be, and was not, carried out as planned, partly because of powerful demands and correctional contingencies inherent in prison settings in general and solitary confinement in particular. The problems proved insurmountable: comparison groups were not comparable, and the integrity of the "treatments" each group received was quickly corrupted. I discuss these and numerous other problems in the next section. The fundamental methodological flaws that plagued the study prevented collection of any meaningful data and ensured that no meaningful conclusions could be drawn.

The Colorado study nonetheless has continued to play an outsized role in contentious policy debates in which proponents of solitary confinement draw on it to support positions that are becoming indefensible. Defenders have characterized the study as "an outstanding example of applied correctional research" that was "planned with great care," employed a "rigorous" design, and produced results that "were about as conclusive as possible" showing that solitary confinement has few or no adverse effects (Gendreau and Labrecque 2016, p. 9).

A year after the study's release, the National Institute of Corrections devoted an entire issue of *Corrections and Mental Health* to discussion of it. One writer (other than the Colorado researchers themselves) who endorsed its results and defended its methodology was Paul Gendreau, a well-known Canadian researcher and long-time prison system employee. Despite not having published primary research data on isolation since the early 1970s, he had defended its use over many decades, for example, in a 1984 article entitled "Solitary Confinement Is Not Cruel and Unusual: People Sometimes Are!" (Gendreau and Bonta 1984). In *Corrections and Mental Health*, Gendreau hailed the Colorado study as a "truly significant contribution to our knowledge base about the effects of prison life for one of the most severe forms of incarceration" and asserted that "in terms of its methodological rigor" no other study "comes close" (Gendreau and Theriault 2011, p. 1). Moreover, despite the deep skepticism voiced by all of the other contributors to the special issue except Gendreau and the study's authors, the journal's editor described the Colorado study as "an important report" because it showed that "administrative segregation is not terribly harmful" (Immarigeon 2011, p. 1).

Similarly, when a brief summary of the study appeared in a scholarly journal (O'Keefe et al. 2013), it was accompanied by commentary written by several prominent clinicians who claimed to have witnessed as much as or more psychological improvement among isolated prisoners than decompensation. They praised the study as "groundbreaking" and described its methodology as "solid" (Berger, Chaplin, and Trestman 2013, pp. 61–63). The authors averred that "the extremes of solitary confinement have been misunderstood" and that "people are resilient and are able to thrive under even difficult environmental conditions."

The respected Irish prison researcher Ian O'Donnell, though more circumspect, offered similar observations. Although O'Donnell acknowledged some limitations, he praised the study's methodology and invoked its results to support some of his own views. "However unpalatable they might appear to some parties," he asserted, the study's findings "must be taken seriously" (2014, p. 120). O'Donnell characterized the study as "valuable" because, he said, it "highlights the individual's capacity to adapt" (p. 122). He defended the Colorado researchers against criticism, noting that it is ethically impossible to study solitary confinement with "sufficient scientific rigour to satisfy everyone" (p. 122). The study's results suggest, he wrote, "that segregation was not highly detrimental to those forced to endure it" (p. 120) and that the harmfulness of this form of penal confinement "may have been over-emphasized" (p. 123).[3]

The Colorado study also figures prominently in correctional policy reviews by recalcitrant prison officials who do not want to modify segregation practices and in litigation over the harmful effects of solitary confinement, where those defending it are eager to find support.[4] For example, the US Government Accountability Office conducted a review of segregated housing practices in the federal Bureau of Prisons (BOP): "BOP HQ officials cited the 2010 DOJ-funded study of the psychological impact of solitary confinement in the Colorado state prison system. This study showed that segregated housing of up to 1 year may not have greater negative psychological impacts than non-segregated housing on inmates. While the DOJ-funded study did not assess inmates in BOP facilities, BOP management told us this study shows that segregation has

---

[3] O'Donnell indicated that the study documented the "benefits" of solitary, ones he suggested derived from "the many hours spent in quiet contemplation" in solitary confinement units. He also suggested that the results buttressed his own belief that "severe forms of trauma are sometimes accompanied by an improvement in functioning" (p. 123).

[4] For example, consider the "Expert Report by Robert Morgan, PhD, Ashker, et al. v. Governor, et al., Case No.:C09-05796 CW (N.D. Cal.)" submitted under oath to a federal district court. Morgan opined that being housed in extremely harsh solitary confinement (the SHU in California's Pelican Bay State Prison) for *ten or more continuous years* does not place inmates at substantial risk of serious mental harm" (p. 1; emphasis added), a position that he supported in part by citing the Colorado study. He described the study as "the most sophisticated study to date on the topic" of the effects of solitary confinement, claimed it showed "an absence of adverse effects for segregated inmates" (p. 1), and cited the results of his own meta-analysis (which was incorporated into Morgan et al. [2016], which I discuss later in this essay) to buttress his defense of long-term solitary confinement. Similarly, see the "Expert Report Provided in the Matter of BCCLA and JHS v. AGC, Court No.:S150415" by Jeremy Mills, PhD, filed in support of the continued use of solitary confinement in Canadian prisons. The Colorado study is described by Mills as "quite likely the most sophisticated longitudinal study to date examining the effects of segregation on mentally ill and non–mentally ill offenders" (p. 13). He also characterized meta-analyses like the Morgan et al. meta-analysis, of which he was a coauthor, as "a hallmark of the scientific process" (p. 12). Mills embraced the Colorado study's conclusions as supportive of his own, which were gleaned from his "clinical experience" working in segregation units on behalf of the Canadian Correctional Service. These included his view that both mentally ill and non–mentally ill prisoners usually need only "a few days" of "a period of adjustment" to get used to solitary confinement. He suggested that prisoners placed in solitary confinement "more frequently" forgo the adjustment period entirely because "they are familiar with the environment" (p. 14). Neither Morgan nor Mills acknowledged the Colorado study's numerous fundamental methodological flaws or indicated that the Morgan et al. meta-analysis on which they relied was based primarily on it.

little or no adverse long-term impact on inmates" (Government Accountability Office 2013, p. 39).

The Colorado study's continuing cachet in prison policy making and important legal circles means that its scientific bona fides bear especially careful analysis. Examining and deconstructing its methodology is a tedious but worthwhile exercise because it illustrates the difficulty of honoring norms of scientific rigor in a setting in which conventional research designs are nearly impossible to implement and necessary trade-offs are especially costly to the quality of the data collected. I turn to that exercise in Section II and to a deconstruction of the Morgan et al. (2016) meta-analysis in Section III.

## II. Interrogating the Colorado Study

Results of the Colorado study appeared in two versions: a lengthy final report to the National Institute of Justice (O'Keefe et al. 2010) and a short article in the *Journal of the American Academy of Psychiatry and Law* (O'Keefe et al. 2013). I mostly discuss the more detailed National Institute of Justice report.[5] I also draw on two depositions, under oath, of Maureen O'Keefe, the lead researcher, in connection with prisoner litigation concerning Colorado's "supermax" facility (where much of the study was conducted). In response to detailed questions, O'Keefe discussed numerous issues not raised in the report or fully addressed in published exchanges following its release.[6]

Why the study was undertaken is unclear. Neither of the primary researchers had prior experience with solitary confinement. Maureen O'Keefe had a master's degree in clinical psychology but no prior involvement in research on the effects of isolation. Kelli Klebe was a psychometrician who also had no direct experience with solitary confinement (O'Keefe 2010, pp. 13–14). Yet they designed the study (pp. 77–79).

The study's impetus may have come from Larry Reid, warden of the Colorado supermax prison that housed prisoners assigned to administra-

---

[5] A number of brief but highly critical commentaries by prison researchers also questioned aspects of the methodology: Grassian and Kupers (2011), Rhodes and Lovell (2011), Shalev and Lloyd (2011), and Smith (2011). See also the response to at least some of these criticisms by Metzner and O'Keefe (2011).

[6] The two depositions are Deposition of Maureen O'Keefe, *Dunlap v. Zavaras*, Civil Action no. 09-CV-01196-CMA-MEH, October 5, 2010; and Deposition of Maureen O'Keefe at 96, 101 *Sardakowski v. Clements*, Civil Action no. 12-CV-01326-RBJ-KLM, October 25, 2013.

tive segregation. O'Keefe indicated that Reid "kept pushing for the study to be done" and served as a member of the study's advisory board (2010, p. 51). A few years before the Colorado study was planned, administrators at a Wisconsin supermax had lost a lawsuit over their use of solitary confinement (*Jones 'El v. Berge*, 164 F.Supp. 2d 1097 [W.D. Wis. 2001]), and Reid apparently wanted to avoid a similar decision. As O'Keefe (2013, p. 44) observed, "I believe [Reid's] concern was that Wisconsin had lost the case and it had severely restricted their ability to use administrative segregation."

The Colorado researchers said that they expected to find that administrative segregation had negative psychological effects: "We hypothesized that inmates in segregation would experience greater psychological deterioration over time than comparison inmates, who were comprised of similar offenders confined in non-segregation prisons" (O'Keefe et al. 2010, p. viii). If so, Warden Reid did not appear to share that view. The Colorado Department of Corrections then housed "three times as many people in solitary confinement as the average state prison system" (*Correctional News* 2012, p. 1). Moreover, O'Keefe (2013, p. 46) acknowledged that Reid "was very pro administrative segregation and all of us on the project felt that way."

Psychologist John Stoner, the mental health coordinator at the Colorado supermax prison, also strongly supported administrative segregation and served as a member of the study's advisory board. He had testified in the Wisconsin case that administrative segregation was not "as detrimental to mental health as others have found it to be" (*Jones 'El v. Berge*, p. 1104). Among other things, Stoner said that he was not troubled by Wisconsin's use of "boxcar" cells with solid metal doors that closed off visual contact and muffled sound because he thought they were "necessary for the protection of staff and other inmates" (p. 1104). He also observed in written testimony that prisoners in isolation who appeared to be seriously mentally ill were likely not as sick as other experts indicated; he speculated that they might be malingering. Although Stoner told the court in *Jones 'El v. Berge* that the isolated housing conditions at the prison were entirely appropriate, the judge disagreed. She held that the Wisconsin facility was unconstitutionally harsh for mentally ill prisoners and ordered them removed.

In any event, the Colorado researchers started out with a seemingly good idea and what appeared to be a reasonable research design. They would identify groups of prisoners housed in administrative segregation

(AS) and in the general population (GP), subdivided into those suffer-ing from serious mental illness (MI) and not (NMI). Their psycholog-ical status would be tracked for 1 year to determine whether and how the different groups were affected by different conditions of confinement.[7] The characteristics of the AS and GP prisoners were not matched at the outset but were expected to be more or less comparable because all had committed rules violations for which they might have received an AS placement.

Assignments to AS were thus not random. The researchers reported that "placement into AS or GP conditions occurred as a function of rou-tine prison operations, pending the outcome of their AS hearing, with-out involvement of the researchers. . . . Inmates who returned to GP fol-lowing an AS hearing were assumed to be as similar as possible to AS inmates and, therefore, comprised the comparison groups" (O'Keefe et al. 2010, p. 17). The prisoners whom prison authorities chose to send to administrative segregation became the treatment group and those re-turned to the general population became the comparison group (again, with each group subdivided into those identified by the prison system as mentally ill and those not).

Unfortunately, the plan fell apart almost immediately. The prison context and "routine prison operations" fundamentally undermined the research design.

## A. Contamination of Treatment and Comparison Groups

The study's implementation was compromised in two fundamental ways. It is important at this juncture to acknowledge the distinction be-tween mere methodological "limitations"—respects in which a study is not perfect—and problems that are so fundamental that they make the resulting data uninterpretable. The two flaws from which the Colorado study suffered were fatal—separately and in combination.

1. *All Participants Were Exposed to the Treatment.* All participants in the study, including those in the comparison group, were initially placed

---

[7] Data for one group of participants—prisoners "with the most acute psychiatric symp-toms" housed at a psychiatric treatment facility where they lived and interacted with one an-other "on their living unit" (O'Keefe et al. 2010, pp. 14–15)—did not bear directly on the issue of whether and how much prisoners were affected by AS. The researchers included them separately "to study inmates with serious mental illness and behavioral problems who were managed in a psychiatric prison setting" (p. 17). The prisoners in this group were not living in conditions remotely comparable to prisoners housed in conventional GP or AS units.

in "punitive segregation," a severe form of solitary confinement, for unspecified but not insignificant periods, before being assigned to administrative segregation or the general population. "At the time leading up to and during their AS hearing," the researchers acknowledged, "inmates have typically been in segregation" (O'Keefe et al. 2010, p. 8).[8] The reason was that Colorado prison officials were required to hold hearings to determine whether prisoners were guilty of infractions and if so whether AS punishment was warranted. Prisoners in Colorado as elsewhere are placed in special housing while they await the outcomes of their disciplinary hearings, often for days or weeks before the process is complete. Thus, the researchers also noted that "offenders reclassified to AS *remain* in a punitive segregation bed until an AS bed becomes available" (O'Keefe et al. 2013, p. 50; emphasis added).

Although this is routine correctional practice, its methodological implications were disastrous. It meant that all members of the comparison group were exposed to a severe dose of the isolation "treatment" before the study began. O'Keefe et al. (2010, p. 9) indicated that the punitive segregation conditions where prisoners were kept while disciplinary proceedings unfolded were so harsh that they were "only intended to be used for a short period of time." This severity distinguished it from AS, which was intended to be used for much longer periods. Here is how they described punitive segregation:

> Punitive segregation offenders remain in their cell for 23 to 24 hours a day, only coming out for recreation and showers, both of which are located in the living unit. Therefore, most do not leave the unit during their segregation time. Services including meals, library, laundry, and even medical and mental health appointments occur at the cell door. If a situation warrants an offender to be out of cell, the offender is placed in full restraints and escorted to a room within the unit

---

[8] Why "typically" is unclear. The report indicates that all prisoners (including the GP comparison groups) were placed in some form of isolation before, during, and shortly after their AS hearings. It is hard to imagine a procedure in which a prisoner would be taken directly out of GP, immediately given an AS hearing, and immediately returned to GP, without having spent time in some form of isolated housing. In fact, the authors reported that AS participants "on average completed their initial test 7 days (SD = 7.3) after their AS hearing," that GP participants on average "were tested 16 days (SD = 18.9) after their hearing," and that "on average, 43 percent of inmates . . . [had] been confined in segregation (40 percent in AS groups and 3 percent in GP groups) for an average of 18.2 days (SD = 18.1)" (p. 30). These figures are mathematically impossible. Moreover, they are at odds with O'Keefe's deposition testimony and with a statement in a more recent published "reflection" on the study (O'Keefe 2017).

where he or she can meet privately. Many offenders do not like being taken out of their cells because of the use of full restraints. Additionally, they may not like leaving their cell because officers may take the opportunity to search the cell for contraband.

Due to the disciplinary nature of punitive segregation, offenders are stripped of most privileges during their stay. Punitive segregation inmates are neither allowed to work nor permitted to participate in programs or education. Furthermore, their televisions are removed, and they cannot order canteen beyond essential hygiene items. (O'Keefe et al. 2010, p. 8)

Punitive segregation prisoners were denied visits, which were considered too labor intensive for prison staff to administer.

In contrast to AS, prisoners in punitive segregation also were denied the opportunity to engage in programming or education and were "unable to begin working their way toward leaving segregation" (O'Keefe et al. 2010, p. 9). Thus, even study participants who wound up in AS likely experienced punitive segregation as a much worse form of treatment.

This initial exposure of all participants to an especially harsh form of solitary confinement in punitive segregation made it impossible to draw meaningful inferences about any separate, subsequent effects of GP versus AS. There can be no comparison group in a study in which all of its participants are subjected to a harsh form of the treatment whose effects are being measured.

It is impossible to know whether or how control group prisoners were damaged by the time spent in punitive segregation and whether those effects continued throughout the study. Nor could anyone know whether the AS prisoners were actually relieved to enter the "treatment" because it was less harsh than punitive segregation. These imponderables could account for participants' psychological reactions, including the reported lack of differences between the AS and GP groups and the reported "improvement" or lack of deterioration of many members of the AS group. This was thus no longer a study of administrative segregation compared with no administrative segregation, but of varying and unspecified amounts of segregation experienced by everyone.

A different kind of analysis might have salvaged something by using the exact periods of overall exposure to administrative segregation–like conditions (including time in punitive segregation) as a continuous variable to estimate whether duration had an effect. However, the amount of time in segregation each prisoner experienced is not reported, so this kind of analysis was apparently not conducted. O'Keefe et al. (2010) treated their data as if they had done a classic treatment versus no treatment study, even though they had not.

The likelihood that initial exposure to punitive segregation conditions had significant negative psychological effects on most participants is more than just speculation. The National Institute of Justice report acknowledged that three of the four groups "showed symptoms that were associated with the SHU syndrome" from the outset (O'Keefe et al. 2010, p. viii), which seems a clear indication that the initial period of segregation adversely affected participants before their AS terms began. High levels of psychological distress measured during or after the prisoners' initial exposure to punitive segregation continued throughout the study. O'Keefe emphasized in a deposition that prisoners in all groups reported "pretty high elevations" of psychological distress (2010, p. 171) and that "clearly, very clearly, the offenders responded with very high elevations. They reported high levels of psychological distress" (p. 201).

Symptoms of distress were so elevated that the researchers wondered, and tried to test, whether the prisoners were malingering: "We had this huge rate of offenders who looked like they could be malingering" (O'Keefe 2013, p. 89). O'Keefe recognized, however, that high scores on a malingering scale "could indicate a lot of psychological problems." In the end, the researchers "didn't really believe that [the prisoners] were malingering" and discarded the results of the malingering scale without analyzing them (p. 89).

Thus, although the researchers acknowledged that most of the participants began the study very much affected by emotional and behavioral trauma, they seem not to have considered that much of that trauma resulted from time spent in the punitive segregation units. Nor did they consider that, when participants "naturally got better as time went on" (O'Keefe 2013, p. 91), it was likely because the conditions of punitive segregation that all of them had experienced were now alleviated, even for those who ended up in AS.

The amount of time that the study participants spent in punitive segregation was problematic, especially because even very brief periods of isolation can have damaging psychological effects. The United Nations Special Rapporteur on Torture, Juan Mendez, has noted that "it is clear short-term solitary confinement can amount to torture or cruel, inhuman, or degrading treatment" and recommended that solitary confinement "in excess of 15 days should be subject to an absolute prohibition"

(2011, p. 23). The United Nations adopted that recommendation in the "Mandela Rules," which defined "prolonged solitary confinement" as lasting "for a time period in excess of 15 consecutive days," and mandated prohibition of such prolonged confinement (Commission on Crime Prevention and Criminal Justice 2015, rules 43.1, 44). The National Commission on Correctional Health Care (2016) also characterized "prolonged solitary confinement" lasting for more than 15 days as "cruel, inhumane, and degrading treatment" because it is "harmful to an individual's health" (p. 260). Yet all of the prisoners in GP and AS experienced a nontrivial duration or dose of isolation that lasted well beyond this potentially damaging threshold. A key table in the National Institute of Justice report indicated that, at the time of their first test interval, participants had spent considerable average times in "Other seg": GP MI prisoners 12.4 days, GP NMI 39.8 days, AS MI 88.9 days, and AS NMI 90.3 days (O'Keefe et al. 2010, table 5).

In her deposition testimony, O'Keefe could not remember exactly how long study participants remained in punitive segregation before their charged disciplinary infractions were resolved. At one point, she said, "When an offender acted out, they were put in punitive seg and generally given notice of a hearing pretty quickly, and then the hearing happened, again pretty quickly after that" (2013, p. 93). Later she "guessed" the time was around "the two week mark" (p. 94). That was not remotely accurate, according to table 5 in the report, except for the GP MI group. O'Keefe later offered another estimate, this time that prisoners were kept in various punitive segregation units "an average of 30 days" before their initial testing session (2017, p. 2). This, too, is much less time than the National Institute of Justice report showed. In any event, it appears that all study participants were subjected at the outset to harsh conditions of punitive segregation for at least twice as long as the Mandela Rules would prohibit, even before the study officially began.

2. *Uncontrolled Cross Contamination.* The second fundamental flaw was as important as the first. It, too, occurred because placement and retention in AS were correctional rather than methodological decisions. The researchers admitted that they "lack[ed] control over the independent variable, which in this case is the conditions of confinement" (O'Keefe et al. 2010, p. 35). There was, in their words, "contamination across groups," because some AS participants "were not confined in segregation for their entire period of participation in the study" and because some GP participants "may have at some time during their study partic-

ipation been placed in punitive segregation or even AS" (p. 35). The researchers also acknowledged that prisoners in the various subgroups "may have [been in] multiple locations within a study period" (p. 35).[9] In fact, not only did participants move between AS and GP, but a number of them were housed in other conditions during the study, including the hospital and "community placement" (p. 36).

Transferring prisoners back and forth between locations and custody statuses is routine correctional practice, but it had disastrous methodological consequences. It meant that some AS prisoners in the study were released into GP for good behavior, some GP prisoners were placed in AS (or punitive segregation) for rule violations, and some members of both groups were transferred to other settings. Having both control and experimental group members move back and forth between treatment and control conditions (and other unspecified places) destroyed the integrity of the two groups and made it impossible to compare their experiences meaningfully.

The contamination occurred differently between groups. By the end of the study, only small and very different numbers of "uncontaminated" participants were left in each group.[10] Methodologically speaking, a true, a natural, or even a quasi experiment cannot be completed if researchers lose control of the integrity of their treatment and comparison groups. The researchers, however, simply aggregated the contaminated prisoners' data into the groups in which they were originally placed.

O'Keefe et al. (2010, p. 35) acknowledged that "one of the challenges of applied research is the researchers' lack of control over the independent variables," but that admission does not ameliorate the problem. They

---

[9] They wrote that "participants remained in their assigned group regardless of their placements throughout the prison system" (O'Keefe et al. 2010, p. 35), but mean by this that individual prisoners were considered to be in those groups for purposes of data analyses even though they did not actually remain housed there.

[10] There were only 26 "pure" cases in the AS MI group (of the original 64), 39 in AS NMI (of 63), 13 in GP MI (of 33), and only 11 in GP MI (of 43) (O'Keefe et al. 2010, p. 35). All the others moved back and forth between treatment, control, and miscellaneous other conditions on an unspecified number of occasions. Thus two-thirds (52 of 76) of the GP control participants spent time in segregation or other non-GP settings during the study period, and their self-reports were used to contrast their prison experiences and reactions with those of the AS prisoners, half of whom (62 of 127) spent unspecified amounts of time in GP or elsewhere. The "pure" cases were pure only in the sense that they were not contaminated by moving back and forth between treatment, control, and other conditions during the study. They were still "contaminated" by being exposed to punitive segregation before the study officially began.

nonetheless asserted that "a significant advantage of this study is the use of comparison groups to determine if [persons in AS] change over time differentially compared to similar groups who are not placed in AS" (p. 59). However, they did not compare similar groups and thus can reach no conclusions about differences in the groups' experiences.

In fact, it is impossible to conclude anything meaningful from the Colorado results. Lovell and Toch (2011, p. 4) in their initial commentary on it correctly concluded that "despite the volume of the data, no systematic interpretation of the findings is possible."

## B. Additional Serious Flaws

The researchers' inability to maintain control of key aspects of their research created numerous additional methodological problems. These problems further negated the possibility that any credible or meaningful findings would emerge from the study.

The additional problems pertained to how the participants were selected and how the various groups were composed, what the researchers recorded (or failed to record) about the experiences of members of the different groups, and questionable data collection procedures. Most stemmed from unyielding correctional realities and some from unwise methodological choices.

1. *Sampling and Group Composition.* The initial sample was drawn from among prisoners deemed eligible for the study by virtue of having received a disciplinary write-up and scheduled hearing to determine whether they would be placed in AS or returned to GP. The initial group of eligible prisoners was much larger than the number selected to participate. The decision about whom to approach was made single-handedly and, as she would characterize it, "haphazardly" by O'Keefe: "I would determine who we used, who we included in our study" (2010, p. 116).

The major consideration for inclusion was proximity to the field researcher: "We had one researcher, so we had to be able to manage her workload" (O'Keefe 2010, p. 116). She described the process as "haphazard selection. . . . We didn't do it in a random fashion, but we didn't necessarily do it in a very targeted fashion either" (p. 116). Participants were drawn from only 10 of Colorado's 26 men's GP prisons (O'Keefe et al. 2013, p. 51). A disproportionate number came from Limon Correctional Facility "[because] it's fairly close" (O'Keefe 2013, p. 66). This was not mentioned in either the National Institute of Justice report or the briefer published version of the study. If there was anything signifi-cantly different about that prison, for example, if its punitive segregation unit (where participants were housed before the study began) was espe-cially harsh or its GP units (to which many participants were returned) were particularly dangerous, troubled, or inhumane, then a dispropor-tionate number of prisoners would have been affected by being held there.[11] There is no way to tell.

There was also unexplained and unnecessary imprecision in the com-position of the groups. In addition to being composed of persons sub-jected to punitive segregation immediately before they entered GP, the GP group began as an amalgam of prisoners who subsequently lived un-der different conditions of confinement. Thus, "thirteen participants in the GP groups were selected from the diversion program (for being at risk of AS placement)" (O'Keefe 2010, p. 30). The report elsewhere im-plied that all of the prisoners were at risk of AS placement because all had AS hearings; apparently that was not true, and some were "diverted" out of the process entirely.

A potentially more serious problem concerned the composition of the AS group. O'Keefe et al. (2010, p. 8) asserted that "Colorado does not house protective custody; therefore, no AS placements occur at the re-quest of inmates." This is a correctional non sequitur. Colorado may not officially house protective custody inmates, but they exist in every American prison system. Protective custody inmates often end up housed in AS, whether or not they formally request it. In the Colorado study, an unusually large group of AS participants were identified as having sex offender needs: 30 percent of the AS NMI prisoners and 44 percent in the full AS group (p. 45). In other prison systems, many, possibly all, such prisoners would be protective custody cases. To be sure, protective cus-tody prisoners are subject to the painful and potentially harmful effects of social and sensory deprivation. However, they are in a very different sit-uation psychologically than prisoners placed in AS for punishment. Pro-tective custody prisoners typically prefer to be housed in AS-type condi-tions instead of what they regard as more dangerous GP environments. As a result, they are likely to be reluctant to voice complaints about living

[11] O'Keefe understood the implications of the sampling methods. Concerning work by others on the effects of administrative segregation, she wrote, "Of particular concern is that sampling procedures are often not discussed, and thus it is impossible to know if the findings were based on a representative sample" (2008, p. 127).

conditions or adverse emotional reactions, lest they be moved. That a third of the AS NMI prisoners and nearly half of the AS group overall in the Colorado study were probably protective custody cases undermined any straightforward interpretation of the data.

Gang members presented a similar problem. Thirty percent of AS MI prisoners and 43 percent of those in the AS NMI group were identified as gang members (O'Keefe et al. 2010, table 9). Being a gang member would ordinarily reduce a prisoner's willingness to report psychological distress because that would be a sign of vulnerability that might be interpreted as weakness.

Thus, nearly three-quarters of both the mentally ill and non–mentally ill AS prisoners were likely protective custody cases or gang members. Yet the researchers ignored the implications of this entirely.

2. *Uncontrolled Differences in GP Conditions.* The control condition—GP—referred to placement in one of 10 different prisons. However, none of the specific conditions of confinement at any of those prisons is described.[12] Variations in GP environments matter because, obviously, unless all GP prisoners experienced the same environment, they were not really in the same condition. If some of the GP environments were so troubled, dangerous, and harsh that they approximated or were worse than conditions in AS, it would be impossible to make meaningful comparisons.

A disproportionate number of study participants were housed in the Limon Correctional Facility (O'Keefe 2013, p. 66). This appears to have been an especially troubled prison when the study was conducted. In 2010, a journalist wrote about "Limon's long history of inmate violence, including two fatal stabbings in five years and the beating death of a correctional officer" (Mitchell 2010).[13] The prison's 5-year violent history encompassed the entire period of the Colorado study from July 2007 through March 2010 (O'Keefe et al. 2010, p. vii). This meant that many study participants came from (and GP comparison group prisoners remained in) an especially harsh and dangerous GP environment, perhaps one as psychologically stressful as an AS unit. In fact, Limon's vi-

---

[12] The published article indicated only that "GP inmates have access to significant out-of-cell time (e.g., >10 hours/day), jobs, and programming" (O'Keefe et al. 2013, p. 51). No additional information about the GP environments was provided.

[13] There were also allegations that in 2008 sex offenders at the prison were targeted by gang members who extorted them to pay "rent" and repeatedly threatened and assaulted them (*Davis v. Zavaras*, 2010 WL 625043 [D. Colorado 2010]).

olent history may have been serious enough to have precipitated recurring violence-related lockdowns (e.g., Associated Press 2007), including in the GP units where some of the control inmates were housed. None of this was commented on or taken into account.

3. *Uncontrolled Differences in AS Conditions.* Colorado study AS participants were ostensibly in the same study condition but were nonetheless exposed to very different conditions of confinement. These differences were not recorded or quantified and thus could not be taken into account. First, as I noted, all study participants experienced varying amounts of a harsh form of prison isolation, punitive segregation, before the study began. For a significant number (apparently, the majority) of the AS prisoners, that continued for a quarter or more of the length of the study. Thus, "When the study began, there was a 3-month average wait for inmates to be transferred to [AS]," which was "due to a shortage of beds. While on the waitlist, AS inmates were held in a punitive segregation bed at their originating facility" (O'Keefe et al. 2010, p. 19).

The median stay in punitive segregation for AS participants was reported as 99 days (which means that half were longer), although a very small group of prisoners were moved "quickly" into AS. Despite these very different periods in prestudy punitive isolation, all AS participants were lumped together for purposes of analysis.[14]

There was additional imprecision about how much and what kind of isolation any one AS participant experienced. Some "were not confined in segregation for their entire period of participation in the study" but were released into GP or other less onerous settings (O'Keefe et al. 2010, p. 19).

However, even beyond this, it is impossible to know exactly what conditions of confinement were experienced by participants who remained in AS throughout the study. The reason is that Colorado's AS program operated a "level" system in which a prisoner's "quality of life" (QOL) varied as a function of behavioral compliance and programming. Changes in QOL were meant to be incentives for compliance with unit rules and eventual reassignment to GP. The average length of AS stay was said to be 2 years, with the expectation that prisoners would spend at least 1 year in AS. However, the minimum stays specified for the QOL program

---

[14] The "distance between when they were ad-seged and when they went to CSP became longer and longer because of the wait list in DOC" (O'Keefe 2010, p. 108). An unspecified but not insignificant number of administrative segregation prisoners "were held in the punitive segregation bed but classified as ad-seg. And that's the—for the study average to be about 90 days, but people could be there pretty short, pretty long" (p. 109).

envisioned much shorter stays: 7 days at level I, 90 at level II, and 90 at level III—187 days altogether—after which prisoners were eligible for consideration for reassignment back to GP (O'Keefe et al. 2010, p. 11).

Providing achievable incentives for good behavior and early release from AS are sensible correctional practices. However, they, too, further compromised any meaningful interpretation of the study results.

This methodological problem was significant because the differences in QOL at different levels of AS were substantial. The researchers acknowledged that "it was expected that [prisoners in AS] might experience varying amounts of isolation based on the amount of time spent at different [QOL] levels" (O'Keefe et al. 2010, p. 40). But these varying amounts of isolation were not documented or taken into account.

O'Keefe acknowledged that the researchers initially wanted information from prison staff on participants' out-of-cell time, "to track every time they left their cell," but could not obtain it because the data "just were not coded consistently or every time" by correctional officers (2013, p. 55). That meant that the researchers were unable to track the basic facts of whether, when, and for how long any one prisoner was at one or another AS level or incorporate these data into their analysis (p. 60). O'Keefe et al. (2010, pp. 40–41) reported that staff records yielded "conflicting information," and "it was often difficult to decipher and/or interpret the records." Thus, "it was not possible to code or use [them] in the study."

4. *Failure to Control or Record Treatment Dose.* There was more to these uncontrolled and unrecorded variations than just minor differences in the amount or duration of isolation. The variations in isolation in the AS condition—including for the relatively few prisoners who stayed in AS continuously—were very significant. The QOL level III AS prisoners were given additional privileges and allowed to have jobs as orderlies or in the barbershop. This permitted significant out-of-cell time, during which the prisoners were presumably unrestrained and in contact with others.[15] These opportunities are rare in prison AS units anywhere and

---

[15] As O'Keefe et al. (2010, p. 12) noted, "Arguably one of the most important benefits of QOL level three is an offender's ability to have more contact with friends and family. While offenders' visits remain noncontact, they are increased to four 3-hour visits per month and four 20-minute phone sessions. . . . One additional benefit is that offenders may now be eligible to work as a porter or barber. . . . Benefits to being offered a job position include the ability to earn money, increased time out of cell, and two additional phone sessions per month."

constitute a significant modification in the nature of the isolation experienced by an unspecified number of AS prisoners. They introduced even more heterogeneity into the "same" condition in the study than already existed.

The researchers also noted that an AS prisoner who acted out could be even more significantly locked down by being placed "on special controls in the intake unit where he can be carefully monitored" and "additional sanctions may be imposed through the disciplinary process" (O'Keefe et al. 2010, p. 13).

None of these and other variations in actual day-to-day conditions of confinement were taken into account. The researchers also did not record and were unable to estimate other basic, important variations in the experiences and treatment of the study participants. These included the number of social or family visits prisoners had, visits from attorneys (O'Keefe 2010, p. 164), and the nature or amount of mental health services the prisoners (including those who were mentally ill) received. As O'Keefe summarized, "We did not look at any facet of segregation or correctional conditions that might affect the outcome of the study. We merely looked at, based on their conditions of confinement—that is, whether they had originally been coded 'AS' or 'GP'—and then noted 'if they reported worse change over time'" (p. 207). But whether a prisoner had originally been coded AS or GP did not indicate what "conditions of confinement" he had experienced in the course of the study.

## C. Miscellaneous Data Collection Problems and Issues

In addition, there were very serious problems with how the Colorado researchers initially structured and eventually implemented the data collection process as well as with the dependent measures they used. Some of these problems were the product of the challenging nature of the prison environment. Others were not.

1. *A Single, Inexperienced Field Researcher.* Almost all the data collection was done by one inexperienced research assistant who had only a bachelor's degree, no graduate training, and no prior experience working with prisoners or in a prison setting. She was single-handedly responsible for conducting five to six separate testing sessions in which she administered between 10 and 12 separate tests with each of 247 participants in 10 different prisons.

The data collection was unusually challenging. O'Keefe noted, "Say when she was at CSP [the AS facility], she might have a whole bunch of [participants] and she would go back and forth checking to make sure that they were all right, and administering the questionnaires when she needed to" (2010, p. 118). Yet no one oversaw her day-to-day work (p. 130). O'Keefe had no recollection of ever observing her administering the tests and indicated Klebe did not (2013, p. 85).

2. *Solicitation and Consent.* When prisoners' participation and consent were solicited, they were told, somewhat misleadingly, that "we're looking at how inmates across the entire DOC are adjusting to prison life" (O'Keefe 2010, p. 199). O'Keefe characterized this as "being cautious without being dishonest" (p. 200). The consent form told prisoners that the "risks of this study to you are very small in contrast with the benefits that are high. This study will help us to figure out what types of men adjust better to prison and how to help those who are struggling with prison life" (O'Keefe 2013, pp. 81–82). This, too, was misleading. The study was not about the types of men who adjust better to prison and how to help them. Moreover, no consideration was apparently given to the possibility that prisoners might want to appear to be "adjusting" rather than "struggling." This would apply with special force to AS prisoners, hoping to advance their QOL level and with that gain additional privileges and earlier release from the unit.

3. *Prison Employee?* The field researcher had to complete "the full CDOC [Colorado Department of Corrections] training academy" and at all times was required "to wear a visible CDOC badge that permitted her unescorted access to the facilities" (O'Keefe et al. 2010, p. 28). Although O'Keefe was "not sure" how the field researcher introduced herself to prisoners, she conceded that "it could be" that prisoners thought the field researcher was a DOC employee (2010, p. 125).

Prisoners in general, and especially in AS units, are typically reluctant to confide in prison staff (including even mental health staff) because of potential adverse consequences. Those consequences can include increased surveillance, placement in degrading "suicide watch" cells, or transfer to or retention in some other form of AS. For these reasons, prisoners frequently avoid admitting that they feel suicidal, depressed, frightened, angry, panicky, out of control, or violent.

That prisoners could reasonably infer that the field researcher/prison employee was checking on their "adjustment" is likely to have dampened their willingness to disclose sensitive feelings. This possibility is nowhere discussed. Despite the fact that while the study was under way, O'Keefe acknowledged awareness of the fraught nature of prisoner-staff relations, especially in AS units: "Administrative segregation facilities are characterized by the complete control exerted over inmates by correctional staff. The typical 'we-they' dynamic between inmates and staff is exacerbated in segregated settings where inmates have almost no control over their environment. Prisoner abuses have been discovered and punished in administrative segregation settings, but in other situations Human Rights Watch found that 'management has tacitly condoned the abuse by failing to investigate and hold accountable those who engage in it'" (2008, p. 126; internal citations omitted).

4. *Undermining Trust.* Little was done to overcome what O'Keefe described as the "we-they" dynamic that she believed was likely to be exacerbated in prison AS units. Two related problems with the Colorado study likely exacerbated the effects of this dynamic. The first was an error of omission: no interviews were conducted to establish rapport with prisoners. O'Keefe indicated that "it was not part of the study to probe and ask them [the prisoners] about themselves" (2013, p. 75). Without rapport-building interactions, prisoners in the study were unlikely to have had much confidence that the field researcher was interested in their well-being or that personal revelations would be handled with sensitivity.

The second problem is more troubling. The field researcher was apparently required (or decided on her own) to challenge prisoners if she thought their answers were "questionable" or "untruthful, or if she found the pattern of their responses abnormal" (O'Keefe et al. 2010, p. 36). There was no explicit or systematic protocol by which this judgment was reached (none is described). In any event, the field researcher reviewed the prisoners' responses on the spot, in their presence, every time they completed a questionnaire. If she was skeptical, the prisoner was asked to redo the test. Prisoners could decide to redo the test or not, but "if the participant said he was being honest and the researcher still did not believe him, she marked the test as questionable" (p. 36).

These practices potentially created very significant data quality problems. They not only jeopardized the development of rapport or trust but also increased the chances that prisoners would give situationally desirable answers. In addition, the problems likely extended to more prisoners than only those who were challenged directly, but to other prisoners who learned through word of mouth that they would be asked to redo their questionnaires if the researcher was skeptical of their answers.

5. *"Untruthful" and Other Questionable Data.* Twelve percent of participants "had a questionable response pattern on any measure at any

time period" (O'Keefe et al. 2010, p. 36). It is unclear whether that figure included all participants who were asked about their answers or only those whose answers were marked "questionable." If challenged prisoners admitted being untruthful and redid the questionnaire, the second versions of their answers were incorporated into the study data. However, even if the field researcher was skeptical and prisoners chose not to redo their questionnaires, "we still included that in the study. . . . In order to increase our statistical power . . . we left those cases in" (O'Keefe 2010, p. 166).

In addition, 23 participants withdrew their consent and dropped out before the study was completed. However, their data were retained and used in the overall analyses (O'Keefe et al. 2010, p. 19). The dropouts constituted nearly 10 percent of the 247 participants. This meant that, in total, more than 20 percent of the participants whose data were included in the study results were adjudged to have given untruthful responses or withdrew from the study.

6. *An AS "Heisenberg Effect"?*  The repeated testing procedure changed the conditions of confinement, especially for AS prisoners otherwise subject to extreme social deprivation. The six interactions of approximately an hour each between the field researcher and the prisoners, no matter how strained or superficial they might have been, increased the otherwise minimal social contact that AS prisoners had with people outside the segregated housing unit.[16] In many prison systems, there are many AS prisoners who get no visits at all. The mere act of repeatedly attempting to measure the effects of severe conditions of isolated confinement can change them, if only slightly, for the better.

7. *Miscellaneous Issues.*  There were other irregular, questionable, and unexplained research decisions and data anomalies. Exactly why prisoners were assigned to AS or GP was not indicated, even though this was how the treatment and control groups were created. Assignment to AS was apparently nearly automatic: no more than "approximately 10 percent of hearings do not result in AS placement" (O'Keefe et al. 2010, p. 17). This raised questions, never addressed, about what accounted for the unusual outcome in the case of the group that was returned to GP.

---

[16] It apparently exceeded the contact AS MI prisoners had with mental health staff: "Offenders with mental illness who are stable are offered a one-on-one session at least once every 90 days," which takes place "in a noncontact booth in the visiting room" (O'Keefe et al. 2010, p. 11).

Nor were reasons discussed for why the NMI prisoners who returned to GP had more disciplinary infractions (average 16 each) than those sent to AS (13.2 average). Nor were reasons discussed for why AS MI prisoners had 70 percent more disciplinary infractions on average than the AS NMI inmates (22 infractions compared with 13.2; O'Keefe et al. 2010, table 9). Nor was there discussion of the effects of exclusion of prisoners from the study who did not read English at an eighth-grade level on the representativeness of the final group of participants, especially with respect to ethnicity and the prevalence of cognitive impairments.

## D.  Troubling Dependent Measures

There were also serious problems in the handling of dependent variables in the study. Dependent measures were said to have been selected on the basis of several important criteria. However, the first two criteria the researchers identified—"(1) use of assessments with demonstrated reliability and validity, (2) use of multiple sources for providing information (e.g., self-report, clinician ratings, files)" (O'Keefe et al. 2010, p. 19)—did not apply to the dependent measures that were actually used in the analyses.

1. *Unvalidated Scales and Instruments.*  Some of the study's scientific bona fides were based on its claimed use of validated and objective assessment instruments. The researchers asserted that "the use of a reliable and valid standardized measure in the present study enabled objective assessment of psychological functioning" (O'Keefe et al. 2013, p. 57).

Indeed, O'Keefe acknowledged that "inaccurate judgments" could be made if instruments were not properly validated (2010, p. 22). However, she later conceded that only "a very low number" of the numerous scales and measures used, perhaps no more than one or two, had been normed or validated with a prisoner population (pp. 144–45).[17]

---

[17] There was no evidence that even the Brief Symptom Index (BSI), on which the researchers relied exclusively in the published version of the study, O'Keefe et al. (2013), had ever been validated with a prisoner as opposed to a "forensic" population. One study that the authors cited to support its psychometric properties (Kellett et al. 2003) concerned the BSI's reliability with persons suffering from intellectual disabilities and did not include a representative sample of prisoners (the "forensic" portion of the sample consisted of 45 "intellectually disabled" convicted persons who were "detained in a maximum security hospital" [p. 129]). The second, Boulet and Boss (1991), was a study of "psychiatric inpatients and outpatients who presented for evaluation at the forensic service of a psychiatric hospital" (p. 434). The third, Zinger, Wichmann, and Andrews (2001), focused on prisoners but did not report reliability or validity data for the BSI.

2. *"Constructs" That Could Not Be Interpreted or Compared.* The near-exclusive reliance on prisoners' self-report assessments was problematic because the researchers chose to separate the various scales into their component parts and then recombine items into eight separate "constructs." Instead of reporting scores on the instruments or scales themselves, only the constructs built from them were presented as standardized composite rather than numerical scores (O'Keefe et al. 2010, p. 22). This meant that the significance of reported overall trends and comparisons between groups was, as Lovell and Toch (2011, p. 4) put it, "difficult to assess because of the degree to which the data have been cooked."

There are a number of unanswered questions concerning construction of composite scales including their basic validity (whether the instruments measured what they purported to measure), whether the various subscales were reliable for this population, and whether the distributions of scores lent themselves to the statistical manipulations and recombinations that occurred. Transformations to the data, the number of instruments, items, and constructs, and the amount of scale and subscale reconstruction that occurred make the results difficult to put in the context of any larger literature using the same self-reported assessments.

3. *Ignoring Behavioral Data.* Researchers who use many rating scales (especially ones not validated for the particular population) generally use other methods of data collection as a validity check. The most basic is a face-to-face interview to establish rapport and acquire background information. When possible, behavioral data (by records reviews or behavioral rating scales completed by others) are included. These different sources of information should be reconcilable, and the interviews provide the glue that binds them. Prison researchers typically take things prisoners say to them very seriously, in part because they contextualize other things being measured or studied. However, no interviews were conducted in the Colorado study, and little or no special effort appears to have been expended to establish rapport. Instead, the researchers engaged in context-free coding and analysis of answers on prepackaged forms associated with tests not typically used with this population. As Lovell and Toch (2011, p. 3) observed, "Readers find themselves swimming in a flood of psychometric data; every so often a clue drifts by, lacking, however, a tether to the context—to what was going on around the prisoners and staff while they carried out this study—we are left to guess what it might mean."

Other kinds of data collection were contemplated including asking corrections officers and clinicians to complete rating scales: "The Brief Psychiatric Rating Scale was completed by clinical staff and the Prison Behavior Rating Scale was completed by correctional officers and case managers" (O'Keefe et al. 2010, p. 26). However, key details about this process were omitted (i.e., exactly who was supposed to complete scales, when, and with what kind of training). In the end, it did not matter. The rating scales were infrequently completed and the responses were too unreliable to be useful. The data were discarded. The researchers ultimately relied only on data from prepackaged, field researcher–administered rating scales.

There was one potential exception. Prison mental health staff kept official accounts of genuine psychiatric emergencies or "crisis events." Any situation that required "immediate psychological intervention is considered a crisis event; crisis events are documented by clinicians" (O'Keefe et al. 2010, p. 42). Because these are typically extreme, clinically significant events, they tend to be reliably recorded. If the prisoners' self-reporting was valid, the results should be more or less consistent with behavioral measures of psychological distress or crisis. In the Colorado study, they were not. Among the 33 GP MI prisoners for whom data were reported, there were only three "crisis events" (on average, one for every 11 inmates). Among the 64 AS MI prisoners, there were 37 "crisis events" (one for every two; O'Keefe et al. 2010, figs. 29, 30). This suggests that at least some mentally ill prisoners were doing much worse in AS than their counterparts were doing in GP.

The researchers dismissed the implications of this incongruity: "Because the number of participants who experienced a crisis event was so small, it was not possible to include this variable as an outcome measure in the change over time analyses" (O'Keefe et al. 2010, p. 42). Thus the significant disparity between self-reports and the behavioral measures was ignored, even though it directly contradicted the study's main finding that AS did not adversely affect the mental health of mentally ill participants. Instead, as they put it, because the mental health crisis data "raise more questions than they provide answers," they were deemed "outside the scope of the current research" (p. 42).

In sum, for all of the above stated reasons, the Colorado study is so methologically flawed that literally no meaningful conclusions can be drawn from it. Drastic compromises necessitated by the complex realities of the prison setting and a series of questionable methodological decisions made by the researchers rendered its results uninterpretable. The Colorado study was not the "most sophisticated" study done to date on the psychological effects of solitary confinement. Its results do not "need to be taken seriously," but cannot be taken for anything at all. Commentators who have praised the study either did not read it very carefully, were unaware of available sources of information on how it was actually conducted, or did not seriously consider the implications of its fundamental flaws.

Ordinarily, a study of this sort would die a quiet death, notwithstanding an occasional prison system's attempt to resuscitate it to defend questionable segregation practices or a scholar overlooking its flaws because its findings comport with his or her own views. However, it has recently been given a second life, figuring prominently in a recently published meta-analysis (Morgan et al. 2016). Its results threaten to live on in another form and to misrepresent the findings of the large, long-established, and frequently reconfirmed literature on the harmful effects of solitary confinement.

III. The Limits and Dangers of Meta-Analysis

Meta-analysis—"a quantitative method of synthesizing empirical research results in the form of effect sizes" (Card 2012, p. 7)—is an important methodological advance that allows researchers to estimate the overall magnitude of relationships between variables. However, it cannot substitute for careful narrative reviews of scientific literature. Meta-analysis comes with substantial limitations, especially for prison research. The prison setting rarely lends itself to collection of meaningful quantitative data capable of generating the kinds of effect sizes on which meta-analyses depend. Most classic book-length treatments of prison life have been primarily ethnographic—not quantitative at all. They contain few if any numerical data, including in the seminal American works by Cressey (1940), Sykes (1958), Toch (1975, 1977), Jacobs (1977), and Irwin (1980) and major comparable British works including Cohen and Taylor (1972) and Crewe (2009).

Similarly, few quantitative effect sizes appear in studies of solitary confinement. This is true of the studies that tell us much of what we know about these institutions, how they operate, and the lengths to which prisoners must go in order to survive inside them, including those from Rhodes (2004), Shalev (2009), Reiter (2016), and Kupers (2017). It is also true of most of the numerous studies of the negative psychological consequences of prison isolation that are discussed in the most-often-cited literature reviews. The nature of the settings and the routine prison operations that govern them make many kinds of conventional research designs impossible to implement.

Because the best prison research is qualitative, or does not lend itself to generating effect sizes, meta-analyses conducted on many important prison topics will be compromised by serious sample bias, resulting in "the drawing of inferences that do not generalize to the population of interest (typically all research conducted on the topic)" (Strube, Gardner, and Hartmann 1985, p. 66).

The concern is not only that meta-analyses on important prison topics almost invariably ignore or underrepresent the larger literature, but also that they privilege certain kinds of studies far beyond their actual scientific merit, and do so in a way that many readers are unlikely to appreciate. One critique rightly observed that readers "might not be motivated to look beyond the meta-analyses themselves due to confidence in the objective, straightforward nature of the tasks of conducting a meta-analysis, reporting findings, and making recommendations" (Coyne, Thombs, and Hagedorn 2010, p. 108). Reducing entire studies to single or multiple effect sizes almost invariably creates a false equivalency between them. Readers can easily be mesmerized by arrays of numbers that appear simply and accurately to represent highly complex and substantially different underlying realities.

The two meta-analyses contained in the Morgan et al. (2016) article suffer from all of these problems and more. They need to be scrutinized carefully because of the stakes involved and the possibility that they will mislead correctional decision makers and policy makers by their "surprising results," ones that, as the authors say, "do not fit with people's intuitive analysis of what happens when you isolate offenders" in solitary confinement. The resulting conclusions are indeed "in marked contrast to the 'fiery opinions'. . . commonly presented in the scientific and advocacy literature" in which solitary confinement "has been likened to torture, with debilitating consequences" (p. 455). They warrant conscientious examination.

## A. Truncating the Scope of Literature Reviewed

The first problem with Morgan et al. (2016) is the tiny number and unrepresentative nature of studies included in its two separate meta-analyses. Literature reviews, whether narrative or meta-analytic, are useful only if they faithfully represent the literature being examined. As Card (2012, p. 10) put it, "If the literature reviewed is not representative of the extant research, then the conclusions drawn will be a biased representation of reality." Morgan et al. (2016) excluded a vast number of published studies, including most of the key works.

The first meta-analysis, "Research Synthesis I," reported that over 90 percent of the published material that they found on the topic was eliminated: "Of the 150 studies located, only 14 (or 9.3 percent) were suitable for analysis according to our inclusion criteria" (Morgan et al. 2016, p. 442). The second meta-analysis, "Research Synthesis II," began with an astonishing 40,589 articles, which were reduced by "trained research assistants" using unspecified methods to 61. A "trained research assistant" then used unspecified methods to reduce that number to 19 (0.05 percent of the initial literature; pp. 442–43).

A meta-analysis that includes so little of the available relevant literature is not a synthesis of much of anything. In addition to the drastic reduction in the sheer number of articles included, the selection criteria used by Morgan et al. (2016) excluded key studies but included questionable other ones. Among the articles excluded is Grassian (1983), regarded as one of the seminal studies on the adverse effects of solitary confinement. Morgan et al. also ignored most of the work discussed in widely cited literature reviews by Haney and Lynch (1997), Haney (2003), Grassian (2006), Smith (2006), and Arrigo and Bullock (2008).

Despite the small numbers of studies included, tables reporting effect sizes seem to suggest that a vast number of studies were taken into account. A closer look reveals something different. Many of the studies have little or nothing to do with the key question of whether and when solitary confinement is psychologically harmful. Morgan et al. (2016) included studies that addressed medical outcomes, and behavioral outcomes such as recidivism and institutional misconduct, that have not been widely studied and are not central to understanding solitary confinement's psychological effects. Thus, despite the drastic reduction in overall number of studies, many of the studies actually included were simply beside the main point.

When the largely irrelevant studies are set aside, only six studies on the psychological effects of solitary confinement remain in the first meta-analysis and 10 in the second. Two in the first were excluded from the second and six others were added.[18] No explanation is given for why different sets of articles appeared in the two meta-analyses. In any event, the truncated set of 12 studies was not remotely representative of the larger scientific literature on the psychological effects of solitary confinement.

## B. Overreliance on the Colorado Study

Even "the most thorough sampling and complete data recovery cannot make up for basic limitations in the data base" (Strube, Gardner, and Hartmann 1985, p. 68). Indeed, "An experiment that is deficient in either statistical conclusion validity, internal validity, or construct validity is meaningless and, therefore, worthless. Consequently, it should not be used" (Chow 1987, p. 266). Notwithstanding these basic methodological truisms, tables 2 and 4 in Morgan et al. (2016) reveal that both meta-analyses relied primarily on the fatally flawed Colorado study. It provided the bulk of the effect sizes on which their overall conclusions were based.

Thus, in the first meta-analysis, I counted 24 of 50 relevant effect sizes on "psychological outcomes" that came from the Colorado study. In the second meta-analysis, 140 of 210 effect sizes came from the Colorado study.[19] Because of its sample size, the weights given to the multiple effect sizes from the Colorado study dwarf those of most of the other studies included.

As tables 2 and 4 in Morgan et al. (2016) make clear, they repackaged the Colorado results in a way that allowed them to dominate the analyses.[20] Thus, when they claimed that their results "are even more compelling when one considers that primary studies with the strongest designs produced much smaller effects," they were referring primarily to the un-

[18] The first (Morgan et al. 2016, table 2) included six studies that explicitly addressed psychological effects of solitary confinement: Ecclestone, Gendreau, and Knox (1974), Suedfeld et al. (1982), Miller and Young (1997), Zinger, Wichmann, and Andrews (2001), Andersen et al. (2003), and O'Keefe et al. (2010). The second (Morgan et al. 2016, table 4) added six studies: Walters, Callagan, and Newman (1963), Miller (1994), Coid et al. (2003), Cloyes et al. (2006), and Kaba et al. (2014); but it omitted Suedfeld et al. (1982) and Andersen et al. (2003).

[19] "Anti-social indicators" such as "re-admission" and "behavior" like re-arrest and "physical health" outcomes were omitted from this calculation of psychological effects.

[20] Zinger, Wichmann, and Andrews (2001) accounted for another four effect sizes in table 2 and 30 in table 4. It too is fundamentally flawed, as I explain in the next section. By my count, it and the Colorado study account for 28 of 50 relevant effect sizes in the first meta-analysis and 170 of 210 in the second.

interpretable O'Keefe et al. (2010) study. However, few if any of the fundamental defects of the Colorado study were even mentioned and none was seriously engaged. Instead, the authors simply described the Colorado study as "the most sophisticated study" ever done on the topic (Morgan et al. 2016, p. 441) and relied on it for the bulk of their conclusions.[21]

## C. Including Other Methodologically Flawed Studies

There are serious problems with a number of the other studies included in the Morgan et al. (2016) analyses. For example, Zinger, Wichmann, and Andrews (2001) accounted for the next-largest number of effect sizes in their meta-analyses. However, there are several problems with how the results of this study were treated and serious issues with how the study itself was conducted, raising questions about whether it should have been included at all. Its sample size is erroneously listed in table 2 as 136. Although 136 was the initial number of participants, only 60 remained at the end of 60 days. The $N$ shown in table 4 is, correctly, the 60 who remained, but that also is misleading. That number includes a majority of prisoners in the "administrative segregation" group (13 of 23) who were there voluntarily. Only 10 involuntary prisoners remained in administrative segregation at the end of 60 days. Thus this study was weighted far too heavily in the first meta-analysis and given a misleading weight in the second.

The results of Zinger, Wichmann, and Andrews (2001) are in any case impossible to interpret. They are based on data from a sample that combined "voluntarily" and "involuntarily" segregated prisoners. Voluntarily isolated prisoners (such as protective custody prisoners who "choose" to be in isolation) control their own fates; at least in theory, they can leave. In addition, in most cases they know that by staying they are at least safe from threats to their well-being elsewhere in the prison system, ones they presumably fear and necessarily want to avoid more than the pain and harm they may endure in solitary confinement. They are thus

---

[21] Morgan et al. (2016) appear to have overweighted the disproportionate number of effect sizes they took from the Colorado study, treating the $N$'s in each group as though their integrity was maintained throughout. However, as I noted, the bulk of the Colorado study participants moved back and forth between groups. Thus the "uncontaminated" cases are far fewer than Morgan et al. cited and used. Because O'Keefe et al. (2010) did not disaggregate their data, Morgan et al. must have relied on the confounded results, treating all participants as if they remained in their original groups for the duration of the study and weighted effect sizes as if this had been the case.

motivated to adapt to their isolation—or to appear to have adapted to it—in ways that involuntarily isolated prisoners are not. They should not be treated as if their experiences represent the effects of solitary confinement on involuntarily segregated prisoners.

A second and more important problem is the significant amount of attrition that occurred. Especially in longitudinal research, participants leave studies for various reasons. This inevitably complicates comparisons over time or between groups because people who remain are likely to be different from those who leave, thereby changing the compositions of the groups in ways that are difficult to specify.[22] This is especially a problem in prison research because prison administrators decide where prisoners are housed, under what conditions, and for how long; they do so on the basis of considerations that have nothing to do with the goals of researchers. In Zinger, Wichmann, and Andrews (2001), the reduction in the number of administrative segregation prisoners after 60 days, from 83 to 23, only 10 of whom were involuntary, means that attrition reduced the number of involuntarily segregated prisoners by 80 percent. The reasons for the attrition were not given.

Attrition is seldom random. That it results largely, if not entirely, from decisions made by prison administrators means that Zinger, Wichmann, and Andrews (2001) wound up with a group that was significantly different, in indeterminate ways, from the group with which they began.[23] They do not report whether and in what ways the prisoners who remained differed from those with whom the study began.[24]

---

[22] Zinger, Wichmann, and Andrews acknowledge this: "Attrition is a major drawback to psychological research in general. The problem with attrition is especially relevant to the evaluation of the psychological effects of segregation" (2001, p. 56). However, they ignored the extent of this problem in presenting and interpreting their results.

[23] If, for example, disproportionate numbers of transferred prisoners were considered too "vulnerable" to remain in administrative segregation, were reacting especially negatively, or were adjusting poorly and were especially effective at convincing the prison administration to return them to the general prison population, those left behind would be, by definition, those least affected by the experience. Alternatively, if those who remained at the end of 60 days were the most recalcitrant and least compliant, perhaps explaining why the prison administrators were less likely to release them, they may have been especially "difficult" prisoners who were less likely to admit vulnerability or weakness in the assessments they underwent. Or if the voluntary administrative segregation prisoners remaining after 60 days were the least willing or able to return to the general prison population, they may have been unlikely to admit that they were suffering lest this jeopardize their continued safekeeping. Any of these possible scenarios could greatly compromise interpretation of the results, and none of them appear to have been considered.

[24] The assertion that "none of the attrition was attributable to prisoners being incapable of participating in the study because of episodes of delusion or hallucination or suicide at-

An additional methodological problem was acknowledged in passing but not fully discussed, either in the published article or in Zinger's (1998) dissertation, on which it was based. "Practice effects" are a common problem in longitudinal studies because they require repeated administration over time of the same tests or measures. Participants may recall the questions and intentionally or inadvertently try to reproduce the same or similar answers, or lose interest and reply with stock, rote answers, or, if the tests include performance measures, improve (because of practice) each time they take the test. If any of these things occurs, the existence of real changes (especially negative ones) will be masked or minimized.

Zinger (1998) himself recognized that "artifacts of repeated testing" likely played a role in producing apparent improvements in functioning and the lack of signs of deterioration and that practice effects may have accounted for prisoners "report[ing] less problems over time" (p. 93). He also observed that it is well known that "participants lose interest in answering repeatedly to identical questions and tend to report less problems over time" (p. 92).[25] Thus, practice effects may have accounted in large part for the findings of "no change" or "improvement" on the measures used and repeatedly administered.

There are also significant problems with several other studies that were included in the already small group that Morgan et al. (2016) considered. For example, Cloyes et al. (2006) did not compare administrative segregation with nonadministrative segregation at all. Instead, all of the prisoners involved in their study were in solitary confinement. The effect size Morgan et al. reported was the only statistical test of differences between groups that appeared anywhere in Cloyes et al. (2006, p. 772). However, it is a $t$-test of differences in Brief Psychiatric Rating Scale scores between two groups of solitary confinement prisoners— those identified as seriously mentally ill or not, both of which were housed in isolation. Data from this study did not belong in the meta-analysis.

---

tempts" (Zinger, Wichmann, and Andrews 2001, p. 71) sets far too high a threshold and does not adequately address the matter. "Episodes of delusion or hallucination or suicide attempts" are hardly the only measures of whether someone is being so adversely affected that he would seek to be transferred elsewhere or, in the opinion of a correctional administrator or mental health staff member, need to be moved.

[25] Zinger, Wichmann, and Andrews (2001) did acknowledge that reports of "better mental health and psychological functioning over time" are "common in studies which rely on studies with repeated measures designs" (p. 74) but then ignored the implications of this for interpretation of results that showed exactly this.

Walters, Callagan, and Newman (1963) arguably does not belong either. It is over 50 years old and, more importantly, the participants were all volunteers. They were not typical of prisoners involuntarily placed in solitary confinement. In addition, the study lasted only 4 days, not long enough to reach a conclusion that the psychological effects of solitary confinement are minimal. The one effect size Morgan et al. (2016) reported, for "anxiety," is .57 with a weight of .726 (table 4, p. 452). Yet the only mention of numerical data for anxiety in Walters, Callagan, and Newman's study was this: "More isolated than non-isolated prisoners reported an increase in anxiety from the pre-test to post-test period ($p =$ .038, Fisher's Exact Probability Test)." It is impossible to calculate an effect size from this statistic.

Another included study, Andersen et al. (2003, table 2), reported only chi-squares and $p$-values. It is not clear how Morgan et al. (2016) managed to calculate effect sizes from those data.

The decision to include Ecclestone, Gendreau, and Knox (1974) is also questionable. The study is more than 40 years old and, more importantly, included only prisoners who volunteered to spend 10 days in isolation. For previously noted reasons, the experience of volunteers is not comparable to that of involuntary administrative segregation prisoners. In addition, the study used an almost indecipherable measure of psychological functioning—the Repertory Grid Technique—which does not appear to have been used in published prison research before or since.[26] Moreover, half of the initial participants "quit the experiment after two days of solitary confinement" (p. 179), which meant that the assignment of participants was no longer "random," the results suffered from significant attrition bias, and the remaining volunteer participants knew that they could leave whenever they wanted. Notwithstanding these problems, Ecclestone, Gendreau, and Knox concluded that isolated confinement was "not more stressful than normal institutional life" (p. 178). Morgan et al. (2016) included this study in both meta-analyses and singled it out as having one of the stronger research designs (along with Zinger, Wichmann, and Andrews [2001] and O'Keefe et al. [2010]).[27]

[26] Description of the nature and scoring of the Repertory Grid Technique was so complicated that it consumed nearly two full pages of text (Ecclestone, Gendreau, and Knox 1974, pp. 180–81).

[27] The studies deemed to have stronger research designs were identified by name only in Morgan et al.'s (2016) Research Synthesis I, although an estimate of the strength of the designs was also apparently used in Research Synthesis II. Morgan et al. concluded that

In sum, Morgan et al.'s (2016) meta-analyses were based on one fundamentally flawed and uninterpretable study (O'Keefe et al. 2010), another with an attrition rate of 80 percent over a 60-day period (Zinger, Wichmann, and Andrews 2001), two that were four decades old and included only volunteers (Walters, Callagan, and Newman 1963; Ecclestone, Gendreau, and Knox 1974), and one (Cloyes et al. 2006) that could not provide an effect size on the impact of AS.

Few readers are intimately familiar with the solitary confinement literature or willing to invest the effort to read and evaluate each of the studies cited in Morgan et al. (2016). Similarly, few are willing to carefully to examine the hundreds of effect sizes included in the two meta-analyses or are able to make judgments about the propriety of the particular statistical techniques used in the calculations.[28] The presentation of a vast array of numerical data in Morgan et al. gives the impression of an objective representation of equally meaningful effect sizes, but it is not the reality. Their conclusion that solitary confinement has modest or no significant negative psychological effects is not at all what a significant preponderance of the relevant empirical research shows and is at odds with findings

---

these studies with "stronger designs" were the ones that showed "less impairment" due to isolated confinement (p. 456). My critical discussion of the individual studies in question shows why.

[28] Morgan et al. (2016) appear to have used statistical methods that require very stringent assumptions and will give misleading results if these assumptions are violated (e.g., Aguinis, Gottfredson, and Wright 2011). Furthermore, the meta-analytic method they used requires a large number of studies to assess these assumptions, and there were not enough studies to assess them. Specifically, they used a random-effects meta-analysis model. This model assumes that the included studies are a random sample from some definable universe of studies. For example, are the prisons represented in Morgan et al.'s meta-analysis a random sample of all US prisons? If not, they cannot claim that their results generalize to this universe. Random-effects meta-analyses also assume that weights and sample sizes are uncorrelated with the effect sizes. If they are correlated, the results will be biased. The correlation between the sample sizes and effect sizes reported in their table 1 indicate that the correlation is about $-.5$, which could severely bias the results. In a random-effects meta-analysis, both the mean and the variance of the effect sizes in the universe are key parameters that need to be estimated and both require confidence intervals. Morgan et al. reported only the sample estimate of the variance and not the confidence interval. However, the confidence interval for the variance requires a strong assumption of normally distributed effect sizes, and the confidence interval is very sensitive to minor violations of this assumption. A large number of studies are needed to assess the normality assumption—much larger than the number used. Morgan et al. also appear to have used a new and unproven method for combining multiple effect sizes from a single study. This method requires at least a moderate number of studies (10–20, the more the better), more than the separate meta-analyses that were used. Finally, Morgan et al. also used extremely crude and inaccurate methods to approximate effect sizes in studies that did not provide enough information to correctly compute an effect size.

that are consistent across many decades, theoretically coherent, and buttressed by a very large and growing literature on the harmful effects of social isolation in contexts other than prison.

Misleading repackaging of bad data can ripple through the field and produce an echo chamber in which motivated commentators repeat each others' flawed conclusions. Thus O'Keefe (2017, p. 5) recently asserted that "a recent meta-analysis found small to moderate adverse psychological effects resulting from [solitary confinement] that were no greater in magnitude than the overall effects of incarceration. These findings are consistent with our Colorado results." She was referring to the Morgan et al. (2016) meta-analysis, whose conclusions were not only "consistent" with the Colorado results but based largely on them.

## IV. Conclusion

These two studies offer several cautionary tales about the fraught nature of prison research, especially on the methodologically challenging and politically charged topic of solitary confinement. The first of these tales is about the potential influence of bad, uninterpretable data on public discourse and correctional policy. Once the results of research that bear the trappings of science enter into public and policy discourse, it is difficult to correct the record, especially when motivated advocates are willing to overlook fatal flaws in the research. Unfortunately, when this transpires, researchers can lose control of the narrative by which their research is described and the manner in which it is applied. For example, O'Keefe has repeatedly and steadfastly defended her Colorado research but has opposed the uses to which others have put it. She was emphatic that she did "not believe in any way and we do not promote the study as something to argue for the case of segregation. . . . My interpretation is that people believe that this study sanctions administrative segregation for mentally ill and non–mentally ill alike. . . . I do not believe that the conclusions lend to that and that is not the intended use of our study" (2013, p. 96).[29] Yet, that is exactly the use to which a number of interested parties have put it.

[29] Two prominent advisory board members, Jeffrey Metzner and Jamie Fellner (2010), published a "post–Colorado study" article that seemed to contravene the study's findings. They conceded that "isolation can be harmful to any prisoner" and noted that the potentially adverse effects of isolation include "anxiety, depression, anger, cognitive disturbances, perceptual distortions, obsessive thoughts, paranoia, and psychosis" (p. 104)—not at all what

The Colorado study is also a stark reminder that attempts to implement conventional experimental or even quasi-experimental research designs in prison environments face a number of often insurmountable obstacles. The ordinary demands of prison operations nearly always doom even the most carefully planned such studies, and certainly anything resembling a traditional experiment. Savvy prison researchers understand that the desire to treat a prison environment as if it were a research laboratory should be resisted. Real people live (and die) in prison, a setting in which the core dynamics between prisoners and staff are governed by forces beyond the researchers' control.

In separate but related ways, both the Colorado study and the Morgan et al. (2016) meta-analyses underscore the pitfalls of allowing the veneer of scientific rigor to substitute for its reality. They also show the limitations of focusing on quantitative outcomes with little or no concern for precisely how and under what conditions data were acquired. The de-contextualized and de-individualized approach to data collection that characterized the Colorado study allowed researchers to treat all participants within each of the study groups as if they were the same, when clearly they—and especially their prison experiences—were not. Ignoring the prison context and individual prisoner trajectories helped render the findings incoherent and uninterpretable.

Similarly, Morgan et al. (2016) illustrate the shortcomings of attempting to apply an otherwise useful approach for summarizing quantitative data to environments as complex and variable as prisons (or especially solitary confinement units). Whatever the benefits of reducing empirical results to effect sizes may be, omitting an entire field's best-known and most in-depth works from consideration because most do not lend themselves to meta-analytic reductions means that nuance and context are inevitably ignored. The compromise in "scientific truth" is far too great.

Some critics of meta-analysis argue that "a literature review should *not* be a formalized or standardized one" (Chow 1987, p. 267; emphasis

---

the Colorado study claimed. Metzner and Fellner's deep concerns led them to recommend that professional organizations "should actively support practitioners who work for changed segregation policies and they should use their institutional authority to press for a nationwide rethinking of the use of isolation" in the name of their "commitment to ethics and human rights" (p. 107). Zinger has become an eloquent critic of the use of solitary confinement in Canada (e.g., Makin 2013) even though defenders of the practice continue to cite his dissertation research to justify its use.

added). As Chow observed, "It is not the case that narrative reviews lack rigor. To the contrary, rigor is maintained by reviewers of the traditional [narrative] approach when they evaluate the validity of individual studies" (p. 268). Meta-analyses, even when done well, risk compromising the richness of the prison data they seek to summarize.

In any event, the magnitude of what can be and often is lost in the course of the compromises made in the kind of research critically discussed in this essay often goes unrecognized. Amid thousands of data entries and hundreds of effect sizes reported in these two studies, there are few references to the core subjectivity, institutional trajectory, or life outcome of a single individual prisoner confined in an isolation unit. Nor is there acknowledgment that the studies focused on human beings rather than on interchangeable data points.

Martha Nussbaum (1995) noted in a different context that regarding people as "fungible" and denying them their subjectivity are powerful ways to ensure their objectification. Objectivity in prison research is a worthy goal, except when it results in objectification of prisoners and others in the prison environment. Feeley and Simon (1992) observed that the era of mass imprisonment occasioned and was facilitated by the emergence of a "new penology" whose key elements—"statistical prediction, concern with groups, strategies of management"—shifted the focus of the prison enterprise "toward mechanisms of appraising and arranging groups rather than intervening in the lives of individuals" (p. 459). This actuarial approach still defines the modern prison. It should not be made worse and reinforced by scholarship that exacerbates rather than alleviates or exposes these depersonalizing tendencies.

Studying only at a distance, as the research criticized in this essay did, requires precisely that kind of objectifying sacrifice. If John Irwin was right, that the close study of people in general and prisoners in particular uncovers their humanity, and I think he was, then the opposite is also true. Studying prisoners at a distance, without trying fully to understand and adequately to convey the conditions in which they live or to gain an "appreciation of their meaning worlds, motivations, and aspirations" (1987, p. 47), leaves us with little insight into basic truths about them. That includes whether and how much they are adversely affected by near-total deprivation of meaningful sensory and social contact.

The insurmountable methodological flaws of the Colorado study and the fundamental inadequacy of the Morgan et al. (2016) meta-analysis should preclude policy makers from using either in debates over the proper use of solitary confinement and the nature of its psychological effects.

REFERENCES

Aguinis, Herman, Ryan Gottfredson, and Thomas Wright. 2011. "Best-Practice Recommendations for Estimating Interaction Effects Using Meta-Analysis." *Journal of Organizational Behavior* 32:1033–43.

American Psychological Association. 2016. *Statement on the Solitary Confinement of Juvenile Offenders.* Washington, DC: American Psychological Association, Public Information Government Relations Office. http://www.apa.org/about /gr/issues/cyf/solitary.pdf.

Andersen, Henrik, D. Setstoft, T. Lillebaek, G. Gabrielsen, and R. Hemmingsen. 2003. "A Longitudinal Study of Prisoners on Remand: Repeated Measures of Psychopathology in the Initial Phase of Solitary versus Non-solitary Confinement." *International Journal of Law and Psychiatry* 26:165–77.

Arrigo, Bruce, and Jennifer Bullock. 2008. "The Psychological Effects of Solitary Confinement on Prisoners in Supermax Units: Reviewing What We Know and What Should Change." *International Journal of Offender Therapy and Comparative Criminology* 52:622–40.

Associated Press. 2007. "Limon Prison under Lockdown after Assault." *Vail (CO) Daily*, September 13. http://www.vaildaily.com/news/limon-prison -under-lockdown-after-assault/.

Association of State Correctional Administrators and the Arthur Liman Public Interest Program. 2016. *Aiming to Reduce Time-in-Cell: Reports from Correctional Systems on the Numbers of Prisoners in Restricted Housing and on the Potential of Policy Changes to Bring About Reforms.* New Haven, CT: Yale Law School.

Barnes, Harry Elmer. 1921. "The Historical Origin of the Prison System in America." *Journal of Criminal Law and Criminology* 12:35–60.

Barte, Henri. 1989. "L'isolement carceral." *Perspectives Psychiatriques* 28:252–55.

Bauer, Michael, Stefan Priebe, Bettina Haring, and Kerstin Adamczak. 1993. "Long-Term Mental Sequelae of Political Imprisonment in East Germany." *Journal of Nervous and Mental Disease* 181:257–62.

Benjamin, Thomas, and Kenneth Lux. 1975. "Constitutional and Psychological Implications of the Use of Solitary Confinement: Experience at the Maine State Prison." *Clearinghouse Review* 9:83–90.

Berger, Ronald, Paul Chaplin, and Robert Trestman. 2013. "Commentary: Toward an Improved Understanding of Administrative Segregation." *Journal of the American Academy of Psychiatry and Law* 41:61–64.

Boulet, Jack, and Marvin Boss. 1991. "Reliability and Validity of the Brief Symptom Index." *Psychological Assessment* 3:433–37.

Brodsky, Stanley, and Forrest Scogin. 1988. "Inmates in Protective Custody: First Data on Emotional Effects." *Forensic Reports* 1:267–80.

Burney, Christopher. 1961. *Solitary Confinement*. New York: Macmillan.

Cacioppo, Stephanie, and John Cacioppo. 2012. "Decoding the Invisible Forces of Social Connections." *Frontiers of Integrative Neuroscience* 6:1–7.

Card, Noel. 2012. *Applied Meta-Analysis for Social Science Research*. New York: Guilford.

Chow, Sui. 1987. "Meta-Analysis of Pragmatic and Theoretical Research: A Critique." *Journal of Psychology* 121(23):259–71.

Cloyes, Kristin, David Lovell, David Allen, and Lorna Rhodes. 2006. "Assessment of Psychosocial Impairment in a Supermaximum Security Unit Sample." *Criminal Justice and Behavior* 33:760–81.

Cohen, Stanley, and Laurie Taylor. 1972. *Psychological Survival: The Experience of Long-Term Imprisonment*. New York: Pantheon.

Coid, Jeremy, Ann Petruckevitch, Paul Bebbington, Rachel Jenkins, Traolach Brugha, Glyn Lewis, Michael Farrell, and Nicola Singelton. 2003. "Psychiatric Morbidity in Prisoners and Solitary Cellular Confinement. I: Disciplinary Segregation." *Journal of Forensic Psychiatry and Psychology* 14:298–319.

Commission on Crime Prevention and Criminal Justice. 2015. *United Nations Standard Minimum Rules for the Treatment of Prisoners*. New York: United Nations Economic and Social Council.

Cormier, Bruno, and Paul Williams. 1966. "Excessive Deprivation of Liberty." *Canadian Psychiatric Association Journal* 11(6):470–84.

*Correctional News*. 2012. "New Colorado Prison Closed Down." November 14. http://correctionalnews.com/2012/11/14/new-colorado-prison-closed-down/.

Coyne, James, Brett Thombs, and Mariet Hagedorn. 2010. "It Ain't Necessarily So: A Review and Critique of Recent Meta-Analyses of Behavioral Medicine Interventions in *Health Psychology*." *Health Psychology* 29:107–16.

Cressey, Donald. 1940. *The Prison Community*. Boston: Christopher Publishing.

Crewe, Ben. 2009. *The Prisoner Society: Power, Adaptation, and Social Life in an English Prison*. Oxford: Oxford University Press.

Dickens, Charles. 1842. *American Notes*. New York: Harper & Brothers.

Ecclestone, C., Paul Gendreau, and Clifford Knox. 1974. "Solitary Confinement of Prisoners: An Assessment of Its Effects on Inmates' Personal Constructs and Adrenal Cortical Activity." *Canadian Journal of Behavioral Science* 6:178–91.

Feeley, Malcolm, and Jonathan Simon. 1992. "The New Penology: Notes on the Emerging Strategy of Corrections and Its Implications." *Criminology* 30:449–74.

Fiorillo, Damiano, and Fabio Sabatini. 2011. "Quality and Quantity: The Role of Social Interactions in Self-Reported Individual Health." *Social Science and Medicine* 73:1644–52.

Foster, Don, Dennis Davis, and Diane Sandler. 1987. *Detention and Torture in South Africa*. New York: St. Martin's.

Franke, Herman. 1992. "The Rise and Decline of Solitary Confinement." *British Journal of Criminology* 32:125–43.

Gendreau, Paul, and James Bonta. 1984. "Solitary Confinement Is Not Cruel and Unusual: People Sometimes Are!" *Canadian Journal of Criminology* 26:467–78.

Gendreau, Paul, and Ryan Labrecque. 2016. "The Effects of Administrative Segregation: A Lesson in Knowledge Cumulation." In *The Oxford Handbook of Prisons and Imprisonment*, edited by John Wooldredge and Paula Smith. New York: Oxford University Press.

Gendreau, Paul, and Yvette Theriault. 2011. "Bibliotherapy for Cynics Revisited: Commentary on *One Year Longitudinal Study of the Psychological Effects of Administrative Segregation*." *Corrections and Mental Health: An Update of the National Institute of Corrections*. https://community.nicic.gov/blogs/mental health/archive/2011/06/21/bibliotherapy-for-cynics-revisited-commentary-on -one-year-longitudinal-study-of-the-psychological-effects-of-administrative -segregation.aspx.

Gendreau, Paul, et al. 1972. "Changes in EEG Alpha Frequency and Evoked Response Latency during Solitary Confinement." *Journal of Abnormal Psychology* 79:54–59.

Government Accountability Office. 2013. *Improvements Needed in Bureau of Prisons' Monitoring and Evaluation of Impact of Segregated Housing*. Washington, DC: US Government Accountability Office.

Grassian, Stuart. 1983. "Psychopathological Effects of Solitary Confinement." *American Journal of Psychiatry* 140(11):1450–54.

———. 2006. "Psychiatric Effects of Solitary Confinement." *Washington University Journal of Law and Policy* 22:325–83.

Grassian, Stuart, and Terry Kupers. 2011. "The Colorado Study versus the Reality of Supermax Confinement." *Correctional Mental Health Report* 13(1):1, 9–11.

Hafner, S., R. Emeny, M. Lacruz, J. Baumert, C. Herder, et al. 2011. "Association between Social Isolation and Inflammatory Markers in Depressed and Non-depressed Individuals: Results from the MONICA/KORA Study." *Brain Behavior and Immunity* 25:1701–7.

Haney, Craig. 1993. "Infamous Punishment: The Psychological Consequences of Isolation." *National Prison Project Journal* 8(2):3–7, 21.

———. 2003. "Mental Health Issues in Long-Term Solitary and 'Supermax' Confinement." *Crime and Delinquency* 49:124–56.

Haney, Craig, and Mona Lynch. 1997. "Regulating Prisons of the Future: The Psychological Consequences of Solitary and Supermax Confinement." *New York University Review of Law and Social Change* 23:477–570.

Hibbert, Christopher. 1963. *The Roots of Evil: A Social History of Crime and Punishment*. Boston: Little, Brown.

Hilliard, Thomas. 1976. "The Black Psychologist in Action: A Psychological Evaluation of the Adjustment Center Environment at San Quentin Prison." *Journal of Black Psychology* 2:75–82.

Hinkle, Lawrence, and Harold Wolff. 1956. "Communist Interrogation and Indoctrination of 'Enemies of the State.'" *Archives of Neurology and Psychiatry* 76:115–74.

Holt-Lunstad, Julianne, Theodore Robles, and David Sbarra. 2017. "Advancing Social Connectedness as a Public Health Priority in the United States." *American Psychologist* 72:517–30.

Hunt, Stephen, Mack Orsborn, Harvey Checkoway, Mary Biggs, Miles McFall, and Tim Takaro. 2008. "Later Life Disability Status Following Incarceration as a Prisoner of War." *Military Medicine* 173:613–18.

Immarigeon, Russ. 2011. "One Year Longitudinal Study of the Psychological Effects of Administrative Segregation: Introduction." *Corrections and Mental Health: An Update of the National Institute of Corrections.* https://community .nicic.gov/blogs/mentalhealth/archive/2011/06/21/one-year-longitudinal-study -of-the-psychological-effects-of-administrative-segregation-introduction.aspx.

Irwin, John. 1980. *Prisons in Turmoil.* Boston: Little, Brown.

———. 1987. "Reflections on Ethnography." *Journal of Contemporary Ethnography* 16:41–48.

Jackson, Michael. 1983. *Prisoners of Isolation: Solitary Confinement in Canada.* Toronto: University of Toronto Press.

Jacobs, James. 1977. *Stateville.* Chicago: University of Chicago Press.

Jones, David. 1976. *The Health Risks of Imprisonment.* Lexington, MA: Lexington Books.

Kaba, Fatos, Andrea Lewis, Sarah Glowa-Kollisch, James Hadler, David Lee, Howard Alper, Daniel Selling, Ross MacDonald, Angela Solimo, Amanda Parsons, and Homer Venters. 2014. "Solitary Confinement and Risk of Self-Harm among Jail Inmates." *American Journal of Public Health* 104:442–47.

Kellett, Stephen, Nigel Beail, David Newman, and Pat Frankish. 2003. "Utility of the Brief Symptom Inventory in the Assessment of Psychological Distress." *Journal of Applied Research in Intellectual Disabilities* 16:127–34.

Koch, Ida. 1986. "Mental and Social Sequelae of Isolation: The Evidence of Deprivation Experiments and of Pretrial Detention in Denmark." In *The Expansion of European Prison Systems,* edited by Bill Rolston and Mike Tomlinson. Working Papers in European Criminology, no. 7. Stockholm: European Group for the Study of Deviance and Social Control.

Kupers, Terry. 2017. *Solitary: The Inside Story of Supermax Isolation and How We Can Abolish It.* Oakland: University of California Press.

Lieberman, Matthew. 2013. *Social: Why Our Brains Are Wired to Connect.* New York: Random House.

Liebling, Alison. 1999. "Doing Research in Prison: Breaking the Silence?" *Theoretical Criminology* 3:147–73.

Lovell, David, and Hans Toch. 2011. "Some Observations about the Colorado Segregation Study." *Correctional Mental Health Report* 13(1):3–4, 14.

Makin, Kirk. 2013. "Canadian Prisons 'Out of Step' on Solitary Confinement." *Globe and Mail,* March 21. https://www.theglobeandmail.com/news/politics /canadian-prisons-out-of-step-on-solitary-confinement/article10103358/.

Masur, Louis. 1989. *Rites of Execution: Capital Punishment and the Transformation of American Culture, 1776–1865.* New York: Oxford University Press.

Mendez, Juan. 2011. *Interim Report of the Special Rapporteur of the Human Rights Council on Torture and Other Cruel, Inhuman or Degrading Treatment or Punishment.* New York: United Nations.

Metzner, Jeffrey, and Jamie Fellner. 2010. "Solitary Confinement and Mental Illness in U.S. Prisons: A Challenge for Medical Ethics." *Journal of the Acad-*

*emy of Psychiatry and Law* 38:104–8. http://www.hrw.org/sites/default/files
/related_material/Solitary%20Confinement%20and%20Mental%20Illness
%20in%20US%20Prisons.pdf.

Metzner, Jeffrey, and Maureen O'Keefe. 2011. "The Psychological Effects of
Administrative Segregation: The Colorado Study." *Correctional Mental Health
Report* 13(1):1–2, 12–14.

Miller, Holly. 1994. "Reexamining Psychological Distress in the Current Conditions of Segregation." *Journal of Correctional Health Care* 1:39–53.

Miller, Holly, and Glenn Young. 1997. "Prison Segregation: Administrative
Remedy or Mental Health Problem?" *Criminal Behaviour and Mental Health*
7:85–94.

Mitchell, Kirk. 2010. "Limon Prison Incentives Keep Inmates in Check." *Denver
Post*, November 24. http://www.deseretnews.com/article/700085422/Limon
-prison-incentives-keep-inmates-in-check.html.

Morgan, Robert, Paul Gendreau, Paula Smith, Andrew Gray, Ryan Labrecque,
Nina MacLean, Stephanie Van Horn, Angelea Bolanos, Ashley Batastini, and
Jeremy Mills. 2016. "Quantitative Synthesis of the Effects of Administrative Seg-
regation on Inmates' Well-Being." *Psychology, Public Policy, and Law* 22:439–61.

National Commission on Correctional Health Care. 2016. "Position Statement:
Solitary Confinement (Isolation)." *Journal of Correctional Health Care* 22:257–
63. http://www.ncchc.org/solitary-confinement.

National Research Council. 2014. *The Growth of Incarceration in the United States:
Exploring Causes and Consequences*. Washington, DC: National Academies Press.

Nowak, Manfred. 2006. "What Practices Constitute Torture?" *Human Rights
Quarterly* 28:809–41.

Nussbaum, Martha. 1995. "Objectification." *Philosophy and Public Affairs* 24:249–
91.

O'Donnell, Ian. 2014. *Prisoners, Solitude, and Time*. New York: Oxford University Press.

O'Keefe, Maureen. 2008. "Administrative Segregation from Within: A Corrections Perspective." *Prison Journal* 88:123–43.

———. 2017. "Reflections on Colorado's Administrative Segregation Study."
*NIJ Journal* 278:1–8. https://nij.gov/journals/278/Pages/reflections-on-colorado
-administrative-segregation-study.aspx.

O'Keefe, Maureen, Kelli Klebe, Jeffrey Metzner, Joel Dvoskin, Jamie Fellner,
and Alysha Stucker. 2013. "A Longitudinal Study of Administrative Segregation." *Journal of the American Academy of Psychiatry and Law* 41:49–60.

O'Keefe, Maureen, Kelli Klebe, Alysha Stucker, Kristin Sturm, and William
Leggett. 2010. *One Year Longitudinal Study of the Psychological Effects of Administrative Segregation*. Final Report to the National Institute of Justice. Washington, DC: US Department of Justice, National Institute of Justice.

Raemisch, Rick. 2017. "Putting an End to Long-Term Solitary." *New York Times*,
October 13. https://www.nytimes.com/2017/10/12/opinion/solitary-confinement
-colorado-prison.html.

Reiter, Keramet. 2016. *23/7: Pelican Bay Prison and the Rise of Long-Term Solitary
Confinement*. New Haven, CT: Yale University Press.

Reyes, Hernan. 2007. "The Worst Scars Are in the Mind: Psychological Torture." *International Review of the Red Cross* 89:591–616. https://www.icrc.org/en/international-review/article/worst-scars-are-mind-psychological-torture.

Rhodes, Lorna. 2004. *Total Confinement: Madness and Reason in the Maximum Security Prison*. Berkeley: University of California Press.

Rhodes, Lorna, and David Lovell. 2011. "Is Adaptation the Right Question? Addressing the Larger Context of Administrative Segregation: Commentary on One Year Longitudinal Study of the Psychological Effects of Administrative Segregation." *Corrections and Mental Health: An Update of the National Institute of Corrections* (June 21). http://community.nicic.gov/cfs-file.ashx/__key/CommunityServer.Components.PostAttachments/00.00.05.95.19/Supermax-_2D00_-T-_2D00_-Rhodes-and-Lovell.pdf.

Rundle, Frank. 1973. "The Roots of Violence at Soledad." In *The Politics of Punishment: A Critical Analysis of Prisons in America*, edited by Erik Wright. New York: Harper.

Scott, George, and Paul Gendreau. 1969. "Psychiatric Implications of Sensory Deprivation in a Maximum Security Prison." *Canadian Psychiatric Association Journal* 14:337–41.

Shalev, Sharon. 2009. *Supermax: Controlling Risk through Solitary Confinement*. Portland, OR: Willan.

Shalev, Sharon, and Monica Lloyd. 2011. "*If* This Be Method, Yet There Is Madness in It: Commentary on One Year Longitudinal Study of the Psychological Effects of Administrative Segregation." *Corrections and Mental Health: An Update of the National Institute of Corrections* (June 21). http://community.nicic.gov/cfs-file.ashx/__key/CommunityServer.Components.PostAttachments/00.00.05.95.21/Supermax-_2D00_-T-_2D00_-Shalev-and-Lloyd.pdf.

Slater, Robert. 1986. "Psychiatric Intervention in an Atmosphere of Terror." *American Journal of Forensic Psychology* 7(1):5–12.

Smith, Peter Scharff. 2006. "The Effects of Solitary Confinement on Prison Inmates: A Brief History and Review of the Literature." In *Crime and Justice: A Review of Research*, vol. 34, edited by Michael Tonry. Chicago: University of Chicago Press.

———. 2011. "The Effects of Solitary Confinement: Commentary on One Year Longitudinal Study of the Psychological Effects of Administrative Segregation." *Corrections and Mental Health: An Update of the National Institute of Corrections* (June 21). http://community.nicic.gov/cfs-file.ashx/__key/CommunityServer.Components.PostAttachments/00.00.05.95.22/Supermax-_2D00_-T-_2D00_-Smith.pdf.

Strube, Michael, William Gardner, and Donald Hartmann. 1985. "Limitations, Liabilities, and Obstacles in Reviews of the Literature: The Current Status of Meta-Analysis." *Clinical Psychology Review* 5:63–78.

Suedfeld, Peter, Carmenza Ramirez, John Deaton, and Gloria Baker-Brown. 1982. "Reactions and Attributes of Prisoners in Solitary Confinement." *Criminal Justice and Behavior* 9:303–40.

Sykes, Gresham. 1958. *Society of Captives*. Princeton, NJ: Princeton University Press.

Toch, Hans. 1975. *Men in Crisis: Human Breakdowns in Prison*. New York: Aldine.
————. 1977. *Living in Prison: The Ecology of Survival*. New York: Free Press.
————. 2003. "The Contemporary Relevance of Early Experiments with Super-max Reform." *Prison Journal* 83:221–28.
Turner, Scott, Laura Cardinal, and Richard Burton. 2017. "Research Design for Mixed Methods: A Triangulation-Based Framework and Roadmap." *Organizational Research Methods* 20:243–67.
Volkart, Reto, Adolf Dittrich, Thomas Rothenfluh, and Paul Werner. 1983. "Eine Kontrollierte Untersuchung uber Psychopathologische Effekte der Einzelhaft" [A controlled investigation on psychopathological effects of solitary confinement]. *Psychologie—Schweizerische Zeitschrift fur Psychologie und ihre Anwendungen* 42:25–46.
Volkart, Reto, Thomas Rothenfluh, W. Kobelt, Adolf Dittrich, and K. Ernst. 1983. "Einzelhaft als Risikofaktor fur Psychiatrische Hospitalisierung" [Solitary confinement as a risk for psychiatric hospitalization]. *Psychiatria Clinica* 16:365–77.
Waligora, Bogusław. 1974. "Funkcjonowanie Czlowieka W Warunkach Izolacji Wieziennej" [How men function in conditions of penitentiary isolation]. *Seria Psychologia I Pedagogika* 34:1–123.
Walters, Richard, John Callagan, and Albert Newman. 1963. "Effect of Solitary Confinement on Prisoners." *American Journal of Psychiatry* 119:771–73.
Zinger, Ivan. 1998. "The Psychological Effects of 60 Days in Administrative Segregation." PhD diss., Carlton University, Department of Psychology.
Zinger, Ivan, Cherami Wichmann, and D. Andrews. 2001. "The Psychological Effects of 60 Days in Administrative Segregation." *Canadian Journal of Criminology* 43:47–83.

*Barry C. Feld*

# Punishing Kids in Juvenile and Criminal Courts

ABSTRACT

During the 1980s and 1990s, state lawmakers shifted juvenile justice policies from a nominally offender-oriented rehabilitative approach toward a more punitive and criminalized one. Pretrial detention and delinquency dispositions had disproportionate adverse effects on minority youths. Despite juvenile courts' convergence with criminal courts, states provided fewer and less adequate procedural safeguards to delinquents than to adults. Developmental psychologists and policy analysts contend that adolescents' compromised ability to exercise rights requires greater procedural safeguards. States' transfer laws sent more and younger youths to criminal courts for prosecution as adults, emphasized offense seriousness over offender characteristics, and shifted discretion from judges conducting waiver hearings to prosecutors making charging decisions. Judges in criminal courts sentence youths similarly to adult offenders. The Supreme Court, relying on developmental psychology and neuroscience research, in *Roper v. Simmons*, *Graham v. Florida*, and *Miller v. Alabama*, emphasized adolescents' diminished responsibility and limited the harshest sentences. However, the court provided states limited guidance on how to implement its decisions. Judicial and legislative responses inadequately acknowledge that "children are different."

The juvenile court lies at the intersection of youth policy and crime policy. How should the legal system respond when the kid is a criminal and the criminal is a kid? During the 1970s and 1980s, structural, economic, and demographic changes in American cities contributed to escalating

Electronically published March 5, 2018
    Barry C. Feld is Centennial Professor of Law Emeritus at the University of Minnesota Law School.

black youth homicide rates. The Great Migration increased the concentration of impoverished African Americans living in inner-city ghettoes. Federal housing, highway, and mortgage policies combined with bank redlining and real estate blockbusting to create poor minority urban cores surrounded by predominantly white affluent suburbs. Beginning in the early 1970s, the United States began to shift from a manufacturing to an information and service economy. The globalization of manufacturing and technological innovations eliminated many jobs of less skilled workers and produced a bifurcation of economic opportunities based on education and technical skills. The economic changes adversely affected blacks more deeply than other groups because of their more recent entry into the manufacturing economy, their vulnerability in the social stratification system, their lower average educational attainment, and their spatial isolation from sectors of job growth. By the 1980s, deindustrialization and white flight left an impoverished black underclass trapped in urban ghettos. The introduction of crack cocaine and the proliferation of guns sparked turf wars over control of drug markets. Black youth homicide rates sharply escalated, and gun violence provided political impetus to transform juvenile and criminal justice policies. By the late 1980s and early 1990s, states adopted get-tough policies to reduce youth crime, punish delinquents more severely, and prosecute more youths in criminal courts.[1]

Competing conceptions of children, as immature and incompetent versus mature and competent, and differing strategies of crime control, treatment, or diversion versus punishment affect courts' substantive goals and procedural means. Ideas about youths' culpability and responsibility affect juvenile courts' decisions to detain and sentence delinquents, transfer youths to criminal court, and sentence children as adults. Views about youths' competence to participate in the legal process influence policies about waiver of *Miranda* rights and the right to counsel, competence to stand trial, and access to a jury trial.

Contemporary juvenile justice policies reflect the harsh legacy of the 1980s and 1990s when lawmakers equated some youths' culpability with that of adults—"adult crime, adult time." Get-tough policies include ex-

[1] Criminal laws of historically unprecedented severity, particularly concerning sentencing of adult offenders and transfer of young offenders from juvenile to adult courts, were enacted in the period 1984–96 (National Research Council 2014; Tonry 2016).

tensive pretrial detention, punitive delinquency sanctions, increased transfer to criminal courts, and severe sentences as adults, all rife with racial disparities. The Supreme Court's trilogy of Eighth Amendment decisions about sentences to death or life without parole, *Roper v. Simmons*, 543 U.S. 551 (2005), *Graham v. Florida*, 130 S. Ct. 2011 (2010), and *Miller v. Alabama*, 132 S. Ct. 2455 (2012), reaffirmed that "children are different," emphasized youths' diminished criminal responsibility, and limited the most severe sentences. However, they provided affected youths with limited relief and provided state courts and legislatures with minimal guidance.

States' get-tough policies affected both delinquents in juvenile courts and youths in criminal courts. In juvenile courts, states held more youths in pretrial detention, especially those charged with drug and violent crimes. Delinquency interventions shifted from emphasizing rehabilitation of young offenders to punishment of them for their crimes. Punitive pretrial detention and post-adjudications dispositions had disproportionate effects on black youths. Despite juvenile courts' increased punitiveness, their procedural deficiencies and youths' developmental limitations heightened risks of excessive, erroneous, and discriminatory interventions. As juvenile courts became more punitive, developmental psychologists questioned whether many juveniles have the ability to exercise their rights under the *Miranda* decision, 384 U.S. 436 (1966), concerning police interrogation and whether some are even competent to stand trial. They doubt whether delinquents have the capacity to waive counsel unaided. And most states deny delinquents the right to a jury trial, which increases the risk of error in guilt determinations.

States' increased punitiveness is also reflected in policy changes to transfer more youths to criminal courts and sentence them as adults. Transfer laws shifted focus from offenders to offenses and increased prosecutors' roles in making adulthood determinations. Despite efforts to get tough, transfer laws failed to achieve their legislative goals and exacerbated racial disparities. The US Supreme Court's decisions in *Roper*, *Graham*, and *Miller* somewhat mitigated the harshest sentences states inflicted on youths, reaffirmed that "children are different," and used developmental psychology and neuroscience to justify its conclusions. However, neither juvenile nor criminal courts provide developmentally appropriate justice for children. Sections I and II discuss juveniles' experiences in juvenile and adult courts. Section III offers reform proposals to enhance fairness and legitimacy.

## I. Delinquents in Juvenile Courts

Social welfare and social control operate in fundamental tension. How do we balance young offenders' best interests with punishment for their offenses? How do we safeguard children and protect communities? The traditional juvenile court asserted a social welfare mission in which children's and society's interests were congruent, but get-tough politicians more recently subordinated welfare to crime control. This imbalance inevitably occurs because states define delinquency jurisdiction on the basis of criminal behavior rather than children's welfare needs, which diverts attention from the criminogenic conditions in which many youths live.

### A. Pretrial and Postconviction Custody Status

Questions about effectiveness of rehabilitation emerged in the 1960s, eroded juvenile courts' interventionist rationale, and evoked a sense of failure among practitioners and the public. In 1974, Robert Martinson's now-famous essay "What Works? Questions and Answers about Prison Reform" concluded that "with few and isolated exceptions, the rehabilitative efforts that have been reported so far have had no appreciable effect on recidivism" (p. 25). "Nothing works" became the conventional wisdom for several decades, undercut efforts to treat offenders, and reinforced conservatives' distrust of government efforts to reduce crime or ameliorate social problems.

Increased rates of violence and homicide in the late 1980s and early 1990s enabled conservative politicians to promote a stereotype of dangerous young super-predators—cold-eyed young killers suffering from moral poverty—rather than traditional images of disadvantaged youths who needed help. On the basis of erroneous demographic projections, they predicted a bloodbath of youth crime, even as juvenile violence declined precipitously after 1991 (Zimring 2013). Relying on those flawed predictions, legislators enacted laws that emphasized suppression of crime through punishment, deterrence, and incapacitation rather than through efforts to rehabilitate children. Juvenile justice shifted from a welfare to a penal orientation and accepted responsibility to manage and control delinquents rather than to treat them. Beginning in the 1970s, just deserts and retribution displaced rehabilitation as rationales for adult and juvenile sentencing policy, focused on offenders' past behavior rather than on preventive considerations, and imposed penalties based on offense or criminal history with little regard for offenders' situations, characteristics, or circumstances.

1. *Preventive Detention of Delinquents.*   Conservatives claimed that ostensibly lenient dispositions in juvenile courts failed to protect the public and emphasized harsher punishment. Detention laws give judges broad discretion to confine youths prior to trial. Judges overuse and abuse detention facilities and disproportionately detain children of color. Reform efforts can reduce unnecessary and inappropriate use of pretrial confinement.

Pretrial detention involves a youth's interim custody status pending trial, the delinquency equivalent of jail. States hold about 20 percent of youths referred to juvenile courts in pretrial detention facilities. This affects between one-quarter and one-third of a million juveniles annually. In 2011, judges detained a larger proportion of youths arrested for violent offenses (25.6 percent) than for property crimes (16.8 percent); but because police arrested so many more youths for property crimes, they confined roughly equal numbers of both. Rates of detention rose and peaked between 1998 and 2007, even as the absolute numbers of youths referred to juvenile courts declined. Courts detained older youths at higher rates than younger juveniles, proportionately more boys than girls, and far more children of color than white youths (Snyder and Sickmund 2006; Sickmund, Sladky, and Wang 2014).

*Schall v. Martin*, 467 U.S. 253, 255–57 (1984), upheld a New York statute that authorized preventive detention if a judge found there was a "serious risk" that the child "may . . . commit an act which if committed by an adult would constitute a crime." The law did not specify the type of current offense, the likelihood or seriousness of any future crime, the burden of proof, or the criteria or evidence a judge should consider to make the prediction. *Schall* held that preventive detention "serves a legitimate state objective, and that the procedural protections afforded pre-trial detainees" satisfy constitutional requirements.

Social scientists question *Schall*'s confidence in judges' prognostication ability. Research comparing statistical versus clinical prediction strongly indicates the superiority of actuarial risk assessment instruments over professional judgments.[2] Judges at an initial appearance often lack information—psychometric tests, professional evaluations, and social histories—

[2] The American Psychiatric Association long has disclaimed psychiatrists' competence to predict future dangerousness because they tend to not use information reliably, to disregard base rate variability, to consider factors that are not predictive, and to assign inappropriate weights to relevant factors (*Barefoot v. Estelle*, 463 U.S. 880, 899–902 [1983]).

on which clinicians would rely. This compounds the fallibility of clinical predictions.

Inadequate and dangerous conditions have characterized detention facilities for decades. Get-tough era policies exacerbated overcrowding as states detained youths to impose short-term punishment or to house those awaiting post-adjudication placement. Studies of conditions of confinement document inadequate physical and mental health care, poor educational programs, lack of treatment services, and excessive use of solitary confinement and physical restraints (Parent et al. 1994). Pretrial detention disrupts youths' lives; weakens ties to family, school, and work; stigmatizes them; and impairs legal defenses. Judges convict and institutionalize detained youths more often than similar youths released pending trial (Barton 2012).

There are racial disparities in rates of detention. States detain black youths more often than similarly situated white offenders (Bishop 2005; Kempf-Leonard 2007; Piquero 2008).[3] Between 1988 and 1991, the peak of the crack cocaine panic, judges detained about half of all black youths charged with drug offenses, twice the rate of white youths (Sickmund, Sladky, and Kang 2014). Race affects detention decisions, and detention adversely affects youths' subsequent case processing and compounds disparities at disposition (Rodriguez 2010; Lieber 2013).

*a. Reform Efforts.* In the late 1980s, the Annie E. Casey Foundation launched the Juvenile Detention Alternatives Initiative (JDAI; http://www .aecf.org), which aimed to reduce use of detention, reduce overcrowding, improve conditions of confinement, and lessen racial disparities. JDAI reforms enlist justice system stakeholders to develop consensus rationales for detention; to adopt risk assessment criteria; to use alternatives to secure detention such as home detention, electronic monitoring, shelter care, after-school, or day reporting centers; and to expedite cases to reduce pretrial confinement (Barton 2012). Stakeholders develop detention criteria based on the current offense, prior record, and other factors. Not all efforts

---

[3] Between 1985 and 2011, juvenile court judges detained about one-fifth of all youths referred to them, including 18 percent of white youths and 26 percent of black youths. Judges detain youths charged with violent offenses at higher rates than youths charged with other crimes. On average, judges detained 22.4 percent of white youths charged with violent offenses compared with 28.4 percent of black youths (Sickmund, Sladky, and Kang 2014). The racial disparities for drug crimes are especially disturbing because, since the 1970s, self-report research has consistently reported that black youths use and sell drugs at lower rates than do white youths (National Research Council 2014).

have been equally successful, but many sites have reduced the numbers of youths detained with no increases in crime or failures to appear. JDAI efforts to reduce racial disparities among detained youths have been less successful, in part because risk assessment instruments include racially biased factors, such as prior record, that make them seem objective and unbiased (Feyerherm 2000; Frase 2009). Some racial disparities may also reflect differences in parental supervision by socioeconomic class: the perceived ability of parents to control their children, to pick them up at a detention center in the middle of the night, or to attend detention hearings (Bishop 2005).

*b. Policy Recommendations.* Juvenile court judges, other justice system stakeholders, and social scientists should develop validated risk-assessment instruments to better identify youths who pose a high risk of offending. Statutes should presume release of all nonfelony offenders and require use of a higher burden of proof—"clear and convincing evidence"—to prove that a youth needs secure detention and that nonsecure alternatives would fail. Other than youths who pose a risk of flight or who have absconded from an institution, states should reserve detention for youths charged with serious crimes such as felonies, violence, or firearms offenses for which commitment to a secure facility would likely follow a conviction. States should bolster detention hearing procedures with a nonwaivable right to counsel and an opportunity to meet with defense counsel prior to the hearing.

2. *Punitive Delinquency Dispositions.* Several Supreme Court decisions, in *Kennedy v. Mendoza-Martinez*, 372 U.S. 144 (1963), *McKeiver v. Pennsylvania*, 403 U.S. 528 (1971), and *Allen v. Illinois*, 478 U.S. 364 (1986), have identified factors with which to distinguish punishment from treatment. Courts examine legislative purpose clauses, use of indeterminate or determinate sanctions, judges' dispositional practices, institutional conditions of confinement, and intervention outcomes to differentiate treatment from punishment (Feld 1988*b*, 1998, 1999). During the get-tough era, lawmakers repudiated juvenile courts' offender-based treatment philosophy, shifted delinquency sanctions toward offense-based punishments, and fostered a punitive convergence between juvenile and criminal courts (Gardner 2012; Feld 2017).

States repeatedly amended their juvenile codes' purpose clauses to endorse punishment (Torbet et al. 1996; Feld 1999). The revisions focused on accountability, responsibility, punishment, and public safety rather than on, or in addition to, a child's welfare or best interests. Accountability became synonymous with retribution, deterrence, and incapacitation, and state courts affirmed punishment as a legitimate element of juvenile courts' treatment regimes (Nellis 2016).

Originally, juvenile courts viewed delinquency as a symptom of a child's needs and imposed indeterminate nonproportional dispositions. *In re Gault*, 387 U.S. 1 (1967), set in motion a shift toward a more criminalized court by providing modest procedural safeguards that legitimated harsher sanctions (Twentieth Century Task Force 1978). During the get-tough era, states amended delinquency sentencing laws to emphasize individual responsibility and justice system accountability and adopted determinate or mandatory minimum sentences. The National Research Council and Institute of Medicine (2001, p. 210) observed that "state legislative changes in recent years have moved the court away from its rehabilitative goals and toward punishment and accountability. Laws have made some dispositions offense-based rather than offender-based and imposed proportional sanctions to achieve retributive or deterrent goals. Strategies for imposing offense-based sentences in juvenile court include blended sentences, mandatory minimum sentences, and extended jurisdiction."

*a. Case Processing.* Several factors influence juvenile court judges' sentencing decisions. States define delinquency jurisdiction on the basis of criminal violations. The same factors that influence criminal court sentences, the current offense and any prior record, also influence juvenile court judges' dispositions (Scott and Steinberg 2008). Another consistent finding is that juveniles' race affects the severity of dispositions (Bishop and Leiber 2012). Several factors account for racial disparities: differences in rates of offending, differential selection, and juvenile courts' contexts—the interaction of urban locale with minority residency. As a result, juvenile courts' punitive sanctions fall disproportionately heavily on African American youths.

Delinquency case processing includes a succession of decisions by police, court personnel, prosecutors, and judges. Compounding effects of disparities produce larger cumulative differences between white youths and children of color.[4] Although the greatest disparities occur at early, less visible stages of the process, differences compound, prior records ac-

---

[4] In 2005, black youths constituted about 17 percent of the population aged 10–17, 30 percent of juvenile arrests, 33 percent of delinquency referrals, 42 percent of juveniles detained, 37 percent of youths charged, and 39 percent of youths placed out of home (Bishop and Leiber 2012, pp. 448–49).

cumulate, and African Americans and other racial minorities make up the largest numbers of youths in institutions.

Judges' focus on the current offense and prior records contributes to racial differences. Black youths commit violent crimes at higher rates than do whites; this accounts for some disparities (Piquero 2008; National Research Council 2013).[5] By contrast, police arrest black youths at higher rates for drug crimes, although white youths use drugs more often (Lauritsen 2005; National Research Council 2013). Prior records reflect previous justice system decisions and mask some racial disparities (Sampson and Lauritsen 1997; Frase 2009).

Justice system decisions amplify racial disparities. Police stop and arrest youths of color more frequently than white youths.[6] Probation officers often attribute white youths' offenses to external circumstances and black youths' crimes to character failings, which affect their referral, detention, and sentencing recommendations (Bridges and Steen 1998; National Research Council and Institute of Medicine 2001). Each stage of the process—court referral, detention, petition, and sentencing decisions—magnifies disparities (National Research Council 2013).

Juvenile courts' contexts also contribute to racial disparities. Urban courts are more formal and sentence all delinquents more severely than do suburban or rural courts (Feld 1991, 1993). They have greater access to detention facilities, detain more minority youths, and sentence all detained youths more severely (Rodriguez 2010). Because more minority youths live in cities, judges detain them at higher rates and sentence them in more formal, more punitive courts (Bray, Sample, and Kempf-Leonard 2005; Snyder and Sickmund 2006).

---

[5] The higher rates of violent offending by black youths reflect their greater exposure to risk factors associated with criminal involvement, many of which are corollaries of living in dire poverty (Loeber and Farrington 1998). Concentrated poverty, limited employment opportunities, broken or unstable families, poor parental supervision, harsh discipline, abuse or maltreatment, failing schools, gang-infested neighborhoods, and community disorder contribute to higher rates of crime and violence in segregated urban areas (Wilson 2009; National Research Council 2014). Some inner-city black youths may be socialized into a code of the street that emphasizes masculinity, risk taking, autonomy, and violent responses to challenges or disrespect (Anderson 1999; Fagan 2000). The presence of gangs can lead to intragang violence over status and intergang violence to settle territorial disputes or perceived disrespect, which further contributes to youth violence (Fagan 2000).

[6] Causes of heightened risks of arrest include deployment of police in minority neighborhoods, racial profiling, aggressive stop-and-frisk practices, and youths' attitudes and demeanor during encounters (Bishop and Leiber 2012).

Get-tough laws have exacerbated racial disparities in confinement. Over the past quarter century, the proportion of white youths removed from home declined by about 10 percent while the black proportion increased by 10 percent. In 1985, states removed 105,830 delinquents from their homes and placed them in residential facilities. The number of youths receiving out-of-home placements increased steadily during the 1990s and peaked at 168,395 delinquents in 1997, a 59 percent increase. Since the late 1990s peak, the number of youths removed from home has declined dramatically. Although we do not know why residential placements have decreased, fiscal considerations may have driven the decline.

Despite the recent drop, the racial composition of youths in confinement changed substantially. By 2012, the proportion of white youths removed from home declined to 57.8 percent of the total—a 10.7 percent decrease—while the proportion of black youths increased to 39.3 percent—a 10.8 percent increase. Notwithstanding overall reduction in youths in confinement, a 1-day count of youths reveals that the racial composition of institutionalized inmates became ever darker. During the past decade, the proportion of white inmates declined from 37.2 percent to 33.8 percent of all institutional residents, the proportion of black inmates hovered around 40 percent, and the proportion of other youths of color increased (Feld 2017).

Congress amended the Juvenile Justice and Delinquency Prevention Act (JJDPA) in 1988 to require states to examine minority overrepresentation in detention and institutions. It amended the JJDPA in 1992 to make disproportionate minority confinement a core requirement and again in 2002 to require states to reduce disproportionate minority contact. States conducted evaluations and confirmed disproportionate minority confinement. Minority juveniles receive disproportionately more out-of-home placements, while whites receive more probationary dispositions. Judges commit black youths to public institutions at rates three and four times that of white youths and send larger proportions of white youths to private residential treatment programs. Black youths serve longer terms than white youths committed for similar offenses (Poe-Yamagata and Jones 2000; National Research Council 2013).

*b. Treatment Programs.* Researchers have evaluated programs in community and residential settings to determine what works, how well, and at what costs (Greenwood and Turner 2012; MacKenzie and Freeland 2012). Correctional meta-analyses combine independent studies to measure effectiveness of different strategies to reduce recidivism or other outcomes. Evaluations have compared generic strategies such as counseling, behavior modification, and group therapy; more sophisticated interventions and replications of brand-name programs such as Functional Family Therapy and Multisystemic Therapy; and cost/benefit appraisals of different treatments. A substantial literature exists on effectiveness of probation and other forms of noninstitutional treatment. Community-based programs are more likely to be run by private (usually nonprofit) service providers, to be smaller and less crowded, and to offer more treatment services than do publicly run institutions.

The Blueprints for Prevention program certifies programs as proven or promising. Proven programs demonstrate reductions in problem behaviors in evaluations with rigorous experimental design, continuing effects after youths leave the program, and successful replication by independent providers (MacKenzie and Freeland 2012; Nellis 2016). Although some proven programs treat delinquents, most aim to prevent school-aged youths' involvement with the juvenile justice system. Mark Lipsey's (2009) ongoing meta-analyses report that treatment strategies such as counseling and skill building are more effective than those that emphasize surveillance, control, and discipline. The Campbell Collaboration conducted meta-analyses of rigorous empirical evaluations of treatment programs for serious delinquents in secure institutions and concluded that cognitive-behavioral treatment reduced overall and serious recidivism (Garrido and Morales 2007; MacKenzie and Freeland 2012). Cost-benefit studies use meta-analytic methods to evaluate program costs and benefits to the individual and community—recidivism reduction, taxpayers, and potential victims. While there is a paucity of high-quality evaluations, research suggests that preschool enrichment and family-based interventions outside of the juvenile justice system provide preventive benefits that exceed their costs and produce improvements in education, employment, income, mental health, and other outcomes (Welsh et al. 2012).

Cumulatively, evaluations conclude that states can handle most delinquents safely in community settings with cognitive-behavioral models of change (MacKenzie and Freeland 2012). The most successful Blueprints programs—Functional Family Therapy and Multisystemic Therapy—focus on improving family problem-solving skills and strengthening parents' ability to deal with their children's behaviors. But effective programs require extensive and expensive staff training, for which most state and local agencies are unwilling to pay. Despite decades of research, "only about 5 percent of the youths who could benefit from these improved programs now have the opportunity to do so. Juvenile justice options in many communities remain mired in the same old tired options of custodial care and community supervision" (Greenwood and Turner 2012, p. 744).

*In re Gault*, 387 U.S. 1 (1967), mandated procedural safeguards in juvenile courts, in part, because of inhumane conditions in some training schools—including inmates beaten by guards, hog-tied, or subjected to prolonged isolation (Krisberg 2012). During the 1960s and 1970s, investigators conducted in-depth ethnographic research in correctional facilities (e.g., Bartollas, Miller, and Dinitz 1976; Feld 1976). They reported violent environments, minimal treatment or educational programs, physical abuse by staff and inmates, make-work tasks, and extensive use of solitary confinement. In the ensuing decades, little changed. States continue to confine half of all youths in overcrowded facilities, more than three-quarters in large facilities, and more than one-quarter in institutions with 200–1,000 inmates (Snyder and Sickmund 2006; MacKenzie and Freeland 2012).

Over the past four decades, juvenile inmates have filed nearly 60 lawsuits that challenge conditions of confinement, assert that they violate the Eighth Amendment's prohibition on cruel and unusual punishment, and deny their Fourteenth Amendment right to treatment (Krisberg 2012; Nellis 2016). Eighth Amendment litigation is proscriptive, defines constitutionally impermissible practices, and delineates the minimum floor below which institutional conditions may not fall. Judicial opinions from around the country describe youths housed in dungeon-like facilities, beaten with paddles, drugged for social control, locked in solitary confinement, housed in overcrowded and dangerous conditions, and subjected to other punitive practices. The Fourteenth Amendment litigation is prescriptive and asserts that the denial of criminal procedural protections imposes a substantive right to treatment and creates a duty to provide beneficial programs (Feld 1999, 2013*b*).

Do institutional treatment programs reduce recidivism, enhance psychological well-being, improve educational attainments, provide vocational skills, or boost community readjustment? Most states do not collect data on programs' effectiveness or recidivism. This complicates judges' ability to distinguish treatment from punishment. Despite these limitations, evaluations of training schools provide scant evidence of effective treatment (Krisberg 2012). Programs that emphasize deterrence or punishment—training schools and boot camps—may increase criminal activity following release (MacKenzie and Freeland 2012). Correctional boot camps, reflecting punitive policies and emphasizing physical training, drill, and discipline, despite their popularity did not reduce recidivism; some studies reported increases (MacKenzie and Freeland 2012). Evaluations of training schools report that police rearrest half or more juveniles for a new offense within 1 year of release (Snyder and Sickmund 2006; Krisberg 2012).

3. *What Should a Responsible Legislature Do?* Justice system involvement impedes youths' transition to adulthood and aggravates minority youths' social disadvantage. Like the Hippocratic Oath, the first priority of juvenile court intercession should be harm reduction—to avoid or minimize practices that leave a youth worse off. Most delinquents will outgrow adolescent crimes without extensive treatment. Interventions should be short-term, community-based, and as minimally disruptive as possible. "The best-known cure for youth crime is growing up. And the strategic logic of diversion and minimal sanctions is waiting for maturation to transition a young man from male groups to intimate pairs and from street corners to houses and workplaces" (Zimring and Tanenhaus 2014, p. 228).

More than four decades ago, Massachusetts's Department of Youth Services (DYS) closed its training schools and replaced them with group homes, mental health facilities, and contracts for services for education, counseling, and job training. Evaluations reported that more than three-quarters of DYS youths were not subsequently incarcerated, juvenile arrest rates decreased, and the proportion of adult prison inmates who had graduated from juvenile institutions declined (Krisberg, Austin, and Steele 1989; Miller 1991). More recently, Missouri replicated and expanded the Massachusetts experiment and used continuous case management, decentralized residential units, and staff-facilitated positive peer culture to provide a rehabilitative environment. Although proponents claim reduction in recidivism rates, no rigorous evaluations demonstrate the initiative's effectiveness (National Research Council 2013). Other states have adopted deinstitutionalization strategies. In one hopeful sign, the California Youth Authority has closed five large institutions and reduced its incarcerated population from about 10,000 juveniles to around 1,600 (Krisberg 2012).

Delinquency prevention programs provide an alternative to control or suppression strategies. Prevention intervenes with children and youths before they engage in delinquency, identifies factors that contribute to offending, and employs programs to ameliorate or counteract them. Interventions apply to individuals at risk of becoming offenders, their families, or communities. Prevention strategies that identify individual risk factors—such as low intelligence or delayed school progress—provide programs to improve cognitive skills, school readiness, and social skills. The Perry Preschool project—an enhanced Head Start Program for disadvantaged black children—aimed to provide intellectual stimulation, improve critical thinking skills, and enhance later school performance. Larger proportions of experimental than control youths graduated from high school; received postsecondary education; had better employment records, earned higher income, and paid taxes; had fewer arrests; and reduced public expenditures for crime and welfare. Other prevention programs address family risk factors such as poor child-rearing techniques, inadequate supervision, lack of clear norms, and inconsistent or harsh discipline. Home visitation, nurse home visitation, and parent management training can produce positive outcomes in the lives of children (Greenwood 2006; Welsh et al. 2012).

David Farrington and Brandon Welsh (2007) provide a comprehensive review of risk factors and effective interventions to prevent delinquency. They identify individual, family, and community-level factors and effective programs to ameliorate delinquency. At each level, they report proven or promising programs to improve youths' lives and recommend risk-focused evidence-based prevention programs.

Peter Greenwood (2006) provides a comprehensive review of prevention programs. He focuses on interventions along the developmental trajectory from infancy and early childhood, through elementary school ages, and into adolescence. Some prevention programs have been adequately evaluated and clearly do not work—for example, Drug Abuse Resistance Education. Many prevention programs have no evidentiary support: they either have not been evaluated or used flawed designs from which researchers could draw no conclusions. Greenwood uses cost-benefit analyses to evaluate various delinquency and prevention programs. While cost-benefit analyses could rationalize delinquency policy and resource allocation decisions, many politicians do not embrace prevention programs because they lack a punitive component and do not demonstrate immediate effects. While highly visible crimes evoke fear and elicit a punitive response, delinquency prevention takes longer to realize and has more diffuse effects. Despite effective programs, delinquency prevention "holds a small place in the nation's response to juvenile crime. Delinquency control strategies operated by the juvenile justice system dominate" (Welsh 2012, p. 409).

During the 1980s and 1990s, lawmakers sharply shifted juvenile courts' emphases from rehabilitative toward punitive policies. They changed juvenile codes' purposes from care and treatment to accountability and punishment. They amended delinquency sentencing statutes to specify length and location of confinement based on the offense. Judges focused primarily on the current offense and prior record when making dispositions. Training schools more closely resembled prisons than clinics and seldom improved delinquents' life chances. Meta-analyses and other evaluations identify effective programs, most of which juvenile justice personnel do not administer.

Tougher handling has fallen most heavily on black youths. At every critical decision, black youths receive more punitive sanctions than white youths. Differences in rates of violence by race contribute to some disparity in justice administration. But many black youths experience very different childhoods and grow up under much worse conditions than do most white youths. Public policies and private decisions created segregated urban areas and consigned children of color to live in concentrated poverty. Race affects decision makers' responses to children of color—the way they see them, evaluate them, and dispose of them. It is not coincidental that the turn from rehabilitation to retribution occurred as blacks gained civil rights and the United States briefly flirted with integration and inclusionary rather than exclusionary racial policies (Feld 1999, 2017).

### B. Juvenile Court Procedures

I emphasize juvenile courts' explicitly punitive turn because it has implications concerning the procedural safeguards they accord children. *McKeiver v. Pennsylvania* denied delinquents a right to a jury and *In re Gault* granted only watered-down safeguards. But punishing delinquents erodes the justifications for fewer safeguards. Progressive Era reformers envisioned the juvenile court as a welfare agency and rejected criminal procedural safeguards—lawyers, juries, and rules of evidence. In 1967, *In re Gault* began to transform the juvenile court from a social welfare agency into a legal institution. *Gault* emphasized juvenile courts' criminal elements—youths charged with crimes facing institutional confinement, the stigma of delinquency, judicial arbitrariness, and high rates of recidivism—and required fundamentally fair procedures. Although *Gault* did not adopt all adult criminal procedural protections, it precipitated a convergence between juvenile and criminal courts. *In re Winship*, 397 U.S. 358 (1970), required states to prove delinquency by the criminal standard of proof—beyond a reasonable doubt—rather than by the lower civil standard of proof of "more probably than not." *Breed v. Jones*, 421 U.S. 519 (1975), described a functional equivalence between juvenile and criminal trials and applied the Fifth Amendment's double jeopardy clause to delinquency prosecutions. However, *McKeiver v. Pennsylvania*, 403 U.S. 528 (1971), posited a benevolent juvenile court that treated delinquents and denied them a constitutional right to a jury trial. Subsequent punitive changes have eroded *McKeiver's* unsupported rationale. The absence of a jury adversely affects accurate fact-finding, the presence and performance of counsel, and chances of wrongful convictions.

Juvenile courts handle about half of the youths referred to them informally without a formal petition or a trial (Snyder and Sickmund 2006; Mears 2012). Court intake workers or prosecutors perform a rapid assessment to determine whether a youth's crime or welfare requires juvenile court attention or whether he or she can be discharged or referred to others for care. Diversion minimizes formal adjudication and provides supervision or services in the community. Proponents of diversion contend that it is an efficient gate-keeping mechanism, avoids labeling minor offenders, and provides flexible access to community resources (Mears 2012). Most youths desist after one or two contacts, and diversion conserves judicial resources for those youths whose crimes or chronic recidivism requires formal intervention.

Critics of diversion contend that it widens the net of social control and exposes youths to informal supervision whom juvenile courts otherwise might have ignored. Probation officers or prosecutors who do preliminary screening make low-visibility decisions that are not subject to judicial review. Many states do not use formal screening or assessment tools; intake constitutes the most significant source of racial disparities in case processing. Although the criteria and administration of diversion raise many significant policy concerns, cases handled informally do not raise the procedural issues of formal adjudication (National Research Council and Institute of Medicine 2001; Mears 2012).

As juvenile courts increasingly punished delinquents, their need for protection from the state increased. *Gault* made delinquency hearings more complex and legalistic. Developmental psychologists question whether younger juveniles possess competence to stand trial and whether adolescents have the ability to exercise *Miranda* rights or to waive counsel. Despite clear developmental differences between youths and adults in understanding, maturity of judgment, and competence, the US Supreme Court and most states do not provide additional safeguards to protect them from their immaturity or provide procedural parity with criminal defendants. States treat juveniles just like adults when formal equality results in practical inequality and use special juvenile court procedures when they provide an advantage to the state.

1. *Police Interrogation.* The Supreme Court has decided more cases about interrogating youths than any other issue of juvenile justice.[7] It repeatedly has questioned juveniles' ability to exercise *Miranda* rights or make voluntary statements but does not require special procedures to protect them. Rather, *Fare v. Michael C.*, 442 U.S. 707, 725 (1979), endorsed the adult standard—"knowing, intelligent, and voluntary under the totality of circumstances"—to gauge juveniles' *Miranda* waivers. While most states' laws equate juveniles' maturity with that of adults, developmental psychologists question adolescents' ability to understand *Miranda* warnings or exercise them effectively. Research on youths' responses to interrogation practices designed for adults highlights how developmental immaturity and susceptibility to manipulation increase the likelihood they will confess falsely.

Before *Miranda* was decided, the Court in *Haley v. Ohio*, 332 U.S. 596 (1948), and *Gallegos v. Colorado*, 370 U.S. 49 (1962), cautioned trial judges to examine closely how youthfulness affected voluntariness of confessions and held that youth, lengthy questioning, and the absence of a lawyer or parent could render confessions involuntary. *Gault* reiterated that youthfulness adversely affects the reliability of juveniles' statements. It ruled that delinquency proceedings "must be regarded as 'criminal' for purposes of the privilege against self-incrimination" (*Gault*, pp. 49–50). It recognized that the Fifth Amendment contributes to accurate fact-finding and maintains the adversarial balance between the individual and the state.

*Fare v. Michael C.* departed from the court's earlier concerns about youths' vulnerability and held that the legal standard used to evaluate

---

[7] *Haley v. Ohio*, 332 U.S. 596 (1948); *Gallegos v. Colorado*, 370 U.S. 49 (1962); *In re Gault*, 387 U.S. 1 (1967); *Fare v. Michael C.*, 442 U.S. 707 (1979); *Yarborough v. Alvarado*, 541 U.S. 652 (2004); *J.D.B. v. North Carolina*, 131 S. Ct. 2394 (2011).

adults' waivers governed juvenile waivers as well. *Michael C.* reasoned that *Miranda* provided an objective basis to evaluate waivers, denied that children's developmental differences demanded special protections, and required them to assert rights clearly. *Miranda*, 384 U.S. 436, 444 (1966), provided that if police question a suspect who is in custody, arrested, or "deprived of his freedom of action in any significant way," they must administer a warning. The court in *J.D.B. v. North Carolina*, 131 S. Ct. 2394 (2011), considered whether a 13-year-old juvenile's age affected the *Miranda* custody analysis. The court concluded that age was an objective factor that would affect how a young person might experience restraint.

Despite *J.D.B.*'s recognition of youths' vulnerability, the vast majority of states use the same *Miranda* framework for juveniles and adults. When trial judges evaluate *Miranda* waivers, they consider offender characteristics such as age, education, IQ, and prior police contacts, and the context of interrogation including location, methods, and length of interrogation. The leading cases provide long lists of factors for trial judges to consider. Appellate courts identify many relevant elements, do not assign controlling weight to any one variable, and provide no meaningful check on judges' discretion. Judges regularly find valid waivers by children as young as age 10, with limited intelligence, with no prior police contacts, and without parental assistance (Feld 2000*a*, 2006*a*, 2006*b*, 2013*c*).

About 10 states presume that most juveniles lack capacity to waive *Miranda* and require a parent or other adult to assist them. Some states require a parent to be present for juveniles younger than 14, presume that those 14 or 16 or older are incompetent to waive, or oblige police to offer older youths an opportunity to consult counsel or parents. Most commentators endorse parental presence, even though many question the value of their participation. Parents' and children's interests may conflict, for example, if the juvenile assaulted or stole from a parent or victimized another sibling, or if the parent is a suspect or has to pay for the child's attorney. Parents may not understand legal rights any better than their children do.

If youths differ from adults in understanding *Miranda*, exercising rights, or being susceptible to pressure, then the law establishes a standard that few can meet. *Miranda* requires police to advise suspects of their rights, but some juveniles do not understand the words or concepts that are used. Psychologists have studied the vocabulary, concepts and reading levels required to understand warnings and concluded that they exceed many adolescents' abilities (Rogers et al. 2008*a*, 2008*b*). Some concepts, such as the meaning of a *right*, the term *appointed* to secure counsel, and *waive*, require a high school education and render *Miranda* incomprehensible to many who lack one. If the youth's reading level or verbal complexity makes a warning unintelligible, then it cannot serve its protective function.

Psychologist Thomas Grisso has studied juveniles' exercise of *Miranda* rights for more than four decades. He reports that many, if not most, do not understand the warning well enough to make a valid waiver. Although age, intelligence, and prior arrests correlate with *Miranda* comprehension, more than half of juveniles, as contrasted with less than one-quarter of adults, did not understand at least one of the warnings, and only one-fifth of juveniles, as compared with twice as many adults, grasped all four warnings (Grisso 1980). Juveniles 15 or younger exhibited poorer comprehension, waived more readily, and confessed more frequently than did older youths. Other research reports that older youths understand *Miranda* as well as adults, but many younger juveniles do not understand the words or concepts (Feld 2013*c*). Adolescents with low IQs perform worse than adults with low IQs, and delinquent youths typically have lower IQs than do those in the general population.

Even youths who understand *Miranda*'s words may not appreciate the function or importance of rights as well as adults do (Grisso 1981). They have greater difficulty conceiving of a right as an absolute entitlement that they can exercise without adverse consequences. Juveniles view rights as something that authorities allow them but that may be retracted or withheld. They misconceive the lawyer's role and attorney-client confidentiality and waive rights at higher rates than do those with better comprehension.

*Miranda* characterized custodial interrogation as inherently compelling because police dominate the setting and create psychological pressures to comply. The differing legal and social statuses of youths and adults make children questioned by authority figures more suggestible and increase their vulnerability. Juveniles may waive rights and admit responsibility because they believe they should obey authority, acquiesce more readily to negative pressure or critical feedback, and accede more willingly to suggestions (Kassin et al. 2010). They impulsively confess to end an interrogation rather than consider long-term consequences (Grisso 1981; Grisso et al. 2003).

The US Supreme Court requires suspects to invoke *Miranda* rights clearly and unambiguously. However, some groups of people—juveniles, females, or members of racial minorities—may speak tentatively to avoid conflict with those in power (Ainsworth 1993). *Davis v. United States*, 512 U.S. 452 (1994), recognized that to require suspects to invoke rights clearly and unambiguously could prove difficult for some. A suspect who thinks he or she has invoked his or her rights but the police disregard this may feel overwhelmed and succumb to further questioning.

About 80 percent of adults and 90 percent of juveniles waive *Miranda* rights. The largest empirical study of juvenile interrogation reported that 92.8 percent waived. Juveniles' higher waiver rates may reflect their lack of understanding or inability to invoke *Miranda* effectively. As with adults, youths with prior felony arrests invoked their rights more often than did those with fewer or less serious police contacts. Youths who waived rights when previously arrested may have learned that they derived no benefit from cooperating, spent more time with lawyers, and gained greater understanding (Leo 2008; Feld 2013*c*, 2013*d*).

Once officers secure juveniles' waivers, they question them just like adults (Kassin 2005; Feld 2006*a*, 2006*b*, 2013*c*). Police employ the same maximization and minimization strategies used with adults. Maximization techniques intimidate suspects and impress on them the futility of denial; minimization techniques provide moral justifications or face-saving alternatives to enable them to confess. Despite youths' greater susceptibility, police do not receive special training to question juveniles and do not incorporate developmental differences into the tactics they employ (Owen-Kostelnik, Reppucci, and Meyer 2006). Techniques designed to manipulate adults, such as aggressive questioning, presenting false evidence, and using leading questions, create heightened dangers when employed with youths (Tanenhaus and Drizin 2003).

Some states require a parent to assist juveniles in the interrogation room, although analysts question their protective role (Grisso 1981; Woolard et al. 2008; Feld 2013*c*). Parents may have marginally greater understanding of *Miranda* than do their children, but both share misconceptions about police practices. Parents did not provide useful legal advice and increased pressure to waive rights, and many urged their children to tell the truth. Parents may be emotionally upset, believe that confessing will produce a better outcome, or think children should respect authority or assume responsibility. If parents are present, police either enlist them as allies in the interrogation or treat them as passive observers. In the vast majority of interrogations that parents attended, they did not participate after police gave their child a *Miranda* warning, sometimes switched sides to become active allies of the police, and rarely played a protective role (Feld 2013c).

*a. Juvenile Vulnerability and False Confessions.* Research on false confessions underscores juveniles' unique vulnerability (Tepfer, Nirider, and Tricarico 2010; Garrett 2011). Younger adolescents are at greater risk of confessing falsely than older ones. In one study, police obtained more than one-third (35 percent) of proven false confessions from suspects younger than 18 (Drizin and Leo 2004). In another, false confessions occurred in 15 percent of cases, but juveniles accounted for 42 percent of all false confessors; two-thirds (69 percent) of those aged 12–15 confessed to crimes they did not commit (Gross et al. 2005). Significantly, research on juveniles who confess falsely involves only the small group of youths prosecuted as adults. This reflects the seriousness of their crimes, the greater pressure on police to solve them, and the longer period available to youths and their attorneys to correct the errors.

Developmental psychologists attribute juveniles' overrepresentation among false confessors to reduced cognitive ability, developmental immaturity, and increased susceptibility to manipulation. They are more likely to comply with authority figures, tell police what they think police want to hear, and respond to negative feedback. The stress and anxiety of interrogation intensify their desire to extricate themselves in the short run by waiving and confessing. The vulnerabilities of youths multiply when coupled with mental illness, mental retardation, or compliant personalities.

*b. Policy Recommendations.* Research on false confessions underscores the unique vulnerability of juveniles. *Miranda* is especially problematic for younger juveniles who may not understand its words or concepts. *Miranda* requires only shallow understanding of the words that developmental psychologists conclude most 16- and 17-year-old youths possess. By contrast, psychologists report that many, if not most, children 15 or younger do not understand *Miranda* or possess competence to make legal decisions.

1. *Mandatory Counsel for Younger Juveniles.* Younger juveniles' limited understanding and heightened vulnerability warrant a nonwaivable right to counsel. The US Supreme Court's juvenile interrogation cases—*Haley, Gallegos, Gault, Fare, Alvarado,* and *J.D.B.*—excluded statements taken from youths 15 or younger and admitted those obtained from 16- and 17-year-olds. The Court's de facto functional line closely tracks what psychologists report about youths' ability to understand the warning. Courts

and legislatures should adopt that functional line and provide greater protections for younger juveniles.

Psychologists advocate that juveniles younger than 16 "should be accompanied and advised by a professional advocate, preferably an attorney, trained to serve in this role" (Kassin et al. 2010, p. 28). More than three decades ago, the American Bar Association endorsed mandatory, nonwaivable counsel for juveniles because it recognized that "few juveniles have the experience and understanding to decide meaningfully that the assistance of counsel would not be helpful" (American Bar Association and Institute of Judicial Administration 1980, p. 92). Juveniles should consult with an attorney, rather than rely on parents, before they exercise or waive rights. If youths 15 or younger consult with counsel, it will somewhat limit police's ability to secure confessions. However, if younger juveniles cannot understand or exercise rights without assistance, then to treat them as if they do enables the state to exploit their vulnerability.

2. *Limiting the Length of Interrogation.*   The vast majority of interrogations are very brief; nearly all last less than an hour, and few take longer than 2 hours (Feld 2013c). By contrast, interrogations that elicit false confessions are usually long inquiries that wear down an innocent person's resistance—85 percent took at least 6 hours—and youthfulness exacerbates those dangers (Drizin and Leo 2004). *Haley* and *Gallegos* recognized that questioning juveniles for 5 or 6 hours rendered their statement involuntary. States should create a sliding-scale presumption that a confession is involuntary and unreliable based on length of interrogation.

3. *Mandatory Recording.*   Within the past decade, legal scholars, psychologists, law enforcement, and justice system personnel have reached consensus that recording interrogations reduces coercion, diminishes dangers of false confessions, and increases reliability (Leo 2008; Garrett 2011; Feld 2013c). More than a dozen states require police to record interrogations, albeit some under limited circumstances, for example, cases involving homicides or very young suspects. Recording creates an objective record and provides an independent basis to resolve credibility disputes about *Miranda* warnings, waivers, or statements. It enables a judge to decide whether a statement contained facts known to a guilty perpetrator or police supplied them to an innocent suspect. Recording protects police from false claims of abuse, enhances professionalism, and reduces coercion. It enables police to focus on suspects' responses, to review details of an interview not captured in written notes, and to test

details against subsequently discovered facts. Recording avoids distortions that occur when interviewers rely on memory or notes to summarize a statement. Police must record all interactions with suspects—preliminary interviews and interrogations—rather than just a final statement—a postadmission narrative. Only a complete record of every interaction can protect against a final statement that ratifies an earlier coerced one or against a false confession contaminated by nonpublic facts that police supplied to a suspect.

2. *Competence to Stand Trial.* *Gault*'s procedural rights are of no value to youths unable to exercise them. The US Supreme Court long has required that a defendant must be competent to preserve the integrity of trials, promote factual accuracy, reduce risks of error, and participate in proceedings. *Dusky v. United States*, 362 U.S. 402 (1960), held that a defendant must possess "sufficient present ability to consult with his lawyer with a reasonable degree of rational understanding . . . [and have] a rational as well as factual understanding of proceedings against him." *Drope v. Missouri*, 420 U.S. 162, 171 (1975), held that "a person whose mental condition is such that he lacks the capacity to understand the nature and object of the proceedings against him, to consult with counsel, and to assist in preparing his defense may not be subjected to a trial." The standard is functional and binary: a defendant either is or is not competent to stand trial.

The standard for competency is not onerous because the more capability it requires of moderately impaired defendants, the fewer who will meet it (Sanborn 2009). Juveniles must understand the trial process, have the ability to reason and work with counsel, and appreciate their situation. If a person understands that he or she is on trial for committing crimes, knows he or she can be sentenced if convicted, and can communicate with his or her attorney, a court likely will find him or her competent. Significant mental illness, for example, psychotic disorders such as schizophrenia, or severe mental retardation typically renders adult defendants incompetent. However, psychotic disorders usually do not emerge until late adolescence or early adulthood, and the American Psychiatric Association's *Diagnostic and Statistical Manual-V* (2013) cautions against diagnosing profound illnesses in younger populations. Despite that reservation, the prevalence of mental disorders among delinquent youths is substantially higher than in the general population: half to three-quarters exhibit one or more mental illnesses (Grisso 2004).

Developmental psychologists contend that immaturity per se—especially for younger juveniles—produces the same deficits of understanding and inability to assist counsel that mental illness or retardation engenders in incompetent adults. Youths' developmental limitations adversely affect their ability to pay attention, absorb and apply information, understand proceedings, make rational decisions, and work with counsel (Scott and Grisso 2005; Scott and Steinberg 2008).

Significant age-related differences appear between adolescents' and young adults' competence, judgment, and legal decision making. Many juveniles younger than 14 were as severely impaired as adults found incompetent to stand trial. Age and intelligence interacted and produced higher levels of incompetence among adolescents with low IQs than adults with low IQs (Sanborn 2009). A MacArthur Foundation study (2006) reported that about one-fifth of 14–15-year-olds were as impaired as mentally ill adults found incompetent; those with below-average intelligence were more likely than juveniles with average intelligence to be incompetent. Some older youths also exhibited substantial impairments (Grisso et al. 2003; Scott and Steinberg 2008).

While incompetence in adults stems from mental disorders that may be transient or treatable with medication, it is less clear how to accelerate legal capacities in adolescents whose deficits result from immaturity and who never possessed relevant knowledge or understanding to begin with. Adolescents deemed incompetent because of mental retardation may be especially difficult to remediate or restore to competence. The prevalence of mental illness among delinquents compounds their developmental incompetence. Analysts estimate that half or more of male delinquents and a larger proportion of female delinquents suffer from one or more mental disorders. Youths suffering from attention-deficit hyperactivity disorder may have difficulty concentrating or communicating with their attorney, and those suffering from depression may lack the motivation to do so (Grisso 2004; Sanborn 2009; Viljoen, Penner, and Roesch 2012).

The issue of competence to stand trial arises both for youths waived to criminal court and for those prosecuted in juvenile court. For youths tried as adults, criminal courts apply the *Dusky/Drope* standard but focus on mental illness rather than developmental immaturity. For youths tried in juvenile courts, about half the states have addressed competency in statutes, court rules, or case law. However, most statutes consider only mental illness or retardation as a source of incompetence rather than developmental immaturity per se (Sanborn 2009; Viljoen, Penner, and Roesch 2012; Feld 2013*b*).

Even after states recognize juveniles' right to a competency determination in delinquency proceedings, they differ over whether to apply the *Dusky/Drope* adult standard or a juvenile-normed standard. Some courts apply the adult standard in delinquency as well as criminal prosecutions because both may result in a child's loss of liberty. Other jurisdictions opt for a relaxed competency standard on the theory that delinquency hearings are less complex and consequences less severe (Scott and Grisso 2005).

Advocates for a lower standard of competence in delinquency proceedings contend that a youth who might be found incompetent to stand trial as an adult or if evaluated under an adult standard in juvenile court should still be found competent under a relaxed standard. They insist that if delinquency sanctions are less punitive than criminal sentences and are geared to promote youths' welfare, then they require fewer procedural safeguards. However, the constitutional requirement of competence hinges on defendants' ability to participate in proceedings and the legitimacy of the trial process, and not the punishment that may ensue. Although delinquency dispositions, especially for serious crimes, may be shorter than criminal sentences, it is disingenuous to claim they are not punitive. *Baldwin v. New York*, 399 U.S. 66 (1969), held that no crime that carried an authorized sentence of 6 months or longer could be deemed a petty offense. While proponents of a watered-down standard argue that a rule that immunizes some incompetent youths from adjudication could undermine juvenile courts' legitimacy (Scott and Grisso 2005; Scott and Steinberg 2008), adjudicating immature youths under a relaxed standard enables the state to take advantage of their incompetence and undermines the legitimacy of the process. Either defendants understand the proceedings and can assist counsel or they cannot; if they cannot perform those minimal tasks, then they should not be prosecuted in any court.

3. *Access to Counsel.*  *Gideon v. Wainwright*, 372 U.S. 335 (1963), applied the Sixth Amendment to the states to guarantee criminal defendants' right to counsel. *Gault* relied on *Gideon*, compared a delinquency proceeding to a felony prosecution, and granted delinquents the right to counsel. However, *Gault* used the Fourteenth Amendment Due Process Clause rather than the Sixth Amendment and did not mandate automatic appointment. *Gault*, like *Gideon*, left responsibility to fund legal services to state and local governments. Over the past half century,

politicians who want to show they are tough on crime and to avoid "coddling" criminals have failed to fund public defenders adequately.

*Gault* required judges to advise the child and parent of the right to have a lawyer appointed if indigent but observed that juveniles could waive counsel. Most states do not use special procedural safeguards—mandatory nonwaivable appointment or prewaiver consultation with a lawyer—to protect delinquents from improvident decisions (Feld 1984, 1993). Instead, they use the adult standard to gauge juveniles' relinquishment of counsel. As with *Miranda* waivers, formal equality results in practical inequality: lawyers represent delinquents at much lower rates than they do criminal defendants (Burruss and Kempf-Leonard 2002; Jones 2004).

Despite statutes and procedural rules that apply equally throughout a state, juvenile justice administration varies with urban, suburban, and rural context and produces justice by geography. Lawyers appear more frequently in urban courts than in more informal rural courts. In turn, more formal urban courts hold more youths in pretrial detention and sentence them more severely. Finally, a lawyer's presence is an aggravating factor at disposition; judges sentence youths more severely when they are represented than when they are not (Feld 1991; Burruss and Kempf-Leonard 2002; Feld and Schaefer 2010*a*).

*a. Counsel in Juvenile Courts.*   When the US Supreme Court decided *Gault*, lawyers appeared in fewer than 5 percent of delinquency cases, in part because judges actively discouraged juveniles from retaining counsel and because courts' informality prevented lawyers from playing an advocate's role. Studies in the 1970s and 1980s reported that many judges did not advise juveniles and most did not appoint counsel (Feld 1989, 1993). Research in Minnesota in the mid-1980s showed that most youths appeared without counsel; rates of representation varied widely among urban, suburban, and rural counties; and one-third of youths whom judges removed from home and one-quarter of those in institutions were unrepresented (Feld 1991). A decade later, about one-quarter of juveniles removed from home remained unrepresented despite law reforms meant to eliminate the practice (Feld and Schaefer 2010*a*, 2010*b*). A study of legal representation in six states reported that only three appointed counsel for a substantial majority of juveniles (Feld 1988*a*). Studies in the 1990s described juvenile court judges' continuing failure to appoint lawyers. In 1995, the US General Accounting Office confirmed that rates of representation varied widely among and within states and that judges tried and sentenced many unrepresented youths. Since the late 1990s, the American Bar Association and the National Juvenile Defender Center (2017) have conducted more than 20 state-by-state assessments; they report that many, if not most, juveniles appear without counsel and that lawyers who represent youths encounter structural impediments to effective advocacy, including heavy caseloads, inadequate resources, and lack of training.

*b. Waivers.*   Several factors account for why so many youths appear in juvenile courts without counsel. Public defender services may be less available or nonexistent in nonurban areas. Judges may give cursory notice of the right to counsel, imply that waivers are just legal technicalities, and be quick to conclude a waiver has been made. If judges expect to impose noncustodial sentences, they may dispense with counsel. Some jurisdictions charge fees to determine a youth's eligibility for a public defender and others base youths' eligibility on their parents' income. Parents may be reluctant to retain or accept an attorney if, as in many states, they may have to reimburse attorney fees if they can afford them (Feld 1999; National Research Council 2013).

The most common explanation for why 50–90 percent of juveniles in many states are unrepresented is that they waive counsel. Judges in most states use the adult standard to gauge juveniles' waivers of counsel and consider the same factors as those for *Miranda* waivers. Many juveniles do not understand their rights or the role of lawyers and waive counsel without consulting a parent or an attorney. Although judges are supposed to conduct a dialogue to determine whether a child can understand rights and represent her- or himself, they frequently fail to give any counsel advisory, often neglect to create a record, and readily accept waivers from manifestly incompetent children. Judges who provide notice often seek waivers to ease their administrative burdens (Feld 1993; Berkheiser 2002; Drizin and Luloff 2007).

*c. Pleas without Bargains.*   Like adult criminal defendants, nearly all delinquents plead guilty. Even though that is the most critical decision a delinquent makes, states use adult standards to evaluate their pleas. Judges and lawyers often speak with juveniles in complicated legal language and fail to explain long-term consequences. A valid guilty plea requires a judge to conduct a colloquy on the record in which an offender admits the facts, acknowledges the rights being relinquished, and demonstrates that she or he understands the charges and potential consequences. Because appellate courts seldom review juveniles' waivers of counsel, pleas made without counsel receive even less judicial scrutiny. Guilty pleas by factually innocent youths occur because attorneys often fail to investigate cases, assume their clients' guilt especially if they have confessed, and avoid adversarial litigation, discovery requests, and pretrial motions that conflict with juvenile courts' ideology of cooperation. Juveniles' emphasis on short-term over long-term consequences and dependence on adult authority figures increase their likelihood of entering false guilty pleas (Singleton 2007; National Research Council 2013).

*d. Counsel as an Aggravating Factor.* Historically, juvenile court judges discouraged adversarial litigants and impeded effective advocacy. Lawyers in juvenile courts may put their clients at a disadvantage when judges sentence them. Research that controls for legal variables—the current offense, prior record, pretrial detention, and the like—consistently reports that represented youths were more likely to be removed from home and incarcerated than unrepresented youths. Law reforms to improve delivery of legal services increased the aggravating effects of representation on dispositions (Feld 1989; Feld and Schaefer 2010a, 2010b).

Several factors contribute to lawyers' negative effects at disposition. Juveniles may not believe lawyers' assurances about confidential communications and withhold important information. Lawyers assigned to juvenile court may be incompetent or make insufficient effort. Public defender offices often send their least capable or newest attorneys to juvenile court to gain trial experience. Lack of adequate funding may preclude investigations that increase the risk of wrongful convictions. Defense attorneys seldom investigate cases or interview their clients prior to trial because of heavy caseloads and limited organizational support. Court-appointed lawyers may place a greater premium on maintaining good relations with judges than on vigorously defending their ever-changing clients. Most significantly, many defense attorneys work under conditions that create structural impediments to quality representation: crushing caseloads, meager compensation, scant support services, inexperienced attorneys, and inadequate supervision (Drizin and Luloff 2007; National Research Council 2013; National Juvenile Defender Center 2017).

Another explanation is that, in most states, the same judge presides at a youth's arraignment, detention hearing, adjudication, and disposition and may appoint counsel if she anticipates a more severe sentence. The US Supreme Court in *Scott v. Illinois*, 440 U.S. 367, 373–74 (1979), prohibited "incarceration without representation" and limited indigent adult misdemeanants' right to appointed counsel to cases in which judges ordered defendants' actual confinement. Finally, judges may sentence delinquents with counsel more severely because the lawyer's presence insulates them from appellate reversal. Juvenile court judges may also effectively penalize youths whose lawyers invoke formal procedures, disrupt routine procedures, or question their discretion in parallel to the adult defendant's trial penalty: those who demand a jury trial receive harsher sentences.

   *e. Appellate Review.*   *Gault* rejected an argument calling for juveniles' constitutional right to appellate review because it did not find that such a right existed for criminal defendants. However, states invariably provide adult defendants with a statutory right to appellate review. By avoiding the constitutional issue, the Court undermined the other rights that it granted delinquents because the only way to enforce them is to use rigorous appellate review (Manfredi 1998). Regardless of how poorly lawyers perform, appellate courts seldom can correct juvenile courts' errors. Juvenile defenders appeal adverse decisions far less frequently than do adults' lawyers and often lack a record on which to base challenges (Harris 1994; Berkheiser 2002). Juvenile court culture may also discourage appeals as an impediment to a youth assuming responsibility.

   Despite the procedural and punitive convergence of juvenile and criminal courts, states do not provide juveniles with additional safeguards, such as mandatory nonwaivable appointment of counsel or prewaiver consultation with a lawyer, to protect them from their own immaturity. Instead, they use adult legal standards that most youths are unlikely to meet. A justice system that recognizes youths' developmental limitations would provide, at a minimum, no waivers of counsel without prior consultation with counsel. A rule that requires mandatory appointment of or consultation with counsel would impose substantial costs in most states. But after *Gault*, all juveniles are entitled to appointed counsel; waiver doctrines to relieve states' fiscal or administrative burdens are scant justifications for denial of fundamental rights. High rates of waiver undermine the legitimacy of juvenile justice because assistance of counsel is the prerequisite to exercise of other rights (Guggenheim and Hertz 1998; Drizin and Luloff 2007). The direct consequences of delinquency convictions, institutional confinement, and use of prior convictions to sentence recidivists more harshly, to waive youths to criminal court, and to enhance criminal sentences make assistance of counsel imperative. Lawyers can represent delinquents effectively only if they have adequate support and resources and specialized training to represent children.

4. *Jury Trial*. States treat juveniles like adults when formal equality produces practical inequality. Conversely, they use juvenile court procedures that provide less effective protection when called on to provide delinquents with adult safeguards. *Duncan v. Louisiana*, 391 U.S. 145 (1968), gave adult defendants the right to a jury trial to assure accurate fact-finding and to prevent governmental oppression. By contrast, *McKeiver v. Pennsylvania*, 403 U.S. 528 (1971), denied delinquents protections deemed fundamental to criminal trials. The presence of lay jurors functions as a check on the state, provides protection against vindictive prosecutors or biased judges, upholds the criminal law standard of proof, and enhances transparency and accountability. *McKeiver* insisted, however, that delinquency proceedings were not criminal prosecutions despite their manifold criminal aspects.

A few states give juveniles a right to a jury trial as a matter of state law, but the vast majority do not (Feld 2003). During the get-tough era states revised their juvenile codes' purposes clauses, opened delinquency trials to the public, imposed collateral consequences for delinquency convictions, and eroded the rationale for fewer procedural safeguards in juvenile proceedings (Feld 1988*b*, 1998). Despite the explicit shift from treatment to punishment, most state courts continue to deny juveniles a jury.

Constitutional procedural protections serve dual functions: they assure accurate fact-finding and protect against governmental oppression. *McKeiver*'s denial of a jury to juveniles fails on both counts. First, judges and juries find facts differently, and when they differ, judges are more likely to convict than are lay people. Second, punitive changes increase the need to protect delinquents from direct and collateral consequences of convictions.

*a. Accurate Fact-Finding.* *In re Winship*, 397 U.S. 358 (1970), held that the seriousness of proceedings and the consequences for a defendant, whether juvenile or adult, required proof beyond a reasonable doubt. *McKeiver*'s rejection of jury trials undermines factual accuracy and increases the likelihood that outcomes will differ in delinquency and criminal trials. Juries and judges agree about defendants' guilt or innocence in about four-fifths of criminal cases, but when they differ, juries acquit more often than judges do (Kalven and Zeisel 1966; Greenwood et al. 1983).

Fact-finding by judges and juries differs because juvenile court judges may preside over hundreds of cases a year while a juror may participate in only one or two cases in a lifetime. Several factors contribute to jurors' greater propensity to acquit. Judges hear many cases, and they may become less meticulous than jurors when they weigh evidence and apply the reasonable doubt standard less stringently. Judges hear testimony from police and probation officers on a recurring basis and form settled opinions about their credibility. Similarly, judges may have opinions about a youth's credibility, character, or the case based on prior contacts from hearing earlier charges or presiding at a detention hearing (Guggenheim and Hertz 1998).

Delinquency proceedings' informality compounds differences between judge and jury. Judges in criminal cases instruct jurors about the applicable law. By contrast, a judge in a bench trial does not state the law; this makes it more difficult for an appellate court to determine whether she correctly understood or applied it. *Ballew v. Georgia*, 435 U.S. 223 (1978), recognized the superiority of group decision making over individual judgments: some group members remember facts that others forget, and deliberations air competing views and promote more accurate decisions. By contrast, judges administer the courtroom, make evidentiary rulings, take notes, and conduct sidebars with lawyers, all of which may divert their attention during proceedings.

The informality of juvenile proceedings compounds the differences between judges' and juries' approaches toward reasonable doubt. When a judge presides at a detention hearing, he or she receives information about the youth's offense, criminal history, and social background that may contaminate impartial fact-finding. Earlier exposure to non-guilt-related evidence increases the likelihood that a judge subsequently will convict and institutionalize the defendant. In bench trials, judges typically conduct suppression hearings immediately before or during trial, a practice that exposes them to inadmissible evidence and prejudicial information (Feld 1984). A judge may know about a youth's prior delinquency from presiding at a detention hearing, prior adjudication, or trial of co-offenders. The presumption that exposure to inadmissible evidence will not affect a judge is especially problematic when the same judge handles a youth's case at several different stages. An adult defendant can avoid these risks by opting for a jury trial, but delinquents have no way to avoid the cumulative risks of prejudice in a bench trial. Critics of juvenile courts' fact-finding conclude that "judges often convict on evidence so scant that only the most closed-minded or misguided juror could think the evidence satisfied the standard of proof beyond a reasonable doubt" (Guggenheim and Hertz 1998, p. 564). As a result, states adjudicate delinquents in cases in which adequate procedural safeguards would preclude convictions. The questionable reliability of some delinquency convictions raises questions about their later use to enhance criminal sentences and impose collateral consequences.

*b. Preventing Governmental Oppression.* *McKeiver* uncritically assumed that juvenile courts treated delinquents rather than punished them. But the Court did not analyze distinctive indicia of treatment or punishment for juveniles when it denied delinquents a right to a jury trial.

The Court long has recognized that juries serve a special role to prevent governmental oppression and protect citizens. In our system of checks and balances, lay citizen jurors represent the ultimate restraint on abuses of governmental power. *Duncan v. Louisiana*, 391 U.S. 145 (1968), decided 3 years before *McKeiver*, emphasized that juries inject community values into the law, increase the visibility of justice administration, and check abuses by prosecutors and judges. The next year, *Baldwin v. New York*, 399 U.S. 66 (1969), again emphasized the jury's role to prevent government oppression by interposing lay citizens between the state and the defendant. *Baldwin* is especially critical for juvenile justice because an adult charged with any offense that carries a potential sentence of confinement of 6 months or longer has a right to a jury trial. Most delinquency dispositions can continue for the duration of minority or a term of years and greatly exceed *Baldwin*'s 6-month line.

The Court in *McKeiver* feared that granting delinquents jury trials would also lead to public trials. However, as a result of changes in the 1980s and 1990s to increase the visibility, accountability, and punishment powers of juvenile courts, about half the states authorized public access to all delinquency proceedings or to felony prosecutions (Torbet et al. 1996). States limited confidentiality protections in order to hold youths accountable and put the public on notice of who poses risks to the community (National Research Council 2013, p. 81).

Youths have challenged *McKeiver*'s half-century-old rationale. Most state appellate courts have rejected their claims with deeply flawed, uncritical analyses that conflate treatment with punishment (Gardner 2012). Few courts analyze purpose clauses, sentencing statutes, judicial sentencing practices, and conditions of confinement to distinguish treatment from punishment. States rejected juveniles' challenges by emphasizing differences in the severity of penalties imposed on delinquents and adult criminal defendants. However, once a penalty crosses *Baldwin*'s 6-month authorized sentence threshold, further severity is irrelevant. By contrast, the Kansas Supreme Court in *In re L.M.*, 186 P.3d 164 (Kan. 2008), concluded that changes eroded the benevolent *parens patriae* character of juvenile courts and transformed it into a system for prosecuting juveniles charged with committing crimes.

    *c. Delinquency Adjudications to Enhance Criminal Sentences.   Apprendi v. New Jersey*, 530 U.S. 466, 490 (2000), ruled that "any fact that increases the penalty for a crime beyond the statutory maximum, other than the fact of a prior conviction, must be submitted to a jury and proved beyond a reasonable doubt." The Court exempted the "fact of a prior conviction" because criminal defendants enjoyed the right to a jury trial and proof beyond a reasonable doubt, which assured reliability of prior convictions. *Apprendi* emphasized the jury's role to uphold *Winship*'s standard of proof beyond a reasonable doubt.

    Juvenile courts historically restricted access to records to avoid stigmatizing youths. But criminal courts need to know which juveniles' delinquent careers continue into adulthood in order to incapacitate them, punish them, or protect public safety (Feld 1999; Jacobs 2014). Historically, criminal courts lacked access to delinquency records because of juvenile courts' confidentiality, sealing or expungement of records, and the difficulty of maintaining systems to track offenders and compile histories across both systems. Despite a tradition of confidentiality, states have long allowed use of some delinquency convictions on a discretionary basis. Most state and federal sentencing guidelines include some delinquency convictions in defendants' criminal history scores, although they vary in how they weight delinquency convictions.

    As a matter of policy, states should not equate delinquency adjudications and criminal convictions for sentence enhancements. Juveniles may cause the same physical injuries or property losses as older actors, but their reduced culpability makes their crimes less blameworthy. Moreover, prior convictions' use to enhance criminal sentences raises questions about the procedures used to obtain those convictions. Juvenile courts in many states adjudicate half or more delinquents without counsel. The vast majority of states deny juveniles the right to a jury trial. Because some juvenile judges may apply *Winship*'s reasonable doubt standard less stringently, more youths are convicted than would be if there were adequate safeguards.

Federal circuits are divided about the question of whether *Apprendi* allows judges to use delinquency convictions to enhance criminal sentences (Feld 2003). State appellate court rulings reflect the federal split of opinion. Until the US Supreme Court clarifies *Apprendi*, defendants in some states or federal circuits will serve longer sentences than those in other jurisdictions on the basis of flawed delinquency adjudications.

The use of delinquency convictions to enhance criminal sentences further aggravates endemic racial disparities. At each stage of the juvenile justice system, racial disparities compound, cumulate, create more extensive delinquency records, and contribute to disproportionate minority confinement. Richard Frase (2009, p. 265) analyzed racial disparities in criminal sentencing in Minnesota and concluded that "seemingly legitimate sentencing factors such as criminal history scoring can have strong disparate impacts on nonwhite defendants."

*d. Collateral Consequences.* Extensive collateral consequences follow from delinquency convictions. Although state policies vary, collateral consequences may follow youths for decades and affect future housing, education, and employment opportunities. States may enter juveniles' fingerprints, photographs, and DNA into databases accessible to law enforcement and other agencies (Feld 2013*b*). Some get-tough reforms opened delinquency trials and records to the public. Media reports on the internet create a permanent and easily accessed record. Criminal justice agencies, schools, child care providers, the military, and others have access to juvenile records automatically or by petition (Jacobs 2014). Expungement of delinquency records is not automatic and requires court proceedings. Delinquency convictions may affect youths' ability to obtain professional licensure, receive government aid, join the military, obtain or keep legal immigration status, or live in public housing (National Research Council 2013; Nellis 2016).

*e. Sex Offender Registration.* Juvenile sex offenders face among the most onerous collateral consequences. Federal sex offender registration and notification laws require states to implement registration and notification standards for individuals convicted as adults or juveniles for certain sex offenses. Some states require lifetime registration; limit where registered offenders can live, work, or attend school; and require neighborhood notification (Zimring 2004; Caldwell 2014; Nellis 2016).

## II. Youths in Criminal Court

During the 1980s and 1990s, lawmakers changed the theory and practice of transfer of youths to adult courts. Each state uses one or more, often overlapping, transfer strategies: judicial waiver, legislative offense exclusion, and prosecutorial direct file (Snyder and Sickmund 2006). Some states' juvenile court jurisdiction ends at age 15 or 16, rather than at 17, which results in about 200,000 chronological juveniles being tried annually in criminal courts. In addition, states transfer another 50,000 youths via judicial waiver (7,500), prosecutorial direct filing in adult courts (27,000), and the remainder with prosecutor-determined excluded offenses (Feld and Bishop 2012). We lack precise numbers because states collect data only on the small number of judicial transfers.

Criminal court judges sentence convicted youths similarly to other adult defendants. Prior to *Roper v. Simmons*, 543 U.S. 551 (2005), *Graham v. Florida*, 130 S. Ct. 2011 (2010), and *Miller v. Alabama*, 132 S. Ct. 2455 (2012), states executed people who committed offenses as youths and sentenced youths to mandatory sentences of life without parole (LWOP). Although the US Supreme Court has rejected the most draconian sentences because of youths' diminished responsibility, states have made only minimal sentencing modifications to acknowledge or implement their reduced culpability and comply with the Court's decisions.

### A. Transfer to Criminal Court

During the get-tough era, legislators shifted control of transfer decisions from judges to prosecutors in order to avoid judges' relative insulation from political pressures. Laws lowered the age for transfer, increased the numbers of "excluded offenses" triable only in adult courts, and strengthened prosecutors' charging powers. Despite the widespread prevalence of judicial waiver statutes, excluded offenses and prosecutors' charging decisions determine the adult status of 85 percent of youths (Juszkiewicz 2000; Amnesty International and Human Rights Watch 2005).

The vast majority of states have judicial waiver laws that specify the ages and offenses for which a judge may conduct a transfer hearing. *Kent v. United States*, 383 U.S. 541 (1966), required judges to hold a procedurally fair hearing including a right to counsel, access to probation reports, and written findings for appellate review, because the loss of juveniles' access to treatment, confidentiality, limited collateral consequences, and the like is a critical action. *Breed v. Jones*, 421 U.S. 519 (1975), applied the Fifth Amendment double jeopardy prohibition to delinquency adjudications and required states to decide whether to prosecute a youth in juvenile or criminal court before proceeding to trial. *Kent* appended a list of criteria for judges to consider, and state courts and statutes incorporated those criteria. Judges have broad discretion to interpret those factors. Studies of judicial waiver document inconsistent rulings, justice by geography, and racial disparities. Judges transfer minority youths more often than white youths especially for violent and drug crimes. In the 75 largest counties in the United States, members of racial minorities constituted more than two-thirds of juveniles tried in criminal courts and the vast majority of those who were sentenced to prison (Poe-Yamagata and Jones 2000; National Research Council and Institute of Medicine 2001).

Some states set their juvenile courts' upper age jurisdiction at 15 or 16 years rather than 17, which results in the largest numbers of youths being tried as adults. In addition, a number of states exclude youths 16 or older charged with murder from juvenile court jurisdiction, and others exclude more extensive lists of offenses. In the 1980s and 1990s, states expanded the lists of offenses excluded to include various crimes against the person, property, drugs, and weapons offenses, to evade *Kent*'s hearing requirement (Feld 2000*b*). Appellate courts uniformly reject youths' claims that prosecuting them for excluded offenses violates the Constitution (Feld and Bishop 2012).

In more than a dozen states, juvenile and criminal courts share concurrent jurisdiction over some ages and offenses, usually older youths and serious crimes, and prosecutors decide where to charge a youth. Appellate courts rely on the doctrine of "separation of powers" and decline to review prosecutors' exercises of executive discretion except under manifestly discriminatory circumstances.

Most direct-file laws provide no criteria to guide prosecutors' choice of forum. Prosecutors lack access to personal, social, or clinical information about a youth that a judge would consider and base their decisions primarily on police reports. Locally elected prosecutors exploit crime issues like get-tough legislators, introduce justice by geography and racial disparities, and exercise their discretion as subjectively as do judges but without being subject to appellate review. Through their charging decisions, prosecutors act as gatekeepers to the juvenile justice system, a role previously reserved for judges (Feld and Bishop 2012; National Research Council 2013).

"Blended sentences," another punitive innovation of the 1990s, provide judges with juvenile and criminal sentencing options. Because juve-

nile courts' jurisdiction ends when youths reach specific ages, judges may
be unable to sentence older offenders convicted of serious crimes appropriately. States increase judges' sentencing powers by allowing juvenile
courts to impose extended delinquency sentences with a stayed criminal
sentence or by giving criminal courts authority to use a delinquency disposition in lieu of imprisonment. Regardless of approach, blended sentencing laws require criminal procedural safeguards, including the right to a
jury trial, to preserve a judge's power to punish. Although states adopted
blended sentences as an alternative to transfer, they had a net-widening
effect. Judges imposed blended sentences on younger, less serious, offenders whom they previously handled as delinquents, subsequently revoked
their probation primarily for technical violations, and doubled the number of youths sent to prison. Prosecutors used the threat of transfer to
coerce youths to plead guilty to obtain a blended sentence, to waive procedural rights, to increase punishment in juvenile courts, and to risk exposure to criminal sanctions (Podkopacz and Feld 2001; Feld and Bishop
2012).

1. *Juveniles in Prison.*  Criminal court judges sentence transferred
youths like adults, which increases their likelihood of subsequent offending. While all inmates potentially face abuse, adolescents' size, physical
strength, lesser social skills, and lack of sophistication increase their risks
of physical, sexual, and psychological victimization. To prevent victimization, some states place vulnerable youths in solitary confinement for
23 hours a day. Prisons are developmentally inappropriate places for youths
to form an identity, acquire social skills, or make a successful transition
to adulthood. Imprisoning them exacts different and greater developmental opportunity costs than are experienced by adults. It disrupts normal development, including completing education, finding a job, forming relationships, and creating social bonds that promote desistance. That
lost ground may never be regained (Mulvey and Schubert 2012; National
Research Council 2013; Deitch and Arya 2014).

2. *Policy Justifications for Waiver.*  States prosecute some youths in
criminal courts as a matter of public safety and political reality. Laws enacted during the get-tough era targeted violent and drug crimes and increased the likelihood and severity of criminal sentences (Zimring 2013).
Judges incarcerate transferred youths more often and for longer sentences
than youths retained in juvenile courts. Although three-quarters of youths
convicted of violent felonies are sent to prison, overall nearly half of all
transferred youths are not convicted or placed on probation, fewer than

25 percent are sentenced to prison, and 95 percent are released from custody by their 25th birthday (Schubert et al. 2010; Deitch and Arya 2014).

Although legislators assumed that the threats of transfer and criminal
punishment would deter youths, studies of juvenile crime rates before
and after passage of legal changes have found no general deterrent effect
(Steiner, Hemmens, and Bell 2006; Steiner and Wright 2006; National
Research Council 2013). Studies of special deterrence report that transferred youths have higher recidivism rates than do those sentenced as
delinquents (Fagan, Kupchik, and Lieberman 2003; Redding 2008). Comparisons of youths transferred to criminal courts with those who remained
in juvenile courts conclude that youths tried as adults have higher and
faster recidivism rates, especially for violent crimes, than do their delinquent counterparts (Centers for Disease Control 2007; National Research
Council 2013).

Although judges do not imprison all transferred youths, they sometimes treat youthfulness as an aggravating rather than a mitigating factor. Comparatively more youths convicted of murder received LWOP
sentences than did adults (Steiner 2009; Feld 2017). Compared with young
adult offenders, judicially waived juveniles convicted of the same crimes
received longer sentences (Kurlychek and Johnson 2004, 2010; Snyder
and Sickmund 2006).

Punitive transfer laws targeted violent crimes that black youths commit more often. Even prior to enactment of the get-tough measures,
studies reported racial disparities in judicial transfer decisions. Subsequently, judges transferred youths of color to adult courts more often
than white youths charged with similar violent and drug crimes (Feld 1998;
Poe-Yamagata and Jones 2000). The vast majority of juveniles transferred to criminal courts and sentenced to prison are youths of color,
primarily blacks (National Research Council and Institute of Medicine
2001).

3. *What Should a Rational Legislature Do?* Expansive transfer policies
generally fail to achieve their publicly stated goals. Equating younger
and older offenders ignores developmental differences and disproportionately punishes less blameworthy adolescents. Transfer does not deter youths because their immature judgment, short-term time perspective, and preference for immediate gains lessen the threat of sanctions.
Youths tried as adults reoffend more quickly and more seriously, thereby increasing the risk to public safety and negating any short-term crime
reduction.

The vast majority of juvenile justice scholars agree that if some youths must be transferred, then it should occur in a judicial waiver process and happen rarely (e.g., Zimring 1998; Fagan 2008; Scott and Steinberg 2008; Feld 2017). States should waive only those youths whose serious and persistent offenses require minimum lengths of confinement that greatly exceed the maximum sanctions available in juvenile court. A retributive policy would limit severe sanctions to youths charged with homicide, rape, robbery, or assault with a firearm or substantial injury. However, severely punishing all youths who commit serious crimes would be counterproductive because youths arrested for an initial violent offense desist at rates similar to those of other delinquents. Chronic offenders may require sentences longer than those available in juvenile court because of persistent criminality and exhaustion of juvenile court resources.

The legislature should prescribe a minimum age of eligibility for criminal prosecution. As the next section explains, the US Supreme Court relied on developmental psychological and neuroscience research that reports a sharp drop-off in judgment, self-control, and appreciation of consequences as well as in competence to exercise procedural rights for youths 15 or younger. The minimum age for transfer should be 16.

A juvenile court hearing guided by offense criteria and clinical considerations and subject to rigorous appellate review is the only sensible way to make transfer decisions. Criteria should focus on offenses, prior record, criminal participation, clinical evaluations, and aggravating and mitigating factors that, taken together, distinguish the few youths who deserve sentences substantially longer than juvenile courts can impose from the vast majority of those who do not. Appellate courts should closely review waiver decisions and develop substantive principles to define a consistent boundary of adulthood. Although waiver hearings are less efficient than prosecutors' charging decisions, it should be difficult to transfer youths. Juvenile courts after all exist to keep youths out of the criminal justice system. An adversarial hearing at which prosecution and defense present evidence about offense, culpability, and treatment prognoses will produce better decisions than will politically motivated prosecutors acting without clinical information (Zimring 1998; Feld 1999; Bishop 2004; Scott and Steinberg 2008).

## B. Sentencing Youths as Adults

The US Supreme Court developed its jurisprudence of youth—"children are different"—in response to get-tough era laws that ignored adolescents' reduced culpability. In a trilogy of cases beginning in 2005, the Court applied the Eighth Amendment prohibition on cruel and unusual punishment to juveniles. *Roper v. Simmons*, 543 U.S. 551 (2005), prohibited states from executing offenders for murder committed prior to 18 years of age. *Graham v. Florida*, 130 S. Ct. 2011 (2010), extended *Roper*'s diminished responsibility rationale and prohibited states from imposing LWOP sentences for nonhomicide offenses and repudiated the Court's doctrine that "death is different." *Miller v. Alabama*, 132 S. Ct. 2455 (2012), extended *Roper* and *Graham*'s diminished responsibility rationale and barred mandatory LWOP sentences for youths convicted of murder and required judges to make individualized culpability assessments.

States annually try upward of 200,000 chronological juveniles as adults. Fallacious predictions of an impending bloodbath by super-predators propelled punitive policies (Bennett, DiIulio, and Walters 1996; Zimring 1998, 2013). States lowered the age for transfer, increased the number of excluded offenses, and shifted discretion from judges to prosecutors. Get-tough transfer laws exacerbated racial disparities. Racial stereotypes taint culpability assessments and reduce youthfulness's mitigating role (Bridges and Steen 1998; Graham and Lowery 2004; Moriearty 2011). Children of color make up the majority of juveniles tried in criminal court and three-quarters of those who enter prison. For adults, states lengthened criminal sentences, adopted mandatory minimums, and imposed mandatory life without parole for homicide and other crimes (Tonry 1996, 2011). Most states' criminal sentencing laws apply equally to juveniles tried as adults in criminal courts, and judges sentence youths to the same prisons.

1. *Capital Punishment for Juveniles.* The Eighth Amendment prohibits states from inflicting cruel and unusual punishments. Prior to *Roper v. Simmons*, the Supreme Court thrice considered whether it prohibited states from executing juveniles convicted of murder. In 1989, *Stanford v. Kentucky*, 492 U.S. 361 (1989), upheld the death penalty for people aged 16 and 17 convicted of murder and allowed juries to assess their personal culpability. In 2005, *Roper* overruled *Stanford* and prohibited states from executing youths for crimes committed prior to age 18.

*Roper* gave three reasons. First, juveniles' immature judgment and limited self-control sometimes cause them to act impulsively and without adequate appreciation of consequences. Second, their susceptibility to negative peer influences and inability to escape criminogenic environments reduce their responsibility. Third, their not fully developed personalities provide less reliable evidence of blameworthiness. Because juveniles' character is transitional, the Court concluded that a great likelihood exists that they can reform. Youths' diminished responsibility undermined retributive justifications for the death penalty. Similarly, the Court concluded that impulsiveness and limited self-control weakened any deterrent effect. *Roper* imposed a categorical ban rather than allowing juries to evaluate youths' culpability individually because the "unacceptable likelihood exists that the brutality or cold-blooded nature of any particular crime would overpower mitigating arguments based on youth as a matter of course, even where the juvenile offender's objective immaturity, vulnerability, and lack of true depravity should require a sentence less severe than death" (pp. 572–73). Because the emotional effects of a brutal murder could overwhelm the mitigating role of youthfulness, *Roper* used age as a categorical proxy for reduced culpability.

*Roper*, and subsequently *Graham* and *Miller*, analyzed youths' reduced culpability within a retributive sentencing framework of proportionality and deserved punishment. Retributive sentencing apportions punishment to a crime's seriousness based on the harm and culpability involved and affects how much punishment an actor deserves. An offender's age has no bearing on the harm caused; children and adults can cause the same injuries. But proportionality requires consideration of an offender's culpability, and immaturity reduces blameworthiness. Youths' inability to fully appreciate wrongfulness or control themselves lessens, but does not excuse, responsibility for causing harms. They may have the minimum capacity to be criminally liable and the ability to distinguish right from wrong but deserve less punishment (Scott and Steinberg 2008).

In response to punitive changes affecting juveniles, in 1995, the John D. and Catherine T. MacArthur Foundation established the Adolescent Development and Juvenile Justice Research Network. Over the following decade, the network conducted research on adolescent decision making, judgment, and adjudicative competence. The research distinguishes between cognitive abilities and judgment and self-control, controlled thinking versus impulsive behaving (Steinberg 2008, 2010, 2014; Monahan, Steinberg, and Piquero 2015).

Youths differ from adults in risk perception, appreciation of consequences, impulsivity and self-control, sensation seeking, and compliance with peers. The regions of the brain that control reward seeking and emotional arousal develop earlier than do those that regulate executive functions and impulse control. Adolescents underestimate the amount and likelihood of risks, focus on anticipated gains rather than possible losses, and consider fewer options. They weigh costs and benefits differently, apply dissimilar subjective values to outcomes, and more heavily discount negative future consequences than more immediate rewards. They have less experience and knowledge to inform decisions about consequences. They prefer an immediate, albeit smaller, reward than do adults who can better delay gratification. In a risk-benefit calculus, youths may view not engaging in risky behaviors differently than adults. Researchers attribute youths' impetuous decisions to a heightened appetite for emotional arousal and intense experiences, which peaks around age 16 or 17 (National Research Council and Institute of Medicine 2011; National Research Council 2013).

2. *Neuroscience and Adolescent Brain Development.* Neuroscientists report that the human brain continues to mature until the early to mid-20s. Adolescents on average do not have adults' neurobiological capacity to exercise mature judgment or control impulses. The relationship between two brain regions, the prefrontal cortex (PFC) and the limbic system, underlies youths' propensity for risky behavior. The PFC is responsible for judgment and impulse control. The amygdala and limbic system regulate emotional arousal and reward-seeking behavior. The PFC performs executive functions such as reasoning, planning, and impulse control. These top-down capabilities develop gradually and enable individuals to exercise greater self-control (Casey, Giedd, and Thomas 2000; Spear 2010; National Research Council and Institute of Medicine 2011).

During adolescence, two processes, myelination and synaptic pruning, enhance the PFC's functions. Myelin is a white fatty substance that forms a sheath around neural axons, facilitates more efficient neurotransmission, and makes communication between different brain regions faster and more reliable. Synaptic pruning involves selective elimination of unused neural connections, promotes greater efficiency, speeds neural signals, and strengthens the brain's ability to process information (National Research Council and Institute of Medicine 2011; Steinberg 2014).

The limbic system controls emotions, reward seeking, and instinctual behavior, expressed in the fight-or-flight response. The PFC and limbic systems mature at different rates, and adolescents rely more heavily on the limbic system involving bottom-up emotional processing rather than on the top-down cognitive regulatory system (Feld, Casey, and Hurd

2013). The developmental lag between the PFC regulatory system and the reward- and pleasure-seeking limbic system contributes to impetuous behavior driven more by emotions than by reason. The imbalance between the impulse-control and reward-seeking systems contributes to youths' poor judgment, impetuous behavior, and criminal involvement (Spear 2010; National Research Council and Institute of Medicine 2011).

*Roper* attributed juveniles' diminished responsibility to greater susceptibility to peer influences. As their orientation shifts toward peers, youths' quest for acceptance and affiliation makes them more susceptible to influence than they will be as adults. Peers increase youths' propensity to take risks because their presence stimulates the brain's reward centers (Spear 2010; National Research Council and Institute of Medicine 2011).

Neuroscience research bolsters social scientists' observations about adolescents' impulsive behavior and impaired self-control. Despite impressive advances, neuroscientists have not established a direct link between brain maturation and behavior or found ways to individualize assessments of developmental differences (Morse 2006; Maroney 2009, 2011; Steinberg 2014).

3. Graham v. Florida: *LWOP for Nonhomicide Juvenile Offenders.* Prior to *Graham v. Florida*, 130 S. Ct. 2011 (2010), the Supreme Court asserted that "death is different." *Graham* extended *Roper*'s diminished responsibility rationale to nonhomicide offenders who received LWOP sentences. *Graham* raised "a categorical challenge to a term of years sentence"—an LWOP sentence applied to the category of juveniles (pp. 2022–23). *Graham* repudiated the court's "death is different" distinction, extended *Roper*'s reduced culpability rationale to term-of-year sentences, and "declare[d] an entire class of offenders immune from a noncapital sentence" (p. 2046). *Graham* rested on three features—offender characteristics, offenses, and sentences. It reiterated *Roper*'s rationale that juveniles' reduced culpability warranted less severe penalties than those imposed on adults convicted of the same crime. Unlike *Roper*, *Graham* explicitly based young offenders' diminished responsibility on developmental and neuroscience research (Monahan, Steinberg, and Piquero 2015).

Focusing on the offense, *Graham* invoked the court's felony-murder death-penalty decisions and concluded that even the most serious nonhomicide crimes "cannot be compared to murder in their 'severity and irrevocability'" (p. 2027). The combination of diminished responsibility and a nonhomicide crime made an LWOP sentence grossly disproportionate.

Finally, the Court equated an LWOP sentence for a juvenile with the death penalty. *Graham* found that no penal rationale—retribution, deterrence, incapacitation, or rehabilitation—justified the penultimate sanction for nonhomicide juvenile offenders. While incapacitation might reduce future offending, judges could not reliably predict at sentencing whether a juvenile would pose a future danger to society.

Although *Graham* adopted a categorical rule, it required states only to provide "some meaningful opportunity to obtain release based on demonstrated maturity and rehabilitation" (p. 2030). It did not prescribe states' responsibilities to provide resources with which to change or specify when youths might become eligible for parole. Parole consideration would not guarantee young offenders' release, and some might remain confined for life. Although *Graham* barred LWOP for juveniles convicted of a nonhomicide crime, many more youths are serving de facto life sentences—aggregated mandatory minimums or consecutive terms totaling 50–100 years or more—than those formally sentenced to LWOPs. Some state courts have found that very long sentences imposed on a juvenile convicted of several nonhomicide offenses did not provide a meaningful opportunity to obtain release. Other courts read *Graham* narrowly, limit its holding to formal LWOP sentences, and uphold consecutive terms that exceed youths' life expectancy.

4. *Mandatory LWOP for Juveniles Convicted of Murder.* When the Court decided *Miller v. Alabama*, 42 states permitted judges to impose LWOP sentences on any adult or juvenile offender convicted of murder. In 29 states, LWOP sentences were mandatory for those convicted of murder, precluded consideration of actors' culpability or degree of participation, and equated juveniles' criminal responsibility with that of adults. Courts regularly upheld mandatory LWOPs and extremely long sentences imposed on children as young as 12 or 13. One of six juveniles who received an LWOP sentence was 15 or younger; for more than half, it was their first conviction. States may not execute a felony murderer who did not kill or intend to kill, but one-quarter to one-half of juveniles who received LWOP sentences were convicted as accessories to a felony murder. Although the US Supreme Court viewed youthfulness as a mitigating factor, many trial judges treated it as an aggravating factor and sentenced young murderers more severely than adults convicted of murder (Amnesty International and Human Rights Watch 2005; Human Rights Watch 2012).

*Miller v. Alabama*, 132 S. Ct. 2455 (2012), extended *Roper* and *Graham* and banned mandatory LWOPs for youths convicted of murder. *Graham* equated a nonhomicide LWOP sentence with the death penalty. *Miller* invoked death penalty cases that barred mandatory capital sentences and required an individualized culpability assessment before a judge could impose an LWOP on a juvenile murderer (e.g., *Woodson v. North Carolina*, 428 U.S. 280 [1976]). *Miller* emphasized that "children are constitutionally different from adults for purposes of sentencing" and "mandatory penalties, by their nature, preclude a sentence from taking account of an offender's age and the wealth of characteristics and circumstances attendant to it" (p. 2467). The Court asserted that once judges considered a youth's diminished responsibility individually, very few cases would warrant an LWOP.

The Court's recognition that children are different reflected a belated corrective to states' punitive excesses, but its Eighth Amendment authority to regulate their sentencing policies is very limited. *Graham* and *Miller* raised as many questions as they answered. Several years after *Miller* held mandatory LWOP unconstitutional, the court in *Montgomery v. Louisiana*, 136 S. Ct. 718 (2016), resolved lower courts' conflicting decisions about *Miller*'s retroactive application to more than 2,500 youths sentenced prior to the decision and ruled that youths who received a mandatory LWOP prior to *Miller* would be eligible for resentencing or parole consideration.

*Miller* gave lawmakers and judges minimal guidance to make culpability assessments. The numerous pertinent factors it described—age, immaturity, impetuosity, family and home environment, circumstances of and degree of participation in the offense, youthful incompetence, and amenability to treatment—effectively enabled judges' subjective discretion. State courts' interpretations and legislatures' responses to *Miller* vary substantially (Moriearty 2015; Drinan 2016).

*Miller* required 29 states to revise their mandatory LWOP statutes to provide for individualized assessments for juveniles. Some states adopted factors identified in *Miller* for judges to consider. A few abolished juvenile LWOP sentences entirely; others replaced them with minimum sentences ranging from 25 years to life with periodic reviews or determinate sentences of 40 years to life (Sentencing Project 2014; Drinan 2016). Other states provide age-tiered minimum sentences for parole consideration: 25 years for youths 14 or younger convicted of murder, 35 years for those 15 or older. None of these changes approximate the American

Law Institute's Model Penal Code's (2017) provision that all juveniles should be eligible for parole consideration after 10 years.

State courts divide over whether *Miller* applies to mandatory sentences other than murder that also preclude consideration of youthful mitigation. Several post-*Miller* courts have approved 25-year mandatory minimum sentences without any individualized culpability assessments; others have found all mandatory sentences violated their state constitutions (Moriearty 2015; Drinan 2016).

## III. Policy Prescriptions

The time is right to reform juvenile courts' jurisdiction, jurisprudence, and procedures. Although most states' juvenile court jurisdiction extends to youths under 18, North Carolina sets the boundary at 16 and 10 states set it at 17. Developmental psychology and neuroscience research strengthens the case to raise the age of jurisdiction to 18 in every state. Indeed, it would be appropriate to extend to young adults aged 18–21 some of the protections associated with juvenile courts: shorter sentences such as a youth discount, rehabilitative treatment in separate facilities, protected records, and the like. Many European countries' criminal laws provide separate young adult sentencing provisions and institutions to afford greater moderation and use of rehabilitative measures (Loeber et al. 2012, pp. 350–51).

States should formally incorporate youthfulness as a mitigating factor in all sentencing statutes. *Roper* and *Graham* adopted a categorical prohibition because the court feared that a judge or jury could not properly consider youthful mitigation when confronted with a heinous crime. There are two reasons to prefer a categorical rule. First, judges and legislators cannot define or identify what constitutes adult-like culpability. Culpability is not an objectively measurable thing, but a subjective judgment about criminal responsibility. Development is highly variable; a few youths may be responsible prior to age 18, but many others may not attain maturity even as adults. Clinicians lack tools with which to assess youths' impulsivity, foresight, and preference for risk or a metric by which to relate maturity of judgment with criminal responsibility. The inability to define, measure, or diagnose immaturity or to identify validly a few responsible youths introduces a systematic bias to overpunish less culpable juveniles. The second reason to adopt a categorical approach is judges' or juries' inability to weigh fairly the abstraction of diminished responsibility against the aggravating reality of a horrific crime. *Roper* rightly feared that jurors could not distinguish between a person's diminished responsibility for causing a harm and the harm itself, whose heinousness might trump consideration of reduced culpability. Treating youthfulness categorically is a more efficient way to address immaturity when every juvenile can claim some diminished responsibility.

The abstract meaning of culpability, the inability to measure or compare moral agency of youths, the administrative complexity of individualization, and the tendency to overweigh harm require a clear-cut alternative. A categorical "youth discount" would give all adolescents fractional reductions in sentence lengths based on age as a proxy for culpability (Feld 1997, 2008, 2013*a*, 2013*e*). While age may be an incomplete proxy for maturity or culpability, no better bases exist on which to distinguish young offenders. A statutory youth discount would require judges to give substantial reductions to youths, affording a sliding scale of diminished responsibility with the largest reductions to the youngest offenders that correspond to their greater developmental differences in judgment and self-control. The youth discount's diminished responsibility rationale would preclude mandatory, LWOP, or de facto life sentences for young offenders. States can achieve their penal goals by sentencing youths to a maximum of no more than 20 or 25 years for even the most serious crimes.

Most youths involved with the juvenile justice system will outgrow their youthful indiscretions without significant interventions. We can facilitate desistance by reinforcing the two-track system—one informal, one formal—proposed by the President's Commission on Law Enforcement and Administration of Justice (1967) a half century ago. For youths who require services, diversion to community resources provides a more efficient and flexible alternative to adjudication and disposition. If states explicitly forgo home removal, they can administer a streamlined justice system using summary processes to make noncustodial dispositions. Diversion raises its own issues because low-visibility decisions contribute to racial disparities at the front end. States can adopt formal criteria, risk assessment instruments, data collection, and ongoing monitoring to rationalize decisions and reduce disparities. Prevention programs that target at-risk youths, families, and communities have demonstrated efficacy, provide cost/benefit returns, and would reduce the number of youths referred to juvenile courts in the first instance.

For youths facing detention and confinement, juvenile courts are criminal courts and require criminal procedural safeguards including the right to a jury. Increasing protections and costs of formal adjudication provide financial and administrative incentives to divert more youths. Although delinquency sanctions are shorter than those imposed by criminal courts, it is disingenuous to claim that they do not pursue deterrent, incapacitative, and retributive goals. Apart from those youths who pose a risk of flight, states should reserve secure detention for those whose offense and prior record indicate that they likely would be removed from home if convicted. Risk assessment instruments, other strategies developed by the Annie E. Casey Foundation's Juvenile Detention Alternatives Initiative, and effective assistance of counsel could reduce pretrial detention and disproportionate minority confinement (Zimring 2014). Juvenile court interventions should keep youths in their communities, avoid out-of-home placements and secure confinement to the greatest extent possible, and use evidence-based programs to rehabilitate and reintegrate them.

The procedural safeguards of juvenile courts should be greatly enhanced to compensate for adolescents' developmental immaturity: automatic competency assessment for children younger than 14 years of age, mandatory presence of counsel during interrogation for those younger than 16, and mandatory nonwaivable counsel for youths in court proceedings. Any system of justice will fail without a robust public defender system to enable youths to exercise rights. Delinquents should enjoy the right to a jury trial to assure reliability of convictions and to increase the visibility and accountability of judges, prosecutors, and defense lawyers. States should strengthen appellate oversight of delinquency proceedings. Records of youths should be easily sealed or expunged to reduce impediments to education and employment. Collateral consequences of delinquency convictions should be eliminated.

For those few youths who should be tried as adults, a judicial hearing guided by offense criteria and clinical considerations and subject to rigorous appellate review is the only sensible way to make transfer decisions. Criteria should focus on serious offenses and extensive prior records, criminal participation, clinical evaluations, and aggravating and mitigating factors that, taken together, distinguish the few youths who might deserve sentences substantially longer than the maximum sanctions that juvenile courts can impose. Appellate courts should closely review waiver decisions and develop substantive principles to define a consistent boundary of adulthood. The legislature should prescribe a minimum age of eligibility for criminal prosecution. Developmental psychological and neuroscience research reports a sharp drop-off in judgment, self-control, and appreciation of consequences as well as in competence to exercise rights for youths 15 or younger. The minimum age for transfer should be 16. Sentences of youths convicted as adults should be substantially reduced—to reflect their diminished culpability. Once judges properly consider youths' generic developmental limitations and diminished responsibility, there would be very few youths or crimes for which prosecution as an adult would be appropriate.

It will take political courage for legislators to enact laws that recognize the diminished responsibility of serious young offenders. It will take even greater political courage when an opponent may charge a lawmaker with being "soft on crime." The get-tough era produced punitive delinquency sanctions, unjust and counterproductive waiver policies, and unduly harsh sentencing laws, all of which had a disproportionate impact on black youths and other children of color. The legislators who enacted them are obliged to undo the damage and adopt sensible policies that reflect our greater understanding of adolescent development—"children are different."

REFERENCES

Ainsworth, Janet E. 1993. "In a Different Register: The Pragmatics of Power-lessness in Police Interrogation." *Yale Law Journal* 103:259–322.
American Bar Association and Institute of Judicial Administration. 1980. *Juvenile Justice Standards Relating to Pretrial Court Proceedings.* Cambridge, MA: Ballinger.
American Law Institute. 2017. *Model Penal Code: Proposed Official Draft.* Philadelphia: American Law Institute.
American Psychiatric Association. 2013. *Diagnostic and Statistical Manual of Mental Disorders.* 5th ed. Washington, DC: American Psychiatric Association.
Amnesty International and Human Rights Watch. 2005. *The Rest of Their Lives: Life without Parole for Child Offenders in the United States.* http://www.amnestyusa.org/www.hrw.org.
Anderson, Elijah. 1999. *The Code of the Street: Decency, Violence, and the Moral Life of the Inner City.* New York: Norton.
Bartollas, Clemens, Stuart J. Miller, and Simon Dinitz. 1976. *Juvenile Victimization: The Institutional Paradox.* New York: Wiley.
Barton, William. 2012. "Detention." In *The Oxford Handbook of Juvenile Crime and Juvenile Justice,* edited by Barry C. Feld and Donna M. Bishop. New York: Oxford University Press.
Bennett, William J., John J. DiIulio, and John P. Walters. 1996. *Body Count: Moral Poverty and How to Win America's War against Crime and Drugs.* New York: Simon & Schuster.

Berkheiser, Mary. 2002. "The Fiction of Juvenile Right to Counsel: Waiver in the Juvenile Courts." *Florida Law Review* 54:577–686.

Bishop, Donna. 2004. "Injustice and Irrationality in Contemporary Youth Policy." *Criminology and Public Policy* 3:633–44.

———. 2005. "The Role of Race and Ethnicity in Juvenile Justice Process." In *Our Children, Their Children: Confronting Racial and Ethnic Differences in American Juvenile Justice*, edited by Darnell Hawkins and Kimberly Kempf-Leonard. Chicago: University of Chicago Press.

Bishop, Donna, and Michael Leiber. 2012. "Racial and Ethnic Differences in Delinquency and Justice System Responses." In *The Oxford Handbook of Juvenile Crime and Juvenile Justice*, edited by Barry C. Feld and Donna M. Bishop. New York: Oxford University Press.

Bray, Timothy, Lisa L. Sample, and Kimberly Kempf-Leonard. 2005. "Justice by Geography: Racial Disparity and Juvenile Courts." In *Our Children, Their Children: Confronting Racial and Ethnic Differences in American Juvenile Justice*, edited by Darnell Hawkins and Kimberly Kempf-Leonard. Chicago: University of Chicago Press.

Bridges, George S., and Sara Steen. 1998. "Racial Disparities in Official Assessments in Juveniles Offenders: Attributional Stereotypes as Mediating Mechanisms." *American Sociological Review* 63:554–70.

Burruss, George W., Jr., and Kimberly Kempf-Leonard. 2002. "The Questionable Advantage of Defense Counsel in Juvenile Court." *Justice Quarterly* 19:37–68.

Caldwell, Michael F. 2014. "Juvenile Sexual Offenders." In *Choosing the Future for American Juvenile Justice*, edited by Franklin E. Zimring and David S. Tanenhaus. New York: New York University Press.

Casey, B. J., Jay N. Giedd, and Kathleen M. Thomas. 2000. "Structural and Functional Brain Development and Its Relation to Cognitive Development." *Biological Psychology* 54:241–57.

Centers for Disease Control. 2007. *Effects on Violence of Laws and Policies Facilitating the Transfer of Youth from the Juvenile to the Adult Justice System.* http://www.cdc.gov.

Deitch, Michele, and Neelum Arya. 2014. "Waivers and Transfers of Juveniles to Adult Court: Treating Juveniles like Adult Criminals." In *Juvenile Justice Sourcebook*, 2nd ed., edited by Wesley T. Church II, David W. Spring, and Albert R. Roberts. New York: Oxford University Press.

Drinan, Cara H. 2016. "The Miller Revolution." *Iowa Law Review* 101:1787–1832.

Drizin, Steven A., and Richard A. Leo. 2004. "The Problem of False Confessions in the Post-DNA World." *North Carolina Law Review* 82:891–1008.

Drizin, Steven A., and Greg Luloff. 2007. "Are Juvenile Courts a Breeding Ground for Wrongful Convictions?" *Northern Kentucky Law Review* 34:275–322.

Fagan, Jeffrey A. 2000. "Contexts of Choice by Adolescents in Criminal Events." In *Youth on Trial: A Developmental Perspective on Juvenile Justice*, edited by Thomas Grisso and Robert Schwartz. Chicago: University of Chicago Press.

———. 2008. "Juvenile Crime and Criminal Justice: Resolving Border Disputes." *Future of Children* 18:81–118.

Fagan, Jeffrey, Aaron Kupchik, and Akiva Lieberman. 2003. "Be Careful What You Wish For: The Comparative Impacts of Juvenile versus Criminal Court Sanctions on Recidivism among Adolescent Felony Offenders." Working Paper no. 03-62, Columbia Law School.

Farrington, David P., and Brandon C. Welsh. 2007. *Saving Children from a Life of Crime: Early Risk Factors and Effective Interventions*. New York: Oxford University Press.

Feld, Barry C. 1976. *Neutralizing Inmate Violence: Juvenile Offenders in Institutions*. Cambridge, MA: Ballinger.

———. 1984. "Criminalizing Juvenile Justice: Rules of Procedure for Juvenile Court." *Minnesota Law Review* 69:141–276.

———. 1988a. "*In re Gault* Revisited: A Cross-State Comparison of the Right to Counsel in Juvenile Court." *Crime and Delinquency* 34:393–424.

———. 1988b. "Juvenile Court Meets the Principle of Offense: Punishment, Treatment, and the Difference It Makes." *Boston University Law Review* 68: 821–915.

———. 1989. "The Right to Counsel in Juvenile Court: An Empirical Study of When Lawyers Appear and the Difference They Make." *Journal of Criminal Law and Criminology* 79:1185–1346.

———. 1991. "Justice by Geography: Urban, Suburban, and Rural Variations in Juvenile Justice Administration." *Journal of Criminal Law and Criminology* 82:156–210.

———. 1993. *Justice for Children: The Right to Counsel and the Juvenile Court*. Boston: Northeastern University Press.

———. 1997. "Abolish the Juvenile Court: Youthfulness, Criminal Responsibility and Sentencing Policy." *Journal of Criminal Law and Criminology* 88:68–136.

———. 1998. "Juvenile and Criminal Justice Systems' Responses to Youth Violence." In *Youth Violence*, edited by Michael Tonry and Mark H. Moore. Vol. 24 of *Crime and Justice: A Review of Research*, edited by Michael Tonry. Chicago: University of Chicago Press.

———. 1999. *Bad Kids: Race and the Transformation of the Juvenile Court*. New York: Oxford University Press.

———. 2000a. "Juveniles' Waiver of Legal Rights: Confessions, Miranda, and the Right to Counsel." In *Youth on Trial: A Developmental Perspective on Juvenile Justice*, edited by Thomas Grisso and Robert Schwartz. Chicago: University of Chicago Press.

———. 2000b. "Legislative Exclusion of Offenses from Juvenile Court Jurisdiction." In *The Changing Borders of Juvenile Justice*, edited by Jeffrey Fagan and Franklin E. Zimring. Chicago: University of Chicago Press.

———. 2003. "The Constitutional Tension between Apprendi and McKeiver: Sentence Enhancements Based on Delinquency Convictions and the Quality of Justice in Juvenile Courts." *Wake Forest Law Review* 38:1111–1224.

———. 2006a. "Juveniles' Competence to Exercise Miranda Rights: An Empirical Study of Policy and Practice." *Minnesota Law Review* 91:26–100.

————. 2006*b*. "Police Interrogation of Juveniles: An Empirical Study of Policy and Practice." *Journal of Criminal Law and Criminology* 97:219–316.

————. 2008. "A Slower Form of Death: Implications of *Roper v. Simmons* for Juveniles Sentenced to Life without Parole." *Notre Dame Journal of Law, Ethics, and Public Policy* 22:9–65.

————. 2013*a*. "Adolescent Criminal Responsibility, Proportionality, and Sentencing Policy: Roper, Graham, Miller/Jackson, and the Youth Discount." *Law and Inequality Journal* 31:263–330.

————. 2013*b*. *Cases and Materials on Juvenile Justice Administration*. 4th ed. St. Paul, MN: West.

————. 2013*c*. *Kids, Cops, and Confessions: Inside the Interrogation Room*. New York: New York University Press.

————. 2013*d*. "Real Interrogation: What Happens When Cops Question Kids." *Law and Society Review* 47:1–35.

————. 2013*e*. "The Youth Discount: Old Enough to Do the Crime, Too Young to Do the Time." *Ohio State Journal of Criminal Law* 11:107–48.

————. 2017. *The Evolution of the Juvenile Court: Race, Politics, and the Criminalizing of Juvenile Justice*. New York: New York University Press.

Feld, Barry C., and Donna M. Bishop. 2012. "Transfer of Juveniles to Criminal Court." In *The Oxford Handbook of Juvenile Crime and Juvenile Justice*, edited by Barry C. Feld and Donna M. Bishop. New York: Oxford University Press.

Feld, Barry C., B. J. Casey, and Yasmin Hurd. 2013. "Adolescent Competence and Culpability: Implications of Neuroscience for Juvenile Justice Administration." In *A Primer on Criminal Law and Neuroscience*, edited by Stephen J. Morse and Adina L. Roskies. New York: Oxford University Press.

Feld, Barry C., and Shelly Schaefer. 2010*a*. "The Right to Counsel in Juvenile Court: The Conundrum of Attorneys as an Aggravating Factor in Dispositions." *Justice Quarterly* 27:713–41.

————. 2010*b*. "The Right to Counsel in Juvenile Court: Law Reform to Deliver Legal Services and Reduce Justice by Geography." *Criminology and Public Policy* 9:327–56.

Feyerherm, William H. 2000. "Detention Reform and Overrepresentation: A Successful Synergy." *Corrections Management Quarterly* 4:44–51.

Frase, Richard. 2009. "What Explains Persistent Racial Disproportionality in Minnesota's Prison and Jail Populations?" In *Crime and Justice: A Review of Research*, vol. 38, edited by Michael Tonry. Chicago: University of Chicago Press.

Gardner, Martin R. 2012. "Punitive Juvenile Justice and Public Trials by Jury: Sixth Amendment Applications in a Post-McKeiver World." *Nebraska Law Review* 91:1–71.

Garrett, Brandon L. 2011. *Convicting the Innocent: Where Criminal Prosecutions Go Wrong*. Cambridge, MA: Harvard University Press.

Garrido, Vincente, and Luz Anyela Morales. 2007. "Serious (Violent and Chronic) Juvenile Offenders: A Systematic Review of Treatment Effectiveness in Secure Corrections." In *Campbell Collaboration Reviews of Intervention and Policy Evaluations*. C2-RIPE, July. Philadelphia: Campbell Collaboration.

Graham, Sandra, and Brian S. Lowery. 2004. "Priming Unconscious Racial Stereotypes about Adolescent Offenders." *Law and Human Behavior* 28:483–504.

Greenwood, Peter W. 2006. *Changing Lives: Delinquency Prevention as Crime-Control Policy.* Chicago: University of Chicago Press.

Greenwood, Peter W., Albert J. Lipson, Allan Abrahamse, and Franklin Zimring. 1983. *Youth Crime and Juvenile Justice in California.* Santa Monica, CA: RAND.

Greenwood, Peter W., and Susan Turner. 2012. "Probation and Other Noninstitutional Treatment: The Evidence Is In." In *The Oxford Handbook of Juvenile Crime and Juvenile Justice,* edited by Barry C. Feld and Donna M. Bishop. New York: Oxford University Press.

Grisso, Thomas. 1980. "Juveniles' Capacities to Waive Miranda Rights: An Empirical Analysis." *California Law Review* 68:1134–66.

———. 1981. *Juveniles' Waiver of Rights: Legal and Psychological Competence.* New York: Plenum.

———. 2004. *Double Jeopardy: Adolescent Offenders with Mental Disorders.* Chicago: University of Chicago Press.

Grisso, Thomas, Laurence Steinberg, Jennifer Woolard, Elizabeth Cauffman, Elizabeth Scott, Sandra Graham, Fran Lexcen, N. Dickon Reppucci, and Robert Schwartz. 2003. "Juveniles' Competence to Stand Trial: A Comparison of Adolescents' and Adults' Capacities as Trial Defendants." *Law and Human Behavior* 27:333–63.

Gross, Samuel R., Kristen Jacoby, Daniel J. Matheson, Nicholas Montgomery, and Sujata Patil. 2005. "Exonerations in the United States: 1989 through 2003." *Journal of Criminal Law and Criminology* 95:523–60.

Guggenheim, Martin, and Randy Hertz. 1998. "Reflections on Judges, Juries, and Justice: Ensuring the Fairness of Juvenile Delinquency Trials." *Wake Forest Law Review* 33:553–93.

Harris, Donald J. 1994. "Due Process v. Helping Kids in Trouble: Implementing the Right to Appeal from Adjudications of Delinquency in Pennsylvania." *Dickinson Law Review* 98:209–35.

Human Rights Watch. 2012. *When I Die . . . They'll Send Me Home: Youth Sentenced to Life in Prison without Parole in California—an Update.* http://www.hrw.org.

Jacobs, James B. 2014. "Juvenile Criminal Record Confidentiality." In *Choosing the Future for American Juvenile Justice,* edited by Franklin E. Zimring and David S. Tanenhaus. New York: New York University Press.

Jones, Judith B. 2004. *Access to Counsel.* Washington, DC: US Department of Justice, Office of Juvenile Justice and Delinquency Prevention.

Juszkiewicz, Jolanta. 2000. *Youth Crime/Adult Time: Is Justice Served?* Washington, DC: Building Blocks for Youth.

Kalven, Harry, and Hans Zeisel. 1966. *The American Jury.* Chicago: University of Chicago Press.

Kassin, Saul. 2005. "On the Psychology of Confessions: Does Innocence Put Innocents at Risk?" *American Psychologist* 60:215–28.

Kassin, Saul, Steven A. Drizin, Thomas Grisso, Gisli H. Gudjonsson, Richard A. Leo, and Allison D. Redlich. 2010. "Police-Induced Confessions: Risk Factors and Recommendations." *Law and Human Behavior* 34:49–52.

Kempf-Leonard, Kimberly. 2007. "Minority Youth and Juvenile Justice: Disproportionate Minority Contact after Nearly 20 Years of Reform Efforts." *Youth Violence and Juvenile Justice* 5:71–87.

Krisberg, Barry. 2012. "Juvenile Corrections: An Overview." In *The Oxford Handbook of Juvenile Crime and Juvenile Justice*, edited by Barry C. Feld and Donna M. Bishop. New York: Oxford University Press.

Krisberg, Barry, James Austin, and Patricia Steele. 1989. *Working Juvenile Corrections: Evaluating the Massachusetts Department of Youth Services*. San Francisco: National Council on Crime and Delinquency.

Kurlychek, Megan, and Brian D. Johnson. 2004. "The Juvenile Penalty: A Comparison of Juvenile and Young Adult Sentencing Outcomes in Criminal Court." *Criminology* 42:485–517.

———. 2010. "Juvenility and Punishment: Sentencing Juveniles in Adult Criminal Court." *Criminology* 48:725–58.

Lauritsen, Janet L. 2005. "Racial and Ethnic Differences in Juvenile Offending." In *Our Children, Their Children: Confronting Racial and Ethnic Differences in American Juvenile Justice*, edited by Darnell F. Hawkins and Kimberly Kempf-Leonard. Chicago: University of Chicago Press.

Leo, Richard A. 2008. *Police Interrogation and American Justice*. Cambridge, MA: Harvard University Press.

Lieber, Michael J. 2013. "Race, Pre- and Post-Detention, and Juvenile Justice Decision Making." *Crime and Delinquency* 59:396–418.

Lipsey, Mark W. 2009. "The Primary Factors That Characterize Effective Interventions with Juvenile Offenders: A Meta-Analytic Overview." *Victims and Offenders* 4:124–47.

Loeber, Rolf, and David P. Farrington. 1998. *Serious and Violent Juvenile Offenders: Risk Factors and Successful Interventions*. Thousand Oaks, CA: Sage.

Loeber, Rolf, David P. Farrington, James C. Howell, and Machteld Hoeve. 2012. "Overview, Conclusions, and Key Recommendations." In *From Juvenile Delinquency to Adult Crime: Criminal Careers, Justice Policy, and Prevention*, edited by Rolf Loeber and David P. Farrington. New York: Oxford University Press.

MacArthur Foundation Research Network on Adolescent Development and Juvenile Justice. 2006. *Development and Criminal Blameworthiness*. http://www.adjj.org.

MacKenzie, Doris Layton, and Rachel Freeland. 2012. "Examining the Effectiveness of Juvenile Residential Programs." In *The Oxford Handbook of Juvenile Crime and Juvenile Justice*, edited by Barry C. Feld and Donna M. Bishop. New York: Oxford University Press.

Manfredi, Christopher P. 1998. *The Supreme Court and Juvenile Justice*. Lawrence: University of Kansas Press.

Maroney, Terry A. 2009. "The False Promise of Adolescent Brain Science in Juvenile Justice." *Notre Dame Law Review* 85:89–176.

————. 2011. "Adolescent Brain Science after *Graham v. Florida.*" *Notre Dame Law Review* 86:765–93.

Martinson, Robert. 1974. "What Works? Questions and Answers about Prison Reform." *Public Interest* 35:22–54.

Mears, Daniel P. 2012. "The Front End of the Juvenile Court: Intake and Informal versus Formal Processing." In *The Oxford Handbook of Juvenile Crime and Juvenile Justice*, edited by Barry C. Feld and Donna M. Bishop. New York: Oxford University Press.

Miller, Jerome. 1991. *Last One over the Wall.* Columbus: Ohio State University Press.

Monahan, Kathryn, Laurence Steinberg, and Alex R. Piquero. 2015. "Juvenile Justice Policy and Practice: A Developmental Perspective." In *Crime and Justice: A Review of Research*, vol. 44, edited by Michael Tonry. Chicago: University of Chicago Press.

Moriearty, Perry L. 2011. "Framing Justice: Media, Bias, and Legal Decision Making." *Maryland Law Review* 69:849–909.

————. 2015. "Miller v. Alabama and the Retroactivity of Proportionality Rules." *University of Pennsylvania Journal of Constitutional Law* 17:929–90.

Morse, Stephen J. 2006. "Brain Overclaim Syndrome and Criminal Responsibility: A Diagnostic Note." *Ohio State Journal of Criminal Law* 3:397–412.

Mulvey, Edward P., and Carol A. Schubert. 2012. "Youth in Prison and Beyond." In *The Oxford Handbook on Juvenile Crime and Juvenile Justice*, edited by Barry C. Feld and Donna M. Bishop. New York: Oxford University Press.

National Juvenile Defender Center. 2017. "State Assessments." http://njdc.info /our-work/juvenile-indigent-defense-assessments/.

National Research Council. 2013. *Reforming Juvenile Justice: A Developmental Approach.* Washington, DC: National Academies Press.

————. 2014. *The Growth of Incarceration in the United States: Exploring Causes and Consequences.* Washington, DC: National Academies Press.

National Research Council and Institute of Medicine. 2001. *Juvenile Crime, Juvenile Justice.* Washington, DC: National Academy Press.

————. 2011. *The Science of Adolescent Risk-Taking: Workshop Report.* Washington, DC: National Academies Press.

Nellis, Ashley. 2016. *A Return to Justice: Rethinking Our Approach to Juveniles in the System.* Lanham, MD: Rowman & Littlefield.

Owen-Kostelnik, Jessica, N. Dickon Reppucci, and Jessica R. Meyer. 2006. "Testimony and Interrogation of Minors: Assumptions about Maturity and Morality." *American Psychologist* 61:286–304.

Parent, Dale G., Valerie Lieter, Stephen Kennedy, Lisa Livens, Daniel Wentworth, and Sarah Wilcox. 1994. *Conditions of Confinement: Juvenile Detention and Corrections Facilities.* Washington, DC: US Department of Justice, Office of Juvenile Justice and Delinquency Prevention.

Piquero, Alex R. 2008. "Disproportionate Minority Contact." *Future of Children* 18:59–79.

Podkopacz, Marcy Rasmussen, and Barry C. Feld. 2001. "The Back-Door to Prison: Waiver Reform, 'Blended Sentencing,' and the Law of Unintended Consequences." *Journal of Criminal Law and Criminology* 91:997–1071.

Poe-Yamagata, Eileen, and Michael A. Jones. 2000. *And Justice for Some: Differential Treatment of Minority Youth in the Justice System*. Washington, DC: Youth Law Center.

President's Commission on Law Enforcement and Administration of Justice. 1967. *The Challenge of Crime in a Free Society*. Washington, DC: US Government Printing Office.

Redding, Richard E. 2008. *Juvenile Transfer Laws: An Effective Deterrent to Delinquency?* Washington, DC: US Department of Justice, Office of Juvenile Justice and Delinquency Prevention.

Rodriguez, Nancy. 2010. "The Cumulative Effect of Race and Ethnicity in Juvenile Court Outcomes and Why Pre-adjudication Detention Matters." *Journal of Research in Crime and Delinquency* 47:391–413.

Rogers, Richard, Lisa L. Hazelwood, Kenneth W. Sewell, Kimberly S. Harrison, and Daniel W. Schuman. 2008a. "The Language of Miranda Warnings in American Jurisdictions: A Replication and Vocabulary Analysis." *Law and Human Behavior* 32:124–36.

Rogers, Richard, Lisa L. Hazelwood, Kenneth W. Sewell, Daniel W. Schuman, and Hayley L. Blackwood. 2008b. "The Comprehensibility and Content of Juvenile Miranda Warnings." *Psychology, Public Policy and the Law* 14:63–87.

Sampson, Robert J., and Janet L. Lauritsen. 1997. "Racial and Ethnic Disparities in Crime and Criminal Justice in the United States." In *Ethnicity, Crime, and Immigration: Comparative and Cross-National Perspectives*, edited by Michael Tonry. Vol. 21 of *Crime and Justice: A Review of Research*, edited by Michael Tonry. Chicago: University of Chicago Press.

Sanborn, Joseph B., Jr. 2009. "Juveniles' Competency to Stand Trial: Wading through the Rhetoric and the Evidence." *Journal of Criminal Law and Criminology* 99:135–213.

Schubert, Carol A., Edward P. Mulvey, Thomas A. Loughran, Jeffrey Fagan, Laurie A. Chassin, Alex R. Piquero, Sandra H. Losoya, Laurence Steinberg, and Elizabeth Cauffman. 2010. "Predicting Outcomes for Youth Transferred to Adult Court." *Law and Human Behavior* 34:460–75.

Scott, Elizabeth S., and Thomas Grisso. 2005. "Developmental Incompetence, Due Process, and Juvenile Justice Policy." *North Carolina Law Review* 83:793–846.

Scott, Elizabeth S., and Laurence Steinberg. 2008. *Rethinking Juvenile Justice*. Cambridge, MA: Harvard University Press.

Sentencing Project. 2014. *Slow to Act: State Responses to 2012 Supreme Court Mandate on Life without Parole*. http://www.sentencingproject.org.

Sickmund, Melissa, A. Sladky, and W. Kang. 2014. *Easy Access to Juvenile Court Statistics: 1985–2011*. Washington, DC: US Department of Justice, Office of Juvenile Justice and Delinquency Prevention.

Singleton, Lacey Cole. 2007. "Say 'Pleas': Juveniles' Competence to Enter Plea Agreements." *Journal of Law and Family Studies* 9:439–55.

Snyder, Howard N., and Melissa Sickmund. 2006. *Juvenile Offenders and Victims: A National Report*. Washington, DC: US Department of Justice, Office of Juvenile Justice and Delinquency Prevention.

Spear, L. P. 2010. *The Behavioral Neuroscience of Adolescence*. New York: Norton.

Steinberg, Laurence. 2008. "A Social Neuroscience Perspective on Adolescent Risk-Taking." *Developmental Review* 28:78–106.

———. 2010. "A Dual Systems Model of Adolescent Risk-Taking." *Developmental Psychobiology* 52:216–24.

———. 2014. *Age of Opportunity: Lessons from the New Science of Adolescence*. New York: Houghton Mifflin Harcourt.

Steiner, Benjamin. 2009. "The Effects of Juvenile Transfer to Criminal Court on Incarceration Decisions." *Justice Quarterly* 26:77–106.

Steiner, Benjamin, Craig Hemmens, and Valerie Bell. 2006. "Legislative Waiver Reconsidered: General Deterrent Effects of Statutory Exclusion Laws Enacted Post 1979." *Justice Quarterly* 23:34–59.

Steiner, Benjamin, and Emily Wright. 2006. "Assessing the Relative Effects of State Direct File Waiver Laws on Violent Juvenile Crime: Deterrence or Irrelevance?" *Journal of Criminal Law and Criminology* 96:1451–77.

Tanenhaus, David S., and Steven A. Drizin. 2003. "Owing to the Extreme Youth of the Accused: The Changing Legal Response to Juvenile Homicide." *Journal of Criminal Law and Criminology* 92:641–705.

Tepfer, Joshua A., Laura H. Nirider, and Lynda M. Tricarico. 2010. "Arresting Development: Convictions of Innocent Youth." *Rutgers Law Review* 62:887–941.

Tonry, Michael. 1996. *Sentencing Matters*. New York: Oxford University Press.

———. 2011. *Punishing Race: A Continuing American Dilemma*. New York: Oxford University Press.

———. 2016. *Sentencing Fragments: Penal Reform in America, 1975–2025*. New York: Oxford University Press.

Torbet, Patricia, Richard Gable, Hunter Hurst IV, Imogene Montgomery, Linda Szymanski, and Douglas Thomas. 1996. *State Responses to Serious and Violent Juvenile Crime: Research Report*. Washington, DC: US Department of Justice, Office of Juvenile Justice and Delinquency Prevention.

Twentieth Century Fund Task Force on Sentencing Policy toward Young Offenders. 1978. *Confronting Youth Crime*. New York: Holmes & Meier.

US General Accounting Office. 1995. *Juvenile Justice: Representation Rates Varied as Did Counsel's Impact on Court Outcomes*. Washington, DC: US General Accounting Office.

Viljoen, Jodi, Erika Penner, and Ronald Roesch. 2012. "Competence and Criminal Responsibility in Adolescent Defendants: The Roles of Mental Illness and Adolescent Development." In *The Oxford Handbook of Juvenile Crime and Juvenile Justice*, edited by Barry C. Feld and Donna M. Bishop. New York: Oxford University Press.

Welsh, Brandon C. 2012. "Delinquency Prevention." In *The Oxford Handbook of Juvenile Crime and Juvenile Justice*, edited by Barry C. Feld and Donna M. Bishop. New York: Oxford University Press.

474 Barry C. Feld

Welsh, Brandon C., Mark W. Lipsey, Frederick P. Rivara, J. David Hawkins, Steve Aos, and Meghan E. Hollis-Peel. 2012. "Promoting Change, Changing Lives: Effective Prevention and Intervention to Reduce Serious Offending." In *From Juvenile Delinquency to Adult Crime: Criminal Careers, Justice Policy, and Prevention*, edited by Rolf Loeber and David P. Farrington. New York: Oxford University Press.

Wilson, William J. 2009. *More than Just Race: Being Black and Poor in the Inner City*. New York: Norton.

Woolard, Jennifer L., Hayley M. D. Cleary, Samantha A. S. Harvell, and Rusan Chen. 2008. "Examining Adolescents' and Their Parents' Conceptual and Practical Knowledge of Police Interrogation: A Family Dyad Approach." *Journal of Youth Adolescence* 37:685–98.

Zimring, Franklin E. 1998. *American Youth Violence*. New York: Oxford University Press.

———. 2004. *An American Travesty: Legal Responses to Adolescent Sexual Offending*. Chicago: University of Chicago Press.

———. 2013. "American Youth Violence: A Cautionary Tale." In *Crime and Justice in America, 1975–2025*, edited by Michael Tonry. Vol. 42 of *Crime and Justice: A Review of Research*, edited by Michael Tonry. Chicago: University of Chicago Press.

———. 2014. "Minority Overrepresentation: On Causes and Partial Cures." In *Choosing the Future for American Juvenile Justice*, edited by Franklin E. Zimring and David S. Tanenhaus. New York: New York University Press.

Zimring, Franklin E., and David S. Tanenhaus. 2014. "On Strategy and Tactics for Contemporary Reforms." In *Choosing the Future for American Juvenile Justice*, edited by Franklin E. Zimring and David S. Tanenhaus. New York: New York University Press.

*Ellen G. Cohn, Amaia Iratzoqui, David P. Farrington,*
*Alex R. Piquero, and Zachary A. Powell*

# Most-Cited Articles and Authors in *Crime and Justice*, 1979–2015

ABSTRACT

*Crime and Justice* has been published by the University of Chicago Press since
1979, originally as a hardcover annual journal and more recently both in print
and electronically. In 2016–17, it was possible to investigate the scholarly
influence of 374 articles published in 44 volumes between 1979 and 2015,
according to Google Scholar and the Web of Science. The most-cited articles
and authors are identified, adjusting the number of citations for time at risk of
citation since publication date and for the number of articles published by
each author. Scholarly influence was also examined by identifying characteristics
of the most-cited articles and by reviewing online access to articles. Articles on
explanations and theories of crime and delinquency were most likely to be cited;
the most-cited article was "Family Factors as Correlates and Predictors of Juvenile Conduct Problems and Delinquency" by Rolf Loeber and Magda
Stouthamer-Loeber (1986). The most-accessed scholar was David P. Farrington;
his most-accessed article was "Understanding and Preventing Bullying" (1993).

Scholarly influence is related to the importance of a given scholar for a
discipline and to the influence of a scholarly work on subsequent publica-

Electronically published March 5, 2018
Ellen G. Cohn is associate professor of criminal justice, Florida International University. Amaia Iratzoqui is assistant professor of criminology and criminal justice, University
of Memphis. David P. Farrington is emeritus professor of psychological criminology, University of Cambridge. Alex R. Piquero is Ashbel Smith Professor of Criminology, University of Texas at Dallas. Zachary A. Powell is a PhD candidate in criminology, University of
Texas at Dallas.

tions in the field. One method of measuring scholarly influence is the use of citation analysis, which is based on the belief that citations indicate influence and that highly cited works are important to the scholars citing them (Meadows 1974); if a work is highly cited, this suggests that others find it important and valuable. Citation analysis provides an objective and quantitative method for investigating the impact of a scholar, work, journal, or academic department (Cohn and Farrington 2005). Citation counts are strongly correlated with other measures of scholarly recognition, such as the receipt of scholarly prizes (e.g., the Nobel Prize), scholarly recognition, leadership of professional associations, peer ratings of professional eminence and departmental prestige, scholarly productivity, and salary (Cohn, Farrington, and Wright 1998). The use of citation analysis to measure scholarly influence and prestige has become an accepted technique in many fields (see Cohn and Farrington [2012] for a detailed review of the literature).

Citation distributions are highly skewed; the vast majority of scholarly articles are rarely or never cited (Hamilton 1990, 1991; Laband and Piette 1994; Meho 2007), while a small number of scholars account for a disproportionately large percentage of all citations (Cohn, Farrington, and Wright 1998; Orrick and Weir 2011). While it is clear that "citation does not necessarily denote approval" (Chapman 1989, p. 341), the evidence suggests that the vast majority of citations are positive or neutral rather than negative (Cole 1975; Garfield 1979; Cohn and Farrington 1994).

This essay explores the scholarly influence of *Crime and Justice: A Review of Research*, a well-known and widely respected annual journal that presents state-of-the-art reviews of research on a wide variety of crime-related issues and problems. The series includes both general volumes, which present summaries and critiques of a number of diverse important topics, and thematic volumes, which deal with a particular topic in criminology. All volumes take an interdisciplinary approach. The editors' original intent was for the series to "help form links of understanding between the various disciplines on which criminological research depends and will continue to depend" (Morris and Tonry 1979, p. ix). However, research into the scholarly influence of the series is limited (Cohn and Farrington 1996).

This essay tracks citations of works published in *Crime and Justice* since its inception in 1979 and explores the journal's influence by identifying the most highly cited authors and articles published in the journal, identifying shared characteristics between the most highly cited articles, and examining online access patterns. Section I discusses the sole previous study that examined citations in *Crime and Justice*. Section II reviews the primary sources of citation data available to criminologists, discussing the advantages and limitations of each source. Section III describes the methodology of this research and explains how information on citations of articles in *Crime and Justice* was obtained from two databases (Google Scholar and the Social Sciences Citation Index), while information on electronic access of these articles was obtained via the JSTOR online database. Section IV outlines the results of the data analyses, including information on the most highly cited articles, the most-cited authors, article characteristics that were correlated with various measures of scholarly influence, and patterns of electronic access of these articles. Finally, Section V presents the conclusions drawn from the results of this study, discusses the contributions this essay makes to the study of citations in the field of criminology and criminal justice, and makes suggestions for future research.

## I. Prior Research

The only previous citation study focusing on *Crime and Justice* was carried out by Cohn and Farrington in 1996. They analyzed the most-cited scholars and works among those published in the 12 general volumes of *Crime and Justice* published between 1979 and 1993; they did not include the six thematic volumes published through 1993. They also analyzed citations of *Crime and Justice* articles in nine major American and international criminology and criminal justice journals and in the Social Science Citation Index. Thematic volumes were omitted in order to avoid skewing the results toward the particular topics covered in those volumes. In an effort to examine changes over time, they separately examined the first six volumes, published between 1979 and 1985, and the second six volumes, published between 1986 and 1993. The topics of all published articles in *Crime and Justice* were also categorized using a classification system that had been developed previously (Cohn and Farrington 1990).

In earlier research examining citations in criminology and criminal justice journals, they used a scoring system that ensured that equal weighting was given to journals with vastly different numbers of citations. For each journal they examined, they identified the 50 most-cited scholars and gave each a score of 51 minus his or her rank; the most-cited scholar therefore had a score of 50 and authors outside the top 50 scored zero (Cohn and Farrington 2012). A scholar's scores in different journals were then added together.

The earlier examination of citations of *Crime and Justice* articles identified the most-cited scholars in each time period and added up the scores for each scholar over the two time periods (Cohn and Farrington 1996). The most-cited scholars overall were Michael J. Hindelang, Alfred Blumstein, and Marvin E. Wolfgang. However, when looking separately at the two time periods, the scores of the most-cited authors between 1979 and 1983 were negatively correlated with their scores between 1986 and 1993. This may indicate changes in influence across the two time periods or changes in the field's substantive interest in topics that these scholars had not previously studied.

The prevalence of citations (the percentage of different articles in which a scholar is cited) was also examined. The most-cited scholars remained the same (Hindelang, Blumstein, and Wolfgang), but the rankings of many other scholars changed considerably across the two time periods. This shows that, for some scholars, many of their works are cited in a few articles, while for others, only one or a small number of works are cited in many different articles. Scholarly influence is likely to be greater in the latter case.

## II. Sources of Citation Data

There are multiple sources of citation data available to criminologists. Two of the most widely used online sources are the Social Science Citation Index (SSCI), a paid service that is part of Thomson Reuter's Web of Science, and Google Scholar (GS), a free resource.

The SSCI lists bibliographic references in journals but does not include citations in books or book chapters. An important advantage of SSCI is that the master list of journals from which citations are taken is available on the Thomson Reuters website, as is a list of changes in journal coverage.

There are, however, some limitations to SSCI as a source of data for citation analysis. First, while the list of journals included is extensive (over 3,000 journals as of August 2016), it is not exhaustive. Some newer journals, such as the *Asian Journal of Criminology*, are not yet included, while others, such as *Crime and Justice*, are included but not fully indexed. The Web of Science has also been criticized for the overrepresentation of journals from North America and western Europe (Meho and Yang 2007). In general, SSCI does not count citations from books, book chapters, technical reports, and similar publications. These coverage limitations may affect citation counts; several studies have found that citation research based on the Web of Science may significantly underestimate total citation counts (Funkhouser 1996; Cronin, Snyder, and Atkins 1997; Nisonger 2004). Another limitation is that the list of journals indexed in SSCI is constantly changing as new journals are added or older ones are removed; while this may not affect an individual research study, it makes longitudinal research extremely difficult. Third, SSCI includes self-citations, which should not be included when studying the influence of a scholar on others in the field and which have traditionally been excluded from citation research (e.g., Cohn and Farrington 1996, 2012).

Google Scholar (GS) is a free online scientific archive launched in November 2004 that includes citations from all types of scholarly literature including journal articles, books, dissertations, technical reports, conference papers, and others (Giles 2005). The inclusion of nonjournal material such as books is considered by some to be a major strength of GS as compared to SSCI (Bauer and Bakkalbasi 2005). However, it is also a weakness, as nonjournal material frequently has not been peer-reviewed and may be of questionable quality. In general, GS tends to produce higher citation counts than SSCI (Bauer and Bakkalbasi 2005; Meho and Yang 2007).

Like SSCI, GS has some well-known limitations. A major concern for citation analysis is that GS does not provide any information as to coverage, such as which journals are included at any given time, which websites or databases are searched, what time periods are covered, or how often GS is updated. The GS website does not give a direct answer to questions regarding the coverage of specific sources (e.g., JSTOR, Elsevier), and when asked what specific journals are covered by GS, the response is, "Ahem, we index papers, not journals" (Google Scholar 2016). Another concern is that the GS software cannot always distinguish authors' names from other elements of text; a test search by Jascó (2008) discovered a variety of false names, and a recent (August 2016) examination of GS by one of the current authors found the names of actual authors replaced by false names such as "First Stage Results," "I. Introduction," "Climate Data," "RSS Tweet," and "Login Cart." Jascó also found that, when setting a custom time range for searching, the number of results inexplicably increases as the time span decreases. One of the current authors confirmed that this problem still exists; for example, an August 2016 search for the term "crime mapping" produced more results when the date range was limited to the years 2000–2015 than when it was expanded to the years 1970–2015 (162,000 compared to 133,000 results). Also, like SSCI, GS includes self-citations.

Additionally, regardless of which source is used, any errors existing in an article's reference list (e.g., spelling mistakes, incorrect or missing initials) are carried over to the database. If a journal permits the use of "et al." in the reference list, those additional authors will not be available in the database. While it is clear that both sources of data have advantages and disadvantages, they are the primary online databases available for citation research. In order to limit the possible inaccuracies, our analysis in this essay uses data from both sources. This is intended to increase confidence in the overall findings and conclusions to the extent that both sources produce similar results (i.e., the same articles and authors appear in the ranking lists from both sources of data).

## III. Methodology

The first part of this research involved identifying the citations of all 374 articles published in the 26 general and 18 thematic volumes of *Crime and Justice* between 1979 and 2015.[1] Scholarly influence was examined by obtaining the total number of citations for each article in both GS and SSCI.

Searches of both databases were conducted in July 2016. However, one concern with the use of online archives such as GS is the unstable nature of the search results (see, e.g., Cohn and Farrington 2012). Because GS constantly updates the databases from which it collects data, the search results will vary depending on the date on which a search is conducted. For both databases, articles were searched using the full title and title fragments and then by the first and last names of the first author, to capture any citations that may have incorrectly cited the work. In all searches, the number of times each article was cited through De-

---

[1] *Crime and Justice* did not publish volumes in calendar years 1982, 1984, or 1994; those volumes appeared in the immediately preceding or following years. Two volumes per year were published in 1983, 1986, 1990, 1992, 1993, 1997, 1998, 1999, 2005, and 2007.

cember 31, 2015, was counted.[2] Articles were ranked on both the total number of citations in GS and the total number of citations in SSCI. GS produced 41,663 total citations of articles published in *Crime and Justice* in the 1979–2015 period, while SSCI produced 6,023 citations for the same period.

Our analysis also identified the most highly cited authors of articles published in *Crime and Justice*. Each author of a coauthored article was examined separately. A scholar's influence was based on the number of citations in GS or SSCI of all articles he or she published in *Crime and Justice*.

One issue that arose was that we discovered that SSCI did not index all issues of *Crime and Justice*. A total of 131 articles in 15 volumes were not indexed in SSCI; for these articles, citation counts were obtained only from GS. The data were imported into Stata for analyses. When comparing GS and SSCI citations, articles with missing data were filtered out, leaving a total of 243 cases with citation counts from both databases.

A number of article characteristics were considered when examining citation patterns. These included the placement of the article in the volume, whether the article was in a general or thematic volume, the "shelf life" of the article (defined as the number of years the article was available for citation, after publication), and its subject classification. Articles were classified using a seven-category system developed by Cohn and Farrington (1990); an additional category was added for a small number of articles that did not fall into any of these seven categories. Table 1 shows the total number of articles on each topic, which included explanations or theories of delinquency or crime; measurement and methodology; general criminology; political, white-collar, and organized crime; police; courts; and corrections. Over one-quarter (26 percent) of all articles in *Crime and Justice* were on topics relating to measurement/methodology and criminal careers.

In addition to citation analysis, one can examine scholarly influence through the frequency of online access of scholarly works. *Crime and Justice* is archived in JSTOR, a digital library of academic journals, books, and primary sources. JSTOR has been collecting usage data since 2008,

---

[2] SSCI and GS do not distinguish among self-citations, co-citations, and citations by independent scholars. Therefore, despite a wealth of literature arguing against self-citations (see, e.g., Cohn and Farrington [2012] for a review), these citations had to be included in our counts.

TABLE 1

Categories of Articles in *Crime and Justice*, 1979–2015

| Category | Number of Articles |
|---|---|
| 1. Explanations/theories of crime/delinquency | 52 |
| 2. Measurement, methodology, criminal careers, crime rates/trends/patterns, victimization, fear of crime | 99 |
| 3. General criminology/criminal justice, crime control/prevention, attitudes/perception of criminal justice | 57 |
| 4. Political crime, organized crime, corporate crime, professional/ white-collar crime, radical/Marxist studies | 19 |
| 5. Police, enforcement, private security, vigilantes, arrest | 21 |
| 6. Sentencing, courts, law, juvenile justice, deterrence, capital punishment | 67 |
| 7. Prisons, jails, private prisons, juvenile facilities, community treatment/corrections, prediction of recidivism, rehabilitation, correctional officers, inmate behavior | 57 |
| 8. Other | 2 |
| Total | 374 |

including all articles in *Crime and Justice* that have been electronically accessed and downloaded. An advantage of examining usage data is that they permit a much broader view of scholarly influence than citation analysis. By definition, citation analysis focuses specifically on the influence of scholarly works on published researchers who cite them in their own publications. However, usage data provide information on how often these works are accessed by a much wider pool of users, including academics, students, and practitioners. This allows an exploration of the use of scholarly works by individuals who are not necessarily accessing these materials as part of a scholarly research project that will result in publication. Usage data may serve as an alternative measure of scholarly influence, showing which articles are most likely to be accessed and downloaded. A comparison of usage and citation data may provide evidence regarding the reliability and consistency of measures of scholarly influence within the field.

*Crime and Justice* may be accessed online via JSTOR in one of three ways. First, individual users may purchase a single article (pay-per-view). Second, individuals may subscribe to JSTOR by purchasing a monthly or yearly JPASS, which allows subscribers unlimited full-text access and a specified number of article downloads. Third, institutions that subscribe to JSTOR may provide access to affiliated individuals (e.g., faculty and students may access JSTOR via their university library site license).

Annual usage information on the 25 most-accessed works in *Crime and Justice* in 2008 and the 50 most-accessed works in each year from 2009 through 2015 was obtained from JSTOR. Articles located on JSTOR could be read via two options, "Read Online" or "Download PDF." JSTOR counts a user clicking on Read Online as an "article view" and Download PDF as a download. The final accession numbers represented the sum of online views and PDF downloads. One point to note is that the same user may have both viewed an article online and downloaded it, thus being counted twice by JSTOR. The files were merged to provide a total count of the number of times each article was accessed over the 8-year period. This produced a total of 90 different articles. It is important to note that the accuracy of the accession information is affected by the fact that JSTOR did not provide accession data on all articles in *Crime and Justice*.

### IV. Results

We present the results of our analysis in this section, showing most-cited articles and authors in SSCI and GS and most-accessed articles in JSTOR. There is substantial concurrence of results between SSCI and GS, especially for the top 10 most frequently cited articles in each. Access patterns for JSTOR are substantially different from both, suggesting a different and probably broader readership. Rolf Loeber, always writing with coauthors, and David P. Farrington, usually as sole author, are the most-cited authors in absolute terms and first and fourth when calculations are adjusted for time elapsed since articles were published. Articles by Loeber and Farrington are ranked first in both SSCI and GS. Farrington's (1993) article "Understanding and Preventing Bullying" is ranked first in JSTOR.

### A. Most-Cited Articles

Table 2 shows the 50 most-cited articles in *Crime and Justice* based on the number of citations in GS. The ranking of each article based on citations in SSCI (when the article is available) is provided for

## TABLE 2

### 50 Most-Cited Articles in *Crime and Justice* Based on Google Scholar Citations

| GS Rank | Article Title | Author(s) | Year | Citations in GS | SSCI Rank |
|---|---|---|---|---|---|
| 1 | Family Factors as Correlates and Predictors of Juvenile Conduct Problems and Delinquency | Loeber, R., Stouthamer-Loeber, M. | 1986 | 1,460 | 1 |
| 2 | Age and Crime | Farrington, D.P. | 1986 | 999 | 2 |
| 3 | Understanding and Preventing Bullying | Farrington, D.P. | 1993 | 795 | *m* |
| 4 | Criminal Deterrence Research at the Outset of the Twenty-First Century | Nagin, D.S. | 1998 | 789 | 4 |
| 5 | Understanding Desistance from Crime | Laub, J.H., Sampson, R.J. | 2001 | 762 | 5 |
| 6 | Modeling Offenders' Decisions | Clarke, R.V., Cornish, D.B. | 1985 | 660 | 10 |
| 7 | Restorative Justice | Braithwaite, J. | 1999 | 639 | 16 |
| 8 | The Criminal Career Paradigm | Piquero, A.R., Farrington, D.P., Blumstein, A. | 2003 | 615 | 3 |
| 9 | Toward a Developmental Criminology | Loeber, R., Le Blanc, M. | 1990 | 564 | 7 |
| 10 | Situational Crime Prevention | Clarke, R.V. | 1995 | 563 | *m* |
| 11 | Public Opinion about Punishment and Corrections | Cullen, F.T., Fisher, B.S., Applegate, B.K. | 2000 | 516 | 8.5 |
| 12 | Procedural Justice, Legitimacy, and the Effective Rule of Law | Tyler, T.R. | 2003 | 513 | 13 |
| 13 | Academic Performance and Delinquency | Maguin, E., Loeber, R. | 1996 | 506 | 8.5 |
| 14 | Collateral Consequences of Imprisonment for Children, Communities, and Prisoners | Hagan, J., Dinovitzer, R. | 1999 | 473 | *m* |
| 15 | Treatment of Drug Abuse | Anglin, M.D., Hser, Y.-I. | 1990 | 453 | 49 |
| 16 | Fear of Crime and Neighborhood Change | Skogan, W. | 1986 | 447 | 27 |

484

| | | | | | |
|---|---|---|---|---|---|
| 17 | Assessing Macro-Level Predictors and Theories of Crime | Pratt, T.C., Cullen, F.T. | 2005 | 440 | 6 |
| 18 | Police Crackdowns | Sherman, L.W. | 1990 | 434 | 17 |
| 19 | Population Growth in U.S. Prisons, 1980–1996 | Blumstein, A., Beck, A.J. | 1999 | 431 | m |
| 20 | Predictors, Causes, and Correlates of Male Youth Violence | Farrington, D.P. | 1998 | 419 | m |
| 21 | Intensive Probation and Parole | Petersilia, J., Turner, S. | 1993 | 387 | m |
| 22 | The Neighborhood Context of Police Behavior | Smith, D.A. | 1986 | 368 | 25.5 |
| 23 | Ethnicity, Crime, and Immigration | Tonry, M. | 1997 | 364 | 59.5 |
| 24 | Situational Crime Prevention: Its Theoretical Basis and Practical Scope | Clarke, R.V. | 1983 | 350 | m |
| 25 | Intoxication and Aggression | Fagan, J. | 1990 | 338 | 31.5 |
| 26 | Crime Placement, Displacement, and Deflection | Barr, R., Pease, K. | 1990 | 336 | 28.5 |
| 27 | Racial and Ethnic Disparities in Crime and Criminal Justice in the United States | Sampson, R.J., Lauritsen, J.L. | 1997 | 334 | 24 |
| 28 | What Have We Learned from Five Decades of Neutralization Research? | Maruna, S., Copes, H. | 2005 | 320 | 11.5 |
| 29.5 | Research in Criminal Deterrence | Cook, P.J. | 1980 | 318 | m |
| 29.5 | Historical Trends in Violent Crime | Gurr, T.R. | 1981 | 318 | m |
| 31 | Delinquency Careers | Blumstein, A., Farrington, D.P., Moitra, S. | 1985 | 314 | 20.5 |
| 32 | Public Opinion, Crime, and Criminal Justice | Roberts, J.V. | 1992 | 307 | m |
| 33 | Why Are Communities Important in Understanding Crime? | Reiss, A.J. | 1986 | 304 | 112.5 |
| 34 | Drugs and Predatory Crime | Chaiken, J.M, Chaiken, M.R. | 1990 | 293 | 40 |
| 35 | The Self-Report Methodology in Crime Research | Junger-Tas, J., Marshall, I.H. | 1999 | 286 | 15 |
| 36 | Community Crime Prevention | Hope, T. | 1995 | 285 | m |
| 37 | The Unprecedented Epidemic in Youth Violence | Cook, P.J., Laub, J.H. | 1998 | 283 | m |
| 38 | Long-Term Historical Trends in Violent Crime | Eisner, M. | 2003 | 282 | 20.5 |
| 39 | Developmental Criminology Updated | Le Blanc, M., Loeber, R. | 1998 | 277 | 19 |
| 40 | Risks and Prices | Reuter, P., Kleinman, M.A.R. | 1986 | 273 | 18 |

TABLE 2 (Continued)

| GS Rank | Article Title | Author(s) | Year | Citations in GS | SSCI Rank |
|---|---|---|---|---|---|
| 41 | Developmental Crime Prevention | Tremblay, R.E., Craig, W.M. | 1995 | 270 | m |
| 42 | Modern Private Security | Shearing, C.D., Stenning, P.C. | 1981 | 269 | m |
| 43 | Imprisonment and Reoffending | Nagin, D.S., Cullen, F.T., Jonson, C.L. | 2009 | 262 | 14 |
| 44 | Interpersonal Violence and Social Order in Prisons | Bottoms, A.E. | 1999 | 257 | m |
| 45 | Crime and Mental Disorder | Monahan, J., Steadman, H.J. | 1983 | 241 | m |
| 46.5 | Sentence Severity and Crime | Doob, A.N., Webster, C.M. | 2003 | 240 | 28.5 |
| 46.5 | Problem-Solving and Community Policing | Moore, M.H. | 1992 | 240 | m |
| 48 | Co-offending and Criminal Careers | Reiss, A.J. | 1988 | 232 | m |
| 49 | The Demand and Supply of Criminal Opportunities | Cook, P.J. | 1986 | 226 | 25.5 |
| 50 | Crime in Cities | Sampson, R.J. | 1986 | 220 | 43 |

NOTE.—GS = Google Scholar; SSCI = Social Science Citation Index; m = article not indexed in SSCI.

comparison.³ The most-cited work, by far, was the 1986 article "Family Factors as Correlates and Predictors of Juvenile Conduct Problems and Delinquency" by Rolf Loeber and Magda Stouthamer-Loeber, with 1,460 citations in GS. This article was also the most-cited in SSCI. The second-most-cited work across both databases was "Age and Crime" by David Farrington. The fact that the prominence of both works remains stable regardless of the source of data greatly increases the level of confidence regarding their influence and importance in the field.

Table 3 shows the 50 most-cited articles in *Crime and Justice* based on the number of citations in SSCI, with the corresponding GS rankings provided for comparison. The number of citations found in SSCI was much lower than in GS, no doubt reflecting the more restricted range of works (usually peer-reviewed journals) covered by SSCI. A comparison of rankings in GS and SSCI shows that overall, there appears to be consistency in the most-cited works across the two sources of data. For example, the 10 most-cited articles according to SSCI were all among the top 17 according to GS. There are some discrepancies between the two sources of data, however. For example, the fifteenth-most-cited work in GS, "Treatment of Drug Abuse," was ranked 49 in SSCI, while "The Neuropsychology of Juvenile Delinquency," which was ranked 11.5 in SSCI, was not among the 50 most-cited works in GS. Additionally, some of the most-cited works in GS were not indexed in SSCI.

Table 4 shows the articles in *Crime and Justice* that were most frequently accessed through JSTOR between 2008 and 2015, with the corresponding ranks in GS and SSCI. It is important to note that while older articles naturally have a greater likelihood of citation simply because of their longer availability, the fact that JSTOR began collecting access data only in 2008 levels the playing field somewhat and places more recent articles on a more equal footing with older works when examining the number of times a work is accessed.

Despite the relatively short time frame for which usage data were available, table 4 does show some overlap between the most-accessed articles in JSTOR and the most-cited articles in GS. Three of the 10 most-cited works according to GS were among the 10 most-accessed articles according to JSTOR. The most-accessed article was David P. Farrington's

---

³ We make the distinction between being ranked outside the top 50 in SSCI and being missing because the article was not indexed in SSCI. Of the 50 most-cited works based on GS, 18 were not indexed in SSCI.

## TABLE 3
### 50 Most-Cited Articles in *Crime and Justice* Based on SSCI Citations

| SSCI Rank | Article Title | Author(s) | Year | Citations in SSCI | GS Rank |
|---|---|---|---|---|---|
| 1 | Family Factors as Correlates and Predictors of Juvenile Conduct Problems and Delinquency | Loeber, R., Stouthamer-Loeber, M. | 1986 | 448 | 1 |
| 2 | Age and Crime | Farrington, D.P. | 1986 | 294 | 2 |
| 3 | The Criminal Career Paradigm | Piquero, A.R., Farrington, D.P., Blumstein, A. | 2003 | 225 | 8 |
| 4 | Criminal Deterrence Research at the Outset of the Twenty-First Century | Nagin, D.S. | 1998 | 190 | 4 |
| 5 | Understanding Desistance from Crime | Laub, J.H., Sampson, R.J. | 2001 | 175 | 5 |
| 6 | Assessing Macro-Level Predictors and Theories of Crime | Pratt, T.C., Cullen, F.T. | 2005 | 171 | 17 |
| 7 | Toward a Developmental Criminology | Loeber, R., Le Blanc, M. | 1990 | 159 | 9 |
| 8.5 | Public Opinion about Punishment and Corrections | Cullen, F.T., Fisher, B.S., Applegate, B.K. | 2000 | 140 | 11 |
| 8.5 | Academic Performance and Delinquency | Maguin, E., Loeber, R. | 1996 | 140 | 13 |
| 10 | Modeling Offenders' Decisions | Clarke, R.V., Cornish, D.B. | 1985 | 132 | 6 |
| 11.5 | What Have We Learned from Five Decades of Neutralization Research? | Maruna, S., Copes, H. | 2005 | 117 | 28 |
| 11.5 | The Neuropsychology of Juvenile Delinquency | Moffitt, T.E. | 1990 | 117 | 55 |
| 13 | Procedural Justice, Legitimacy, and the Effective Rule of Law | Tyler, T.R. | 2003 | 106 | 12 |
| 14 | Imprisonment and Reoffending | Nagin, D.S., Cullen, F.T., Jonson, C.L. | 2009 | 98 | 43 |
| 15 | The Self-Report Methodology in Crime Research | Junger-Tas, J., Marshall, I.H. | 1999 | 97 | 35 |
| 16 | Restorative Justice | Braithwaite, J. | 1999 | 91 | 7 |
| 17 | Police Crackdowns | Sherman, L.W. | 1990 | 86 | 18 |

| | | | | | |
|---|---|---|---|---|---|
| 18 | Risks and Prices | Reuter, P., Kleiman, M.A.R. | 1986 | 83 | 40 |
| 19 | Developmental Criminology Updated | Le Blanc, M., Loeber, R. | 1998 | 79 | 39 |
| 20.5 | Delinquency Careers | Blumstein, A., Farrington, D.P., Moitra, S. | 1985 | 70 | 31 |
| 20.5 | Long-Term Historical Trends in Violent Crime | Eisner, M. | 2003 | 70 | 38 |
| 22 | The Effects of Parental Imprisonment on Children | Murray, J., Farrington, D.P. | 2008 | 66 | 56 |
| 23 | Determinants of Penal Policies | Tonry, M. | 2007 | 64 | 98 |
| 24 | Racial and Ethnic Disparities in Crime and Criminal Justice in the United States | Sampson, R.J., Lauritsen, J.L. | 1997 | 63 | 27 |
| 25.5 | The Neighborhood Context of Police Behavior | Smith, D.A. | 1986 | 58 | 22 |
| 25.5 | The Demand and Supply of Criminal Opportunities | Cook, P.J. | 1986 | 58 | 49 |
| 27 | Fear of Crime and Neighborhood Change | Skogan, W. | 1986 | 52 | 16 |
| 28.5 | Crime Placement, Displacement, and Deflection | Barr, R., Pease, K. | 1990 | 50 | 26 |
| 28.5 | Sentence Severity and Crime | Doob, A.N., Webster, C.M. | 2003 | 50 | 46.5 |
| 30 | Drug Abuse in the Inner City | Johnson, B.D., Williams, T., Dei, K.A., Sanabria, J. | 1990 | 48 | 70.5 |
| 31.5 | Intoxication and Aggression | Fagan, J. | 1990 | 46 | 25 |
| 31.5 | After the Epidemic | Cook, P.J., Laub, J.H. | 2002 | 46 | 88 |
| 33.5 | Sexual Predators and Social Policy | Lieb, R., Quinsey, V., Berliner, L. | 1998 | 43 | 73 |
| 33.5 | Youth Gangs | Spergel, I.A. | 1990 | 43 | 75 |
| 35 | Penal Policy in Scandinavia | Lappi-Seppälä, T | 2007 | 42 | 110 |
| 36 | Gender, Race, and Sentencing | Daly, K., Tonry, M. | 1997 | 39 | 89 |
| 37.5 | What Recent Studies Do (and Don't) Tell Us about Imprisonment and Crime | Spelman, W. | 2000 | 38 | 93 |
| 37.5 | The Road to Dystopia? Changes in the Penal Climate of the Netherlands | Downes, D., van Swaaningen, R. | 2007 | 38 | 117.5 |
| 40 | Drugs and Predatory Crime | Chaiken, J.M., Chaiken, M.R. | 1990 | 37 | 34 |
| 40 | Crime and Work | Fagan, J., Freeman, R.B. | 1999 | 37 | 66 |
| 40 | Penal Communications | Duff, R.A. | 1996 | 37 | 86 |

TABLE 3 (*Continued*)

| SSCI Rank | Article Title | Author(s) | Year | Citations in SSCI | GS Rank |
|---|---|---|---|---|---|
| 42 | Juvenile Offenders in the Adult Criminal Justice System | Bishop, D.M. | 2000 | 36 | 60.5 |
| 43 | Crime in Cities | Sampson, R.J. | 1986 | 34 | 50 |
| 44.5 | The Purposes, Practices, and Problems of Supermax Prisons | Kurki, L., Morris, N. | 2001 | 33 | 113 |
| 44.5 | Rape and Attrition in the Legal Process | Daly, K., Bouhours, B. | 2010 | 33 | 122.5 |
| 47 | Intermediate Sanctions | Tonry, M., Lynch, M. | 1996 | 32 | 84 |
| 47 | The Construct of Psychopathy | Harris, G.T., Skilling, T.A., Rice, M.E. | 2001 | 32 | 101 |
| 47 | Multiple Homicide | Fox, J.A., Levin, J. | 1998 | 32 | 111 |
| 49 | Treatment of Drug Abuse | Anglin, M.D., Hser, Y.-I. | 1990 | 30 | 15 |
| 50.5 | Crime and Conflict | Daly, M., Wilson, M. | 1997 | 29 | 103.5 |
| 50.5 | Trust, Welfare, and Political Culture | Lappi-Seppälä, T. | 2008 | 29 | 132 |

NOTE.—GS = Google Scholar; SSCI = Social Science Citation Index.

# TABLE 4
## Most-Accessed Articles in *Crime and Justice* Based on JSTOR

| JSTOR Rank | Article Title | Author(s) | Year | Accessions in JSTOR | GS Rank | SSCI Rank |
|---|---|---|---|---|---|---|
| 1 | Understanding and Preventing Bullying | Farrington, D.P. | 1993 | 41,445 | 3 | *m* |
| 2 | The Effects of Solitary Confinement on Prison Inmates: A Brief History and Review of the Literature | Smith, P.S. | 2006 | 37,967 | X | X |
| 3 | Multiple Homicide: Patterns of Serial and Mass Murder | Fox, J.A., Levin, J. | 1998 | 34,483 | X | 47 |
| 4 | Youth Gangs: Continuity and Change | Spergel, I.A. | 1990 | 29,769 | X | 33.5 |
| 5 | Restorative Justice: Assessing Optimistic and Pessimistic Accounts | Braithwaite, J. | 1999 | 25,572 | 7 | 16 |
| 6 | Private Prisons | Harding, R. | 2001 | 18,309 | X | X |
| 7 | Juvenile Offenders in the Adult Criminal Justice System | Bishop, D.M. | 2000 | 17,323 | X | 42 |
| 8 | Situational Crime Prevention | Clarke, R.V. | 1995 | 17,146 | 10 | *m* |
| 9 | Adjusting to Prison Life | Adams, K. | 1992 | 15,223 | X | *m* |
| 10 | Trafficking for Sexual Exploitation | Lehti, M., Aromaa, K. | 2006 | 15,043 | X | X |
| 11 | Public Opinion, Crime, and Criminal Justice | Roberts, J.V. | 1992 | 13,506 | 32 | *m* |
| 12 | Public Opinion about Punishment and Corrections | Cullen, F.T., Fisher, B.S., Applegate, B.K. | 2000 | 12,633 | 11 | 8.5 |
| 13 | Sociological Perspectives on Punishment | Garland, D. | 1991 | 12,578 | X | *m* |
| 14 | Hate Crimes: A Critical Perspective | Jacobs, J.B., Potter, K.A. | 1997 | 12,196 | X | X |
| 15 | Gun Self-Defense and Deterrence | Ludwig, J. | 2000 | 12,056 | X | X |
| 16 | Guns, Youth Violence, and Social Identity in Inner Cities | Fagan, J., Wilkinson, D.L. | 1998 | 11,528 | X | *m* |
| 17 | Understanding Prison Policy and Population Trends | Caplow, T., Simon, J. | 1999 | 11,510 | X | *m* |
| 18 | Community Crime Prevention | Hope, T. | 1995 | 11,398 | 36 | *m* |
| 19 | Crime and Justice in Eighteenth- and Nineteenth-Century England | Hay, D. | 1980 | 11,126 | X | *m* |

TABLE 4 (*Continued*)

| JSTOR Rank | Article Title | Author(s) | Year | Accessions in JSTOR | GS Rank | SSCI Rank |
|---|---|---|---|---|---|---|
| 20 | Age and Crime | Farrington, D.P. | 1986 | 11,125 | 2 | 2 |
| 21 | Why Has US Drug Policy Changed So Little over 30 Years? | Reuter, P. | 2013 | 10,346 | X | X |
| 22 | Family Factors as Correlates and Predictors of Juvenile Conduct Problems and Delinquency | Loeber, R., Stouthamer-Loeber, M. | 1986 | 10,310 | 1 | 1 |
| 23 | Women's Imprisonment | Kruttschnitt, C., Gartner, R. | 2003 | 10,279 | X | X |
| 24 | The Prevalence of Drug Use in the United States | Mieczkowski, T.M. | 1996 | 10,027 | X | X |
| 25 | Gender, Race, and Sentencing | Daly, K., Tonry, M. | 1997 | 9,976 | X | 36 |
| 26 | Collateral Consequences of Imprisonment for Children, Communities, and Prisoners | Hagan, J., Dinovitzer, R. | 1999 | 9,958 | 14 | *m* |
| 27 | The Criminal Career Paradigm | Piquero, A.R., Farrington, D.P., Blumstein, A. | 2003 | 9,826 | 8 | 3 |
| 28 | Problem-Solving and Community Policing | Moore, M.H. | 1992 | 9,664 | 46.5 | *m* |
| 29 | Prevention of Youth Violence | Howell, J.C., Hawkins, J.D. | 1998 | 9,474 | X | *m* |
| 30 | Race, Ethnicity, and Criminal Justice in Canada | Roberts, J.V., Doob, A.N. | 1997 | 9,291 | X | X |
| 31 | Preventing Substance Abuse | Hawkins, J.D., Arthur, M.W., Catalano, R.F. | 1995 | 9,211 | X | *m* |
| 32 | Prison Suicide and Prisoner Coping | Liebling, A. | 1999 | 8,780 | X | *m* |
| 33 | Juvenile and Criminal Justice Systems' Responses to Youth Violence | Feld, B.C. | 1998 | 8,596 | X | *m* |
| 34 | Racial and Ethnic Disparities in Crime and Criminal Justice in the United States | Sampson, R.M., Lauritsen, J.L. | 1997 | 8,197 | 27 | 24 |
| 35 | Abolishing the Death Penalty Worldwide: The Impact of a "New Dynamic" | Hood, R., Hoyle, C. | 2009 | 7,934 | X | X |
| 36 | Predictors, Causes, and Correlates of Male Youth Violence | Farrington, D.P. | 1998 | 7,748 | 20 | *m* |
| 37 | Restorative and Community Justice in the United States | Kurki, L. | 2000 | 7,645 | X | X |

| # | Title | Author | Year | | | |
|---|-------|--------|------|---|---|---|
| 38 | Probation in the United States | Petersilia, J. | 1997 | 7,339 | X | X |
| 39 | Understanding Desistance from Crime | Laub, J.H., Sampson, R.J. | 2001 | 7,010 | 5 | 5 |
| 40 | Gang Violence in the Postindustrial Era | Hagedorn, J.M. | 1998 | 6,632 | X | m |
| 41 | Parole and Prisoner Reentry in the United States | Petersilia, J. | 1999 | 6,350 | X | m |
| 42 | Assessing Macro-Level Predictors and Theories of Crime: A Meta-Analysis | Pratt, T.C., Cullen, F.T. | 2005 | 6,193 | 17 | 6 |
| 43 | The Law and Criminology of Drunk Driving | Jacobs, J.B. | 1988 | 5,969 | X | m |
| 44 | Sexual Predators and Social Policy | Lieb, R., Quinsey, V., Berliner, L. | 1998 | 5,619 | X | 33.5 |
| 45 | Drugs and Drug Policy in the Netherlands | Leeuw, E. | 1991 | 5,301 | X | m |
| 46 | Prison Labor and Prison Industries | Hawkins, G. | 1983 | 5,111 | X | m |
| 47 | Attacking Crime: Police and Crime Control | Sherman, L.W. | 1992 | 5,031 | X | m |
| 48 | The Effects of Overcrowding in Prison | Gaes, G.G. | 1985 | 4,885 | X | X |
| 49 | Situational Crime Prevention: Its Theoretical Basis and Practical Scope | Clarke, R.V. | 1983 | 4,878 | 24 | m |
| 50 | Police Organization in the Twentieth Century | Reiss, A.J. | 1992 | 4,570 | X | m |
| 51 | Interpersonal Violence and Social Order in Prisons | Bottoms, A.E. | 1999 | 4,453 | 44 | m |
| 52 | Procedural Justice, Legitimacy, and the Effective Rule of Law | Tyler, T.R. | 2003 | 4,048 | 12 | 13 |
| 53 | What Have We Learned from Five Decades of Neutralization Research? | Maruna, S., Copes, H. | 2005 | 3,986 | 28 | 11.5 |
| 54 | Money Laundering | Levi, M, Reuter, P. | 2006 | 3,839 | X | X |
| 55 | Ethnicity, Crime, and Immigration | Tonry, M. | 1997 | 3,821 | 23 | X |
| 56 | Does Gentrification Affect Crime Rates? | McDonald, S.C. | 1986 | 3,742 | X | X |
| 57 | Drug Abuse in the Inner City: Impact on Hard-Drug Users and the Community | Johnson, B.D., Williams, T., Dei, K.A., Sanabria, H. | 1990 | 3,704 | 30 | 30 |
| 58 | Prison Management Trends, 1975–2025 | Riveland, C. | 1999 | 3,533 | X | m |
| 59 | The Purposes, Practices, and Problems of Supermax Prisons | Kurki, L., Morris, N. | 2001 | 3,530 | X | 44.5 |
| 60 | Biology and Crime | Mednick, S.A., Volavka, J. | 1980 | 3,528 | X | m |
| 61 | The Effects of Parental Imprisonment on Children | Murray, J., Farrington, D.P. | 2008 | 3,429 | 22 | X |

TABLE 4 (*Continued*)

| JSTOR Rank | Article Title | Author(s) | Year | Accessions in JSTOR | GS Rank | SSCI Rank |
|---|---|---|---|---|---|---|
| 62 | Treatment of Drug Abuse | Anglin, M.D., Hser, Y.-I. | 1990 | 3,129 | 15 | 49 |
| 63 | Criminalizing the American Juvenile Court | Feld, B.C. | 1993 | 2,726 | X | m |
| 64 | A Critique of Marxist Criminology | Sparks, R.F. | 1980 | 2,486 | X | m |
| 65 | Restoration in Youth Justice | Walgrave, L | 2004 | 2,435 | X | X |
| 66 | Understanding Theories of Criminal Victimization | Meier, R.F., Miethe, T.D. | 1993 | 2,342 | X | m |
| 67 | Understanding the Effects of Wrongful Imprisonment | Grounds, A.T. | 2005 | 2,183 | X | X |
| 68 | The Construct of Psychopathy | Harris, G.T., Skilling, T.A., Rice, M.E. | 2001 | 2,175 | X | 47 |
| 69 | Community and Problem-Oriented Policing | Reisig, M.D. | 2010 | 2,031 | X | X |
| 70 | Imprisonment and Reoffending | Nagin, D.S., Cullen, F.T., Jonson, C.L. | 2009 | 1,754 | 43 | 14 |
| 71 | Police Organization Continuity and Change: Into the Twenty-First Century | Mastrofski, S.D., Willis, J.J. | 2010 | 1,752 | X | X |
| 72 | Understanding Trends in Personal Violence: Does Cultural Sensitivity Matter? | Kivivuori, J. | 2014 | 1,577 | X | X |
| 73 | The Social, Psychological, and Political Causes of Racial Disparities in the American Criminal Justice System | Tonry, M. | 2010 | 1,496 | X | X |

| | | | | GS | SSCI | |
|---|---|---|---|---|---|---|
| 74 | The Influence of Gun Availability on Violent Crime Patterns | Cook, P.J. | 1983 | 1,369 | X | m |
| 75 | Intensive Probation and Parole | Petersilia, J., Turner, S. | 1993 | 1,300 | 21 | m |
| 76 | Academic Performance and Delinquency | Maguin, E., Loeber, R. | 1996 | 1,242 | 13 | 8.5 |
| 77 | Juvenile Justice: Shoring Up the Foundations | Moore, M.H., Wakeling, S. | 1997 | 1,219 | X | X |
| 78 | Firearms Regulation: A Historical Overview | Bellesiles, M.A. | 2001 | 1,214 | X | X |
| 79 | Modeling Offenders' Decisions: A Framework for Research and Policy | Clarke, R.V., Cornish, D.B. | 1985 | 1,210 | 6 | 10 |
| 80 | Organized Crime, Transit Crime, and Racketeering | Kleemans, E.R. | 2007 | 1,185 | X | X |
| 81 | Fear of Crime and Neighborhood Change | Skogan, W. | 1986 | 1,173 | 16 | 27 |
| 82 | Criminal Deterrence Research at the Outset of the Twenty-First Century | Nagin, D.S. | 1998 | 1,150 | 4 | 4 |
| 83.5 | Sex Offender Recidivism | Soothill, K. | 2010 | 1,135 | X | X |
| 83.5 | Youth Justice in Canada | Doob, A.N., Sprott, J.B. | 2004 | 1,135 | X | X |
| 85 | Women, Crime, and Penal Responses: A Historical Account | Zedner, L. | 1991 | 1,132 | X | m |
| 86 | Public Opinion and Youth Justice | Roberts, J.V. | 2004 | 1,125 | X | X |
| 87 | Developmental Crime Prevention | Tremblay, R.E., Craig, W.M. | 1995 | 1,111 | 41 | X |
| 88 | Long-Term Historical Trends in Violent Crime | Eisner, M. | 2003 | 1,094 | X | X |
| 89 | Drugs and Consensual Crimes: Drug Dealing and Prostitution | Hunt, D.E. | 1990 | 1,051 | X | X |
| 90 | Crime and Public Transport | Smith, M.J., Clarke, R.V. | 2000 | 1,019 | X | X |

NOTE.—GS = Google Scholar; SSCI = Social Science Citation Index; $m$ = article not indexed in SSCI; X = article not ranked in the top 50.

"Understanding and Preventing Bullying," which was accessed over 41,000 times between 2008 and 2015. This article was ranked 3 in GS but was missing in SSCI. John Braithwaite's "Restorative Justice: Assessing Optimistic and Pessimistic Accounts" was the fifth-most-accessed work and ranked 7 in GS, and "Situational Crime Prevention" by Ronald V. Clarke was the eighth-most-accessed work according to JSTOR and ranked 10 in GS. There was less overlap with SSCI, possibly because of missing articles. None of the 10 most-cited works according to SSCI were among the 10 most-accessed articles and only three were among the 25 most-accessed works.

Overall, however, many of the most-accessed articles in JSTOR were unranked or were ranked far lower in GS and SSCI. Approximately 62 percent (56 of 90) of the most-accessed articles were unranked in GS and approximately 34 percent (31 of 90) were unranked in SSCI.[4] Similarly, many of the most-cited works in GS or SSCI were unranked or ranked lower on the basis of accessions data. The most-cited work in both GS and SSCI (Loeber and Stouthamer-Loeber 1986) was ranked 22 in JSTOR and the second-most-cited work in GS and SSCI (Farrington 1986) was ranked 20 in JSTOR. The lack of overlap between JSTOR and the GS and SSCI citation ranks remained regardless of JSTOR accession rank, possibly because of the different time periods covered.

Tables 5 and 6 show the correlations between various article characteristics and two different measures of scholarly influence: the raw numbers of citations and the unweighted ranks in both GS and SSCI. Multiple correlations were run substituting each paper topic in the model (e.g., theory, methods). Given the degree of missingness in the SSCI variables, the correlations were run on the basis of 243 of the 374 articles for which SSCI information was available. Importantly, the numbers of citations in GS and SSCI were very highly correlated, indicating reliability between these measures. Several patterns emerge from these analyses. First, and perhaps most interesting, for GS, rank was significantly more correlated with paper topics than were raw citation counts. The number of citations in GS was significantly related to only articles on theory (positive) and courts (negative), suggesting that articles relating to criminological theory were most likely to be cited. In contrast, rank in GS was significantly correlated with all but one of the paper topics (criminology/criminal jus-

[4] Approximately 37 percent (31 of 90) of the most-accessed articles in JSTOR were not indexed in SSCI.

## TABLE 5

### Correlations Based on Raw Numbers of Citations

|  | Number of Authors | Volume Type | Citations in GS | Citations in SSCI | Shelf Life |
|---|---|---|---|---|---|
| Volume type | .001 | | | | |
| Cites in GS | .095 | −.195** | | | |
| Cites in SSCI | .148* | −.363** | .933** | | |
| Shelf life | −.210** | −.295** | .237** | .264** | |
| Theory paper | .069 | −.059 | .318** | .282** | .038 |
| Methods paper | .121* | .071 | −.059 | .064 | −.104* |
| Crim/CJ paper | −.040 | .038 | −.052 | −.013 | .106* |
| CJ topics paper | .078 | .029 | −.100 | −.069 | −.014 |
| Police paper | −.067 | .050 | .033 | .020 | .146** |
| Courts paper | −.109* | −.063 | −.124* | −.091 | −.143** |
| Corrections paper | −.074 | −.035 | .0006 | −.040 | .041 |

NOTE.—GS = Google Scholar; SSCI = Social Science Citation Index.
* $p \le .05$.
** $p \le .01$.

tice). As expected, the direction of the significant relationships reversed when ranks were examined, because low ranks correspond to high numbers of citations. Interestingly, the relationship between paper topics and influence was far less evident using SSCI data. Theory articles were pos-

## TABLE 6

### Correlations Based on Ranks

|  | Number of Authors | Volume Type | GS Rank | SSCI Rank | Shelf Life |
|---|---|---|---|---|---|
| Volume type | .001 | | | | |
| GS rank | −.072 | .253** | | | |
| SSCI rank | −.120 | .565** | .882** | | |
| Shelf life | −.210** | −.295** | −.386** | −.363** | |
| Theory paper | .069 | −.059 | −.248** | −.228** | .038 |
| Methods paper | .121* | .071 | .107* | .137* | −.104* |
| Crim/CJ paper | −.040 | .038 | .037 | −.003 | .106* |
| CJ topics paper | .078 | .029 | .116* | .052 | −.014 |
| Police paper | −.067 | .050 | −.108* | −.067 | .146** |
| Courts paper | −.109* | −.063 | .161** | .138* | −.143** |
| Corrections paper | −.074 | −.035 | −.118* | −.124 | .041 |

NOTE.—GS = Google Scholar; SSCI = Social Science Citation Index.
* $p \le .05$.
** $p \le .01$.

itively correlated with number of citations in SSCI, and the correlation remained significant when ranks in SSCI were examined. No other paper topics were correlated with the SSCI raw citation counts. SSCI rank was positively correlated with methods and courts articles; however, the relationship between number of citations and each of these paper topics was nonsignificant.

Similar results appeared when other journal characteristics were examined. Type of volume was significantly related to citations and ranks in both GS and SSCI, indicating that thematic volume articles were less likely to be cited than general volume articles. The number of authors of an article was positively correlated with raw citations in SSCI, indicating that multiple-authored articles were more likely to be cited. Finally, shelf life was significantly associated with citations and ranks in both GS and SSCI. As expected, older articles tended to accumulate more citations and to be more highly ranked.

It appears that the relationship between scholarly influence and article characteristics varies on the basis of the measure of scholarly influence employed (raw number of citations versus ranks), perhaps in part because the average number of citations per article is increasing (see, e.g., Cohn 2011; Cohn, Farrington, and Iratzoqui 2014). Therefore, rank may be a more stable and accurate measure of scholarly influence than raw citation counts, the latter of which may be more reflective of a recent trend toward more inflated reference lists than an increase in influence of a scholar from one time period to the next.

## B. The Issue of Missing Data

One issue with this study is that the Web of Science (SSCI) did not index all volumes of *Crime and Justice*; information on citations of 131 articles published during the years 1979–83, 1988–89, part of 1990, 1991–95, and part of 1998 and 1999 was missing. This meant that comparisons between GS and SSCI could be made for only 243 of the 374 articles published in *Crime and Justice*. The extent of "missingness" resulting from the indexing instability inherent in SSCI raises the question of the scholarly influence of those missing articles. To address this, missingness was examined in two ways. First, a "missingness" variable (where 0 = present for the 243 cases; 1 = missing for the 131 cases) was created to identify articles missing in SSCI. Pairwise correlations revealed that this variable was significantly correlated with nearly every other variable in the study other than citations and rank in SSCI.

Second, the articles were examined across several variables, exposing a number of significant differences between missing and present articles. Articles that were missing tended to have a longer shelf life, which is somewhat obvious since all the missing volumes were pre-2000. Missing articles also were significantly more likely to cover topics related to criminology/criminal justice or police and significantly less likely to cover topics related to courts. The relationship between missingness and topic may be linked to shelf life; criminology/criminal justice and police topics were positively associated with shelf life (i.e., older articles were more likely to be on these topics), while courts topics were negatively correlated (so that older articles were less likely to be on this topic). Additionally, articles that were missing had fewer authors, on average. Again, given that they are older, this is not surprising; research suggests that solo authorship is declining and multi-authored articles are becoming increasingly more prevalent (see, e.g., Sever 2005; Tewksbury, De-Michele, and Miller 2005; Tewksbury and Mustaine 2011; Lemke, Johnson, and Jenks 2015). This was also true in *Crime and Justice*. Finally, articles missing in SSCI were ranked significantly lower on GS than articles that were present in SSCI. This finding may suggest that articles that are more recent and more likely to appear in searches of SSCI are more likely to be cited in GS.

## C. Most-Cited Scholars

Table 7 presents the 50 most-cited scholars in GS based on the number of citations of the articles they authored in *Crime and Justice* between 1979 and 2015. The 10 most-cited scholars were David P. Farrington, Rolf Loeber, Ronald V. Clarke, Michael Tonry, Alfred Blumstein, Magda Stouthamer-Loeber, Phillip J. Cook, Robert J. Sampson, Francis T. Cullen, and John H. Laub. However, it is important to note that these scholars authored different numbers of *Crime and Justice* articles, which influenced their opportunities for citations. Therefore, the average number of citations per article is also shown in this table.

In addition, a mean rank was also generated for the scholar's rank based on his or her average number of citations per article. A scholar's mean rank was not always similar to his or her ranking based on the raw number of citations. For example, while David Farrington was ranked first on the basis of his raw citation count, he authored a large number of articles in *Crime and Justice*, lowering his mean rank based on citations per article to 33. On the basis of mean rank, Magda Stouthamer-Loeber

## TABLE 7
## Most-Cited Scholars Based on Citations in Google Scholar

| Rank | Author | Citations in GS | Number of Articles | Citations per Article | Mean Rank |
|---|---|---|---|---|---|
| 1 | David P. Farrington | 4,136 | 19 | 217.7 | 33 |
| 2 | Rolf Loeber | 2,817 | 5 | 563.4 | 3 |
| 3 | Ronald V. Clarke | 1,939 | 7 | 277.0 | 28 |
| 4 | Michael Tonry | 1,699 | 30 | 56.6 | 50 |
| 5 | Alfred Blumstein | 1,477 | 5 | 295.4 | 25 |
| 6 | Magda Stouthamer-Loeber | 1,460 | 1 | 1,460.0 | 1 |
| 7 | Phillip J. Cook | 1,371 | 10 | 137.1 | 43 |
| 8 | Robert J. Sampson | 1,316 | 3 | 438.7 | 12 |
| 9 | Francis T. Cullen | 1,296 | 6 | 216.0 | 34.5 |
| 10 | John H. Laub | 1,241 | 4 | 310.3 | 23 |
| 11 | Daniel S. Nagin | 1,159 | 4 | 289.8 | 26 |
| 12 | Joan Petersilia | 1,006 | 7 | 143.7 | 41 |
| 13 | Marc Le Blanc | 915 | 3 | 305.0 | 24 |
| 14 | Jeffrey Fagan | 908 | 4 | 227.0 | 29 |
| 15 | Lawrence W. Sherman | 733 | 4 | 183.3 | 37 |
| 16 | Albert J. Reiss | 721 | 4 | 180.3 | 38 |
| 17 | John Braithwaite | 691 | 2 | 345.5 | 15 |
| 18 | Alex R. Piquero | 681 | 3 | 227.0 | 29 |
| 19 | Derek B. Cornish | 660 | 1 | 660.0 | 2 |
| 20 | John Hagan | 659 | 2 | 329.5 | 18 |
| 21 | Julian V. Roberts | 586 | 5 | 117.2 | 44 |
| 22 | Wesley G. Skogan | 577 | 2 | 288.5 | 27 |
| 23 | Peter Reuter | 576 | 7 | 82.3 | 47 |
| 24 | Mark H. Moore | 535 | 6 | 89.2 | 46 |
| 25.5 | Bonnie S. Fisher | 516 | 1 | 516.0 | 4.5 |
| 25.5 | Brandon K. Applegate | 516 | 1 | 516.0 | 4.5 |
| 27 | Tom R. Tyler | 513 | 1 | 513.0 | 6 |
| 28 | Eugene Maguin | 506 | 1 | 506.0 | 7 |
| 29 | Kenneth Pease | 484 | 3 | 161.3 | 39 |
| 30 | Ronit Dinovitzer | 473 | 1 | 473.0 | 8 |
| 31 | Anthony N. Doob | 458 | 6 | 76.3 | 49 |
| 32.5 | M. Douglas Anglin | 453 | 1 | 453.0 | 9.5 |
| 32.5 | Yih-Ing Hser | 453 | 1 | 453.0 | 9.5 |
| 34.5 | Clifford D. Shearing | 443 | 2 | 221.5 | 31.5 |
| 34.5 | Phillip C. Stenning | 443 | 2 | 221.5 | 31.5 |
| 36 | Travis C. Pratt | 440 | 1 | 440.0 | 11 |
| 37 | Susan Turner | 432 | 2 | 216.0 | 34.5 |
| 38 | Allen J. Beck | 431 | 1 | 431.0 | 13 |
| 39 | Anthony E. Bottoms | 428 | 3 | 142.7 | 42 |
| 40 | Josine Junger-Tas | 392 | 5 | 78.4 | 48 |
| 41 | Douglas A. Smith | 368 | 1 | 368.0 | 14 |
| 42 | Mark A. Kleiman | 365 | 2 | 182.5 | 37 |
| 43 | Robert Barr | 336 | 1 | 336.0 | 16 |
| 44 | Janet L. Lauritsen | 334 | 1 | 334.0 | 17 |

TABLE 7 (*Continued*)

| Rank | Author | Citations in GS | Number of Articles | Citations per Article | Mean Rank |
|------|--------|-----------------|--------------------|-----------------------|-----------|
| 45.5 | Heith Copes | 320 | 1 | 320.0 | 19.5 |
| 45.5 | Shadd Maruna | 320 | 1 | 320.0 | 19.5 |
| 47.5 | Ted R. Gurr | 318 | 1 | 318.0 | 21 |
| 47.5 | Cheryl L. Jonson | 318 | 3 | 106.0 | 45 |
| 49 | Soumyo D. Moitra | 314 | 1 | 314.0 | 22 |
| 50 | Cheryl M. Webster | 302 | 2 | 151.0 | 40 |

NOTE.—GS = Google Scholar.

was the most-cited scholar, based on her coauthorship with Rolf Loeber of "Family Factors as Correlates and Predictors of Juvenile Conduct Problems and Delinquency," which was the most-cited article in *Crime and Justice*.

Table 8 identifies the most-cited *Crime and Justice* authors based on their adjusted citations in GS. Many of the most-cited articles were published before 2000 and so were at risk of citation for a relatively long time. This system standardizes the number of citations of an article by that article's shelf life, or number of years since publication; the concept is similar to adjusting an offender's rate of offending by his or her "street time" or number of days on the street (Piquero et al. 2001). This removes the bias resulting from publication date and allows more recently published works to be considered alongside much older articles. It is important to note, however, that while the use of shelf life to standardize risk of citations by years in print eliminates the advantage of older works in having more time to accumulate citations, it may also penalize them because citations tend to decrease with time since publication (Cohn, Farrington, and Iratzoqui 2017). Therefore, while using raw citation counts may provide an advantage to older articles, standardization by years at risk of publication may provide an advantage to more recently published works.

The 10 most-cited scholars based on adjusted citations were largely consistent with results in table 7, although the order changed slightly; the only change was the presence of Daniel S. Nagin instead of Magda Stouthamer-Loeber. The use of adjusted citations allows Nagin's relatively recent works (all but one of which were published after 2000) to compete on a level field with the article by Stouthamer-Loeber, which was published in 1986 and therefore had many more years at risk of citation. Because of the adjustment, some authors who were not among the

# TABLE 8

## Most-Cited Scholars Based on Adjusted Citations in Google Scholar

| Rank | Author | Adjusted Citations in GS | Number of Articles | Mean | Mean Rank |
|------|--------|--------------------------|--------------------|------|-----------|
| 1 | David P. Farrington | 226.25 | 19 | 11.91 | 29 |
| 2 | Michael Tonry | 135.27 | 30 | 4.51 | 49 |
| 3 | Francis T. Cullen | 127.51 | 6 | 21.25 | 18 |
| 4 | Rolf Loeber | 112.16 | 5 | 22.43 | 14 |
| 5 | Daniel S. Nagin | 105.26 | 4 | 26.32 | 9 |
| 6 | Alfred Blumstein | 89.23 | 4 | 22.31 | 15 |
| 7 | John H. Laub | 85.38 | 4 | 21.35 | 16 |
| 8 | Ronald V. Clarke | 76.65 | 7 | 10.95 | 31 |
| 9 | Robert J. Sampson | 75.71 | 3 | 25.24 | 13 |
| 10 | Phillip J. Cook | 69.04 | 10 | 6.90 | 41 |
| 11 | Alex R. Piquero | 58.18 | 3 | 19.39 | 20 |
| 12 | Joan Petersilia | 52.05 | 7 | 7.44 | 39 |
| 13 | Peter Reuter | 49.07 | 7 | 7.01 | 40 |
| 14 | Magda Stouthamer-Loeber | 48.67 | 1 | 48.67 | 1 |
| 15 | Cheryl L. Jonson | 47.93 | 3 | 15.98 | 26 |
| 16 | Lawrence W. Sherman | 43.03 | 4 | 10.76 | 33 |
| 17 | Marc Le Blanc | 42.37 | 3 | 14.12 | 27 |
| 18 | Jeffrey Fagan | 41.91 | 4 | 10.48 | 34 |
| 19 | Travis C. Pratt | 40.00 | 1 | 40.00 | 2 |
| 20 | John Braithwaite | 39.85 | 2 | 19.93 | 19 |
| 21 | Tom R. Tyler | 39.46 | 1 | 39.46 | 3 |
| 22 | Anthony N. Doob | 36.33 | 6 | 6.06 | 45 |
| 23 | Julian V. Roberts | 34.02 | 5 | 6.80 | 42 |
| 24 | John Hagan | 33.46 | 2 | 16.73 | 25 |
| 25.5 | Bonnie S. Fisher | 32.25 | 1 | 32.25 | 4.5 |
| 25.5 | Brandon K. Applegate | 32.25 | 1 | 32.25 | 4.5 |
| 27 | Tapio Lappi-Seppälä | 29.47 | 6 | 4.91 | 47 |
| 28.5 | Heith Copes | 29.09 | 1 | 29.09 | 6.5 |
| 28.5 | Shadd Maruna | 29.09 | 1 | 29.09 | 6.5 |
| 30 | Ronit Dinovitzer | 27.82 | 1 | 27.82 | 8 |
| 31 | Albert J. Reiss | 26.15 | 4 | 6.54 | 43 |
| 32 | Joseph Murray | 26.00 | 1 | 26.00 | 10 |
| 33.5 | Allen J. Beck | 25.35 | 1 | 25.35 | 11 |
| 33.5 | Cheryl M. Webster | 25.35 | 2 | 12.68 | 28 |
| 35 | Eugene Maguin | 25.30 | 1 | 25.30 | 12 |
| 36 | Mark H. Moore | 25.22 | 6 | 4.20 | 50 |
| 37 | Anthony E. Bottoms | 24.92 | 3 | 8.31 | 37 |
| 38 | Josine Junger-Tas | 23.69 | 5 | 4.74 | 48 |
| 39 | Kathleen Daly | 23.19 | 2 | 11.60 | 30 |
| 40 | Manuel Eisner | 21.69 | 2 | 10.85 | 32 |
| 41 | Derek B. Cornish | 21.29 | 1 | 21.29 | 17 |
| 42 | Brandon C. Welsh | 20.47 | 4 | 5.12 | 46 |
| 43 | Wesley G. Skogan | 19.54 | 2 | 9.77 | 35 |
| 44 | Kenneth Pease | 18.91 | 3 | 6.30 | 44 |

TABLE 8 (*Continued*)

| Rank | Author | Adjusted Citations in GS | Number of Articles | Mean | Mean Rank |
|------|--------|------|------|------|------|
| 45 | Susan Turner | 18.38 | 2 | 9.19 | 36 |
| 46 | Janet L. Lauritsen | 17.57 | 1 | 17.57 | 21 |
| 47.5 | M. Douglas Anglin | 17.42 | 1 | 17.42 | 22.5 |
| 47.5 | Yih-Ing Hser | 17.42 | 1 | 17.42 | 22.5 |
| 49 | Ineke Haen Marshall | 16.82 | 1 | 16.82 | 24 |
| 50 | Leena Kurki | 15.76 | 2 | 7.88 | 38 |

NOTE.—GS = Google Scholar.

most-cited scholars based on total numbers of citations (table 7) do appear here, such as Daniel Nagin and Alex R. Piquero.

It is important to note that in tables 7 and 8, the mean ranks are based on the 50 most-cited scholars. It is therefore possible that some scholars with higher average numbers of citations per article are excluded because they did not have enough raw citations to be ranked among the top 50. For example, Jan M. Chaiken and Marcia R. Chaiken coauthored one article in *Crime and Justice*, which received a total of 293 citations in GS. Because the fiftieth-most-cited scholar in table 7 received 302 citations, they did not appear in that table. However, because the Chaikens authored only one article, their mean number of citations also was 293, which was greater than that of some of the most-cited scholars who did appear in table 7.

Similarly, Shawn Bushway coauthored one article in *Crime and Justice* in 2008, which received a total of 46 citations. His adjusted citation count was 5.75, which was far too low to appear in table 8. However, since he authored only one article, his mean number of adjusted citations was also 5.75. Again, this was greater than some of the most-cited scholars who did appear in table 8. Therefore, the mean rankings cannot solely be used to judge influence without considering the total citations of articles published in *Crime and Justice*.

## V.  Conclusion

This essay has examined the citations of the 374 articles published in the 44 volumes of *Crime and Justice* between 1979 and 2015, according to both Google Scholar and the Web of Science (Social Science Citation

Index), characteristics of the most-cited articles, and online access data between 2008 and 2015, according to JSTOR. This study also gives insight into the relative merits of Google Scholar and the Web of Science as sources of information on citations. While citation counts from the two sources generally resulted in similar overall rankings, the actual numbers of citations varied greatly, depending on which source was used. For example, the article by Loeber and Stouthamer-Loeber (1986), which was the most highly cited work according to both sources, had 1,460 citations through December 2015 according to GS but only 448 citations when SSCI was used. Similarly, the second-most-cited work, Farrington's (1986) article "Age and Crime," had 999 citations according to GS but only 294 according to SSCI. GS clearly has significantly greater coverage than SSCI. However, the lack of information regarding the sources of citation information used by GS limits its usefulness as a reliable source of citation data. Conversely, the limited coverage of SSCI means that citation counts based on SSCI may be significantly underestimated. Specifically, the fact that a large number of articles in *Crime and Justice* were not indexed in SSCI not only affected the utility of SSCI for this study but also highlights the effects that SSCI's coverage limitations may have on citation analysis in general.

Ultimately, the use of multiple sources of citation data may prove useful in identifying the most-cited scholars and works in a serial publication like *Crime and Justice*. The findings from these analyses provided two important insights. First, it is apparent that articles published in *Crime and Justice* generally have a high citation rate. The total numbers of citations of *Crime and Justice* articles through 2015 were 41,663 in GS and 6,023 in SSCI, suggesting that this serial publication is highly influential in the field. In agreement with this, *Crime and Justice* had the highest impact factor (4.94) out of 57 criminology journals in 2015, according to Thomson Reuters Journal Citation Reports. Second, analyses of the citation patterns of these articles also revealed that certain factors were more highly correlated with our two measures of influence (i.e., raw numbers of citations and ranks). In both GS and SSCI, the most-cited articles tended to be older and to cover topics related to criminological theory, while the top-ranked articles tended to cover topics relating to methods, courts, and other criminal justice topics, in addition to the above factors.

It also appears that while there is some basic similarity between the most-cited articles in *Crime and Justice*, at least when using GS data, and the most-accessed articles, according to JSTOR, the overlap is limited. This may be due in part to the limited information provided by JSTOR; it would be useful to examine access data for all articles in *Crime and Justice*, not just the top 50 most accessed each year. However, the differences between the results obtained from an examination of citations and those obtained from usage data suggest that accessions may better capture current usage of articles than citations.

It is interesting to note the large number of older articles that were among those most accessed according to JSTOR. Of the 90 most-accessed articles, approximately 63 percent (57 of 90) were published prior to 2000. The most-accessed article, Farrington's "Understanding and Preventing Bullying," was published in 1993. One possible explanation for this is that the 2009 Campbell Collaboration report on antibullying programs (Farrington and Ttofi 2009) is the second-most-downloaded review on the Campbell Collaboration website, with over 36,000 downloads between 2008 and 2015. This may have led readers of the review to access Farrington's 1993 article on bullying. Additionally, current events may lead to renewed interest in older essays. The large number of accessions of Smith's 2006 essay on solitary confinement began in 2013 and may have been due in part to the national attention on California's solitary confinement practices after prisoners staged a statewide hunger strike in that state. Similarly, the recent concerns about mass shootings, particularly those committed in schools, may have contributed to the high number of accessions of Fox and Lewin's 1998 essay on serial and mass murder.

It would be instructive to replicate this research over time as topics of interest within the field of criminology and criminal justice change. It is anticipated that theoretical issues, particularly those relating to developmental and life course criminology more generally, will remain topics of importance to the field. Several of the most-cited scholars identified by the earlier research were leading researchers in this area, and several of the most-cited works focused on issues such as family influences, age and crime, desistance from crime, developmental criminology, and the criminal career paradigm (Cohn and Farrington 1996). It will be interesting to see if these trends continue.

REFERENCES

Anglin, M. Douglas, and Yih-Ing Hser. 1990. "Treatment of Drug Abuse." In *Drugs and Crime*, edited by Michael Tonry and James Q. Wilson. Vol. 13

of *Crime and Justice: A Review of Research*, edited by Michael Tonry. Chicago: University of Chicago Press.

Bauer, Kathleen, and Nisa Bakkalbasi. 2005. "An Examination of Citation Counts in a New Scholarly Communication Environment." *D-Lib Magazine* (11). http://dlib.org/dlib/september05/bauer/09bauer.html.

Braithwaite, John. 1999. "Restorative Justice: Assessing Optimistic and Pessimistic Accounts." In *Crime and Justice: A Review of Research*, vol. 25, edited by Michael Tonry. Chicago: University of Chicago Press.

Chapman, Anthony J. 1989. "Assessing Research: Citation-Count Shortcomings." *Psychologist* 8:336–44.

Clarke, Ronald V. 1995. "Situational Crime Prevention." In *Building a Safer Society: Strategic Approaches to Crime Prevention*, edited by Michael Tonry and David P. Farrington. Vol. 19 of *Crime and Justice: A Review of Research*, edited by Michael Tonry. Chicago: University of Chicago Press.

Cohn, Ellen G. 2011. "Changes in Scholarly Influence in Major International Criminology Journals, 1986–2005." *Canadian Journal of Criminology and Criminal Justice* 53:157–88.

Cohn, Ellen G., and David P. Farrington. 1990. "Differences between British and American Criminology: An Analysis of Citations." *British Journal of Criminology* 30:467–82.

———. 1994. "Who Are the Most Influential Criminologists in the English-Speaking World?" *British Journal of Criminology* 34:204–25.

———. 1996. "*Crime and Justice* and the Criminal Justice and Criminology Literature." In *Crime and Justice: A Review of Research*, vol. 20, edited by Michael Tonry. Chicago: University of Chicago Press.

———. 2005. "Citation Research in Criminology and Criminal Justice." In *Encyclopedia of Criminology*, edited by Richard A. Wright and J. Mitchell Miller. New York: Routledge.

———. 2012. *Scholarly Influence in Criminology and Criminal Justice*. New York: Nova Science Press.

Cohn, Ellen G., David P. Farrington, and Amaia Iratzoqui. 2014. *Most-Cited Scholars in Criminology and Criminal Justice, 1986–2010*. New York: Springer.

———. 2017. "Changes in the Most-Cited Scholars and Works over 25 Years: The Evolution of the Field of Criminology and Criminal Justice." *Journal of Criminal Justice Education* 28:25–51.

Cohn, Ellen G., David P. Farrington, and Richard A. Wright. 1998. *Evaluating Criminology and Criminal Justice*. Westport, CT: Greenwood.

Cole, Stephen. 1975. "The Growth of Scientific Knowledge: Theories of Deviance as a Case Study." In *The Idea of Social Structure: Papers in Honor of Robert K. Merton*, edited by Lewis A. Cose. New York: Harcourt Brace Jovanovich.

Cronin, Blaise, Herbert Snyder, and Helen Atkins. 1997. "Comparative Citation Rankings of Authors in Monographic and Journal Literature: A Study of Sociology." *Journal of Documentation* 53:263–73.

Farrington, David P. 1986. "Age and Crime." In *Crime and Justice: An Annual Review of Research*, vol. 7, edited by Michael Tonry and Norval Morris. Chicago: University of Chicago Press.

————. 1993. "Understanding and Preventing Bullying." In *Crime and Justice: A Review of Research*, vol. 17, edited by Michael Tonry. Chicago: University of Chicago Press.

Farrington, David P., and Maria M. Ttofi. 2009. "School-Based Programs to Reduce Bullying and Victimization." *Campbell Systematic Reviews* 2009(6):1–149.

Funkhouser, Edward T. 1996. "The Evaluative Use of Citation Analysis for Communications Journals." *Human Communication Research* 22:562–74.

Garfield, Eugene. 1979. "Is Citation Analysis a Legitimate Evaluation Tool?" *Scientometrics* 1:359–75.

Giles, Jim. 2005. "Start Your Engines." *Nature* 438:1–2.

Google Scholar. 2016. "Search Tips: Content Coverage." https://scholar.google.com/intl/en/scholar/help.html#coverage.

Hamilton, David P. 1990. "Publishing by—and for?—the Numbers." *Science* 250:1331–32.

————. 1991. "Research Papers: Who's Uncited Now?" *Science* 251:25.

Jascó, Péter. 2008. "Savvy Searching: Google Scholar Revisited." *Online Information Review* 32:102–14.

Laband, David N., and Michael J. Piette. 1994. "A Citation Analysis of the Impact of Blinded Peer Review." *Journal of the American Medical Association* 272:147–49.

Lemke, Richard, Lee M. Johnson, and David Jenks. 2015. "Perceptions of the Trend of Collaborative Publications: Results from a Survey of Criminal Justice and Criminology Department Chairs." *Journal of Criminal Justice Education* 26:1–21.

Loeber, Rolf, and Magda Stouthamer-Loeber. 1986. "Family Factors as Correlates and Predictors of Juvenile Conduct Problems and Delinquency." In *Crime and Justice: An Annual Review of Research*, vol. 7, edited by Michael Tonry and Norval Morris. Chicago: University of Chicago Press.

Meadows, Arthur J. 1974. *Communication in Science*. London: Butterworths.

Meho, Lokman I. 2007. "The Rise and Rise of Citation Analysis." *Physics World* 20(1):32–36.

Meho, Lokman I., and Kiduk Yang. 2007. "Impact of Data Sources on Citation Counts and Rankings of LIS Faculty: Web of Science versus Scopus and Google Scholar." *Journal of the American Society for Information Science and Technology* 58:2105–25.

Moffitt, Terrie E. 1990. "The Neuropsychology of Juvenile Delinquency: A Critical Review." In *Crime and Justice: A Review of Research*, vol. 12, edited by Michael Tonry and Norval Morris. Chicago: University of Chicago Press.

Morris, Norval, and Michael Tonry. 1979. "Introduction." In *Crime and Justice: An Annual Review of Research*, vol. 1, edited by Norval Morris and Michael Tonry. Chicago: University of Chicago Press.

Nisonger, Thomas E. 2004. "Citation Autobiography: An Investigation of ISI Data Base Coverage in Determining Author Citedness." *College and Research Libraries* 65:152–63.

Orrick, Erin A., and Henriikka Weir. 2011. "The Most Prolific Sole and Lead Authors in Elite Criminology and Criminal Justice Journals, 2000–2009." *Journal of Criminal Justice Education* 22:24–42.

Piquero, Alex R., Alfred Blumstein, Robert Brame, Rudy Haapanen, Edward Mulvey, and Daniel Nagin. 2001. "Assessing the Impact of Exposure Time and Incapacitation on Longitudinal Trajectories of Criminal Offending." *Journal of Adolescent Research* 16:54–74.

Sever, Brion. 2005. "Ranking Multiple Authors in Criminal Justice Scholarship: An Examination of Underlying Issues." *Journal of Criminal Justice Education* 16:79–100.

Smith, Peter S. 2006. "The Effects of Solitary Confinement on Prison Inmates: A Brief History and Review of the Literature." In *Crime and Justice: A Review of Research*, vol. 34, edited by Michael Tonry. Chicago: University of Chicago Press.

Tewksbury, Richard, Matthew T. DeMichele, and J. Mitchell Miller. 2005. "Methodological Orientations of Articles Appearing in Criminal Justice's Top Journals: Who Publishes What and Where." *Journal of Criminal Justice Education* 16:265–79.

Tewksbury, Richard, and Elizabeth Mustaine. 2011. "How Many Authors Does It Take to Write an Article? An Assessment of Criminology and Criminal Justice Research Article Author Composition." *Journal of Criminal Justice Education* 22:12–23.